PORTRAYING PERSONS WITH DISABILITIES

AN ANNOTATED BIBLIOGRAPHY OF

FICTION

FOR CHILDREN AND TEENAGERS

SERVING SPECIAL NEEDS SERIES

ACCEPT ME AS I AM
Best Books of Juvenile Nonfiction on
Impairments and Disabilities
by Joan Brest Friedberg, June B. Mullins, and Adelaide Weir Sukiennik

BOOKS FOR THE GIFTED CHILD
*by Barbara H. Baskin and Karen H.
Harris*

**BOOKS FOR THE GIFTED CHILD,
Volume 2**
by Paula Hauser and Gail A. Nelson

**BOOKS TO HELP CHILDREN COPE WITH
SEPARATION AND LOSS, 2nd Edition**
by Joanne E. Bernstein

**BOOKS TO HELP CHILDREN COPE WITH
SEPARATION AND LOSS, Volume 3**
An Annotated Bibliography
*by Joanne E. Bernstein and Masha
Kabakow Rudman*

CHALLENGING THE GIFTED
Curriculum Enrichment and Acceleration Models
*by Corinne P. Clendening and Ruth
Ann Davies*

CREATING PROGRAMS FOR THE GIFTED
A Guide for Teachers, Librarians, and
Students
*by Corinne P. Clendening and Ruth
Ann Davies*

HEALTH, ILLNESS, AND DISABILITY
A Guide to Books for Children and
Young Adults
by Pat Azarnoff

HIGH/LOW HANDBOOK, 3rd Edition
Encouraging Literacy in the 1990s
By Ellen V. LiBretto

**MORE NOTES FROM A DIFFERENT
DRUMMER**
A Guide to Juvenile Fiction Portraying
the Disabled
*by Barbara H. Baskin and Karen H.
Harris*

NOTES FROM A DIFFERENT DRUMMER
A Guide to Juvenile Fiction Portraying
the Handicapped
*by Barbara H. Baskin and Karen H.
Harris*

PARENTING THE GIFTED
Developing the Promise
by Sheila C. Perino and Joseph Perino

**PORTRAYING PERSONS WITH
DISABILITIES**
An Annotated Bibliography of Fiction
for Children and Teenagers,
3rd Edition
by Debra E. J. Robertson

**PORTRAYING PERSONS WITH
DISABILITIES**
An Annotated Bibliography of
Nonfiction for Children and Teenagers,
2nd Edition
by Joan Brest Friedberg, June B. Mullins, and Adelaide Weir Sukiennik

REACHING CHILDREN AT RISK
Multimedia Resources
*by Grady Sue L. Saxon, Margaret
Cothran, and Sarah Hoehn*

SERVING THE OLDER ADULT
A Guide to Library Programs and Information Sources
by Betty J. Turock

AN ALL NEW VOLUME IN THE TRADITION OF
NOTES FROM A DIFFERENT DRUMMER AND
MORE NOTES FROM A DIFFERENT DRUMMER

PORTRAYING PERSONS WITH DISABILITIES

AN ANNOTATED BIBLIOGRAPHY OF

FICTION

FOR CHILDREN AND TEENAGERS

THIRD EDITION

DEBRA E. J. ROBERTSON

R. R. BOWKER
A REED REFERENCE PUBLISHING COMPANY
New Providence, New Jersey

Published by R. R. Bowker, a Reed Reference Publishing Company
Copyright © 1992 by Reed Publishing (USA) Inc.
All rights reserved
Printed and bound in the United States of America

No part of this publication may be reproduced or transmitted
in any form or by any means, or stored in any information
storage and retrieval system, without prior written permission
of R. R. Bowker, 121 Chanlon Road, New Providence, New Jersey 07974.

Library of Congress Cataloging-in-Publication Data

Robertson, Debra.
    Portraying persons with disabilities : an annotated bibliography
of fiction for children and teenagers / Debra E. J. Robertson. — 3rd
ed.
        p.   cm. — (Serving special needs series)
    Includes indexes.
    ISBN 0–8352–3023–6
    1. Children's stories—Bibliography.   2. Young adult fiction—
Bibliography.   3. Handicapped—Juvenile literature—Bibliography.
4. Handicapped in literature—Bibliography.   I. Title.   II. Series.
    Z1037.9.R63   1992
    [PN1009.A1]
    016.80883'93520816'083—dc20   91–39177
                                                                        CIP

ISBN 0 - 8352 - 3023 - 6

9   780835   230230

For Mom,
who fought the school board
for accommodation;
Dad,
who mended unrestricted braces and crutches;
and my sons and their generation
of "special" classmates

CONTENTS

PREFACE

It takes 13 years for American children to complete their public school education. The first mainstreaming programs in response to the 1975 Education of All Handicapped Children Act (P.L. 94–142) are at least that old and many recent graduates do not recall a time when "special" kids were excluded from their schools. Many students who have some physical or mental impairment to cope with in their lives now also have opportunities for intellectual challenges, social interactions, and new expectations that segregation denied them.

I'm sure this change has occurred, not because of the citations gathered in this book from professional resources regarding the impact of P.L. 94–142. Those articles show that many jurisdictions have created the "least restrictive environment" intended by the law, while others have had to be taken to court to address the narrowest interpretation of "accommodation." I'm sure of the change because in April 1990, my second-grade son described this class discussion of *A Special Trade* by Sally Wittman.

> "...Then Mrs. McKinley asked, 'If a person has a handicap, does that mean that they are stupid?' And everyone said, 'No-o-o-o!' She asked, 'If a person has a handicap, does that mean that they can't have a job? 'No-o-o-o!' And after she asked more questions we answered like that, I said 'I should know all this, because my mom's handicapped!' "

> "What did Mrs. McKinley say then?" I asked.

> "She said, 'James's mother has trouble with walking so she uses braces and crutches.' And then she asked, 'If a person is handicapped, does that mean that they are a very special person?' and the class said, 'Y-e-e-e-s!' "

I know first-hand the pitfalls of trying to live up to the billing of "a very special person," but this glowing summary came after a week's involvement with Wittman's characters of Bartholomew and Nelly and their long-term relationship. I believe James's classmates will take away more than the label "special" to apply to the next—or first—person they meet who lives with a disability. They have a model of acceptance from their teacher and James; a positive, vicarious experience from the story; and insights for interpersonal interactions from the discussion. All these outcomes are due to a literature-based reading program spearheaded by the California Department of Education and available in our district through Houghton Mifflin's text editions of stories from various children's publishers.

Those schoolchildren also know where they can get more stories to read because Mrs. McKinley added that "If you go down to the public library across from the high school, you'll see Mrs. Robertson working. She can help you because her job is to be the librarian for our part of town." When children come in for more stories, I use *Notes from a Different Drummer* (R. R. Bowker, 1977) and *More Notes from a Different Drummer* (R. R. Bowker, 1984), both by Barbara H. Baskin and Karen H. Harris, to identify other titles that are as well done as *A Special Trade*.

The preface of *More Notes from a Different Drummer* (pp. x-xii) summarizes the history of these works and their usefulness in mainstreaming efforts as follows:

> *Notes from a Different Drummer*, the predecessor of this volume, was written to assist educators addressing the issue who needed access to juvenile fiction on impairment. This earlier book identified, described, and critiqued works written between 1940 and 1975 that contained disabled characters. *More Notes from a Different Drummer* extends that effort—examining juvenile titles written during the early critical years of the mainstreaming experiment and containing characters with impairments.
>
> . . .It is Chapter 3, An Annotated Guide to Juvenile Fiction Portraying the Disabled, 1976–1981, in which each book is individually assessed, that forms the heart of this work. . . .
>
> In *More Notes from a Different Drummer*, we have attempted to define and examine a field of inquiry, describe its contents, organize our findings, and provide both a qualitative and quantitative analysis.

The nonfiction complement to Baskin and Harris's analysis was *Accept Me As I Am* (R. R. Bowker, 1985). These three titles serve now as the foundation for Bowker's 1992 series Portraying Persons with Disabilities, which includes this volume on fiction and a companion book on nonfiction.

The annotated entries in Chapters 3 through 7 of this volume extend coverage of juvenile fiction from 1982 through 1991. They encourage teachers, reading resource staff, special education professionals, and librarians to take a closer look at juvenile fiction containing characters with physical, mental, and emotional impairments. The annotations identify specific impairments and plot themes related to featured characters who are disabled. Although we discourage the use of "labels" for people in our diversified society, standard terms for disabling conditions have been used to provide subject access as an important aspect of this bibliographic work.

This guide also employs two features of *Accept Me As I Am* to increase its usefulness. Annotations are grouped by broad disability categories and full annotations are not included for seriously flawed titles. This is intended to increase the series' utility in ready reference work. A discussion of evaluation guidelines and a bibliography summarizing recommended titles from the Different Drummer guides is included in Chapter 1 to simplify collection development using those tools.

Aside from these changes, the scope is still:

> . . .works of fiction addressed to a juvenile audience. Books written for a readership ranging from infants to adolescents are included. Picture books containing a story, therefore, are part of this study, as are junior novels. . . .
>
> Books written in foreign countries but distributed domestically have been considered within our purview if their U.S. copyright date is within the span of years encompassed by this work. Such novels influence attitudes here and are part of the American literary scene. Out-of-print books are likewise considered important since many can be found in children's collections where they may continue to affect readers for many years. (*More Notes. . .* p. xi)

First-person texts or "live-action" illustrations were considered fiction if the author credit was someone other than the narrator, or the photographs had been posed to illustrate a fabricated story rather than a true-life event. Folklore has been outside the range of these studies, acknowledging that "a comprehensive report and analysis of myths and legends involving disability would require a separate, extensive volume." (*Notes. . .* p. ix) Also,

> Those novels issuing from sectarian presses that expound a particular religious belief and should most properly be considered supplements to Sunday School curricula are outside our concern. . . . However, books that feature religious characters or settings as a natural aspect of the story are a part of this collection. (*More Notes. . .* p. xi)

Children's publishing became a fast-growing business in the 1980s and early 1990s, as the educational mainstreaming effort was producing its first graduates. On one hand, more marginal or poorly edited writing seems to stay in print, but young, first-time authors who have a different perspective on society may be getting their chance in this expanding market. Characters that are well drawn in fiction tend to have foibles as well as strengths, so we hope new fiction utilizes a broader sample of society's diversity. Not every impairment portrayed has to be critical to the action. Not every disability in a story should be a metaphor for the protagonist's development. Juvenile fiction will feel much closer to the truth when it's what disabled characters think, say, and do that makes them stand out, not what they can't do.

When I was in high school, a group of disgruntled beachgoers were trying to salvage the rainy Saturday. "Let's go anyway." "Let's play pool at Sue's." "How about the show?" When "I haven't been skating in ages!" got the most enthusiastic response, I suggested that someone could swing by my place on the way. "Why?" asked a couple of the planners.

"Well, it's so noisy at a skating rink, we can't really talk. And, it's not as much fun to watch as other things." They were so shocked, I could tell they'd expected me to say that I needed more money, or couldn't wear shoe skates without some socks.

I guess, this decade, I'm on the lookout for children's fiction that is as honest as those public school friends were when they said, "Oh I forgot! Not about you—about your braces!" "We're so used to your doing everything else with us. . . ." Like today's mainstreamed students, we'd learned how to share the "least restrictive environment" with a bit of "accommodation." I think we were on our way to Sue's when I told them about the time I tried my little sister's clamp-on skates—but had to lengthen my crutches three inches for the experiment.

ACKNOWLEDGMENTS

Special thanks to Dr. Margaret Mary Kimmel, Dr. Elizabeth Segal, Dr. Joan Brest Friedberg, and Dr. Blanche Woolls for keeping my mind and career lively with projects like this book's proposal when I had too little to do in Pittsburgh, Pensylvania. When I had too much to do in Fresno, California, wise encouragement from Zena Sutherland, Joanna Long, and Patti Campbell helped me complete this project anyway. Ladies, my deepest respect and appreciation to all of you. Additional thanks go to my ALSC associates and friends who share their opinions about books for children and teenagers through various review media, committees, and book discussions. I miss you Amy, April, Betty, Carla, Carol, Chris, Colleen, Connie, Grace, Jean, Jill, Marilyn, Megan, Pat, Peggy, Sara, Susan, Theresa, Vaun, and all.

Interlibrary loan and branch loan staff of the San Juaquin Valley Library System and members of the OCLC ILL component located needed books. Joe Hoyt, Mary Vega, Kristi Tillery, and the staff of Cedar Clinton Library were especially helpful.

Thanks, too, to the agencies and institutions that prepared me to research and form opinions regarding the literature discussed here: Ventura Unified School District, Ventura County Easter Seal Society, Chapman College, University of Southern California, University of Pittsburgh, National Information Center for Special Educational Materials, Los Angeles County Public Library System, Ventura County Public Library, and Fresno County Free Library.

Several plot summaries were outlined by staff members of the Fresno County Free Library: Karen Bosch Cobb, Julie Rothenflu, and Deb Jensen.

Publisher Marion Sader, managing editor Judy Balsamo, and the rest of the staff at R. R. Bowker have supported my efforts and converted many batches of manuscript into this reference tool, and I thank them.

Financial assistance from Kenneth and Audrey Jackson, James and Anabel Robertson, Marion Sachs, and Wilbur and Anne Rubottom literally allowed me to keep on my feet (in repaired prosthetics) during this project. My love and thanks to them and my son, James Kenneth Robertson, for generosity and patience. Lillie Banuelos, whose day care for Ian Jackson Robertson kept both my baby and my book growing in healthy stages, also was instrumental in this project's completion.

My greatest debt, though, is to Dr. Steven D. Robertson: indexer, bibliographer, research assistant, data entry person, proofreader, mail handler, and meal coordinator. Without his professional and personal contributions, this work would not exist. Steve, when people ask how many children we have after 12 years together, let's respond honestly, "Two boys, a dissertation, and an annotated bibliography."

ABBREVIATIONS

REVIEW SOURCES

BCCB	Bulletin for the Center for Children's Books	HB	Horn Book Magazine
BF	Bookfinder	KR	Kirkus Reviews
BL	Booklist	SLJ	School Library Journal

DATES

Ja	January	Sp	Spring
F	February	Su	Summer
Mr	March	MS	Midsummer
Ap	April	Fl	Fall
My	May	W	Winter
Je	June	MW	Midwinter
Jl	July		
Ag	August		
S	September		
O	October		
N	November		
D	December		

1

NOTES FROM A DIFFERENT DRUMMER, REPRISE

In 1975, the passage of Public Law 94-142 (Education of All Handicapped Children Act) ensured a free and appropriate public education, in the "least restrictive environment" possible, for children in the United States. As of 1978, it was a national requirement that public schools be opened to students whose physical or mental disabilities had previously excluded or segregated them from "mainstream" educational settings or opportunities. Although implementation of this law is uneven and the courts have had to settle disputes regarding its interpretation, the intent to accommodate disabled students beside their nondisabled peers has become a reality for many in the 1980s. This effort is referred to as "mainstreaming in education," and early contributors to its success were Barbara H. Baskin and Karen H. Harris, authors of *Notes from a Different Drummer: A Guide to Juvenile Fiction Portraying the Handicapped* (R. R. Bowker, 1977).

Published in 1977, *Notes from a Different Drummer* outlined the historic roles society had cast for disabled people. The tremendous changes in Western attitudes during this century together with civil rights activism in the United States set the scene for P.L. 94-142 and its focus on schools. Schools naturally emphasize books as learning aids, so Baskin and Harris prepared an annotated bibliography of juvenile fiction titles written between 1940 and 1975 that portrayed characters with physical and emotional impairments.

Many of those portrayals were stereotyped or supported traditional social responses to disability. Pitfalls included childlike treatment, romanticization, spread or association of one limitation with another, differential patterns of avoidance, and use of disability in humorous or figurative expressions. Literary treatment of disability often used artificial scenarios in which a disabled

1

person overcame a significant ailment in no time at all through the agency of faith or pious suffering or death that subsequently enlightened all who had known them. Because the social patterns of the era did not offer many outlets for disabled individuals, readers rarely had personal experiences to balance the negative or stilted portrayals they absorbed through fictional characterizations in their books.

Baskin and Harris defined these hazards, identified titles that included portrayals of various disabilities, summarized the plots, analyzed the literary qualities of the works, and demonstrated each title's usefulness in building a fair or balanced perception of exceptional people.

At that time, terminology was in flux: the word "handicapped" was contained in the text of the law but became eclipsed by the favored term "disabled." Since then, "special," "exceptional," "challenged," and other coined adjectives that did not have the negative connotation of "crippled" or "handicapped" have been in vogue. In an effort to model sensitivity to the harmful social pattern of defining a person by disability or limitations, Baskin and Harris arranged their work in alphabetical order by author, with index terms for the type of physical or emotional impairment portrayed. In a 1984 publication, they extended the coverage through 1981 with *More Notes from a Different Drummer: A Guide to Juvenile Fiction Portraying the Disabled* (R. R. Bowker). An increase in the number of favorable reviews from the late 1970s indicates that publishing houses and children's book reviewers were becoming sensitive to flaws that Baskin and Harris had identified and that the houses and the reviewers were seeking a broader spectrum of human diversity in their mainstream literature for children.

During the creation of a bibliography of nonfiction titles that would complement the Baskin and Harris books, another organization scheme evolved. In *Accept Me as I Am: Best Books of Juvenile Nonfiction on Impairments and Disabilities* (R. R. Bowker, 1985), Joan Friedberg, Adelaide Sukiennik, and June Mullins made the distinction of "using labels to serve rather than demean." Carefully phrased reviews provide a valuable model for shifting attitudes about individuals whose lives are affected by various impairments and disabilities. However, indexing becomes cumbersome and subject access is awkward when concise terms are avoided because of their latent linguistic power as labels. *Accept Me as I Am* was arranged by classifications grouped as physical problems, sensory problems, cognitive and behavior problems, and multiple/severe and various disabilities. The new work *Portraying Persons with Disabilities* continues to use those classifications.

The following summary of the most highly recommended titles from *Notes . . . and More Notes . . .* by Baskin and Harris has been organized in the same manner.

When more than one type of disability is portrayed in a story, whether a main character's problem or incorporated in a supporting role, the title is listed under each appropriate category of disability. Baskin and Harris consciously resisted ranking the books they covered or arranging titles by physical or mental disabilities. It is difficult to compromise with sound precedent, but two changes in children's publishing and library services for children have led to this restructured, retrospective summary of *Notes . . .* and *More Notes. . . .*

First, the alarming frequency with which titles are going out of print in the 1990s follows patterns dictated by new tax laws. Publishers no longer can afford to store inventories of backlisted titles, and reprinting orders are small, so even new children's books go out of print quickly. This summary of the best from *Notes . . .* and *More Notes . . .* offers selectors a manageable tool for replacement when titles come back into print. This list can also help to refer children to "good books" in a collection, but attentive and even assertive measures have to be taken to see that a copy in decent condition is still available. My associates in acquisitions and veteran children's booksellers tell me that publishers may not know there is a market for a particular title until it is backordered by the hundreds.

The second development in library education and children's literature that affects this volume is the lack of trained specialists in juvenile and young adult services. A trend of cutting positions for children's librarians and sparse response to recruitment for positions that do exist has caused concern in the Association for Library Services to Children. Professionals who do have training in youth services are often forced into a "generalist" or administrative assignment. This limits their availability to caregivers, parents, teachers, and children who would most benefit from a librarian's knowledge of the literature. Major bibliographic tools are not always user friendly, and the subject terms used in card or computerized public catalogs do not always identify fictional works by the disability portrayed. This booklist is organized for library staff, counselors, parents, and educators who want to provide reader's guidance to high-quality juvenile literature that portrays characters who have particular disabilities and impairments.

Anyone who wants to build skills in literary criticism or who seeks a model for perceptive comparisons of portrayals of impairments and disabilities would do well to study the less positive or negative reviews included in *Notes . . .* and *More Notes . . . .* Baskin and Harris provided insightful and erudite analysis of juvenile fiction published between 1940 and 1981. They encouraged readers to consider the flaws and strengths of each title before selecting it for a particular collection or reader. That is an ideal use for those bibliographies, and this retrospective booklist is intended to redirect selectors to excellent (*) or positive choices summarized and analyzed in full in *Notes . . .* (1977) and *More Notes . . .* (1984). Each entry in the list is followed by a page number where the full annotation may be found. Numbers preceded by an N indicate a page in *Notes . . .*; numbers preceded by an M indicate a page in *More Notes. . . .*

BOOKS DEALING WITH PHYSICAL PROBLEMS

HEALTH PROBLEMS

* Annixter, Jane, and Paul Annixter. Pseud. J.L. Comfort. *The Runner.* Holiday, 1956. 220pp. Reading Level: Grades 5–8.
  Disability: Orthopedic impairment; also General health problems. N109
* Carpelan, Bo. *Bow Island.* Trans. by Sheila LaFarge. Delacorte, 1968. 140pp. Reading Level: Grades 7–9.
  Disability: Mental retardation; also General health problems. N140
  Corbin, William. *The Golden Mare.* Illus. by Pers Crowell. Coward, 1955. 122pp. Reading Level: Grades 4–6.
  Disability: General health problems. N152
* Corcoran, Barbara. *A Dance to Still Music.* Illus. by Charles Robinson. Atheneum, 1974. 192pp. Reading Level: Grades 7–9.
  Disability: Hearing impairment; also Emotional disturbances; General health problems. N153
* Forman, James. *The Shield of Achilles.* Farrar, 1966. 211pp. Reading Level: Grades 10–12.
  Disability: Orthopedic impairment; also General health problems. N181
* Hamilton, Virginia. *The Planet of Junior Brown.* Macmillan, 1971. 210pp. Reading Level: Grades 8–10.
  Disability: Emotional disturbances; also General health problems. N198
  Hodges, C. Walter. *The Namesake.* Illus. by author. Coward, 1964. 269pp. Reading Level: Grades 7–9.
  Disability: Orthopedic disabilities; also Emotional disturbances; General health problems. N207
  Hunter, Edith Fisher. *Sue Ellen.* Illus. by Bea Holmes. Houghton, 1969. 170pp. Reading Level: Grades 4–6.
  Disability: Mental retardation; also General health problems. N215
* Lee, Virginia. *The Magic Moth.* Illus. by Richard Cuffari. Seabury, 1972. 64pp. Reading Level: Grades 4–6.
  Disability: General health problems. N232
* Little, Jean. *Mine for Keeps.* Little, Brown, 1962. 186pp. Reading Level: Grades 4–6.
  Disability: Neurological disabilities; General health problems. N238
  Ormsby, Virginia. *Mountain Magic for Rosy.* Illus. by Paul E. Kennedy. Crown, 1969. 137pp. Reading Level: Grades 4–6.
  Disability: General health problems. N262

* Excellent selection.

* Rinaldo, C. L. *Dark Dreams*. Harper, 1974. 154pp. Reading Level: Grades 8–10.
Disability: Mental retardation; also General health problems. N282

Rosevear, Marjorie. *The Secret Cowboy*. Messner, 1955. 155pp. Reading Level: Grades 4–6.
Disability: General health problems. N286

* Tate, Joan. *Ben and Annie*. Illus. by Judith Gwyn Brown. Doubleday, 1974. 79pp. Reading Level: Grades 5–8.
Disability: General health problems. N313

Thrasher, Crystal. *The Dark Didn't Catch Me*. Atheneum, 1975. 182pp. Reading Level: Grades 5–8.
Disability: Cosmetic impairment; General health problems; also Mental retardation. N322

Winthrop, Elizabeth. *A Little Demonstration of Affection*. Harper & Row, 1975. 152pp. Reading Level: Grades 7–9.
Disability: General health problems. N345

* Yolen, Jane. *The Transfigured Hart*. Illus. by Donna Diamond. Crowell, 1975. 86pp. Reading Level: Grades 5–8.
Disability: General health problems. N358

ORTHOPEDIC/NEUROLOGICAL DISABILITIES

Adler, Carole S. *Down by the River*. Coward, 1981. 206pp. Reading Level: Grades 8–10.
Disability: Neurological disabilities. M57

* Alcock, Gudrun. *Turn the Next Corner*. Lothrop, Lee & Shepard, 1969. 160pp. Reading Level: Grades 4–6.
Disability: Orthopedic impairment. N103

Alexander, Lloyd. *Westmark*. Dutton, 1981. 184pp. Reading Level: Grades 5–8.
Disability: Orthopedic impairment; also Hearing impairment; Speech & language impairment. M60

* Annixter, Jane, and Paul Annixter. Pseud. J.L. Comfort. *The Runner*. Holiday, 1956. 220pp. Reading Level: Grades 5–8.
Disability: Orthopedic impairment; also General health problems. N109

* Armer, Alberta. *Screwball*. Illus. by W.T. Mars. World, 1963. 202pp. Reading Level: Grades 4–6.
Disability: Orthopedic impairment. N110

* Barber, Elsie Oakes. *The Trembling Years*. Macmillan, 1949. 237pp. Reading Level: Grades 8–10.
Disability: Orthopedic impairment. N115

Berry, Barbara. *Just Don't Bug Me*. Illus. by Joe E. DeVelasco. Follett, 1970. 125pp. Reading Level: Grades 7–9.
Disability: Orthopedic impairment. N119

---

* Excellent selection.

* Blume, Judy. *Deenie.* Bradbury, 1973. 159pp. Reading Level: Grades 7–9.
  Disability: Orthopedic impairment. N121

Bodker, Cecil. *Silas and Ben-Godik.* Trans. by Sheila La Farge. Delacorte, 1978.
191pp. Reading Level: Grades 4–6.
Disability: Orthopedic impairment; Visual impairment. M90

* Bodker, Cecil. *Silas and the Black Mare.* Trans. by Sheila La Farge. Delacorte, 1978.
152pp. Reading Level: Grades 4–6.
Disability: Orthopedic impairment; Visual impairment. M91

Bodker, Cecil. *Silas and the Runaway Coach.* Trans. by Sheila La Farge. Delacorte,
1978. 245pp. Reading Level: Grades 4–6.
Disability: Orthopedic impairment. M92

Brancato, Robin. *Winning.* Knopf, 1977. 211pp. Reading Level: Grades 8–10.
Disability: Neurological disability; Orthopedic impairment. M98

Branscum, Robbie. *The Ugliest Boy.* Illus. by Michael Eagle. Lothrop, Lee & Shepard, 1978. 126pp. Reading Level: Grades 5–8.
Disability: Orthopedic impairment. M102

Bykov, Vasil. *Pack of Wolves.* Trans. by Lynn Solotaroff. Crowell, 1981. 179pp.
Reading Level: Grades 8–10.
Disability: Orthopedic impairment. M126

Christopher, Matt. *Sink It, Rusty.* Illus. by Foster Caddell. Little, Brown, 1963.
138pp. Reading Level: Grades 4–6.
Disability: Orthopedic impairment. N147

Churchill, David. *It, Us and the Others.* Harper & Row, 1978. 119pp. Reading Level:
Grades 5–8.
Disability: Orthopedic impairment. M140

Coleman, Hila. *Accident.* Morrow, 1980. 154pp. Reading Level: Grades 7–9.
Disability: Neurological disabilities; Orthopedic impairment. M144

* Corcoran, Barbara. *Me and You and a Dog Named Blue.* Atheneum, 1979. 179pp.
Reading Level: Grades 7–9.
Disability: Orthopedic impairment. M153

* Corcoran, Barbara. *A Row of Tigers.* Atheneum, 1969. 165pp. Reading Level: Grades
7–9.
Disability: Orthopedic impairment. N155

Corcoran, Barbara. *Sasha, My Friend.* Illus. by Richard L. Shell. Atheneum, 1972.
203pp. Reading Level: Grades 7–9.
Disability: Orthopedic impairment; Neurological disabilities. N156

Courlander, Harold. *The Son of the Leopard.* Illus. by Rocco Negri. Crown, 1974.
55pp. Reading Level: Grades 4–6.
Disability: Orthopedic impairment; Visual impairment. N157

Cummings, Betty Sue. *Hew Against the Grain.* Atheneum, 1977. 174pp. Reading
Level: Grades 7–9.
Disability: Emotional disturbances; Neurological disabilities; Orthopedic impair-
ment. M158

---

* Excellent selection.

* Curry, Jane Louise. *The Bassumtyte Treasure.* Atheneum, 1978. 130pp. Reading
Level: Grades 4–6.
Disability: Orthopedic impairment; Visual impairment. M166

Dank, Milton. *Red Flight Two.* Delacorte, 1981. 185pp. Reading Level: Grades
8–10.
Disability: Emotional disturbances; also Orthopedic impairment. M172

de Angeli, Marguerite. *The Door in the Wall.* Illus. by author. Doubleday, 1949.
121pp. Reading Level: Grades 4–6.
Disability: Orthopedic impairment. N163

DeJong, Meindert. *The Wheel on the School.* Harper & Row, 1954. Reading Level:
Grades 4–6.
Disability: Orthopedic impairment. N165

* DePaola, Tomie. *Now One Foot, Now the Other.* Illus. by author. Putnam, 1981. unp.
Reading Level: Grades K–3.
Disability: Neurological impairment. M174

Duncan, Lois. *Ransom.* Doubleday, 1966. 188pp. Reading Level: Grades 7–9.
Disability: Orthopedic impairment. N169

Dyer, Thomas A. *A Way of His Own.* Houghton, 1981. 154pp. Reading Level: Grades
4–6.
Disability: Orthopedic impairment. M189

* Fanshawe, Elizabeth. *Rachel.* Illus. by Michael Charlton. Bradbury, 1975. unpaged.
Reading Level: Grades K–3.
Disability: Orthopedic impairment. N176

Fassler, Joan. *Howie Helps Himself.* Illus. by Joe Lasker. Whitman, 1975. unpaged.
Reading Level: Grades K–3.
Disability: Orthopedic impairment. N177

Fitzgerald, John D. *The Great Brain.* Illus. by Mercer Mayer. Dial, 1967. 175pp.
Reading Level: Grades 5–8.
Disability: Orthopedic impairment. N179

Forbes, Esther. *Johnny Tremain.* Illus. by Lynd Ward. Houghton, 1943. 256pp.
Reading Level: Grades 5–8.
Disability: Orthopedic impairment; also Cosmetic impairments N180

Forman, James. *The Shield of Achilles.* New York: Farrar, 1966. 211pp. Reading
Level: Grades 10–12.
Disability: Orthopedic impairment; also General health problems. N181

Friermood, Elisabeth Hamilton. *The Luck of Daphne Tolliver.* Doubleday, 1961.
239pp. Reading Level: Grades 7–9.
Disability: Orthopedic impairment. N183

Garfield, Leon. *Black Jack.* Illus. by Anthony Maitland. Pantheon, 1968. 243pp.
Reading Level: Grades 7–9.
Disability: Emotional disturbances; also Orthopedic impairment. N186

* Excellent selection.

Garfield, Leon. *Footsteps.* Delacorte, 1980. 196pp. Reading Level: Grades 5–8.
Disability: Orthopedic impairment. M201

Garfield, Leon. *Smith.* Illus. by Anthony Maitland. Pantheon, 1967. 218pp. Reading Level: Grades 7–9.
Disability: Orthopedic impairment; also Visual impairment. N187

Garst, Shannon. *Red Eagle.* Illus. by Hubert Buel. Hastings, 1959. 145pp. Reading Level: Grades 4–6.
Disability: Orthopedic impairment. N189

Girion, Barbara. *A Handful of Stars.* Scribner, 1981. 179pp. Reading Level: Grades 7–9.
Disability: Neurological disabilities. M214

Green, Phyllis. *Walkie-Talkie.* Addison Wesley, 1978. 96pp. Reading Level: Grades 4–6.
Disability: Emotional disturbances; Neurological disabilities. M222

Griese, Arnold A. *At the Mouth of the Luckiest River.* Illus. by Glo Coalson. Crowell, 1969. 65pp. Reading Level: Grades K–4.
Disability: Orthopedic impairment. N193

Griffiths, Helen. *The Mysterious Appearance of Agnes.* Also published as *Witch Fear.* Illus. by Victor G. Ambrus. Holiday, 1975. 160pp. Reading Level: Grades 7–9.
Disability: Emotional disturbances; also Neurological disabilities. N194

Harnishfeger, Lloyd. *Prisoner of the Mound Builders.* Illus. by George Overlie. Lerner, 1973. 141pp. Reading Level: Grades 5–8.
Disability: Orthopedic impairment. N203

Hermes, Patricia. *What If They Knew?* Harcourt, 1980. 121pp. Reading Level: Grades 4–6.
Disability: Neurological disabilities. M239

Hodges, C. Walter. *The Namesake.* Illus. by author. Coward, 1964. 269pp. Reading Level: Grades 7–9.
Disability: Orthopedic impairment; also Emotional disturbances; General health problems. N207

Hunt, Irene. *No Promises in the Wind.* Follett, 1970. 247pp. Reading Level: Grades 8–10.
Disability: Orthopedic impairment. N213

* Hunter, Mollie. *The Stronghold.* Harper & Row, 1974. 259pp. Reading Level: Grades 8–10.
Disability: Orthopedic impairment. N216

Jewett, Eleanore M. *The Hidden Treasure of Glaston.* Illus. by Frederick T. Chapman. Viking, 1946. 307pp. Reading Level: Grades 7–9.
Disability: Orthopedic impairment; Emotional disturbances. N218

Jones, Adrienne. *The Beckoner.* Harper & Row, 1980. 243pp. Reading Level: Grades 10–12.
Disability: Emotional disturbances; Orthopedic impairment. M257

* Excellent selection.

Judd, Denis. *Return to Treasure Island.* St. Martin's, 1978. 209pp. Reading Level: Grades 8–10.
Disability: Orthopedic impairment; also Speech and language impairments. M261

Kerr, M.E. (pseud for Meaker, Marijane) *Little Little.* Harper & Row, 1981. 183pp. Reading Level: Grades 8–10.
Disability: Orthopedic impairment. M268

Kingman, Lee. *Head Over Wheels.* Houghton, 1978. 186pp. Reading Level: Grades 8–10.
Disability: Neurological disabilities. M271

Klein, Norma. *A Honey of a Chimp.* Pantheon, 1980. 152pp. Reading Level: Grades 4–6.
Disability: Orthopedic impairment. M273

Konigsburg, Elaine L. *Father's Arcane Daughter.* Atheneum, 1976. 118pp. Reading Level: Grades 5–8.
Disability: Neurological disabilities; Hearing impairment. M275

Lasker, Joe. *He's My Brother.* Illus. by author. Whitman, 1974. 40pp. Reading Level: Grades K–3.
Disability: Neurological disabilities. N229

Lasker, Joe. *Nick Joins In.* Illus. by author. Whitman, 1980. unp. Reading Level: Grades K–3.
Disability: Orthopedic impairment; also Learning disabilities. M277

Lawrence, Mildred. *The Touchmark.* Illus. by Diane Hollinger. Harcourt, 1975. 186pp. Reading Level: Grades 5–8.
Disability: Orthopedic impairment. N230

* Lee, Mildred. *The Skating Rink.* Seabury, 1969. 126pp. Reading Level: Grades 8–10.
Disability: Speech and language impairments; also Orthopedic impairment. N231

Lee, Robert C. *It's a Mile from Here to Glory.* Little, Brown, 1972. 150pp. Reading Level: Grades 5–8.
Disability: Orthopedic impairment; Cosmetic impairment. N232

L'Engle, Madeline. *Camilla Dickinson.* Also published as *Camilla.* Crowell, 1965. 282pp. Reading Level: Grades 10–12.
Disability: Orthopedic impairment. N233

Levenkron, Steven. *The Best Little Girl in the World.* Contemporary, 1978. 196pp. Reading Level: Grades 8–10.
Disability: Emotional disturbances; Orthopedic impairment. M283

* Little, Jean. *Mine for Keeps.* Little, Brown, 1962. 186pp. Reading Level: Grades 4–6.
Disability: Neurological disabilities; General health problems. N238

Little, Jean. *Spring Begins in March.* Illus. by Lewis Parker. Little, Brown, 1966. 156pp. Reading Level: Grades 4–6.
Disability: Neurological disabilities. N239

Lowry, Lois. *Autumn Street.* Houghton, 1980. 188pp. Reading Level: Grades 5–8.
Disability: Neurological disabilities; Emotional disturbances; Orthopedic impairment. M298

---

* Excellent selection.

MacKellar, William. *The Soccer Orphans.* Dodd, Mead, 1979. 157pp. Reading Level: Grades 5–8.
Disability: Orthopedic impairment; Hearing impairment. M305

McHargue, Georgess. *The Horseman's Word.* Delacorte, 1981. 259pp. Reading Level: Grades 7–9.
Disability: Neurological disabilities. M302

Mohr, Nicholasa. *In Nueva York.* Dial, 1977. 192pp. Reading Level: Grades 10–12.
Disability: Orthopedic impairment; Special health problems. M324

Myers, Walter Dean. *The Legend of Tarik.* Viking, 1981. 185pp. Reading Level: Grades 7–9.
Disability: Orthopedic impairment; Visual impairment; Emotional disturbances. M329

Norton, Andre. *Scarface.* Illus. by Lorence Bjorklund. Harcourt, 1948. 263pp. Reading Level: Grades 7–9.
Disability: Cosmetic impairment; also Orthopedic impairment. N256

Nourse, Alan B. *The Bladerunner.* McKay, 1974. 245pp. Reading Level: Grades 10–12.
Disability: Orthopedic impairment. N257

O'Dell, Scott. *The Captive.* Houghton, 1979. 211pp. Reading Level: Grades 7–9.
Disability: Orthopedic impairment. M338

* O'Dell, Scott. *Sing Down the Moon.* Houghton, 1970. 137pp. Reading Level: Grades 5–8.
Disability: Orthopedic impairment. N259

Oppenheimer, Joan. *On the Outside Looking In.* Scholastic, 1973. 191pp. Reading Level: Grades 7–9.
Disability: Orthopedic impairment. N261

Ottley, Reginald. *The Bates Family.* Harcourt, 1969. 175pp. Reading Level: Grades 5–8.
Disability: Orthopedic impairment. N262

Paterson, Katherine. *Of Nightingales That Weep.* Illus. by Haru Wells. Crowell, 1974. 170pp. Reading Level: Grades 8–10.
Disability: Orthopedic impairment. N266

Peyton, K. M. *Flambards.* Illus. by Victor G. Ambrus. World, 1967. 206pp. Reading Level: Grades 8–10.
Disability: Orthopedic impairment; also Visual impairment. N269

* Peyton, K. M. *The Right-Hand Man.* Illus. by Victor G. Ambrus. Oxford Univ. Pr., 1977. 218pp. Reading Level: Grades 8–10.
Disability: Orthopedic impairment; also Special health problems. M353

Phelan, Terry Wolfe. *The S. S. Valentine.* Illus. by Judy Glasser. Four Winds, 1979. 40pp. Reading Level: Grades 4–6.
Disability: Orthopedic impairment. M357

Phipson, Joan. *Birkin.* Illus. by Margaret Horder. Harcourt, 1965. 224pp. Reading Level: Grades 7–9.
Disability: Orthopedic impairment. N270

---

* Excellent selection.

Phipson, Joan. *A Tide Flowing.* Atheneum, 1981. 156pp. Reading Level: Grades 7–9.
Disability: Neurological disabilities. M358

Pieper, Elizabeth. *A School for Tommy.* Illus. by Mina G. McLean. Child's World, 1979. 32pp. Reading Level: Grades K–3.
Disability: Orthopedic impairment. M362

* Platt, Kin. *The Boy Who Could Make Himself Disappear.* Chilton, 1968. 216pp. Reading Level: Grades 8–10.
Disability: Emotional disturbances; Speech and language impairments; also Orthopedic impairment. N271

Pollowitz, Melinda. *Cinnamon Cane.* Harper & Row, 1977. 154pp. Reading Level: Grades 5–8.
Disability: Neurological disabilities. M367

Potter, Bronson. *Antonio.* Illus. by Ann Grifalconi. Atheneum, 1968. 41pp. Reading Level: Grades 4–6.
Disability: Orthopedic impairment. N273

Rabe, Bernice. *The Balancing Girl.* Illus. by Lillian Hoban. Dutton, 1981. unp. Reading Level: Grades K–3.
Disability: Orthopedic impairment. M371

Raskin, Ellen. *The Westing Game.* Dutton, 1978. 185pp. Reading Level: Grades 7–9.
Disability: Neurological disabilities. M373

Reynolds, Pamela. *A Different Kind of Sister.* Lothrop, Lee, & Shepard, 1968. 192pp. Reading Level: Grades 7–9.
Disability: Mental retardation; also Cosmetic impairment; Orthopedic impairment. N279

Richard, Adrienne. *Wings.* Little, Brown, 1974. 209pp. Reading Level: Grades 7–9.
Disability: Orthopedic impairment. N281

* Rinkoff, Barbara. *The Watchers.* Knopf, 1972. 130pp. Reading Level: Grades 5–8.
Disability: Neurological disabilities. N283

Robertson, Keith. *Ice to India.* Illus. by Jack Weaver. Viking, 1955. 224pp. Reading Level: Grades 7–9.
Disability: Orthopedic impairment; Cosmetic impairment. N284

Rodowsky, Colby. *P.S. Write Soon.* Franklin Watts, 1978. 149pp. Reading Level: Grades 4–6.
Disability: Orthopedic impairment. M384

* Sachs, Elizabeth-Ann. *Just Like Always.* Atheneum, 1981. 160pp. Reading Level: Grades 5–8.
Disability: Orthopedic impairment. M395

Salassi, Otto L. *On the Ropes.* Greenwillow, 1981. 248pp. Reading Level: Grades 7–9.
Disability: Orthopedic impairment; also Cosmetic impairment. M396

Savitz, Harriet May. *On the Move.* Day, 1973. 142pp. Reading Level: Grades 7–9.
Disability: Orthopedic impairment. N292

Sherburne, Zoa. *Why Have the Birds Stopped Singing?* Morrow, 1974. 189pp. Reading Level: Grades 7–9.
Disability: Neurological disabilities. N294

* Excellent selection.

Shotwell, Louisa R. *Roosevelt Grady.* Illus. by Peter Burchard. World, 1963. 151pp. Reading Level: Grades 4–6.
Disability: Orthopedic impairment. N295

Sivers, Brenda. *The Snailman.* Illus. by Shirley Hughes. Little, Brown, 1978. 118pp. Reading Level: Grades 4–6.
Disability: Orthopedic impairment; Cosmetic impairment; also Hearing impairment. M413

* Slepian, Jan. *The Alfred Summer.* Macmillan, 1980. 119pp. Reading Level: Grades 7–9.
Disability: Neurological disabilities; Mental retardation; Speech & language impairments. M416

* Slepian, Jan. *Lester's Turn.* Macmillan, 1981. 139pp. Reading Level: Grades 7–9.
Disability: Neurological disabilities; Mental retardation; Orthopedic impairment. M418

Small, Mary. *And Alice Did the Walking.* Photog. by Lionel Jensen. Oxford Univ. Pr., 1978. unp. Reading Level: Grades 4–6.
Disability: Orthopedic impairment. M420

* Smith, Doris Buchanan. *Tough Chauncey.* Illus. by Michael Engle. Morrow, 1974. 222pp. Reading Level: Grades 5–8.
Disability: Orthopedic impairment. N298

Smith, Vian. *Tall and Proud.* Illus. by Don Stivers. Doubleday, 1966. 181pp. Reading Level: Grades 5–8.
Disability: Orthopedic impairment. N300

Smucker, Barbara. *Runaway to Freedom.* Illus. by Charles Lilly. Harper & Row, 1977. 152pp. Reading Level: Grades 5–8.
Disability: Orthopedic impairment. M423

* Southall, Ivan. *Let the Balloon Go.* Illus. by Ian Ribbins. St. Martin's, 1969. 142pp. Reading Level: Grades 4–6.
Disability: Neurological disabilities. N303

* Stein, Sara Bonnet. *About Handicaps: An Open Family Book for Parents and Children Together.* Photog. by Dick Frank. 47pp. Walker, 1974. Reading Level: Grades K–3 (and Adults).
Disability: Neurological disabilities; also Orthopedic impairment. N306

* Stewart, Agnes Charlotte. *Elizabeth's Tower.* Phillips, 1972. 222pp. Reading Level: Grades 5–8.
Disability: Orthopedic impairment. N307

Sutcliff, Rosemary. *Blood Feud.* Dutton, 1976, 144pp. Reading Level: Grades 7–9.
Disability: Orthopedic impairment; also Visual impairment; Hearing impairment. M438

* Sutcliff, Rosemary. *Warrior Scarlet.* Walck, 1958. 207pp. Reading Level: Grades 7–9.
Disability: Orthopedic impairment; also Visual impairment. N311

---

* Excellent selection.

* Sutcliff, Rosemary. *The Witch's Brat.* Walck, 1970. 143pp. Reading Level: Grades 4–6.
  Disability: Orthopedic impairment. N312
Tavo, Gus. *Ride the Pale Stallion.* Knopf, 1968. 180pp. Reading Level: Grades 5–8.
  Disability: Orthopedic impairment. N315
Tolan, Stephanie S. *Grandpa—And Me.* Scribner, 1978. 120pp. Reading Level: Grades 4–6.
  Disability: Neurological disabilities; also Hearing impairment. M443
Trevor, Meriol. *The Rose Round.* Dutton, 1964. 176pp. Reading Level: Grades 7–10.
  Disability: Orthopedic impairment. N325
Uchida, Yoshiko. *A Jar of Dreams.* Atheneum, 1981. 131pp. Reading Level: Kindergarden–Grade 3.
  Disability: Orthopedic impairment. M447
Uchida, Yoshiko. *Journey Home.* Illus. by Charles Robinson. Atheneum, 1978. 131pp. Reading Level: Grades 4–6.
  Disability: Orthopedic impairment. M448
Underhill, Ruth M. *Antelope Singer.* Illus. by Ursula Loering. Coward, 1961. 280pp. Reading Level: Grades 4–6.
  Disability: Orthopedic impairment. N327
* Walter, Mildred Pitts. *Ty's One-man Band.* Illus. by Margot Tomes. Four Winds, 1980. unp. Reading Level: Grades K–3.
  Disability: Orthopedic impairment. M456
Weik, Mary Hays. *The Jazz Man.* Illus. by Ann Grifalconi. Atheneum, 1966. 42pp. Reading Level: Grades 4–6.
  Disability: Orthopedic impairment; also Mental retardation. N337
Weiman, Eiveen. *Which Way Courage.* Atheneum, 1981. 132pp. Reading Level: Grades 7–9.
  Disability: Orthopedic impairment. M458
Whitney, Phyllis A. *Mystery of the Haunted Pool.* Illus. by H. Tom Hall. Westminster, 1960. 223pp. Reading Level: Grades 5–8.
  Disability: Orthopedic impairment. N339
Whitney, Phyllis A. *Nobody Likes Trina.* Westminster, 1972. 187pp. Reading Level: Grades 7–9.
  Disability: Orthopedic impairment. N340
Witter, Evelyn. *Claw Foot.* Illus. by Sandra Heinen. Lerner, 1976. 66pp. Reading Level: Grades 4–6.
  Disability: Orthopedic impairment. M468
* Wittman, Sally. *A Special Trade.* Illus. by Karen Gundersheimer. Harper & Row, 1978. unp. Reading Level: Grades K–3.
  Disability: Orthopedic impairment. M469
Yolen, Jane. *Dream Weaver.* Illus. by Michael Hague. Collins, 1979. 80pp. Reading Level: Grades 4–6.
  Disability: Visual impairment; Orthopedic impairment. M475

* Excellent selection.

BOOKS DEALING WITH SENSORY PROBLEMS

HEARING IMPAIRMENTS

Alexander, Lloyd. *Westmark*. Dutton, 1981. 184pp. Reading Level: Grades 5–8.
Disability: Orthopedic impairment; also Hearing impairment, Speech and language impairment. M60

Allan, Mabel Esther. *Ship of Danger*. Abelard-Schuman, 1974. 153pp. Reading Level: Grades 7–9.
Disability: Hearing impairment. N105

Arthur, Catherine. *My Sister's Silent World*. Photog. by Nathan Talbot. Children's Pr., 1979. 31pp. Reading Level: Grades K–3.
Disability: Hearing impairment. M68

* Baker, Margaret J. *The Sand Bird*. Illus. by Floyd Garet. Nelson, 1973. 158pp. Reading Level: Grades 4–6.
Disability: Hearing impairment. N114

Bunting, Eve. *The Waiting Game*. Lippincott, 1981. 56pp. Reading Level: Grades 5–8.
Disability: Hearing impairment. M125

* Corcoran, Barbara. *A Dance to Still Music*. Illus. by Charles Robinson. Atheneum, 1974. 192pp. Reading Level: Grades 7–9.
Disability: Hearing impairment; also Emotional disturbances; General health problems. N153

Christopher, Matt. *Football Fugitive*. Illus. by Larry Johnson. Little, Brown, 1976. 119pp. Reading Level: Grades 4–6.
Disability: Hearing impairment. M138

Cowley, Joy. *The Silent One*. Illus. by Hermann Greissle. Knopf, 1981. 136pp. Reading Level: Grades 4–6.
Disability: Hearing impairment; Speech and language impairments; Special health problems. M157

DeJong, Meindert. *Journey from Peppermint Street*. Harper & Row, 1968. 242pp. Reading Level: Grades 4–6.
Disability: Hearing impairment; Speech and language impairments. N164

Fine, Anne. *The Summer-House Loon*. Crowell, 1978. 127pp. Reading Level: Grades 7–9.
Disability: Visual impairment; also Hearing impairment. M195

Garner, Alan. *The Stone Book*. Illus. by Michael Foreman. World, 1976. 60pp. Reading Level: Grades 4–6.
Disability: Hearing impairment. M207

Hanlon, Emily. *The Swing*. Bradbury, 1979. 209pp. Reading Level: Grades 4–6.
Disability: Hearing impairment. M232

Harris, Rosemary. *The Bright and Morning Star*. Macmillan, 1972. 254pp. Reading Level: Grades 7–9.
Disability: Hearing impairment. N204

* Excellent selection.

Hightower, Florence. *Dreamworld Castle*. Houghton, 1978. 214pp. Reading Level: Grades 5–8.
Disability: Special health problems; also Hearing impairment. M241

Kerr, M.E. (pseud. for Meaker, Marijane) *Gentlehands*. Harper & Row, 1978. 183pp. Reading Level: Grades 8–10.
Disability: Hearing impairment. M267

King, Clive. *Me and My Millions*. Crowell, 1976. 180pp. Reading Level: Grades 5–8.
Disability: Learning disabilities; also Hearing impairment. M

Konigsburg, Elaine L. *Father's Arcane Daughter*. Atheneum, 1976. 118pp. Reading Level: Grades 5–8.
Disability: Neurological disabilities; Hearing impairment. M275

Levine, Edna S. *Lisa and Her Soundless World*. Illus. by Gloria Kamen. Human Sciences, 1974. 40pp. Reading Level: Grades K–3.
Disability: Hearing impairment. N236

Litchfield, Ada B. *A Button in Her Ear*. Illus. by Eleanor Mill. Whitman, 1976. unp. Reading Level: Grades K–3.
Disability: Hearing impairment. M292

Litchfield, Ada B. *Words in Our Hands*. Illus. by Helen Cogancherry. Whitman, 1980. unp. Reading Level: Grades K–3.
Disability: Hearing impairment. M293

MacKellar, William. *The Soccer Orphans*. Dodd, 1979. 157pp. Reading Level: Grades 5–8.
Disability: Orthopedic impairment; Hearing impairment. M305

Montgomery, Elizabeth Rider. *The Mystery of the Boy Next Door*. Illus. by E. Gold. Garrard, 1978. 48pp. Reading Level: Grades K–3.
Disability: Hearing impairment. M325

Morganroth, Barbara. *Will the Real Renie Lake Please Stand Up?* Atheneum, 1981. 164pp. Reading Level: Grades 7–9.
Disability: Hearing impairment. M327

Ogan, Margaret, and George Ogan. *Water Rat*. Funk & Wagnalls, 1970. 118pp. Reading Level: Grades 5–8.
Disability: Hearing impairment; Speech impairment. N260

Ray, N. L. *There Was This Man Running*. Macmillan, 1981. 151pp. Reading Level: Grades 5–8.
Disability: Hearing impairment. M375

* Riskind, Mary. *Apple is My Sign*. Houghton, 1981. 146pp. Reading Level: Grades 4–6.
Disability: Hearing impairment. M379

* Robinson, Veronica. *David in Silence*. Illus. by Victor Ambrus. Lippincott, 1966. 126pp. Reading Level: Grades 5–8.
Disability: Hearing impairment. N285

Rosen, Lillian. *Just Like Everybody Else*. Harcourt, 1981. 155pp. Reading Level: Grades 7–9.
Disability: Hearing impairment. M386

* Excellent selection.

Roth, David. *The Hermit of Fog Hollow Station*. Beaufort, 1980. 96pp. Reading Level: Grades 4–6.
Disability: Special health problems; also Hearing impairment. M391

Sivers, Brenda. *The Snailman*. Illus. by Shirley Hughes. Little, Brown, 1978. 118pp. Reading Level: Grades 4–6.
Disability: Orthopedic impairment; Cosmetic impairment; also Hearing impairment. M413

Smith, Vian. *Martin Rides the Moor*. Illus. by Ray Houlihan. Doubleday, 1964. 181pp. Reading Level: Grades 5–8.
Disability: Hearing impairment. N300

Spence, Eleanor. *The Nothing Place*. Illus. by Geraldine Spence. Harper & Row, 1972. 228pp. Reading Level: Grades 4–6.
Disability: Hearing impairment. N305

Sutcliff, Rosemary. *Blood Feud*. Dutton, 1976, 144pp. Reading Level: Grades 7–9.
Disability: Orthopedic impairment; also Visual impairment; Hearing impairment. M438

Tolan, Stephanie S. *Grandpa—And Me*. Scribner, 1978. 120pp. Reading Level: Grades 4–6.
Disability: Neurological disabilities; also Hearing impairment. M443

Vinson, Kathryn. *Run with the Ring*. Harcourt, 1965. 225pp. Reading Level: Grades 7–9.
Disability: Visual impairment; also Hearing impairment. N329

* Wahl, Jan. *Jamie's Tiger*. Illus. by Tomie de Paola. Harcourt, 1978. unp. Reading Level: Grades K–3.
Disability: Hearing impairment. M451

Zelonky, Joy. *I Can't Always Hear You*. Illus. by Barbara Bejna and Shirlee Jensen. Raintree, 1980. 31pp. Reading Level: Grades K–3.
Disability: Hearing impairment. M480

VISUAL IMPAIRMENTS

Allan, Mabel E. *The View beyond My Father*. Dodd, 1977. 192pp. Reading Level: Grades 7–9.
Disability: Visual impairment. M61

Anderson, Paul. *The Boy and the Blind Storyteller*. Illus. by Yong Hwan Kim. William R. Scott, 1964. 91pp. Reading Level: Grades 4–6.
Disability: Visual impairment. N107

Armer, Alberta. *Steve and the Guide Dogs*. Illus by J.D. Kocsis. World, 1965. 190pp. Reading Level: Grades 5–8.
Disability: Visual impairment. N110

* Bawden, Nina. *The Robbers*. Lothrop, Lee & Shepard, 1979. 155pp. Reading Level: Grades 4–6.
Disability: Special health problems; Visual impairment. M81

---

* Excellent selection.

Bawden, Nina. *The Witch's Daughter*. Lippincott, 1966. 181pp. Reading Level: Grades 4–6.
Disability: Visual impairment. N116

* Bethancourt, T. Ernesto. *The Dog Days of Arthur Cane*. Holiday, 1976. 160pp. Reading Level: Grades 7–9.
Disability: Visual impairment. M85

Bodker, Cecil. *Silas and Ben-Godik*. Trans. by Sheila La Farge. Delacorte, 1978. 191pp. Reading Level: Grades 4–6.
Disability: Orthopedic impairment; Visual impairment. M90

* Bodker, Cecil. *Silas and the Black Mare*. Trans. by Sheila La Farge. Delacorte, 1978. 152pp. Reading Level: Grades 4–6.
Disability: Orthopedic impairment; Visual impairment. M91

Borland, Kathryn, and Helen Speicher. *Good-By to Stony Crick*. Illus. by Deanne Hollinger. McGraw-Hill, 1975. 138pp. Reading Level: Grades 4–6.
Disability: Visual impairment; also Mental retardation. N124

Bouchard, Lois Kalb. *The Boy Who Wouldn't Talk*. Illus. by Ann Grifalconi. Doubleday, 1969. 74pp. Reading Level: Grades K–3.
Disability: Visual impairment. N127

Butler, Beverly. *Gift of Gold*. Illus. by Doris Reynolds. Dodd, 278pp. Reading Level: Grades 8–10.
Disability: Visual impairment; also Mental retardation; Speech and language impairments. N136

Butler, Beverly. *Light a Single Candle*. Dodd, 1962. 242pp. Reading Level: Grades 7–9.
Disability: Visual impairment. N136

Carrick, Malcolm. *"I'll Get You!"* Illus. by author. Harper & Row, 1979. 188pp. Reading Level: Grades 4–6.
Disability: Mental retardation; also Visual impairment. M133

Clewes, Dorothy. *Guide Dog*. Illus. by Peter Burchard. Coward, 1965. 159pp. Reading Level: Grades 7–9.
Disability: Visual impairment; also Cosmetic impairment. N150

* Corn, Anne L. *Monocular Mac*. Illus. by Diane Dawson. National Association for Visually Handicapped, 1977. 31pp. Reading Level: Grades K–3.
Disability: Visual impairment. M156

Courlander, Harold. *The Son of the Leopard*. Illus. by Rocco Negri. Crown, 1974. 55pp. Reading Level: Grades 4–6.
Disability: Orthopedic impairment; Visual impairment. N157

* Curry, Jane Louise. *The Bassumtyte Treasure*. Atheneum, 1978. 130pp. Reading Level: Grades 4–6.
Disability: Orthopedic impairment; Visual impairment. M166

* Dickinson, Peter. *Annerton Pit*. Little, Brown, 1977. 175pp. Reading Level: Grades 7–9.
Disability: Visual impairment. M178

---

* Excellent selection.

* Dickinson, Peter. *Tulku*. Dutton, 1979. 286pp. Reading Level: Grades 8–10.
Disability: Visual impairment. M179

Ericsson, Mary Kentra. *About Glasses for Gladys*. Illus. by Pauline Batchelder
Adams. Melmont, 1962. 31pp. Reading Level: Grades K–3.
Disability: Visual impairment. N172

Fine, Anne. *The Summer-House Loon*. Crowell, 1978. 127pp. Reading Level: Grades
7–9.
Disability: Visual impairment; also Hearing impairment. M195

Garfield, James B. *Follow My Leader*. Illus. by Robert Greiner. Viking, 1957. 191pp.
Reading Level: Grades 4–6.
Disability: Visual impairment. N185

Goodsell, Jane. *Katie's Magic Glasses*. Illus. by Barbara Cooney. Houghton, 1965.
43pp. Reading Level: Grades K–3.
Disability: Visual impairment. N191

Griffiths, Helen. *The Wild Horse of Santander*. Illus. by Victor G. Ambrus. Doubleday, 1966. 182pp. Reading Level: Grades 7–9.
Disability: Visual impairment. N195

Hark, Mildred, and Noll McQueen. *Mary Lou and Johnny*. Illus. by Taylor Oughton.
Watts, 1963. 228pp.Reading Level: Grades 4–6.
Disability: Visual impairment. N201

* Heide, Florence Parry. *Sound of Sunshine, Sound of Rain*. Illus. by Kenneth Long-
temps. Parents Magazine, 1970. unp. Reading Level: Grades 4–6.
Disability: Visual impairment. N204

* Holman, Felice. *Slake's Limbo*. Scribner, 1974. 117pp. Reading Level: Grades 7–9.
Disability: Visual impairment. N211

Johnson, Annabel, and Edgar Johnson. *The Black Symbol*. Harper & Row, 1959.
207pp. Reading Level: Grades 7–9.
Disability: Visual impairment. N220

* Keats, Ezra Jack. *Apt. 3*. Illus. by author. Macmillan, 1971. unp. Reading Level:
Grades K–3.
Disability: Visual impairment. N223

L'Engle, Madeline. *The Young Unicorns*. Farrar, 1968. 245pp. Reading Level: Grades
7–9.
Disability: Visual impairment. N234

Litchfield, Ada B. *A Cane in Her Hand*. Illus. by Eleanor Mill. Whitman, 1977. unp.
Reading Level: Grades K–3.
Disability: Visual impairment. M292

* Little, Jean. *From Anna*. Illus. by Joan Sandin. Harper, 1972. 201pp. Reading Level:
Grades 4–6.
Disability: Visual impairment. N237

Little, Jean. *Listen for the Singing*. Dutton, 1977. 215pp. Reading Level: Grades 7–9.
Disability: Visual impairment. M294

---

* Excellent selection.

MacLachlan, Patricia. *Through Grandpa's Eyes*. Illus. by Deborah Ray. Harper & Row, 1980. unp. Reading Level: Grades K–3.
Disability: Visual impairment. M308

* Mathis, Sharon Bell. *Listen for the Fig Tree*. Viking, 1974 175pp. Reading Level: Grades 7–9.
Disability: Visual impairment; also Emotional disturbances; Speech and language impairments. N247

Micklish, Rita. *Sugar Bee*. Illus. by Ted Lewin. Delacorte, 1972. 195pp. Reading Level: Grades 4–6
Disability: Visual impairment. N248

Milton, Hilary. *Blind Flight*. Watts, 1980. 138pp. Reading Level: Grades 4–6.
Disability: Visual impairment. M319

Mulcahy, Lucille. *Magic Fingers*. Illus. by Don Lambo. Nelson, 1958. 124pp. Reading Level: Grades 4–6.
Disability: Visual impairment. N250

Myers, Walter Dean. *The Legend of Tarik*. Viking, 1981. 185pp. Reading Level: Grades 7–9.
Disability: Orthopedic impairment; Visual impairment, Emotional Disturbances. M329

Naylor, Phyllis. *Jennifer Jean, the Cross-Eyed Queen*. Illus. by Harold K. Lamson. Lerner, 1967. unp. Reading Level: Kindergarden–Grade 3.
Disability: Visual impairment. N251

* Paterson, Katherine. *The Great Gilly Hopkins*. Crowell, 1978. 148pp. Reading Level: Grades 4–6.
Disability: Visual impairment. M345

Peyton, K. M. *Flambards*. Illus. by Victor G. Ambrus. World, 1967. 206pp. Reading Level: Grades 8–10.
Disability: Orthopedic impairment; also Visual impairment. N269

* Raskin, Ellen. *Spectacles*. Illus. by author. Atheneum, 1969. unp. Reading Level: Grades K–3.
Disability: Visual impairment. N275

Rayson, Steven. *The Crows of War*. Atheneum, 1974. 269pp. Reading Level: Grades 10–12.
Disability: Visual impairment; also Emotional disturbances. N276

Renick, Marion. *Five Points for Hockey*. Illus. by Charles Robinson. Scribner, 1973. 132pp. Reading Level: Grades 4–6.
Disability: Visual impairment. N277

Reuter, Margaret. *My Mother is Blind*. Photog. by Phillip Lanier. Children's Pr., 1979. 31pp. Reading Level: Grades K–3.
Disability: Visual impairment. M379

Sutcliff, Rosemary. *Blood Feud*. Dutton, 1976, 144pp. Reading Level: Grades 7–9.
Disability: Orthopedic impairment; also Visual impairment; Hearing impairment. M438

* Excellent selection.

* Sutcliff, Rosemary. *Warrior Scarlet*. Walck, 1958. 207pp. Reading Level: Grades 7–9.
  Disability: Orthopedic impairment; also Visual impairment. N311
* Taylor, Theodore. *The Cay*. Doubleday, 1969. 137pp. Reading Level: Grades 5–8.
  Disability: Visual impairment. N316
  Thomas, William E. *The New Boy is Blind*. Illus. with photographs. Messner, 1980.
  64pp. Reading Level: Grades 4–6.
  Disability: Visual impairment. M441
  Vinson, Kathryn. *Run with the Ring*. Harcourt, 1965. 225pp. Reading Level: Grades
  7–9.
  Disability: Visual impairment; also Hearing impairment. N329
  Whitney, Phyllis A. *Secret of the Emerald Star*. Illus. by Alex Stein. Westminster,
  1964. 233pp. Reading Level: Grades 5–8.
  Disability: Visual impairment. N341
  Wilder, Laura Ingalls. *Little Town on the Prairie*. Illus. by Garth Williams. Harper &
  Row, 1941. 307pp. Reading Level: Grades 4–6.
  Disability: Visual impairment. N342
  Wilder, Laura Ingalls. *These Happy Golden Years*. Illus. by Garth Williams. Harper
  & Row, 1943. 289pp. Reading Level: Grades 4–6.
  Disability: Visual impairment. N343
  Witheridge, Elizabeth. *Dead End Bluff*. Illus. by Charles Geer. Atheneum, 1966.
  186pp. Reading Level: Grades 5–8.
  Disability: Visual impairment. N347
  Wosmek, Frances. *A Bowl of Sun*. Illus. by author. Children's Pr., 1976. 47pp.
  Reading Level: Grades K–3.
  Disability: Visual impairment. M474
  Yolen, Jane. *Dream Weaver*. Illus. by Michael Hague. Collins, 1979. 80pp. Reading
  Level: Grades 4–6.
  Disability: Visual impairment; Orthopedic impairment. M475

BOOKS DEALING WITH COGNITIVE AND BEHAVIOR PROBLEMS

EMOTIONAL DISTURBANCES

Bauer, Marion Dane. *Tangled Butterfly*. Houghton, 1980, 162pp. Reading Level:
Grades 8–10.
Disability: Emotional disturbances. M78
Branscum, Robbie. *Toby, Granny and George*. Illus. by Glen Rounds. Doubleday,
1976. 104pp. Reading Level: Grades 4–6.
Disability: Emotional disturbances. M100

---

* Excellent selection.

* Bridgers, Sue Ellen. *Notes for Another Life*. Knopf, 1981. 250pp. Reading Level: Grades 7–9.
Disability: Emotional disturbances. M106

Bunting, Eve. *Blackbird Singing*. Illus. by Stephen Grammell. Macmillan, 1980. 92pp. Reading Level: Grades 5–8.
Disability: Emotional disturbances. M122

* Burch, Robert. *Simon and the Game of Chance*. Illus. by Fermin Rocker. Viking, 1970. 128pp. Reading Level: Grades 7–9.
Disability: Emotional disturbances. N134

* Corcoran, Barbara. *A Dance to Still Music*. Illus. by Charles Robinson. Atheneum, 1974. 192pp. Reading Level: Grades 7–9.
Disability: Hearing impairment; also Emotional disturbances; General health problems. N153

Cummings, Betty Sue. *Hew Against the Grain*. Atheneum, 1977. 174pp. Reading Level: Grades 7–9.
Disability: Emotional disturbances; Neurological disabilities; Orthopedic impairment. M158

Dank, Milton. *Red Flight Two*. Delacorte, 1981. 185pp. Reading Level: Grades 8–10.
Disability: Emotional disturbances; also Orthopedic impairment. M172

Dengler, Marianna. *A Pebble in Newcomb's Pond*. Illus. by Kathleen Garry-McCord. Holt, 1979. 160pp. Reading Level: Grades 7–9.
Disability: Emotional disturbances; Special health problems. M175

Donovan, John. *Remove Protective Coating a Little at a Time*. Harper, 1973. 101pp. Reading Level: Grades 7–9.
Disability: Emotional disturbances. N168

Duncan, Lois. *Killing Mr. Griffin*. Little, Brown, 1978. 243pp. Reading Level: Grades 8–10.
Disability: Emotional disturbances; Special health problems. M183

Garfield, Leon. *Black Jack*. Illus. by Anthony Maitland. Pantheon, 1968. 243pp. Reading Level: Grades 7–9.
Disability: Emotional disturbances; also Orthopedic impairment. N186

Green, Phyllis. *Walkie-Talkie*. Addison Wesley, 1978. 96pp. Reading Level: Grades 4–6.
Disability: Emotional disturbances; Neurological disabilities. M222

Griffiths, Helen. *The Mysterious Appearance of Agnes*. Also published as *Witch Fear*. Illus. by Victor G. Ambrus. Holiday, 1975. 160pp. Reading Level: Grades 7–9.
Disability: Emotional disturbances; also Neurological disabilities. N194

* Hamilton, Virginia. *The Planet of Junior Brown*. Macmillan, 1971. 210pp. Reading Level: Grades 8–10.
Disability: Emotional disturbances; also General health problems. N198

* Hamilton-Paterson, James. *The House in the Waves*. Phillips, 1970. 157pp. Reading Level: Grades 8–10.
Disability: Emotional disturbances; also Cosmetic impairment. N199

---

* Excellent selection.

Heide, Florence Parry. *Growing Anyway Up*. Lippincott, 1976. 127pp. Reading Level: Grades 7–9.
Disability: Emotional disturbances. M236

Heide, Florence Parry. *Secret Dreamer, Secret Dreams*. Lippincott, 1978. 95pp. Reading Level: Grades 7–9.
Disability: Emotional disturbances. M237

Hodges, C. Walter. *The Namesake*. Illus. by author. Coward, 1964. 269pp. Reading Level: Grades 7–9.
Disability: Orthopedic impairment; also Emotional disturbances; General health problems. N207

Hunt, Irene. *Up a Road Slowly*. Follett, 1966. 192pp. Reading Level: Grades 7–9.
Disability: Mental retardation; Emotional disturbances. N214

Jewett, Eleanore M. *The Hidden Treasure of Glaston*. Illus. by Frederick T. Chapman. Viking, 1946. 307pp. Reading Level: Grades 7–9.
Disability: Orthopedic impairment; Emotional disturbances. N218

Jones, Adrienne. *The Beckoner*. Harper & Row, 1980. 243pp. Reading Level: Grades 10–12.
Disability: Emotional disturbances; Orthopedic impairment. M257

Kelley, Salley. *Trouble with Explosives*. Bradbury, 1976. 117pp. Reading Level: Grades 4–6.
Disability: Speech and language impairments; Emotional disturbances. M262

* Kerr, M. E. *Dinky Hocker Shoots Smack!* Harper & Row, 1972. 198pp. Reading Level: Grades 8–10.
Disability: Emotional disturbances. N223

Kerr, M. E. *Is That You, Miss Blue?* Harper & Row, 1975. 170pp. Reading Level: Grades 8–10.
Disability: Emotional disturbances; also Multiple disturbances. N224

Levenkron, Steven. *The Best Little Girl in the World*. Contemporary, 1978. 196pp. Reading Level: Grades 8–10.
Disability: Emotional disturbances; Orthopedic impairment. M283

Levoy, Myron. *Alan and Naomi*. Harper & Row, 1977. 192pp. Reading Level: Grades 7–9
Disability: Emotional disturbances. M286

Levoy, Myron. *A Shadow Like a Leopard*. Harper & Row, 1981. 184pp. Reading Level: Grades 7–9.
Disability: Special health problems; Emotional disturbances. M287

Lowry, Lois. *Autumn Street*. Houghton, 1980. 188pp. Reading Level: Grades 5–8.
Disability: Neurological disturbances; Emotional disturbances; Orthopedic impairment. M298

Lutters, Valerie A. *The Haunting of Julie Unger*. Atheneum, 1977. 193pp. Reading Level: Grades 5–8.
Disability: Emotional disturbances. M300

* Excellent selection.

* Mathis, Sharon Bell. *Listen for the Fig Tree*. Viking, 1974 175pp. Reading Level: Grades 7–9.
  Disability: Visual impairment; also Emotional disturbances; Speech and language impairments. N247

McKillop, Patricia A. *The Night Gift*. Illus. by Kathy McKillop. Atheneum, 1976. 156pp. Reading Level: Grades 5–8.
  Disability: Cosmetic impairment; Emotional disturbances. M306

Myers, Walter Dean. *The Legend of Tarik*. Viking, 1981. 185pp. Reading Level: Grades 7–9.
  Disability: Orthopedic impairment; Visual impairment; Emotional disturbances. M329

* Neufeld, John. *Lisa, Bright and Dark*. Phillips, 1969. 125pp. Reading Level: Grades 8–10.
  Disability: Emotional disturbances. N281

Ney, John. *Ox Under Pressure*. Lippincott, 1976. 253pp. Reading Level: Grades 8–10.
  Disability: Emotional disturbances; Speech and language impairments. M334

* Oneal, Zibby. *The Language of Goldfish*. Viking, 1980. 179pp. Reading Level: Grades 7–9.
  Disability: Emotional disturbances. M341

Pfeffer, Susan Beth. *About David*. Delacorte, 1980. 167pp. Reading Level: Grades 7–9.
  Disability: Emotional disturbances. M354

* Platt, Kin. *The Boy Who Could Make Himself Disappear*. Chilton, 1968. 216pp. Reading Level: Grades 8–10.
  Disability: Emotional disturbances; Speech and language impairments; also Orthopedic impairment. N271

Platt, Kin. *Hey, Dummy*. Chilton, 1971. 169pp. Reading Level: Grades 7–9.
  Disability: Mental retardation; Emotional disturbances. N271

Potter, Marian. *The Shared Room*. Morrow, 1979. 192pp. Reading Level: Grades 4–6.
  Disability: Emotional disturbances. M370

Rayson, Steven. *The Crows of War*. Atheneum, 1974. 269pp. Reading Level: Grades 10–12.
  Disability: Visual impairment; also Emotional disturbances. N276

Rees, Lucy. *Horse of Air*. Methuen, 1980. 211pp. Reading Level: Grades 8–10.
  Disability: Emotional disturbances. M377

Ruby, Lois. *What Do You Do in Quicksand?* Viking, 1979. 199pp. Reading Level: Grades 8–10.
  Disability: Emotional disturbances. M393

Sachs, Marilyn. *The Bear's House*. Illus. by Louis Glanzman. Doubleday, 1971, 81pp. Reading Level: Grades 4–6.
  Disability: Emotional disturbances. N289

* Excellent selection.

Sherburne, Zoa. *Stranger in the House*. Morrow, 1963. 192pp. Reading Level: Grades 7–9.
Disability: Emotional disturbances. N294

Stern, Cecily. *A Different Kind of Gold*. Illus. by Ruth Sanderson. Harper & Row, 1981. 123pp. Reading Level: Grades 4–6.
Disability: Emotional disturbances. M433

* Taylor, Theodore. *Teetoncey*. Doubleday, 1974. 153pp. Reading Level: Grades 5–8.
Disability: Emotional disturbances. N317

Terris, Susan. *The Drowning Boy*. Doubleday, 1972. 189pp. Reading Level: Grades 7–9.
Disability: Emotional disturbances. N318

Van Leeuwen, Jean. *Seems Like This Road Goes on Forever*. Dial, 1979. 214pp. Reading Level: Grades 7–9.
Disability: Emotional disturbances. M449

Warwick, Dolores. *Learn to Say Goodbye*. Farrar, 1971. 179pp. Reading Level: Grades 7–9.
Disability: Emotional disturbances. N332

Windsor, Patricia. *The Summer Before*. Harper & Row, 1973. 241pp. Reading Level: Grades 7–9.
Disability: Emotional disturbances. N344

Wolitzer, Hilma. *Toby Lived Here*. Farrar 1978. 147pp. Reading Level: Grades 5–8.
Disability: Emotional disturbances. M469

LEARNING DISABILITIES

Anderson, Margaret J. *Searching for Shona*. Knopf, 1978. 159pp. Reading Level: Grades 4–6.
Disability: Learning disabilities. M64

* Gilson, Jamie. *Do Bananas Chew Gum?* Lothrop, Lee & Shepard, 1980. 158pp. Reading Level: Grades 4–6.
Disability: Learning disabilities. M213

King, Clive. *Me and My Millions*. Crowell, 1976. 180pp. Reading Level: Grades 5–8.
Disability: Learning disabilities; also Hearing impairment. M270

Lasker, Joe. *Nick Joins In*. Illus. by author. Whitman, 1980. unp. Reading Level: Grades K–3.
Disability: Orthopedic impairment; also Learning disabilities. M277

* Pevsner, Stella. *Keep Stompin' Till the Music Stops*. Bradbury, 1977. 136pp. Reading Level: Grades 4–6.
Disability: Learning disabilities; also Speech and language impairments. M352

MENTAL RETARDATION

Borland, Kathryn, and Helen Speicher. *Good-Bye to Stony Crick*. Illus. by Deanne Hollinger. McGraw-Hill, 1975. 138pp. Reading Level: Grades 4–6.
Disability: Visual impairment; also Mental retardation. N124

---

* Excellent selection.

Branscum, Robbie. *For Love of Jody*. Lothrop, Lee & Shepard, 1979. 111pp. Reading Level: Grades 4–6.
Disability: Mental retardation. M99

* Bridgers, Sue Ellen. *All Together Now*. Knopf, 1979. 238pp. Reading Level: Grades 7–9.
Disability: Mental retardation. M105

Brown, Roy. *Escape the River*. Also published as *The River*. Seabury, 1972. 160pp. Reading Level: Grades 5–8.
Disability: Mental retardation. N131

Brown, Roy. *Find Debbie!* Seabury Pr., 1976. 160pp. Reading Level: Grades 8–10.
Disability: Emotional disturbances; Mental retardation. M118

Byars, Betsy. *Summer of the Swans*. Illus. by Ted CoConis. Viking, 1970. 142pp. Reading Level: Grades 5–8.
Disability: Mental retardation. N137

* Carpelan, Bo. *Bow Island*. Trans. by Sheila LaFarge. Delacorte, 1968. 140pp. Reading Level: Grades 7–9.
Disability: Mental retardation; also General health problems. N140

* Carpelan, Bo. *Dolphins in the City*. Trans. by Sheila LaFarge. Delacorte, 1976. 145pp. Reading Level: Grades 7–9.
Disability: Mental retardation. M131

Carrick, Malcolm. *"I'll Get You!"* Illus. by author. Harper & Row, 1979. 188pp. Reading Level: Grades 4–6.
Disability: Mental retardation; also Visual impairment. M133

Christopher, Matt. *Long Shot for Paul*. Illus. by Foster Caddell. Little, Brown, 1966. 151pp. Reading Level: Grades 4–6.
Disability: Mental retardation. N146

Cleaver, Vera, and Bill Cleaver. *Me Too*. Lippincott, 1973. 158pp. Reading Level: Grades 7–9.
Disability: Mental retardation. N148

* Clifton, Lucille. *My Friend Jacob*. Illus. by Thomas Di Grazia. Dutton, 1980. unp. Reading Level: Grades K–3.
Disability: Mental retardation. M142

* Cummings, Betty Sue. *Let a River Be*. Atheneum, 1978. 195pp. Reading Level: Grades 8–10.
Disability: Mental retardation; Special health problems. M160

* Friis-Baastad, Babbis. *Don't Take Teddy*. Trans. by Lise Somme McKinnon. Scribner, 1967. 218pp. Reading Level: Grades 4–6.
Disability: Mental retardation. N184

Garrigue, Sheila. *Between Friends*. Bradbury, 1978. 160pp. Reading Level: Grades 5–8.
Disability: Mental retardation; also Speech and language impairments. M208

Grollman, Sharon Hya. *More Time To Grow*. Illus. by Arthur Polonsky. Beacon, 1977. 39pp. Reading Level: Grades K–3.
Disability: Mental retardation. M227

* Excellent selection.

Hirsch, Karen. *My Sister*. Illus. by Nancy Inderieden. Carolrhoda Books, 1977. unp. Reading Level: Grades K–3.
Disability: Mental retardation. M242

Holman, Felice. *A Year to Grow*. Norton, 1968, 100pp. Reading Level: Grades 7–9.
Disability: Mental retardation. N212

Hunt, Irene. *Up a Road Slowly*. Follett, 1966. 192pp. Reading Level: Grades 7–9.
Disability: Mental retardation; Emotional disturbances. N214

Hunter, Edith Fisher. *Sue Ellen*. Illus. by Bea Holmes. Houghton, 1969. 170pp. Reading Level: Grades 4–6.
Disability: Mental retardation; also General health problems. N215

Kemp, Gene. *The Turbulent Term of Tyke Tiler*. Illus. by Carolyn Dinan. Faber & Faber, 1977. 118pp. Reading Level: Grades 4–6.
Disability: Speech and language impairments; also Mental retardation. M263

Levitin, Sonia. *A Sound to Remember*. Illus. by Gabriel Lisowski. Harcourt, 1979. unp. Reading Level: Grades K–3.
Disability: Mental retardation; Speech and language impairments. M285

Lipsyte, Robert. *Summer Rules*. Harper & Row, 1981. 150pp. Reading Level: Grades 7–9.
Disability: Mental retardation. M290

* Little, Jean. *Take Wing*. Illus. by Jerry Lazare. Little, Brown, 1968. 176pp. Reading Level: Grades 5–8.
Disability: Mental retardation. N239

* Mazer, Harry. *The War on Villa Street*. Delacorte, 1978. 182pp. Reading Level: Grades 7–9.
Disability: Mental retardation. M316

Platt, Kin. *Hey, Dummy*. Chilton, 1971. 169pp. Reading Level: Grades 7–9.
Disability: Mental retardation; Emotional disturbances. N271

Reynolds, Pamela. *A Different Kind of Sister*. Lothrop, Lee & Shepard, 1968. 192pp. Reading Level: Grades 7–9.
Disability: Mental retardation; also Cosmetic impairment; Orthopedic impairment. N279

* Rinaldo, C. L. *Dark Dreams*. Harper, 1974. 154pp. Reading Level: Grades 8–10.
Disability: Mental retardation; also General health problems. N282

Rodowsky, Colby. *What About Me?* Franklin Watts, 1976. 136pp. Reading Level: Grades 7–9.
Disability: Mental retardation; Special health problems. M385

Shyer, Marlene F. *Welcome Home, Jellybean*. Scribner, 1978. 152pp. Reading Level: Grades 5–8.
Disability: Mental retardation. M411

* Slepian, Jan. *The Alfred Summer*. Macmillan, 1980. 119pp. Reading Level: Grades 7–9.
Disability: Neurological disabilities; Mental retardation; Speech and language impairments. M416

* Excellent selection.

* Slepian, Jan. *Lester's Turn*. Macmillan, 1981. 139pp. Reading Level: Grades 7–9.
  Disability: Neurological disabilities; Mental retardation; Orthopedic impairment.
  M418

Smith, Doris Buchanan. *Up and Over*. Morrow, 1976. 224pp. Reading Level: Grades
  8–10.
  Disability: Mental retardation. M421

* Smith, Gene. *The Hayburners*. Illus. by Ted Lewin. Delacorte, 1974. 64pp. Reading
  Level: Grades 7–9.
  Disability: Mental retardation. N299

Southall, Ivan. *Hill's End*. St. Martin's, 1963. 174pp. Reading Level: Grades 5–8.
  Disability: Mental retardation. N302

Thrasher, Crystal. *Between Dark and Daylight*. Atheneum, 1979. 251pp. Reading
  Level: Grades 7–9.
  Disability: Mental retardation; Speech and language impairments. M442

Thrasher, Crystal. *The Dark Didn't Catch Me*. Atheneum, 1975. 182pp. Reading
  Level: Grades 5–8.
  Disability: Cosmetic impairment; General health problems; also Mental retarda-
  tion. N322

* Walker, Pamela. *Twyla*. Prentice-Hall, 1973. 125pp. Reading Level: Grades 8–10.
  Disability: Mental retardation. N330

Weik, Mary Hays. *The Jazz Man*. Illus. by Ann Grifalconi. Atheneum, 1966. 42pp.
  Reading Level: Grades 4–6.
  Disability: Orthopedic impairment; also Mental retardation. N337

Wolff, Ruth. *A Crack in the Sidewalk*. Day, 1965. 288pp. Reading Level: Grades 7–9.
  Disability: Mental retardation. N349

* Wrightson, Patricia. *A Racecourse for Andy*. Illus. by Margaret Horder. Harcourt,
  1968. 156pp. Reading Level: Grades 5–8.
  Disability: Mental retardation. N357

SPEECH AND LANGUAGE IMPAIRMENTS

Alexander, Lloyd. *Westmark*. Dutton, 1981. 184pp. Reading Level: Grades 5–8.
  Disability: Orthopedic impairment; also Hearing impairment; Speech and language impairments. M60

Callen, Larry. *The Deadly Mandrake*. Illus. by Larry Johnson. Little, Brown, 1978.
  163pp. Reading Level: Grades 5–8.
  Disability: Speech and language impairments. M127

Callen, Larry. *Sorrow's Song*. Illus. by Marvin Friedman. Little, Brown, 1979. 150pp.
  Reading Level: Grades 4–6.
  Disability: Speech and language impairments. M128

Chambers, Aidan. *Seal Secret*. Harper & Row, 1980. 122pp. Reading Level: Grades
  5–8.
  Disability: Speech and language impairments. M136

---

* Excellent selection.

Cowley, Joy. *The Silent One*. Illus. by Hermann Greissle. Knopf, 1981. 136pp. Reading Level: Grades 4–6.
Disability: Hearing impairment; Speech and language impairments; Special health problems. M157

DeJong, Meindert. *Journey from Peppermint Street*. Harper & Row, 1968. 242pp. Reading Level: Grades 4–6.
Disability: Hearing impairment; Speech and language impairments. N164

* Fleischman, Paul. *The Half-a-Moon Inn*. Illus. by Kathy Jacobi. Harper & Row, 1980. 88pp. Reading Level: Grades 5–8.
Disability: Speech and language impairments. M196

* Friis-Baastad, Babbis. *Kristy's Courage*. Trans. by Lise Somme McKinnon. Harcourt, 1965. 159pp. Reading Level: Grades 4–6.
Disability: Cosmetic impairment; Speech and language impairments. N185

Garrigue, Sheila. *Between Friends*. Bradbury, 1978. 160pp. Reading Level: Grades 5–8.
Disability: Mental retardation; also Speech and language impairments. M208

Greene, Constance C. *The Unmaking of Rabbit*. Viking, 1972. 125pp. Reading Level: Grades 4–6.
Disability: Speech and language impairments. N192

* Henry, Marguerite. *King of the Wind*. Illus. by Wesley Dennis. Rand McNally, 1948. 175pp. Reading Level: Grades 4–6.
Disability: Speech and language impairments. N206

Holland, Isabelle. *Alan and the Animal Kingdom*. Lippincott, 1977. 190pp. Reading Level: Grades 4–6.
Disability: Speech and language impairments; also Special health problems. M243

Judd, Denis. *Return to Treasure Island*. St. Martin's, 1978. 209pp. Reading Level: Grades 8–10.
Disability: Orthopedic impairment; also Speech and language impairments. M261

Jupo, Frank. *Atu, the Silent One*. Illus. by author. Holiday, 1967. unp. Reading Level: Grades K–3.
Disability: Speech and language impairments. N222

Kelley, Salley. *Trouble with Explosives*. Bradbury, 1976. 117pp. Reading Level: Grades 4–6.
Disability: Speech and language impairments; Emotional disturbances. M262

* Lee, Mildred. *The Skating Rink*. Seabury, 1969. 126pp. Reading Level: Grades 8–10.
Disability: Speech and language impairments; also Orthopedic impairment. N231

* Mathis, Sharon Bell. *Listen for the Fig Tree*. Viking, 1974 175pp. Reading Level: Grades 7–9.
Disability: Visual impairment; also Emotional disturbances; Speech and language impairments. N247

Ney, John. *Ox Under Pressure*. Lippincott, 1976. 253pp. Reading Level: Grades 8–10.
Disability: Emotional disturbances; Speech and language impairments. M334

---

* Excellent selection.

Ogan, Margaret, and George Ogan. *Water Rat*. Funk & Wagnalls, 1970. 118pp. Reading Level: Grades 5–8.
Disability: Hearing impairment; Speech and language impairments. N260

* Pevsner, Sheila. *Keep Stompin' Till the Music Stops*. Bradbury, 1977. 136pp. Reading Level: Grades 4–6.
Disability: Learning disabilities; also Speech and language impairments. M352

* Platt, Kin. *The Boy Who Could Make Himself Disappear*. Chilton, 1968. 216pp. Reading Level: Grades 8–10.
Disability: Emotional disturbances; Speech and language impairments; also Orthopedic impairment. N271

Rounds, Glen. *Blind Outlaw*. Illus. by author. Holiday House, 1980. 94pp. Reading Level: Grades 4–6.
Disability: Speech and language impairments. M392

* Slepian, Jan. *The Alfred Summer*. Macmillan, 1980. 119pp. Reading Level: Grades 7–9.
Disability: Neurological disabilities; Mental retardation; Speech and language impairments. M416

Stanek, Muriel. *Growl When You Say R*. Illus. by Phil Smith. Whitman, 1979. unp. Reading Level: Grades K–3.
Disability: Speech and language impairments. M431

BOOKS DEALING WITH MULTIPLE/SEVERE AND VARIOUS DISABILITIES

MULTIPLE/SEVERE DISABILITIES

* Hull, Eleanor. *Alice with the Golden Hair*. Atheneum, 1981. 186pp. Reading Level: Grades 7–9.
Disability: Multiple disabilities. M247

Kerr, M.E. *Is That You, Miss Blue?* Harper & Row, 1975. 170pp. Reading Level: Grades 8–10.
Disability: Emotional disturbances; also Multiple disabilities. N224

Lee, Mildred. *The People Therein*. Houghton, 1980. 269pp. Reading Level: Grades 10–12.
Disability: Multiple disabilities. M279

VARIOUS DISABILITIES

Bach, Alice. *A Father Every Few Years*. Harper & Row, 1977. 130pp. Reading Level: Grades 5–8.
Disability: Special health problems. M73

* Excellent selection.

Bates, Betty. *The Ups and Downs of Jorie Jenkins*. Holiday, 1978. 126pp. Reading Level: Grades 4–6.
Disability: Special health problems. M77

* Bawden, Nina. *The Robbers*. Lothrop, Lee & Shepard, 1979. 155pp. Reading Level: Grades 4–6.
Disability: Special health problems; Visual impairment. M81

Clewes, Dorothy. *Guide Dog*. Illus. by Peter Burchard. Coward, 1965. 159pp. Reading Level: Grades 7–9.
Disability: Visual impairment; also Cosmetic impairment. N150

Cowley, Joy. *The Silent One*. Illus. by Hermann Greissle. Knopf, 1981. 136pp. Reading Level: Grades 4–6.
Disability: Hearing impairment; Speech and language impairments; Special health problems. M157

* Cummings, Betty Sue. *Let a River Be*. Atheneum, 1978. 195pp. Reading Level: Grades 8–10.
Disability: Mental retardation; Special health problems. M160

* Danziger, Paula. *The Pistachio Prescription*. Delacorte, 1978. 154pp. Reading Level: Grades 7–9.
Disability: Special health problems. M173

Dengler, Marianna. *A Pebble in Newcomb's Pond*. Illus. by Kathleen Garry-McCord. Holt, 1979. 160pp. Reading Level: Grades 7–9.
Disability: Emotional disturbances; Special health problems. M175

Forbes, Esther. *Johnny Tremain*. Illus. by Lynd Ward. Houghton, 1943. 256pp. Reading Level: Grades 5–8.
Disability: Orthopedic impairment; also Cosmetic impairment. N180

* Friis-Baastad, Babbis. *Kristy's Courage*. Trans. by Lise Somme McKinnon. Harcourt, 1965. 158pp. Reading Level: Grades 4–6.
Disability: Cosmetic impairment; Speech and language impairments. N185

Hightower, Florence. *Dreamworld Castle*. Houghton, 1978. 214pp. Reading Level: Grades 5–8.
Disability: Special health problems; also Hearing impairment. M241

* Hamilton-Paterson, James. *The House in the Waves*. Phillips, 1970. 157pp. Reading Level: Grades 8–10.
Disability: Emotional disturbances; also Cosmetic impairment. N199

Holland, Isabelle. *Alan and the Animal Kingdom*. Lippincott, 1977. 190pp. Reading Level: Grades 4–6.
Disability: Speech and language impairments; also Special health problems. M243

Jones, Rebecca C. *Angie and Me*. Macmillan, 1981, 113pp. Reading Level: Grades 4–6.
Disability: Special health problems. M258

Lee, Robert C. *It's a Mile from Here to Glory*. Little, Brown, 1972. 150pp. Reading Level: Grades 5–8.
Disability: Orthopedic impairment; Cosmetic impairment. N232

* Excellent selection.

Levoy, Myron. *A Shadow Like a Leopard.* Harper & Row, 1981. 184pp. Reading Level: Grades 7–9.
Disability: Special health problems; Emotional disturbances. M287

McKillop, Patricia A. *The Night Gift.* Illus. by Kathy McKillop. Atheneum, 1976. 156pp. Reading Level: Grades 5–8.
Disability: Cosmetic impairment; Emotional disturbances. M306

Mohr, Nicholasa. *In Nueva York.* Dial, 1977. 192pp. Reading Level: Grades 10–12.
Disability: Orthopedic impairment; Special health problems. M324

Norton, Andre. *Scarface.* Illus. by Lorence Bjorklund. Harcourt, 1948. 263pp. Reading Level: Grades 7–9.
Disability: Cosmetic impairment; also Orthopedic impairment. N256

Paulsen, Gary. *The Foxman.* Nelson, 1977. 125pp. Reading Level: Grades 7–9.
Disability: Cosmetic impairment. M346

* Peyton, K. M. *The Right-Hand Man.* Illus. by Victor Ambrus. Oxford Univ. Pr., 1977. 218pp. Reading Level: Grades 8–10.
Disability: Orthopedic impairment; also Special health problems. M353

Pfeffer, Susan Beth. *Starring Peter and Leigh.* Delacorte, 1979. 200pp. Reading Level: Grades 7–9.
Disability: Special health problems. M356

Radley, Gail. *Nothing Stays the Same Forever.* Crown, 1981. 148pp. Reading Level: Grades 4–6.
Disability: Special health problems. M372

Reynolds, Pamela. *A Different Kind of Sister.* Lothrop, Lee & Shepard, 1968. 192pp. Reading Level: Grades 7–9.
Disability: Mental retardation; also Cosmetic impairment; Orthopedic impairment. N279

Robertson, Keith. *Ice to India.* Illus. by Jack Weaver. Viking, 1955. 224pp. Reading Level: Grades 7–9.
Disability: Orthopedic impairment; Cosmetic impairment. N284

Roth, David. *The Hermit of Fog Hollow Station.* Beaufort. 1980. 96pp. Reading Level: Grades 4–6.
Disability: Special health problems; also Hearing impairment. M391

Salassi, Otto L. *On the Ropes.* Greenwillow, 1981. 248pp. Reading Level: Grades 7–9.
Disability: Orthopedic impairment; also Cosmetic impairment. M396

Sivers, Brenda. *The Snailman.* Illus. by Shirley Hughes. Little, Brown, 1978. 118pp. Reading Level: Grades 4–6.
Disability: Orthopedic impairment; Cosmetic impairment; also Hearing impairment. M413

Thrasher, Crystal. *The Dark Didn't Catch Me.* Atheneum, 1975. 182pp. Reading Level: Grades 5–8.
Disability: Cosmetic impairment; General health problems; also Mental retardation. N322

* Excellent selection.

Towne, Mary. *First Serve*. Illus. by Ruth Sanderson. Atheneum, 1976. 214pp. Reading Level: Grades 5–8.
   Disability: Cosmetic impairment. M445
Winthrop, Elizabeth. *Marathon Miranda*. Holiday, 1979, 155pp. Reading Level: Grades 4–6.
   Disability: Special health problems. M467

* Excellent selection.

2

TWO STEPS FORWARD, ONE STEP BACK: STEREOTYPES ABANDONED AND REVIVED IN THE 1980S

He drew a circle that shut me out—
Heretic, rebel, a thing to flout.
But Love and I had the wit to win:
We drew a circle that took him in!
                    —Edwin Markham[1]

DRAWN WITHIN THE CIRCLE

Juvenile fiction published in the United States from 1982 through 1991 followed the trend of American mass media in presenting a broader view of human diversity than had previously been depicted. Sentimental situations with simplistic solutions were eclipsed by more complex explorations of character and interpersonal relationships affected by specific impairments. Shifting attitudes are reflected and will continue to be affected by characterizations through many media formats, not just the juvenile books produced during the 1980s and identified in this volume. Popular culture has drawn a wider circle around Americans with disabilities in contemporary society.

FILM AND VIDEO IMAGES

The movie industry honored the productions of *Terms of Endearment, Children of a Lesser God, Rain Man, Born on the Fourth of July,* and *My Left Foot* during the 1980s. Actors portraying characters with disabilities in these well-known films won high praise—some of them Academy Awards—for their performance. In *Dominick and Eugene,* Tom Hulce gave a superb inter-

33

pretation of a twin brother whose mental abilities were impaired by an abusive father. Admittedly, a rash of horror series made teen idols out of two psychotic killers (Jason and Freddie Krueger), and *Freak Show* offended March of Dimes supporters who heard about it. Still, mainstream cinematic sensitivities are improving.

Marlee Matlin and Chris Burke were praised for debut performances that convincingly portrayed characters experiencing the same impairments that these actors cope with in real life. Burke's role in the television series "Life Goes On" is often developed along insightful new lines, but some writers still saddle "Corky" with mythic, "nature's child" extrasensory abilities. *Junior Scholastic* summarized Corky's characterization this way.

> Corky, like actor Chris Burke who plays him, has Down's syndrome. Down's syndrome causes mental retardation and some physical abnormalities. People who have this condition are born with it. . . .
>
> Viewers of "Life Goes On" know that Corky is caring and affectionate. He works twice as hard as everyone else and still gets lower grades, but he's determined to graduate from a regular high school. His part-time job in his dad's restaurant helps his family and contributes to his sense of self-esteem. His extracurricular activities round out his personality. Corky has participated in the Special Olympics, gone swimming with dolphins, and run for school office.[2]

Television movies have showcased Emmy-award-winning artists Mickey Rooney in *Bill: On His Own* and Marlo Thomas in *Nobody's Child.* Though critics recognize that there seems to be an illness-of-the-week formula at work in some network or studio productions, other scripts show family drama, romance, humor, and personal development touching these special individuals' life. During the 1980s, the Media Access Awards gained visibility, and Tom and Jack Ritter's annual review of outstanding portrayals of disabilities was produced by KCET for many PBS stations across the country. PBS's Wonderworks series for children featured a futuristic challenge to NASA from a youth in a wheelchair—"Walking on Air." Now available in video due to the tremendous influx of titles in that format this past decade, library VHS collections should make a point of adding this excellent portrayal.[3]

"From the Heart," a performing arts gala concluding 1989's First International Very Special Arts Festival, was aired on a major network supported by corporate funding. Earlier, Special Olympic events had received coverage. Whitney Houston's performance for the special athletes' opening ceremonies in Los Angeles was as moving as her rendition of the national anthem at 1991's war-worried Super Bowl—the audience was just smaller. Audience coverage is broadened by cable channels like ESPN, Lifetime, and Discovery, who increase visibility for wheelchair sports and features on people who adapt activities or technologies to accommodate their special needs.

When "Home Magazine" initiated morning television broadcasts, one feature showed how mothers had "mainstreamed" their children's school yard to avoid the isolated clumps of special versus regular play groups that had been evident earlier. By integrating the equipment so that able-bodied students could share slides, swings, and other play areas with disabled class-mates who needed customized seating and ramps, these women established a new socialization pattern on campus. The children, of course, merely thought it was exciting to have new equipment, and so their mutual pleasure was not overshadowed by the calculated effort it took to break down some significant barriers to interpersonal relations on campus. Human interest spots such as this continue to be a feature of broadcast journalism, but they are intangible after airing—either you saw it or you didn't; still, this is a trend that makes an impact.

In 1989, two rock climbers (one paralyzed) inched up a natural stone wall in Yosemite, California, while news-watchers held their breath. The com-pleted ascent was commemorated in a political cartoon by Dennis Renault, who drew the famous cliff behind a universal access sign (stick figure in wheelchair) on a post to identify "El Capitan, 3,500 ft.," as a handicapped-accessible location. This wealth of images and increasing video access to old and new movies make it more likely that young people will have vicarious experiences with disabling conditions. The best screenplays and documentar-ies show that physical and mental impairments can affect an individual's ways of living without handicapping that person's life.

ADVERTISING AND PRINT MEDIA: "SEE IT TO BELIEVE IT!"

One indicator of change in American popular culture is how often advertisers through the 1980s have featured differently abled people in their packaging, television spots, or publications. When Wheaties introduced a "Search for Champions" campaign to identify outstanding amateur athletes, the first winner featured on the famous package was George Murray, an outstanding wheelchair athlete. In 60 seconds or less, Du Pont introduced thousands of television viewers to a man whose basketball skills, self-reliance, and high-tech prosthesis were in evidence when he pulled sweatpants off his artificial legs to compete with strangers on an outdoor court.

McDonald's commercials have casually introduced wheelchair users as part of the after-school crowd and have presented scenes from Ronald Mc-Donald Charities that include youngsters with special needs. In January 1990, Burger King launched animated ads, a newsletter, children's meal prizes, and posters that featured the Kids Club, whose inventive member, "Wheels," uses a turbowheelchair. That fall, Target's newspaper inserts pic-tured a model seated in a wheelchair in one group that featured girls' back-to-school fashions. Every few months, one of that chain's weekly ads has included different models in appropriately scaled wheelchairs, and a walker. It is encouraging to see how consciousness raising has generated a commercial niche for portrayals of adults and children with disabilities.

Periodicals have a longer history of including pieces that show physically or mentally challenged individuals, but there has been an uneven tone to their portrayals. Inspirational features still lionize the sufferer or the caregiver who is dealing with a disabling condition. While trying to create structure for a short piece of journalism, writers may leave out facets of the person's life that would ground it in the mainstream experience. Some writers have not abandoned terminology that implies patronizing bias, yet others will use the latest euphemistic jargon they are acquainted with. But whether it is a local account of coping with terminal illness, a feature in the teen magazine *Sassy* about getting to know a blind girl, or a *Parade* magazine cover story on Bree Walker and her daughter (who shares the television broadcaster's genetic impairment), the public is given new perspective on that faceless percentage of the general population that is called "disabled."

NONFICTION PUBLICATIONS ON DISABILITIES

When how-to books appealed to the yuppie decade's self-improvement drive, there was a definite shift in the wording of titles given to works that presented disabilities. Although it is not unusual to find terms like "tragedy," "heartbreak," and "meeting the needs" in the titles of older books on this kind of subject, recent publications take a much more positive and "self-actualizing" approach. Note the lack of pity and increasingly assertive tone in the following chronology of titles from 1981 to 1988.

A Difference in the Family: Living with a Disabled Child, by Helen Featherstone. (Penguin Books, 1981)

Taking on the World: Empowering Strategies for Parents of Children with Disabilities, by Joyce Slayton Mitchell. (Harcourt Brace Jovanovich, 1982)

On Becoming a Special Parent: A Mini-Support Group in a Book, by Marcia Routburg. (Parent/Professional, 1986)

No Apologies: A Guide to Living with a Disability, Written by the Real Authorities— People with Disabilities, Their Families and Friends, compiled by Florence Weiner. (St. Martin's, 1986)

In Time and With Love: Caring for the Special Needs Baby, by Marilyn Segal. (Newmarket Press, 1988)

Growing Up Proud: A Parent's Guide to the Psychological Care of Children with Disabilities, by James E. Lindemann and Sally J. Lindemann. (Warner, 1988)

Books that focused on mainstreaming in education also had titles that indicated transition from fighting an uphill battle to get P.L. 94-142 passed to seeing it as a manageable process with standard approaches that should be utilized to ensure the education of handicapped children in the least restrictive setting possible.

No Easy Answers: The Learning Disabled Child at Home and at School, by Sally L. Smith. (Winthrop, 1979, and Bantam, 1980)

Negotiating the Special Education Maze: A Guide for Parents and Teachers, by Winifred Anderson, Stephen Chitwood, and Deidre Hayden. (Prentice Hall, 1982)

Making Regular Schools Special, by John Henderson, with chapter contributions by Arthur Murphy and Robert Mignone. (Schocken, 1986)

The Special Education Handbook: A Comprehensive Guide for Parents and Educators, by Kenneth Shore. (Teachers College Pr., 1986)

TWO STEPS FORWARD

A trend toward portrayal of greater human diversity, including active characterizations of individuals with physical or mental or emotional impairments has been demonstrated within these media formats. Authors, illustrators, and editors selecting manuscripts for publication have been exposed to these trends, and so have children who will be the audience for the juvenile literature identified in this volume. The trend is to draw a larger circle around the handicapped-access stick figure to include people of all types, with strengths and weaknesses of their own. When that larger circle is emphasized, one hardly notices the small circle of the wheel that was drawn to identify a limitation.

ONE STEP BACK WITH TINY TIM: CURRICULUM TRENDS IN THE 1980s

> *"Children's literature constantly lags behind grown-up literature in its sensitivity to intellectual revolutions."*
> —Clifton Fadiman[4]

Individualized instruction, learning centers, and magnet schools were important educational innovations during the same years that P.L. 94-142 was being implemented. In California, one magnet school option was a "back to basics" curriculum, which anticipated the National Reading Initiative. Unfortunately, this curriculum trend can undermine attitudinal changes that facilitate the mainstreaming process by relying on "classic" or recommended reading lists, which reintroduce the Tiny Tim stereotype. California's new language arts framework called for literature-based reading instruction, including a list of "recommended readings in literature, kindergarten through grade eight." California Media and Library Educators Association had expressed their opposition to a prescriptive list and had lobbied instead for state support of adequate, trained staff in the elementary schools of California. Public librarians pointed out that the pooled resources of many branches could not address even one school's student body demand for specific titles. Early drafts of the "Honig list" introduced a motive for compromise: because there obviously was going to be a list, library professionals wanted to have a say about what was on it. By 1988, the final annotated bibliography of 1,010 "classical and contemporary works of fiction, nonfiction, poetry and drama" was published by the California State Department of Education.[5]

Many professionals have contributed to the various tools and texts that have been generated by this shift, and legal compliance committees have examined them before acceptance. Blocks of books, including long-out-of-print titles placed on the list, are available through vendors in order to build collections.

There is nothing bad about any of this progression, but children who "read to the list" are likely to be as limited as students who "study to the test." Many reading awards will be given, and higher test averages will be gained, but incentive for reading books too new for the list is blunted the way skills or knowledge not measured on the test is slighted. Other states and districts are also adopting recommended or "classic" lists that demonstrate multicultural or legal compliance sensitivity. The best of these still will need review and revision to include portrayals of disabilities that can maintain the momentum gained during P.L. 94-142's implementation. In 1984, Baskin and Harris concluded that:

> ". . . literature about disability is plentiful and varied. Some books intentionally or inadvertently deliver derogatory messages about people with impairments; others combine inspired, insightful writing with honest, accurate presentation (often accompanied by quality illustrations) to produce an abundance of valuable materials that can be used to facilitate the mainstreaming process."[6]

Because excellent books have been identified that were published since 1940, recommended reading lists should include these to balance dated portrayals of disabilities that will be encountered in "classics" such as *A Christmas Carol, Heidi, Little Women, Pollyanna, A Secret Garden, Treasure Island,* and on into more demanding titles such as Shakespeare's *Richard III, Of Mice and Men, The Glass Menagerie,* and *Nicholas Nickleby.* My experience is that recommended reading lists can quickly become restricted reading lists. Even children have only so much time, and what was to be an exciting pathway out of illiteracy can become an ever-narrowing funnel toward a core of books that have merit but often lack immediacy for readers. Children's literature has fiction "classics" that tend to incorporate portrayals of disabilities that are seriously flawed, as pointed out by author Jean Little in her autobiography *Little by Little: A Writer's Education.*

> "Remembering how I had never found a cross-eyed heroine in a book, I decided to search for books about children with motor handicaps. I did not for one moment intend to limit my students to reading about crippled kids. I knew that they completely identified with Anne Shirley and Homer Price, that they actually became Bambi, Piglet and Wilbur. I did not think they needed a book to help them adjust. I did believe, however, that crippled children had a right to find themselves represented in fiction.
> "I began to feel angry on their behalf. Why couldn't there be a happy ending without a miracle cure? Why wasn't there a story with a child in it who resembled the kids I taught?"[7]

Baskin and Harris praised Jean Little's books about children who had disabilities. They extended the argument that crippled children had a right to find themselves in fiction by proposing that *all* children could benefit from reading about characters who cope with special needs *and* that they should be encouraged to do so to ensure the success of P.L. 94-142. Will focus on "basics" or "classics" send young audiences toward Tiny Tim, right past Jean Little's Anna or the other contemporary characterizations described in this volume? Books that accurately portray a disability as part of a characterization should be featured in school curricula, and those that perpetuate stereotypes in which a person is defined by an impairment should be seriously reconsidered.

The Day They Came to Arrest the Book, by Nat Hentoff, helps put the complex question of intellectual freedom into perspective by describing a challenge to Mark Twain's *The Adventures of Huckleberry Finn.* When minority rights and social justice seem undermined by Huck's point of view, some students read it as racist trash, and others as a thought-provoking satire. I am not proposing that classics with stereotypical characterizations should be purged from collections and reading lists. Instead, their presence on lists should be justified and balanced by including titles written with modern sensitivity. When today's children get a qualitative directive to "Read One of These Good Books," it implies sanction of what is portrayed in those books. If the reading is a classroom experience that includes discussions, comparisons, or lectures that can place the work in its appropriate social setting, the exposure can be wonderful. But passive lists do not carry the warning "These titles may contain a social bias that violates current federal law."

If a community's response to the national reading initiative or literature-based education movements of the 1980s was to adopt reading lists for students from kindergarten through high school, then some questions should be asked about them.

1. Who has agreed that these titles have literary merit and child appeal instead of just longevity in school files or visibility in media adaptations?
2. What cultural baggage such as dated language, attitudes, literary clichés, and conventions or stereotypes will be encountered in these titles?
3. How many of the titles on this list are from 1940 on, and how many contain portrayals of disabilities that have been identified by the bibliographies in Bowker's series?
4. Can this list be improved by striking the titles that reviewers found seriously flawed and/or supplementing it with recent titles that can promote the type of attitudinal change Baskin and Harris campaigned for to facilitate the mainstreaming process?
5. Are young readers encouraged to develop analytical skills as well as decoding and comprehension skills so that exposure to actions or attitudes in print is not equal to acceptance of them?
6. Who is available to guide young readers to other titles that may touch them personally, once a recommended list has helped to interest them in books?

My experience in school libraries, in public libraries, as a member of two of California's committees for legal compliance review of textbooks, and during two years on the Association for Library Services to Children's Notable Books Committee have led me to develop these guidelines. However, the courage to share these considerations comes from memories of little Debbie, who, like Jean Little's students, only found books that made her think she had to be as hopeful as Pollyanna, as good as the Little Lame Prince, or as much a blessing to others as Tiny Tim since she could never climb Heidi's mountain or recover in some secret garden.

Legislation and popular culture have taken two steps forward. Let's avoid a well-intended step back. Mainstreaming efforts have momentum as long as educators and parents can focus resources on accommodating students in the least restrictive environment possible. We must keep their reading resources as rich as possible with accurate portrayals and honest role models.

NOTES

1. Edwin Markham, "Outwitted," *Modern American Poetry,* new & enl. ed., edited by Louis Untermeyer. New York: Harcourt, Brace & World, 1962, p. 106.

2. Dorothy Scheuer, "How Real Is What You See on TV?" *Junior Scholastic* (February 1991): pp. 2–4.
3. Leonard Maltin, *Leonard Maltin's TV Movies and Video Guide, 1991 ed.* New York: Signet, 1990.
4. Clifton Fadiman, *The World Treasury of Children's Literature: Book Three.* Boston: Little, Brown, 1985, p. 604.
5. Janet McWilliams, *Celebrating the National Reading Initiative.* Sacramento: Bureau of Publications, California State Department of Education, 1989, p. 78.
6. Barbara H. Baskin and Karen H. Harris, *More Notes from a Different Drummer: A Guide to Juvenile Fiction Portraying the Disabled.* New York: Bowker, 1984, p. 49.
7. Jean Little, *Little by Little: A Writer's Education.* New York: Viking, 1987, pp. 223–224.

3

TRENDS IN FICTION, 1982–1991

*I think it is at best confusing to lump people with
diseases such as epilepsy and diabetes with people
who are paraplegics, blind, or otherwise physically
disabled. In fact, it is not terribly sensible to lump all
physically disabled people together.*
—Dorothy M. Broderick[1]

ACCESS POINTS

In this volume, the annotated books are grouped into four major categories:
physical problems, sensory problems, cognitive and behavior problems, and
multiple/severe and various disabilities. For each character in the book,
indexing terms for health impairments, physical limitations, and mental or
emotional disabilities were assigned if the conditions could be specifically
identified. If not, the annotations were included in the chapter on various
disabilities.

Plot elements common to these works were also indexed by terms such as
"Medication," "Surgery," and "Terminal illness." Segregating health care
institutions by physical treatment (Hospitalization), custodial or psychiatric
treatment (Institutionalization), and geriatric care (Nursing homes) was an
awkward decision. However, as in *Psychology Index* and *Medical Subject
Headings,* some terms had to be selected for clarity even though we would
like to avoid emotionally loaded terms and labeling in general usage. Though
authors may have referred to a character's "therapy," a distinction has been
made here between psychiatric care (Counseling) and physical rehabilitation
(Rehabilitation therapy).

The relationship of the protagonist to the character with a disability is indexed by the terms "Friendship," "Mothers," "Brothers and sisters," and other labels for family members. Though indexing does not identify same-age friends as different from intergenerational friends, plot summaries clarify the protagonist's interactions with any disabled character.

The analysis portion of an annotation indicates if a book is written in first person or includes passages from the disabled character's point of view. These access points aid comparison of juvenile fiction identified in review media from 1982 to 1991. To provide an overview of titles that can expose readers to aspects of living with physical, emotional, or mental impairment, some discussion of trends and patterns as well as current literary criticism is in order.

TRENDS AND PATTERNS

The subject index of this volume provides a rough chart of how often modern authors have developed characterizations that represent particular disabling conditions. Between 1982 and 1991, orthopedic and neurological impairments and emotional disturbances were the most frequently portrayed disabilities in fiction for children and teenagers. Cynthia Voight's *Izzy, Willy Nilly* and Chris Cutcher's *The Electric Horse Game* stand out as young adult novels that address the social readjustment of suddenly disabled teens. Congenital conditions are explored for middle grades in *Golden Daffodils* by Marilyn Gould and *Margaret's Moves* by Bernice Rabe. Most authors identify the cause of paralysis or neurological impairment, but some are lax in presenting an authentic portrayal of the disability or disease the character is said to have.

Though authors made a point of including exact terminology for orthopedic and neurological conditions, emotional disturbances were rarely labeled. Occasionally, characters were revealed through their journal or comments addressed to psychiatric care providers. *Sex Education* by Jenny Davis, *Life Without Friends* by Ellen Emerson White, *The Hunger Scream* by Ivy Ruckman, and *Up Country* by Alden R. Carter used this introspective first-person recounting.

Often, writers used a case study progression of behavioral change observed by a friend or family member. This gave the story suspense, but accurate depiction of the disturbance sometimes slowed the plot and made the dialogue stiff. Other writers skillfully integrated foreshadowed details of the disturbance, believable pace in plot development, and unique characterizations that developed during the novel. Richard Peck's *Remembering the Good Times* and Jean Thesman's *The Last April Dancers* are examples of compelling novels that are not clumsy with case study exposition. These titles show both the progression of an emotional disturbance that leads to suicide and the way that act affects other major characters.

Suspense novels and mysteries show a new restraint in their use of characters with an emotional disturbance. Whereas protagonists used to see their mad assailant destroyed, current villains are neutralized in the climactic scene, then paired with appropriate psychiatric support during the denouement. Often, emotional scars are revealed or foreshadowed so readers may convert their dread of criminally insane characters into sympathetic relief. Joan Lowery Nixon is particularly skilled at this blend of sensationalism and sensitivity, as demonstrated in *Secret, Silent Screams*. Avi tweaks the reader's conscience when his protagonist seems to pressure a deluded man toward violence in *Wolf Rider*.

Missing children and sexual abuse received a great deal of media coverage in the 1980s; these two connected issues seem to have rendered authors anxious to add a plot twist that reassured readers there were no sexual overtones in the incidents they portrayed. Three novels dealt with male kidnappers who had mental blocks about the accidental deaths of young loved ones. The most successful use of this mistaken identity/emotional disturbance conclusion was in *The Twisted Window* by Lois Duncan.

Conversely, when it indeed was sexual abuse that caused a child to experience a personality shift, authors were honest about the lingering effects of such abuse. *Gillyflower* (Ellen Howard, 1986), *The Boy in the Off-White Hat* (Lynn Hall, 1984), and *Mac* (John MacLean, 1987) portrayed characters with profound emotional disturbance due to sexual abuse. Emotional disturbance caused by suppressed memories of such abuse is portrayed in *Sacred Circle of the Hula Hoop* by Kathy Kennedy Tapp.

Increasingly, health impairments have been defined or developed beyond vague mention of "invalid," "frail," or "bedridden" characters. AIDS, allergies, Alzheimer's disease, and cancer, in particular, are more evident in literature that was produced for children and teenagers during the 1980s than in earlier periods covered. M. E. Kerr's *Night Kites,* for young adult readers, and *Losing Uncle Tim,* a picture book by MaryKat Jordan portray AIDS patients from a younger, male relative's point of view. Gloria D. Miklowitz used three points of view in *Goodbye Tomorrow* (1987); *Alex, the Kid with AIDS* (Linda Walvoord Girard, 1990) shows the dynamics of mainstream education and social acceptance of a student with this health impairment.

Anorexia nervosa and bulimia were also front-page news items that made their way into American fiction for juvenile readers. Authors have successfully researched and projected the impact of recently discovered health hazards on family and other relationships. One example is *Anything to Win,* also by Gloria D. Miklowitz, which examines the risks related to steroid use.

Most of the stories that deal with terminal illness involved cancer, Alzheimer's disease, or strokes (cerebral hemorrhage). In *After the Rain,* Norma Fox Mazer portrays a girl who invests herself in the life of her terminally ill grandfather. In *Sheila's Dying* (Alden R. Carter, 1987) and *Heartbeat* (Norma Fox Mazer and Harry Mazer, 1989), subdued romance blossoms between visitors at the bedside of dying teens. In *One Green Leaf,* Jean Ure presents an athletic young man's decision to discontinue his chemotherapy in order to enjoy a relatively relaxed quality of life during the time remaining to him.

Successful chemotherapy is rarely presented, but *Invincible Summer* (Jean Ferris, 1987), *No Dragons to Slay* (Jan Greenberg, 1983), and *Will You Be My POSSLQ?* (Eve Bunting, 1987) offer welcome views of lengthy remissions. Difficult recovery from stroke and some communication problems that can result from such neurological impairments are portrayed in Katherine Paterson's *Park's Quest,* Betty Levin's *The Trouble with Gramary,* and a little gem called *The Canada Geese Quilt* (Natalie Kinsey-Warnock, 1989).

Few titles have attempted to incorporate portrayal of multiple handicaps, and no deaf-blind fictional character was encountered during the extensive survey of reviews and books within the scope of this bibliography. The role of multiple handicapped characters has been limited to a sibling of the protagonist or a sibling of a central character. In *The King of Hearts' Heart* (Sam Teague, 1987), the protagonist's girlfriend's brother dies of complications from his multiple birth defects. In *God, the Universe, and Hot Fudge Sundaes* (Norma Howe, 1989), a girl goes through a crisis of faith when her seriously disabled sister dies. Though a baby brother also dies in *Loving Ben* (Elizabeth Laird, 1989), most of the plot takes the main character beyond that point in her life.

In contrast to all those funerals, *Captain Coatrack Returns* (Joseph McNair, 1989) shows an older sister adjusting to a new relationship with her brother. He is enrolled in special education and establishes interests that go beyond the one-on-one these siblings had nurtured for five years while their parents drifted around in a benevolent haze of guilt and grief over their son's multiple birth defects. *Inside Out* (Ann M. Martin, 1984) also describes special education options for an autistic sibling, with realistic limits on the family's expectations. In *Why I'm Already Blue,* by Terry Farish, the taboo mystery of the handling of personal hygiene and elimination for a friend in a wheelchair is even hinted at. These daring insights are evidence of the pendulum swing needed to shift portrayals toward normalization, instead of idealization of special needs characters.

Historical fiction is where this pendulum swing is most evident. Some authors present stereotypic, negative attitudes to create an authentic sense of place and time. *Hide Crawford, Quick!* (Margaret W. Froelich, 1983) shows a family in shock over their newborn's missing lower leg. In *A Blue-Eyed*

Daisy (Cynthia Rylant, 1985), the protagonist muses on the impact of her father's arm injury and a schoolmate's seizures. Epilepsy, diabetes, and mental retardation are portrayed in various time periods. The narrator or protagonist generally provides a sensitive (i.e., modern) viewpoint to counter the historical bias shown through dialogue and dramatic episodes.

Visual and hearing impairments, speech problems, and cosmetic impairments are still being used to help distinguish various members of crowded casts. "Less fortunate" characters with such disabilities are frequent beneficiaries of a protagonist's blossoming ethics and good intentions. Carefully crafted fiction does not rely on these cardboard characters, however, so there are usually as many flaws in the writing style of those authors as there are in the blind/wise, deaf/clever, ugly/loving, and stammering/shy stereotypes they perpetuate.

The best writing allows readers to project how the featured impairment affects the disabled character. *Gideon Ahoy!* by William Mayne and *Tell Me How the Wind Sounds* by Leslie Davis Guccione accurately and vividly focus the reader's perceptions on those of the hearing impaired characters. Several novels, like Ian Strachan's *The Flawed Glass* and Marc Talbert's *Toby,* make the valid point that communication problems can cause misjudgment of a person's mental abilities.

Mental retardation and learning disabilities are hard to index if a character is described only as "dull" or "slow." *Probably Still Nick Swanson* by Virginia Euwer Wolff makes an impressive distinction between these cognitive problems. For elementary grades, *And Don't Bring Jeremy* (Marilyn Levinson, 1985) or the historical fiction reader *Stay Away from Simon!* by Carol Carrick show how bias against a cognitive impairment can be overcome. *Where's Chimpy?* by Bernice Rabe or *Different, Not Dumb* by Margot Marek can be excellent discussion starters for younger children.

Titles that handle controversial topics such as nursing homes, hospice care, and euthanasia will also initiate valuable discussion. Robert Cormier's *The Bumblebee Flies Anyway* is intriguing, distressing, and exhilarating in its presentation of a terminal care/research facility and several outstanding characterizations. Physicians were drawn into mercy death pacts in *Doc* by Richard Graber, *Going Backwards* by Norma Klein, and *The Rain Catchers* by Jean Thesman.

Temporary hospital stays were also portrayed in several titles. A curious fantasy, *Voyages* (Doris Buchanan Smith, 1989), merged trauma, origami and Norse mythology. The ambitious science fiction novel *Eva* (Peter Dickinson, 1989) projected the ultimate transplant and rehabilitation. Realistic rehabilitation from a spinal injury was presented in *Wheels for Walking* (Sandra Richmond, 1985), a novel with autobiographical details in it.

First-person accounts by a protagonist who has some impairment are often written for young adults. For younger readers, disabled central characters tend to be a grandparent, a sibling, or a newly acquired friend. Parents are often eliminated by some health impairment from an active role in the protagonist's life, which initiates or escalates character development.

Afternoon of the Elves (Janet Lisle, 1989) and *Daphne's Book* (Mary Downing Hahn, 1983) each have a rather bleak ending because a child's valiant efforts to provide for an incapacitated guardian are insufficient. In *Crazy Quilt* (Jocelyn Riley, 1984) and *Fran Ellen's House* (Marilyn Sachs, 1987), optimistic endings from previous stories about these dysfunctional families are balanced by exploring the stresses that a mother's release from psychiatric care and the presence or absence of outpatient counseling offer the reunited families. *The Big Way Out* (Peter Silsbee, 1984) counters Riley's and Sachs's portrayals of abandoned wives with suffering daughters by depicting a successful doctor whose psychotic, yet controlling, behavior makes his son consider violence as the solution.

From patricide to suicide, congenital conditions to accidents, euthanasia to successful medical intervention, such books for children and teenagers offer a broad view of life experiences and the various types of disabilities that can affect people. Most portrayals are in young adult novels; however, picture books have also incorporated an impressive number of characters with various impairments.

ILLUSTRATIONS

Themes for bibliotherapy and purposive texts once dominated other production values at well-intentioned small presses like A. Whitman and Twenty First Century Books. From 1982 to 1991, better book design, a higher quality of binding, and closer attention to pairing illustrations with the text have resulted in significant improvements in picture books and middle readers. Contrasting the weak drawings by Charles Robinson for *Grandma Drives a Motor Bed* (Diane Johnston Hamm, 1987) with *I'm Deaf and It's Okay* (Lorraine Aseltine et al., 1986) or *There's a Little Bit of Me in Jamey* (Diana M. Amadeo and Judith Friedman, 1989) demonstrates that progress. In addition, readers of transitional fiction (books to be used between easy readers and longer, chapter books) have been targeted by the Kids on the Block series. Though the illustrations for Kids on the Block stories have a cartoonish style, they are inviting and the format accommodates a lot of information at the back of the book, so that the story does not dwell on each impairment.

In *See You Tomorrow, Charles* (Miriam Cohen, 1983), Lillian Hoban illustrates how her classic cast of primary grade characters get to know a blind student. Ted Rand's paintings for *Knots on a Counting Rope* (Bill Martin Jr. and John Archambault, 1987) are expressive and exciting, with no conventional images of a blind child with eyes closed. Other artists have complemented the tone and action of texts with illustrations that range from Daniel Pinkwater's bold designs for *Uncle Melvin* to Lambert Davis's softly rendered scenes in *The Bells of Christmas* (Virginia Hamilton, 1989). For *One Light One Sun* (Raffi, 1988), illustrator Eugenie Fernandes extended the song's text by detailing a bright, busy neighborhood where one youngster uses a wheelchair. The text for *No Trouble for Grandpa* by Carol A. Marron never mentions that David, who is sure his baby sister will be too hard for his grandfather to care for, uses a wheelchair.

Many picture books deal with the aging grandparent and the various physical and mental impairments that may affect such characters. Alzheimer's disease is a tragic decline for a child to witness, but *Always Gramma* (Vaunda Micheaux Nelson, 1989) offers a poetic, yet credible story. Death of a newborn is another important portrayal offered in *Last Week My Brother Anthony Died* by Martha Whitmore Hickman.

Successful pairing of text and illustration or an attractive, accurate representation on the cover are two strengths reviewers look for in books for children and teenagers. Other aspects, such as plot, characterization, and the author's writing style are evaluated as well. Though guidelines to avoid stereotyped portrayals of characters with disabilities may be agreed on as an ideal, reviews may both praise and criticize some of the same works of fiction. In acknowledgment that a uniform opinion is rarely available, a closer look at what is written about these books for children and teenagers follows.

LITERARY CRITICISM

> *Soon I became aware that there were almost (well,
> not quite) as many books about children's
> literature as there were books of children's
> literature, and that anyone who wished to handle
> the literature wisely would have to become familiar
> with a learned corpus of astonishing proportions.*
> —Clifton Fadiman[2]

During the 1980s, a tremendous increase in the amount of publishing for children became evident, and juvenile fiction generated a proportionate amount of review literature. That there is "more" by no means ensures that there are "better" portrayals of disabilities, because attitudinal changes toward a new ideal are still being integrated with each of the writer's, the editor's, or the reviewer's life experiences. This conflict has surfaced in literary evaluation of children's fiction. Reviewers of *Uncle Melvin* and *Gideon Ahoy!* did not agree at all on those books' merits or faults. Browsing through *Book Review Digest* for titles to be read and evaluated for this volume will reveal that opinion was divided on many of them.

In October 1990, the *Voice of Youth Advocate (VOYA)* editor, Dorothy M. Broderick, recounted how battlelines were drawn when a reviewer whose criteria for "treatment of persons with disabilities" colored the review submitted for a new title so much that the "subscribers would know almost nothing about the content of the book." That reviewer stressed criteria that supported "the *ideal*—to have characters with disabilities be a part of the story. Period. No melodramatics, no apologies, no superheroics. . . ." The reviewer concluded that "The criteria are debatable, of course, so you may want the input of other reviewers who are less radical, perhaps, in their notion of acceptable portrayal of characters with disabilities." [3]

This curiously polarized incident resulted in the reviewer's resignation rather than a revised review. I believe a sufficiently informative review could have indicated the historically correct, though disappointingly "crippled," characterization without compromising the reviewer's ideals. Constructive discussion of a book's merits and flaws depends on the tenet that any perspective has value because it is correct in the eyes of that reader. Though there can be no "right" answer to defend to the death, consistent guidelines have value. Conflicts are likely to arise when any ideal is applied too strictly to a piece of fiction, which, after all, is an art form that requires subjective evaluation.

The annotations in this volume are from one perspective: one person's experience modified by that person's synthesis of several reviewers' opinions. Misinterpretation of comments or lack of availability of the actual book may have affected some analysis. Broderick acknowledged "that we all bring a lot of adult garbage to everything we read," and it is likely that this bibliographer's ideals will be evident. Quotations are included to help users sample the reality of a portrayal's value or a writer's skill.

These annotations also contain full summaries and, unlike any book-talk, "give away" the ending of each story. Student readers should not be encouraged to browse through this bibliography, but book selectors should use it to build a suitable collection or to locate a particular fiction request for a reading audience. That way, the reality of a staff person's own resources (space, money, or time) and personal experience (none, little, or lots) can be accommodated by the ideological guidelines used to prepare this bibliography. After all, accommodation is the key word in a successful mainstreaming process.

NOTES

1. Dorothy M. Broderick, "Fiction: Reality or Ideology?" *VOYA* 13 (October 1990):203–204.
2. Clifton Fadiman, *The World Treasury of Children's Literature: Book Three.* Boston: Little, Brown, 1985, p. 622.
3. Broderick, "Fiction: Reality or Ideology?" p. 203.

ADDENDUM: THE 1990s ARE HERE

After the deadline for this book, more than one hundred 1990–1991 titles were selected in a supplementary survey of review media. Thirty additional book review summaries were included in the body of this volume, and for the titles listed below multiple review sources were identified. The descriptive quote with each title is from the first source cited. Each title still needs further exposure in the review literature or the author's examination to be evaluated.

Baird, Thomas. *Smart Rats.* HarperCollins, 1990. "It causes brain damage during pregnancy and deterioration of joints." KR 15 090. SLJ S90.

Brooks, Bruce. *Everywhere.* HarperCollins, 1990. "Turley's grandfather has a heart attack." KR 1 Ag90. HB Ja-Fe91.

Byers, Rinda M. *Mycca's Baby.* Orchard/Watts, 1990. "Helping the vague old lady next door." KR 15 Fe90. "Mycca bluntly describes Maudie as forgetting everything, including Rose, who takes care of her every day." BCCB Ap90.

Carter, Alden R. *Robodad.* Putnam, 1990. "A brain aneurism has left Sharon's father disastrously altered." KR 1 D90. SLJ Ja91.

Clements, Bruce. *Tom Loves Anna Loves Tom.* Farrar, 1990. "When a girl comes to stay with her ailing aunt . . . Aunt Barbara suddenly dies." KR 15 Je90. SLJ O90.

Close, Jessie. *The Warping of Al.* HarperCollins, 1990. "His bedridden grandma. . . ." KR 15 S90. SLJ S90.

Cohen, Barbara. *Laura Leonora's First Amendment.* Lodestar, 1990. "A boy with AIDS forces all of them to confront their different superstitions." KR 1 N90. SLJ Ja91.

Cohen, Barbara. *The Long Way Home.* Lothrop, Lee & Shepard, 1990. "Mom has had a mastectomy and is undergoing chemotherapy." KR 15 S90. SLJ O90.

Collins, Pat Lowery. *Waiting for Baby Joe.* Whitman, 1990. "Little brother arrives two months early . . . he needs a heart operation." KR 15 S90. HB N-D90.

Cross, Gilbert B. *A Witch Across Time.* Atheneum, 1990. "On the mend from the anorexia." KR 15 Ja90. "Where she is sent for deppression and anorexia." BCCB Fe90.

DeFelice, Cynthia. *Weasel.* Macmillan, 1990. "With the help of Ezra—a strange, tongueless hermit . . ." KR 15 Mr90. SLJ Je90.

Degens, T. *On the Third Ward.* HarperCollins, 1990. "The newest of the tubercular inhabitants of the Hessian State Hospital for Children." KR 15 S90. HB N-D90.

Dyjak, Elisabeth. *I Should Have Listened to Moon.* Houghton, 1990. "The senile old woman . . . comes to live with Nadine's family." KR 1 Ap90. BCCB MS90.

Feuer, Elizabeth. *Paper Doll.* Farrar, 1990. "Jeff, whose mild cerebral palsy affects his walk." KR 15 Je90. BCCB S90. HB S-090

Fosburgh, Liza. *The Wrong Way Home.* Bantam, 1990. "Her mother's steady deterioration from Huntington's chorea." KR 1 Jy90. BCCB N90. SLJ Jy90.

Gleitzman, Morris. *Two Weeks with the Queen.* Putnam, 1991. "His younger brother's inoperable cancer." KR 1 Fe91. BCCB Ap91.

Goldin, Barbara Diamond. *Cakes and Miracles: A Purim Tale.* Viking, 1990. "Blind Hershel . . . prays for a way to be of more help." KR 1 D90. SLJ Mr91.

Gruenberg, Linda. *Hummer.* Houghton, 1990. "The mother's mental illness is sensitively described." KR 15 Fe90. BCCB Mr90.

Hall, Lynn. *Halsey's Pride.* Scribner, 1990. "An epileptic teen-ager . . . confronts her own worst fears about her condition." KR 1 Fe90. BCCB MS90.

Holland, Isabelle. *The Unfrightened Dark.* Little, Brown, 1990. "Blind since the car accident that killed her parents four years ago. Now she has a guide dog." KR 1 Ja90.

Katz, Welwyn Wilton. *Whalesinger.* Macmillan, 1991. "Marty may have a marginal learning disability." KR 1 Ja91. BCCB Fe91.

Kehret, Peg. *Sisters, Long Ago.* Dutton, 1990. "Her sister Sarah's leukemia." KR 1 Fe90. BCCB Fe90.

King, Buzz. *Silicon Songs.* Delacorte, 1990. "Loving uncle Pete . . . is dying of brain cancer." KR 1 Je90. BCCB Je90.

LeGuin, Ursula K. *Tehanu: The Last Book of Earthsea.* Atheneum, 1990. "A young child . . . has been viciously abused and maimed by her own parents." KR 15 Ja90. BCCB Ap90. HB My-Je90.

McCuaig, Sandra. *Blindfold.* Holiday, 1990. "His blind brother Joel." KR 15 Ap90. BCCB O90.

Mayerson, Evelyn Wilde. *The Cat Who Escaped from Steerage.* Scribner, 1990. "She proves to immigration officials that her deaf cousin is intelligent and can communicate." KR 15 O90. HB Ja-Fe91. SLJ Fe91.

Mazer, Harry. *Someone's Mother Is Missing.* Delacorte, 1990. "She's still too deeply depressed to pick up her old life." KR 15 S90. SLJ S90.

Mazer, Norma Fox. *Babyface.* Morrow, 1990. "When Dad has a heart attack." KR Ag90. SLJ O90.

Meyer, Carolyn. *Killing the Kudu.* Macmillan, 1990. "Two new friends help a disabled teen-ager develop a sense of self-worth." KR 15 O90. SLJ N90.

Paterson, Katherine. *Lyddie.* Lodestar/Dutton, 1991. "Abandoned by their mother, whose mental stability has been crumbling . . ." KR 1 Ja91. SLJ Fe91.

Paterson, Katherine. *The Tale of the Mandarin Ducks.* Lodestar, 1990. "Shozor, the one-eyed servant. . . . Although the jacket describes this as a folk-tale, LC classifies it as fiction." KR 1 Ag90. HB N-D90.

Pirner, Connie White. *Even Little Kids Get Diabetes.* Whitman, 1991. "A preschooler tells how it was discovered, when she was only two, that she has this common disease." KR 1 Ja91.

Powell, E. Sandy. *Geranium Morning*. Carolrhoda, 1990. "A girl whose mother is dying." KR 15 Mr90.

Radin, Ruth Yaffe. *Carver*. Macmillan, 1990. "A sixth grader who has been blind since the age of two." KR 15 Mr90. BCCB Je90.

Sachs, Marilyn. *At the Sound of the Beep*. Dutton, 1990. "Sad derelicts and crazies." KR 1 Ap90. "Indigent park-dwellers." BCCB Mr90.

Sauer, Jim. *Hank*. Delacorte, 1990. "Emily, an odd child who is unaccountably disturbed by some trauma. . . . Hank catches meningitis from Arthur and dies." KR 15 Mr90. BCCB Mr90.

Schwandt, Stephen. *Guilt Trip*. Atheneum, 1990. "Fall guy for an unbalanced killer." KR 1 Fe90.

Semel, Nava. *Becoming Gershona*. Viking, 1990. "Her newly blind grandfather." KR 1 Jy90. HB Ja-Fe91.

Shaw, Diana. *What You Don't Know Can Hurt You*. Little, Brown, 1990. "Barrie . . . is driven to a number of irrational acts, including the harassment and (later) attempted suicide." KR 1 Ja90.

Stolp, Hans. *The Golden Bird*. Dial, 1990. "Daniel, who is only 11, is in a hospital dying of cancer." KR 15 Mr90. ". . . is comforted by a number of mystical visitations." BCCB Ap90.

Stover, Marjorie Filley. *Midnight in the Dollhouse*. Whitman, 1990. "Melissa's fall from a tree leaves her with a permanent limp." KR 1 Ja90.

Stowe, Cynthia. *Home Sweet Home, Good-Bye*. Scholastic, 1991. "Charlie's mother . . . has some sort of breakdown." KR 15 Fe90. "Charlie performs some irrational acts." BCCB Ap90.

Taylor, Theodore. *Tuck Triumphant*. Doubleday, 1991. "When 'Chok' arrives he's not a baby but a six-year-old—and profoundly deaf." KR 15 Fe91. SLJ Mr91.

Tomalin, Ruth. *Long Since*. Faber, 1990. "She has taught a deaf boy, believed to be 'daft,' to read." KR 15 Mr90.

Whelan, Gloria. *Hannah*. Knopf, 1991. "Blind Hannah, nine, has never been to school." KR 1 Fe91.

Winthrop, Elizabeth. *Luke's Bully*. Viking, 1990. "Arthur's problem is that he can't see: he's near-sighted." KR 15 Je90. "The Thanksgiving play in which Arthur is cast as a horse—with blinders, to mask the new glasses—lends humor." BCCB S90.

Zeier, Joan T. *The Elderberry Thicket*. Atheneum, 1990. "Her helping a 'retarded' boy learn to read (modern readers will recognize dyslexia)." KR 1 S90. SLJ 090.

4

BOOKS DEALING
WITH PHYSICAL PROBLEMS

This chapter classifies titles in two sections: Health Impairments and Ortho-pedic/Neurological Impairments.

Citations are alphabetical by author in each of these two main sections.

Health Impairment descriptions include conditions such as allergies, can-cer, diabetes, eating disorders, organ failure, and other diseases that affect the blood or immune system.

Books annotated in the Orthopedic/Neurological Impairments section focus on conditions such as cerebral palsy, epilepsy, missing limbs, motor impairments, paralysis, and spina bifida.

Short entries describe secondary characters or additional disabilities dis-cussed at length in a full annotation that has been classified in some other chapter. "See" references are noted.

HEALTH PROBLEMS

■ Adler, Carole S. *The Shell Lady's Daughter.* Coward-McCann, 1983. 140pp. (0-698-20580-4) Reading Level: Grades 7–9.
Disability: Health impairment

Kelly Allgood stays with her grandmother and ill grandfather the summer her mother attempts suicide. *See full annotation* Chapter 6: Emotional Disturbances.

■ Aiello, Barbara, and Jeffrey Shulman. *Friends for Life.* Illus. by Loel Barr. Twenty-First Century, 1988. 48pp. (0-941477-03-7) Reading Level: Grades 3–5. (BL 15 Mr89)
Disability: AIDS

The Woodburn School Video Club is making a movie, and the club's sponsor is Natalie Gregg. Amy Wilson is in the group, and though she is shy, the members pick her title for Robbie Jenkins's plot in "The Purple Slime from Seldon Swamp."

While working on their props, Amy and club members overhear Robbie's parents demanding that the assistant principal both confirm reports that Mrs. Gregg has AIDS and "get her out of the school and away from our children." All the members of the Video Club drop out due to rumors and fears about Natalie's illness.

Amy sees a television message from a guy who "reminded me of an old sea captain. I couldn't tell whether he was a soldier or a doctor. He looked like both." She looks in the mailbox, and, just as the TV message proclaimed, a pamphlet about AIDS had been delivered that day. Amy reads the pamphlet, talks with her parents, and tells several lies to visit Natalie and her husband. Amy cannot bring herself to listen to Natalie's explanation, then goes to a Video Club meeting at which Robbie is ready to vote Mrs. Gregg out.

Later, Amy attends an AIDS information meeting with her parents. There, a doctor, while attempting to assure those gathered that "AIDS is not spread by casual contact," is interrupted by the unruly audience. Amy goes to the podium with a video she helped the club to make that afternoon. It is called "Friends for Life," and it records the way Natalie discussed her illness with club members and responded to their questions. Amy gives a T-shirt with a "Friends for Life" logo on it to Natalie.

Several students drop out of the club, and some new members join. The "Friends for Life" video wins an Honorable Mention award in a fifth- and sixth-grade contest. Natalie becomes too ill to attend meetings, but she visits with Amy. Natalie shares a quote from Robert Kennedy about standing up for an ideal and sending ripples of hope out into the world.

Analysis: Part of the Kids on the Block series, this title incorporates the question-and-answer portion in a video presentation instead of in a separate interview with the young protagonist at the end. The information is accurate yet defers to parents at several points in the questioning for specific discussion about how sex can transmit AIDS. Natalie has contracted AIDS from her husband, who had shared a needle with an infected person during a period of his life when he was using drugs. Natalie is asked about her feelings of anger and betrayal and responds that she and her husband are "going to see this thing through together . . . One of the worst things about AIDS is that it's such a . . . lonely disease. People don't want to be near you—even your friends."

Natalie's advice is that "The best thing to do is to be a responsible person. Don't do drugs. Don't have sex until you're grown up. Learn the facts. Talk to your parents." The subplot of Amy's changing from being a "quiet little" thing to speaking up for what she thinks is right is rather slight character development, and the lies are an odd way to show her new assertiveness. Paired with *Losing Uncle Tim* in most collections, lower-graders could have vicarious experiences with two children's views of the personal and social impact of this disability.

■ Aiello, Barbara, and Jeffrey Shulman. *Hometown Hero: Featuring Scott Whittaker.* Illus. by Loel Barr. Twenty-First Century, 1989. 56pp. (0-941477-84-5) Reading Level: Grades 4–6.
Disability: Asthma

Scott Whittaker keeps a journal at his doctor's suggestion. Between Thanksgiving and Christmas, his entries record his plans for a sports banquet and the friendship he strikes up with a homeless man he meets at the library. When the banquet speaker cannot make the engagement, Scott invites his new friend, who has revealed that he was the championship quarterback in a well-known game, to come as a featured guest. Scott loans the man a shirt and tie from his father's closet.

Scott's karate club makes a presentation, and then the hometown hero is introduced as the evening's speaker. Scott does not see the fellow at the library any longer and later hears that the man has a job in a nearby town. For Christmas, packages arrive for Scott's family, including the returned shirt and tie.

Analysis: Scott tells about the options he has for managing his life to avoid asthma episodes. His diary is one way to identify both triggers and successful methods of treatment. He mentions the types of weather and activities that are a strain on his health and does deep-breathing exercises each evening. The standard section of questions for Scott follows the pattern of other titles in the Kids on the Block series.

The social consciousness of this book overloads the plot a bit, but a classmate's negative reaction to a sports has-been bum contrasts with Scott's acceptance of the withdrawn man. Scott's mother makes it clear that homeless people can be working or mentally ill or any age and still need to live in shelters. Scott's adult friend is hostile at first, and frequently he gets a vacant look or makes oblique references to his past. Although he may be emotionally disturbed, he is able to get a job and keep it for a while without any apparent professional assistance.

The illustrations are bland, and the cover picture of a grubby, football-carrying adult with young Scott, outside the library, has no relation to any scene from the story. The questions and answers at the back are the strongest part of the book.

■ Aiello, Barbara, and Jeffrey Shulman. *A Portrait of Me.* Illus. by Loel Barr. Twenty-First Century, 1989. 56pp. (0-941477-05-3) Reading Level: Grades 4–6.
Disability: Diabetes

Christine Kontos is 11 when she reads her 15-year-old brother Ari's report on immigration and Ellis Island. She recalls how disenchanted she has been with "old country" ways and having to eat meals left over from her grandparents' Greek restaurant. Christine regrets the frequent fights she now has with her older brother because Ari had supported Christine through her adjustment to taking insulin injections by helping her learn to "give shots" to citrus fruit he drew faces on.

When Christine's new personal priorities for a dance recital and a performance of the Joffrey ballet conflict with her family's commitment to the restaurant and a Greek Orthodox celebration, she feels her brother lives in the past, and "That's why he hates me." After their dog is struck by a car and dies, Ari admits he feels that memories are important because they are the only thing that lasts during a lifetime of changes. Christine is inspired by Ari's report to create a personal piece for her dance recital that includes Greek folk dance, ballet, and rock music.

Analysis: As in other books in the Kids on the Block series, information on Christine's health impairment is incorporated into a first-person account. Because Christine's independence versus family relationships is the real theme of the story, her references to the accommodations she makes for her disability are more oblique than those in the other titles in this series.

The story has a one-paragraph episode when Christine feels tired and dizzy, takes the "candy cure," and admits "I should have eaten all my lunch. I was just so busy." Other than this scene, Christine's point of view consistently ignores daily routine, like the blood tests she performs "two or three times a day by pricking my finger" and using a test strip and meter. The "Meet Christine" frontispiece lists favorite friends and activities and then includes:

Yuck!:
    Arguing with Ari
    Greek leftovers
    A messy fridge
    ("Who moved my insulin NOW?")

Other details on how diabetes affects Christine are presented at the end of the book in a question-and-answer format that tries to maintain a chatty exchange in language suited to the protagonist's age. Downplaying her routine is consistent with her comment at the end that "after a while, you get used to treating your diabetes. It just becomes a part of your life that you don't think about that much."

Too little attention is paid to siblings other than Ari, since Christine does introduce two sisters and two other brothers, who then play no role at all in the story she tells. The author avoids crowding out action with minor characters and details of Christine's special health need in this slim novel, but those are indeed the unique elements of the story, which could have offered readers insights and given the story some depth. The wise grandfather diagnoses the sibling conflict between Ari, who has adolescent fears of change and holds on too tightly to his roots, and Christine, who in learning to cope with her physical difference pursues independence so fiercely that she cuts off her family.

The illustrations serve best as diagrams in the last section and are awkward in presenting the dance Christine so proudly performs for her family. All Kids on the Block series stories should be considered for purchase when a collection of "transitional" fiction (short, illustrated, chapter books) is needed. However, Christine's self-portrait is skimpy on literary merit, gets heavy with a "be proud of your roots" message, and features cartoonish drawings that lack proportion, consistency, and grace. An additional choice for large collections or when the entire series is desired.

■ Alcock, Vivien. *The Stonewalkers.* Delacorte, 1983. 151pp. (0-440-08321-4) Reading Level: Grades 5–8. (BCCB Je83)
Disability: Health impairment

Poppy Brown is known as a liar, and her various foster mothers are not willing to dismiss her stories with the easy excuse that she has had a hard life. Her father died when she was 3, and her mother's health is so poor that she is often hospitalized.

"When Poppy was five, her mother had gone into the hospital for so long that when at last Poppy was allowed to see her, she did not recognize her and would have walked past the pale, gaunt woman in the bed, had not Foster-Mother Allen caught hold of her arm and told her to go and kiss her mother. She had sat uncomfortable on the chair, while her mother gazed at her pleadingly, as if she wanted something. But Poppy had already given her the flowers."

When Poppy's mother gets a job as a live-in cook, Poppy tends to call her Mother Brown, as she would have in a foster home. Poppy sees lightning bring a statue to life and has adventures combating the army of stone characters that becomes animated by an ancient chain. Poppy is 12 years old and her only companion is another girl named Emma. The girls and a little lost boy named Rob are surrounded by stonewalkers from gardens and graves. The heartless and powerful figures are intrigued by Rob's tears and the children's frail bodies. Their night of terror ends in a mine where the figures smash into each other while trying to climb up a ledge to reach the fleeing girls.

When Rob tells the police his story, it is ignored in their effort to find the missing girls. Mrs. Brown regrets being so unfeeling toward Poppy.

"It was I who was wicked, she thought now, though I never meant to be. I wanted to be a good mother, to bring her up to know right from wrong, to be a credit to me. But I was so tired! Always so tired and my bones aching! Each time I came out of the hospital, I'd ask for her back right away. Wait till you're stronger, they'd say, but I wanted her back there and then, my own daughter!"

When they are reunited, Poppy starts on her resolution to try to be friends with her mother, by calling out, "Mom!"

Analysis: This fantasy has realistic scenes and emotions threaded through its suspenseful action. Both Poppy and her mother want to improve their relationship, and what is lacking between them is much the same as what is lacking in the stonewalkers.

■ Amadeo, Diana M. *There's a Little Bit of Me in Jamey.* Illus. by Judith Friedman. Whitman, 1989. 32pp. (0-8075-7854-1) Reading Level: Grades 3–4. (BCCB MS89)
Disability: Leukemia

Brian wakes to find his brother, Jamey, has been rushed to the hospital. Jamey has been hospitalized before, because of leukemia. "This means that some of the cells in Jamey's blood aren't normal. They're growing too fast." Brian makes his first visit to the hospital, where he has to wear a mask and gown and see intravenous (IV) lines and blood test procedures for Jamey. Brian brings his old-timer baseball card of Joe Garagiola, but Jamey is too tired to appreciate the gift.

After a week, Jamey returns home. Brian feels frustrated by all the warnings he has been given and all the special attention Jamey gets. After a talk with his mother, Brian and his parents spend more time together. Jamey loses his hair in "big clumps" as a side effect of chemotherapy. "The medicine that was in the IV can cause hair to fall out." When Jamey becomes completely bald, he jokes, "Just call me Joe Garagiola."

Jamey does not want to return to the hospital for a scheduled radiation treatment. Mom promises there would be "no needles this time," and Brian comes along for moral support. Jamey does not improve. One night their parents wake Brian to discuss a bone marrow transplant that the doctors hope would help. Brian's father shows "a bandage over his hipbone. 'This is where they take the marrow from.' " The doctors felt that Brian's cells could be the best match to give Jamey a chance to live. Brian sets aside his worries about getting sick from Jamey's cells or that the transplant would hurt and never stop hurting.

The test shows Brian to be a perfect match, so the transplant is completed.

"Dad was sitting by Jamey's bed. He was watching the tube leading to Jamey's wrapped arm.

'Are my cells in there?' I asked.

'Yes,' Dad said proudly. 'And I do believe that Jamey is stronger already!'

'How do you feel?' Jamey asked me.

'Like I slid hard into home plate,' I admitted.

But I didn't mind. Because of that little bit of me in Jamey, he may come home, to stay."

Analysis: This candid story was written by a nurse who points out, "Young cancer patients as well as their siblings, parents, and friends need to be reassured that feelings of fear, confusion, and anger are normal reactions to the disease." She presents this theme in an unsentimental way, and the duo-tone book design complements each episode in the touching account. The boys are subdued by their circumstances, but persistent hints of personality come out in Brian's comments about trading cards and playing baseball. Brian's father is proud of Brian's willingness to help, but the emotional echo of this story comes from textless pictures of the brothers walking away from the hospital hand in hand. The last page is a rear view in sepia, foreshadowed by the title page's front view. The inviting color cover shows the boys with their arms around each other's shoulders, grinning at the reader, Jamey wearing a cap on his still-bald head.

■ Arnold, Katrin. *Anna Joins In.* Illus. by Renate Seelig. Abingdon, 1983. 32pp. (0-687-01530-8) Reading Level: Grades K–3. (SLJ Ja84)
Disability: Cystic fibrosis

Anna has a difficult pattern to her days because she has cystic fibrosis. Sometimes her sister or her friends make her feel bad because she cannot do everything they can. When Mother has to strike Anna's back to loosen congestion in her lungs or when Anna must use special equipment at home, she wishes she did not have this health problem. Anna argues with a friend at school, but they make up in time for a Halloween party.

Analysis: This translation from a German publication is often stiff in its dialogue, and it mixes tenses in some scenes. The text blocks are large and somewhat cluttered, with decorative drawings of Mimi and Doodel, Anna's stuffed toys, mimicking the action. The other watercolor washed drawings are lively, with childlike details.

The symptoms and treatment of cystic fibrosis are clearly presented, sometimes through Anna's action and sometimes by her parents' or her doctor's comments. The details of Anna's physical accommodation and emotional reactions to the illness are what will appeal to readers, because the subplot of a patched-up friendship is too slight to really carry interest. The double-page spread of a Halloween party seems a weak climax, but it does show Anna joining in.

■ Bach, Alice Hendricks. *Waiting for Johnny Miracle.* Harper & Row, 1980. 240pp. (0-06-020348-X) Reading Level: Grades 8–12. (BF, vol. III) *Disability:* Cancer

Theo and Becky Maitland are identical twins. At 17, their athletic activities on the basketball team and Becky's body-conscious boyfriend keep Becky from complaining about pain in her right leg. A month after her first trouble with the leg, she is rushed for treatment, and a tumor on her right thigh is diagnosed as malignant. Becky begins chemotherapy and attempts to adjust to the stress of her condition. Her boyfriend runs out on her when he learns she is ill.

At the hospital, she makes friends in the cancer unit and interacts with patients. Surgery to remove the tumor and replace the affected bone with a metal rod leads to a two-month convalescence. Becky's roommate, Mariela, has a form of leukemia that will not respond to treatment. When Theo comes to visit Becky at winter break, the twins conspire to remove Mariela's dread of dying while still a virgin. The twins smooth over their own relationship and look forward to Becky's return home.

Analysis: This book has a mature tone in the language used and contains vivid descriptions of the pain, death, and discomforts that Becky and her mother are exposed to in the hospital. It also presents the story of a critical illness and its impact on an entire family. Though it has a publication date earlier than the stated scope of this volume, I wished to include this summary to supplement coverage provided in the Baskin and Harris volumes.

■ Bates, Betty. *Tough Beans.* Illus. by Leslie Morrill. Holiday, 1988. 89pp. (0-8234-0722-5) Reading Level: Grades 3–5. (BCCB Ja89) *Disability:* Diabetes

Nat is playing baseball when he collapses and is taken to the hospital. He learns that he has diabetes and must therefore restrict his diet and be careful about his medication. In fourth grade, his best friend is an Asian girl named Cassie, and his foe is the bullying new boy named Jasper. When Cassie's family moves away, Nat is upset. Then Nat learns why Jasper has such a mean streak, and they become friends.

Analysis: Information about diabetes is the core of this story, and other plot elements are not integrated as well as they might be. Characterizations are functional and the writing can seem choppy. Despite its stylistic flaws, Nat's willingness to cope with his health impairment and Jasper's failings makes him a character worth meeting.

■ Bawden, Nina. *Henry.* Illus. by Joyce Powzyk. Lothrop, 1988. 119pp. (0-688-07894-X) Reading Level: Grades 4–6. (BCCB Mr88)
Disability: Health impairment

During World War II, a family is evacuated to the English countryside. The youngest, a boy named Charlie Jones, finds a baby squirrel that gets named Henry, and the creature becomes a part of the family. Charlie's older sister enjoys her school holidays with her family and meets their neighbors.

Mrs. Jones is ill and tries to hide from her family the terminal nature of her condition. Charlie's older brother and sister discuss this. Visits from school create gaps in Charlie's sister's knowledge of the family and their friends so she feels left out. When she comes home at Christmas, she doubts her mother was as "lonely as I'd been at school when the letter came about Mrs. Jones and there was no one to talk to about it . . . with no one around me who knew her."

There is a caged-off part of a room where the family keeps Henry, but the sister takes him for a walk, assuming Henry has matured and that he will return to the house as he always had in the past. She is blamed for losing Henry, because he stays free after that, but the family adjusts to his absence.

Analysis: This closely observed animal story has additional depth from its subplots in which two families adjust to a parent's absence. Charlie is so young that he has no memory of his father, and an amusing episode of trouble in the three-holed privy helps resolve Charlie's worries that his father will not like him. Maturation and acceptance of realities one would rather dismiss are themes that Henry, Mrs. Jones, and the hardships of wartime introduce in this recommended novel.

■ Benjamin, Carol Lea. *Nobody's Baby Now.* Macmillan, 1984. 157pp. (0-02-708850-2) Reading Level: Grades 7–10.
Disability: Geriatric impairments

Liv Singer turns 15 and has big plans to lose weight and to gain a romance in her life. She imagines passionate responses for every friendly conversation she has with Brian. She has to give up her room when her maternal grandmother, Minnie, needs somewhere to stay until a nursing home can be located. Liv also gives up a lot of her usual pursuits with school friends to talk and read to Minnie, because Minnie has stopped speaking. "There's got to be more to life than being clean and avoiding salt, even when you're very old . . ." When Minnie does respond to Liv's poetry, conversation, and scrapbook sharing, the woman cries over her husband's death, two years previously.

" 'You know, tootsie,' she said in this calm voice, as if she had never stopped talking at all, 'no one's said "I love you" to me since my Sidney died.' "

Running for exercise in the park and being careful when she applies makeup give Liv a new look. Brian does not seem to notice, and when he does, he is uncomplimentary. Liv wants to prove to her parents that Minnie is well enough to stay with them by helping her walk downstairs. They do not make it, Minnie is injured, and she loses control of her bowel in their humiliating trek. Liv decides that Minnie can reminisce at the nursing home, where she will have better care than in their home. She plays an old guessing game with Brian and helps romantic matters along by kissing him.

Analysis: Many young adult novels show the teen protagonist's taking a dim view of the parents' decision to place a grandparent in a nursing home. Liv has her scheme, but it is certainly more realistic than some of the abduction scenarios that other titles use. The humor is so well integrated with this story's serious elements that many readers will enjoy Liv's account of the difficult weeks when she found and lost and found her grandmother.

■ Bess, Clayton. *Big Man and the Burn Out.* Houghton, 1985. 197pp. (0-395-36173-7) Reading Level: Grades 7–12. (BCCB F86)
Disability: Sickle-cell anemia

Jess Judd lives with his grandmother and her husband, Sid. He has no friends and assumes his grandmother hates him. His English teacher, Mr. Goodban, tries to encourage him, but Jess is doing so poorly in science that he is afraid he will be held back in eighth grade like the blond boy, Meechum. When Meechum is injured while defending Jess in a fight, Jess meets Meechum's family at the hospital. Jess is surprised to learn that Meechum's father and his brother, Jamie, are black.

Both boys need to select science projects. Jess decides to incubate a goose egg, and just when he's ready to give up on it, the gosling imprints him as its parent. Meechum tells Jess that Jamie is really his stepbrother and that the little boy has sickle-cell anemia. Meechum and Jamie spend a day with Jess and show him their "Frankenstein tree." The wild apricot tree has many kinds of fruit branches grafted onto it, so it makes an excellent science project for Meechum. For the first time since his mother died, Meechum is given a chance to have his schoolwork judged by the unbiased Mr. Goodban instead of supercritical instructors.

Meechum and Jess are skinny-dipping at the creek, when Jess's grandmother sees them. She is warned by Sid that she has to be less condemning of Jess or the boy will leave. The gosling that Jess hatched is brought to its emaciated mother to coax the mother goose off her ruined nest. Jess shares this successful effort with his grandmother and Sid.

Analysis: Jess is burdened by the fact that his mother abandoned him, leaving him with her own strict mother. Jess's grandmother is so concerned about controlling Jess that their relationship has deteriorated to the point where only Sid can smooth things between them. The themes of foster parenting, nurturing love, and complex genetic mixes are developed in the boy's home situations and science projects.

Homosexual preferences are alluded to in Mr. Goodban's living arrangement and in several of Jess's interactions with schoolmates. The viewpoint of the story shifts between characters and even the mother goose. However, the characterizations are strong enough to carry all this complexity and deal fairly with the strengths and weaknesses of each person.

■ Branfield, John. *The Fox in Winter.* Atheneum, 1982. 158pp. (0-689-50219-2) Reading Level: Grades 7–9. (BCCB Ap82)
Disability: Health impairment

Fran's mother is a district nurse in Cornwall. Tom Treloar is an elderly patient who brightens up when Fran comes along with her mother for a visit. A friendship develops, and Fran does not mind the way the old fellow plays on her sympathy, becoming a personal responsibility. When Tom dies, Fran is upset, but she has learned a lot about the man's life, and she values the time she spent building the friendship.

Analysis: This touching story of an intergenerational friendship reveals more about Tom's life and character than Fran's. The plot may not move enough to engage all readers' interest, but rewarding characterization, subtle relationships, and a colorful setting are offered.

■ Bunting, Eve. *Our Sixth-Grade Sugar Babies.* Lippincott, 1990. 147pp. (LB 0-397-32452-9) Reading Level: Grades 5–7. (KR 1 N90; BCCB N90)
Disability: Dementia

Eleven-year-old Vicki wants to prove she is responsible enough to be in charge of her half-sister. A school project to care for a five-pound bag of sugar ("Babe") introduces new obligations and problems for Vicki. When the handsome seventh-grade neighbor Vicki has a crush on asks her to go to the library, "Babe" is left with old Mr. Ambrose. Mr. Ambrose loses track of the dressed-up bag of sugar and becomes distressed when Vicki scolds him. Subsequent to this, Mr. Ambrose disappears, and Vicki takes responsibility for her actions.

Analysis: Authentic dialogue and introspection make Vicki's character interesting, and the plot moves well. Vickie's self-centeredness in taking advantage of Mr. Ambrose's kindness and then faulting him for neglecting her odd "child" is believable. Mr. Ambrose is portrayed as being vague about things, and easily distressed and disoriented. Vicki's compassion and her efforts to avoid a tragedy make this story a valuable addition to collections.

■ Bunting, Eve. *Will You Be My POSSLQ?* Harcourt, 1987. 181pp. (0-15-297399-0) Reading Level: Grades 7–9. (BCCB N87)
Disability: Cancer

Jamie tells the story of her first year in college at UCLA. She meets a sophomore named Kyle. When his roommate moves out, Kyle suggests that he come share Jamie's apartment. The financial motivations for this arrangement are clarified in the Census Bureau's acronym, "POSSLQ," for "persons of the opposite sex sharing living quarters."

Jamie is hesitant about falling in love again because her previous boyfriend deserted her after kidney surgery for cancer. She is also sensitive about the issue of premarital sex because her older sister has been propelled into marriage by an unplanned pregnancy. A younger sister decides to avoid such a complication in her relationship by refusing her boyfriend's persistent sexual advances.

When Jamie realizes that she has fallen in love with Kyle, she asks him to move out of her apartment. Kyle surprises her by remaining loyal even after she confesses that she is under treatment for cancer, and he agrees to put physical distance between them because he loves her too.

Analysis: This is a believable young adult novel that stands out because of its portrayal of celibacy as an option within a love relationship and because it presents oncologic treatment and care for a patient in remission.

Jamie's concerns are no longer focused on life and death but on the quality of the life she has. The pediatric care patients whom Jamie visits introduce a variety of conditions and characterizations. Bunting's pleasant romantic novel has a clear message about sexual activity, but, while delivering it, she shows that cancer is not always fatal.

■ Carrick, Carol. **The Elephant in the Dark.** Illus. by Donald Carrick. Houghton, 1988. 135pp. (0-89919-757-4) Reading Level: Grades 3–7. (KR 1 088)
Disability: Health impairment

Early in the 19th century, an elephant is placed in the care of a lonely boy named Will. At 12, he is the only child of impoverished Maddy, whose dreamy, artistic ways and poor health set them outside society in their small Massachusetts town. At first, Will is overwhelmed by the beast he cleans and cares for, but eventually he learns the commands she responds to and begins to trust her. Bullies that had once taunted Will are impressed to see huge Toong Talong protect the boy and obey him.

Maddy's terminal illness and death make Will turn to the elephant for comfort. When Toong Talong's new owner comes to claim her (by paying overdue room and board to Will's employer), orphaned Will follows them out of town. The new owner loses control of the elephant, but Will is nearby to keep her from being shot. Will is hired to accompany the little troupe and care for the beast he has come to love.

Analysis: This is a heartwarming historical novel based on a real elephant that was exhibited in rural areas of the United States. Maddy's illness is crucial to both the plot and Will's sympathetic characterization. Apparently she dies of tuberculosis, and this is an accurate portrayal of the time period and the neglect their poverty causes. Many drawings add to the story and make this an inviting package for upper-grade or reluctant older readers.

■ Carter, Alden R. **Sheila's Dying.** Putnam, 1987. 207pp. (0-399-21405-4) Reading Level: Grades 9–12. (BCCB MS87)
Disability: Cancer

Jerry is a junior in high school with a committee to chair, a hedonistic buddy to hang around with, and an insecure coach to put up with. When Sheila, the dramatic girl he has been dating, is diagnosed as having cancer, he chooses to stand by her. Her grandmother drinks and cannot cope with the surgery and the medical procedures designed to help Sheila. It seems to be up to Jerry and Sheila's argumentative friend Bonnie to see the dying girl through. At times Jerry wonders how he got involved, because he was ready to break up with Sheila before she got sick. When he gets benched for being late to the junior varsity game and forgets to pick up his little sister because of spending time with Sheila, Jerry finally lets his mother know how bad things are.

Other classmates do not pay a visit, but a Native American student named Mike brings a talisman for Sheila. Bonnie is so fierce that Jerry thinks of her as "Tiger Shark" but she is insightful about Sheila:

"Mike's a very perceptive guy, and he knows we're losing somebody pretty special." Suddenly the Tiger Shark had to turn away and take a deep breath to get control. "Sheila's never given a damn about surface stuff. Mike's an Indian. So what? I'm a stuck-up, brainy bitch. So what? You're a handsome, arrogant jock. So what? She cared about what was inside of us. Made us her friends. . . . And I'm talking about her like she was already dead!"

Jerry is vulnerable too, and when he gets kicked off the basketball team he goes drinking with Phil. Bonnie and his sister help him stay out of more trouble. Sheila makes plans to attend a Valentine's Day celebration but things do not go well, and Sheila cries, "I can't eat; I can't stay awake; I can't deal with people. And I look like a scarecrow. I'm done. I'm finished."

Sheila unnecessarily tries to do chores at home and is desperate about her grandmother's not having someone to take care of her any longer. Bonnie and Jerry get help from a social worker who tells them, "You young people have been trying to handle too much on your own. . . . someone from the hospital should have picked up on the home situation . . ."

The doctor has in his bag no miracle to offer, so Sheila's pain intensifies as the tumor in her intestine grows back and causes a blockage. Morphine for pain and time for "the cancer to eat her guts" are all that is left after surgery. Sheila talks to Bonnie and Jerry a few times as they keep loyal watch up through her last breath. Bonnie's crush on Jeff and his judgmental view of the Tiger Shark has turned into a love that Sheila would have approved of.

Analysis: Excellent structure and well-realized characters make this an outstanding novel. What drinking and sex there are provide the same credibility as Jerry's coarse or angry descriptions. Like *Stotan!,* this title presents a young man's efforts to deal with the terminal illness of a classmate. Highly recommended, this portrayal spends lots of time at the bedside, so Sheila's physical, spiritual, and emotional battles are not slighted, even though it is Jeff's story.

■ Charlton, Michael. **Wheezy.** Illus. by Michael Charlton. Bodley Head, 1988. 26pp. (0-370-31150-7) Reading Level: Grades 2–3. (BCCB F89) *Disability:* Asthma

William has asthma that causes physical problems and makes him feel left out of all the fun that other children have. He may not have a pet, he may not play sports, and he often feels lonely and in pain. His doctor explains what causes the asthma attacks and that medical inhalers can help relieve the symptoms. When his teacher suggests that William start a scrapbook, the book presents each page of it and a cartoon as well.

Analysis: The page design becomes cluttered with narrative, William's scrapbook, and each cartoon, but a lot of information is available for lower-grade readers. The emotional content is on target, and the expressive cover William drew for his scrapbook will gain sympathy for breathing disorders.

■ Charnas, Suzy McKee. **The Golden Thread.** Bantam, 1989. 224pp. (0-553-05821-5) Reading Level: Grades 7–9. (BCCB My89) *Disability:* Coma

Valentine knows she has magical powers, like her grandmother, who now is affected by a long, comatose illness. An alien, Bosanka, is stranded and demands that Val and her friends join their psychic power to send Bosanka back to her home in space. Val talks to Gran's spirit before the old woman dies. Bosanka learns that her people have become sea creatures, and she chooses to take the form of a dolphin to be able to join them.

Analysis: This sequel to *The Silver Glove* lets its fantasy elements overshadow the story and its characterizations. Occult powers and mystic purposes are part of Gran's illness. Science fiction fans satisfied with speculative mediocrity will read this if it is available.

■ Christiansen, C. B. **A Small Pleasure.** Atheneum, 1988. 134pp. (0-689-31369-1) Reading Level: Grades 7–12. (BCCB MS88) *Disability:* Cancer; Emotional disturbance

Wray Jean is determined to earn enough merit points for School Leadership Council to really be somebody. It is part of her three-year plan to change herself, and baton twirling, memorizing the name of everyone in the yearbook, and joining the right secret club are all part of it. Her best friend, Poe, accepts a different club's invitation to join, and Wray Jean is uncomfortable with the Cats' initiation and the news that she may be losing leadership points for joining. Wray Jean also has an after-school job and a boyfriend named Rusty that claim her time.

Often, sayings from her Uncle Raymond bolster Wray Jean's drive, but lately she is upset when her mother says Wray Jean reminds her of Raymond. Raymond is in a group home, suffering severe depression. Wray Jean knows that he had a successful real estate business and was engaged to a lovely woman before his breakdown. Now he makes ceramics and says he has lost everything, so Wray Jean is uneasy about being compared with her disturbed uncle.

Daddy Dean often had a gardening or woodworking project going, and Wray Jean used to join him in his work, but his cancer, originally treated by surgery, returns, and Daddy Dean is forced to rest in bed more and more. One of Wray Jean's teachers regularly asks how her father is doing, and she responds with a score from 1 to 10. It is all relative, because Daddy Dean's health fails rapidly, and what would have been a bad day before becomes the best that one could hope for weeks later.

Wray Jean keeps assuring herself there will be a time "when things are back to normal." Her mother cannot respond when Wray Jean tells of silly fears that a call to the guidance office would mean that Daddy Dean had died. That evening, he does die. Wray Jean's older sister Kayla flies home, and Wray Jean sees the doctor, wondering why he did not do something.

"We did everything we could," he tells me, as though he can read my mind. "It spread too quickly. We couldn't operate. Chemotherapy would have just made his last days miserable."

On the day of the funeral, an unsigned note arrives that upsets Wray Jean. It says, "Death has not captured your father. I've seen him!" She keeps the note but burns the envelope, almost certain it is from her "crazy" Uncle Raymond.

When Rusty comes to see her, Wray Jean tries to break off with him for a while, but Rusty stands by her through the grief. Poe becomes Wray Jean's confidant about the details of Daddy Dean's illness and death. At Christmas, Wray Jean wonders "what will happen if I don't develop a hardness, a way of dealing with Daddy Dean's death and Uncle Raymond's decline." She shuts the door on her grief, pulls the curtains on memories, and locks her feelings in a hidden place. But all this denial and the busy schedule she has built for herself become too taxing. On the night of a dance, she is crowned queen and breaks down in hysterics.

Mama and Dr. Peck assume it is exhaustion, but Wray Jean knows she is disappointed by the results of her overachiever plans. She puts on an old workshirt of her father's and goes to the basement to work on a bookcase Daddy Dean had started. Her mother asks, "Do you know who you remind me of?" and Wray Jean braces herself to be compared again with Uncle Raymond, who went crazy with disappointment over a lost love and wants to work for a ceramic shop now. Wray Jean is delighted when her mother says, "You remind me of your father." Wray Jean turns down her faculty adviser's suggestion that she run for vice president.

Analysis: Small-town life in eastern Washington State is sketched in with credible episodes from Wray Jean's life during a difficult year. Raymond's character is always revealed through secondhand comments. Daddy Dean is gentle and perceptive, fades away, and leaves Wray Jean with the life goal of being happy. She had a very close relationship with him, playful and loving. These memories are nicely integrated with the message elements of the story regarding success versus happiness. Recommended for a wide audience.

■ Cleaver, Vera. *Sweetly Sings the Donkey.* Lippincott, 1985. 160pp. (LB 0-397-32157-0) Reading Level: Grades 6–9. (KR 1 F89)
Disability: Health impairment; Emotional disturbance

Lily is 14 when her father inherits land in Florida, but the family finds out that there is no home on the property. Her mother wants things to be nice, but her father is too ill to pursue many types of employment. He keeps his sickness a secret from Lily's mother and lets everyone assume he is just lazy. He buys a secondhand store and is a cordial host to his customers, but few people buy things. Lily takes matters into her own hands and assembles a team of builders and advisers to work on a house for her family. She makes friends with the operator of the gas station and learns how to refinish furniture from her own father's shop.

Just before the house is completed, Lily's mother runs off with a well-to-do charmer who has been befriending the family. The near-silent older son admits that he once walked in on his mother and a salesman making love. Lily takes her father and siblings to the home she and her friends have constructed. Lily then determines that the man at the gas station needs to get out more and that she is just the person to see that he does.

Analysis: Cleaver always can present with insight independent rural ladies in stressful situations. Lily is well drawn, and her interview with her father establishes the clear choice he made to keep his health impairment to himself. Ironically, he lost his wife anyway. Once the mother is gone, there is less pretending and deception for every member of the family. Manipulating the men in her life is a legacy Lily inherited from her mother, but at least she uses it to good purpose. Recommended for most collections, this is not as good as *Where the Lilies Bloom* but will please the same readership.

■ Corcoran, Barbara. *The Potato Kid.* Atheneum, 1989. 172pp. (0-689-31589-9) Reading Level: Grades 3–7. (KR 1 N89)
Disability: Heart attack

Ellis is 14 and resentful of the way her mother's philanthropy is always directed at others. The summer that a needy child from northern Maine comes to visit, Gramps has a heart attack. This makes Ellis responsible for 10-year-old Lilac. They are often in disagreement with each other, but the initial antagonism turns into friendship.

Lilac's mother was widowed four years earlier but is making plans to remarry. She wants Lilac to be adopted, so the little girl's future is settled when Gramps recovers enough to have her come out to his home.

Analysis: Plot and characterizations are developed in a pleasant way. Gramps's illness, treatment, and recovery are important to what happens to Lilac but not central to the story. An entertaining additional choice for large collections.

■ Craig, Mary Francis. *The Sunday Doll.* Dodd, 1988. 138pp. (0-396-09309-4) Reading Level: Grades 5–8. (BCCB MS88)
Disability: Cerebral hemorrhage; Emotional disturbance; Orthopedic impairment

When Emmy turns 13, she dreads changing into a teenager because she does not like most of the older kids she knows. Aunt Harriet sends her a birthday gift—an Amish doll that seems like a faceless omen of bad times. Emmy's family excludes the young girl from news of her sister's boyfriend's suicide. This is consistent with the way they have shielded Emmy from unsettling scenes in movies. Emmy wants to be treated differently from this, but she is sent to stay with Aunt Harriet. While there, Emmy learns about family ghosts in the house and helps to cope with Aunt Harriet's most recent "spells." Aaron works at Aunt Harriet's, and Emmy follows his advice to act grown-up and in control when her parents continue to be secretive about the suicide and her sister's guilt-ridden grief.

Aunt Harriet has a stroke and the doctor reprimands the family for not having taken more medical precautions. Emmy, Aaron, and Aunt Harriet have an understanding about accepting situations as they are that will help Emmy when she returns to her home.

Analysis: Emmy sees that her own frustrations with imperfect parents are part of an adjustment that everyone has to make on growing up. She knows that Aunt Harriet was mourning her own husband when Emmy first came to visit. Being distracted by Emmy's troublemaking helped the woman to stop her own grieving. Emmy learns to cope with real life as it presents itself instead of adapting truth to fit a movie version of life. Her parents wonder what good can come of that type of open communication: "What could you have done about it except be upset?" But Emmy answers, "I could have CARED."

Aunt Harriet's illness is dealt with realistically. Her doctor's anger that an ambulance was not called clashes with Aaron's point that independent Harriet had already drawn up a document in order to avoid extensive medical procedures. "You know how she feels about your swinging bottles and oxygen tanks and scurrying nurses."

Academic pressure about SAT scores and parental expectation overwhelm Geoff Wheaton. When his desperate request that Emmy's sister leave school and home to run away with him is turned down, he hangs himself. Aaron curses both the waste that that sort of pressure causes and the ripples of pain that such an unnatural death brings to others. Aaron is a war veteran with a limp, whom Emmy's friend considers an old hippie. Emmy finds herself influenced by Aaron's views. "He wasn't out to live my life for me. But his words had a way of sticking in my head like a goat's head thorn in a sock."

This recommended story has narrative suspense and depth, and it incorporates the characterizations of several disabled characters well.

■ Cross, Gillian. **Born of the Sun.** Holiday, 1984. 229pp. (0-8234-0528-1) Reading Level: Grades 7–10. (BCCB Mr85) *Disability:* Cancer

Paula is taken out of school to accompany her famous father on an expedition to find a lost Incan city in Peru. The group includes a photographer, Paula's mother, and a guide. The jungle adventure is made even more hazardous when Paula's father makes irrational decisions, causing the death of one of their party. Paula's mother admits that her husband has cancer that has spread to his brain. She had hoped that he would be well enough to complete this challenge.

A native healer operates on the man's skull and treats him for the rest of his illness. When they return to England, Paula tells the whole story and shares photographs with a friend. Though her father seems well, he will probably not complete the book he intended to write. The secret city and the secret cure intrigue her listener, and he plans to take the journey himself some day.

Analysis: There is great strength in the story's setting, and multiple themes are developed in this novel. Characters indicate that their dialogue switches to Spanish in logical places, but it is not actually presented in both languages. The mother's motivation for taking the risks of an expedition with her ill husband are clear.

". . . 'Matteo told me that the cancer had spread into the whole of his body. And that there was no hope of a cure. Not so late. Only that Karel's life could be spun out—a little—if he had massive, disfiguring surgery. And drugs. Powerful drugs, all the time, to keep him out of pain."

". . . Should I have made him stay at home and spend the rest of his life—the tiny rest of his life—in a hospital bed, drugged into silliness and eaten up with despair because of what he had missed? He would have withered away. I would have had to watch him vanish in front of my eyes, until he was not Karel at all."

Paula learns a lot about life from her close brushes with death in this exciting adventure. Readers will muse over the believability of the healing with Paula and her friend.

"Do you think it was all in the mind? You know, like faith healing? Or was it that green stuff the old man covered him with?"

"I think—" Paula hesitated. "I think perhaps it was both together. Mind and body. I'm not sure you can separate them."

■ Crutcher, Chris. *Stotan!* Greenwillow, 1986. 183pp. (0-688-05715-2) Reading Level: Grades 8–12. (BCCB Je86)
Disability: Cancer; Leukemia

Walker Dupree keeps a journal during four months of physical and emotional challenge. He and three friends are the last swim team for Frost High School, and, as seniors, they want this year to prove their strength, endurance, and commitment. Their Korean coach, Max, sets the first part of Christmas vacation as Stotan Week—a Stotan being a cross between Stoic and Spartan—and the boys push beyond exhaustion and pain to reach an ecstatic level of achievement. They live together that week, in Lion's apartment over a bar, and they share stories of experiences when they had to act like Stotans.

Lion was orphaned at 14. Nortie lives with an abusive, racist father, who drove his brother to suicide. Walker is dating Devnee but feels attracted to a former swim team competitor named Elaine. Jeff has powerful athletic abilities and self-confidently pursues his challenges. However, after Christmas break, Jeff's performance is limited, and he collapses while swimming. He is hospitalized for what proves to be a terminal illness.

Walker tries to deal with all these situations and to sort out his feelings about being a writer. When Nortie is beaten by his father for dating a black, Walker arranges for Nortie to live at his house. When Walker sees baseball players distributing neo-Nazi newspapers, he finds a way to keep them from harassing Nortie. With Max's help, Walker tries to find a realistic perspective on romantic complications and Jeff's illness. The three swimmers do well at a state meet, where they complete three legs of a four-man relay as a tribute to Jeff. Walker comes to some conclusions about life, about facing the truth, and about his calling to be a "Stotan observer" who can pass some of that truth on to others through writing.

Analysis: This sports novel has lots of motivation in its plot, subplots, and character development. From Jeff's sarcastic attitude in the beginning, to Lion's loyal support of his hospitalized friend, there is an honest tone in the interactions. With all the problems of unrequited love, racism, domestic violence, and coming-of-age, the terminal illness gets stirred in with little detail. Leukemia that will not respond to treatment is Jeff's apparent health impairment. The value of such a portrayal is that strength and youth are no guarantee against impairment or death. This title can be recommended to teens who will feel that it addresses their interests and stretches their perceptions about life.

■ Dacquino, Vincent T. *Kiss the Candy Days Good-bye.* Delacorte, 1982. 129pp. (0-440-04546-0) Reading Level: Grades 6–8. (BCCB D82) *Disability:* Diabetes

When Jimmy is in seventh grade, he is paired with the team captain to work out in wrestling. But Jimmy is worried that he is losing weight despite a big appetite, and he misses his friend, Margaret, to confide in. Jimmy finally goes to Margaret's neighborhood to tell her all his symptoms but learns that she has moved. On the way home he feels weak and dizzy, then passes out. At the hospital, the doctors diagnose Jimmy as having diabetes mellitus. After tests and insulin injections, Jimmy acknowledges that his life will be different, but at least he can still wrestle.

Margaret and her cousin Santiago visit Jimmy's family at their mountain cabin. Too much exertion causes Jimmy to have an insulin reaction, so he eats some candy and laughs off the incident. Jimmy's brother helps him determine to be truthful about his physical condition so that friends can help if he really needs it. Jimmy returns to school with a new friend, Santiago.

Analysis: Lots of information on symptoms and the hazards of untreated diabetes are incorporated in this story line, but it weakens the literary value because characterization and plot have to serve this informative purpose. Jimmy is a sympathetic character, narrating a hard part of his life in great detail. Since the story shows Jimmy's renegotiating his social relationships and becoming more honest in sharing his needs and feelings with others, this is a good discussion starter for support groups and mainstreamed classrooms.

■ Delton, Judy. *I'll Never Love Anything Ever Again.* Illus. by Rodney Pate. Whitman, 1985. 32pp. (LB 0-8075-3521-4) Reading Level: Grades PS–3. (BCCB MS85)
Disability: Allergies

This is a boy's first-person ramble through memories of his dog, Tinsel, and bitter realizations that his pet will have to be given away. Because the boy has developed allergic reactions, Mother has found a home for Tinsel on a farm where visits will be allowed.

Analysis: The narrator's feelings of betrayal and anger can overwhelm the insights about his condition that this situation story offers. Banishment of the dog is the only physical adjustment to his newly diagnosed condition that is revealed. He describes a bout of infection, fever, sore throat, and watering eyes and then exclaims, "I don't care if I miss school! I don't care if I die! No one else is getting my dog!"

The ill child comforts himself, "I don't want to *visit* Tinsel . . . Still, I've never been in the country to stay. It might be fun to see a real farm." However, allergy sufferers will wonder how fast his allergic reactions will hit him on a farm in June. No plot, and expressive line drawings with clumsy blue washes make this weak for picture book audiences, but readers may have their sympathies stirred.

■ Duffy, James. *Doll Hospital.* Scholastic, 1989. 160pp. (0-590-41860-2) Reading Level: Grades 3–5. (BCCB F89)
Disability: Health impairment

Alison is 8 and, for as long as she can remember, her health has been so poor that she is often hospitalized. Her 13-year-old brother, Christopher, helps her create a doll hospital. The dolls are able to talk to each other and to Alison and Christopher. Alison becomes ill from too much activity with her dolls, and she is hospitalized. By Christmas, her condition is improved, and doctors hope she will be able to return to school.

Analysis: Oddly old-fashioned, and weak as a fantasy, this does offer a pleasant characterization of brother and sister accommodating a sibling's differences. Most other sibling stories are of same-sex children. Perhaps the hazard of stereotypic sex roles's taking over keeps more authors from exploring this type of relationship. Christopher is nurturing and playful, not just aping a manly role of provider and protector in his relationship with Alison.

Christopher wants to be a doctor when he grows up and is faithful in his attendance at Alison's bedside during her treatment with an experimental procedure. The doctor, hospital staff, and other patients know Alison's favorite doll's adventures and personalities, supposedly due to the little girl's absorption with acting out all her fantasies. Hospital staff members encourage Alison's coping game by presenting her doll with a little doctor's coat as a going-home present. Alison's loss of weight and her fatigue are stopped by the intravenous medications and chemotherapy she receives, but the realistic situation can be obscured more than softened for audiences by Alison's persistent interactions with and, apparently, through her dolls.

■ Dunlop, Beverly. *The Poetry Girl.* Houghton, 1989. 216pp. (0-395-49679-9) Reading Level: Grades 6–8. (BCCB Ap89)
Disability: Health impairment; Emotional disturbance

In New Zealand, the Kondrotovitch family faces many hardships, which 12-year-old Natalia records. From 1947 to 1949, her Russian immigrant father is subject to depression, harsh with his child, and argumentative with his wife. Financial insecurity, moving twice, social persecution, and her frequent poor health figure in Natalia's account. Also, she inserts and repeats passages of poetry, which help her cope with her misery. When her father attempts suicide, additional changes take place. Natalia deals with the rejection and isolation her differences in appearance, health, and background bring.

Analysis: Historical fiction cannot be criticized for accurate portrayals of abhorrent social practices. The bigotry and cruelty shown by Natalie's classmates and instructors is balanced, ironically, by the harshness of her own father. As Mr. Kondrotovitch responds to his environment with self-destruction, Natalia develops poetic self-confidence to cope with her physical, educational, and financial limitations.

■ Ethridge, Kenneth E. *Toothpick.* Holiday, 1985. 118pp. (0-8234-0585-0) Reading Level: Grades 6–9. (BCCB F86)
Disability: Cystic fibrosis

Glenwood High School has a new student, Janice Brooks. Jamie Almont's friends nickname her "Toothpick" as a put-down because she is so thin. Jamie is thin, too, and used to the critical tone most of his classmates use. Janice's open friendliness embarrasses Jamie, and when they spend time together, Jamie is wide open for more teasing. Janice gets straight A's and offers to help Jamie with his math. Jamie confides in Janice about his crush on Ginger. Janice shares some advice, and Jamie finds that relaxing, being himself, and not being afraid of what other people say make life more comfortable, if more unconventional.

Janice is frequently absent from school, because she was born with cystic fibrosis. When Janice is hospitalized, Jamie looks up the term, finds out that it is an incurable condition, and that affected people rarely live beyond their teens. He feels he has had all the benefits from their friendship and makes special efforts to contact and cheer Janice. He plans a date with Ginger, listens when Janice needs to talk about dying, records happenings at school that Janice is missing, and gets suspended for a fight with a bully who insulted "Toothpick."

Janice's mother invites Jamie to visit her daughter in the intensive care unit. He makes an empty spirited promise that they will write a book together the coming summer. Janice dies, and Jamie is given Janice's folder of notes from school with a message from her and a happy face doodle.

Analysis: The friendship theme of this story comes through in natural dialogue, recognizable characters, and touches of humor. Janice seems so upbeat to Jamie because she wants to be seen that way, yet passages reveal her "bad days" too. Jamie feels he has been callous but comes to understand that their casual friendship was just what Janice wanted so as to balance herself against the realities of her progressive condition. This is a nicely written middle school novel portraying without melodramatics a health impairment that causes the death of a young person.

■ Eyerly, Jeannette. *Seth and Me and Rebel Make Three.* Lippincott, 1983. 213pp. (LB 0-397-32043-4) Reading Level: Grades 7–9. (BCCB S83)
Disability: Cerebral hemorrhage

When Ryan is 17 he gets an apartment with his friend Seth. A runaway named Rebel shelters with them and becomes a burden. When Tamsin meets Rebel at the apartment she stops talking to Ryan. Ryan loses his job, Grandpa has a stroke and moves in, Seth moves out, and Rebel is pregnant by a previous lover. When Ryan uses Seth's car to take Rebel back to Colorado, he saves the life of a famous orchestra conductor who has had a heart attack. There is a news story about Ryan's heroism, and he gets his job and his girl back. The conductor also offers to pay for Ryan's first year of college.

Analysis: Grandpa's stroke is one of many plot devices that crowd this story. Though Ryan and Rebel are adequate characterizations, the rest of the cast is unconvincing.

■ Ferris, Jean. *Invincible Summer.* Farrar, 1987. 167pp. (0-374-33642-3) Reading Level: Grades 7–10. (BCCB MS87)
Disability: Cancer

Seventeen-year-old Robin lives on a farm in Iowa and is dating steadily for the first time. Her best friend is delighted, but Robin feels Ivan is a reckless driver and rather insensitive. She starts feeling tired when exams come up, so she gets a medical evaluation and then has tests that may confirm acute lymphocytic leukemia. She meets an aggressive patient named Rick, who is having chemotherapy that includes steroids: "They mess up my moods. I'm not usually like this. If you want to get up and walk out, I'll understand."

Rick tells her his rich father has spared no expense in getting him cured and then jokes about wanting to avoid her room because he has told her his life story in "the old stranger-on-the-bus syndrome." Instead, he introduces her to the classic movie *Casablanca,* and they become friends—then lovers.

Rick attends Jefferson agricultural college and when he visits Robin's farm, Mr. Gregory enjoys the student's good sense and good company. Rick is hospitalized for the final time, and Robin drops her classes to be with him as much as possible. Her chemotherapy seems to be effective, but she muses on an old game of "What's the Worst that Could Happen?" Whether she dies soon or lives, whether there is an afterlife or not, she resolves that there is still nothing to worry about.

Analysis: This touching story is accurate in its portrayal, and Robin's viewpoint is maintained throughout. The hardback cover does not foreshadow the mood but does proclaim this as a romance. Rick is different from other boys Robin has met, and his clever banter is so charming that readers will know she is not falling in love just because she feels sorry for him. After all, he supports her with compassion and wit instead of pity through her own treatment.

Other medical conditions and impairments are mentioned in the hospital scenes. Rick is on a moody train of thought when he claims:

> "Everybody's so frightened of cancer. It's like having a curse put on you. I'd rather have cancer than be blind or have no arms. I might get cured of cancer. There's no cure for blindness or no arms."
>
> "There's artificial arms," she said, wanting for some reason to reassure him. "You could still function."
>
> "I don't want to just function. I want to be whole. More than whole. Is there a word for being more than whole, better than normal? I've been sick for so long I don't want to be only *better,* I want to be clear on the other side of better. Where nothing can touch me again."

Fans of *Only Love* will appreciate this title, because there is less contrivance, and it would complement *Sheila's Dying* in all young adult collections.

■ Ferris, Jean. *The Stainless Steel Rule*. Farrar, 1986. 170pp. (0-374-37212-8) Reading Level: Grades 6–12. (SLJ My86)
Disability: Diabetes

In her junior year of high school, Kitty relies on her friends Fran and Mary for stability, because her artist father treats her more like a room-mate and she never knew her mother. The three girls are on the swim team, and both Fran and Kitty know how to help Mary when she shows signs of low blood sugar from her diabetes.

Mary begins dating Nick, a water-polo-playing senior new to the school. When he convinces Mary to use biofeedback instead of insulin injections for her diabetes, she goes into a diabetic coma. Kitty did not tell Mary's foster mother in time and feels responsible when Mary almost dies. Kitty's grade-school friend Casey dates Kitty and is supportive through all this. She feels her father is ready to grow up when yet another of his live-in nude models leaves him.

Analysis: The title is based on opinionated Fran's "stainless steel rule" that one should never do something for someone else's own good. Some-where between the themes of loyalty and romantic love versus mature affection, Mary is shown to be a fool and Nick is shown to be a sadistic braggart. This may be interesting reading but it is not sympathetic to the true nature of Mary's disability or the likelihood of her adjustment to its limitations. Mary is so devoted to charming, manipulative Nick that she throws out the proper number of empty syringes to fool her mother, who does count them when Kitty reveals Mary is going to stop taking her medicine. In the end, Mary is emotionally isolated because she is afraid to risk loving again and physically isolated because of new health restrictions resulting from her coma.

Nick's behavior is analyzed by Mary's foster mother as being rooted in his own mother's death shortly after he was born. Since she got her information from Mary, this speculation seems contrived in order to counter all the things Fran and Kitty know about just plain mean Nick.

Simplistic in its development of characters with emotional disturbances (Kitty's Dad is really an adolescent stuck in the drug-fogged 60s) and physical impairment, this book is an additional choice for larger collec-tions.

■ Fox, Paula. *The Village by the Sea*. Orchard/Franklin Watts, 1988. 148pp. (LB 0-531-08388-8) Reading Level: Grades 5–8. (BCCB J1Ag88)
Disability: Heart disease; Emotional disturbance

"Are you afraid? Emma asks her father about the heart bypass surgery that is scheduled. He tells her how he copes with the fear, and her mother tells her that thousands of people have had this type of surgery. Emma agrees to keep a journal of her two weeks on Long Island with Aunt Bea and Uncle Crispin so she can share events with her father when he's feeling better. Father describes Bea as "a terror," and mother summarizes the cause as envy, but there is no one else Emma can stay with while her parents are concerned with hospitalization and recuperation.

Emma is taken aback by Aunt Bea's harsh words and demanding ways. Uncle Crispin is a musician, who can smooth things over for Emma and take the sting out of Bea's verbal barbs. On the beach, Emma makes a new friend, named Bertie, and the two girls begin to construct small buildings out of whatever they can gather. The village grows and occupies the girls for many happy hours.

Aunt Bea's complaints and rages allow Emma to identify several events that Bea holds grudges about. Bea is a recovering alcoholic, and one of the plastic deer from her old, hidden liquor bottles makes a nice addition to the miniature village by the sea. Uncle Crispin tells Emma he thinks the village is wonderful. Aunt Bea finds and destroys the girls' creation. Emma is so angry she considers lashing out. Instead, she and Bertie make plans for meeting in the city that fall, and Emma feels better.

When Emma rereads an early journal entry, she sees that Aunt Bea completed Emma's aborted description of Aunt Bea: "a sad bad old woman." Emma can accept that as her aunt's secret, and she then dismisses the burden of her own anger at the disturbed woman's actions.

Analysis: The childlike games at the shore are as genuine as the dark opening passage about fear of heart surgery. Uncle Crispin and Aunt Bea have an interdependence that Emma recognizes, and she assumes they will return to comfortable "hibernation" once she is not there to stir up Bea's resentments about stepmothers, half-brothers, stunted art careers, and lost property. Bertie calls Bea "Lady Bonkers," and there is evidence that Bea's hostile resentments are severe enough to be considered an emotional disturbance. At one point, Emma observes,

> Aunt Bea was wearing not one but two of the old robes she had found in the thrift shop and the buckles were missing from the sandals on her feet. Her face was flushed as though she'd been running. Maybe she didn't drink brandy anymore, but something in her mind was making her drunk.

When her family discussed Bea's problem as "envy," Emma's father admitted, "I envy anyone with a healthy heart." His appearance after the surgery includes the details that "his skin was rosy. He even looked a little plump." The parallel theme of recovery from a literally "broken heart" adds depth to Emma's experiences with Bea's "broken heart." This type of sophisticated structure in plot, stunning control of language, and skillful creation of character distinguish this novel for a wide audience.

■ Galvin, Matthew. *Gran-Gran's Best Trick: A Story for Children Who Have Lost Someone They Love.* Illus. by Michael Chesworth. Magination, 1989. 24pp. (0-945354-19-3) Reading Level: Grades K–3. (SLJ F90) *Disability:* Cancer

A nameless girl recalls how her grandfather used to play with her and go fishing before he became ill with cancer. She shares what her parents have told her and makes her own observations about the man's failing health.

"It's horrible. Gran-Gran's skinny. Except his face—it's puffy. (If something is growing inside of him, why is he getting so thin?) He's really pale, and all his hair fell out, except for a few little grey curly ones. Mom and Dad say it's the medicine that doctors gave him to kill the cancer. Something about it eating the cancer, which is good, but also eating part of him, which is bad. Stupid medicine! Why can't it tell the difference between the cancer and my Gran-Gran?"

After her grandfather's death and funeral service, the girl visits Gran-Gran's home and recalls how he would make her feel better after a fall by saying, "Hey, that was a good trick! Can I see that one again?" She can't just laugh about this new trick of Gran-Gran's until it doesn't hurt so much.

Her grandmother gives the girl a book that Gran-Gran had written in about himself. She reads and recalls her grandfather's active days, then determines to share those memories with her baby sister. "Then she will know Gran-Gran like I do, even though he's gone."

Analysis: Part of a series called Books to Help Parents Help Their Children, the jacket summary states that learning "how those we love never leave our hearts" is love's best trick. The text can seem lengthy by dealing with the child's reaction to a terminal illness through many stages of uncertainty and loss. However, nice book design and variety in the black-and-white sketches that accompany the story make the title an appealing choice for bibliotherapy.

Not as poetic as *My Grandson Lew* or as nicely structured as *Nana Upstairs, Nana Downstairs,* this book's specific details about cancer and its treatment make it a good supplement for collections.

■ Getz, David. *Thin Air.* Henry Holt, 1990. 120pp. (0-8050-1379-2) Reading Level: Grades 5–8. (KR 1 D90; BCCB Ja91) *Disability:* Allergies; Asthma; Blindness

Jacob enters sixth grade in Manhattan and is dismayed to find out that his new classmates are already doing a disability awareness paper on how they would want to be treated if they had a chronic health impairment like Jacob's. Asthma attacks and even a near-deadly taste of pistachios are not as frustrating to Jacob as being singled out at school and overprotected at home. He assures his new principal that 40 absences last year is not enough reason for him to transfer into the special class. He makes friends with schoolmate Cynthia and with Theodore, a blind newspaper vendor. For Jacob, mainstreamed education and a new understanding with his family provide a happy ending.

Analysis: As in *The Kidnapping of Kevin Kowalski,* an overprotective mother is foiled, but in this portrait, Jacob is the astute observer of his own predicament. Humorously expressing his disdain of his brother's attentions and his mother's inescapable precautions, Jacob's character is a very successful portrayal. Though the plot incorporates Jacob's stressful episodes of asthma and allergic reactions, these do not overburden the story line. Highly recommended for middle grade audiences.

■ Giff, Patricia Reilly. *The Gift of the Pirate Queen.* Illus. by Jenny Rutherford. Delacorte, 1982. 164pp. (0-440-02970-8) Reading Level: Grades 3–6. (BCCB D82)
Disability: Diabetes

Grace O'Malley accidentally breaks the glass bell of her teacher, Mrs. Raphael. It has been a hard year, because Grace's mother died of cancer, and Mrs. Raphael's harsh ways make Grace decide to secretly buy a replacement. She is taken to get it by Fiona, her father's cousin, who has come from Ireland to visit and help with the family only so long as she is needed and wanted. Grace likes Fiona's story of a courageous historical figure also named Grace O'Malley, but the 11-year-old Grace does not feel brave at all when Fiona compares her with the pirate queen.

Amy, Grace's little sister, has diabetes but is careless about her restricted diet. When Amy has to be taken to the hospital, she herself jokes about getting a box of candy. Grace responds that she hates Amy for taking risks she knows she should avoid and for frightening her family. Father visits the next day and brings home a message from Amy to Grace. Amy finds it hard to stay on her diet and sometimes wants to pretend she does not have diabetes. Father admits that he has been avoiding mention of his wife, as if running away from the truth could mean she was still alive somewhere.

Grace realizes that being "everyday brave" should apply as well to her own situation at school, and she confesses to Mrs. Raphael about the bell.

Mrs. Raphael is surprised that her sixth-grade students fear her, and she indicates that she would like to regain the perspective she had years before as a teacher. Grace asks Fiona to stay as part of the family. Fiona gives Grace a photograph of Mrs. O'Malley and Fiona together in Ireland. Grace has learned that there are many kinds of courage, and she now has a photograph to help her recall her mother.

Analysis: Amy is having believable problems with the restrictions related to her diabetes. The entire family is caught in a pattern of denial since Mrs. O'Malley's terminal illness. Grace is a well-developed character, and the lesson she learns is presented in a skillfully written story. This title is recommended for all graduates of the Cleary books and fans of Giff's stories about Casey Valentine and her friends.

■ Girard, Linda Walvoord. *Alex, the Kid with AIDS.* Illus. by Blanche Sims. Whitman, 1991. 32pp. (0-8075-0245-6) Reading Level: Grades 3–5. (KR 15 D90; BCCB F91)
Disability: AIDS

Michael is in Mrs. Timmer's fourth-grade class, and the students are informed that a new student, Alex, has AIDS. The school nurse indicates that Alex contracted AIDS from a blood transfusion and that if he should have a cut or a nosebleed, "we had better be extra careful not to touch the blood in case we had a scratch or cut, too." Michael understands there is no danger from being seated next to Alex, but the entire class tends to ignore the new boy. Alex is aware that adults make allowances for his behavior because of his illness, but he oversteps Mrs. Timmer's standards of acceptable performance when he and Michael make fun of the playground supervisor in a poem.

Admitting that she has been treating Alex as a visitor instead of just one of the class, Mrs. Timmer gives Alex a choice between continuing to receive special treatment or actually interacting as the other students in the class do.

Analysis: This excellent story has realistic characters that develop and change over the course of a relatively short period. Instead of being a spiritless how-to list or a here-is-the-truth-about-AIDS story, this book portrays lots of learning experiences in an unforced plot and with a light touch. When Alex does get a cut, the teacher uses rubber gloves to clean and bandage what is termed "no big scratch and no big deal." Alex uses manipulative socialization skills and crude humor but makes responsible choices and even gets invited to a sleepover. It is a relief to see some faults addressed in a portrayal that goes far beyond the "tragic victim" mode.

Bright cartoon illustrations present a racially mixed classroom. The title may seem a bit bald, but it captures the casual tone of this highly recommended work.

■ Graber, Richard. **Doc.** HarperCollins, 1986. 160pp. (0-06-022064-3)
Reading Level: Grades 7–10. (BCCB D86)
Disability: Alzheimer's disease; Emotional disturbance

Brad Bloodworth is reluctant to see his grandfather's symptoms from Alzheimer's disease as a steady decline. His grandfather had founded the hospital that Brad's father works in, is highly respected, and is known as "Doc." Doc talks his grandchildren into helping him disconnect life support equipment for Dr. Feathers, who was his partner and with whom he shared a pact to avoid any "long and fruitless death after a stroke." After the hospital's hearing, Doc begins confusing the days of the week, is hostile toward Aunt Susan, and has irrational fits of anger.

At their summer cottage, Doc's behavior includes tantrums, forgetting to dress, and incontinence in a public place. Brad and his sister, P.J., have friendships that are affected by Doc's actions, and P.J. voices her wish that Doc "would just die." Brad's friend Lance has been under psychiatric care but mixes alcohol with his medication. He is killed in a boating wreck, and Brad's family goes home from the cape early. Doc's confusion is so profound that he wanders off in the night. Brad finds him at an intersection where a crash takes place. After providing medical care, Doc loses consciousness and dies. From a canoe, Brad spreads Doc's ashes over the water, while his father and girlfriend wait.

Analysis: Brad's experiences during his sophomore and junior year are believable and presented skillfully. Brad's father and aunt are honest with him about his grandfather's past failings as well as his illness, but Brad has to accept these facts to gain perspective on his grandfather's life and death.

The portrayal of Doc's condition does not overshadow other action and characterizations. Lance, shown to be the disturbed child of an alcoholic, suffers a dramatic consequence for his emotional instability and persistent rejection of friendship and medical advice. This and the heroic death of Doc can seem contrived, but the characters have depth.

The mission to honor Dr. Feathers' euthanasia pact introduces an ethical dilemma that echoes in P.J.'s wish that her grandfather would just die. Feelings of guilt and early grief for a personality that is gone while the body still exists are explored. Other complexities in human relationships are developed that make this book a recommended title for mature readers.

■ Grant, Cynthia D. *Phoenix Rising; Or, How to Survive Your Life.* Atheneum, 1989. 160pp. (0-689-31458-2) Reading Level: Grades 7–10. (BCCB F89)
Disability: Cancer

Jessie is 17 years old when she finds the diary her older sister kept while she was being treated for cancer. Helen wrote about her fear, anger, and resignation to the fact that her disease was terminal. The family is shown completing those same stages of grief and coping with the loss in various ways. Reading the diary helps Jessie adjust to Helen's death.

Analysis: Sad tales are popular with teen readers, but this one has few other plot elements to balance the death story. Helen is allowed to complain in her diary but is idealized in her family's recollections. There are better examinations of bereavement and terminal illness, although they may be more complex reading than this straightforward novel.

■ Greenberg, Jan. *No Dragons to Slay.* Farrar, 1983. 152pp. (0-374-35528-2) Reading Level: Grades 7–10. (BCCB Mr84)
Disability: Cancer

A lump is discovered on Thomas's hip and is diagnosed as a malignant tumor. Three weeks of radiation followed by chemotherapy offers a 30 percent chance of cure. It also disrupts Thomas's school and soccer activities, postpones his parents' trip to Europe, and puts new stress on family members. The physical discomforts of therapy include skin too sensitive for clothing, weakness, hair loss, and nausea.

After this treatment, Thomas must choose between still another biopsy or an experimental drug. He opts for the drug and its antidote, which makes him too ill to leave bed for a week. Eager to be away from his parents and the long sequence of treatments, Thomas goes to help excavate a prehistoric Indian community. Here he makes new friends, one of whom is critically injured in a landslide. Thomas faces his fears about death and, one year later, is headed for Dartmouth.

Analysis: The doctor warned Thomas Newman that "The next eighteen months will be hell." Complex family relationships are convincingly revealed during that stressful time. Mr. Newman reacts to Thomas's decision to cut a hole in his pants that exposes the radiated skin, and he wonders why Thomas does not use a wig. It seems that Thomas is flaunting his illness, but once Thomas and his father admit how frightened they both are, these small evidences of illness no longer cause angry exchanges between father and son.

Mrs. Newman has only one child and finds it difficult to balance her need to protect her son with his need to keep his independence and pursue outside interests. Thomas feels his illness has separated him from school-mates. He does not return to the academic world until he has spent time making literal and emotional discoveries while digging at the Indian site.

Analysis: This situation has been given a convincing and sympathetic portrayal. Although the structure of the story has weak points, the author has avoided sentimentality and uses humor to draw readers into one teenage boy's life. There is no denying that that life is a fragile thing, once readers go through Thomas's challenges with him. Even with a satisfying ending, the story is not unwisely optimistic. Thomas needs to go five years without a recurrence of the cancer, in order to be free of it, but he chooses to spend those years studying for a future, rather than staying angry and fearful that there may be no future for him.

■ Griffith, Helen V. *Georgia Music.* Greenwillow, 1986. 22pp. (LB 0-688-06072-2) Reading Level: Grades PS–4. (BCCB D86)
Disability: Health impairment

A girl visits her grandfather for the summer in rural Georgia. He lets her join him in the routines that keep the garden going, give him an afternoon rest, and fill the evening with mouth organ music. Whenever they hear the mockingbird call, they joke about the "Sassy old bird."

Next summer the cabin becomes overgrown, and grandfather just sits because he is "mighty tired." He agrees to return to Baltimore with his daughter and granddaughter, so the girl assumes he is sicker than he will say. In the city, he "sat in a chair looking worried and sad." The little girl asks for a tune from the mouth organ, and when grandfather just looks at it, she tries it herself. He is pleased, and he listens while she teaches herself all the songs he played for her the summer before. When she begins to imitate the sounds of "cricket chirps and tree frog trills and bee buzzes and bird twitters," her grandfather chuckles, recalling the "Sassy old bird." They share a laugh over the memories brought back by the girl's performance of "Georgia music."

Analysis: This picture book has loose, watercolor scenes of the action that pair well with the low-key text. The gentle unfolding of setting and character has sensory richness. A specific ailment is unstated, and unimportant, in this excellent story for read-aloud or read-alone pleasure. The book encourages children to interact with others even if they seem aloof or severely withdrawn. Such small heroics deserve kindly recognition.

■ Griffiths, Helen. *Rafa's Dog.* Holiday, 1983. 107pp. (0-8234-0492-7) Reading Level: Grades 4–6. (BCCB Ap84)
Disability: Heart condition

Rafa and his younger sister stay with their aunt and uncle while Mama prepares for the arrival of her third child. The delivery may be dangerous because Mama has a heart condition. Rafa finds a stray dog and names it Moro. Mama dies and the children return to Madrid. Rafa misses his dog, so he takes some money to go claim Moro. Papa agrees that Rafa can keep the dog.

Analysis: This story uses the foreshadowed death of Rafa's mother to create the opportunity for a city boy to meet a village dog. Risking a third pregnancy is discussed briefly, but the death scene is poignant. Rafa is calmed by his father, then focuses his affection on the dog when his mother is in danger. It is a natural conclusion that the dog would remain a strong attachment during Rafa's grief. To broaden the settings offered in a collection, this story of contemporary Spain may help.

■ Guernsey, JoAnn Bren. *Five Summers.* Clarion, 1983. 181pp. (0-89919-147-9) Reading Level: Grades 6–9. (BCCB Je83)
Disability: Cancer

When Mandy is 12, her grandmother comes to stay on the family's farm. Grandma is outspoken and demanding, causing friction between Mandy's parents. The 80-year-old is so critical of everything that everyone is relieved when she makes arrangements to live in a nursing home instead.

Next summer, Mandy's aunt and uncle are killed in a car accident, and their son, Chicky, comes to the farm. While her parents look into getting a foster home for Chicky, Mandy is shadowed by the 5-year-old cousin. Chicky says he follows Mandy so much because he wants a younger mother—one who will not die. Chicky is registered for kindergarten in the fall and stays as part of the family.

When Mandy is 14, her mother has a mastectomy and undergoes chemotherapy. Grandmother returns to help at the farm, and Mandy enjoys a closer relationship with her father. The next summer, Mandy fantasizes about Peter, an 18-year-old musician who is working at the farm. Chicky is sent away to camp and Grandma returns, signaling that Mandy's mother requires further medical care. Mandy's oldest brother is in Vietnam, and her other brother, Greg, is trying to avoid being drafted. Mandy dates Peter, and they come to an understanding about waiting for each other during the years he is in college.

Mandy's mother suffers a second mastectomy, but by the next summer her condition has become inoperable. Mandy runs away, calls home, and learns that Grandma has died. Mandy becomes so depressed that she tells Peter to stop visiting her. Chicky goes to stay with another aunt, because

Mandy's mother is ill from the frequent chemotherapy. Mandy visits Grandma's grave with her mother, and she imagines the caustic woman advising her to shape up. Mandy realizes Grandmother knew she loved her. Mandy and her mother face their fears about the cancer and express their love.

Analysis: A convincing story of family life and the relationships that are established through five stressful summers is presented here. The 1960s are conveyed through concerns about the draft and medical options for Mandy's mother. The ill woman copes with her repeated surgeries and enjoys life even though she is weakened by chemotherapy. Mandy's maturation between 12 and 17 is believable, and this is a recommended title.

■ Guthrie, Donna. *Grandpa Doesn't Know It's Me.* Human Sciences, 1986. 29pp. (0-89885-302-8) Reading Level: Grades PS–3. (BCCB MS86)
Disability: Alzheimer's disease

Elizabeth has spent a lot of time with her Grandpa. He taught her to ride a bicycle and used to take her biking through their neighborhood. She has noticed the changes in both his memory and his ability to take care of himself safely. He moves into Elizabeth's home when his condition becomes worse. The doctor has explained that Grandpa has a brain disease that makes him forget, and he will not get better. People at the day care center help Elizabeth's parents two times a week. Elizabeth also helps see that Grandpa is safe, even though he becomes confused and cannot recall her name.

Analysis: Alzheimer's disease causes disorientation and other conditions described in this book. The book is useful in exposing very young children to this problem, and the story avoids an unrealistic resolution. Other stories may touch on a child's grief process, but this plot deals with the child's feelings of rejection and confusion that can result from early behavior changes brought on by the disease. The illustrations are dull line drawings in peach tints, so picture book audiences may not respond, but bibliotherapy needs can be met with this title.

■ Hartling, Peter. *Crutches.* Lothrop, 1988. 163pp. (0-688-07991-1) Reading Level: Grades 5–8.
Disability: Amputation; Health impairment

In 1945, Crutches has a recurrence of malaria that interrupts his repatriation to Germany. *See full annotation* Chapter 4: Orthopedic/Neurological Impairments.

■ Hensley, Jr. Sam. *Family Portrait.* Franklin Watts, 1988. 256pp. (0-531-10611-X) Reading Level: Grades 9–12. (KR 1 O88)
Disability: Cerebral hemorrhage

Jeff "Ice" Waters is on a college football scholarship the year he meets Stacy Cottrell. He grew up with his uncle Forrest and sees many contrasts between his own family life and Stacy's. Forrest was often drunk and unable to hold a job, but when he has a stroke, Jeff stands by him. However, a second stroke kills Forrest, so Jeff continues with his college career, comfortable with his new loyalties to Stacy's family.

Analysis: Jeff is willing to sacrifice his schooling to care for Forrest. This is a vehicle for contrasting characterizations, and Forrest's physical limitations are a small part of his portrayal. *The Trouble with Grammary* is a more powerful selection, but this one will provoke thought on family values and obligations.

■ Hermes, Patricia. *Be Still My Heart.* Putnam, 1989. 144pp. (0-399-21917-X) Reading Level: Grades 6–9. (KR 15 D89)
Disability: AIDS

Allison works on the yearbook and enjoys time with her best friend, Leslie. She is not impressed by come-ons from Ronald Hamburger but is sorry to see her crush, David, start dating Leslie.

Their teacher, Mrs. Adams, is married to a man who contracted AIDS by a blood transfusion years ago. Allison is intimidated about sexiness, risking AIDS, and the way everyone is acting toward Mrs. Adams. Allison's grandmother explains the medical situation and the paranoid reactions. Mr. Adams visits school and discusses his disease with the students. When David sees how compassionate Allison is about this he is attracted to her. Allison gets her first kiss.

Analysis: A little romance and a lot of inner turmoil make this a pleasant young adult novel. Allison is believable even though the plot seems developed to accommodate the disease. The information about AIDS is accurate, and the characterizations of Mr. and Mrs. Adams are clear.

■ Hermes, Patricia. *You Shouldn't Have to Say Good-bye.* Harcourt, 1982. 117pp. (0-15-299944-2) Reading Level: Grades 5–7. (BCCB Mr83)
Disability: Cancer

When Sarah is 13, her mother becomes ill. She does not go to a doctor immediately but later finds out she has terminal cancer from a quick-spreading melanoma. Sarah resists her mother's lessons on how to do laundry and take care of the house. Sarah rejects the books her mother recommends and purchases as gifts. Before Christmas, a party taxes Mother's strength and she returns to the hospital. Sarah goes to her friend Robin's house. They each plan to make daring changes in their gymnastics programs but resist the risk-taking at the last minute because their parents are able to attend the show.

Sarah and her mother talk about the show and Sarah's temptation to do something dangerous. On the day before Christmas, Sarah's parents suggest an early exchange of presents; Sarah gets angry because all the family rituals are being spoiled. Before the gifts can be opened, Mother dies. Father says that the one thing Sarah's mother wanted was to be able to watch her daughter grow up. Sarah's mother has left a book, written during her illness, for Sarah to read so she can learn all the things her mother wanted to be able to tell Sarah.

Analysis: This memorable story features both a close relationship between mother and daughter and consistent characterization. Robin's mother has agoraphobia, yet is improved enough to attend the gymnastics show. Robin and Sarah distract themselves from their emotional strains by planning forbidden stunts. Sarah's mother helps her daughter recognize that risk-taking is an escape from the inner threats one is afraid to face. Sarah's father is supportive and honest. No flowery sentimentality screens the ending, when Sarah reads her mother's bald statement that "What we're going through stinks."

■ Herzig, Alison Cragin, and Jane Lawrence Mali. *A Season of Secrets.* Little, Brown, 1982. 193pp. (0-316-35889-4) Reading Level: Grades 4–6. (BCCB D82)
Disability: Epilepsy

On the last day of school, 6-year-old Benji faints again, and Brooke and Jason, his teenage sister and brother, wonder all summer long what is wrong with him. Their parents provide no explanations. A new neighbor seems to be doing experiments on the bats in his barn, and there is concern about a health hazard. Brooke and her friend Izzie get summer work painting a house.

Benji has a little office in his room that he transforms into a home for a pet bat named Lucifer. He tells Brooke his secret so she will help him keep his mother out. Brooke also is told her parents' secret that Benji has epilepsy and must take medication to avoid any more fainting spells or seizures.

When the neighbors become alarmed by Benji's seizure and the death of a dog, they are ready to blame the bats for spreading rabies. Brooke speaks out about her brother's condition.

"What you've got is like having nosebleeds, every now and then, for no reason. Nosebleeds look yucky, but then they stop and you're fine. Your thing is called epilepsy. Okay? It's different, but it's the same. Yucky-looking, but you're fine. Okay?"

Izzie's mom shares her observation that epilepsy "Scares you half to death and hardly amounts to a hill of beans." She knows because her sister "has epilepsy. It's a damn nuisance, but it never slowed her down any. Six children, a whiner for a husband, and runs the gas station in Biloxi."

Brooke discovers that Benji had such trouble swallowing his pills that he used the summer's supply to make the scales on a clay dinosaur. By Labor Day, he has attended a birthday party without social ostracism and has learned to swallow his new capsules.

Analysis: Except for the parents' supersecrecy, this is an excellent story with believable characterization and humorous elements to balance the mysteries. Brooke is very close to her precocious brother, so readers learn how preoccupied the little boy is both with fears about his true condition and with the new neighbor who has trained bats and pigs for the army. Bats are sympathetically portrayed, as is epilepsy, and they are both given better reputations because of Benji's endearing character.

The wild creature is released in a parallel theme to Benji's new freedom from his family's overprotectiveness and secrets. Fans of Lowry's *Anastasia* and other preteen family stories will enjoy this book.

■ Hickman, Martha Whitmore. *Last Week My Brother Anthony Died.* Illus. by Randie Julien. Abingdon, 1984. 26pp. (0-687-21128-X) Reading Level: Grades K–2. (BCCB F85) *Disability:* Birth defects

Julie had looked forward to the birth of her baby brother and, because of his weak heart, was very careful around him once he came home from the hospital. When surgery failed to correct his problem, Anthony died. Julie asks her mother if they will have another baby, and her mother is not sure. The little girl realizes that even a new baby would not take the place of Anthony, and she discusses her feelings with the minister when he visits. Mr. Miller tells Julie that she will feel better soon, and he invites her to have some ice cream. Julie wonders if Anthony would mind that she is having fun, then decides to order two scoops—one for her and one for Anthony.

Analysis: A perceptive story told with warmth and gentle childlike observations introduces readers to Julie's grief and initial adjustment to

Anthony's death. She knows that "you can miss a person you didn't even used to know" and shares her memories of anticipation during the pregnancy and her bonding during Anthony's four weeks of life. Mr. Miller offers comfort with a story of his only daughter's death rather than with doctrinal dogma. This first-person account could be an excellent script for reader's theater, although the illustrations are not strong enough for picture book sharing in a group setting.

■ Holl, Kristi D. *Hidden in the Fog.* Atheneum, 1988. 132pp. (0-689-31494-9) Reading Level: Grades 4–8. (KR 1 My89)
Disability: Health impairment

Nikki tries to be noble and to help her family out because her mother is chronically ill. After surgery, counseling, recovery, and becoming disabled once more in an accident, Nikki's mother still relies on her daughter for what help the girl can give around their riverboat hotel. When Nikki is feeling the pressure of her mother's work too much, she finds another job, but Dad says she may not take it. When Nikki speaks up for herself, her father tells her she is too bossy. Nikki is persistent though, and they come to a compromise.

Analysis: Nikki is put upon and knows it. Her mother's ailments are obscure, so the plot and characterizations seem manipulated. This is only for large collections in which a Mississippi River story of self-sacrifice and initiative may be needed. A better choice would be *Sweetly Sings the Donkey* by Cleaver.

■ Holl, Kristi D. *The Rose Beyond the Wall.* Atheneum, 1985. 180pp. (0-689-31150-8) Reading Level: Grades 5–9. (BCCB 085)
Disability: Cancer

There are many changes in Rachel Lincoln's life when she is 12. Her grandmother has surgery for a malignant tumor and comes to the Lincolns' home when she is released from the hospital. Rachel's parents and older brother, Brent, act as if both a speedy recovery is expected and Grandma will be at their house only until she is well enough to go home again. However, Rachel remembers that Nurse Carlson indicated this was a terminal condition that would require hospice or home care. Grandma says that she has promised not to spend her life selfishly and that God has cured her. Rachel sees her grandmother's reactions to the chemotherapy and gets angry at God because Grandma seems sicker.

When the chemotherapy is stopped, Rachel realizes that it is not because Grandma is cured, but because there is no more hope. Mr. Lincoln does not want Rachel talking to Grandma about her illness, and Mrs. Lincoln refuses to listen to funeral plans. Grandma says she needs to talk about these things, and Rachel is the one she shares poetry and last requests with. Rachel keeps talking to Grandma, even after it seems the woman does not hear anymore. Grandma's death is followed by a funeral that would have pleased the old woman and by Rachel's spending time with a friend she had nearly alienated by being too possessive.

Analysis: This book gets into the storyline a lot of information on home care for terminally ill patients. However, the prolonged denial stage of grief unrealistically keeps Mr. and Mrs. Lincoln's characters shallow and forces Rachel to be Grandma's wise confidant. While this may be done to give readers an active character to read about, it reduces the book's literary quality.

The potential of religious comfort is explored, as Grandma spends time with a minister and comes to view death as a new beginning, hence the title reference to a poem that tells of a rose that grew through a crack in a wall to a beautiful world on the other side.

In the end, Rachel believes her grandmother is still blooming, somewhere new. When Rachel applies what she has learned about the risk of losing any interaction with a person you love if you hold on to them too tightly, her friendship with John is restored. This is an adequate presentation of the stresses and the changes in life-style and philosophy that dealing with a terminal illness can raise in a family.

■ Hooks, William H. *A Flight of Dazzle Angels.* Macmillan, 1988. 176 pp. (0-02-744430-9) Reading Level: Grades 7–10.
Disability: Orthopedic impairment; Epilepsy

Annie Earle helps her brother cope with an epileptic condition that causes him to be considered feebleminded. *See full annotation* Chapter 4: Orthopedic/Neurological Impairments.

■ Howe, James. *A Night Without Stars.* Atheneum, 1983. 178pp. (0-689-30957-0) Reading Level: Grades 4–7. (BCCB Je83)
Disability: Heart disease; Orthopedic impairment; Cosmetic impairment

Eleven-year-old Maria Tirone faces open-heart surgery. Her older brother works and is trying to save up for college but spends time and money to distract his sister from her fears about hospitalization. Maria also has another brother, Joey, and a baby sister. Mother's comments about the surgery are limited to "Ai, Maria, Maria," and observations about the doctors' looks and faith in God. In addition, Maria's silly sixth-grade friends, parents, doctor's jargon, and hospital roommates cannot answer her questions about the operation. She is drawn to another patient, Donald, who has had many corrective surgeries because of burn damage.

Donald's appearance horrifies Maria at first, and the other patients call him "Monster Man." Donald tells Maria about his life, his abusive mother, the fire, repeated surgeries, and his current foster parents. He describes being anesthetized as "A night without stars. That's what it's like. No stars. Just black, black, blackness. And it holds you. And becomes your only friend." After Maria reaches out to comfort and thank him, he cries "Not because he was afraid and not because he was alone. But because Maria had touched his arm. And he had let her."

After surgery, Maria's intensive care unit nurse prepares her parents for the shock of visiting by summarizing: "She may have black and blue marks from surgery. She has a tube running into her nose to deliver oxygen, and tubes coming from her chest. . . . Don't let them frighten you."

Lorna Barthels works with Maria and Donald in the playroom four days after their surgeries. Maria finds out that Donald is 11 also, that he lives in a rural area north of the hospital, and that he writes poems. While they work with art materials, "Maria watched him out of the corner of her eye. She tried to make believe she'd never seen him before; she wanted to know if the sight of him would still make her feel sick. But it was too late, she was used to him already. She knew he was strange-looking, ugly even, but so what? He was different, that's all."

Maria finds out more specifics about her operation and adjusts to her scar. Other patients tease her about spending time with Donald, but they keep in touch even after their hospital stay is over.

Analysis: Maria's fears and adjustments regarding her surgery provide a limited plot, but complex, well-realized relationships enhance this excellent piece of fiction. Characterizations give each patient a personality that is independent from each one's respective health impairment. The book goes a long way to break down the type of ignorance that Maria suffered from before her hospitalization. Recommended for most collections, the action is firmly set in a time of soap operas, 8-track recordings, and "Saturday Night Fever"-flavored Queens.

■ Howe, Norma. *God, the Universe, and Hot Fudge Sundaes.* Houghton, 1984. 182pp. (0-395-35483-8) Reading Level: Grades 7–10. (BCCB MS84)
Disability: Birth defects

Alfie is a bright senior, involved in the Math Club and science. She has an 11-year-old sister who uses a wheelchair, an aunt who is a trained nurse living with them, a mother who is deeply involved in charismatic Christian fellowship, and a father whose puns cannot mask his alienation from his wife. Alfie goes along with her mother's worship and beliefs until the church leadership pressures her to quit playing Dungeons and Dragons in Math Club and to give up her student assistant position in science.

When a creationist suit against the state of California is tried in Sacramento, Alfie gets permission to attend as a project for MGM (Mentally Gifted Minor) credit. She meets a graduate student who challenges her to side with the evolutionist view that creation belongs in religious instruction, not in science textbooks. Alfie puzzles through the courtroom arguments, the teachings of her church, and the conviction that it would be fair to include both theories because no one has ever witnessed either to know which is true.

One day, Alfie is summoned from the courthouse because her sister's heart problems have reached a terminal stage. Friends from church are supportive, and Alfie watches her mother rely on teachings of their faith to cope with her loss. Alfie's father and aunt withdraw from participation in funeral plans, and Alfie decides she needs to go back to southern California to retrieve a secret crucifix Francie had treasured as a gift from Jesus. However, Alfie's old house has been torn down, and her quest is hopeless.

Alfie's dad moves out, takes Alfie to a favorite family spot for a hot fudge sundae, and initiates divorce. Mother recognizes that Alfie's beliefs are different from her own and that they will have to create a new relationship not based on Francie's needs or church dogma.

Analysis: Alfie reveals that her parents separated after her sister's death and that she has recently rejected a lot of the teachings that her mother holds convictions for. Then, her flashback interjects oblique references about Francie's health impairment and the strain it has caused on family relationships since the 11-year-old was born. Francie appears in several scenes: cheating at board games, delighted and deliciously frightened by Alfie's and Gregg's efforts to lift her chair onto Alfie's special lookout, innocently trusting her mother's desire to take Francie to healing meetings, and uncertain about the source of her mysterious answer from Jesus.

The author impressively handles strong characterizations with opposite orientations of faith. Alfie even questions her mother about genetic counseling and abortion in light of Francie's difficult life. This type of character exploration is deeper than *God's Radar,* another excellent look at convictions and conventions of evangelical, fundamental Christianity's alienating family members. Alfie's recognition of spiritual strength and elation are balanced with her observations about the socially extreme elements of her mother's "spirit-filled" church experiences. This controlled writing style is also used to imply that Alfie was so accustomed to Francie's condition that the specifics of her impairment rarely surfaced in conversation or thought.

> Kurt turned sort of pale. "Jesus! Your sister? She *died?* Well what happened? Uh, how *old* was she?"
> "She was eleven. She's been sick a long time." I told him how she was born with this disease, and how she had other health problems as well, like her heart. The doctors always said she would probably die from the heart trouble before the other. It turned out they were right.
> Kurt didn't say anything during my explanation. And when I finished, he just shook his head and said softly, "God, that's rough!"

The casual oaths of nonbelievers lend authenticity to the dialogue and add ironic depth to this unsentimental exploration of a young person's struggle to come to terms with God, the universe, and hot fudge sundaes. Alfie's friendships, romantic interests, academic pursuits, role in the family, and faith are deeply affected by the impaired health and terminal illness of a younger sister. There is some contrived action (especially with both the block and tackle to lift Francie and Kurt's reappearances), but Alfie's story can be recommended because the book is as fair in its portrayals of health, sickness, youth, maturity, and faith in God or evolution as Alfie would like to be.

■ Howe, Norma. *In with the Out Crowd.* Houghton, 1986. 196pp. (0-395-40490-8) Reading Level: Grades 6–9. (BCCB Ja87)
Disability: Alzheimer's disease; Health impairment

Robin Tweedy-Boyd is a self-absorbed 16-year-old whose secure place in the social elite of her school erodes after she turns down the school quarterback. She knows that smoking, drinking, and sex are part of the social scene, but she has her own ideas about romance with a "real boyfriend." Her friend Jennifer tells her that old friends feel Robin is judging them by not participating.

Christmas vacation gives Robin time to interact with her grandfather, a doctor with Alzheimer's disease, and her grandmother. Grandmother gives everyone a Christmas dinner assignment, and Robin's is to bring a guest for dessert. When Emory, who had the brunt of fourth-grade teasing because he cried all the time, reveals some things about his life, Robin regrets some of her snobbish behavior.

A tentative reentry with her old social crowd turns into humiliation when Robin's popularly endorsed scheme to embarrass the principal is used against her. Emory spends time with Robin and says he understands why she puts him down when her old friends see them together.

On their fiftieth anniversary, Robin's grandmother and grandfather take her to Venice as their escort. Grandfather's lack of interest and recollections distress his wife. Robin sees the real tragedies of adult life, which puts her adolescent social strife in perspective. Emory persuades her to volunteer in the hospital and to help in his campaign for student body president; he then invites her to the senior ball.

Analysis: Adolescence is a time of establishing independence, and this is a good look at the stress of being strong enough to resist peer pressure. Robin and her classmate Muriel turn away from alliances with "in" crowd members and discover the benefits of deeper relationships. Part of Robin's development comes through her reactions to her grandfather's change of personality, her grandmother's grief, and Emory's mother's terminal illness. Though not all these characters are as well portrayed as Robin, she is a believable teen in transition.

■ Hughes, Monica. *Hunter in the Dark.* Atheneum, 1983. 131pp. (0-689-30959-7) Reading Level: Grades 6–9. (BCCB MS83)
Disability: Cancer

Mike drives alone to set up camp for hunting. He recalls the events of the last year that make him want to find a stag to bring home as a trophy. Shortly after his sixteenth birthday, he collapsed playing basketball and was treated in the hospital for an "anemic" condition. When his hair fell out, he knew that the doctor and his parents had withheld information.

Through various incidents, Mike is persuaded by his friend Doug to return to school, to plan a hunting trip, and to try to participate in activities. Mike's parents restricted Doug's visits until, in retaliation, Mike refused his treatment. When Mike was in remission, his father taught him to drive and bought him a car. After another hospitalization, Mike sets out on his hunting trip. When he tracks the stag, he decides not to take its life and still feels he has had a perfect day.

Analysis: Unlike *Tracker* by Paulsen, the hunting analogy in this story deals with an ill protagonist's fight to face the realities of his own condition. The parents are ineffectual in expressing their own feelings and in preparing Mike for an uncertain prognosis. The doctor did not override Mike's parents' wish for secrecy until Mike looked up his medication at the library and learned it was for acute lymphocytic leukemia. Both how realistic this situation would be and the advisability of anyone going hunting alone are small flaws in an otherwise empathic story.

■ Irwin, Hadley, and Ann Irwin. *What About Grandma?* Atheneum, 1982. 165pp. (0-689-50224-9) Reading Level: Grades 6–9. (BCCB MS82) *Disability:* Health impairment

Grandma breaks her hip, and her daughter, Eve, and 16-year-old grand-daughter, Rhys, come to help her move into a nursing home. During their month-long visit, Grandma insists she wants to keep her things and does not want to sell her home. Rhys is caught in the middle of the women's arguments.

She enjoys getting out to go golfing and meets Lew. Lew's grandmother is Grandma Wyn's best friend, Virene. When Virene and Lew come to visit, Rhys worries that Lew seems interested in Eve.

Eve asks Rhys to gently inform Grandma that a room is reserved for her at the nursing home. Rhys is also confided in by Grandma, who does not know how to tell her own daughter, Eve, that she is terminally ill. Rhys feels overburdened and forces the women to communicate directly about the situation.

Eve and Rhys stay, caring for Grandma in the home she loves. Rhys talks with Grandma about dying, and together they burn some old letters. Virene and another friend of Grandma's, named Wid, visit as Grandma's failing health requires her to stay in a hospital bed on the sun porch. Lew returns to medical school, and Rhys does not know if she will ever see him again. Grandma dies, but Rhys has resolved that a part of Grandma "would live in me."

Analysis: This perceptive story has strong characterizations that allow the author to focus on both relationships between mothers and daughters and long-term friendships. Aging and terminal illness are dealt with realistically. The doctor warns Eve that home care is difficult and demands a lot of work. The emotional growth that Rhys experiences provides most of the story's momentum, but the sad plot has memories of happy times and love scattered thoughout to lighten the mood.

■ Jordan, MaryKate. *Losing Uncle Tim.* Illus. by Judith Friedman. Whitman, 1989. 32pp. (0-8075-4756-5) Reading Level: Grades K–3. (BCCB N89) *Disability:* AIDS

Daniel recalls his close relationship with his Uncle Tim, who runs an antique store. For Daniel, certain items in the shop have special memories of times they spent playing together outdoors and indoors. Their cozy visits on cold days were interrupted by Uncle Tim's becoming so tired sometimes that "he fell asleep right while he was talking." The boy's mother explained that "Uncle Tim's body was getting worn out from a disease called AIDS."

"The next time I went to visit Uncle Tim, he looked different to me, somehow, because now I knew he had AIDS. It was the first time I had ever looked at somebody and known he was probably dying."

Daniel notices that his uncle loses weight and strength until he looks old. One day, after the boy sees an assistant helping Uncle Tim, he runs home, pounds on his pillow, then confides in his father:

"Uncle Tim can't even walk to the bathroom . . . And maybe I'm going to get AIDS from being over there so much. . . .

. . . I hug him. Sometimes we have dinner together."

Daniel's father repeats the doctor's assurances that caring for Tim and getting close were safe.

The next day, Tim suspects his nephew of throwing their checkers match, and the boy admits, "I thought maybe if I didn't win so much you might not die." After a talk, Tim won and gave his nephew the checkers set. The next three days, Tim is in a coma, and the boy is comforted to find out that greetings and comments he had been making even though Tim was asleep may have been heard.

Tim dies and the family has a funeral and reads his will. Three special items from the shop that Daniel had loved are left to him. His memories of Uncle Tim teach Daniel that no matter what he chooses to do with his life, it should be something that he loves.

Analysis: This straightforward account includes Daniel's reactions and information from his parents. Its bland dialogue has some philosophical comments about the sun always shining somewhere, and "The hardest part of having Tim die is not having his body here to hug." What lends momentum to the episodic sequence of events is the relationship between Daniel and his favorite "grown-up." Interestingly, Daniel and Tim never talk to each other about the illness.

Illustrations in soft colors, bordered in brown, face text blocks of greatly varied lengths that are decorated with small drawings of items from the antique shop. The figures are drawn with adequate expression and consistency but are stiffly posed. These flaws can be overlooked in a book for young audiences that not only complements AIDS education but deals with grief over the terminal illness of a close relative. There are many picture books on the death of a grandparent, but few present the demands of terminal care for a younger adult. This title will be useful in most collections for that reason, even if the survival rate or incidence of AIDS dramatically changes in the future.

■ Kerr, M. E. *Night Kites.* HarperCollins, 1986. 192pp. (LB 0-06-023254-4)
Reading Level: Grades 8–12. (BCCB My86)
Disability: AIDS

Erick Rudd is in his senior year, has an innocent girlfriend, named Dill, and an older brother, named Pete. Pete teaches, travels on writing grants, and hopes to sell his novel outline to a Hollywood producer. When Pete comes to visit, he is ill, and later he is hospitalized with AIDS. Erick's mother has known that Pete was homosexual, but Erick is angry that he was not told sooner, because he thinks of it simply as "just another way of being."

Erick's parents have Pete come live at home when his illness makes him lose his job and apartment. Although the household members all make adjustments to Pete's homosexuality and support him through chemotherapy, they evade all references to death. A gathering of Pete's family and friends is planned but is marred by one guest's homosexual lover and the employment agency servers' refusal to come to the home of someone with AIDS.

Erick loses contact with his girlfriend, and his best friend, Jack, because he responds to the advances of Jack's love, Nicki. Nicki hears about Pete's illness and angrily breaks off her relationship with Erick. When he goes to talk to her, she is busy flirting with her next conquest.

Analysis: The title image comes from Erick's memory of Pete flying a kite with battery-powered lights through evening darkness. He admires Pete's ability to be his own person and is intrigued by Nikki, whose sensuous style is in high contrast to Erick's designer-jeaned classmates. Erick is propelled through emotional changes when the unconventional people in his life introduce options for sexual activity that have some harsh consequences. Coarse jokes, a scheme to "get laid," and Erick's and Jack's frustration with virginity contribute to foreshadowed events and character development.

Though the story contains humorous aspects, it is generally a serious, insightful novel that includes the health impairment brought on by AIDS as one of its complex themes.

Action is firmly established in the mid-80s by mention of real-life clothing brands, TV shows, songs, and rock performers. The story line accurately presents medical knowledge and social issues for that time period. Three different characters recall Michelle, Pete's girlfriend of nine years earlier. Readers get a concentrated impression of a pretty girl in a wheelchair who dated a homosexual man so both of them could have a "safe" social niche. Pete's comments show that Michelle had been a loyal friend, mature enough to push him out of "the closet" and independent and confident enough in her own sexuality to get married.

Pete's health fails rapidly, during which time the apprehensions of friends, family, and neighbors are addressed. The possibility of physical contagion is shown to generate fear, but appropriate assurances are made regarding AIDS. Besides outsiders' attention to physical infection, the possibility that Erick might pursue homosexual relationships causes his father to misinterpret an exchange between Jack and Erick. This type of confrontation helps develop the characters and rounds out the portrayal of a "perfect family" that is "coming apart at the seams."

■ Klass, Sheila S. *Alive & Starting Over.* Scribner, 1983. 144pp. (0-684-17987-3) Reading Level: Grades 7–9. (BCCB F84)
Disability: Hemophilia; Heart disease

Her father has remarried, and 15-year-old Jessica Van Norden is considering going to boarding school to avoid potential conflicts with her stepmother. Grandma is hospitalized for a heart attack, and Jessica cares for her empty apartment. Jessica has a friend, Jason, who supports her through these changes. She also spends time with a new student, Peter, who trusts Jessica not to pity him because of his hemophilia. When Grandma is released, she goes to live in a nursing home. Peter is injured in a motorcycle accident, and Jessica suggests that Jason visit the recuperating patient to play chess. Everyone seems to be getting a new start, and Jessica is confident of her decision to attend a boarding school that is not too far away from her family or the two boys.

Analysis: This book is an enjoyable first-person description of Jessica's various relationships and the ways in which each helps her understand her own needs. The plot structure is not as strong as the characterizations. As a child, Jessica had allergies that were complicated by Grandma's presence, and Grandma's preoccupation with her health, together with her overbearing manner still irritates Jessica. This time though, a psychiatrist's suggestion is not needed that Jessica seek more "space."

Peter observes most of the restrictions that hemophilia places on his life, but his one outlet, motorcycle riding, results in an accident. The serious nature of such an injury under the circumstances is indicated when both of Jessica's parents donate blood and Jessica visits Peter in the hospital. Peter does not like to discuss any kind of illness and is reluctant to admit he has a health impairment. This tendency to conceal a condition puts his relationship with Jessica and his life at risk.

This is a sequel to *To See My Mother Dance,* and readers may like to find out more about Jessica here.

■ Klass, Sheila S. **To See My Mother Dance.** Scribner, 1981. 154pp. (0-684-17227-5) Reading Level: Grades 6–8. (BCCB My82)
Disability: Asthma

Jessica was 1 year old when her mother, Karen, ran off to a hippie commune. Karen's father had a detective find his daughter. Jessica grows up hearing her grandmother rail against her own irresponsible daughter, and she develops asthma and creates a fantasy mother who is a successful dancer, always there for Jessica's intimate confidences.

When Father announces his plans to marry Martha, Grandmother's advice is that Jessica make things so tough on Martha that she won't stay.

Jessica gets her first kiss from Jason and offers to sleep with him just to hurt her father and Martha. He declines. Jessica's friend Sylvia is at odds about her clothing, her hair, the shape of her nose, and her own overbearing stepmother. Jessica's friend Brookie drinks herself into a stupor to get her mother to recognize her own alcoholism.

Martha locates Karen, Jessica's mother, in San Francisco and arranges for them to meet. The reunion is far from Jessica's imagined conversations, because Karen is vague and distant, and life is not glamorous at the Children of the Lotus commune. Because her mother does not even say good-bye, Jessica believes Martha's observations that Karen's heavy drug use made her change. Jessica suggests that she go to boarding school after the wedding so she can sort out realities on her own.

Analysis: Strong characterizations fill this story, but the problems Jessica and her friends deal with serve only to introduce more topics to ponder than resolutions. The title refers to Jessica's desire to see her mother dancing professionally—a career she daydreams about to justify her mother's abandoning her father and never trying to reestablish contact with Jessica. Emotional trauma triggers allergic reactions, and stress, such as Father's bringing home potential mothers, results in Jessica's asthma attacks. Jessica's manipulative behavior is understandable, because Grandmother is her role model as well as chief persecutor.

■ Klause, Annette Curtis. **The Silver Kiss.** Delacorte, 1990. 198pp. (0-385-31060-X) Reading Level: Grades 8–12. (KR 1 O90)
Disability: Cancer

Zoe's mother is dying of cancer, her father excludes Zoe from his hospital vigil, and her best friend prefers to bemoan trivial changes instead of allowing Zoe to confide any feelings or events concerning the terminal illness. One night, Zoe meets Simon in a park and is drawn into a romantic relationship. Simon is immortal, and Zoe is slowly introduced to his mystical life as a vampire. Simon has been seeking revenge on his brother across the centuries, because his evil vampire counterpart was responsible for the death of their mother. Revelations and confrontations build to a startling conclusion for Zoe.

Analysis: Extremely good characterization and restrained, though vivid, presentation of the more lurid elements of this plot make it a winner. It is good that the somewhat erotic fantasy is not undermined by converting Zoe's experience into a stress-provoked delusion. Readers will appreciate the author's skill at integrating a magical tale with a realistic problem.

■ Klein, Norma. *Going Backwards.* Scholastic, 1986. 182pp. (LB 0-590-40328-1) Reading Level: Grades 7–10. (BCCB O86)
Disability: Alzheimer's disease; Anorexia nervosa

Charles Goldberg does not mind babysitting for his 10-year-old brother, Kaylo, but being in charge of his grandmother too is getting to him. She came to live in their 12-room apartment in Manhattan after Dr. Goldberg's father died, and Alzheimer's disease has disoriented her more and more lately. Granny asks, "What's your father's name?" every 20 minutes, and she will not stay in bed, even after repeated doses of tranquilizers.

Charles recalls how alert and lively his grandmother used to be. He feels fat and socially inept because, though he is a 16-year-old senior who has been offered early acceptance at Cornell, he still has not dated. The Goldbergs' housekeeper, a black woman named Josie, prods Charles and helps him to talk things out.

Charles's friend, Kim, has an elderly grandfather whose vision is failing, but the Korean gentleman has no memory problems. One of Charles's classmates from the fine arts school that he and Kaylo attend is a dancer named Wendy. She and her parents meet the Goldbergs on a picnic at which Granny loses bladder control. Wendy also lives with a grandmother who has experienced the disorientation of Alzheimer's disease. Charles takes Wendy to a show, and she reveals that she is a recovering anorectic, who has learned that part of her illness stems from her distrust of men and her fear of sex. The two have so little self-confidence or experience that they initiate a tentative romance with each other.

Kaylo is frightened by Granny one night when she begins writing her life story on the walls of his closet, in Hebrew, with a green magic marker. Mrs. Goldberg pressures her husband to find full-time care for Granny that will not be such a drain on all family members. She is particularly concerned that Kaylo's talent as a pianist not be undermined by recent emotional distress as evidenced by his nightmares of witches sitting on his bed.

Charles and his father talk late at night because of insomnia, and Dr. Goldberg enlists Charles as moral support on a visit to a nearby nursing facility that he hopes will not be a "hellhole." Their visit is not reassuring, but Granny's appearance at breakfast in only a pajama top prompts action. The evening before she is to be moved, Granny dies in her sleep. Dr. Goldberg is violent in his grief.

Charles begins his freshman year of studies, and by Thanksgiving has lost weight and his virginity. His father dies, and he goes home to comfort his mother. Josie wants to know about Charles's girlfriend, and he shows her a picture of Lorraine, an athletic black girl six months older than him. Mrs. Goldberg confides that Granny received a fatal dose of pills the night of her death and that Dr. Goldberg had undermined his health and refused care ever since. Charles imagines a place where his loved ones are alive and visiting Josie on some idyllic rural property that Charles would like to buy for her.

Analysis: One family's reaction to the effects of Alzheimer's disease is the focus of the action. Charles's first-person account of the other elements of his life add some humor and present the provocative minor themes of sexuality and filial devotion. Granny's former abilities and personality have been established in recollections about shell gathering and tennis playing, in addition to a moving account of her resourcefulness in getting her family established in the United States.

Dr. Goldberg's motivations about euthanasia are clear, and, because he is a pathologist, the situation is foreshadowed. Mrs. Goldberg makes this admission: "I think that must be the bravest thing anyone can do, to kill someone you love to spare them suffering. My mother just asked if we could leave some pills near her bed so she could take them herself when she was dying of cancer. But that only works if the person is mentally competent, which Gustel certainly wasn't."

Wendy's portrayal depends on her curious drive to tell Charles everything her therapy has revealed about herself on their first date. Her romance with Charles is a period of groping, physically and emotionally, for what she feels her mother is lacking in a "stay at home" marriage. Charles tells that Wendy and Kim establish a strong, serious relationship in their first year at the same college. Kim and Wendy create an interracial couple, which echoes Charles's relationship with Lorraine, though Josie is the only character who comments on the potential social implications.

The thought-provoking themes and convincing characterizations are presented in a clear style. Only Kaylo, the precocious pianist, seems to be drawn too young for fifth grade in his speech patterns and interactions with his mother. This may foster that stereotype of gifted students as social dunces. Otherwise, Klein uses even a brief revelation that Charles's aunt and uncle "have one son, Beal, who's retarded and sequestered in some special school in Maine" to add dimension to Charles's musings on family interaction. Young adults are often interested in both the type of introspection and the vicarious experiences with social and emotional situations that Klein offers in this story.

■ Lasky, Kathryn. *Home Free.* Macmillan, 1985. 245 pp. (0-02-751650-4)
Reading Level: Grades 8–10.
Disability: Cancer

Sam loves the reservoir and the eagles that he photographs with an old man who is dying from cancer. *See full annotation* Chapter 6: Emotional Disturbances.

■ Leonard, Alison. *Tina's Chance.* Viking, 1988. 187pp. (0-670-82430-5)
Reading Level: Grades 7–10. (BCCB D88)
Disability: Huntington's chorea

Tina's mother died when Tina was 2, but nobody tells her anything about that part of her family history. At 15, Tina finds some family records and photographs, and she pursues a quest that takes her to Aunt Louise's home. When she arrives, she falls ill. Aunt Louise is a nurse and allows her niece to recover in the home Louise shares with her lover, Diana. Tina adjusts to this new situation and to the knowledge that she and her aunt are at risk from a genetic condition called Huntington's chorea. It is a 50-50 chance that this life-threatening disease will manifest itself as it did in Tina's mother.

Analysis: From Great Britain, this import *(Tinker's Career)* has been effectively retitled but still suffers from shifting points of view and tedious details of Tina's plight. Readers who find the mystery suspenseful or the health risk intriguing may overlook plot elements that are too coincidental. Louise is familiar with the effects of a genetically transmitted disease, has been drawn to medicine as a career, and has established a love relationship in which childbearing is not one of the expectations. Louise's ways of coping with an uncertain future are not forced on Tina. Fans of Sallis's *Secret Places of the Stairs* can weep over this hidden family misery mystery as well.

■ Little, Jean. *Mama's Going to Buy You a Mockingbird.* Viking, 1985.
213pp. (0-670-80346-4) Reading Level: Grades 4–8. (BCCB Je85)
Disability: Cancer

Aunt Margery is taking care of 11-year-old Jeremy and his younger sister,
Sarah, at the family's lakeside cabin. When their mother and father join
the group, Jeremy learns that his father's surgery has revealed cancer that
must be treated. Jeremy dreads returning to school, where his father had
been a teacher, because of gossip and his father's request that Jeremy
befriend a sixth-grade classmate named Tess.

Many changes at home due to Father's continued hospitalization and
terminal illness burden Jeremy's family emotionally and financially.
Jeremy sets himself a goal of reading a difficult book that his father
recommended, Kipling's *Kim.* When Jeremy's runaway cat is returned by
Tess, he wants to tell Father about the friendship that has been established. However, Jeremy's father dies that afternoon. "The doctor said it
was a blessing. It was very sudden. One minute we were talking. The next,
he was gone . . . gone."

Adjusting to life now that Mother will be the head of the household is
difficult for Jeremy. He withdraws and wonders why he does not react
more strongly to his father's death. The family relocates to an apartment
in a building owned by Tess's grandfather. Tess confides that her mother
abandoned her at the age of 7. Jeremy decides to forget his father the way
Tess tries to forget her own mother because it hurts too much to remember. Jeremy feels that they have formed a new type of family, and he
decides to stop putting on the affectation at school that he is indifferent
toward Tess.

Christmas celebrations overwhelm Jeremy with memories of his father.
The ritual of filling stockings makes Jeremy offer his mother some special
items, including a ceramic owl that had become a mascot for Jeremy and
his father during the difficult summer and the hospitalizations.

Analysis: Jean Little uses bickering siblings and realistic school dynamics to balance this serious story of virulent cancer and the adjustments a
family makes to cope with a sudden loss. The title refers to Mother's shift
to provider and is integrated into the story when she comforts Sarah with
the old song, "Mama's Going to Buy You a Mockingbird." A soft watercolor cover of Jeremy with his arm around Sarah, both looking at Hoot
the owl while the cat perches on the sofa, invitingly portrays the book's
emotional tone and important characters.

Sarah foreshadows her father's death when she repeats her aunt's comment that "Daddy had left something too late and now there's only a

fifty-fifty chance." This type of clarification that not all cancer follows the pattern shown here helps to avoid stereotyping without intruding on the story. This skilled work of fiction is highly recommended and will find a wide age range of readers.

■ Lorentzen, Karin. *Lanky Longlegs.* Trans. by Joan Tate. Illus. by Jan Ormerrod. Atheneum, 1983. 90pp. (0-689-50260-5) Reading Level: Grades 3–5. (BCCB Je83)
Disability: Health impairment

Di dislikes the nickname of "Lanky Longlegs" that her new classmate, Martin, has coined. She makes him abandon it when he wants to come visit her new puppies. When he calls her Lanky Longlegs again, she refuses to let him buy one of the puppies. He shows her the leash and collar that had been purchased for his own dog before it was killed by a car.

Mike, Di's brother, has a blood disease that causes his hospitalization. When he comes home, he no longer laughs, and Di's mother quits her job to be with him. During the next hospital stay, Mike dies, and Di dreams about him.

Di does not want to return to school until her friend Helen steps in. Martin gives Di a leash and collar for the puppy she had chosen to keep.

Analysis: This earnest tale is translated from a Norwegian story published in 1976. The believable action and everyday events soften its sad theme of death and adjustment to loss. Di discusses heaven with her mother, but a particular faith is not the focus of this wistful production.

■ Lyon, George Ella. *Red Rover, Red Rover.* Orchard, 1989. 131pp. (LB 0-531-08432-9) Reading Level: Grades 6–9. (BCCB S89)
Disability: Ulcers

Sumi is 11 when her grandfather dies of a bleeding ulcer that has been misdiagnosed. Her older brother goes away to school, and Sumi feels abandoned in a world of change. When her menstrual period begins, her mother only gives her help with cleaning up and pads. Sumi associates the mysterious bleeding with her grandfather's unrecognized ailment instead of simply a new and normal pattern in her life until a schoolmate gives her more information.

When Sumi receives a Peter, Paul, and Mary album for Christmas, she finds she can share her brother's love of music even though she does not play an instrument as masterfully as he does. She decides to lose weight, survives a crush on one of her teachers, and reflects on many of the new complexities of her life as she matures during the 1960s.

Analysis: Sumi's grandfather was having difficulty with various signs of aging but could still perform athletic feats for his grandchildren. The entire family is alarmed when he drives off the road after passing out at the wheel. An examination is followed by treatment with yeast cakes, which does not address the true ailment. His sudden death is a great shock to Sumi, and the rest of the story shows how it seemed to trigger a year of change and maturation.

The historic setting is vague until Peter, Paul, and Mary's music is mentioned, so readers can be confused about why Sumi's mother is so reluctant to give Sumi the information she needs. Also, Sumi seems very unsophisticated for her age, until one learns that she was growing up in an earlier time period. On the other hand, Sumi records poetic musings that are precocious. Though they present wise insights, their tone does not fit Sumi's character all the time.

■ McDaniel, Lurlene. *Goodbye Doesn't Mean Forever.* Bantam, 1989. 166pp. (paper 0-553-28007-4) Reading Level: Grades 8–10.
Disability: Cancer

Jory Delaney is in her senior year of high school but cannot settle her college plans or enjoy her former party-girl style because her best friend is battling cancer. Though Melissa's disease is in remission, her clinic visits and newly grown-in hair are reminders of recent chemotherapy. Melissa is a Semifinalist for a National Merit Scholarship and continues to work toward a college education in law. Jory admires Melissa and considers Melissa's mother and brother her second family. Melissa's brother is in college, but Jory has been in love with him for years. Michael attends classes, has two jobs, has taken his absent father's role with Melissa, and considers Jory his sister's rich friend. Jory dates schoolmates and escorts whom her mother coerces her into attending social functions with.

When tests show that Melissa's white blood cell count is up again, the doctors consider the 50-50 chance of success in the use of Michael's bone marrow as a transplant. Jory stands by Melissa during the sick girl's decision, and she supports the family during the actual procedure.

A classmate named Lyle works with Jory on a carnival to raise funds for donations of blood, because Melissa's system seems to be rejecting the transplant. One night Jory goes to a party, argues with Lyle, and drives drunken Michael to a special place Melissa had pointed out. While comforting each other, Michael's intimacies stop short of sexual relations with Jory, which makes her feel rejected. He is sobered and apologetic, so their interactions are strained for the final weeks of Melissa's life.

Melissa contracts meningitis just as her transfusions become effective.

Lyle's family had been through therapy while his mother was under treatment for cancer, and he often encourages Jory to open up about her feelings. Jory avoids his concern, even though he supports her when she grows faint during the funeral. One day Jory goes to Lyle's home unannounced because she is ready to talk with him about her loss.

Jory selects a college and tries to improve her academic standing so she can transfer to a campus nearer Lyle in her sophomore year. On a hot air balloon flight, Michael and Jory share Melissa's last letters, feel the presence of her spirit, and see a new day dawning.

Analysis: The poor-little-rich-girl themes established in the book *Too Young to Die* are also present in this companion novel for Jory's characterization. Her alienation from busy, materialistic parents is softened when Mrs. Delaney donates $5,000 to the carnival. Jory's defensive pattern with her mother makes losing her best friend and confidant that much harder. Denial of Melissa's serious condition makes Jory erratic, and suppressed anger makes her drive recklessly several times.

When Jory's mother inquires about Melissa, Jory's harsh response is: "She gets chemo every six weeks. She gets stuck with needles and has her bone marrow sucked out, and sometimes she gets so sick, she throws up for hours."

Michael blames himself and rages against the doctors who hold out hope that seems to get snatched away like Charlie Brown's football held by perverse Lucy. When it seems that the bone marrow has not been a compatible option for Melissa, Michael summarizes:

"The first time she was in the hospital, I thought I'd go nuts. . . . Every day, I'd go in and see what the chemo was doing to her. It invaded her, turned her inside out, and made her hurt so bad. All the doctors said was 'It's normal. It's always this way.' I hated those doctors, and I hated what their 'cure' was doing to her."

Lyle's mother has experienced remission for years, and he intends to become a doctor, so his compassionate use of counseling techniques is believable. The ballooning scene on the cover is a good introduction to this perceptive story. Though the writing style shifts tone at times, this is a more worthwhile addition to collections than the rash of love-and-death titles this author penned for series from Willowisp Press.

■ McDaniel, Lurlene. *Too Young to Die.* Bantam, 1989. 166pp. (paper 0-553-28008-2) Reading Level: Grades 8–10.
Disability: Cancer

Jory Delaney asks her best friend, Melissa Austin, "IF you make Brain Bowl, and IF you date Brad, will you confess that this could possibly be the best school year of your life?" But, just when Melissa makes the team's first cut, and Brad admires her waist-length black hair, school authorities are ready to report Melissa as a victim of child abuse. However, the bruises on her legs are not evidence of anything wrong at home. There, Melissa's life with big brother Michael and Mom is so loving that Jory often visits their family rather than go home to her empty mansion. The doctor puts Melissa in the hospital for tests and diagnoses lymphocytic leukemia. Treatment with chemotherapy, hoped-for remission, and a program of maintenance are outlined for Melissa.

In the hospital, Melissa meets a boy named Richter Davis, who has had an amputation of one leg below the knee due to osteogenic sarcoma. His track career was halted, but he has been in remission and is being fitted for a new prosthesis to avoid skin ulcers. He is open about chemotherapy and gives Melissa advice and sympathy:

"Too bad about your hair."

"What about it?"

"The chemo will take it. It'll take it all."

In a symbolic act against fate, Melissa has Jory cut her hair before treatments start. Ric comforts Melissa and helps her use imaging to "turn on your inner healing reserves." Melissa gets sores on her face, contracts a secondary infection, loses weight, and loses her hair. Rick is discharged from the hospital but says he wants to keep in touch. Michael gives his sister a blank book to keep as a journal of "this whole stinking experience." Melissa says, "I'd rather think of it as portable bathroom walls, where I can write all kinds of dirty words about these last few weeks." She tells him that his hot air balloon is the image she calls up to use her alpha cells in fighting the leukemia.

Four-year-old Rachael comes to Melissa's room, innocently revealing her own experiences with leukemia, chemotherapy, "mission," and relapse. "I used to think if they stuck me with needles everything inside would leak out. But that was when I was only three and I was still a baby." Melissa is released on outpatient care but not allowed to return to school until Christmas. Jory accompanies Melissa to the PSAT, and Melissa scores in the top percentile. She buys a short, dark hairpiece. Brad never contacted Melissa in the hospital, but she is still upset to see him with another girl around school. Faculty and students make Melissa feel excluded and edgy, but she stays on the Brain Bowl team.

Melissa starts dating Ric, and he asks her to sleep with him during spring break. She is curious about sex but not committed to Ric. Rachael dies, Melissa reevaluates her life goals, and she breaks up with Ric. She encourages him to pursue his options in athletics because she is going to stick to her original plans. She confronts the Brain Bowl advisers with their bias against her because of her health problem, and they name her as a member of the final team.

Jory gives a custom-made human hair wig to Melissa, which makes her look as she did before the illness. Michael is impressed by the generosity of Melissa's "rich little friend." Melissa goes off to Brain Bowl competition.

Analysis: Melissa's case history is nicely blended with a romance or two. Jory and Rachael and Ric are adequately developed minor characters. Like Bunting's *Will You Be My POSSLQ?* this book incorporates the theme of life beyond cancer therapy.

In the sequel, *Goodbye Doesn't Mean Forever,* Melissa has a relapse and a bone marrow transplant that are foreshadowed here. The hopeful outlook of this story makes it a good addition for most collections.

■ McDonnell, Christine. *Just for the Summer.* Illus. by Diane deGroat. Viking/Kestrel, 1987. 117pp. (0-670-80059-7) Reading Level: Grades 3–5. (BCCB S87)
Disability: Health impairment

Lydia's father is hospitalized during the summer, and Lydia goes to stay with her aunts, Connie and May. Lydia has two friends in the neighborhood, named Emily and Ivy. They undertake various projects, and Lydia works on a miniature diorama. Lydia is concerned for her father and wishes to be the best at something. The summer is highlighted when Lydia wins a prize for her diorama.

Analysis: This simple presentation of episodes in a girl's life does not detail the father's treatment or ailment. As in Fox's *Village by the Sea,* a girl must spend her summer away from home because her father is under medical care. The illustrations are pleasant, and they break up the text for students who are intimidated by chaptered books. Lydia's worries and the activities that help to distract her from them are developed in a competent manner.

■ McDonnell, Margot B. *My Own Worst Enemy.* Putnam, 1984. 192pp. (0-399-21102-0) Reading Level: Grades 7–9. (BCCB N84)
Disability: Heart disease; Emotional disturbance

Todd recalls the year his father had heart bypass surgery and his grandfather came to live at their home. Robbie, a new student, seems to be stealing both Todd's position on the baseball team and Kelly, the girl Todd liked. When Todd begins tutoring Robbie in math, Todd's grandfather and Robbie become friends. Todd's father becomes so depressed after surgery that he has to be admitted to a mental hospital.

After Todd challenges Robbie to a showdown, he realizes that Robbie is not his enemy but wants his friendship. They try to lose their virginity with willing partners after Robbie breaks up with Kelly. Robbie's father moves away suddenly, pursued as usual by gambling debts. Todd becomes so distressed about losing his friend during a visit with his father, that the man comes out of his isolation and begins to recover. Todd receives a note from Robbie that answers some of his questions.

Analysis: The theme of jealousy that is developed in this book is incorporated into the father-son relationship. Todd resents his father's workaholic perfectionism, not recognizing the same traits in himself until his grandfather points them out. Todd shifts from feeling that his father ruined his own health and deserves the consequences to expressing his hope that his father will not leave him like his best friend did. Though Todd's father is presented as such a demanding person that a physical impairment could make him clinically depressed, it is less credible when Todd's heartfelt comments turn things around.

■ McGraw, Eloise Jarvis. *The Seventeenth Swap.* McElderry, 1986. 105pp. (0-689-50398-9) Reading Level: Grades 4–6. (BCCB Ja86) *Disability:* Orthopedic impairment; Neurologic impairment

Eric lives in a poor section of town and works three afternoons a week as a companion for Jimmy, who is 8 and uses a wheelchair. When Jimmy shows Eric a sale announcement for a pair of red-and-black cowboy boots, Eric hatches a complex plan of exchanged goods and services to earn the purchase price. Once the gift is delivered, Eric realizes that he has made an additional swap—he has grown up enough to set a goal and achieve it, ready to put forth his best effort even if he might fail.

Analysis: The plot seems stretched, and some may feel this offers padded introspection rather than suspense. However, the boys interact naturally, and Jimmy's desire for the boots is insightful. Since Eric's father, a librarian who lost his position, has settled for a dull, safe job, Eric's seventeenth swap of attitude shows real independence. Eric's motivation to get the boots relates to Jimmy's legitimate desire to cover his "dumb legs" and at least look good. It is important that readers interpret all these as gestures of sincere friendship and not as pity-driven good deeds.

■ Mahy, Margaret. *Memory.* McElderry, 1988. 278pp. (0-689-50446-2) Reading Level: Grades 8–12. (BCCB Ap88) *Disability:* Alzheimer's disease; Emotional disturbance

Nineteen-year-old Jonny Dart gets drunk and into a brawl on the fifth anniversary of his sister's death. He tries to find Bonny, the girl who was playing with them the evening of the accident, because he is haunted by memories of the night Janine fell off a dangerous ridge during an old game with their "Pythoness." Bonny's parents are political activists in New Zealand, fighting for Maori land rights, but Bonny has gone back to their old neighborhood to study. Jonny wanders the depressed community and encounters a confused old woman. He intends only to see that she gets home safely, but the chaos in her dwelling makes him stay.

Jonny finds many cats, litter, and unhygienic messes at Tap House, Sophie's home, that he sets straight. Since Sophie has no healthy food in the place, he helps her draw money from her bank account to buy groceries. He keeps intending to leave as soon as possible, but ". . . she had really caught his attention. Collapsing little by little in her collapsing house she still battled on with everything she had." Jonny sees lots of evidence of Sophie's declining mental abilities.

> He went on tidying up, fascinated by the surface of a life even more incoherent than his own. A cake of soap sat cosily in the sugar bowl, where it fit very well; a series of tiny newspaper parcels carefully sealed with Scotch tape proved to hold one used tea bag apiece. . . . Once upon a time, probably in the beginning, when her memory was just beginning to let her down, Sophie had fought back by making many lists.

Jonny and his sister had been tap dancing performers featured in television commercials for chicken. In his old neighborhood, Jonny runs into Nev, the boy who plagued him about his dancing and who is still a brutal bully. When Jonny leaves Sophie, he stops at a pub and finds evidence that Nev has been stealing from Sophie and taking "rent" payments from the easily misled woman. Jonny uses his dancing ability to confront Nev and two other toughs. The righteous fight to defend Sophie releases lots of the hostility that had been getting Jonny in trouble since his sister's death. Bonny is at the scene when police stop the fight. Jonny finally asks her about the memory/fear that has been disturbing him for years.

> "You see . . ." he began haltingly, "sometimes I think I pushed her, I sort of remember doing it."
> "You know you didn't," Bonny said in a very matter-of-fact voice. "Really, you must know you didn't."
> "It just seemed I must have pushed her. . . . I knew I must have done something to make it happen . . . well, not *knew,* I just *believed* I had. I could remember not doing it, but I could remember doing it, too."

Sophie's needs are made public during the fight, and appropriate care is scheduled. Bonny stops for a meal with Sophie every day, and after six weeks, Jonny comes to visit. He describes his hospitalization for a broken shoulder and his family sessions with "some sort of shrink." Sophie is on a waiting list for 24-hour care, so Jonny suggests that he come live with her to help out while he is not at work at a nearby construction site. Bonny tries to be aloof, but Jonny plans to win her heart away from her engineer boyfriend.

Analysis: Well-crafted writing reveals the complex problems that Jonny and Sophie are having. Parallel themes of distress caused by flawed memory can be too obvious, but overall this offers poignant portrayals. The superrealistic portraits on the cover show a bruised Matt-Dillon-ish youth looking at a placid old woman, with the bizarre silhouette of Tap House behind them. Unlike *Doc* or *Going Backwards,* the male protagonist here is hopeful that he can help Sophie, because, instead of just watching her decline from active grandparent to incompetent stranger, he finds a stranger and improves her living conditions. This title is highly recommended because Jonny shares his impressions of Sophie's courage and dignity while dealing with humiliating realities like wet beds, naked encounters, and dead birds in the kitchen.

■ Manes, Stephen. *I'll Live.* Avon/Flare, 1982. 160pp. (0-380-81737-3) Reading Level: Grades 8–10. (BCCB F83)
Disability: Cancer

Barbra Feingold has just moved to California from New York City when she meets Dylan Donaldson at the hospital. Dylan is visiting with his father, Al, who is determined to take an overdose of sleeping pills at the appropriate time instead of having his wife and son face hard decisions during his terminal care. Dylan falls in love with Barbra and continues his hang-gliding activities despite his preoccupation with his father's illness.

After Al dies, Barbra tells Dylan she is in love with someone else. Dylan attempts suicide during a flight but survives. He decides that he still wants to live and gains insight about his father's choice.

Analysis: Terminal illness is stressful for families, and euthanasia and suicide are complexities of the situation that many consider. This book, however, uses the serious theme to engage the readers' interest but does not then develop the characters well enough to resolve all that the issues have stirred up. Graber's *Doc* and Klein's *Going Backwards* are stronger choices, but they deal with Alzheimer's disease and lack the sports and romance.

■ Marino, Jan. *Eighty-Eight Steps to September.* Little, Brown, 1989. 154pp. (0-316-54620-8) Reading Level: Grades 5–8. (KR 1 Ap89)
Disability: Leukemia

Fifth-grader Amory Martin, her 13-year-old brother, Robbie, 15-year-old sister, Susan, and their parents move to a new home that is too small for their dog. When Baron goes to live with relatives, Robbie is distressed, but Amy softens their loss with a new puppy she names Sam. Robbie and Amy work on a doghouse for Sam, but they argue over its color and whom the dog should sleep with indoors.

At the beginning of summer, Robbie's camp physical leads to tests and eventual hospitalization in Boston. Amy feels abandoned to her least favorite baby-sitter when Mother arranges to be with Robbie daily. Amy assures herself and her friend, Celie, that when Robbie comes home, everything will be fine again. She is sure Robbie will be able to beat her up the eighty-eight steps that are called the "88s" once he is well. Only when Robbie asks Amy to bring Sam for a visit does she admit to herself that Robbie will not be coming home. His death and funeral occur before school starts in September. The evening of Susan's birthday party, Amy finally cries and talks to her father about missing Robbie. She goes down the 88s and feels Robbie's presence at the bottom. She tells her father to fix the doghouse she had destroyed and prepares to paint it yellow, Rob's preference, but with a blue roof, the way he had originally wanted.

Analysis: In 1948, families had fewer medical options in the treatment of cancer, so the rapid progression of Robbie's leukemia is authentic. Robbie looks thin and pale to Amy when she visits, but he is animated by the dog. Sibling adoration and annoyance are both nicely portrayed, as in the he/she argument about Sam's gender that becomes a standard taunt between Robbie and Amy. Robbie's terminal illness is not described, but its impact is evident in the emotional stresses, school episodes, baby-sitter conflicts, and best-friend interactions that fill out the other subplots of this novel.

Amy's uncle has to wear a brace for a spinal injury, which makes his wife too busy to "save" Amy from her mean baby-sitter early in the summer. The wrenching scene of father trying to comfort his daughters, Mother screaming out her son's name, and little sister breaking up the doghouse will remain with readers. This honest historical fiction will supplement collections and could be used in bibliotherapy.

■ Martin, Ann M. *With You and Without You.* Holiday, 1986. 179pp. (0-8234-0601-6) Reading Level: Grades 5–7. (BCCB My86)
Disability: Heart disease

The O'Hara family is told that Father's ill health is due to heart disease. Six months to a year is all the time that they can expect to have together, and when Father returns from the hospital, he tells Liza he feels lucky that they will have time to say anything they need to in preparation for the death. Liza is 12, and she narrates the story of this year and how it affects her parents, older brother, Brent, and younger sisters, Carrie and Hope.

Liza has acute stage fright but invites her father to see the Christmas pageant she participates in. Her friend Denise lost her own father several years before, so Liza has an understanding confidant. Nonetheless, when Father dies in late spring, Liza feels that the rest of the family is betraying him by making changes, having social outlets, and being happy. She refuses to visit the grave and passes through the stages of grief at a gradual pace. A date with Marc and the seasonal Christmas celebrations help to lift her sadness. An epilogue summarizes the progress each family member makes toward future plans and education. After graduation, Liza visits her father's grave for the first time.

Analysis: Mr. O'Hara has a degenerating heart ailment that will not respond to medical intervention. He is a gentle, understanding father, wise in his approach to death and truthful about his sadness. Since he had expressed his regrets about not being able to see his children grow up, it makes a nice closure to the story when Liza goes to the cemetery to tell him all the news. This portrayal may not be as informative about heart conditions as others, but it is important to the theme of acceptance of loss due to terminal illness. This theme is well developed without overwhelming the other plot elements of family and friendship interactions. A strong choice for middle school readers.

■ Martin, Katherine. *Night Riding.* Knopf, 1989. 197pp. (LB 0-679-90064-0)
Reading Level: Grades 5–8. (BCCB D89)
Disability: Tuberculosis

Prin is 11 when her father is admitted to the West Tennessee Tuberculosis Hospital. Mama tries to keep their trucking business going, but the customers are unaccustomed to dealing with a woman. Financial worries mount because Mom is pregnant and she will not be allowed to return to her teaching job. The pregnancy has complications, so Mama must rest, and Aunt Map comes to help out.

Prin misses her father and takes care of his horses, sometimes riding out at night, against house rules. She meets a teenage neighbor, named Mary Faith, spies on the girl and her brother, and tries to avoid their intimidating father, B. Z. Hammond. Rumors, condescending revelations from Prin's older sister, Jo Lynn, and Mom's guarded comments help Prin determine that motherless Mary Faith is "expecting." Prin sees B.Z. kick

Mary Faith and throw her down the porch steps. Mary Faith tells Prin her baby died, and she invites Prin into her bedroom to see some drawings. B.Z. storms into the bedroom with his pants undone, and Prin senses the sexual threat he poses to herself and Mary Faith.

Though Prin is not yet 12 and too young to visit her father, she hides in the car one time her mother goes to the hospital. Daddy comes down to the lobby, and father and daughter sneak a hug in the elevator. Prin goes night riding, and B.Z. threatens her again. Daddy's horse tramples B.Z. to death. Mary Faith helps Prin get back to the house, and her family conspires to keep B.Z.'s attempted assault a secret. A social worker places Mary Faith in a home out of town, and the sheriff takes the horse away to be destroyed as a killer.

Analysis: "Tuberculosis is something in the lungs that makes it hard to breathe, makes you weak. Your grandmama had it, too, back when they didn't know how to do for it." Her eyes went to the window again.

"She died from it," Jo Lynn said.

"That was a long time ago, before you were born," Mama said. "This is 1958, and there's all kinds of things they can do now, medicines and rest."

This outstanding novel is vividly set in the rural South, during a time when medical practices and social interactions were both limited. Prin's summer is full of change that she is not prepared for because little girls in the conservative 50s are told only certain, nice things. She becomes adept at spying and eavesdropping and trying to breach her mother's preoccupation with family difficulties. Prin's aunt, mother, and sister choose to ignore Mr. Hammond, like other unpleasant social realities, instead of intervening.

The story's plot and characterizations are impressive, and Daddy's place in the family is clearly defined, though he is absent. His return from the hospital and the birth of the baby are being planned for at the end of the story. After six more months' bed rest, perhaps he will be able to ride the horse Prin makes arrangements to get for him. The sexual menace and the reality of incest presented here may still be taboo in some conservative areas, but most collections will want this excellent work of fiction.

■ Mazer, Norma Fox. *After the Rain.* Morrow, 1987. 290pp. (0-688-06867-7) Reading Level: Grades 6–9. (BCCB My87)
Disability: Cancer

Rachel is in high school, but she has adult brothers because her parents had her late in life. She often writes to her brother Jeremy, who drifts from job to job and lover to lover, even though he rarely responds with even a postcard. Her settled brother has a daughter nearly her own age. Rachel's grandfather, Izzy, is diagnosed with terminal cancer, and she feels drawn to spend more time with him. The opinionated old man is hard to love, but the more time Rachel spends walking with him in the afternoons, the more she enjoys his company. When his condition worsens, she wants to be with him at the hospital. Her parents try to get her to go to school, but she wants only to get her assignments in order to just keep up with classwork.

She has a premonition and is with Izzy the evening he dies. Her mourning is aided when Lewis, her boyfriend, helps her search for Izzy's handprint and initials on a bridge he made in his youth.

Analysis: Grandpa's physical distress never undermines his dignity as a character. His biases are clearly the product of a different age, so his harsh judgment of Jeremy and Uncle Leonard can be understood. Jeremy speaks of his own life being disrupted by the Vietnam War.

Rachel is able to develop a relationship with her grandfather after she knows that he is dying. The memories she reviews, her jealousy of her niece's easy tears, and her quest with Lewis are all credible and moving introspection. The variety of writing is impressive, since Rachel's journal, letters, and even body-language interactions with Lewis help reveal the action. A Newbery Honor book, this title should be in all collections.

■ Mazer, Norma Fox, and Harry Mazer. *Heartbeat.* Bantam, 1989. 165pp. (0-553-05808-8) Reading Level: Grades 7–10. (BCCB MS89) *Disability:* Viral infection

Tod begins his senior year in high school planning to go to college and take prelaw courses. His widowed father is not impressed by that or anything Tod has to do or say. Tod's best friend, Amos, is the class clown at his own school but asks handsome Tod to speak for him to a girl named Hilary. Tod knows that girls like him, and he fantasizes about certain classmates, but he is scared of female rejection when it comes to dating. His defensive sneer and insecure silences make Tod seem stuck-up. He dreads speaking to Hilary for Amos but does it because Amos once rescued Tod from drowning.

Hilary repairs cars and is slowly won over by Tod's attempts to get to know her, but Tod has to find a way to let Amos learn that Tod and Hilary have become a couple. The three attend a fair together, and Amos winds up with Hilary. Hilary compares her feelings for Tod and for Amos. Tod confides in a younger schoolmate named Jen and surprises himself by kissing her. Both his mood swings and his self-absorption come into focus when he realizes, "he had been acting just like his father. . . . First the screwing up, then the depression and self-pity, then mania and turning to other women for comfort."

When Hilary and Tod are restablished as a couple, Tod tries to get Jen and Amos together. Hilary accepts a concert date with Amos rather than have to be the one to tell him about her relationship with Tod. After she has enjoyed the evening and Amos's company, she wonders ". . . why can't I love him and Amos, too?" Amos gives a locket to Hilary, though she tries to refuse it. When Tod sees Amos, he senses that Amos knows Hilary has chosen to be Tod's girl.

Amos is hospitalized with a rare virus and, during the weeks it takes to identify the terminal infection, Hilary and Tod visit their friend. Rather than keep up the sham of treating each other as casual acquaintances while they are with Amos, the two really do break up for the duration of Amos's illness. When Amos is moved to intensive care, Hilary and Tod share some of their grief. On their next visit to Amos, the ill boy takes each of his friends' hands and then brings their hands together. Amos dies of heart failure.

After the funeral, grief and guilt get in the way of Hilary's and Tod's old relationship. Tod writes to his grandmother in England and is invited for a visit. He is hopeful that Hilary and he will get back together "Someday . . ."

Analysis: Like *Sheila's Dying* and *One Green Leaf,* this novel convincingly explores the strains on relationships when a young friend's health is undermined. The hospital scenes here are less credible than in *Invincible Summer.* Hospital policy on visitors and casual access to the intensive care area are suspiciously lax in this book. But this weakness is balanced by well-drawn characters and good pace. When the point of view shifts to Hilary or when Tod is imagining what he should say, passages are in italics. This device allows readers to see how complexities and misinterpretations affect communications between Tod and all his loved ones.

Amos's attitude toward medical tests and the equipment in his room is masked by his characteristic humor. All three friends suppress their real feelings in an effort to help each other to cope with the stress: Hilary pushes aside her unhappiness to comfort Amos; Tod gives up his claim to Hilary's time and love; and Amos keeps inside himself whatever anger, adjustment, or acceptance he feels about his condition.

Because high disclosure is not part of Amos's character, the final scene that shows his subtle acknowledgment that Tod and Hilary have been brought together and separated by their loyalty to him seems genuine instead of melodramatic. Highly recommended, this romance does not gloss over the complexities of family relationships and friendships.

■ Miklowitz, Gloria D. *Anything to Win.* Delacorte, 1989. 160pp. (0-385-29750-5) Reading Level: Grades 7–12. (BCCB O89)
Disability: Health impairment

Senior Cam Potter is captain of the football team but needs to be heavier to be considered for a scholarship from the state college. Thirty pounds seems an impossible goal, until anabolic steroids are introduced into his training program. Cam experiences ethical and emotional dilemmas and meets an athlete whose health has become impaired by steroid use. Weighing the promise against the reality, Cam chooses to stop the drug use.

Analysis: A list of risks related to steroid abuse is provided in an introduction. Not only does the list give an informational tone to the book, but also it becomes a checklist of changes that Cam experiences and observes in others. This lessens its effectiveness as fiction, but the story is accessible reading with a clear message.

■ Miner, Jane Claypool. *This Day Is Mine: Living with Leukemia.* Illus. by Vista III Design. Crestwood, 1982. 63pp. (LB 0-89686-173-2) Reading Level: Grades 4—12.
Disability: Leukemia

Cheryl is in the hospital for three weeks before she can pressure a doctor into telling her that the tests show she has leukemia. At 16, she views this as the end of her life and is angry at her parents for avoiding the truth. She runs away to her Aunt Martha's rather than go back to school and be treated differently. She cuts her knee, and the bleeding will not stop, so she is hospitalized for four more days. Cheryl makes peace with her parents and visits with the patient in the room next door. Cindy Lou has a different type of leukemia, is in the terminal stages of her illness, and will be under treatment, away from her family, until she dies. Yet the girl copes: "I never talk about tomorrow. But this day has been good. This day is mine."

Analysis: Cheryl's feelings about her uncertain future and her desire for a relatively "normal" life are clearly developed. The pat solution of inspiration from a younger and wiser patient will please reluctant readers, for whom this text has been designed. As part of the Crisis series, this title may be used for curriculum support. However, the marginal illustrations and incomplete presentation of realistic treatment and prognosis undermine its value for most collections.

■ Montgomery, Robert. *Rabbit Ears: A Sports Novel.* New American Library, 1985. 159pp. (paper 0-451-13631-4) Reading Level: Grades 7–10. (BL Ag84)
Disability: Cancer

Jason enjoys baseball and works with a talented new student at their Catholic high school. The boy has skill in pitching but loses control when hecklers unnerve him. Jason refers to this as a case of "rabbit ears" and helps the pitcher improve. Jason has a girlfriend named Marcia. He also likes a girl named Izzy, who often comes to visit his father. Jason's father is under treatment for cancer due to agent orange exposure. During both practice time and the first games of the season, Jason's team heckles its new teammate even louder than the opposition, and Jason's team wins. Jason's father is in great pain after attending the second game because he skipped taking his medication. The veteran loses use of his legs, is hospitalized, then returns home for the terminal stages of his illness.

Jason and Izzy pair off more, Marcia starts seeing a fellow named Thomas, and Izzy's old boyfriend starts dating around. When Jason's father's cancer is in remission, Jason worries that his father will linger with only rare moments of lucidity. Also, the possibility of genetic damage bothers the boy. Jason almost blows the championship and a chance to impress a sports scout, but he hits a three-run homer in the eighth inning.

Analysis: Sports stories rarely focus on significant personal growth in the main characters. Besides the play-by-play and team strategies that are incorporated here, Jason's family members and his ambivalent love life are developed. The father's progression from power hitter to bed-ridden patient is moving, even though one wonders how he recovers enough to go to Houston for the final game. For collections in which original paperback titles are popular, this story offers something more than the rest.

■ Myers, Walter Dean. *Scorpions.* Harper & Row, 1988. 216pp. (LB 0-06-024365-1) Reading Level: Grades 6–9. (BCCB MS88)
Disability: Asthma

Jamal's older brother, Randy, has been jailed, and his mother is trying to scrape together $500 for a new lawyer. Jamal and his sister, Sassy, are the only ones at home, unless their father comes by for one of his infrequent visits. At school, the Scorpions gang members hassle Jamal, and he is pressured into flaunting a gun to claim leadership of the group so that proceeds of their crack running can go toward Randy's defense. During a desperate showdown, Tito uses the gun. He is charged as a juvenile delinquent and allowed to go to Puerto Rico to stay with his father.

Analysis: Myers presents a stunning view of one friendship in Harlem that is subjected to social pressures and underworld dangers that are hard to associate with children just 12 years old. At one point, Jamal is traveling across town when Tito has so much trouble breathing that his black friend tries to get some police officers to let them ride public transit without the fare money. Tito's asthma does not flare up at every possible emotional point in the story, but it is nicely integrated as one aspect of the boys' vulnerability and concern for each other.

■ Naylor, Phyllis Reynolds. *The Dark of the Tunnel.* Atheneum, 1985. 216pp. (0-689-31098-6) Reading Level: Grades 7–10. (BCCB MS85) *Disability:* Cancer; Emotional disturbance

Craig Sheldon lost his father three years before and has been living with his uncle, his mother, and his younger brother, Lonnie. During his senior year, his mother is diagnosed with pancreatic cancer and begins chemotherapy. Craig meets John Motto, an artist known as "Cougar," who lives on a mountain. Cougar confides that he suffered a nervous breakdown after the war, the death of his brother, and a loss of property to county development. When civil defense drills threaten Cougar's mountain retreat and fallout shelter plans make use of Craig's tunnel hideout, public opinion is split on the value of such efforts.

Mrs. Sheldon's treatment is not effective, and she dies after a few days of semiconsciousness. Craig is angered that medical research is not funded as well as military planning and development are, and he convinces his uncle to write to the governor to reject the current defense plans. Some missing dynamite blows up at Cougar's home, killing the artist and causing panic in the community below. The townspeople recognize that the chaos created by this relatively small explosion is nothing compared with the emergency situations a nuclear war would result in. Did Cougar commit suicide, or did he lose his life trying to teach the people this lesson?

Analysis: So many tragedies in one life, in addition to the threat of global distruction, can make for bleak reading. Well-written scenes and dialogue convey the issues effectively, and readers will understand why Craig is convinced that it is better to face reality than to spend energy pretending. When the terminal nature of Mrs. Sheldon's illness is recognized, the men in her family face their regrets. The explosion that gives citizens a dry run to demonstrate their emergency preparedness needs makes them face the futility of planning for nuclear attack rather than for peace. The eventuality of Cougar's death is foreshadowed by his disclosures about an earlier emotional disturbance. He is remembered by his sister and Craig in the final scene, and this offers balance to the pat portrayal of a talented, but disturbed individual.

■ Nelson, Vaunda Micheaux, and Kimanne Uhler. **Always Gramma.** Putnam, 1988. 32pp. (0-399-21542-5) Reading Level: Grades K–3. (BCCB Ja89)
Disability: Alzheimer's disease

A little girl is distressed by the changes she sees in her grandmother. Once Gramma taught her granddaughter a fun springtime song about a red robin "bob bob bobbin' along" and could fix a wonderful cake. But after a while, the woman becomes unable to remember important phone messages or be trusted with a lighted cigarette. When Gramma gets frustrated, she yells, and the little girl is frightened to see her grandfather put locks on the door so Gramma cannot wander away from home alone. Gramma does not get well, her problems are too much for Grampa to take care of every day, and she is placed in a nursing home.

At the nursing home, family members visit regularly, though Gramma does not recognize them. The little girl knows she loves her Gramma and will always remember the things they did together. It is now nearly spring, so the girl waits for that red robin.

Analysis: Pleasant watercolor compositions may seem scrubby or overworked in places but are well integrated within this excellent story. Though the child is never told the name of Gramma's illness, the progression of forgetfulness, disorientation, irrational behavior, and violence associated with Alzheimer's disease is clear and moving. The author keeps a child's viewpoint, shifting from the past tense to describe memories of how Gramma used to be and what happened to mark her stages of illness to the present tense and a hopeful comment at the end about springtime. Because picture books must be brief, this method of compressing events subtly allows readers to see the characters reacting and sharing their feelings about a very difficult type of loss. Recommended for most collections, this sweet recollection of a special personality will touch grandchildren of all ages.

■ Nichols, Joan Kane. **All But the Right Folks.** Stemmer, 1985. 100pp. (0-88045-065-7) Reading Level: Grades 5–8. (SLJ N85)
Disability: Asthma; Enuresis

Marv Johnson stays with his maternal grandmother while his father is on a photography assignment over the summer. Marv is stunned to find out that his mother, who died of a drug overdose, was white. His grandmother, Helga, and Uncle Billy host Marv's visit to New York City, and Marv decides he likes the way Helga deals with his special problems of asthma and bedwetting. With neighborhood children, Marv pretends that Helga is merely his caregiver instead of a relative.

Uncle Billy has a drug habit, and Marv is injured in a robbery at Helga's place of employment. Marv's father visits, and the boy is confused by his father's bitter comments about whites—isn't Marv himself white? While visiting one of Helga's friends in Connecticut, Marv recognizes Billy as the driver from the robbery and is kidnapped. He fights his fear in order to avoid an asthma attack, and he escapes. His father is proud of his son, who gets media attention. Helga clarifies that Marv's mother was active in the civil rights movement and died from a first-time drug experience at a party. Marv plans to visit again the following summer and finds out that a dual heritage also confuses German Helga sometimes because Helga's own mother, a Jew, died at Auschwitz.

Analysis: Self-confidence is the theme of this story, and once that is established, Marv does better with his enuresis and asthma. The plot perpetuates the stereotypic Vietnam veteran as a maladjusted drug user, as have other portrayals available. Because the mixed-heritage situation is not unique but its representation in children's literature is, this title may be acquired to reflect ethnic diversity in a collection.

■ Nixon, Joan Lowery. *The Specter.* Delacorte, 1982. 184pp. (0-440-08063-0) Reading Level: Grades 7–10. (BCCB S82)
Disability: Hodgkin's disease; Emotional disturbance

Dina is under treatment in the hospital for Hodgkin's disease when she meets a 9-year-old patient named Julie. The little girl has survived a car accident that killed her parents. At 17, Dina feels drawn to the orphaned girl, who does not seem able to mourn her parents but insists that the man who killed her father is after her also. Dina was orphaned long ago, and since her cancer is in remission, she is to be released from the hospital. A retiring nurse's aide, named Mrs. Cardenas, agrees to take both girls for foster care in her home.

Dina tries to evoke Julie's memories, but the little girl's behavior and comments are more and more suspicious. Julie is jealous when Dina spends time with anyone else, especially a new acquaintance, Dave. While Dina is looking for more clues in Julie's room, the girl allows the house to fill with gas from an unlit oven. Fearing that Julie intentionally tried to kill both herself and Dina, the older girl looks for an opportunity to get the child to speak with Dina's psychologist. Julie shows to Dina items from her treasure box that make it clear that the man who died in the accident was not Julie's father. Dina tries to get the girl to the hospital, where a psychologist and the detective who is investigating the car crash can help the disturbed child. On the way, Julie grabs Dina around the neck, reenacting the way she caused the crash that killed her own mother and the man she thought of as Bill Sikes.

Dina is able to keep from crashing, and travelers offer them assistance. Dina realizes that for the first time since her diagnosis, she was fighting to live, once Julie threatened their safety.

Analysis: In this thriller, Dina compassionately aligns herself with Julie against the probing of a detective and the prodding of psychological counseling. Dina does not intend to look toward a future that cannot promise her long life, familial relationships, or a cure for her health impairment. The trauma of working through Julie's fears and facing accidental death helps Dina value the life she still has.

Nixon keeps the mystery of Julie's background and motivations unraveling while Dina's dread of Sikes's threatening presence shifts to fear of the disturbed little girl's capacity for violence. Physical abuse and deep emotional scars lead Julie to cause an accident that she intended should kill her mother, her mother's lover, and herself.

Fans of the old movie *The Bad Seed* will love this story, but the ending is not judgment from a bolt of lightning. Early on, Julie tells her doctor, "I get the impression that her head is so filled with terrible thoughts that the fear has pushed her into a corner of her own mind, and she's afraid to come out." This plot allows Julie's deeper needs to be addressed once her father is located and she has appropriate medical care available. Dina's readjustment signals that she has worked through her anger and is ready to both see an old friend and pursue a relationship with Dave. Her doctor is visibly moved by this breakthrough.

Because these portrayals have more depth than some other writers' attempts at standard "problem" novels that present the same disabilities, this is recommended for most collections. The cover, depicting a screaming child behind a dark, torn screen, is a compelling image.

■ Okimoto, Jean Davies. ***Jason's Women***. Atlantic Monthly, 1986. 210pp. (0-87113-061-0) Reading Level: Grades 7–10. (BCCB N86) *Disability:* Cancer

Jason Kovak is 16 years old when he states his philosophy of life for the position of "consultant." His imagination runs wild until the job turns out to be that of a handyman for Bertha Jane Fillmore, an elderly woman who has sponsored a Vietnamese girl named Thao Nguyen. Jason's parents are divorced and unaware of his loneliness or his fantasy life. Jason responds to an ad for a date, deals with the robbery of a fast-food restaurant, supports Bertha's opinions and civic interest, and learns about Thao's hard life.

When Jason meets his dream date, he is disappointed. Bertha has been visiting a clinic, but Jason did not realize how seriously ill she was until he notices that she is wearing a wig. Thao explains that the cancer no longer can be treated, and that Bertha has come home to die. Jason has made a campaign sign, which he now posts for voters after Bertha dies. "Vote for Bertha Jane Fillmore—Save the Snow Leopard—Plant Christmas Trees— No Bombs."

Analysis: Jason's emotional turmoil is lightened with humor. The parents are stereotypic self-centered figures, but Bertha and Thao are well-developed characters. When Jason meets the "dark-eyed beauty" of the ad, he determines she is neither "classy" nor "sharp" and bows out of the situation without revealing who he is.

It may be as hard for readers to believe that Jason never realized Bertha was ill as it was for him. "How could I have not known! A friend—my friend is sick," he confides. But his relationship with her is much more credible, and the last scenes reveal how her illness affects him. "Bertha Jane had a lot of tubes in her—she looked so little and frail and she had on the wig. I felt like smashing everything in sight. I couldn't stand seeing her that way." The story line gets cluttered, but the overall impression is that Jason learned a lot from the women in his life.

■ Paulsen, Gary. *Tracker.* Bradbury, 1984. 96pp. (0-02-770220-0)
Reading Level: Grades 5–8. (BCCB My84)
Disability: Cancer

John Borne has grown up on his grandparents' small farm, where he enjoys chores and deer hunting. When John is 13, his grandfather is diagnosed with a terminal illness. Memories of death and bargains against death crowd John's thoughts. Sent out for the first day of deer season, he is alone, haunted by the feeling that things are not right without his grandfather there. When John tracks a doe but cannot "give her death" at the first chance, he determines to get close enough to touch her. After tracking so long that both the boy and the doe are exhausted, John reaches out to "own-love-touch" the doe. His mystical experience becomes a metaphor for becoming resigned to his grandfather's approaching death. After tracking for two days and a night, John returns home, saying, "A thing changed in hunting, in everything . . ." John's grandfather reacts with a new touch of pride in John's accomplishment.

"He walked one down. Ain't that something?" . . . "I'll take that with me," his grandfather went on. "That's something I'll just take with me."

Analysis: This is a slim novel, dense with poetic elements and difficult philosophical musings. Sophisticated readers will find that it presents a view of death as a part of living. Medical efforts to "stop the cancer" are summarized early in the book.

> The doctors had done tests and more tests and worked with chemicals and knives and finally had sent John Borne's grandfather home to die in peace on the small farm at the edge of the woods.

The real theme of this book is John's quest for peace regarding this death.

■ Paulsen, Gary. *The Voyage of the Frog.* Orchard, 1989. 143 pp. (LB 0-531-08405-1) Reading Level: Grades 7–10.
Disability: Cancer

David's uncle Owen gives him a sailboat named the *Frog* and instructions to scatter his ashes at sea. A storm sends David hundreds of miles south of Ventura, California, to Baja California. David faces danger and isolation, finds Uncle Owen's written ship's log, and encounters a pod of dancing whales. When a research vessel cannot tow the *Frog* home, David sends his parents a message that he is safe, and he starts the long, difficult sail north.

Analysis: As in *Tracker,* a young man works through his grief and regard for life in a sporting adventure/quest. Again, Paulsen summarizes the medical efforts to deal with cancer, but Uncle Owen's backache is diagnosed as terminal cancer, and tumors are found in his brain within one week.

"David hated hospitals, and it was worse when he saw Owen lying in bed. He looked weak, caved in, dead already, dead and done, and when David saw him he was overwhelmed with the change."

David regurgitates at the smell and scene, but Owen is understanding. During the voyage, David recalls other times with Owen and gains insight about his uncle's life and death from reading the log entries. The survival story is full of suspense and may prove a popular addition to collections.

■ Peck, Richard. *Remembering the Good Times.* Delacorte, 1985. 181pp. (0-385-29396-8) Reading Level: Grades 7–10.
Disability: Emotional disturbance; Geriatric disabilities; Hyperactivity

Polly is lovingly referred to as "the third oldest woman in Slocum Township, but when it comes to meanness, she's Number One." *See full annotation* Chapter 6: Emotional Disturbances.

■ Plummer, Louise. *The Romantic Obsessions and Humiliations of Annie Sehlmeier.* Delacorte, 1987. 181pp. (0-385-29574-X) Reading Level: Grades 6–9. (BCCB D87)
Disability: Dementia

The Sehlmeier family migrates from Utrecht, Holland, to Salt Lake City, Utah. Annie is 17 and makes adjustments to life in America. She and her younger sister both get a crush on the same boy. Also, their grandmother's failing memory causes problems for the family. In the end, Annie and her sister realize that the boy they were fighting over is not as special as his charming ways led them to believe.

Analysis: With a different slant on sibling rivalry and boy-girl relations, this contemporary story may please middle-graders. It contains unconvincing elements, like the father's impression that Dutch will be part of the American curriculum, just as English is in Holland. Annie's fluency in English is peppered with misquotes, which heightens the humor and reminds readers that she is still out of step with some of American culture, including many of its idioms. Grandmother is a doubly displaced person, for her disorientation and memory loss severely hamper adjustment to a new home. The family problems are not allowed to overwhelm the action, yet they add depth to this little romance.

■ Porte, Barbara Ann. *Harry's Dog.* Illus. by Yossi Abolafia. Greenwillow, 1983. 48pp. (0-688-02556-0) Reading Level: Grades 1–3. (BCCB MS84)
Disability: Allergies

Harry longs for a pet but his father is allergic to fur. When a dog named Girl is hidden in Harry's room, his father develops the usual symptoms of sneezing, watery eyes, and runny nose. Girl is discovered, prompting Harry to fabricate many stories about how he got her and why he cannot possibly take her back. Father reaches for another tissue once the real story is told, but his sister, Aunt Rose, arrives just then with a solution in mind. Since she always wanted a dog but could not have one because of her allergic brother, she would like to have Girl stay at her house. Harry will care for the dog, two blocks away. Harry also decides that since his father always wanted a dog too, a goldfish from the pet shop would be an acceptable substitute now.

Analysis: This humorous story in an easy-to-read format presents a sympathetic view of coping with the limitations imposed by health impairments. Aunt Rose could not have a dog because of Father's allergies, and now the same ailment is keeping Harry from having one. Wise compromise gives Aunt Rose a dog when she is an adult, and it rewards Harry with a dog he can "room" away from his father's allergic reactions. Cartoon-style line drawings make the book great fun for young readers.

■ Rabinowitz, Ann. **Knight on Horseback.** Macmillan, 1987. 197pp. (0-02-775660-2) Reading Level: Grades 6–8. (BCCB D87)
Disability: Asthma

On a family tour of English cultural and historic places, 13-year-old Eddy Newby is sick from frequent bouts of asthma. He meets an antique dealer while straying through London. Later, a cloaked man follows Eddy from site to site. A performance of Shakespeare's *Richard the Third* and a look at a book of English royalty identify the phantom. The ghost of Richard III mistakes the American boy for his son Edward. Eddy is guided through the combat of a 500-year-old battle and returns a toy knight to its proper place in a time-shifted castle. He has to be rescued from its high point of crumbling stone once he rejects Richard's hold on him for his own family's needs.

Analysis: This ghost story has momentum and good scenes involving time travel. The ghost of Richard III is revealed in a role that is quite different from that of Shakespeare's villain. Eddy has nightmares and asthma attacks that his sister, Kate, helps him through. He will not tell his protective parents, because "Sometimes the worry seemed to him to have a weight and mass all its own. Dragging him under." After his two-week adventure, his mother comments on how big and healthy he looks. His father has been diagnosed as having angina and tells Eddy, "Nothing to worry about so long as I take it easier. Keep pills by me. But I'll need your help." Eddy comes to a new understanding with his father so they can keep the man's health problem a secret from Kate and Mother, knowing "how they worry."

■ Radley, Gail. **CF in His Corner.** Four Winds, 1984. 128pp. (0-02-777390-6) Reading Level: Grades 7–8. (BCCB My84)
Disability: Cystic fibrosis

Jeff is 14 and his brother Scotty is 7 when Mom has Jeff baby-sit all summer while she works. Supposedly, Scotty suffers from asthma, but both boys suspect that it is really some other ailment. Scotty's symptoms are outlined in a pamphlet on cystic fibrosis (CF) that Jeff finds in his mother's room. Jeff decides Scotty has a right to know the truth about his condition and that CF has no cure. Mom always tries to make things seem pleasant, even when they are not, so Jeff knows he is risking her anger. When Scott runs away and becomes ill, Jeff has to admit that he has told the little boy about CF. Mom is angry and unforgiving about Jeff's betrayal of her trust until Scotty's doctor and she agree that a child suffering from a fatal disease should be provided with the truth.

Analysis: Scotty has stomachaches and has to have his back pounded morning and night to clear his lungs. Because asthma is not described this way in the encyclopedia, Jeff and Scotty conclude that he must be sick with some other ailment. The plot shifts focus from the mystery of Scotty's illness to the dilemma of telling the full truth, regardless of consequences. Since CF is featured in the title, this theme about Jeff's decision to reveal the truth actually supplants the story that readers may think they are getting. Little information on the disease is provided, though Scotty is comforted to know that there are not only lots of kids like him but also clubs for children with CF.

■ Reading, J. P. *The Summer of Sassy Jo.* Houghton, 1989. 182pp. (0-395-48950-4) Reading Level: Grades 6–9. (BCCB Je89)
Disability: Allergies; Emotional disturbance

Sara Jo spends the summer before her freshman year of high school with her mother, stepfather, and preschool-age half-sister. Sara Jo cannot bring herself to call Joleen "Mother," because the woman, an alcoholic, had abandoned "Sassy Jo" when the girl was only 5. Four years later, Joleen tried to make contact with Sara Jo and remarried. When Sara Jo's father died, Aunt Mimi became Sara Jo's legal guardian. Sara feels alienated from her strict aunt and Joleen's new family.

Swimming next door with a younger girl named Katie, shopping for clothing that Aunt Mimi would not have approved of, and falling in love with L. T. are the highlights of Sara Jo's summer. Katie is very sheltered, has allergies, and is bound by many house rules. When Sara Jo's irresponsible actions and superdefensive style rupture the friendship, she regrets her cruelty. Once the girls are reunited, they have even more in common, because Katie has a boyfriend she met at Vacation Bible School.

Joleen tries to overcome Sara Jo's hostility too soon, but by the end of the summer, Sara Jo realizes that she wants to stay with her mother, her funny half-sister, and her kind stepfather. Sara Jo knows that her father was a demanding and judgmental husband and father, but she cannot dismiss her resentment toward Joleen because "I don't know why you left me." The woman replies, "I was a drunk. I couldn't even take care of myself, and I did a lot of irresponsible things, but leaving you was the very worst thing I've ever done."

Sara Jo's mother attends meetings of Alcoholics Anonymous and has just had surgery that rules out plans for a larger family. Sara Jo decides to live in her mother's home and attend a local high school, where she intends to be true to L. T.

Analysis: Many unsatisfactory relationships constitute Sara Jo's life at the beginning of the summer. Her self-centered reactions and bitter retorts earn Sara Jo even more disappointments when she accidentally injures her half-sister, is "quarantined" from Katie, and foils many possible reconciliations with Joleen. Aunt Mimi's reaction to seeing Sara Jo and L. T. kissing in the kitchen helps define the strait-laced fuss-budget from Boston who cannot cope with the adolescent struggle for independence. The author nicely reveals Sara Jo's distrustful character and the personalities that have bruised Sara Jo's emotional development.

Joleen's relationship with her new husband and younger daughter are in high contrast with Sara Jo's memories. When Joleen calls her older daughter by a pet name from the past, Sara Jo recoils.

Katie struggles with her own parents' overprotective rules, and Sara Jo's humor and friendship helps the younger girl. Allergies figure in some of the restrictions that Katie lives with, but her parents realize that too many rules are potentially to blame for the weepy, "neurotic" behavior Katie develops over the summer. There is a sweet ending for everyone that does not undermine the believability of Sara Jo's maturation and her hard-won battle with hatred for past wrongs.

■ Roberts, Willo Davis. *Sugar Isn't Everything: A Support Book, in Fiction Form, for the Young Diabetic.* Atheneum, 1987. 190pp. (0-689-31316-0) Reading Level: Grades 5–7. (BCCB Ap87)
Disability: Diabetes

Amy hides the snacks she keeps eating yet does not gain any weight. As thirsty as she always is for juice, it is not surprising she spends so much time going to the bathroom. When she collapses and is hospitalized, it is suspected that she has diabetes. She wonders, "How come Jan and Matt and her mother and dad were all right, and only she had diabetes?" Then, Ginny, who has had diabetes for two years, comes to share Amy's room. Ginny got lost in the woods and did not get her insulin, but she tells Amy that the usual routine is something "You get used to."

Amy wonders, "What would happen if she didn't do the things they told her, if she refused to give shots and stick her finger to make it bleed for a test, and if she ate candy bars. What would happen then?"

By the end of summer, "She was, she supposed, getting somewhat used to the insulin shots before breakfast in the morning and before supper in the evening. Jan refused to stay in the room with her when she gave the shots. Amy didn't really want anyone to watch, to see how she had to psych herself up to do it; yet a part of her resented the aversion Jan obviously felt. If SHE had to do it twice a day, the least Jan could do was learn to accept it as something routine, not disgusting." Matt, her older brother, is much more supportive, learns to give shots, and goads Amy into exercising enough that her blood sugar will drop so she can have occasional ice cream and sweets.

At a ball game, Amy overhears her friends have "a chocolate fit, and we didn't want to eat it in front of you—" but Amy lets herself feel isolated and goes home, miserable. On her bed a pamphlet that discusses dealing with anger catches her eye, and she gains perspective on all the financial and emotional stress her parents are experiencing. When Gram is healed enough to move out of Amy's room, she gives Amy an alarm watch to "keep track of when it's time for blood testing and insulin shots."

Arrogant Coby hopes to get an athletic scholarship and pushes himself too hard in a baseball game. Amy knows about his diabetes and snatches a candy bar from a friend to help Coby. Coby's score makes Amy's team lose the championship, but he calls her and that makes her feel grown-up at 11½.

Analysis: Amy's experiences are a case study in adjustment to diabetes. She has a supportive older brother, a pesty little sister, and normal preadolescent worries that help and hinder the process. Gram uses a walker during her visit but picks up her active life of travel and work as soon as her convalescence is over. All the characterizations are believable, but there are few plot elements to fill out the story beyond its "support book" purpose.

■ Rodowsky, Colby F. *Julie's Daughter.* Farrar, 1985. 231pp. (0-374-33963-5) Reading Level: Grades 7–10. (BCCB S85)
Disability: Cancer

Mary Rose October, called "Slug," is 17 before she meets her mother, Julie. Slug is curious and willing to accept her mother's invitation to live together after Grandmother Gussie's burial. It is an uneasy reunion until Julie and Slug join with neighbors to provide home care for a dying elderly artist. The artist—named Harper Tegges—and Julie and Slug each take turns narrating the story.

When Harper reveals that she, too, left an infant daughter to be raised by the father, Slug is overwhelmed by disappointment in this woman she so admired. Slug returns in time to take her next shift caring for Harper, and Julie asks that Slug be as forgiving toward her own mother as she has been toward the artist. When Harper dies, Julie and Slug set things straight in the artist's house, then share an embrace at home.

Analysis: This book has a sophisticated structure, gives two adult females' viewpoints, and has strong language in it. Though younger readers may not find it accessible, persistent readers will be rewarded by a convincingly developed story of abandonment that leads to either bitterness or forgiveness.

Harper is reluctant to seek medical attention, and, after surgery for a brain tumor, insists on dying in her own bed. She is a well-drawn character, and the neighbors involved in her home care show the strains of such an effort. All the characters are allowed to grow, and Harper's death is sensitively portrayed.

■ Roy, Ron. *Where's Buddy?* Illus. by Troy Howell. Clarion, 1982. 95pp. (0-89919-076-6) Reading Level: Grades 3–5. (SLJ Ja83)
Disability: Diabetes

While vacationing at the shore, Mike is left in charge of his younger brother, Buddy, because their parents go to an antique auction on business. Their father writes out a schedule to be sure that Buddy gets his snack, his lunch, and his insulin shot on time. Buddy talks Mike into letting him play with a friend, and Mike swaps favors with the boy's sister, Loni, so he can join in the community football game. The game runs long, and Mike gets back to his house late. He cannot find Buddy and so mobilizes friends and acquaintances to find the missing playmates before Buddy's diabetic reaction can endanger the little boy's life.

Mike and Loni look for their brothers along the sea cliff, where there is a cave. The boys' bikes are there, and the tide is covering the cave entrance. Mike is able to revive Buddy with a drink of cola. The little boy had fallen asleep due to an insulin reaction during a picnic lunch. All four children leave through the flooded tunnel.

Mike's parents realize they were expecting him to set aside his own plans for Buddy's needs, and Mike realizes that he had not fulfilled his responsibilities. Buddy knows how to monitor his own condition and administer his own shots but learns he may not just do everything he wants.

Analysis: Twelve-year-old Mike stars in this suspenseful story, which incorporates information about his brother's condition and its requirement for food and medication at specific times of the day. Mike acknowledges that his family spoils Buddy despite doctor's orders. "When the doctor warned the family to treat Buddy like any other kid, nobody listened. Even aunts, uncles, and cousins back home treated Buddy as if he were a little prince. Mike had been guilty, too. Now, if Buddy didn't get his way, out came the lower lip and down came the tears."

This novel not only presents the physical accommodations that are necessary in the life of a diabetic person, but it also touches on hazards in adjusting family roles and relationships to cope with disability.

■ Ruby, Lois. *This Old Man.* Houghton, 1984. 192pp. (0-395-36563-5)
Reading Level: Grades 7–10. (BCCB Ja85)
Disability: Geriatric impairment; Emotional disturbance

Greta goes to live in a group home after her mother, a prostitute, calls a social services agency in to protect her 16-year-old daughter. At the group home, Greta establishes a friendship with Pammy, who is 15 and expecting a baby. Greta does well in school and starts to revise the severe way she dresses. Her weekly sessions with a counselor help her address her fears that her mother's pimp will find her.

One night she follows Wing, a Chinese-American boy, to a hospital in San Francisco's Chinatown. She begins a nightly vigil in the hall outside "Old Man's" room, while the 91-year-old eats dinner prepared to his demands and delivered by his honored grandson, Wing. Wing also introduces Greta to life in Chinatown, from unassimilated cultural patterns to an "FOB" (fresh off the boat) hoodlum cousin.

One day, Greta runs into her mother's pimp, but the Chinese woman he is visiting in the hospital distracts him so Greta can get away.

In sessions with her counselor, Greta works through her feelings about her mother, her mother's pimp, a need for ethnic or family identity, and her fascination with Wing's grandfather. On realizing that her mother's pimp is not really looking for her and that she has friends and enough brains to help her get away from him if he were, Greta stops having her nightmares. Though she cannot understand what Wing's grandfather tells her when they are alone together, she is pleased that the crotchety old man wanted to share something with her and that he knows she wrote him a poem.

Analysis: Greta has a bleak background to overcome, so she builds a "family" for herself. All of the girls in the home have problems: overeating, running away, teenage pregnancy. Greta offers clearheaded support to Peggy, who nearly gives birth at home and then signs adoption papers so the baby can be raised as its father's little brother. After Greta's mother hides from her pimp, Greta realizes that they love each other in an interdependent way that she has no role in. Love-hate relationships are presented also in the way Wing wants to be the one to serve dinner to his grandfather, despite the man's domineering ways. The author handles each of these complex characterizations very well.

When Wing buys ashes to spread under grandfather's bed, there is an improvement in the man's health. This corresponds to earlier comments that grandfather did not want to get well and did not trust the modern methods used by his Chinese-American doctor. A broken hip results from daily exercises in the hospital room, but the old gentleman is discharged to be cared for at home in the end. This may interest readers of Yep's historical fiction, *Children of the Serpent,* because it shows how an aristocratic Chinese man came to America to work on the railroads and to found a patriarchal extension of Chinese culture in San Francisco. Greta feels that he and his son have every right to avoid the English language and American ways because the dream of prosperity has not proved true for them. Underworld pressures and Old World ways are depicted in vivid episodes.

■ Ruckman, Ivy. *Hunger Scream.* Walker, 1984. 188pp. (0-8027-6514-9)
Reading Level: Grades 5–8.
Disability: Anorexia nervosa

By the end of summer, high school senior Lily Jamison is nearing her weight loss goal. She is also intent on reestablishing her friendship with Daniel, a black neighbor who is back from a difficult freshman year at Stanford. Lily is pleased with the changes in her appearance and resists all comments that advise her to change her eating and exercise patterns. Lily feels that her fashion illustrator mom wants to control her and that her father shows affection only for her little sister, June.

When Lily's girlfriend, Erica, and Daniel tell her that she is too thin, Lily binges, vomits, and punishes herself with another five-pound weight loss goal. She feels she is exercising discipline and establishing control in the only area of her life her parents do not rule. A veteran cheerleader, Lily is disappointed by her coach's suggestion that she not try out, and she is embarrassed by students' jeers when she does. Lily hides for two days. As a result, her mother arranges for counseling with Dr. Coburn, a female specialist on weight problems. Socializing with the sophomore squad and its heavy male member, Franklin, threatens Lily. She uses laxatives after snacking at Erica's and flirting with Daniel, and she postpones her counseling sessions.

Lily, the Jamisons, and Dr. Coburn share impressions about Lily's life, personal motivations, and condition, which is diagnosed as anorexia when she goes below 88 pounds. Lily's focus on a fashion-model-thin appearance and fantasies about Daniel turn into a death wish when he brings a date to the Jamisons' Christmas party. She is admitted to the university hospital, given intravenous medication, and not allowed visitors. Her

treatment and counseling proceed, with Lily earning privileges by con-
tracting to gain pounds. She does not intend to go above 110 but understands "the fact that her anorexia was a plea for attention and independence." In her next family therapy session, Lily decides to discuss sex and
is released from the hospital. She uses her new assertiveness and invites
Daniel over for a nostalgic marshmallow roast.

Analysis: This book clearly defines anorexia nervosa and a classic case
history follows. It is told from shifting points of view, which break up the
flow of the story but allow readers to balance Lily's negative, control-
obsessed impressions with concerned outsiders' observations. A standard
"problem novel" approach limits the character development and crowds
out subplots of friendship, romance, and Daniel's need to reevaluate his
career and education goals. Lily's body image problems and state of denial
are clearly shown when she reflects:

"Of course she'd read about anorexia! It was discussed in all the magazines. Besides, when that singer died of it, her mother had circled all the
newspaper articles for her to read. What was wrong with Snell and her
parents? She wasn't about to diet herself to death. She understood nutri-
tion, knew what felt right for her. She wasn't stupid!"

The need to "know thyself" is the story's theme, but its bibliotherapeutic value is contained in its depiction of one teen's impaired
health, complex needs, and treatment. No easy cure is promised, and
family therapy and behavior modification are incorporated in several
scenes.

■ Ruckman, Ivy. *This Is Your Captain Speaking.* Walker, 1987. 139pp.
(0-8027-6434-6) Reading Level: Grades 6–8. (BCCB N87)
Disability: Terminal illness

Tom is a junior in high school with an older brother who is known as quite
an athlete. Tom gets along with his mother pretty well but compares
himself with his brother. When Tom's interest in a classmate named
Carmela is reciprocated, he spends more and more time with her. He also
donates volunteer time at a retirement home, where he is popular with
staff and patients. He is especially fond of Roger, a former sea captain.
When Roger dies, Tom has to adjust to his grief as he builds his self-
confidence.

Analysis: Intergenerational friendship and adjustment to grief are
themes that are capably presented. The light romance and Tom's maturing
self-image balance the prominent elements of old age, death, and elective
euthanasia.

■ Sachs, Marilyn. *Just Like a Friend.* Dutton, 1989. 154pp. (0-525-44524-2)
Reading Level: Grades 6–9. (KR 15 O89)
Disability: Heart attack; Emotional disturbance

Patti is 14, and she and her friends enjoy being pals with Patti's pretty
mother. Vi was only 17 when Patti was born and is a girlish companion
for shopping, snacking, and having fun. When Patti's father has a heart
attack, Vi becomes hysterical and unable to cope with the accommodations that must be made. Vi's mother is closer to the ill man's age and
comes to help out at the house.

Seeing Vi's being shielded from conflict between her own self-indulgent
patterns and the new needs of the family makes Patti angry, but she does
not express her feelings. She finds a new friend, whose home life is quite
different. Patti decides that being pretty and spoiled or loved for your
weaknesses does not compose the future she wants. The girl is ready to
accept her mother the way she is, but she chooses to become more intellectual and apply her good sense in the future.

Analysis: Sachs is a skilled writer, and each character's conflicting
needs and motivations are revealed very gracefully. Dad knew what he
was getting when he married, and his child-wife is not expected to change.
Instead, he becomes friends with Vi's mother to share activities they have
in common. The cover of a young woman soulfully draped across a
younger girl's shoulders captures the story quite well. There are hazards
in not getting along with one's parents, but this shows that Vi's spoiled
childhood and limited role in the family present frustrations for her
daughter, even though it seems mother is "just like a friend."

■ Sakai, Kimiko. *Sachiko Means Happiness.* Illus. by Tomie Arai. Chil-
dren's Book Pr., 1990. 32pp. (0-89239-065-4) Reading Level: Grades
K–5. (KR 1 D90; HB Ja-F91; BCCB Ja91)
Disability: Alzheimer's disease

Sachiko tells of the day her grandmother did not even recognize her and
how she resented being told to watch the old woman. The woman (also
named Sachiko) becomes more confused as they walk together. At first,
Sachiko is angered when her grandmother insists that she is only 5 years
old and must find her home. Realizing that no matter how disoriented her
tearful grandmother has become, she is still the person young Sachiko
loves, the girl comforts her grandmother as if she really were another
child. Sachiko resolves the woman's distress by inviting her home, as a
new friend might.

Analysis: Exploring the frustrations a 10-year-old girl might feel in dealing with an Alzheimer's patient, the author describes a dramatic episode that may be beyond the perceptions of the usual picture book audience. However, group discussion could allow lower-grade schoolchildren to grasp the more subtle elements of the story as well as the characterizations. Here, young Sachiko develops empathy for her grandmother's disorientation and the grandmother's resulting fear of being surrounded by strangers. For young children who would not find themselves in a caretaker role, *Always Gramma* may be more helpful for dismissing concerns about the behavior changes that Alzheimer's disease causes.

The illustrations are well matched to the tone of the story, and the Japanese family is portrayed honestly in this impressive work from a small press that focuses on the ethnic diversity in the world.

■ Sallis, Susan. *Secret Places of the Stairs*. Harper & Row, 1984. 151 pp. (LB 0-06-025142-5) Reading Level: Grades 7–10.
Disability: Asthma

Gideon tries to keep a tough image but admits to Cass that he has asthma. *See full annotation* Chapter 7: Multiple/Severe Disabilities.

■ Scoppettone, Sandra. *Long Time between Kisses*. Harper & Row, 1982. 224pp. (LB 0-06-025230-8) Reading Level: Grades 7–9. (BCCB MS82)
Disability: Health impairment

When Billie is 16, she is living with her divorced mother in Manhattan. Her father pursues fame as a jazz musician and escapes from his musical failures through frequent drug use. Billie is frustrated with her parents, referring to them as The Mother and The Father. Rebellious attitudes mount until she cuts her hair and dyes it purple. Her boyfriend breaks off with Billie, but she has already fallen in love with Mitch, who has an incurable health impairment.

Billie helps her friend Elissa and an old man she meets. Elissa's Aunt Ruthie appreciates Billie's loyalty and loving generosity. When Mitch recounts his efforts to leave behind a girlfriend rather than become a burden to her, Billie finds Mitch's lost love and unselfishly reunites Mitch with his lady.

Analysis: Scoppettone is a skilled writer, who balances the bleak elements of her story with an essentially sweet characterization. Billie is distressed at home but gets personal satisfaction from having Mitch rely on her. She is honest about his limitations, yet insightful about the way he distances himself from reminders of his former life. Through Billie's kindness, Mitch learns that his life does not have to be as constrained as he once believed.

This is a modern version of the Heidi story, with Billie supporting Mitch until he can love again on his own. Billie is emotionally orphaned, and Mitch (though not miraculously healed) restores his broken spirit through time spent with Billie. For younger readers than those targeted by Klein's *My Life as a Body*, this story of love found and forwarded has similar appeal.

■ Simon, Norma. *The Saddest Time.* Illus. by Jacqueline Rogers. Whitman, 1986. 37pp. (0-8075-7203-9) Reading Level: Grades K–3. (BCCB Ap86)
Disability: Health impairment

Michael visits his favorite uncle, frightened to learn the young man is dying. His mother assures him that most people do not die so young and that there is no need to worry. The funeral is difficult for Michael until he hears stories about his uncle and determines to help his aunt.

The principal of Fleetwood School informs Teddy Baxter's classmates that Teddy has been killed in an accident. The class remembers Teddy and writes letters to the boy's parents.

Emily knew that her grandmother was seriously ill, but the woman's death makes Emily sad and angry. Her grandfather stays after the funeral and helps Emily do things and remember things that make the little girl adjust better to her loss.

Analysis: Three scenarios of death include the terminal illness of an older person and a younger person. Simple pencil drawings and comments in italics that explain death accompany the text. This is recommended for most collections and is intended to help young children who may be confused by TV and movie scenes in which an actor dies and then seemingly comes to life again on another program.

■ Skorpen, Leisel Moak. *Grace.* Harper & Row, 1984. 87pp. (LB 0-06-025799-7) Reading Level: Grades 6–8. (BCCB D84)
Disability: Dementia

One summer, 12-year-old Sara establishes a daily routine of caring for the neighbor woman who had been the butt of local pranksters, Sara included. Since she had promised to apologize and then stay away from Mrs. Craig's property, Sara keeps her visits a secret. Even when she has bought food, cashed a check, cleaned house, and read aloud to Mrs. Craig for weeks, no one knows because Mom has gone back to work. When Mrs. Craig dies, her estranged daughter is the only one at the funeral, but Sara goes out to the McPherson farm and digs up a lilac that had been planted during Mrs. Craig's childhood there. Sara imagines that she can see Mrs. Craig as little Grace McPherson, with her father, once the lilac is planted at Grace's grave.

Analysis: The writing style is full of ellipses and odd combinations, such as "Sara knows she shouldn't but doesn't see how she can't, and so she does." This and a sudden shift to the present tense on page 28 of the narrative seem contrived rather than careless. Sara is at loose ends this summer, without her mother or her friends who have a sudden interest in boys. But that potential boredom does not make it easier to believe that Sara instantly reverses her first impression, that Grace was "like . . . violent. . . . I'll bet you she's crazy. . . . Someone should lock her up before she really hurts somebody." Sara never realizes that Grace's "dour" Scottish personality and stubbornness have already led the old woman to hurt herself, since she is not receiving medical care and has alienated her only living child.

Sara may have been able to fill her summertime and matured in her view of life because of helping Grace, but reliving old memories with a woman in failing health should not be considered the most constructive thing one can do about old age. When Sara's father, a doctor, assures Sara that "Old age isn't a disease—like the measles," it seems a weak insight. The plot offers Mrs. Craig's daughter no opportunity to mend bridges with her mother, who gives all her personal treasures to Sara. Sara accepts the legacy as secretly as she helped out in the house.

This book can give a fanciful look at a short friendship across the generations.

■ Slepian, Jan. *The Broccoli Tapes.* Philomel, 1989. 157pp. (0-399-21712-6) Reading Level: Grades 5–7. (BCCB Ap89)
Disability: Health Impairment

Sara and her brother Sam rescue a wild cat in the lava field near their rented home in Hawaii. Sara and Sam tame the cat, name it Broccoli after its favorite leftovers, and meet a boy named Eddie Nutt. Eddie's father runs a pet shop and owns a prize female cat. Eddie's mother deserted the family but sends word that she wants Eddie to live with her and her new husband. Eddie's father assumes his son does not want to be with him and Eddie in turn is sure his father does not love him.

For herself and her classmates back in Boston, Sara creates tape-recorded messages that record her experiences. Some messages she sends, some she makes for herself, and some she erases as soon as she has made the recording. The family's five-month stay is interrupted when Grandma is hospitalized, then dies. Broccoli also dies, and the children take her kittens to the pet shop to foster with a pure-bred mother. This plan serves as good publicity for Eddie's father, and it introduces the lonely man to a newswoman Eddie refers to as "Miss Hawaii." Sara sees that the little family they created for Broccoli's kittens is a success, and she prepares to return to Boston.

Analysis: Well-rounded portrayals and compelling action are described in Sara's account of her visit to Hawaii. The use of recorded episodes gives strength to the dialogue, to introspection, and to Sara's sixth-grade viewpoint but sometimes seems disjointed. The multiple themes of loss, reconciliation, and being willing to be hurt in order to be open to love are clearly, and gracefully, developed.

Sara feels excluded from her mother's and uncle's concern for Grandma. Only her aunt tells the children that Grandma's condition is terminal, while the other adults keep talking of the woman's recovery. On a visit to the hospital, Sara reflects that "She wasn't scary, but she wasn't Grandma, either. Yellowy eyes, yellowy face, funny smell." She also wonders how her mother and uncle get "into a giggling fit" that Mom says is "Just letting off steam."

Psychological growth shows Sara's development from an aloof new kid at school to her first kiss, a commitment to "something special" she feels with Eddie. Slepian's sensitivity toward vulnerable Sam and insecure Eddie comes through as it did in her books about Lester and Alfred. Here the boys' emotional adjustments and lessons in communicating love are as authentic as the physical challenges this author has explored in other stories. Highly recommended, Broccoli's story has appeal for *Where the Red Fern Grows* animal lovers and general readers as well.

■ Slepian, Jan. **Something Beyond Paradise.** Philomel, 1987. 180pp. (0-399-21425-9) Reading Level: Grades 7–10. (BCCB MS87) *Disability:* Dementia

Franny, 16, lives in Honolulu, but a dance scholarship lures her to New York. She finds it difficult to make up her mind or inform her mother of her decision to leave "paradise". Because Franny is the one most often successful in dealing with her irrational grandmother, there is additional pressure on Franny to stay. She is distracted from her decision when her friend Akiko leaves a squalid home to pursue "Instant Bliss" at the "House of Regis." The probation period that Akiko is placed on by her cult leads Franny to plan a rescue for her friend with Aled, who works at the home. Franny's mother encourages Akiko to build her own identity and not give control of her life over to someone else. Akiko points out that

Franny and her mother have the same type of loving coercion in their life. Akiko returns to the group home. Franny takes leave of her grandmother and invites Aled to go to New York with her.

Analysis: Franny knows her grandmother's scattered memories mix with odd behavior every day. These circumstances have been Franny's to bear because her mother has a love interest and friends who want nothing to do with their home life. Franny's mother finds the letter from New York, so Franny is free from introducing the subject of her big decision. Franny's mother takes a more responsible role in her mother's disability so that Franny can have a future of her own. Excellent writing and complex relationships are presented in this title.

■ Snyder, Carol. *Ike and Mama and the Seven Surprises.* Lothrop, 1985. 160pp. (0-688-03732-1) Reading Level: Grades 3–6. (BCCB Mr85) *Disability:* Tuberculosis; Orthopedic impairment

Ike is facing his bar mitzvah studies without his father. For a month, Papa has been hospitalized far from their home on Manhattan Island. Only Mama is allowed to visit because tuberculosis is so contagious. Papa does get out for fresh air on a hospital boat, though, and Ike and his friends find a way to see him. Ike tries to cheer Papa by reciting the blessing he has been studying with cousin Jake.

Times are hard for the family, with a new puppy, a newly arrived immigrant cousin, and no earnings from Papa while he recuperates. Still, Mama finds the ingredients for a special pastry and organizes Ike's bar mitzvah to take place near enough to Papa so that he can hear the ceremony.

Analysis: The plot is presented in short chapters with period details that should engage the interest of an upper-elementary audience. It will be clear to readers that this happened long ago, when Fords were called "flivvers" and gas meters needed 50 cents to get the lights to come back up. The dialogue for the nurse is stilted when compared with the English, Yiddish, and Hebrew-peppered exchanges between Ike and his family. As the title suggests, Ike is expecting seven surprises once he saves the life of the dog, and this gives the action some suspense and structure.

Cousin Jake is described as a "fine grown-up man who just did not grow to be very tall." It is interesting to read that the doctors at the immigration building had placed a tag on Jake's back that said "L" for limp, just as they would have tagged a person who had a weak heart with an "H." When Jake cannot find work, it is mentioned as an economic situation, not as a problem resulting from his limp. His enthusiasm for his new country, language, and family is clear.

Ike comes to appreciate his cousin Jake for what this wise and generous man did in the past, as well as the way he helps the family now. It is important to keep Papa's place open for him, meanwhile, but there is no doubt that Jake will be the main source of income for this family until Papa overcomes his illness.

■ Stren, Patti. *I Was a Fifteen-Year-Old Blimp.* Harper & Row, 1985. 192pp. (LB 0-06-026058-0) Reading Level: Grades 6–9. (BCCB N85) *Disability:* Bulimia

Gabby, at 15, knows that she is overweight, but her self-image plummets when she overhears the boys at school rate her a zero. Her mother insists that Gabby abandon a crash diet in favor of a well-balanced program. When Gabby gains two pounds, her friend Nicole shares the "dancer's secret" of laxative use and induced vomiting. Gabby confides in Mel, a sympathetic boy who saves her from humiliation at a dance. Gabby is depressed, binges, vomits, and continues this pattern until Dr. Baber suggests she attend Camp Blossom for overweight girls.

Camp counselor Bunny is slim but recovering from bulimia. When Bunny shares the fact that she still feels "fat inside," even after a year of therapy, Gabby admits that she fears gaining weight and has continued vomiting. Bunny helps Gabby control her bulimia. After camp, slim Gabby is a sensation at her 16th birthday party. She chooses to dance with Mel, over the "cool" schoolmates who had ignored her before she lost weight.

Analysis: When characters share opinions or information on bulimia it can stall the progress of the story, but most readers find this a satisfying book. The plot presents an accurate progression and provides honest recognition that this disorder requires extensive therapy. When Gabby has mixed emotions about her newfound popularity, her father agrees that counseling will help her face these insecurities. One does worry about Nicole and those dancers though, because sustaining their "secret" may undermine their health in ways this book does not define.

■ Stretton, Barbara. *You Never Lose.* Knopf, 1982. 237pp. (LB 0-394-95230-8) Reading Level: Grades 6–9. (BCCB Mr83) *Disability:* Cancer

The summer before his senior year, Jim Halbert finds out that his father is dying of cancer. Mr. Halbert is a football hero and coach, so his illness affects the entire school. Jim is at a loss as to how to react either to his class's unit on "Death, the Final Taboo" or to sympathetic comments from students and faculty. Most of all, Jim is uneasy with his father, who has always seemed distant and demanding.

Jim's father insists on maintaining his coaching duties, even though he falls down on the field and is knocked out by a hard pass he goads Jim into throwing. Jim's girlfriend, Mimi, seems more interested in her campaign to give the coach a great season record for his last year than in Jim. A new girl, Agnes, is friendly, she and Jim make love, and she skips school to visit Coach Halbert in the hospital with Jim. After an opening season win, Jim realizes he wants to go tell his father about the game instead of being with Mimi and the fans for a celebration. Jim and his father talk about the thrill of football; afterward Jim goes to be with Agnes.

Analysis: Jim fills many introspective passages with his memories, needs, and feelings about adjustments he must make, so the plot gets bogged down. Jim is believable, but the dialogue is stilted, especially with "Gus" (Agnes) who is abrupt and sometimes caustic. At one point, Jim finds his father sobbing in the hospital rest room, so Jim leaves without letting the man know he was observed. Jim's mother has things to share about Coach Halbert's need to hide weaknesses. Jim's teacher drops his unit on death after his own feelings about his father's suicide give him insight about Jim's stressful situation. This is not a first choice for father-son relationship stories but may serve in a large collection.

■ Taha, Karen T. *A Gift for Tia Rosa.* Illus. by Dee deRosa. Gemstone, 1986. 40pp. (0-87518-306-9) Reading Level: Grades 2–3. (BCCB Ap86) *Disability:* Health impairment

Eight-year-old Carmelita has good friends next door, whom she calls Tia Rosa and Tio Juan. Tia Rosa has just come home from the hospital, and Carmelita notices many changes in her. Tia Rosa gives the little girl a piece of jewelry as a remembrance of her, but Carmelita is puzzled and refuses to believe her father's comment that Tia Rosa will not be getting well. When Tia Rosa dies, Carmelita is hard to console and will not touch the knitting they used to do together. In the end, she works out her grief by interacting with Tio Juan and completing Tia Rosa's pink baby blanket for the new grandbaby, Rosita.

Analysis: While the cause of Tia Rosa's illness is unclear, this book makes childlike observations about an invalid's failing health that are insightful. Carmelita smells the difference in her friend's room and wonders why Tia must stay in bed all the time. Though this book is narrowly focused on one child's experience with death and grief, it is adequate for collections when portrayals of Hispanic characters, cross-generational friendships, and health impairments are needed.

■ Talbert, Marc. *Thin Ice.* Little, Brown, 1986. 207pp. (0-316-83133-6) Reading Level: Grades 4–7. (BCCB Ja86)
Disability: Diabetes

Martin's parents are separated, his father lives in Alaska, and things get so tough at home and school that Martin runs off. Because it was Martin's job to give his sister, Franny, her insulin shots, she goes into insulin shock. However, Martin becomes able to restore his friendship with his best friend Barney and face his responsibility at home.

Analysis: The author creates raucous scenes of classroom interaction and presents dialogue that incorporates more adolescent vulgarisms than may be necessary. So many problem situations are used in the plot that the theme of mending relationships by abandoning pride and fear of embarrassment becomes obscured. Franny is important to the story, but her big scene is as a victim, not a capable person with a health impairment.

■ Taylor, Theodore. *Sweet Friday Island.* Scholastic, 1984. 149pp. (0-590-33174-4) Reading Level: Grades 7–9. (BCCB F85)
Disability: Diabetes; Emotional disturbance

Peg recalls a camping trip she took with her father when she was an adolescent. They could not be discouraged from going to the deserted Mexican area called Sweet Friday Island. They were astonished to see that someone was on the island and that that person was threatening their lives. Their boat became useless after this enemy slashed it. Their clothes were slashed also. Things disappeared from their campsite, and boulders fell off a cliff above them. Dad's insulin was stolen, and Peg had to smoke the crazed thief out of hiding. Years later, Peg learns that their "deserted" island had been occupied by an insane man whose son chose to leave him to roam Sweet Friday Island, rather than have him placed in an institution.

Analysis: Dramatic action and suspense make for a fast-paced plot. Unfortunately, portrayals of the mentally ill are a stock element of mystery. The son's decision in this book indicates that Peg and her father made Jane Eyre's mistake of entering a crazy person's turf. Look elsewhere for information on caretaking and guardianship of mentally disturbed individuals. In this story, however, Peg's father is a lively example of the activities a person can pursue, even though dependent on insulin. A diabetic condition is this survival mystery's unique offering in characterization.

■ Terris, Susan. *Nell's Quilt*. Farrar, 1987. 162pp. (0-374-35504-5)
Reading Level: Grades 7–9. (BCCB N87)
Disability: Anorexia nervosa

Farm life in 1899 is hard for Nell and her family, but she has a harder time facing the idea of being bartered for good shoes and a secure home in town with Anson Turner. Her grandmother died six months before, leaving a legacy of women's suffrage campaigning and the pieces of an unfinished crazy quilt. Nell's aversion to the arranged marriage with a widower leads her to work on the quilt, endlessly, and to stop eating. She undermines all the virtues of health, strength, and dependability that Anson had been interested in. She also makes her parents suffer for trying to control her future instead of helping her with her dream of going to Boston.

Nell is 18, still in high school, and interested in Rob Hoffman as a special friend. Her sister Eliza is a year younger and has "been delicate since her bout with rheumatic fever." After a year of waiting, Eliza and Anson make wedding plans, but Nell's health becomes so poor she obviously cannot wed. In a final exercise of destructive control, Nell takes the quilt she has labored over and dyes it black. She wraps herself in it and expects to die, but at the last moment realizes she is not "Wednesday's child" and must put aside her woe, because she is really "Thursday's child" with "far to go."

Analysis: Casting a character with anorexia nervosa in a historical piece is commendable, but Nell's anger and her manipulation of everyone around her can seem overdrawn. Nell has undermined her health, first from a nervous loss of appetite, then as a punishment for her parents, and, finally, as a symbol that since all her energies are expected to go into domestic efforts, the quilt will grow while Nell forces herself to waste away. The author uses complex themes and shifts dated chapters from first-person accounts to third-person observations and then back for the climax.

The dramatic ending omits mention of how hard it will be for Nell to regain her health. Her new motivation is based on her old, competent self-image's desire to look after some kittens, as well as her mother, and to change things for Anson's little girl, Jewel, as well as Ludie, who is married to a brute. In her current condition as a "Scarecrow," these ambitions present "a long way to go." Readers may be satisfied with the foreshadowed return of Rob Hoffman and Anson's engagement to Eliza, but reading through Nell's year can be a trial.

■ Thesman, Jean. **Appointment with a Stranger.** Houghton, 1989. 182pp. (0-395-49215-7) Reading Level: Grades 7–9. (BCCB S89) *Disability:* Asthma

Keller is at a new school, shy, uncomfortable, and afraid she may have an asthmatic attack in public. There is a pond near her grandfather's house, where she meets Tom, who does not attend her school. Keller is relaxed with Tom and falls in love. As she meets more classmates and finds out about the town, she comes to realize that Tom is a ghost. Drew, a boy from school, helps Keller establish some friendships, and Keller discovers some details about Tom's death.

Analysis: Embarrassment and apprehension are authentic character traits for Keller regarding her asthma. But the Gothic quality of the story relies on Keller's vulnerable, shy persona, and limits her characterization. The fantasy elements and Tom's mysterious appearances do not blend smoothly in this novel.

■ Thesman, Jean. **The Rain Catchers.** Houghton, 1991. 182pp. (0-395-55333-4) Reading Level: Grades 8–12. (KR 15 F91; BCCB Mr91) *Disability:* Cancer; Arthritis

At 14, Gray pieces together a broader view of her family history. She was raised by her grandmother after her father was murdered and her mother was left to focus on success in the business world. Grandmother's household includes her elderly cousin, Olivia, who has cancer and has asked for a mercy death if her condition worsens. This request is honored by Grandmother and Belle, a black doctor who was supported through her medical studies by Grandmother. Gray is friends with Colleen, whose father could disclose Belle's actions. Colleen is feeling so pressured by her father and stepbrother that she wants to live with Grandmother too. At Grandmother's home, afternoon tea is a ritual for recounting personal histories. Gray visits her mother to learn another side of that tragic story.

Analysis: Complexities abound, but the well-realized characterizations in this household of women make the novel compelling. As in *Going Backwards* and *Doc,* a mercy death at the hands of a physician provides a suspenseful but weak element in the story. The women's motivation is clear, but Dr. Clement is too easily put off the track.

Belle's great empathy with Olivia's choice is supposed to come from her own experiences in nursing Grandfather during a terminal illness, practicing medicine, and dealing with her own painful arthritis. A strong writing style and judicious introduction of a romantic interest for Gray make this story recommended for young adult collections.

■ Thomas, Karen. *Changing of the Guard.* Harper & Row, 1986. 186pp. (LB 0-06-026164-1) Reading Level: Grades 6–8. (BCCB Je86)
Disability: Dementia

For two years, Caroline has been grieving for her grandfather. She still resists new relationships and goes by Grandpa's rigid opinions. At 16, she has family concerns and a new acquaintance, Maddy, to make decisions about. Caroline's father is out of work and her grandmother is becoming senile. Caroline sets aside her suspicions and resentments to become friends with Maddy.

Analysis: Caroline's grief colors her interpersonal interactions as well as her self-image. Her concern for her grandmother is believable, and the characterization is consistent. The plot is rather flat and drawn out, but the writing style is adequate.

■ Thurman, Chuck. *A Time for Remembering.* Illus. by Elizabeth Sayles. Simon & Schuster, 1989. 24pp. (0-671-68573-2) Reading Level: Grades PS–3.
Disability: Health impairment

After his grandfather's funeral, a little boy honors the man's last request. He recalls times spent with the understanding man, including the last hospital visit. His grandfather had removed the wilted blooms from a plant to help it grow stronger and asked for private time with the boy.

"He gave the boy one of the wilted flowers and asked him to keep it for a while. He asked the boy to sit by the fire someday after he died and remember things about him. Then, when the boy was finished remembering, he was to throw the flower into the fire."

Once their last hug is remembered, the boy burns the flower and goes to join his parents.

Analysis: Color illustrations extend this touching story by lending emotional content to the simple text. The spread that pictures the boy and his parents walking to the hospital indicates the overwhelming feelings such a visit can evoke. The next picture is softened, for the boy is at his grandfather's side, with the flowered plant evident in the corner. Next, an intimate portrait of the hug includes the flower in the boy's hand.

It is good to have a picture book that depicts a hospitalized person as being approachable, instead of in quarantine. There are medical reasons to exclude children (and plants) from hospitals, so this may not be a common experience. However, this story reflects the increased family interaction that hospice care has recently introduced into institutions. This book has a binding that detracts from its presentation by stitching through and swallowing up gutter portions of double-page spreads. Still, it is a nice addition to parental shelf offerings.

■ Todd, Leonard. *The Best Kept Secret of the War.* Knopf, 1984. 165pp. (LB 0-394-96569-8) Reading Level: Grades 5–7. (BCCB My84)
Disability: Geriatric impairment

Ten-year-old Cam is worried about his father, who is serving in World War II. His best friend, Tal, thinks Cam is too proud of his father. When Jeddah runs away from Tal's father's nursing home, Cam helps him hide. Tal's father just wants Jeddah back in the home because of the money the business brings in. The home operator also bothers Cam's mother. Cam is able to resolve the situation.

Analysis: This tightly constructed historical novel has good characterizations and pace. The nursing home owner has an eye for profits and a lonely wife but skirts the villainous stereotype. Jeddah has initiative that is greater than his physical resources, and his character is portrayed a believably and is given a central role in the story. Readers will enjoy this simple tale.

■ Ure, Jean. *One Green Leaf.* Delacorte, 1989. 192pp. (0-385-29751-3) Reading Level: Grades 6–9. (BCCB My89)
Disability: Cancer

When Robyn was 11, she left a private school and became close friends with David, Abbey, and Zoot. Abbey has trouble getting to know people. David is straightforward and considers religious doctrine "mumbo jumbo or some kind of con trick." Robyn and Zoot are more outgoing, and their friendship sees them through various classroom plots.

Five years later, Abbey and David pair off, but the four-way friendship is not shaken until David develops a limp and is hospitalized. Everyone misses the athletic, popular student, and the diagnosis of a cancerous tumor requiring amputation of his leg is difficult to accept. Abbey tries to rally everyone to "be positive"; Robyn's father, who is a doctor, shares with her information about treatment. The characters recall a woman who had the same surgery and now climbs mountains, and Zoot tells of an amputee who "plays golf, rides his bike, goes swinning . . . everything, practically."

Abbey rejects the prayerful concern of schoolmates and faculty, because she and David consider religion a sham. "Yesterday she had been worried about the bomb and nuclear waste and radiation: today all she could think about was David."

Abbey goes to speak with a teacher about college and strikes up a friendship that Robyn resents. Robyn, though, is busy with cast members in a production of *Much Ado About Nothing.* Visits with David show that his personality is changed. Robyn's mother explains, "He has to come to terms with a whole new concept of himself." A plan to take David's dog, Max, to visit him in the hospital seems a good idea to Robyn. "After all, even crying was better than showing no feelings at all. At least if he cried, it meant that he CARED; and as long as he cared, then that meant he had a reason for living."

Robyn is reprimanded for unthinkingly reminding David of what he was afraid of losing, just when he had emotional walls in place to protect himself. "Try to understand and be patient. Not feel hurt at being excluded, not think that he's given up just because he seems withdrawn. If he's self-absorbed it's because that's what's necessary for survival. He'll come back to you when he's ready; when he feels strong enough. But he has to do it at his own pace. Just bear with him. That's the best support you can give him at the moment"

David walks out on the field to get Max during a game and is cheered by schoolmates. When Robyn visits David's mother to arrange a homecoming party, the woman reveals that David will have no more chemotherapy, though other types of treatment are being given. The class vamp gets David to dance at the party, and Robyn agrees with her mother that "there is such a thing as being too considerate," toward the self-conscious David.

Robyn notices that David acts unkindly toward Abbey once he is back into school routine. On school break, Robyn witnesses David in a betrayal of Abbey by being with another girl. While David is celebrating his improved prosthesis, Robyn confronts him with too much truth about his bid for loveless sex and his subconscious ways of distancing Abbey. When the girls are in college, they keep in contact and recall their dead friend, David.

Analysis: This polished novel deals not only with David's illness and personal adjustment but also with the grief and change that his friends undergo. Lots of British terms and grade distinctions may be hard for some readers, and both coarse language and teasing about homosexuals are used to set the tone for this friendship that incorporates four well-realized individuals. Highly recommended, this perceptive novel allows Robyn to vent her bias against chemotherapy and enables David's mother to express her intention that David's quality of life should not be undermined by treatment that cannot ensure survival.

■ Walker, Alice. *To Hell with Dying.* Illus. by Catherine Deeter. Harcourt, 1988. 32pp. (0-15-289075-0) Reading Level: Grades 2–5. (BCCB Ap88; HB MS88)
Disability: Diabetes

"Mr. Sweet was a diabetic and an alcoholic and a guitar player and lived down the road from us on a neglected cotton farm." Memories of Mr. Sweet and the way his near-fatal bouts with illness could be reversed by Alice's family are listed. The whole family enjoys Mr. Sweet and his guitar music. "Sometimes he would cry and that was an indication that he was about to die again. And so we would all get prepared, for we were sure to be called upon."

At least ten times in the history of her family, Mr. Sweet Little's doctor advised Alice's father that:

> . . . the children had best not see the face of implacable death (I didn't know what "implacable" was, but whatever it was, Mr. Sweet was not!). My father pushed him rather abruptly out of the way saying, as he always did and very loudly, for he was saying it to Mr. Sweet, "To hell with dying, man, these children want Mr. Sweet"—which was my cue. . . .

When Alice is 24 and leaves her studies at the university to see Mr. Sweet through a dying spell, he cannot respond in the old way. "He was like a piece of rare and delicate china which was always being saved from breaking and which finally fell." She is given Mr. Sweet's guitar and realizes that he was her first love.

Analysis: Walker's prose gives strong images and provides clear emotional impact. However, it is not a good text for a picture book. The audience for this extravagantly illustrated adult short story is uncertain, so its portrayal of an eccentric black man worn down by the woes of his life may be lost in some collections.

The confusion that children already have about death may be compounded by Walker's admission: "It did not occur to us that we were doing anything special: we had not learned that death was final when it did come. We thought nothing of triumphing over it so many times, and in fact became a trifle contemptuous of people who let themselves be carried away. It did not occur to us that if our own father had been dying we could not have stopped it, that Mr. Sweet was the only person over whom we had power."

This story is a bit of wish fulfillment, for Walker was not really able to leave her studies, pay for transportation, and be with Mr. Sweet during his last illness. Though the story is a good introduction to serious writing by a skilled author, this presentation does not succeed in accessibility to an elementary school audience.

■ Westall, Robert. *The Promise.* Scholastic, 1991. 176pp. (0-590-43760-7) Reading Level: Grades 6–10. (KR 1 F91; HB Mr-Ap91; BCCB Ap91) *Disability:* Health impairment

World War II has just begun when 15-year-old Bob becomes friends with Valerie. Her health is so poor that she misses school a lot, and Bob's visits are erratic because the war effort, air raids, and plane-spotting distract him. When Valerie dies, her ghost makes contact with Bob, insisting that he keep his promise to find her if she ever gets lost. The war provides Bob with a way to keep his promise.

Analysis: Ghost stories have wide readership, and the romantic-looking but misleading cover may appeal to additional browsers. The real rewards here are Westall's authentic setting and realistic characters instead of Gothic cardboard cutouts. Valerie reacts to her parents' overprotection, her adolescent uncertainties, and her sexual stirrings. Once she is a ghost, her insecurities make her a compelling though demanding presence in Bob's life. Enjoyable and well written.

■ Willey, Margaret. *The Bigger Book of Lydia.* Harper & Row, 1983. 256pp. (LB 0-06-026486-1) Reading Level: Grades 7–10. (BCCB Ja84) *Disability:* Anorexia nervosa; Short stature

Lydia Bitte's father dies when she is 10, "killed beneath the wheels of a huge produce truck with brake failure. After the funeral Lydia's mother, Agnes, fell quickly into a trancelike slumber, wandering into and out of her bed like a sleepwalker. . . . But Lydia . . . pulled a thick, empty notebook from her father's desk" and titled it *The Bigger Book.* Small, frail things like the Bitte family members seemed prone to danger and death, so Lydia gathers in her notebook all the memories that she could of her father and information on growth and size.

A friend of the family, Claudine, moves in to help out, and her robust style leads Lydia's sister, Rita, to call the little woman "Queen." Claudine moves out when Agnes Bitte recovers somewhat, and Lydia takes on the family budgeting. By the time Lydia is 13, her mother is working full-time and leaves household matters to Lydia.

Lydia avoids students who make reference to her size and is cool to teachers, especially ones who use "nicknames like 'Peanut' and 'Shrimp.' " She is obsessed that her wardrobe should never accentuate her stature or petite frame. When Lydia is a sophomore in high school, she dates a six-foot-tall musician named Eddy Erron. He is 20 years old and calls her "Littlebit." She does not tell him how she hates the pet name, is puzzled by their relationship, resists his sexual demands, and is attracted to his brother, Fred, who is dating Wanda. Though Lydia decides to avoid both the brothers, she becomes friends with six-foot-tall Wanda.

Claudine's niece, Michelle, has been treated unsuccessfully for anorexia nervosa and comes to live with the Bittes. Lydia subconsciously reacts to Michelle's emaciated appearance and eating habits by gaining eight pounds. When she tells Michelle this, the two girls, with opposing obsessions, strike a bargain that Michelle will try to eat more to help Lydia lose weight. Agnes has a boyfriend who Michelle predicts will disrupt the family by becoming its father. Lydia does not enjoy her junior year because of a rigid art teacher, and she considers quitting school.

Against Michelle's therapist's advice, the girl's father demands that she return home. At the same time, Lydia's friendship with Wanda is ruptured because Fred has betrayed Wanda and is pestering Lydia. During the two weeks before Michelle's father is to arrive, Lydia and Michelle mope around until Claudine tells them to face their troubles and value their friendship. Lydia encourages Michelle by deciding to go back to school, finds *The Bigger Book,* and gives it to Michelle, hoping the gift will help her friend recover. When Michelle sees her father, she senses that his oppressive, self-assured manner has shifted to a nervous concern for her. Claudine feels that her niece will be able to continue to gain weight.

Analysis: A complex psychological study, with strong characterizations and believable development, is presented in this account of Lydia's maturation from 10-year-old worrywart to talented young woman who can put a pushy male in his place. Some of the dialogue is stiff, maybe sappy at times of high personal disclosure, but the comments or impressions about stature, size, and "craziness" are true to the point of view of the character expressing them.

Lydia is vulnerable, Agnes is frail, Claudine has strength, and Michelle has been wounded by her parents. Michelle admits that she has hurt them as well and realistically refuses to promise Lydia she will get well. Lydia wanted to tell Michelle that she looked better, but she could not do it. Michelle's face was saggy and pale from sleeping so much and from three days without food. She looked terrible.

Because the author takes the time to develop a multifaceted story, without pat solutions, readers are sure to respond to the self-image obsessions that make life so difficult for two teen girls.

■ Williams, Barbara. **Beheaded, Survived.** Franklin Watts, 1987. 150pp. (0-531-10403-6) Reading Level: Grades 6–9. (BCCB D87)
Disability: Diabetes; Emotional disturbance

Jane and her older sister, Courtney, are on a tour of historic sites in England and Wales with 30 other teenagers. Jane makes journal entries that describe the events and her interest in Lowell, who writes letters constantly but has little to say to fellow travelers. Sometimes he answers the group leader's question, as in "divorced, beheaded, died, divorced, beheaded, survived" to describe the fate of Henry VIII's wives. At Becket's grave, Jane and Lowell are both moved to tears, which opens communication between them with the agreement that there will be no personal questions.

Moody Lowell is 16 but already a senior because he skipped a few grades. Fourteen-year-old Jane is impressed by his vocabulary and wide range of knowledge, but gets annoyed when he compares her with "plain" Jane Austin. Once Jane reads some of Austin's novels, she changes her opinion of Lowell. Courtney wants to protect her sister, and since her boyfriend, Scott, is Lowell's roommate, Lowell's discarded letter to a pregnant girl named Chris gets passed on to Jane. When confronted, Lowell refuses to go into details at first, but he later confides that his mother had been terminally ill with leukemia for a year and that the day of her funeral, his father announced he was going to marry his secretary, who was already pregnant. Jane helps Lowell see that by being unforgiving, he has let his hatred nearly drive him to suicide.

Jane tries to conceal her diabetes from other teenagers on the tour, afraid that they would treat her differently if they knew about it. Her sister interrupts time that Jane wants to spend with Lowell by reminding Jane to get enough rest and making unspoken threats to tell him about Jane's diabetes if Jane does not maintain a healthy routine. One evening, Jane binges on chocolate and cookies, then forces herself to vomit as she has heard bulimics do. Another day, she skips breakfast to go with Lowell to visit a castle. He wants to give her a poem, so she pushes herself to get to the romantic destination even though the exertion is taking a toll. She feels hot, then panics and runs away, but Courtney and Scott arrive in time to give Jane breath mints and a banana. Her hypoglycemic reaction is under control when Lowell asks:

"Why didn't anyone tell me she has diabetes?"

Scott shrugs. "She made Court promise not to tell. She's a lot like my sister. Doesn't want anyone to think she's different."

Jane has to catch her flight to California, but at the airport she gets to say good-bye to her summer love. Lowell gives her roses and a note that both points out he is a compulsive letter-writer and is signed, "I love you." On his flight to Phoenix, Lowell writes to his father that he wants to talk about the past year and plans to study premed at Stanford. He also writes to his stepmother, "It's okay about the baby."

Analysis: Jane's journal entries record most of the action, with Lowell's letters and poems interspersed. Details of the tour complement the plot structure and characterizations in this story. Courtney is a consistently drawn character who tries to monitor Jane's health while letting the younger girl enjoy as much independence as possible. The tour leaders are ridiculed by their charges, but an affectionate bond is also established.

Jane is active yet knows the limitations of her health impairment. When she argues with Teresa, another girl on the tour, about martyrdom and natural death, Teresa tells of her grandmother's natural death that "took her exactly four years and seven months—in this bizarre nursing home with demented old people walking around in their underwear and slobbering." Teresa's plans to become a nun, save the orphans, win the Nobel peace prize, and die in her 80s prompts Jane to write:

> I sigh. As a rule, I don't worry too much about my illness and when or how I might die. . . . What if the cure doesn't come until after I've already developed all those problems that diabetics can get? Liver ailments. Heart attacks. Blindness. Amputations. Not to mention those two kinds of spells that I've already had—diabetic comas and hypoglycemic reactions. When I have a hypoglycemic reaction (Courtney keeps reminding me), I yell at people and throw things and act like an escapee from your basic horror movie.
>
> My cousin Paul, who had diabetes, died at seventeen, before he even graduated from high school.

Lowell sees Jane crying at this point and realizes that he is not the only person in the world with problems. He stops trying to fly home from the tour, and focuses on building a friendship with Jane. He writes to his father, his stepmother, his doctor, his dead mother, and "To Whom It May Concern." All of these attempts to get in contact with his feelings of betrayal and grief end in an ellipse, and the reader never knows which letters get mailed or destroyed. His volatile mood swings and Jane's ability to draw out his story are credible.

When Lowell writes that he has decided to attend Stanford and become a doctor, his motivation to be near Jane to help with her health problems is clear.

This title is highly recommended, because special needs are just part of the well-rounded portrayals that are presented with natural dialogue in an appealing setting.

■ Wolitzer, Hilma. **Wish You Were Here.** Farrar, 1984. 179pp. (0-374-38456-8) Reading Level: Grades 6–8. (BL 15 S84)
Disability: Asthma

Bernie Segal has an older sister, Celia, and a younger sister, Grace. His mother is planning to remarry, and Bernie wants to go live with his paternal grandfather rather than see Nat Greenberg take his father's place. Bernie has several ways to earn money for the airfare to Florida (only $99), but his asthma makes yard work and other physical chores out of the question. When he helps Celia learn her role for a high school production of *Member of the Wedding,* she pays him $1 per hour. He even offers comfort when she cuts her hair too short in order to resemble her character, Frankie.

When Bernie's mother finds his paid ticket to Florida, they discuss his feelings of disloyalty to his father who's been dead for two years. Bernie's grandfather comes for the wedding, so Bernie's plans to avoid the celebration are foiled, and they talk about grief and memories. Nat and Bernie begin a relationship, and Bernie takes his father's name, Martin, as a middle name.

Analysis: Bernie's lively first-person narration incorporates both passages from *Member of the Wedding* and a tentative romance of his own in addition to the main plot regarding his mother's remarriage. Bernie's asthma is just one aspect of his well-developed characterization. Insights on grief are provided by Rabbi Stein and a family psychologist as well as Bernie's mother and grandfather. Grace still draws pictures that express her anger and depression. Bernie's showdown with Nat, in which he tells the man that his cheery attitude is what most makes Bernie dislike him, is one example of this author's ability to mix serious themes with humorous action.

■ Wright, Betty Ren. **The Summer of Mrs. MacGregor.** Holiday, 1986. 160pp. (0-8234-0628-8) Reading Level: Grades 5–8. (BCCB D86)
Disability: Heart disease; Cerebral hemorrhage; Emotional disturbance

Twelve-year-old Caroline feels invisible at home, where her 15-year-old sister, Linda's, failing health overshadows all interaction between family members. Her father died of the same heart condition, so every opportunity for treatment for Linda has been assiduously pursued. Linda tries to postpone rehospitalization, but she and her mother leave for treatments all summer in Boston. This gives Caroline new responsibility at home with her stepfather, Joe. In addition, Caroline has a job across the street helping an old man who should use a walker due to a recent stroke.

A visitor in the neighborhood introduces herself as Mrs. Lillina Taylor MacGregor, aspiring photographer. But there is no film in her camera. Lillina, a tall redhead, strikes "Miss America" poses and discloses about herself one unlikely detail after another with sophisticated aplomb. Caroline is convinced that this 17-year-old has a rich husband but wants to pursue her life as a writer and model as soon as she returns home to New York. Lillina encourages Caroline's dim hopes to earn $100 for spending money, to accept Grandmother's offer of air fare to London, and to visit her best friend there for Christmas.

Lillina describes her independent, 13-year-old sister, Eleanor, to Caroline, who begins to measure her own reactions to life by "what Eleanor would do." When the man across the street needs medical attention, Caroline is the one to discover it and handle the situation. That same evening, she confronts Lillina as a thief. Caroline visits with Lillina's "aunt" and finds out that Lillian Taylor, a high school sophomore from Michigan, has been stealing money from the family she has been staying with. Caroline locates her friend, confronts her with the truth, and deals maturely with the hysterical scene Lillian causes.

Linda's treatment has been completed, with little improvement, but Joe is so enlivened by the family's reunion that he sets up a gazebo outdoors for Linda. Caroline is not the same "good old" girl that she used to be, but she intends to turn her dreams into reality and avoid her former invisibility. Lillian will stay in town long enough to begin psychiatric counseling.

Analysis: This story of a 12-year-old's summer maturation includes many portrayals of disability. It is clear to the reader that Lillina is not reliable, so Caroline's credulity is hard to accept. The final scene between the girls shows that emotional disturbances do not always manifest in psychotic delusions but should be given medical attention nonetheless. The stroke patient has not adjusted to his limitations, and by refusing to use the walker, he risks his life. Linda is revealed in one chapter and by various comments, as a near-angelic invalid. Caroline points out that before Linda became sick, she was still considered the perfect student, so some character development is provided. The most telling quote is when Linda says:

"Mr. Jameson would be better than—oh, you know . . ."
    Better than blood tests and hospital trays and feeling weak all the time and having shots and not being able to breathe at night.

The family tension about Linda's condition will not change, but Caroline has found a new role to play that will be healthy for her should Linda's condition worsen.

■ Zindel, Paul. *Begonia for Miss Applebaum.* Harper & Row, 1989. 192pp. (LB 0-06-026878-6) Reading Level: Grades 7–10. (BCCB Ap89) *Disability:* Cancer

Zelda and Henry take turns recording on the word processor their impressions of family, school, and visits with Miss Applebaum. Miss Applebaum was a science teacher, but has retired. Cancer has undermined Miss Applebaum's health, but the wise old lady sets an eccentric pattern for her last days, and Henry and Zelda help her enjoy them. What starts with the gift of a begonia from two former students turns into a friendship between three outsiders.
    Analysis: The format of alternate voices is standard for Zindel fans, and Miss Applebaum is a character worth knowing. Like Zelda and Henry, readers may gain insights on life from a close encounter with death.

ORTHOPEDIC/NEUROLOGICAL IMPAIRMENTS

■ Adler, C. S. *Eddie's Blue-Winged Dragon.* Putnam, 1988. 144pp. (0-399-21535-2) Reading Level: Grades 4–6. (BCCB D88) *Disability:* Cerebral palsy; Learning disabilities; Speech impairment

Eddie is in the sixth grade and has saved a $5 reward to buy a birthday present for his little sister. He takes it to school so his friend Gary can use it to pay for a troll that is on display at Gary's father's secondhand shop. The school bully chokes Eddie and steals his money before school. Eddie can not defend himself well because cerebral palsy affects his motor skills and speech. Eddie gives Gary his workbook assignment so the slow student can go out to recess. Gary offers to sneak the troll out of the store and let Eddie pay it off later.
    At home, Eddie's grown brothers encourage him, and he gets an anonymous loan for the present. The troll was sold, though, and Gary substitutes a brass dragon with glass wings. Gary did not notice that it was

worth $15 instead of $5. Eddie tries to earn more money by collecting cans and locates the bully's hideout in the woods.

To Eddie's sister, the brass dragon seems alive so she gives it back to Eddie. It gives Eddie some odd dreams, and when he takes it to school in his backpack, it comes alive and takes revenge on Eddie's teacher. Gary's father also gets a taste of the dragon's vengeance. The bully captures Eddie and ties him up in the hideout, but Eddie escapes. A fire destroys the woods, and Eddie fears it was the dragon's uncontrollable power. Instead, he finds out that the bully has confessed that the destruction is his own fault.

Gary, Eddie, and Eddie's sister return the dragon to the shop, and Gary's father is much nicer. Eddie decides to show his teacher what he is capable of by winning a composition contest. When he is chosen as a finalist, he refuses an offer to have someone else read his work in the competition. When it is Eddie's turn, he takes a conversational tone with the audience and announces:

> "Mine's real short." They all laughed. "But you're going to have to listen hard, because I don't speak that clearly. Okay? . . . "
> "Now I'm a slow sort of guy. You've all seen me walk down the hall; so you know that. And lots of times people don't have patience enough to let me finish what I want to say, but when I read a book, boy, am I fast. Just call me speedy, when I read a book . . ."

Eddie wins the competition and uses the prize money to buy the dragon back.

Analysis: This is a pleasant fantasy with suspense and several clearly drawn characters. Gary's father exploits his son, yet demeans him as a "dummy" and is biased against Eddie because of both boys' disabilities. Eddie's teacher is not tolerant of his presence in her class, and even when he does well in class participation, she does not listen closely enough to understand his correct responses. When Eddie suggests that he could help Gary with social studies, the teacher responds, "If you researched the answers and Gary wrote them down, I'd get good work out of both of you." Since Eddie's right hand is not affected by cerebral palsy, he has to agree that his handwriting is bad and Gary's is neat. This comment by his teacher shows that she is not totally unreasonable about her student's special needs.

When his plans to go to college and become a psychologist are challenged by his teacher's low expectations due to his unclear speech, Eddie applies himself to the contest. The goal of reading his own composition also helps Eddie see that his schoolmates accept him because the prize is awarded by popular vote. This is a good contrast to the scenes with the cruel bully, when Eddie knows his disability makes him an easy victim.

Perceptions about other people's reactions to Eddie can be supersensitive, because the book is written from his point of view. Eddie describes his teacher as mean, revises that to crabby, then surmises that she does not like teaching or is afraid of people with disabilities.

> Eddie had seen visitors look scared when they came into the Center for the Disabled. They'd sneak looks at kids in wheelchairs and braces, with droopy heads and spastic limbs and hands and feet that turned backwards, and draw away if any got too close.

The cover painting of a glowing dragon beside Eddie's bed features a slender boy with his left side in the foreground. It is very inviting and conforms to what you find out about Eddie, yet it does not stress the disabled boy's differences either. This title is highly recommended, and, like *Golden Daffodils,* offers a view of mainstreaming for a child who has to cope with cerebral palsy.

■ Aiello, Barbara, and Jeffrey Shulman. *It's Your Turn at Bat.* Illus. by Loel Barr. Twenty-First Century, 1988. 48pp. (0-941477-02-9) Reading Level: Grades 3–5.
Disability: Cerebral palsy

Mark Riley is a fifth-grader who wishes he did not have to write a report about sewing machines. He would much rather help a girl from class learn about Roberto Clemente for her sports writing topic. After talking to a woman at the senior center about the center's sewing machine, Mark moves from his wheelchair to a seat where he can guide the material while the woman uses her hands to treadle for him.

The Wildcats need new baseball jerseys to boost morale, and, as designated hitter and fund-raising chairman, Mark is deeply involved with the team. When the collected jersey money is missing, the team members yell at Mark and even at his twin brother, Michael. Mark knows it is his responsibility as team manager to handle problems and is dismayed to be the prime theft suspect. Mark's scheme to get the jerseys in time for the game by having the senior center lady make substitutes falls through. The day of the game, pizza delivery shirts with machine-appliqued letters serve as uniforms, thanks to Mark's adult friends.

When the money is found in Mark's pack and his classmate gives an excellent report on her favorite sports personality, Mark realizes that he should not be so hasty in jumping to conclusions or judging other people.

Analysis: This title from the Kids on the Block series features Mark Riley, a character developed for an award-winning puppet presentation. These stories involve children from the same school and baseball team, so other special needs are casually referred to from time to time. The illustrations use strong black line drawings in cartoon style. Mark's headgear and his lightweight wheelchair that he refers to as his "cruiser" are consistently represented in the drawings.

Some things introduced casually into the story are intended to raise questions. Conversation-style answers are provided at the end of the story.

For example, Mark emerges as a sports fan and a member of the team. So a number of inevitable questions, including "But how can you play baseball in a wheelchair?" and "Can you play other sports?" are answered in the back of the book.

Important insights are clearly and sometimes humorously conveyed by Mark's responses to these questions. "The words that we use to describe other people always matter. Words can hurt just as much as sticks and stones. They can give you the wrong idea about people before you even have a chance to meet them—and that can be a real handicap."

The Kids on the Block series titles are designed to provide helpful words and positive perceptions by vicarious exposure to various conditions. Though this informational aspect and the slim format restrict well-rounded characterization in the story, they enhance the book's usefulness with readers who are just starting longer fiction.

■ Aiello, Barbara, and Jeffrey Shulman. *Trick or Treat or Trouble.* Illus. by Loel Barr. Twenty-First Century, 1989. 56pp. (0-941477-07-X) Reading Level: Grades 4–6.
Disability: Epilepsy

Brian and his friends take up a dare to trick or treat at the scariest house in town. Recent construction at the spooky place has stirred up stories of bodies in the basement. In addition, a sign announces that the mansion is operating as a funeral home. On Halloween night, Brian is deserted on the porch by his pals, but his hostess gives him hot chocolate. Police officers return with the frightened trick or treaters, and the woman gives the overimaginative children a tour of her business.

"This is where they make monsters!"

"No, it isn't," Mrs. Fremont replied firmly. "This is not some monster movie, and I am not a modern-day Dr. Frankenstein." She shook her head just a little bit, as if to say, "Where do they get these ideas?" Then, she continued: "We treat a body with great care and respect. I believe that when a person dies, the spirit moves on to a new life. But it's hard to say goodbye to a spirit. Since the body is all that's left, we prepare it for a last goodbye."

There is a power failure, but the children regain their composure and bid farewell to their hostess. That night, Brian sleeps peacefully with the light off.

Analysis: The Kids on the Block series features a section of questions and answers at the end to clarify references made throughout the story. Brian mentions that he uses medication to treat his epilepsy and that some people are frightened of his condition. His friends are aware of his special health needs, and they accommodate them. Examples of what should and should not be done for a person experiencing a seizure are given. Brian answers the question "How did you find out you had epilepsy?" by recounting that he had a seizure in his second-grade classroom, which was followed by an electroencephalogram.

For students just beyond beginning reading, this could be an independent experience with a mildly suspenseful holiday story. It does try too hard to give insights on the unwarranted fear of death in American culture. Since the story is already strained to include Brian's asides about his physical impairment, calculated elements like the sexual and ethnic balance of the group of friends make it more purposive than other titles in the series. Like the rest of the series, though, it is a sensitively constructed exposure to a young protagonist with a specific disability.

■ Alcock, Vivien. *Travelers by Night.* Delacorte, 1985. 182pp. (LB 0-385-29406-9) Reading Level: Grades 4–6.
Disability: Cerebral hemorrhage

When the circus closes and an elderly animal trainer has a stroke, two children kidnap his elephant to save its life. *See full annotation* Chapter 7: Various Disabilities.

■ Anderson, Mary. *Catch Me, I'm Falling in Love.* Delacorte, 1985. 134pp. (0-385-29409-3) Reading Level: Grades 7–9. (BCCB D85)
Disability: Brain damage; Orthopedic impairment

Amelia has been in a cast, but when it comes off she still has a limp. Her mother suggests she see a chiropractor, but Amelia is not very interested until she finds that the practitioner is young, handsome, and kind. Amelia falls in love instantly, convinces herself that the affection is mutual, and confesses her feelings. She is gently rebuffed, then discovers that a teacher at her school has a crush on her.

Analysis: Chiropractic information is not very gracefully integrated into the text or dialogue. The plot deals with the frequent problem of romantic fantasies initiated by a patient's interaction with the health care provider. The element about a teacher's crush is less credible. Also, Amelia's father is recuperating from a brain injury, which is a novel complication for such a slight story.

■ Auch, Mary Jane. *Kidnapping Kevin Kowalski.* Holiday, 1990. 124pp. (0-8234-0815-9) Reading Level: Grades 5–8. (KR 15 Ap90; BCCB My90) *Disability:* Orthopedic impairment

Kevin returns from a rehabilitation program after a serious bike accident. His mother is overprotective and Kevin seems so passive that his best friends, Ryan and Mooch, are startled by the change in him. They hope he will still attend scout camp, so they determine that an overnight stay in the woods may help Kevin regain his independent spirit. The friends kidnap Kevin so that his mother cannot proscribe their adventure. While swimming in dangerous waters, Kevin saves his friends. The overnight disappearance affects all three families and makes a clear point to Mrs. Kowalski that Kevin needs more freedom to fully heal.

Analysis: Good story telling and distinct characterization of the boys and their families make this a recommended selection. Though Ryan and Mooch are loyal to Kevin, their former leader, they are anoyed by his new limitations. Ryan determines that Kevin needs to be removed from his mother's babying restrictions and forciably placed into the challenging environment of the woods—hence the kidnapping. The author foreshadows that Kevin is more capable than he knows, so readers will accept the results of Ryan's and Mooch's gamble with their friend's safety.

Youngsters want their friendships to be unchanging and generally believe that adults are too cautious, so this book contains an accurate presentation of juvenile ethics. If Kevin's mother had placed new restrictions on her son based on medical advice rather than parental nearsightedness, his friends' actions would have been irresponsible. This story shows a difference between the way a disability can be accommodated and the way it can become a handicap.

As presented, the boys' drastic solution and its unplanned test of Kevin's abilities constitute a humorous, appealing story for middle-graders. The title and a cover that shows an all-terrain vehicle with the boys crossing a creek will also appeal to students who are looking for some action in their books.

■ Baird, Thomas. **Where Time Ends.** Harper & Row, 1988. 230pp. (LB 0-06-020360-9) Reading Level: Grades 8–10. (KR 15 O88)
Disability: Orthopedic impairment

In the near future, biological warfare isolates three boys and a girl in the Adirondack Mountains. Doug and his best friend, Loop, are both interested in Ernie as a girlfriend. Ernie is sometimes exasperated by her younger brother, Orin. His injury in a motorcycle wreck has made him bitter about his limitations. All four are backpacking and reliant on Doug's knowledge of the wilderness to survive. He leads them to find his grandfather, a local environmentalist.

They meet Ed, who is a sympathetic listener to the temperamental Doug. Ed's folk music soothes Orin. Loop and Ernie pair off and have a night together. The group finds evidence that some biological species will survive the recent conflict.

Analysis: The twist on a nuclear holocaust setting is that Russia and America have abandoned one type of weapon, only to escalate to another type of global threat. This future view may have a woman president but seems a rehash of bleak stories we have seen before. Orin's physical and emotional needs are featured to showcase Ernie's devotion and Ed's earthy, pot-mellowed qualities. Consider this for large collections in which William Sleator's *House of Stairs* is popular.

■ Beatty, Patricia. **Be Ever Hopeful, Hannalee.** Morrow, 1988. 216pp. (0-688-07502-9) Reading Level: Grades 5–8. (BCCB N88)
Disability: Amputation

In 1865, the Civil War ends, and Hannalee Reed and her young brother, Jem, return to Georgia from the Yankee mill where they have been working. Hannalee's older brother, Davey, returns from a Yankee hospital, "but he wasn't the Davey Reed we used to know. This one was thin and ragged and hungry and—worst of all—one-armed." Davey intends to make a new life for his family in Atlanta. Hard times in the struggling major city disillusion Davey. He cannot compete for carpentry work due to his disability, and drinking comes easy to a wounded veteran. He begins working for a rough character named Garson Redmond.

In the North, Hannalee was disguised as a boy named "Hannibal Sanders." A Union officer comes into the Atlanta dry goods shop that Hannalee works at and frightens her with questions about Hannibal.

Later, she finds out he is the son of the lady Hannalee had boarded with. The Yankee mother had her son trace "Hannibal," and he found out from Davey's lost love, Hannalee's true identity. Davey is accused of murder, but a black girl named Delie witnessed the event, and Hannalee persuades her to speak up about Davey's innocence. Since Redmond was involved with the violent "Regulators," Delie has reason to be afraid of reprisal if she comes forward. Henry Brackett is so impressed with Hannalee's brave ways and pretty looks that he promises he will come courting her some day. Hannalee thinks that is as romantic as Davey going to inform his mourning girlfriend that he is not dead.

Analysis: Hannalee's and her mother's resentments toward Yankees are worn down by the kindness of their employers and the justice of the new order, which allows a black to speak in court. Hannalee is true to her well-drawn character from *Turn Homeward, Hannalee.* Davey's character is far less developed. When compared with Miz Amalie's determination to turn the few skills she had from her privileged youth into a candy store business, Davey's discouragement and long adjustment to telegraph key operating as a substitute vocation look self-centered. He has Hannalee send his sweetheart a letter that says he is dead, and the girl goes into deep mourning. When Hannalee gives evidence that the faithful lover is in failing health, Davey goes to see her. Hannalee thinks, "Look at Davey's and Rosellen's love. That could be a ballad." This really is Hannalee's story, and her heroic determination is developed when her brother's social role as provider is undermined by his disability. This historical novel has extensive author notes about the period and will serve large collections well.

■ Beckman, Delores. *Who Loves Sam Grant?* Dutton, 1983. 160pp. (0-525-44055-0) Reading Level: Grades 6–8. (BCCB Mr83)
Disability: Orthopedic impairment

Samantha was happy with her football star boyfriend, Bogie, but when he jilts her, she is ready to do anything to get him back. Her best friend has problems with an alcoholic mother, who attempts suicide, but Sam is too preoccupied with Bogie and a stolen parrot he gives her to be much of a friend. The boy next door, who had polio, wins Samantha's regard with his cheerfulness and courage. Sam realizes that she has been used by Bogie to cover for him with lies.

Analysis: This dated little story is told in a lively style, with good dialogue. The relationships touch on ethical concepts, friendship values, and overcoming one's handicaps, but in a patterned plot. This would be an additional choice for large collections.

■ Bellairs, John. *The Mummy, the Will, and the Crypt.* Illus. by Edward Gorey. Dial/Dutton, 1983. 168pp. (LB 0-8037-0030-X) Reading Level: Grades 5–6. (BCCB Ap84)
Disability: Brain tumor

John decides to solve the puzzle of a lost will and win the $10,000 reward. At 12 years of age, he is burdened by worries about his father, who has been shot down in Korea and remains missing. Also, Grandmother has just had surgery for a brain tumor and may require a second operation. This very real situation is then peppered with clues about the will and with fantasy elements such as a murdering witch who controls an evil force.

Analysis: Grandmother's condition is critical to John's motivation, but not the plot. Fans of *The Curse of the Blue Figurine* might want to read more about these characters in this sequel, full of action and arcane objects. Unfortunately, they will also encounter lots of coincidence, contrivance, and stereotyped characters.

■ Berry, James. *A Thief in the Village and Other Stories.* Orchard, 1988. 148pp. (LB 0-531-08345-4) Reading Level: Grades 6–10. (BCCB MS88)
Disability: Orthopedic impairment

Nine short stories set in Jamaica portray young characters and village life. In one, prejudices against a reclusive man with one foot make him the prime suspect in repeated thefts. Two children watch their coconut grove and expose the true poacher, revising their opinion of the disabled man in the process. Another tale features the difficulties that a boy with a pet mongoose faces at the hands of bullies. He is an easy target because of a mobility impairment.

Analysis: Complex family relationships and vivid language make this anthology stand out. The portrayals are insightful and realistic in terms of the subsistence society and island culture presented. Recommended because it can broaden the world outlook of young audiences.

■ Blackwood, Gary L. *The Dying Sun.* Atheneum, 1989. 213pp. (0-689-31482-5) Reading Level: Grades 8–12. (BL 15 Je89)
Disability: Amputation

In the twenty-first century, glaciers and posttechnological decay change the United States so much that rural life takes place only in harsh outposts. Deciding to risk life on a farm in Missouri, the Simpsons leave their 16-year-old son, James, to his "comfort" in the hot, terrorist-ridden city that spreads along the Mexican border. James's friend Robert's foot is blown off by a bomb, military draft is instituted, the boys trek across barren country with Sunny Shanahan, and they try to adapt to hard work and long winters. Robert sets off for a more temperate area, Sunny is attacked by wild dogs, and James gets to know his cousin, Judith. James stays to make the best of a bleak future.

Analysis: Futuristic stories often focus more on the scientific and social details of their story, but James does grow as a character. Robert's physical loss helps make up the boy's mind about traveling, and Robert makes a realistic (if not admirable) choice about living where the living is easier though still dangerous. This supplemental science fiction work with its message about the value of working the land may be useful in some collections.

■ Blos, Joan. *Brothers of the Heart.* Scribner, 1985. 162pp. (0-684-18452-4) Reading Level: Grades 7–9. (BCCB Ja86)
Disability: Orthopedic impairment

Shem Perkins is crippled, yet accompanies his family from New England to Michigan in the 1830s. When his father speaks harshly to him, Shem runs away. He serves as a clerk in Detroit, then joins a wilderness expedition. A Native American woman becomes his loving friend. She is elderly and recalls her long-dead husband as a "brother of the heart" to Shem's maturing character. By the time she dies, Shem returns to his family, strengthened by arduous frontier life.

Analysis: Written in a mannered style and using historical speech patterns, the text can sound forced. The use of letters and journal entries helps give a good picture of a sympathetic protagonist. Shem overcomes his handicap and becomes self-reliant, strong, sensible, and compassionate. A historical, and somewhat idealized, view of disability is provided in this work by a Newbery Medal winner.

■ Bradford, Ann, and Kal Gezi. *The Mystery of the Missing Dogs.* Illus. by Mina Gow McLean. Child's World, 1980. 24pp. (0-89565-143-2) Reading Level: Grades 2–3.
Disability: Orthopedic impairment

A rural neighborhood is upset because many dogs are missing from their homes. Several young children scout around for clues, visiting their new friend at his grandparents' home. The friend uses a wheelchair, but the others have gotten used to it in order to include him in their activities. All the children go out to a shed, where they discover many dogs and the men who hoped to profit from kidnapping pets. When the children get rewards, they give the money to the boy to buy a motor for his wheelchair. "If we hadn't come back to see you, we'd never have found the dogs."

Analysis: A direct response to legal compliance and early mainstreaming markets, this slight story features an artificially balanced cast. If this title is already in a collection, it will be a comfortable read for students who like both *Nate the Great* and *"Something Queer . . ."* mysteries but are not ready for Corbett's *"Trick"* books.

■ Bridgers, Sue Ellen. **Permanent Connections.** Harper & Row, 1987. 320pp. (LB 0-06-020712-4) Reading Level: Grades 7–10.
Disability: Emotional disturbance; Orthopedic impairment

Uncle Fairlee recuperates from a hip replacement operation with help from his nephew, Rob. *See full annotation* Chapter 6: Emotional Disturbances.

■ Bunting, Eve. **The Wall.** Illus. by Ronald Himler. Houghton, 1990. 32pp. (0-395-51588-2) Reading Level: Grades K–2. (KR 15 Mr90; BCCB MS90)
Disability: Amputation

On a visit to the Vietnam War Memorial with his father, a little boy finds his grandfather's name and leaves a picture of himself at the base of the wall. Other visitors to the memorial include a teacher, her class, and a disabled veteran.

Analysis: Simple text conveys information and impressions related to the memorial. Watercolor illustrations represent the characters and the mementos left at the wall with quiet dignity. The legless veteran is one of the strong images that make this book an outstanding choice for picture book collections.

■ Burns, Peggy. **Nothing Ever Stays the Same.** Lion, 1989. 128pp. (paper 0-7459-1249-4) Reading Level: Grades 6–9. (BCCB S89)
Disability: Cerebral hemorrhage

Sandie's parents are divorced, and she lives with her grandparents. Gram has a stroke, and Sandie goes to live with her mother. There is a lot of anger and distrust in the relationship. Sandy relies on faith in Jesus Christ to help face her problems.

Analysis: Sandie is not given much opportunity to interact with her grandmother after the stroke. It is clear that she is being sent to the family member who will not find her presence too inconvenient. Sandie's personal commitment to Christian principles does not bend the plot line with fatalism or optimism, but the story maintains its subtle strengths of characterization.

■ Caseley, Judith. ***Apple Pie and Onions.*** Illus. by Judith Caseley. Greenwillow, 1988. 32pp. (0-688-06763-8) Reading Level: Grades K–3. (KR 15 Ja88)
Disability: Geriatric impairment

Rebecca enjoys her grandmother's stories of her immigrant childhood. They walk through Grandma's neighborhood happily until the woman stops by a friend's wheelchair and chatters in a foreign language. Rebecca is mortified and turns away, insisting that there be no more stories. Grandma tells one more about the time her father embarrassed her on the subway. He was wearing dirty work clothes and carrying a sack of onions, so Grandma pretended she did not know him. Once home, Grandma's father kissed her, and her mother used the onions in a stew.

Rebecca and her grandma get home and use the apples they have bought to make pie.

Analysis: Part of Rebecca's discomfort stems from the amused reaction of strangers who watch her grandmother's animated conversation with an elderly friend. Realistically, part of it is also from Rebecca's uncertainty about being associated with Hattie, who must use her wheelchair to get about the old neighborhood. Hattie is comfortable, Grandma is comfortable, and by the end of the book Rebecca is comfortable too. What a nice way to help children broaden their judgmental little opinions. Recommend this title for most picture book collections, because its stylized pictures reinforce the unsentimental story well.

■ Caseley, Judith. ***Harry and Willy and Carrothead.*** Illus. by Judith Caseley. Greenwillow, 1991. 24pp. (LB 0-688-09493-7) Reading Level: Grades PS–2. (KR 1 F91; BCCB Ap91)
Disability: Missing limbs

Harry was born with one hand, something his parents accepted in their wonderful baby. At 4, Harry begins using a prosthesis, and at 5, he handles new schoolmates' curiosity in a friendly way. When Harry senses how much Oscar is distressed by the nickname "Carrothead," he intervenes.

Analysis: In this direct and nicely illustrated story, Harry is clearly just one of the kids. The way in which empathy can strengthen a friendship is made evident. Harry's parents' attitude sets an accepting tone that readers will absorb. Because Harry is described as a good ball player, maybe fans of Olympic gold medalist Jim Abbott will project a future in pro sports for this fictional character, so effectively introduced.

■ Cheatham, Karyn Follis. *The Best Way Out*. Harcourt, 1982. 168pp. (o.p.) Reading Level: Grades 6–10.
Disability: Orthopedic impairment; Learning disabilities

Haywood Romby had expected to be the only high school graduate in his family, until he was bused to Gill Memorial Junior High and had to repeat seventh grade. Getting up for the 16-mile ride is exhausting and boring; often he does not bother catching the bus at its first stop near his home. One day he catches the other bus, and the tips of two fingers get cut off in the bus door due to a fight with Phillip. Haywood is so distressed about the appearance of his hand, his dread of the bus, and the principal's comment that he should use a tutor to catch up in school, that the 13-year-old ditches more and more, fights Phillip again, and gets suspended for drinking enough "warm-up" whiskey to pass out on the bus.

Mrs. Bennett has developed an auxiliary education program at Gill called SHOP—Student High (School) Orientation Program. Haywood resents it, because his friend Leon was placed in "special ed even though he got his glasses. Say he's a slow learner. He's the best catcher on the church softball team!" But when Mrs. Bennett visits the Romby home, Haywood's father agrees that Haywood, too, should try the special class or just drop out and get a job. Mr. Romby has only a sixth-grade education himself, and Haywood agrees to take a part-time janitorial position to learn how an education can lead to "work without sweat." Haywood's stepmother had a son who died after dropping out of school and getting involved with drugs and street violence. Mr. Romby says Haywood had better not hurt her again that way.

Haywood is surprised to see Leon and the other students succeeding at assignments and completing projects with confidence and enthusiasm that lots of the kids in regular classes lack. He is still angry though and creates a collage caricature of Mrs. Bennett. When she compliments him on its artistic quality and enters it in an art show, Haywood is stunned. Haywood is asked to transfer to a new SHOP program closer to his home, makes friends, and earns special privileges like going to a party at Mrs. Bennett's home. His collage wins honorable mention in a citywide art show, and he rethinks the way he has been "trying to live up to a bad reputation instead of living it down." Haywood is impressed by what Mrs. Bennett and her husband have achieved academically and financially, and he promises to go to summer school and improve his grades enough to skip ahead to his proper grade level.

Analysis: Haywood's adjustment problems are complex, and this is a deep portrayal that can foster cross-cultural understanding. From the white, middle-class point of view, what could be bad about enrolling black students in a school where teachers, facilities, and academic progress have proved superior to an inner-city campus? Plenty, according to Haywood, and the physical stress of a 16-mile ride, coupled with loss of status when he could not do the course work his age mates were succeeding at, was just the beginning. His injured hand and his foiled efforts to hide the disfigured digits compose an emotional blow, for he learns to fear the bus and all the failure it represents. Depression is Haywood's real ailment once the bandages come off his hand. "It seemed that sleep was his biggest interest. He couldn't get enough of it." Since Haywood allows his slight physical loss to "cripple" him, the SHOP experience is ironically suited to his needs. One teacher had warned him, "don't use that as another excuse to slack off around here. Your grades are low and there's no excuse for it. So if you think anyone at Gill owes you something because of what happened, think again."

The portrayal of Leon is brief but provides insights about special education and mainstreaming since "Gill hadn't had a special ed class until the busing started." That implied slur on the abilities of "inner-city" students is sensitively dealt with in this novel.

■ Christian, Mary Blount. ***Growin' Pains.*** Macmillan, 1985. 180pp. (0-02-718490-0) Reading Level: Grades 5–9. (BCCB Ja86)
Disability: Brain damage

Ginny Ruth, at 12 years old, is determined to escape her bleak life in Clemmons, Texas, of 1947. She blames her "Maw" for being so harsh and stingy that her merry, fun-loving father ran off three years earlier. On Christmas Eve, she overcomes her aversion to Mr. Billy Gaither's spastic walk, shakes, and drooling long enough to wish him "Merry Christmas." He returns the kindness with small Christmas treats, and a friendship develops. Books from another neighbor, Miss Marnie, widen Ginny Ruth's outlook, and she starts to view Maw and rural life in Clemmons with new eyes. Her poetry is kept in a notebook, and though her hard-working mother does not understand Ginny Ruth's need to write, she does recognize her need to dream of education and of travel beyond Clemmons.

When Ginny Ruth becomes ill from multiple bee stings, she is cared for in the home of her maternal grandparents. That relationship had been severed when Maw married a boy from out of town, but Ginny Ruth helps mend the rift. Ginny Ruth also learns that her father took all Maw's savings with him, and she gains new insight about blending a free-spirited temperament from Paw with Maw's practical nature. Ginny Ruth publishes her first piece in a newspaper, and Maw gives her daughter earnings from picking cotton so she can establish a college fund.

Analysis: The circumstances of Mr. Billy Gaither's injury are curious: he was kicked in the head by a cow soon after returning home from World War I. The first descriptions of his motor impairments are harsh because they are Ginny Ruth's perceptions, and she associates losing her father with the day she was punished for saying, "I wonder what terrible sin Mr. Billy has committed to be visited upon by such wrath." But Ginny Ruth also recalls her mother's words as well as the "fearful switching: 'A man's got his pride, Ginny Ruth. Even a man as tormented as Mr. Billy wants to do for himself what he can.' " These sensitive observations balance well with the young girl's early impressions and her friends' ridicule of Mr. Billy's mannerisms. The first poem revealed in the plot is:

> Crippled man and half-growed girl,
> We're the same, aren't we?
> Trapped in unloved bodies,
> We both need to be free.

Sometimes, the regional details slow the story, but this protagonist wants to be a writer, so making such observations helps define her character. Ginny Ruth finds a satisfying outlet for her restlessness and talent, thanks to interaction with Miss Marnie and Mr. Billy Gaither. The mutual regard that builds between the man with brain damage and the fatherless girl is clear when she shares her poetry with him and he indicates that it helps him "walk right—inside." Gaining a mature view of Mr. Billy also helps Ginny Ruth understand things that her mother has always done or said, that used to seem too practical or uncompromising to her daughter. A fine selection for most collections.

■ Christian, Mary Blount. *Mystery at Camp Triumph.* Whitman, 1986. 128pp. (0-8075-5366-2) Reading Level: Grades 4–6.
Disability: Muscular dystrophy

A boy with muscular dystrophy keeps his mental and physical "wheels" turning to help solve the mystery of camp accidents. *See full annotation* Chapter 5: Visual Impairments.

■ Corcoran, Barbara. *Child of the Morning.* Atheneum, 1982. 112pp. (0-689-30876-0) Reading Level: Grades 6–9. (BCCB Je82)
Disability: Epilepsy

Susan Bishop was injured in a volleyball game and has had "little spells" of unconsciousness and occasional falls in the year since her concussion. The people in her small town are unwilling to hire her for the summer before her junior year in high school, but she gets work doing odd jobs at the local theater. She is asked to be in three dance numbers in an upcoming production but fears the headaches that precede her spells are increasing. Her doctor, who is retiring soon, has prescribed only some pain relief. During a rehearsal, Susan blacks out, falls, and is treated by the new doctor in town, who refers her to a neurologist in Boston. It takes three months to find a medication that will control the seizures without severe side effects. Susan is relieved to know she can deal with her condition, and she decides to continue in dance.

Analysis: Sketchy characterizations combine with a plot line that depends on an unskilled doctor and unassertive parents in this novel. Once Susan is relieved of her euphemistic "spells" and given the honest terms of "epilepsy" and "seizures" to deal with, appropriate action can be taken to accommodate her physical needs. Susan chooses a career in dance, so her adjustment is nicely realized.

■ Corcoran, Barbara. *I Am the Universe.* Atheneum, 1986. 136pp. (0-689-31208-3) Reading Level: Grades 5–8. (BCCB D86)
Disability: Brain tumor

Kit is 12 when her interest in writing focuses on a contest. Her third-grade brother is failing school in spite of a high IQ. Her mother's headaches are caused by a brain tumor. When their mother becomes hospitalized for surgery, Kit and her older brother motivate their gifted sibling to get A's by paying him. The little boy wants to buy his mother a gift, so he does the assignments he used to ignore.

The stress of wondering about Mother's condition and Kit's disappointment in being named runner-up for the contest tempt her to throw eggs at cars and houses. The police and Kit's father take action, and Kit is punished. She makes prayerful vows and spends time "ESPing the surgeon to get it right." Mother's tumor is benign, and the family is relieved. Kit's interview with an author is helpful in showing Kit that she should write from her own experience. Mother comes home from the hospital, and Kit is thanked for helping the family through some hard weeks.

Analysis: Kit narrates her stress-filled story and includes many clever observations about herself and her family. The baby sister, gifted brother, and best friend are clearly delineated characters. Mother is defined by Kit's worries about the situation and her memories of better times. When mother's headaches give the woman a "dreamy little smile . . . I wondered if the pills were habit-forming. What if she got addicted?" Also, Kit faces her fears about her mother's appearance and any changes that might have taken place because of the surgery.

The emotional tension is well examined, and Kit's contest story comes out of her emotional turmoil, so it is believably less successful than a two-year-old story that the visiting author preferred. The cover of the book shows a very young-looking Kit in three views, guarding the home where her father and siblings are. Its mystical feel is close to Kit's philosophy once she decodes gifted Daniel's comment: "I Am the Universe." Recommended for most collections, especially for Anastasia Krupnik followers.

■ Crutcher, Chris. *The Crazy Horse Electric Game.* Greenwillow, 1987. 160pp. (0-688-06683-6) Reading Level: Grades 7–12. (BCCB My87) *Disability:* Neurological impairment; Speech impairment

Willie Weaver is an athletic 16-year-old who gains particular status in Coho, Montana, as champion pitcher against the Crazy Horse Electric team. Willie has a waterskiing accident, is resuscitated by his girlfriend, and is left to cope with speech and motor impairments from the resultant brain damage. He uses a cane to return to school after two months and avoids speaking because it takes him too long to form the words he is thinking of. His identity as a champ is undermined so much that in six months, his relationships with family and friends decay to the point that he runs away.

Arriving in San Francisco, Willie is befriended by Lacey, a black bus driver and pimp, who takes him home to Oakland and sends him to One More Last Chance (OMLC) High School. One night Willie hits Lacey with his cane to stop the pimp from beating Angel, his "whore." Willie stays on working at odd jobs for Lacey and is the hero of a gang-related fire.

Willie's interactions with André and Lisa, who are OMLC staff members, address his emotional needs, and he sees how bitter and paranoid he had been in Coho. He plays basketball and is offered a chance to try some "rehab things" with Lisa, who is writing a paper, and her boyfriend, Sammy, who teaches oriental disciplines such as T'ai Chi Ch'uan. After 18 months, Willie earns a Comeback Cowboy award and speaks well at his graduation, then goes home, unannounced. He learns that everyone thought he was dead, his parents have divorced, his mother has remarried, and his father is stuck in an alcoholic depression. Willie gets permission to enter his family's old home, goes to the room where his baby sister died of sudden infant death syndrome (SIDS) six years earlier, and then returns to Oakland.

Analysis: The author depends on an unlikely plot, yet avoids sentimentality in this tale of overcoming one's handicaps. The pat element of a near-illiterate, black pimp with a heart of gold offers a much weaker characterization than Willie's. Willie is adjusting not only to his physical impairments but also to the reactions of those around him and to his own, revised self-image. As a counterpart to Voigt's *Izzy, Willy-Nilly,* which portrays a girl cheerleader's realignment of expectations and relationships, Crutcher portrays a young male athlete's efforts to find a new life fit for the realities of his physical limitations and the social trials they cause him. Unlike Izzy, who puts a "good face" on her withdrawal and regrets, Willy's actions to heal himself put his loved ones at risk. He has to use Sammy's philosophy and André's advice to deal with his guilt about the changes back home.

It is clear that Willie's injury and his subsequent disappearance were not the first blows to his parents' marriage and that his baby sister's death from SIDS had not been addressed successfully in family counseling sessions. A "mythic" legacy of athletic prowess from Willie's grandfather and father turns into an emotional trap for Mr. Weaver, and after 18 months he becomes a "mean" drunk at the local bar.

Readers may find Willie's omniscient, present-tense flashbacks involving enough so that they will accept that he knows what other characters were experiencing or what they thought while he was unconscious. The tough dialogue and dramatic action have enough appeal to recommend this title despite its flaws.

■ Dank, Gloria Rand. *The Forest of App.* Greenwillow, 1983. 163pp. (0-688-02315-0) Reading Level: Grades 4–6. (BCCB Ja84)
Disability: Orthopedic impairment

The forest of App is a fantasy world, where a dwarf, elf, and witch-child find a crippled boy. He is named Nob, and he comes to live in their cottage, hidden from dwellers of nearby villages. Creatures come and go in the forest, talking about various things. A unicorn needs to be rescued and protected from cruel hunters. The little group from the cottage is joined by an old wizard and assorted fantasy folk to drive the hunters away from the forest.

Analysis: Since crippled or blind outcasts are often mythic characters, Nob is in classic company among these magical folk. This promising fantasy delivers humor and wonder but is a bit crowded with characters for the slow-moving plot.

■ Dickinson, Peter. *Healer.* Delacorte, 1985. 184pp. (0-385-29372-0)
Reading Level: Grades 6–9. (BCCB My85)
Disability: Amputation; Various disabilities

Barry is 16 when he sets out to rescue his former schoolmate, Pinkie Proudfoot. She is only 10 but has the power to heal the people that visit the Foundation. Barry believes the procedures and rituals exploit Pinkie, but he is not sure whether it is all a fraud or not. He senses Pinkie's ability to strengthen people with her touch. He also learns that Pinkie's granddad is helped by Pinkie's ability, though he uses a wheelchair and is a double amputee: "Got what's called a phantom limb, young man. Went and stood on a land mine at Alamein. Came to the hospital and found the surgeons had been having a go at my legs, sawn off anything the mine had left. Left leg never got the message, though. Thinks it's still there. Bloody rum thing, the human mind. You're looking at a man that's haunted by his own left leg, supposed to be buried out in the sands of Egypt forty years back. Shut my eyes, and there it is. I can move it around, wiggle the toes—doing that now. Reach out and scratch my shin, only the bloody thing's not there and my hand goes clean through the itch."

Mr. Freeman manipulates the staff of the Foundation and the Harmony Sessions, but Barry feels that the man is convinced of the power of Pinkie's gift and relies on the organization of "the spheres" to protect Pinkie's "harmony flow."

When Barry gets evidence that Mr. Freeman is giving Pinkie drugs and has sent her mother to America to avoid interference, Barry makes a plan. Granddad helps them, but Mr. Freeman stops them. In a struggle with a guard dog, Barry wounds it, and it kills Mr. Freeman. Police investigators, journalists, and a social worker ply Barry with questions, but the important one he still cannot answer: "Did you ever see Pinkie heal anyone, Barry?"

Analysis: Both fantasy and adventure elements are blended in a powerful story. Characterizations are well-rounded, from the saintly Pinkie to her villainous stepfather. Pinkie knows that Barry has a violent alterego they both call Bear. Such an original story is fun to recommend, and the ambivalent ending regarding Pinkie's powers leaves readers with an occult shiver.

■ Dunlop, Eileen. *The Valley of the Deer.* Holiday, 1989. 139pp. (0-8234-0766-7) Reading Level: Grades 6–9. (BCCB N89)
Disability: Orthopedic impairment; Neurological impairment

When she is 13, Anne Farrar and her parents and older sister rent a home in Deer, Scotland. In 1953 the area is scheduled to be flooded so Anne's archaeologist parents spend a year excavating an ancient burial mound. They find a skeleton, and Anne finds an old family Bible in which she reads about Alice Jardyne, who died in 1726. A note indicates that Alice was "blotted out of the Book of Life," so Anne investigates in the cemetery and in local documents. She finds a charm stone and envisions Alice being hounded through a wood in her bare feet. Anne reads that "Alys" was accused of witchcraft in the "Parish of Deer." Anne gets upset when she is cast as a witch for entertainment purposes during the upcoming pagent highlighting local history.

Returning to studies at her private girls' school, Anne is distracted by Alice's terrifying fate and her parents' decision that she will board at school once they finish their work nearby. Anne writes her landlord, who is descended from Alice's family. His wife, Joscelyn, invites Anne to visit so the young woman can tell her about Alice. Joscelyn uses "a wheeled invalid chair" because she had polio seven years before. She asks Anne to call her Polly and confides that while recuperating from polio, she went through some family papers and found items that belonged to Alice.

"Alice's mother was the local wise woman, quite famous for her healing skills and she taught Alice. Alice Jardyne had a spinal deformity, she had a hump on her left shoulder, and a withered left arm. She was very well educated for a woman of her time, but she lived in a very superstitious age, and in an isolated, uncouth part of the world, where it was more than a disadvantage to be different from your neighbours—it was downright dangerous."

A storm makes Anne Polly's willing guest. Polly's husband, John, comes home and thanks Anne for the girl's stories that made Polly happy. That night, Anne reads Alice's spells for healing and finds one that used the charm stone found in the Grey Mound of Deer. It once cured "palsy," which Anne knows is the old word for polio.

After her performance as a witch in a slashed tartan makes her feel disloyal to Alice, Anne leaves the crowd to wait in Witches Cottage. While there, Alice's memories of Midsummer Eve flood Anne and the modern girl runs to the mound where the charm stone was found. Anne knows that she has experienced Alice's last moments, and this experience makes her uncomfortable with the nameless archaeological finds of her parents.

Polly tries to help Anne accept that the power of suggestion gave her vivid dreams of Alice, but Anne is convinced that the charm stone's power should be used to heal Polly. Their friendship suffers from Anne's persistent belief in the charm stone spell.

Anne gives the charm stone to her mother to inventory with the rest of the archaeological items. Her dread of boarding at school once her parents move is soothed by a plan to live with Polly for the three years remaining in her schooling. The minister tells Anne how Alice was freed by the courts but stoned by her neighbors, and Anne shifts her career choice from archaeology to medicine, because "There's a vaccine now, and in a few years there won't be any new cases of polio, thank goodness. But there are other illnesses where they haven't even begun to find cures. I think I'd like to have a part in finding them."

Analysis: Hints of supernatural awareness, hidden cupboards, and ancient artifacts add suspense and ambiguity to this novel. Polly's needs and emotional tension are incorporated into the story from Anne's early, romantic viewpoint, and then revised.

Believable or not, this is a compelling story with a fully developed cast of characters. It offers insight into two time periods and how differences in physical ability affected the lives of two women. Highly recommended, this has an attractive cover that shows Anne's first vision of desperate Alice as the background to Anne's profile while she examines the charm stone in her own palm.

■ Evernden, Margery. *The Kite Song.* Lothrop, 1984. 192pp. (0-688-01200-0) Reading Level: Grades 5–8.
Disability: Emotional disturbance; Amputation; Muteness

War veteran Clem makes no mention of his artificial leg, so his young cousin is surprised to see it one morning before Clem gets dressed. *See full annotation* Chapter 6: Emotional Disturbances.

■ Eyerly, Jeannette. *Angel Baker, Thief.* Lippincott, 1984. 246pp. (LB 0-397-32097-3) Reading Level: Grades 7–9. (BCCB D84)
Disability: Paralysis; Cerebral palsy

Angel began stealing presents for her younger brother and sister because her father was gone and her mother was often ill. The habit grew until Angel had to enroll in a correctional institution and be on probation and assigned to foster care in the Gardiners' home. Angel finds friends but gets pressured into stealing something by the members of an exclusive "club." She is caught when she tries to return the item. Her court hearing includes the testimony of Tony, a boy who was involved, so the judge does not make Angel return to an institution. When Father finds a job in Colorado, he moves his family there for a happier future.

Analysis: One of the pressures in Angel's home situation is that her little sister has cerebral palsy. When she meets handsome Jurgen Crenshaw, she has no reason to expect that this rich boy, who uses braces and crutches, will lead her into more delinquent behavior. Jurgen's physical limitations are addressed by the specially constructed wing of his parents' house, but he fulfilled his need to rebel and control things by founding the Contra Mundum group. Since he is "against the world," it is not surprising that he selfishly abandons Angel even though he knew her record would make his "initiation" ritual a serious offense. Since the author focuses on Angel's case history rather than her characterization, other portrayals are a better first choice than this one.

■ Farish, Terry. *Why I'm Already Blue.* Greenwillow, 1989. 152pp. (0-688-09096-6) Reading Level: Grades 4–6. (SLJ O89)
Disability: Muscular dystrophy

Lucy is 12 when her older sister, Jane, goes away for nurses training. Their alcoholic father, James, and persevering mother, Dell, are always at odds. Lucy tries to smooth things between them, and her neighbor, Gus, offers supportive ideas and sympathetic insight. Gus uses a wheelchair and often tries to deflect people's attention with humor.

Gus's mother is protective of his health, but he takes risks with Lucy. They run away to a unique Thanksgiving gathering at Lucy's family's cabin. Jane is there with a foster child because she was overwhelmed by her studies. Another stranger, Lance, takes special interest in Gus's mother. James and Dell finalize their separation. Jane points out that Dell depends on Lucy to make family troubles bearable.

Analysis: The family dynamics at Lucy's home have been disruptive for years. Her friendship with Gus is so much a part of her life, that she takes his special needs for granted. She recalls in detail the day he got his first wheelchair. Lucy knows his routine so well that "She imagined Gus, after Teresa got him in his hospital bed with the help of a lift she could crank up. She would make Gus comfortable on his side and bend his knee the way he liked and switch on his tensor lamp so he could read."

In the course of this book, Lucy interprets some of Gus's coping behaviors and faces the debilitating progression of his disease. The changes in Lucy's life include her new awareness of Gus's unique struggle to be as active as possible. Most of the time, she knows Gus can accomplish what he needs to. Lucy tells Jane in a letter that there are steps at James's apartment, but Gus "probably will sweet-talk" the landlord "into building us a ramp so I don't have to haul Gus's chair up the steps." Characterizations have depth, and the small events of the story enable both Lucy and the reader to gain insight on interrelationships.

■ Fine, Anne. *The Granny Project.* Farrar, 1983. 167pp. (0-374-32763-7)
Reading Level: Grades 5–6. (BCCB O83)
Disability: Dementia

Natasha and Henry Harris have four children and care for Gran, who is
incontinent and at times irrational, demanding, capricious, and querulous.
The children make their own plan to avoid Gran's placement in one of
Great Britain's "homes" for the elderly. Their efforts are well intended,
but eventually they must strike a compromise with their parents. Gran dies
soon after the Harris adults and children design a pattern for sharing her
care at home.

Analysis: Many novels allow juvenile protagonists to exercise more
compassion and ingenuity than their parents in plots that deal with grandparents who need around-the-clock care. This undermines the characterizations of the parents in most cases. Here the tragic mother spouts prov-
erbs in Russian at her children, and the father emerges as a pushover. The
writing is adequate and the dialogue crisp, so large collections may want
this title for its portrayal of geriatric complications in a person's life and
family relationships.

■ First, Julia. *The Absolute, Ultimate End.* Franklin Watts, 1985. 156pp.
(0-531-10075-8) Reading Level: Grades 6–8.
Disability: Epilepsy

Maggie Thayer overcomes her negative reactions to the special students at
her school and campaigns for funds to continue the mainstreaming program. *See full annotation* Chapter 5: Visual Impairments.

■ Fox, Mem. *Wilfrid Gordon McDonald Partridge.* Illus. by Julie Vivas.
Kane-Miller, 1985. 32pp. (0-916291-04-9) Reading Level: Grades PS–2.
Disability: Dementia

Wilfrid Gordon McDonald Partridge lives next door to a nursing home
and makes friends with all of the boarders there. He especially likes
96-year-old "Miss Nancy Alison Delacourt Cooper because she has four
names just as he did." He shares secrets with Miss Nancy, and when his
parents call her a "poor old thing" who has "lost her memory," Wilfrid
sets out to find some for her.

Each of the boarders describes a memory differently, so Wilfrid selects
gifts for Miss Nancy that match all of their abstract terms. Miss Nancy
examines the gifts, one by one. "What a dear, strange child to bring me

all these wonderful things," thinks Miss Nancy. Then she starts to remember.

Each item—a warm egg, a shell, a medal, a puppet, and a football—triggers a memory for Miss Nancy to share with Wilfrid. "And the two of them smiled and smiled because Miss Nancy's memory had been found again by a small boy, who wasn't very old either."

Analysis: This is a wonderful little story of intergenerational friendship. Wilfrid does not view Miss Nancy as a "poor old thing" and sets out to give her a memory or two because his parents say that is what she has lost. If you need to examine the emotions of a child who may be worried about behavior changes due to severe memory loss, use *Always Gramma* or *Something for Grandpa.*

For read-aloud entertainment, this book has large spreads, amusing figures, a variety of colors, and great white space in the layouts. It will also please one-on-one listeners because of the conspiratorial tone and the very young hero, who is able to do so very much for his good friend.

■ Fox, Paula. *One-Eyed Cat.* Bradbury, 1984. 216pp. (0-02-735540-3)
Reading Level: Grades 4–7. (BCCB O84)
Disability: Arthritis, rheumatoid; Cerebral hemorrhage

When Ned Wallis is 11, he lives with his father, his mother, and a bullying housekeeper named Mrs. Scallop. His mother is often bedridden by rheumatoid arthritis.

His father puts Uncle Hilary's gift—an air rifle—into the attic because he feels Ned is not old enough to use it. Ned sneaks the gun out of the house, fires at a shadow on the barn, and becomes convinced that someone at the window saw him do it. Guilt mounts for Ned when Mr. Sully, the man he does odd jobs for, says a gray, one-eyed cat that comes around was probably used for target practice by some boy. Mr. Sully feeds the cat, and Ned begins to join him in caring for the animal.

Uncle Hilary writes peculiar letters recounting his worldwide adventures and invites Ned for Christmas vacation, but Ned wants to stay with the cat and his mother, who grows ever weaker from her bouts with severe pain. Mr. Sully has a stroke; Ned finds him and then cares for the cat while the man is in the hospital. Ned becomes ill for several days and worries even more about the cat, then can not find the animal. Ned's mother is ill, Mr. Sully seems weaker every time Ned visits, and the boy makes a confession about the injured cat on the visit before Mr. Sully dies.

After Mrs. Wallis starts gold salt injections and regains the ability to walk around, Ned bumps into her at an abandoned house. They share confidences about guilty feelings and the strain of trying to live up to Reverend Wallis's goodness.

Analysis: A carefully crafted tale, and a Newbery Honor Book, *One-Eyed Cat* describes two physical disabilities. The time setting is the mid-1930s, and medical care for arthritis and stroke is accurately portrayed. Ned never expects Mr. Sully to recover but is a faithful visitor and friend. Other opinions of the time are examined when Ned covers his uneasiness about the cat by telling his mother how the insensitive Mrs. Scallop blames Mrs. Wallis's poor health on Ned's birth. He needs no reassurances but is told, "Your birth made me healthy. I felt so strong! It was a long, long time before I got sick. Life has its surprises."

Ned hears from his uncle, who plans to visit Father Damien at Molo-kai. Ned "had homework to do for Monday but what he was thinking about mostly was sickness, his mother's and Mr. Sully's. He didn't want a colony of lepers on his mind, too." This type of introspective honesty helps define Ned's character. Besides her physical weakness and courage in the face of so much pain, Ned's mother reveals an emotional complexity. She talks about the year she ran away to a cabin to deal with her unworthiness but returned to spare 3-year-old Ned from sleepless wandering through the house. Right and wrong, guilt and redemption, love, suffering, and death—they are all here for the reader who can take time to meet Fox's memorable cast.

■ Froelich, Margaret Walden. *Hide Crawford Quick.* Houghton, 1983. 168pp. (0-395-33884-0) Reading Level: Grades 5–8. (BCCB S83) *Disability:* Missing limbs; Mental retardation

During World War II, the Prayther family awaits the birth of a fifth child on Thanksgiving Day. Though it turns out to be their first boy, he is not named after the father, and Mother has trouble preparing the birth announcement. Twelve-year-old Gracie senses something is odd, but the middle child, Lizzie, is the first to say something. "How come this baby is broke? You should take him back, Mama, and get a different one." Crawford "had only one pink foot. His other leg ended just below the knee."

The house is in an uproar because of the new baby, and Gracie sees her parents' relationship become strained. At school, she is worried that her best friend may visit with a present for Crawford, so she withdraws from the friend and insults her. Older sister Roberta is desperate to keep her own friends from seeing the baby, demanding that Gracie "Hide Crawford, quick." Because Crawford's bed is in Gracie's room, she takes responsibility for soothing him. She also acts on her idea of taking the baby to a local woman known as a healer.

By Christmas, Roberta is adamant that the family not take Crawford anywhere, and they stay home from the holiday program at their one-room school. Gracie sneaks out to help a retarded friend, Burniss, to start her song for the program. If Gracie had not discovered that the slow girl could remember all the words of songs she heard on the radio, Burniss would not have been given any part in the program.

Crawford runs a high fever and goes into convulsions while the family is gathered for Christmas. Gracie yells at them to do something, accusing them of not caring about the baby enough to save his life. Her father responds to Gracie's apology about yelling by saying, "My God, Gracie, it's time somebody screamed at all of us."

Analysis: Any new baby can cause uproar in a household, but Crawford's arrival causes emotional strain for all the members. Apparently shock and self-pity motivate Mr. Prayther's extreme depression about his son's deformity. Guilt figures into Mrs. Prayther's reactions, and Gracie wonders if the family is being punished for not attending church regularly.

The first time Gracie sees Crawford's leg, she vomits. The uncomfortable weeks between Thanksgiving and Christmas are described from Gracie's point of view and filled with details of the period, like "ho-supporters," jewel tea ceramics, Toni home permanents, and wringer washers that can strip the buttons off a shirt. In historical fiction, use of period details and language needs to include enough information to give an understanding of what something is in context. This author slides over many elements of Gracie's life, creating confusion for readers removed from that era by three generations.

Daily events distract Gracie from the greater problem—Lizzie's fear of an aggressive chicken, Roberta's starting her period and getting a permanent, Father making plans for spring chickens—but they clutter the story somewhat. The clearest subplot consists of Gracie's efforts to help Burniss to do her best, when no one expected the mentally retarded girl to be able to contribute anything. Gracie's kindness to Burniss is forced at the beginning, but then, Burniss's singing ability intrigues Gracie. The teacher is quick to judge Burniss as incapable of any task, but Gracie sticks up for her.

Lizzie repeats a comment early in the story that " 'Burniss should be put away.' Gracie finished the thought in her own head. It means there's something wrong with you and you won't do in the world, so they shut you up someplace." Emotionally, the Praythers were having Crawford "put away," and it was by confronting their angry and anguished focus on his disability instead of his life that the family is healed. This title can be recommended to middle school girls who may appreciate a family story from the 40s.

■ Gondosch, Linda. *The Best Bet Gazette*. Illus. by Patricia Henderson. Dutton, 1989. 128pp. (0-525-67287-7) Reading Level: Grades 3–5. (SLJ N89)
Disability: Polio

Ten-year-old Judy liked to write articles for her "Best Bet Gazette." She often made up details or revised the facts in order to create headlines that would sell. She and her next-door neighbor, Dylan, walked to school with Ralph, a cowboy-crazy 6-year-old. Judy was teased for having a boyfriend and worried that the daughter of a reporter for the town paper would be appointed head of the school publication in the fall. School activities and summer events did not distract Judy from her objective of convincing her teacher that she could put out a great newspaper. Instead, the teacher pointed out that Judy changed events and projected things that might happen instead of reporting the truth.

Ralph got ill, and when it was announced that he had polio, Judy was shunned because she was "covered with polio germs and my mother says I'm not allowed to play with you—ever." Judy turned her worries about Ralph and the panic that gripped the neighborhood into a backyard carnival to benefit the local chapter of the Polio Foundation. The carnival softened even Noreen, one of the classmates who could always think of a teasing word to rhyme with "Judy." When Noreen won the raffle drawing, she gave Ralph her year's worth of riding lessons. Ralph came home from the hospital the same day Judy found out she was made editor in chief for her sixth-grade year.

Analysis: This period story has lots of details from the early 50s—from Slinky toys to news of Dr. Salk's tests. The school scene uproar and dialogue are lively. Judy's energy and good intentions are rewarded. Ralph's recovery includes his use of a leg brace and crutches. Sometimes the leg hurts, but his nurse expects further improvement. Readers who enjoyed *Meet Molly* or *Ellen Tibbits* may also want to see Judy through her eventful summer.

■ Gorman, Carol. *Chelsey and the Green-Haired Kid*. Houghton, 1987. 110pp. (0-395-41854-2) Reading Level: Grades 5–8. (SLJ MS87)
Disability: Orthopedic impairment

Chelsey is 13 when she witnesses a murder at a local basketball game. She knows that the only other witness was a tough new boy in school, named Jack. The two overcome their differences to pursue their own investigation of this drug-related violence. At one point, punk-haired Jack sits in Chelsey's lap so they can make a quick getaway in her wheelchair. Eventually, they capture two men who have been dealing drugs from a pizza parlor.

Analysis: Chelsey was injured in an automobile accident when she was 3. Because she accepts her wheelchair and the inconveniences it causes, people around her learn to do the same. Chelsey attends basketball games, even though she cannot sit in the bleachers. She wastes no time or effort on self-pity, and she curbs other people's patronizing tone with humor. For a bit of action adventure, this is a younger, and more liberated, version of *Ironsides* episodes. Younger fans of Joan Lowery Nixon and Lynn Hall will appreciate Chelsey's story.

■ Gould, Marilyn. **Golden Daffodils.** Harper, 1982. 172pp. (LB 0-201-11571-9) Reading Level: Grades 4–7. (BL 15 Mr83)
Disability: Cerebral palsy; Epilepsy; Paraplegia

Janis Ward has been attending a special school because she has cerebral palsy, but in fifth grade, she starts class in a mainstreamed public school. Her cousin Rhoda is in the class, and Rhoda and the teacher are too helpful. On the other hand, Cheryl and Garth are cruel in their teasing. Classmate, Barney Fuchs, has an older brother who was injured during Vietnam combat, uses a wheelchair, and has become a bitter recluse. One of Cheryl's taunts leads Janis to challenge Cheryl and Garth to a handball competition against Janis and Barney.

Janis visits Barney's brother, David, and his caustic attitude softens enough for him to offer some handball pointers. Janis practices a lot and finds ways to compensate for her weaker side and limp. Janis visits her old school and decides that she has outgrown some of the modified activities and studies it offered her. One morning, a fight between Garth and Barney at the handball court disrupts Janis's adjustment to school.

On a weekend visit to their grandparents (who live in the same beach town) Janis and Barney go swimming. Janis has to be assisted by her grandfather when she goes beyond the depth she can cope with to follow Barney. The morning of Junior Olympics Day, Janis is so intent on the challenge match in handball that she forgets to take her anti-seizure medicine. After a tough game, Janis and Barney win, but as the announcement of their victory is made, Janis feels a seizure begin.

Recovering at home, Janis talks with her father about the unfair situation she is in and is cheered by cards from her class. Barney visits her and delivers a blue ribbon from the handball game and a daffodil. They plan to play handball against each other when Janis is ready to do her best to beat Barney.

Analysis: This pleasant story has many insights to offer both on mainstreaming in education and on the difference between having a disability and allowing it to handicap one's life. At times the dialogue is stiff and the message slows the plot, but Janis, her friends at her old school, and Barney's brother, David, are all developed as individuals who deal with their impairments in different ways.

When David and Janis first meet, he asks,

"And how does cerebral palsy feel? As rotten as paraplegia?"

Janis pulled up her nose at the word rotten. Her cheek tensed. "I don't think I feel rotten," she said a little belligerently.

Then she hesitated. She wanted to find the exact words to describe how she felt. There was no point in lying to David.

"I think I feel . . . very inconvenienced and at times very frustrated. Especially when my body won't do what I want it to do. But deep inside I feel fine . . . I even feel normal. And that's the real me, the person inside.". . .

"But my friend Tina—she's in a wheelchair, too—she says it best. She says, 'I'm a person like everyone else except I happen to have a disability, but that doesn't make me a disabled person.' "

When Janis wants to go beyond her limits at the beach, her grandfather delivers this maxim, "Life is not a game of follow the leader. You don't do something just because someone tells you to. You have to know what's right for you." Readers will enjoy Janis's classroom adjustments and will root for her against the obnoxious jeers of classmates. The cover is a watercolor scene from the handball game, showing David cheering from his wheelchair in the sideline audience.

■ Gray, Patsey. *Barefoot a Thousand Miles*. Walker, 1984. 92pp. (0-8027-6528-93) Reading Level: Grades 7–9. (BCCB My84)
Disability: Paraplegia

An Apache adolescent sets out on a quest from Arizona to California. He is hitchhiking to find the tourists who were given his dog, Quick, in a cruel prank. When Jim hops a train, he encounters a criminal and jumps off near Yuma. A wheelchair-bound young man named Clyde becomes Jim's friend and helper. Jim reaches Santa Barbara but is told that his dog jumped out of the tourists' car in Los Angeles. Jim continues his search at the stockyards, where he finds Quick's tracks and the injured, but still pregnant, dog. Jim returns, feeling he has earned the honor name of E-dhah in this pursuit that proved his resourcefulness and diligence.

Analysis: This is an adequate story cluttered with unlikely encounters.

The characterization is not impressive, so Jim's friend in the wheelchair lacks depth. He was injured while working as a forest ranger and is bitter about the loss of his health and his girlfriend. Since Jim relies on Clyde's transportation, it is interesting to note the disabled man's use of hand controls and his confident driving (speeding and talking) habits.

■ Greenberg, Jan. *Exercises of the Heart.* Farrar, 1986. 160pp. (0-374-32237-6) Reading Level: Grades 7–10. (BCCB N86)
Disability: Cerebral hemorrhage

Roxie Baskowitz has had to deal with guilt over both her panic at age 10, when her mother suffered a stroke, and the loss of her father to a heart attack three years later. At 15, Roxie is impatient with her mother's impaired speech and movement. She attends a private school and is embarrassed by the differences between her home life and that of her wealthy friend, Glo. When Glo is in a car crash, the police negotiate with Mrs. Baskowitz, the only adult available. Roxie sees that her mother handles the situation well. Glo is willing to let their schoolmate, Tony, take the blame for the car crash, though he will lose his scholarship and have to face court proceedings to protect her. Then Glo sees that the pattern of letting someone else take on your troubles is what has led her mother to become an alcoholic. Roxie shifts from being at odds with her mother about most things, to an understanding that any person's capabilities or weaknesses are not judged correctly by appearances only.

Analysis: Roxie tells her story with first-person details about school, boy-girl encounters, best friend loyalty, and adolescent-parent conflict. She may focus on her mother's limited speech as a reason for poor communication, but insightful readers will recognize other barriers in their relationship. When Mrs. Baskowitz begins dating, Roxie is resentful and rude. This is a natural expression of the unresolved feelings Roxie has about her father's death and her mother's ability to go on with a "normal" life. Mother may have to express herself in simple ways, but she is shown to be decisive about life's complications. Until Roxie learns that Glo's family situation is troubled, she is uncooperative toward her mother and unappreciative of her friend, John. These engaging characterizations and the story line that brings new perceptions to Roxie are well integrated.

■ Guernsey, JoAnn Bren. *Journey to Almost There.* Clarion, 1985. 166pp. (0-89919-338-2) Reading Level: Grades 6–9. (BCCB F86)
Disability: Parkinson's disease

Alison O'Brien is 15 when her grandfather's Parkinson's disease becomes so severe that her mother is considering placing him in a nursing home. Since Alison has her learner's driving permit and her grandfather has a valid driver's license, she takes him on a cross-country trek to see her father. On the way, Grandfather O'Brien's condition deteriorates, and he gets delusions of little people that leave him alone only when he is asleep. He is taking sleeping pills and medication for his Parkinson's symptoms and for allergic reactions. He picks up a hitchhiker, who complains about an alcoholic mother. He drives recklessly and finally has to be hospitalized.

The delusions were the result of mixing too many types of drugs, so after that gets straightened out, Alison and her grandfather continue their trip to her father's last known address. However, he has been warned by Alison's mother that they were on the way, and, rather than face them with the truth about his failed art career, he has left a note for each of the travelers. Alison reads her note, calls her mother, expresses her love, and accepts her mother's compliment on the determination it took to make the drive.

Choosing to drive back instead of fly, Alison and her grandfather share more about his failures and successes at fathering. Alison's father has never matured, and Alison knows that her grandfather was important and reliable when she and her mother needed help. She clarifies the family feelings she has, and he agrees to stay with Alison and her mother. Now, they are not on their way to "almost there," but on their way to "almost home."

Analysis: This is an uneven story, but wishful thinking exists in abundance among children who feel estranged from a single parent. Alison's anger with her mother's controlling ways and her hope to reunite with an artistic father she barely knows are sympathetic needs. The plot device about Mr. O'Brien's improper medication is unique, and the characterizations are consistent. The language gets coarser when Rita, the hitchhiker, is along, and we learn that Alison's parents married because they were expecting a baby already, but these elements are not enough to call this a "mature" novel. It can be a supplemental choice for middle school collections.

■ Hamilton, Virginia. *The Bells of Christmas.* Illus. by Lambert Davis. Harcourt, 1989. 60pp. (0-15-206450-8) Reading Level: Grades 4–6. (BCCB N89)
Disability: Orthopedic impairment

In Ohio, just off the National Road, two days before Christmas 1890, time is passing slowly for Jason. He wants snow to come for a sleigh ride with his cousin and best friend, Tisha Bell. When his family involves Jason in the holiday preparations, waiting for the Bells to arrive still occupies his imagination.

Jason's father and uncle are woodworkers, and Papa uses a "wheel-a-chair" and a wood peg that "worked as well as the true right" leg. Papa and two of Jason's older brothers plan to start their own business. Papa tells that a cow path was built up into a road 50 years before and that covered wagons had come along by the hundreds when he was a boy. The recollection includes an unspoken reference to how Papa lost his leg, and Jason is warned to "Stay out of the way of the Road."

Jason's 13-year-old friend, Matthew, punches him after a teasing comment about Tisha. The boys make up and bring the wheeled chair back from the barn. They wonder what Uncle Levi Bell has made as Christmas presents. Christmas morning, Jason gets a train from his father, and his sister gets a beautiful walking doll made by Aunt and Uncle Bell. Snow has made the National Road a perfect place for "sleighs . . . full of laughing, talking, shouting Christmas folks." Tisha and her family arrive with Christmas packages. Uncle Levi's "grand surprise" for Papa is an artificial leg made of oak.

> "It's a great wonder . . . to have a mechanical leg and foot. Papa, you look just like everybody!"
>
> The grown-ups laughed at that. I was not too embarrassed. Tisha knew what I meant. So did Papa. It was a good son that wanted his papa to be just like folks. Oh, I liked him fine in his wheel-a-chair or on his peg leg. He was only different to me because he was such a fine carpenter and woodworker. But his two true feet did look the marvel. And then I just swelled up with pride at my papa and Uncle Levi.

The family enjoys a wonderful Christmas dinner and church service, recalling years past and "sleighing toward 1900!"

Analysis: Jason's account of two days provides a look at loving relationships in a prosperous black family during the late 1800s. Warm, muted colors are used in one illustration for every spread. The text is displayed in a wide block, which may be a bit uncomfortable for readers, but the large format and cream-colored stock complement the story's antique feel. This recommended title successfully showcases Hamilton's skilled writing and introduces an active amputee in a well-realized historical setting.

■ Hamm, Diane Johnston. *Grandma Drives a Motor Bed.* Whitman, 1987. 32pp. (LB 0-8075-3025-5) Reading Level: Grades PS–3. (BCCB D87)
Disability: Paralysis

From a young boy's point of view, the reader sees Grandma, Grandpa, and their family and friends. Grandma sometimes has enough energy to type letters. Some days Grandma has lots of visitors, who tell her their troubles. Sometimes she can sit up in a wheelchair—maybe to watch her grandson Joel swing—but it wears her out. Usually, Grandma is in a motor bed that she can make go up and down with a control box. She jokes, "The only thing my motor bed won't do is wash the dishes."

She does exercises with a helper who "lifts Grandma's arms and legs and makes her roll her head." "I don't want to get flabby muscles!" Grandma tells Joel. When she looks as if she needs a hug, Joel gives her one. Joel hears her say quietly, "Sometimes I feel like I'm never going to get better." And Joel has been told that "Maybe Grandma will get better and maybe she won't. Nobody knows."

So, for now, he drives five hours with Mama to get to Grandma's house for visits and to give Grandpa a brief vacation. "Mostly Grandpa takes care of Grandma. But when he goes downtown, Grandma takes care of herself." When Joel hears Grandpa holler at Grandma and gets scared, his Mom explains that anyone "may get frustrated and grumpy. Grandpa loves Grandma very much."

Though Joel is aware of the frustrations and limitations in his grand-parents' life, he enjoys his interaction with them and takes special pleasure in being allowed to use the controls of the motor bed.

Analysis: This slight story line offers lots of unique exposure to an invalid grandparent who still has social outlets, family interactions, and sensual as well as surly exchanges with her husband. These insights are the real value of this book, because the illustrations are awkward, and the faces sometimes detract from the nice compositions and good variety of page designs. Sepia has been added to the line drawings, but it is so uniform that it looks like a child colored the drawings with a pale felt pen. Though it is weak as a picture book, the author has characterized both a realistic couple dealing with aging and illness and the family members helping them do so.

■ Hartling, Peter. *Crutches.* Lothrop, 1988. 163pp. (0-688-07991-1) Reading Level: Grades 5–8. (BCCB N88)
Disability: Amputation; Health impairment

In 1945, Austria is a bleak landscape of destroyed buildings and displaced persons. Thomas is nearly 13 when he attaches himself to a one-legged man who has a trailer and survival skills. For two years, the man has been called "Crutches." Thomas continues to search for his Aunt Wanda, but they find out she has died. Along the way, Crutches locates shelter and food for them, and he interprets the odd political and social relationships that threaten them.

Curfew, the black market, international troops, crowded transport trains, German officers pursued as criminals, and other realities of postwar living concern Crutches and Thomas. Crutches has a recurrence of malaria, and wood for burning is too scarce to help him fight the chills. When Crutches is hospitalized, Thomas is sent to a children's barracks because the authorities know that Crutches is not really Thomas's uncle. Thomas makes friends who put in a good word to allow Crutches and Thomas to stay together for the last leg of their repatriation. Thomas and Crutches are assigned to a home in a town that was left untouched during the war, and Crutches "organizes" gifts to help them celebrate Christmas.

Moving four times in eight months, Thomas was still able to go to school. They receive a letter from Bronka, a Jewish woman who is traveling to Jerusalem to live. Crutches grows moody. He admits that the Red Cross has located Thomas's mother and that the past two weeks have been their parting time together. Thomas meets his mother at the train station, and Crutches slips away without good-byes but with plans to visit.

Analysis: An outstanding import with effective translation presents this unique portrait of a disabled German veteran of World War II. While serving in Hitler's army on the Russian border, Crutches's leg was amputated due to gangrene. The phantom pain from his amputation and a recurrence of malaria are detailed in this portrayal. Crutches is agile and respected as a clever survivor who can "organize" many types of supplies from the crumbled, militarized society around him. When Thomas says he thinks Crutches is falling in love with his nurse, Crutches replies that it is merely the style he has developed for dealing with nurses because they are so often dragons. The man's machinations and preference for the nickname of Crutches are part of his persona for survival. Bitter toward Hitler and the wartime circumstances, Crutches is still open to affectionate concern for Bronka and Thomas.

Crutches is returning to a homeland that has lost the war, but without criminal charges against him for carrying out Hitler's orders against civilians. Recommended for all collections, this title won the Batcheldeor award the year it was published.

■ Hartling, Peter. *Old John*. Trans. by Elizabeth D. Crawford. Lothrop, Lee & Shepard, 1990. 120pp. (0-688-08734-3) Reading Level: Grades 5–8. (KR 15 Ap90; BCCB MS90; HB J1-Ag90)
Disability: Cerebral hemorrhage

Laura and Jacob Schirmer listen to their father's pointing out the problems that may attend inviting their maternal grandfather, Old John, to live with the family. Still, the eccentric, loving man is made welcome, and Mr. Schirmer's underlying affection for his father-in-law is evident. At 75, Old John acts with a lot of independence and little forethought at times, but there is humor in even the most troublesome episodes that his presence introduces. When he suffers a stroke, his personality shifts, and his family copes with his physical decline.

Analysis: Vivid characterizations and a humorous "what-next?" thread make this a rewarding book. Old John has his own opinions about everything from drunks to swimming suits to living with a new love. The honest narration throughout indicates that the stroke makes John a bit paranoid and even more unpredictable and irresponsible. Family stresses are not slighted, but, as in *The Trouble with Gramary,* a rollicking individual is accommodated by a loving family to the end. The skilled story telling has been well translated, so that this German setting for universal themes will be very welcome to most collections.

■ Hassler, Jon. *Jemmy*. Atheneum, 1980. 180pp. (0-689-50130-7) Reading Level: Grades 7–9. (BCCB O80)
Disability: Amputation

Jemmy Stott is beginning her senior year of high school when her alcoholic father demands that she quit school to care for her 11-year-old brother, Marty, and six-year-old sister, Candy. When she goes to school to initiate the withdrawal she gets stranded in a Minnesota blizzard. Otis Chapman finds her in his barn, and he and his wife care for her. Otis is working on a mural and asks Jemmy to pose as a model because of her Chippewa heritage.

The Chapmans encourage Jemmy's interest in art and invite the Stotts for Christmas. Mr. Stott takes Marty to town instead, and the boy gets trapped in an unheated building. Two of Marty's fingers have to be removed due to frostbite, and he refuses to return to school. Jemmy and the Chapmans help Marty face his fears of ridicule. Otis reveals to Jemmy that he is a recovering alcoholic, and he gives her father the job of painting the Chapmans's barn.

Mr. Stott accomplishes little on the project, and Mr. Chapman tells him off. Mr. Stott faces the truth of Otis's words and begins to drink less, starts to paint his own home, and is kinder to his children. Jemmy sees the mural and recognizes herself and Otis in the characters it presents. She knows she will continue to paint and that the Chapmans have also influenced her father during their six-month acquaintance.

Analysis: This book is recommended for its convincing setting and characterization of Jemmy. It is a relief that Jemmy's white father is the one with the alcohol problem instead of perpetuating the association of alcoholism with her Indian heritage. She takes pride in her Chippewa background due to Otis's research on the lore of the Maiden of Eagle Rock to commemorate Minnesota's Indian heritage.

Marty is ready to use his injury as an excuse to avoid school and social pressure. He also associates losing his fingers with the humiliation of his father's drunken behavior. Jemmy and the Chapmans help him view the physical loss as an inconvenience and support him in dealing with his emotions about his father's weakness. Middle school readers will see Jemmy broaden her expectations and will find the bittersweet ending satisfying.

■ Henriod, Lorraine. ***Grandma's Wheelchair.*** Illus. by Christa Chevalier. Whitman, 1982. 32pp. (LB 0-8075-3035-2) Reading Level: Grades K–3. (SLJ My82)
Disability: Orthopedic impairment

Thomas spends weekday mornings with his grandmother. He is 4 years old, and she uses a wheelchair. Together they can do a lot of things. Thomas helps her dust the top shelf of the bookcase and folds some of the clothes. When her wheelchair needs to be fixed, they accomplish it together. Thomas has an older brother, who brags about all that he does in kindergarten. Thomas knows that his own busy time with Grandma is special too.

Analysis: Thomas and his grandmother get along fine, and they make no big deal of it. Society may have prepared audiences to pity Grandma, but she is so busy taking care of Thomas and her house with loving, humorous, and capable style, that this story can give new insights about physical limitations.

Unfortunately, the book is an example of a strong text and illustrations with some appeal that are undermined by consistently careless layout. At one point the roly-poly charm of Thomas's sitting in his grandmother's lap in the wheelchair is destroyed by the cut-and-paste white rectangle of the text. This book deserves to be reissued with page designs that make the most of its casual tone and naive artwork. Until then, it can be used for read-aloud sessions or as a flannel-board script for copies of the best drawings.

■ Holl, Kristi D. *The Haunting of Cabin 13.* Atheneum, 1987. 117pp. (0-689-31321-7) Reading Level: Grades 4–6. (BCCB My87) *Disability:* Paraplegia

While vacationing with her family and friend, Laurie discovers mysterious notes in Cabin 13. Apparently, someone is posing as the ghost of Eleanor, a girl who died the summer before, and Laurie wants to solve this mystery before their visit is over.

The campers in the cabin next door are two brothers, Kevin and Matt, and their dad. Fourteen-year-old Matt uses a wheelchair because his spine was injured in an accident at the camp two years before. Laurie and her friend Jenny are 13 years old, but Jenny has an easier time talking to boys. Laurie is able to set aside her shyness with Matt, because he seems like someone who could be a friend.

Laurie corners a girl who just delivered one of the notes and learns that Eleanor's half-sister has been trying to startle coworkers into revealing more about the circumstances of Eleanor's death. She shows Laurie notes that Eleanor made, and Laurie breaks the code of the messages. When the camp director is exposed as being involved in Eleanor's death and stock-piling artifacts to plant on the campground to make it more famous, Matt chases him in the wheelchair.

Laurie exchanges addresses with Matt, encourages him on his career goals in art, and senses that Eleanor's presence is now gone from the camp.

Analysis: A mild ghost story and formulaic mystery will appeal to steady fans with undemanding standards. Laurie also solved a mystery the year before, when Jenny disappeared into a deluded old woman's mansion, and her reputation as a successful sleuth is one reason that Eleanor's sister keeps writing the notes. Very convoluted thinking here, but at least the author takes time to have characters talk these angles out.

Matt's injury establishes a motive for his father or brother to be harassing the campground. It also shows the difference between Jenny's superficial ease at making conversation and Laurie's pensive character. When Kevin introduces his brother as an artist, and Matt demurs, saying he scribbles "a little to keep busy," Jenny is patronizing.

> "I'm sure that's very nice for you." She smiled prettily up at Kevin, then turned back to Matt. "Maybe if you get bored, you could do crafts. I know people like you can make billfolds and things like that."

"Jenny!" Laurie was aghast. "I'm sure if he wants to be an artist, he will be." She smiled awkwardly at Matt, wincing at the sparks of anger that showed in his eyes.

"I'm sorry," Jenny said. "I just meant that even if you're crippled, you can still make a contribution to society."

Matt does not break his angry silence to put Jenny down but allows Laurie to distract him with questions about his nature drawings. At 13, it is believable that Laurie would prefer making a "friend" to Jenny's boy-crazy posing, but her reason for feeling relaxed around Matt hints at the old asexual stereotype of disabled people. Matt explains that he had had nightmares until returning to the scene of his accident. His physical therapist suggested that going to the camp was like getting back on a horse after a fall. These little grace notes of characterization make this slight book a good choice for large collections.

■ Holland, Isabelle. *The Empty House.* Lippincott, 1983. 128pp. (LB 0-397-32006-X) Reading Level: Grades 7–9. (BCCB D83)
Disability: Epilepsy; Orthopedic impairment; Emotional disturbance

Betsy is 15 when she and her younger brother, Roddy, stay at Aunt Marian's. Their father is jailed on unfair tax fraud charges, and their mother travels out of England where she lives with their stepfather. Betsy's father gave her $5000 in case his assets were frozen, and she and Roddy try to conceal it. They also discover a reclusive pair in a spooky-looking "empty" house. Miranda Whitelaw uses a wheelchair and pursues her painting and needlepoint while in a world of her own. Her elderly mother, Ellen, decided to secretly keep her emotionally disturbed daughter with her after psychiatric treatment was unsuccessful.

Roddy keeps his epilepsy a secret from his aunt, but Betsy tells her new acquaintance, Ted, about Roddy's need for medication to avoid seizures. When the medicine is gone, Roddy insists that he has outgrown his need for it. Betsy discovers that Ted's father, Larry, is the journalist who attacked her father consistently in the press. She and Ted argue; the next morning, the paper announces that the children are visiting their aunt. Larry and some reporters press in on the children at the shore, and Roddy suffers a seizure in the water.

Betsy and Roddy take refuge at Ellen's, where the older woman reveals that the knight featured in Miranda's paintings is Betsy's father. His business dealings with the Whitelaws included rescuing them from a swindler; this casts new suspicions on why he is being condemned so quickly now. Ted makes amends with Betsy. Betsy's father's case is reopened,

Betsy and Ted are a couple, and Roddy learns to make friends of his own instead of being so dependent on Betsy.

Analysis: Roddy's and Miranda's impairments are introduced seemingly to lend a Gothic touch to this logical, romantic mystery. But the author goes on to develop relationships, touching on the way a physical or emotional disability makes other family members respond in a protective way. A difference is implied between the way Ellen shields Miranda from the world and the way Betsy encourages Roddy to make his own way.

Betsy's first-person narration has a credible tone, and readers will enjoy the steady progress she makes in proving the adult world wrong about her father.

■ Hooks, William H. *A Flight of Dazzle Angels.* Macmillan, 1988. 176pp. (0-02-744430-9) Reading Level: Grades 7–10. (BCCB O88)
Disability: Orthopedic impairment; Epilepsy

In a small southern town, in the early 1900s, Annie Earle Roland seems the mainstay of her family, even though she has a clubfoot. Her father has died, her mother is an invalid, and her brother's epileptic condition labels him "feebleminded." Though the Rolands have money, it is at risk because of an ambitious and vicious aunt.

Annie Earle depends on the friendship of the family's black housekeeper and the housekeeper's granddaughter, Queen Esther. She also is assisted by a young lawyer who is more enlightened than most of the townfolk.

Analysis: Gothic romance is comfortable reading for many young adults. In addition to a trip made for getting magic from a root woman and the literal and sexual "storm" Annie shares with a logger, there is harassment from the "bad-old-boy" son of the local sheriff. The social disdain Annie Earle experiences because of her birth defect has not squashed her determination. Perhaps her mother and brother had to be portrayed with health impairments also in order to lend credibility to this story of a handicapped female doing so much on her own in the South of 1908. The story and the prose are overdone, but the strength of Annie Earle's character can probably rise above these.

■ Howard, Ellen. *Circle of Giving.* Atheneum, 1984. 112pp. (0-689-31027-7) Reading Level: Grades 5–7. (BCCB Ap84)
Disability: Cerebral palsy

In the 1920s, Jeannie and Marguerite expected their brand-new neighborhood in California to be "glamorous" with "movie stars and stuff." But all the new neighbors seem alike, with dads who work and moms who stay home with the children. Marguerite, 12 years old and suddenly without a fawning circle of old friends, complains about the dull sameness of the homes and the families in them.

When the house across the street is purchased by a famous pianist, things get interesting on Stanley Avenue. Alert to the differences in Mrs. Hanisian's family and drawn to her severely disabled daughter Francie, Marguerite and Jeannie open their eyes to the interesting differences among the other new neighbors.

"How come we didn't think about the funny way Mr. and Mrs. Mendenhall talk, or Mrs. Lord's drawl, for that matter? How come we never noticed Sammy goes to church on Friday evenings, or heard that Lloyd's relatives live in England?" Jeannie wondered. By the time Christmas comes, all the homesick families have revealed their special qualities, and they join in a holiday celebration. Since they are too far from their grandparents, aunts, and uncles, the Stanley Avenue residents form a family of their own.

A turning point in the interaction between all the characters occurs when Francie presents her mother with a gift that shows the little girl has learned to write. Marguerite's desire to learn piano is fulfilled, and Mrs. Hanisian is grateful for the time and interest she took in helping Francie learn. One mother in the neighborhood has taught school and offers to help Francie study. Marguerite will assist but will also have enough time now to play with her new friends on the block.

Analysis: Jeannie tells this story of adjustment, friendship, and individuality set in Los Angeles's boom years. Marguerite's adolescent yearnings and shyness fit a girl of 12. Social bias against people of various abilities, colors, religions, financial stations, and ethnic mixes surfaces on Stanley Avenue. Jeannie's observations, some snatches of gossip, and the dialogue establish strong impressions of character and place.

For historical regional fiction that portrays severe physical limitation that conceals mental prowess, this title is highly recommended.

■ Howard, Ellen. *Edith, Herself.* Illus. by Ronald Himler. Atheneum, 1987. 130pp. (0-689-31314-4) Reading Level: Grades 5–7. (BCCB My87) *Disability:* Epilepsy

In the late 1800s, Edith tries to "keep the blackness in her head at bay." When her mother dies, her oldest sister, Alena, and brother-in-law, John, take her to be raised with their son, Vernon, who is the same age as Edith.

John's parents live with them, and Edith is intimidated by the old woman's harsh ways and unhealthy smell. John kills a nest of mice, and Edith has a "fit." John's mother interprets it as punishment from God because Edith treasures her doll and some other things from her home so highly. John insists that there is nothing wrong with Edith's ability to learn and has her start school with Vernon. On the first day, Vernon wets his pants because he forgot to use the privy at recess, and Edith helps him avoid a punishment. Edith makes friends but still worries about having fits. When one occurs at school, Edith decides to never return, but Vernon and Rosa are accepting, and she decides she does not care what the others think.

Analysis: From Edith's point of view, she knows about her "fits" only from others' descriptions of them, so is very upset by the shame and ignorance surrounding epilepsy at that time. The emotional strain that brings on Edith's seizures fits an old stereotype, but the characterizations are all strong enough to overcome this weakness. Skilled writing makes this short historical novel a good introduction to one little girl who has a lot to adjust to. She is at first mortified by Vernon's open comments, then supported by him in her resolution to face taunting schoolmates: "They shan't laugh at me, she thought. I won't let them!"

It is especially appealing that Edith decides to defend herself before Vernon, Rosa, and an older boy on horseback can intervene for her in order to get past some bullies. Highly recommended, this title shows that just as Edith needs her peers to develop tolerance, Edith herself learns to show some toward John's ill mother.

■ Howe, James. *A Night Without Stars.* Atheneum, 1983. 178pp. (0-689-30957-0) Reading Level: Grades 4–7.
Disability: Orthopedic and neurological impairments

Maria Tirone meets many other patients when she undergoes open-heart surgery. *See full annotation* Chapter 4: Health Problems.

■ Jones, Rebecca C. *Madeline and the Great (Old) Escape Artist.* Dutton, 1983. 112pp. (0-525-44074-7) Reading Level: Grades 4–7. (BCCB D83)
Disability: Epilepsy

Madeline was on the softball team in Chicago before her parents' divorce, and the coach gave her a journal to keep when she moved to Sycamore to live with her mother and grandmother. It is hard for Madeline to think of reasons to like Sycamore, especially after she suffers a seizure in class. In the hospital, her roommate is Mary Gibson, an old lady recovering from her third heart attack. After tests and an explanation from the doctor, Madeline is given pills to take every night in order to control the seizures.

Madeline's father is not willing to have her come for a weekend visit as they had planned, because he is so uncertain about her medical condition. Madeline wants to escape the embarrassment of facing people who saw her "fit," because she knows they saw her lose control of everything, including her bladder. Madeline fakes a seizure, is sent home from the hospital again, and then complains she is too ill to go to school. Classmates and school staff either ignore her or are so solicitous that Madeline is uncomfortable. She decides to run away with Mary Gibson. They make a plan, but the old lady's credit card has expired, and personal credit will not be accepted at the bus depot.

Madeline realizes that their schemes of living together in the city were foolish. She admires the lady for wanting to return to her nursing home on her own instead of being found and taken back. Madeline decides to face the hard adjustment of returning to school. She continues to visit Mary, even though a stroke results in the woman's frequent confusion about who Madeline is.

Analysis: These characters have complex personalities with strengths and weaknesses. Mary Gibson manipulates Madeline to go along with her runaway scheme, intending to get away from the nursing home just for a diversion from her roommate. Their conversations are often affected by Mary's poor hearing, but the author handles the dialogue well. This direct little adventure includes Mary's reminiscence about a girl from her own past who had "fits" and was institutionalized when her parents died. Madeline looks closely at her medication, stamped PD 362.

"I thought of the girl being carted off to the insane asylum, and I looked again at the capsule in my hand. She could have used that little bugger."

These touches of humor, the slim format, and an active watercolor cover showing Madeline pushing Mary in her wheelchair and "go" hat invite readers to an excellent novel on both adjustments to limitations and special friendships.

■ Jones, Toeckey. *Skindeep.* Zolotow/Harper, 1986. 250pp. (LB 0-06-023052-5) Reading Level: Grades 9–12. (BCCB N86)
Disability: Orthopedic impairment

Rhonda is attending college in South Africa when she meets a bald-headed student named Dave. Her original dismissal of him as "an obvious weirdo" turns into attraction, and they have an affair. Dave is usually friendly and jocular, but some comments make him act angry, and he breaks off with Rhonda for three days. Political violence and the pressures of apartheid have made Rhonda want to leave for London as soon as she finishes four years of university. Her best friend, Lynn, is Jewish and wants to go to Israel.

Rhonda and Dave take a romantic trip together to Capetown. While shopping, they come across a beggar woman and her daughter, whom Dave recognizes. He disappears for a while and when he returns, he tells Rhonda that the crippled colored woman is his mother. Rhonda's racism is so inbred that she reacts with revulsion to this disclosure. Dave accuses her of being only "skindeep" and leaves to rejoin his colored family.

Rhonda is ill when she returns home, and Lynn helps her find Mrs. Schwartz, Dave's adoptive mother. Mrs. Schwartz relates how "Dawie's" mother gave him up for adoption to protect her son and because of her ambitions that his white looks would let him pass as part of the privileged class. Rhonda visits the Schwartz family again and hears that Dave refuses his mother's and adoptive parents' advice to return to the university. Rhonda sees Dave once more, but does not agree that they should pursue a future together. Rhonda spends three years at university, active in student antiapartheid protests. Dave stays in contact with his adoptive parents, without revealing much about his black liberation activities, because they are so dangerous.

Analysis: Though this is written according to the pattern of many young adult romances, the institutionalized racism of South Africa gives a tragic motivation to the plot that makes it valuable for intercultural understanding. Rhonda is 18, and Dave is the first boyfriend whom she feels physically attracted to. When she analyzes her reactions and her family's reversal of their opinion of Dave and the fact that their responses stem from social conditioning, she sets out to change things for her country, if not herself.

Dave's melodramatic abandonment of Rhonda in Cape Town is tempered by the revelation that his mother's injury in a hit-and-run accident has been kept a secret for three years. That he comes across her begging, with his sister, is therefore a double shock for him. The colored woman's injuries were obviously not cared for well, and her options for employment were reduced by her physical handicap as well as the social limitations of her race. But she has ambitions for her children, as well as a sacrificial love that Mrs. Schwartz helps Rhonda to understand.

The contemporary, yet foreign setting gives this portrayal its value. Though we do not observe the mother's character much in the story, her past decisions, injury, and current efforts to make the most of the limited life options she has can break down the apathetic views that may be held by some readers.

■ Kinsey-Warnock, Natalie. *The Canada Geese Quilt.* Illus. by Leslie W. Bowman. Dutton, 1989. 60pp. (0-525-65004-0) Reading Level: Grades 3–5. (BCCB Ja90)
Disability: Cerebral hemorrhage

In Vermont, "Ariel spends hours walking through the fields and woods, drawing wildflowers and birds." Her grandmother encourages this artistic effort and uses one of Ariel's sketches to plan a quilt for the baby that Mama is expecting. Then Grandma suffers a stroke. "She can't walk very well and it's hard for her to pronounce words," but Mama is most distressed when the woman seems to have given up and "isn't even trying to get better."

Ariel talks to her grandmother, even if she gets no response, and she lures the woman out on a short walk to enjoy some migrating butterflies. Grandma begins to talk, and Ariel asks that she teach her how to complete the baby's quilt. One day, all of the sewing and Grandma's weakness get to Ariel, who says, "I want to be outside. I hate that quilt and I hate you!"

Grandma's observation is "Good for you. Ever since I got home, you and your folks have been tiptoeing around here like you were on eggshells, afraid to say or do anything that might upset me. You're the first person to get mad, and I'm glad of it. You're mad because I got sick and it made you scared. I get mad, too, because I can't do some of the things I used to."

When Mama goes to have the baby, Grandma keeps busy sweeping and baking. After Grandma announces that the baby is a boy, she gives Ariel a quilt done in nighttime colors from the sketch of the Canada geese. She had completed Ariel's quilt before the stroke.

Analysis: Ariel has a year of new worries that develops her character in many ways. This slim book has the power of Rylant's *A Blue-Eyed Daisy* and the artistry of *Sarah, Plain and Tall.* Grandma's illness, her treatment with therapy and home care, and her slow recovery are believable. When the emotional pressure is vented and Grandma says she's glad, it is very affective. Readers will benefit from this honest work and, like Ariel, may find it easier to face the mortality of a loved one after working through Grandma's stroke.

■ Klein, Norma. *My Life as a Body.* Knopf, 1987. 304pp. (LB 0-394-99051-X) Reading Level: Grades 9–12. (BCCB O87)
Disability: Orthopedic and neurological impairments

During her senior year in private school, Augie meets Sam and is asked to tutor him. Sam uses a wheelchair. His halting responses in class make

Augie think he has mental impairments and should not be eligible for admission to their final year of progressive, college-preparatory classes.

Augie is the only child of two professors, and her tuition at the expensive school is covered by a merit scholarship. Her best friend, Claudia, is outspokenly homosexual except when she is trying to get to know a new girl she has a crush on. Augie thinks of herself as a "repressed, intellectual, peculiar" teenager, and when her counselor suggests that working with Sam might address Augie's own "superciliousness," Augie agrees that she is "inwardly contemptuous" and judgmental. Claudia's feminist advice covers tutoring, sexual fantasies, masturbation, and a prediction of Augie's first love affair: "You'll get a sense of self and then you'll go on to whatever."

Sam's mother tells Augie what Sam was like before he was hit by a car and that the family did not want to enroll him in special education or to have a home tutor. "I want you to treat Sam as the same person he was and the person he will become, not just the person he is now." Augie meets Sam's father and realizes that there are stresses in the family that existed before the accident. She starts an oil painting of Sam for her portfolio and is pleased that he chooses to be shown seated in his wheelchair.

After the holiday break, Sam recovers his mental acuity and speech abilities. Sam and Augie celebrate with drinks, Augie lets her anger out, and their friendship deepens. Since Sam needs no further tutoring, Augie invites him to her home, and they become lovers. After three months, the affair is discovered, and their parents try to intervene in the relationship.

Augie begins art school and makes new friends. She is "afraid of clinging to Sam too much, just out of fear of the unknown." Insecurities and loneliness take their toll on Augie, and by Christmas she is confused as to how to respond to Sam's gift of a blue fur coat.

During a defensive long-distance call with Sam, Augie finds out he is using crutches some of the time. She leaves town before he gets home, even though he had asked her to stay an extra day so he could see her. A painful phone conversation ends without the usual "I love you."

By spring break, Augie realizes that Sam wants a wife and companion and that she is not ready to fill the roles. Sam transfers to UCLA and the lovers break up.

Analysis: The title comes from an English assignment that Sam and Augie share after reading some Virginia Woolf. Klein lets her protagonist reveal all the intimacies and self-deprecating impressions that both thrill and plague her character during the course of her senior and freshman years. The dialogue is kept natural, even when indicating Sam's speech impairments. Using dashes for Sam's awkward phrases, the author also has Augie perceive that "He spoke all his sentences slowly with funny little stops at the wrong places, but by now I was used to that."

Though Augie questions her motivations and interprets and reinterprets everything Sam does or says, their relationship is a healthy blend of mutual regard and sexual attraction. When the young man thanks Augie for the part her love played in his recovery, she refers to the mental improvements "that would've happened anyway." But he insists that she helped him to beat the "emotional deadness I felt."

Sometimes Augie's "constant inner debate" and the story's uneven plot development may make readers impatient, but they will be rewarded by strong style and honest characterizations of many interesting individuals.

■ Knowles, Anne. *Under the Shadow.* Harper & Row, 1983. 128pp. (LB 0-06-023222-6) Reading Level: Grades 5–8.
Disability: Muscular dystrophy; Orthopedic impairment

Cathy is 15 when she moves to Beamsters, a historic house in the English countryside. She surprises herself by falling in love with the house and the surrounding property. A boy lives with his mother in a nearby cottage, and when she meets him, she feels awkward because no one warned her that he was in a wheelchair due to muscular dystrophy. Old houses are too hard for Mark to maneuver in, but he has studied a lot about the history of Beamsters and wants to write stories about it. However, his mother is too busy to take dictation. Cathy offers Mark her tape recorder and the suggestion that Mrs. Anderson simply type up her son's dictation since he sometimes feels too weak to use his hands.

As Cathy and Mark spend time together, she becomes familiar with his physical limitations, his imaginative nature, his frustrations, and the grumpy rudeness he reverts to in order to cope. She also determines to buy a horse so that Mark can have the freedom of riding that he has sampled only once in a special program called "Riding for the Disabled." Cathy locates a pony that is for sale because the rider injured her hand and wants nothing to do with horses anymore.

Fiona's injury is dismissed by Mark as "One miserable wonky hand. She could help that all right. If she'd do her physio I'm sure she could get more movement in it. She just doesn't try."

Cathy concludes that Fiona does not "hate the idea of riding because she's damaged her hand. I think she doesn't want her hand to get better because she's scared silly to ride." Mark feigns helplessness so Fiona will help him with the horse, risking a fall to make Fiona reveal that she has worked through her fears during secret morning sessions with the pony.

Cathy is rewarded with friendship, Mark learns his rude humor is as unfair to others as outsiders' patronizing tone is to him, and the bees return to "the Beemaster's home."

Analysis: This is one of the best imports from England, especially because the characters are developed beyond the pat function of an audience for sermons on how to treat a cripple. Mark makes plenty of caustic observations about his situation and reenacts certain social interactions that distressed him.

"The worst part of being in this thing," Mark went on, "is that people find it so embarrassing that they either pretend I don't really exist, like a bad smell in someone's bathroom, or they treat me like one of the more sickening characters out of Dickens, which is worse." When Mark cannot place Cathy into either of those categories, a friendship blossoms. The bees' returning to the property is not a forced metaphor of restoration, but a pleasant reward for the research Mark has done on the old house and the support Cathy offered in getting his book ready to submit to a publisher.

Mark is very prickly, but his comments are tempered with wit, imagination, and a high level of self-disclosure with Cathy, which he admits is because "I get scared sometimes, and I need someone to talk to who isn't going to get fussed the way Mother does." This portrayal is sometimes calculated to fly in the face of British stereotypes that have lingered too long in juvenile literature. "Sometimes Katy-cat, there's enough resentment in me to split the whole world at the seams."

Most of the British slang and terms can be understood in context, and they do help to establish the setting. The horse scenes may not be as profuse as fans of that genre like, but the cover, showing Mark relaxed and confident, astride the pony while Cathy leads him past the old building and cottage, is great. Though the story is about teenagers, upper-grade and middle school students will enjoy this recommended book.

■ Lelchuk, Alan. *On Home Ground.* Illus. by Merle Nacht. Gulliver/Harcourt, 1987. 64pp. (0-15-200560-9) Reading Level: Grades 5–7. (BCCB O87)
Disability: Orthopedic impairment

In 1947, Aaron lives with his Russian Jewish immigrant father. Aaron's special friend is Burt, a young veteran injured in the war. Burt takes Aaron to see a Brooklyn Dodgers game, and Jackie Robinson impresses Aaron with his ability.

Ten-year-old Aaron revises his opinion of his own father during a country visit. Aaron's father may not seem at ease in the city, but, galloping on a huge horse, he is as "at home" as Burt in Brooklyn, or Jackie Robinson on the playing field.

Analysis: Aaron gives his first-person account of events and interactions by using sports details and appealing observations. The time period is well realized, and the prose is strong enough for reading aloud. Burt's combat-related injuries do not interfere with his friendships and are consistent with the historical context.

■ Levin, Betty. *The Trouble with Gramary.* Greenwillow, 1988. 198pp. (0-688-07372-7) Reading Level: Grades 6–8. (BCCB Mr88)
Disability: Cerebral hemorrhage

Merkka Weir's family is crowded living over grandmother's welding yard. If Gramary would compromise with the right people in town, maybe they could move to a nice house that is for sale. Merkka is frustrated when her grandmother's eccentric ways and scrap-metal projects collide with their fishing village's efforts to become a tourist attraction.

For a while, Merkka is busy with a dog named Jet, who has to be rescued from the sea, and then with a flock of island sheep. She tries to write a winning entry for a contest, only to see her best friend win instead. A big surprise is that everyone but Merkka knows her mother is going to have a baby.

Gramary decides to move out and marry a man Merkka suspects of trying to drown Jet. He explains the situation, Merkka misunderstood, and Merkka adjusts to the marriage. Gramary's metal sculptures become hot items for art collectors and dealers. Ironically, her projects are a boost to town development, and Gramary donates proceeds to help unemployed townfolk.

Gramary has several strokes, and Merkka helps interpret for her when her words become scrambled. Though she has medication, Gramary has spells that leave her less and less able, and she dies in Merkka's arms.

Analysis: Merkka's first-person comments or writing efforts introduce each chapter. There are two major plots, each with a separate resolution, because the story starts out with Merkka's efforts with the dog and sheep, then shifts to her involvement in Gramary's reluctant art career. There is subtle humor in the auction scenes, when avaricious dealers snap up pieces of equipment that Gramary was repairing and her smaller pieces of sculpture gleaned from all over town.

After the first stoke, Merkka believes her grandmother just hurt her eye.

Gramary was seated on the bottom step of the busboat, her legs spread wide, her hands clutching her face.

Staring into Gramary's face, it was hard to tell whether she was actually crying or just recovering from some kind of blow. The weeping eye kept twitching, and something wasn't right about Gramary's cheek. All the way down to her mouth.

"What happened?" asked Merkka.

Gramary tried to look at her, but her eye wouldn't stay still. "Moment," Gramary got out. "Time."

Gramary didn't seem to know how to step up into the busboat.

When Merkka tells her mother about Gramary's injury she says, "It was something else mysterious and terrible that had come inside of Gramary like the tide after a storm." Gramary "jumbles" her words, saying "deep" for "sleep," and Merkka learns to use association to decode snatches of song or rhyming words that Gramary often substitutes for terms she means to use.

This book has realistic impact when it focuses on Merkka's family dynamics and succeeds in establishing a clear setting on a storm-swept coastline.

■ Levinson, Marilyn. *And Don't Bring Jeremy.* Illus. by Diane de Groat. Henry Holt, 1985. 128pp. (0-8050-0554-4) Reading Level: Grades 4–6. (BCCB O85)
Disability: Neurological impairment

Adam is a sixth-grader who hopes to improve his baseball game and gain the approval of the coach's son, Eddie. Eddie is the best player but has been mean to and manipulative of the boys he plays with. When Adam is invited to join Eddie for pizza, he warns Adam, "Don't bring Jeremy." Jeremy is Adam's seventh-grade brother, who has a neurological impairment that hampers his motor and mental capabilities. Adam feels that is is hard being Jeremy's brother, not only because of the way Jeremy acts, but also because their mother insists that Jeremy be treated just like everybody else.

During a game, Jeremy misses a ball, simply walks away, and gets Adam so mad that the younger boy punches his brother. Jeremy makes friends with a little boy named Tommy, who enjoys his imaginative games. But Jeremy's mother does not approve of her seventh-grader playing with someone so much younger. Jeremy has a garden, but Adam and Eddie mess it up. In retaliation, Jeremy destroys Adam's baseball cards.

Jeremy also stands up to Eddie, who calls him a "retard." Eddie's cruel pranks escalate, and he throws suspicion on Jeremy for the damage. Adam finds out that Jeremy was babysitting with Tommy and getting paid for it, so has an alibi against Eddie's claims. Jeremy and Adam try to get Eddie to tell the truth, until Eddie's father steps in and succeeds. The brothers see that Eddie has a tough time with his father, and they feel sorry for him. Jeremy offers to help Adam repair the stage sets for a play, and the younger boy accepts his brother's limited, but appreciated help.

Analysis: Friendship themes often appear in juvenile literature, but this title also explores the strains on a relationship between brothers, due to their different physical and mental capabilities. Adam has new peer concerns, which make him question his mother's tireless efforts to see that Jeremy pursues "normal" activities. Jeremy is able to express his frustrations when Adam seems to get all the attention because he is more capable in baseball. This is a truthful presentation of the way a disability amplifies typical family conflicts, whether they are rooted in sibling rivalries or arise from parental expectations.

The accompanying line drawings are pleasant and portray the emotional content as well as the action of the story. The sports details will appeal to baseball fans without intruding on other plot developments. Some turns of the plot are predictable, but this will seem a small flaw to upper-grade, or reluctant middle-school, readers.

■ Levinson, Riki. *DinnieAbbieSister-r-r!* Illus. by Helen Cogancherry. Four Winds, 1987. 90pp. (0-02-757380-X) Reading Level: Grades 2–4. (BCCB My87)
Disability: Paralysis

Two brothers and their preschool sister have lively family fun in Bensonhurst, Brooklyn. The boys attend yeshiva and are "full of beans"—leaping, hopping, and playing stickball in their neighborhood. When Mother wants one of them to come home, she always calls out "DinnieAbbieSister-r-r!"

One day, Abbie becomes too ill to go to school, and for weeks, Abbie's door is not open and the doctor makes many visits. When Abbie is carried downstairs, the family celebrates, but Dinnie whispers, "Abbie's feet look funny, Mama." Dinnie skips school the next day because he wants Abbie to be able to go with him. Mr. Simon starts coming to the house.

> He rubbed Abbie's legs up and down.
> Dinnie and I watched through the window.
> "What's he doing, Dinnie?" I asked, as quietly as I could.
> "He's trying to wake up Abbie's legs," Dinnie whispered."

The therapy continues, and Abbie can stand, then walk "funny—up and down, up and down—with a little skip in between." When there is a special presentation at their school, Abbie sings solo. During summer, Jenny joins in the stickball game and scores by running for Abbie.

Analysis: One year in a Jewish family's life is presented with period detail, economical prose, and many expressive pencil drawings. The most dramatic event is Abbie's being able to stand on a chair after his illness. His recovery is probably from polio, and the accommodations that his siblings make are subtle yet heartwarming.

The story is told in the first person from a 5-year-old's point of view, so the episodes are necessarily simple. For children just beginning to read novels, this period piece is entertaining as well as inviting.

■ Likhanov, Albert. *Shadows Across the Sun.* Trans. by Richard Louie. Harper & Row, 1983. 150pp. (LB 0-06-023869-0) Reading Level: Grades 7–9. (BCCB MS83)
Disability: Polio

Lena is home from her boarding school to recuperate from pneumonia. Because she is in a wheelchair due to polio, she often watches her neighbor Feyda working on a pigeon cote. She also learns that Feyda's father has a drinking problem and that his mother must replace money missing from her job or be fired. Friends rally to offer the needed money in time, but Feyda's new problem is that the neighborhood is scheduled to be razed for high-rise redevelopment. Lena hears that a friend from school has died, and Feyda barely saves the distraught Lena from being run over by a bus.

Feyda moves, establishing a new life at school and with his family, but he returns to visit Lena. She has returned to the school, so Feyda decides to take his pigeons to her and rebuild the cote there. The two kiss and decide to stay just friends since it would not be sensible to keep seeing each other "at least, until we're grown up."

Analysis: The alternating viewpoints of Lena and Feyda provide a sometimes didactic account of family life in Russia. Clearly, Lena's complex feelings about her disability are affected by the state-run school for crippled children and her natural adolescent longings. Thankfully, the characters leave a window open for a serious relationship once they have completed their education and people stop questioning their maturity.

■ Lowry, Lois. *Us and Uncle Fraud.* Houghton, 1984. 148pp. (LB 0-395-36833-X) Reading Level: Grades 4–6. (BCCB D84)
Disability: Coma; Learning disabilities

Uncle Claude comes for a visit, and Louise records the reactions of her family. Father, known for his rudeness, talks about Claude's perpetual need for money. Mother catches herself referring to her younger brother as a "considerate boy." Fourteen-year-old Tom calls him "Uncle Fraud."

Louise is 11 and Marcus is 10. They enjoy Claude's visit, because he has brought a box that he tells them has something priceless and fragile in it. Before Claude leaves town, he tells of his travels to many countries and of learning all kinds of languages. He promises the children that there is a treasure hidden in their house, and he gives them some secret words to learn in order to help them find it. A silver robbery gets first-page coverage just before Claude leaves, and the two children share their suspicions that Claude did it.

Flooding rains endanger the town and surrounding farms. Louise and Marcus have almost given up their treasure hunt, but Louise visits the library to find out if there is such a thing as jeweled Russian Easter eggs. Marcus searches for bones in the cemetery, and just as Louise catches up to him, a falling limb casts Marcus into the floodwater. Louise calls for help from a man she sees in the graveyard, and Tom arrives on his bike in time to reach Marcus. However, a surge of water sends Marcus up on shore and sweeps Tom downstream, where he is injured against the bridge.

Tom has two broken arms and a fractured skull. He stays in a coma for months, and his family takes turns talking to him all day long. When Louise and Marcus are running out of news, stories, and songs, they recite Uncle Claude's secret message. A nurse coming on duty overhears them and asks Mother why the children were speaking Russian. Louise and Marcus go to the nurse's home, where her husband translates, "I love you."

Tom comes out of his coma and returns home. Father has restored Tom's bike, and Marcus volunteers to keep up Tom's newspaper route. Louise helps solve the case of the missing silver and decides that Uncle Claude's "lie" should be balanced against the gift he wanted to give and the good times Marcus and she shared in pursuit of the treasure.

Analysis: Uncle Claude is perceived in many ways, but it is mostly through Mother's recollections. It is clear that Claude knows a lot of things. When the children learn the translation of the phrase they have chanted, Claude's knowledge of languages is verified. This helps break down the hatred for Uncle Claude that Louise allowed her disappointment to cause.

When Mother recalls Claude's childhood betrayals and foibles, readers will hear the tone of acceptance and love that builds to the firm statement, "You know Claude is different. You know he has flaws. He can't seem to hold a job, he has no money, and sometimes he drinks too much. But he never hurts anyone. He tries so hard, still, to create worlds for himself, worlds where he is rich and where he can give wonderful gifts. It's all in his imagination—but imagination itself is a gift, Louise."

Tom's injuries heal, but he does not awaken. Mother explains to Louise and Marcus that a coma is "a very very deep sleep. Tom can't open his eyes yet, and he can't speak, of course, but maybe he can hear us." The family makes every effort to "keep talking because it may be the thing that wakes him up." Louise notices that Tom seems smaller as the months pass. "We became accustomed to it, the bizarre act of talking to a motionless, sleeping figure in a bed."

Tom's recovery is summarized, "He had to learn to walk and to talk and to read, as if his life had begun all over again." His use of a wheelchair is alluded to when he suggests that Marcus do the paper route, "until I'm better." After a bit of sibling banter, Louise thinks, "Tom hadn't changed. . . . We loved Tom, and we had not truly known that before."

Many families draw closer, change their behaviors, and cherish the casual times together once they have been through a life-threatening crisis. This account avoids being the stereotypic inspiration tale, because the author has taken time to develop each character. Her use of dialogue and the communication on notes "passed through" the wall between Louise's and Marcus's rooms is exceptional.

Lowry's characters experience a bit of mystery, the terror of the storm, and the suspenseful tragedy of Tom's coma, but they find joy even in a flawed world, which adds up to a perfect family story for upper graders.

■ Marron, Carol A. *No Trouble for Grandpa.* Illus. by Chaya Burstein. Raintree, 1983. 31pp. (0-940742-27-6) Reading Level: Grades K–3. (BL 1 Ja84)
Disability: Orthopedic and neurological impairments

David warns his grandfather that baby sister Amy's joining them for an overnight visit is a bad idea. Grandpa never gets angry at any of the troublesome things Amy does though. When a stranger picks her up in a shop, David tells the man to put her down. The man ignores David until the boy shouts that his sister is afraid and wants to be put down. David earns a hug from Amy, and the three go home. When Amy is in bed with her new frog, David beats Grandpa at checkers.

Analysis: This little story about adjusting to a younger sibling has an unstated message about life in the mainstream for a boy in a wheelchair. The conversations with Grandpa about babies being a lot of trouble imply that David and his wheelchair do not give much trouble. When the man in the store ignores David, the boy has every right to get angry, but his focus is on his sister's endangerment, not on the man's insensitivity to either child's rights.

Bright watercolor illustrations include some double-page spreads that will carry well at storytime. Like *One Light, One Sun*, the text is generic, but the casual inclusion of a special needs child gives the book significance.

■ Mayne, William. ***All the King's Men.*** Delacorte, 1988. 182pp. (0-385-29626-6) Reading Level: Grades 4–6.
Disability: Orthopedic impairment; Short stature

In a group of medieval dwarves at court, Joachim has no knees, Hubert has chronic allergies, Roberto is clever but malicious, Rafe cannot hear or speak, and Fonso is "one of God's children and an idiot." *See full annotation* Chapter 7: Various Disabilities.

■ Miklowitz, Gloria D. ***Close to the Edge.*** Dell, 1984. 160pp. (0-440-91381-0) Reading Level: Grades 7–9.
Disability: Arthritis

Jenny knows Hannah has arthritis and thinks the lady is valiant to live on her own and perform with a band that provides entertainment for patients in hospitals and nursing homes. *See full annotation* Chapter 6: Emotional Disturbances.

■ Miner, Jane Claypool. ***New Beginning: An Athlete Is Paralyzed.*** Illus. by Vista III Design. Crestwood, 1982. 63pp. (LB 0-89686-174-0) Reading Level: Grades 5–9.
Disability: Spinal injury

At 17, Steve hopes his future includes playing pro football or becoming a coach. When the season starts, he is injured by a tackle. He wakes up in a hospital, unable to move his legs, and numb below the waist. The doctor confirms Steve's fears that it is a permanent condition. After a short stay in the hospital, Steve goes home in a wheelchair. He spends four months refusing visitors, watching TV from his bed, and ignoring his school assignments. When his coach takes over as tutor, Steve starts doing course work to try to keep up his studies. The coach also insists that Steve try for a job as cashier at a nearby store. Steve is hired, his boss installs ramps before his first day of work, and he bluffs a shoplifter into returning a candy bar and then coaches the boy in basketball at the Y. Steve feels good about himself and even considers playing sports again, as a wheelchair athlete.

Analysis: Part of the Crisis series, this book is clearly for reluctant readers. Each spread has a sketchy illustration, occasionally in color. The story includes more social insights than information about physical limitations. Steve's injury seems to be paraplegia, but he ignores all the doctor's explanations except "... afraid we can't operate ... seems to be permanent." At several points in the story, there is mention that Steve's arms ache from using the wheelchair, but by the end, "he was really glad they'd taught him how to handle the wheelchair well in the hospital."

Curriculum support can make use of the entire series, but this title stands out for public libraries because Steve has some depth of characterization within the otherwise simplistic presentation. Though the action and adjustment have been distilled to fit a short, illustrated format, some of Steve's insights are valuable. "It was the first time he'd been in a wheelchair. It felt so weird. He saw waists, not faces."

When Steve begins work, it is to prove he is not lazy and because his coach has told him, "You're as useless as you feel." On the job, "A few people gave Steve funny looks. He had to expect that. He just smiled at them and acted natural. It helped."

His successful interactions with children include this impression: "Somehow having Buddy help on curbs made Steve feel better instead of worse. That was the good thing about little kids. They took you as they found you, without looking funny or trying too hard."

■ Moeri, Louise. *Journey to the Treasure.* Scholastic, 1986. 186pp. (paper 0-590-33561-8) Reading Level: Grades 5–7. (BCCB Mr86) *Disability:* Missing limbs

Victoria's grandfather is pursuing his boyhood dream of retrieving a treasure he saw hidden by bandits when he was a child. Victoria and Trevor set out to rescue him. They face the deprivations of a desert trail, the appearance of a bear, a landslide, and a cave-in. Trevor uses an artificial leg to negotiate all these physical trials.

Analysis: Since "problem novels" are often where we find heroes with disabilities, this action adventure is rather disarming. It is not well edited and the cover does not portray the children's ragged condition. It portrays loyal Trevor, fighting for survival, and deals with his disability well along the way.

■ Muldoon, Kathleen M. *Princess Pooh.* Illus. by Linda Shute. Whitman, 1989. 32pp. (0-8075-6627-6) Reading Level: Grades K–3. (SLJ N89) *Disability:* Orthopedic and neurological impairments

Patty Jean is so bitter about the way her 10-year-old sister, Penelope, orders everybody around, gets presents from strangers, and "just sits in her throne with wheels" that the younger sister thinks of Penny as "Princess Pooh." Mother has both girls do Saturday chores, but one day Penelope goes to therapy, so Patty folds the clothes, thrilled to take the "Princess's" place and swap bathroom "maid" duties. Patty Jean was outraged when Penelope came home so tired from therapy that she was put to bed, leaving the younger girl to do additional chores.

One summer day, the girls were amusing themselves in the yard. All Patty's friends were away at camp, but her family could not afford to send Patty because "the Princess got new braces." While Penny reads "so I can win a prize in the summer reading program," Patty goes rolling off in the "throne." She falls forward out of the chair, has to wait in traffic halfway across the street, notices people turning quickly away from her, and is taunted by some boys. She is unable to catch up to the ice cream truck and is stuck in the rain. She drags the wheelchair home and finds her parents looking for her. She is surprised they were not looking for the "throne." Patty asks her sister some questions that help her to decide "maybe Princess isn't a good name for her, after all. Maybe it's nicer that she's just Penelope Marie and that I am her sister, Patty Jean Piper."

Analysis: Sibling rivalry can be amplified by a special needs child in the family. This unique book takes the viewpoint of an oppressed younger sibling to explore the emotional strains that physical limitations can cause in a household. The author is trying to address "painful feelings" in a piece of bibliotherapy, but other qualities of this book make it good for large collections. Penny is a bland character, but some details like the way her wheelchair is hard to use sometimes or the fact that she folds the clothes can help stretch readers' assumptions about disabled people.

By the end of the story, readers should recognize that Patty's impressions of Penny only led to jealousy. Color caricatures of the scenes barely temper these exaggerations. For example, when "Patty Jean the Servant" carries packages while Dad wheels Penny through the mall and Mom carries the crutches, Penny has one item in her lap and can wave to others "like she's some kind of movie star." Not until Patty has her distasteful experiences in the wheelchair does she think to ask if her sister might like walking better than sitting. Once the "throne" has lost its glory, Patty Jean is willing to readjust her perspective on Penny's life. This book can open discussions about ability versus disability, pity versus fear, and sibling adjustment to the accommodations a family makes for a disabled member.

■ Newman, Robert. *The Case of the Frightened Friend.* Atheneum, 1984. 168pp. (0-689-31018-8) Reading Level: Grades 5–8. (BCCB Ap84)
Disability: Cerebral hemorrhage

Peter Wyatt, an investigator for Scotland Yard, and his young friend Andrew try to find out about a schoolmate named Cortland. Cortland has not returned from vacation, something Peter Wyatt feared might happen. Peter Wyatt is assisted by Andrew and Sara as he solves the case.

Analysis: A series mystery with poisoning, murder, and spy secrets will appeal to many. Cortland's father has died and his grandfather has suffered a stroke. More than a portrayal, this is a plot device that adds much to the characterizations. It gives Cortland a reason to feel vulnerable and to be in need of the clever team of Andrew, Sara, and Peter Wyatt.

■ Newth, Mette. *The Abduction.* Trans. by Tiina Nunnally and Steve Murray. Farrar, 1989. 248pp. (0-374-30008-9) Reading Level: Grades 9–12. (BCCB N89)
Disability: Orthopedic and speech impairments

Her first day as a woman, Osuqo looks forward to marriage with Poq, but strangers in a ship kidnap the young Inuit couple from Greenland. The ocean venture had been commanded to locate unicorns or to trade for the expensive horn believed to be a curative. The English queen had requested the expedition, but the ship's backers and crew have come from Norway. There, a serving girl named Christine waits for news of the ship and her father. He had hoped, by working on a sailing ship, to earn enough for a proper dowry for Christine. She reflects on this unspoken need: "Otherwise, what man would take a poor sailor's daughter with a crippled arm, ugly as the work of the devil?"

Changes in weather and temperature give Christine pain in her arm, but she performs work alongside her mother at a merchant's fine home. The merchant's wife is hostile toward both of them and especially the crippled girl.

On board the ship, Osuqo is raped and Poq is beaten. When Osuqo tries to jump overboard, she is losing so much blood that a sailor stops and tends her. When she wakens, she defensively pushes a man overboard before realizing it was the helpful stranger. When the ship returns to port, the captain incites the crowd to kill his prisoners for murdering Christine's father, but the merchant insists that law and justice will prevail "even for insane heathens."

Christine is put in charge of "the creatures" from Greenland. The master's son, Henrik, is a scholar who has compassion for the foreigners.

He studies their language and discovers that they understand Icelandic and may be descendants of Norwegian colonists. But his mother, other merchants, and the religious leaders of the town stir up fears of witchcraft. Christine feels the animosity: "A cripple like me isn't used to kindness from people. That had never bothered me. But the fact that people now shunned me as if I were in league with Satan himself made me sick with fear."

Henrik uses the captain's log to defend the Inuits in their murder trial, but the threat of witchcraft charges escalates. Osuqo often withdraws to fond memories of her people, but she and Poq are humiliated in repeated examinations. She collapses after they are forced to be baptised.

Henrik tries to speak up when his father intends to give the man and woman as a wedding present to Henrik's cruel sister and her groom. Henrik stammers his case, but his father cuts him off with a threat to send the youth to sea to learn some manners. Christine sees Henrik's good intentions subdued by the power his father has to force him to waste his life in hard labor or a minor job in some small store. Accused of witchcraft, Poq and Osuqo paddle to open sea in their kayak instead of the boat Henrik had provided.

Analysis: A complex and compelling story, *The Abduction* is based on historical documents. The point of view shifts between Christine and Osuqo, and both girls' impressions of the tragic events are convincing. As in *The Valley of the Deer,* social disfavor and suspicion of any physical difference are portrayed. Henrik's speech impairment undermines his ability to persuade his father, and the stuttering becomes even more pronounced when he is agitated. This award-winning novel should be available in most collections because the author takes the trouble to show how ethnocentric "discoveries" harmed individuals and societies during Europe's age of exploration.

■ Nixon, Joan Lowery. *The Other Side of Dark.* Delacorte, 1986. 186pp. (LB 0-385-29481-6) Reading Level: Grades 7–10. (BCCB O86) *Disability:* Coma

Stacy McAdams wakes from a long dream, calling her mom. A nurse is there instead, and Stacy is appalled to see that she has a different body, tall and with firm breasts. Stacy was 13 when a gunshot wound put her in a semiconscious state for four years. Her mother was killed in the same incident, and Stacy is determined to remember the face of their assailant so she can be a witness against him. The press covers Stacy's recovery as a "Sleeping Beauty" feature before police can take precautions about revealing there is a witness in a murder case that has charged no one in four years.

Stacy is uncomfortable with the clothing styles of the day, the high school version of her best friend from seventh grade, and being alone at home so much. She learns her father works two jobs to pay the medical bills, and her sister got married without any of the festivities and details they had planned as girls. She hates the gunman for the lengthening list of losses he has incurred for her family.

Stacy is introduced to Jeff, a new boy in town, and he offers to tutor her in math so she can enter high school in the fall. A male calls on the phone, hinting that she should not try to remember anything about the shooting. At a party, she sees many of the kids she knew four years before and is offered a spiked drink by Jarrod Tucker. While Jeff is helping her repel Jarrod's efforts to get Stacy into his car, Stacy identifies Jarrod as the person who shot her. Jarrod drives off but is apprehended.

Jeff takes Stacy home and is kind to her during the days before the hearing. She distrusts Jeff because there is something secretive about him and because Jarrod has threatened her with harm from "a friend." Stacy is alone in the house when the news announces that Jarrod has escaped from protective medical care. She hides in the treehouse, and he stalks her. When he admits how the murder took place and explains that he has set up a defense of insanity, Stacy pulls free, shoving the treehouse on top of him. Stacy takes up the gun but resists killing Jarrod, even though she knows the justice system will take a long time and may fall short on her need for revenge.

Stacy finds out that Jeff is an undercover agent, assigned to the high school and "loaned" to her case. She is disappointed, because she was beginning to care about him and have physical attractions that were novel to her previous 13-year-old experience. He explains that he acted cold because he does not want to be her "first boyfriend" but would like to have a longer lasting relationship.

Analysis: Stacy is not just set up as the poor amnesiac target of a crazed stalker in this mystery. The scenario of her semicoma and the treatment with minor surgery that triggers her waking is based on factual medical experience. If these explanations had not been provided, the story would have been seriously flawed, for the character's physical maturation would have been delayed and long rehabilitation required if she were truly in a coma for four years. Stacy even meets her physical therapist, an energetic lady, proud of keeping Stacy's body in good health all this time and insistent that Stacy keep up a regimen of exercise.

Stacy's father speaks to her directly about his concern that she has not mourned her mother. Stacy has suppressed her grief inside her anger toward the faceless gunman. When Jarrod is recognized, then has to be picked out in a lineup, and later must be identified in court, Stacy learns that trials and retrials and probation may prolong the time until she sees

Jarrod punished. After the action of this book is over, Stacy will still need to have several good cries and find ways to deal with the hatred, but Nixon has developed a support group of well-drawn characters that readers will believe can help pull Stacy through. It is uncommon to explore the reactions of a victim of violent crime, and this aspect adds to what is already a gripping mystery.

■ Paterson, Katherine. **Park's Quest.** Lodestar, 1988. 160pp. (0-525-67258-3) Reading Level: Grades 5–8. (BCCB Ap88)
Disability: Cerebral hemorrhage

Park has little to connect him with his father other than his aristocratic full name, Parkington Waddell Broughton V, a hidden photograph, and some books. His mother is reluctant to speak of any relatives or her marriage to a pilot who lost his life during a second tour of duty in Vietnam. Park pursues his own quest for information: reading his father's books, locating his father's name on the Vietnam War Memorial, and visiting his grandfather's faded estate in Virginia.

Embedded in the text are Arthurian daydreams that parallel Park's desires to discover more about his father and to find himself an heir to greatness. During his visit, however, Park mistakes his uncle for a hired hand, is irritated by the presence of a Vietnamese woman and her mouthy daughter, and is terrified by his grandfather's physical disabilities that resulted from a stroke.

A midnight disturbance brings Park to his grandfather's room.

> There was a lamp on beside the bed, casting its light on a pillow. An empty pillow. Park's heart jumped for the ceiling. Then he saw him. The old man was on his feet, his swaying body humped over the metal frame of a walker. The sobbing cut off abruptly as the head twisted up sideways to look at the intruder.
>
> Park opened his mouth, but it was stone dry. He meant to say something. Are you all right? What's the matter? Can I help? Anything.
>
> Haaa. The wail, for it was a wail, almost inhuman, the cry of some wretched animal in pain. Haaaa. Park turned and fled from the sound of it.

This encounter colors Park's fantasies with self-blame and guilt-ridden efforts to restore the family honor.

The boy's shifting perceptions of his grandfather contrast with two other characters'. Patronizing comments by the woman hired as nurse and housekeeper reveal that the elderly man has lost adult, if not human, status. An unlikely romp with the wheelchair shows that the girl, Thanh, views this man as a personality worth discovering and entertaining, despite his inability to communicate desires.

Since Park's discomfort with the visit is heightened by his lack of experience in a rural setting, he focuses on learning to use a rifle as a way to prove himself his father's son. Target practice with his uncle leads to an unsupervised shot that accidentally injures a crow. Thanh attacks him, crying "Murderer," and Park perceives combat as a life-shattering reality instead of a glorified legend.

His personal quest for information is resolved when a photograph of Thanh's father reveals the familiar features of Parkington Broughton IV. The denouement allows Park to unravel the family secrets for his new-found sister, as well as to decode his grandfather's remorseful cry.

Analysis. Paterson creates strong, spare prose but may be overreaching the abilities of her audience by shifting into and out of Park's fantasy life of Arthurian metaphor. The elements of Park's mystery that deal with self-concept and adolescent needs are believable. The elderly character whose loss of communication skills and mobility leads to loss of social stature as well is honestly portrayed. The depiction of a nurse who says, "We'd be better off dead, wouldn't we? Poor old thing" is well balanced by Thanh's role as patient advocate, wheeling Grandfather's chair off the porch and through the yard.

However, the other characters' guilt-laden pattern of withholding information from the children is extreme. Park's mother did not even tell him that his uncle and seriously ill grandfather would host his visit. The uncle is so well-intentioned that he searched refugee camps for his brother's foreign-born daughter, married the widow, works the family farm in the face of social ostracism, and yet does not sense his nephew's and stepdaughter's need to know the truth. These character inconsistencies make Park's motivation stagger and may make the reader grow impatient with his quest.

■ Paton Walsh, Jill. *Torch.* Farrar, 1988. 176pp. (0-374-37684-0)
Reading Level: Grades 7–12.
Disability: Orthopedic impairment

Oppressed children in a posttechnological future trek through corrupted Euro- and Afro-communities in search of The Games that their torch was created to light. One of their members has been trained for the legendary races and is intent on winning. Slavers capture him, he establishes a reputation for himself, and he resists rescue by his comrades. Only when he is told to throw a race so his master can profit on bets, does the runner rebel. He wins, cuts his own hamstrings, and is beaten and thrown on the trash heap for dead. The troop nurses him, but he avoids any assistance once they resume walking across country.

The girl who is recounting the adventure comes to know the runner better, and he begins training her to race. The band forms its own shore community, and the members pair up into couples. Perhaps they and their children will begin a tradition of games that is worthy of the Torch.

Analysis: Olympic "what-ifs?" are nicely presented. Various terrors that the fleeing children feel and the mystical attributes of the Torch keep up the pace throughout this quest novel. The runner is egocentric and has no personality at the beginning, but once the physical ability he most prizes is sacrificed for honor, he develops humanity. That's really the point of his subplot, so the narrow characterization is quite effective. There are "games" to participate in, but politics, religion, the economy, and blood lust have corrupted all the competitions the children locate. This is a good addition to collections in which speculative fiction has a big audience.

■ Paulsen, Gary. *Dancing Carl.* Bradbury, 1983. 105pp. (0-02-770210-3) Reading Level: Grades 5–7.
Disability: Neurological impairment

Helen is courted by Carl, who dances alone on the ice. *See full annotation* Chapter 6: Emotional Disturbances.

■ Payne, Bernal C. *The Late, Great Dick Hart.* Houghton, 1986. 133pp. (0-395-41453-9) Reading Level: Grades 5–7. (BCCB F87)
Disability: Brain tumor

Tom loses his best friend, Dick. Dick was 12 years old when he died from a brain tumor. For six months, Tom visits the gravestone. Then he meets Dick himself, seemingly alive and as full of mischief as Tom can recall. A fifth-dimension duplicate of their town seems to exist, where the former populace lives on. Tom visits the ageless Dick and the parallel town and is seen by another ex-resident. Dick is unable to persuade Tom to stay and share their longevity, because Tom prefers life at home.

Analysis: The fantasy transition is unexpected after a realistic beginning. Since Dick is not a ghost, and Tom does not awaken from a dream or go through an out-of-body journey, the author's life-after-death scenario seems odd. The first portion of the book could involve readers, but the second part may just puzzle them.

■ Payne, Sherry Neuwirth. *A Contest.* Illus. by Jeff Kyle. Carolrhoda, 1982. 37pp. (0-87614-176-9) Reading Level: Grades 3–4. (BL 1 Se82)
Disability: Cerebral palsy

Mike starts fifth grade in a public school where it is difficult to get around in his wheelchair. He is afraid to ask for help in the cafeteria and rest rooms, especially after a classmate snatches his cap and calls him a "spaz." Mike talks to his father and teacher about how things are going for him since he left his special school. His teacher selects classroom activities that Mike can excel in, and his classmates respond by sitting with him at lunch and asking about his other interests. Randy loses to Mike in arm wrestling and checkers; then the boys pair up at the community center for pool playing. Mike enjoys the rest of his year and learns both to ask for help when he needs it and to dismiss the stares his differences attract.

Analysis: Mike's account of his first year in mainstreamed education is a pleasant illustrated story that will appeal to students who are too old for *See You Tomorrow Charles* and too young for *Golden Daffodils.* The advice Mike gets from his father is insightful without seeming forced. Mike's point of view reveals the linear plot, but his character is not flat. Mike learns to admit his needs as well as showcase his strengths. When Randy throws his first match with Mike because he is afraid of hurting the disabled youth, Mike credits his wheelchair with building up muscles. Later, Randy challenges to a game of pool the boys who ridicule Mike, knowing that a wheelchair is no reason to prejudge the abilities of his friend.

Dark paper with drawings in sepia and white detail some of the action and focus on the characters' expressions. Mike's isolation shifts to his being part of the group in the compositions as well as the text.

■ Rabe, Bernice. *Margaret's Moves.* Illus. by Julie Downing. Dutton, 1987. 105pp. (0-525-44271-5) Reading Level: Grades 4–6. (BCCB My87)
Disability: Spina bifida

Margaret is 9 years old and wishes for a canopy bed like the one her older neighbors, the twins, have. She saves some money of her own and then gets angry when her younger brother, Rusty, takes advantage of her chance to win something from the new mall. She blames her wheelchair for slowing her down in getting the prize—a baseball mitt. She makes a game of setting the table and breaks her mother's jam jar, so gives up her savings to replace it. After her father treats her to a basketball game where the athletes all use lightweight wheelchairs, Margaret decides she would prefer getting a sports model wheelchair instead of a canopy bed.

Margaret's parents are still paying off loans on several surgeries Margaret has had to correct problems caused by spina bifida. Margaret's current chair is okay for getting around, and her parents feel it is more important to invest in a waterbed that will keep Margaret from getting pressure sores. Margaret resolves to follow her doctor's directions better so as to avoid the sores, tries to get her parents to change their mind, and finds ways to earn her own money. She tells an elderly friend in the park about her aspirations, and he encourages her to work toward her own goal.

Margaret and Rusty play together less and squabble a lot more than they used to, but when their father goes out of the country for a summer work assignment, they find ways to help their mother at home. Frequent trips to the local grocery store lead Margaret to ask for a job straightening up the displays and bins. Balancing things is her special talent, and the shopkeeper pays Margaret and Rusty for their help. Margaret also sells lemonade in the park and sings with her best friend for park visitors. When Margaret's grandmother and aunt are planning a wedding, Margaret suggests the park as a location. Preparing to be the flower girl, Margaret coaches her 2-year-old brother Tad about being the ring bearer.

When the waterbed is delivered to Margaret's home, she buys her neighbor's discarded canopy at a garage sale, and her grandfather helps suspend it over her wide new bed. Margaret persuades her father to visit a showroom and to take a loaner wheelchair home for the wedding weekend. She enjoys the extra mobility and freedom the lightweight chair gives her.

Margaret's father has been restoring an old sports car, and Margaret's friend in the park has a rich buddy who is interested in buying it. Margaret gets a finder's fee that brings her much closer to the purchase price of a sports model wheelchair, and her parents are so impressed with the loaner chair that they support her new priority.

Analysis: The prequel to this novel is a picture book called *The Balancing Girl.* This longer format allows family dynamics and details of Margaret's disability to be incorporated into the story. Characterizations are adequate, and Margaret's point of view is consistently maintained. The sibling stresses and financial pinch are introduced smoothly, but the dialogue is occasionally stiff, and some of Margaret's physical challenges and the accommodations made for them are presented in a self-conscious instead of subtle way.

When Margaret has the loaner chair, she is pleased to be able to pop the front wheels up over low steps that would have been a barrier before. When her friends are walking and talking, she can wheel along fast enough to hear all of their conversation.

Clearly, Margaret's special needs affect her whole family. Besides financial strains and the necessary physical accommodations described, Margaret's mother serves as an officer on the national spina bifida board, and both parents attend a conference for parents of special needs children. Though Rusty has new social outlets in sports that Margaret is not a part of, she adjusts to the change and enjoys playing catch with Tad. Margaret's mobility needs are the focus of this summertime story, and no details on her personal hygiene or her education are included. The episodic plot pulls all the little events of Margaret's summer together in a satisfying conclusion.

This book is recommended for the same children who are reading about Ramona or Fudge and their families, because Rabe maintains an authentic tone in her unique portrayal, adding a touch of humor and lots of self-reliance.

■ Raffi. *One Light, One Sun.* Illus. by Eugenie Fernandes. Crown, 1988. 32pp. (0-517-56785-7) Reading Level: Grades PS–2. (SLJ MS88) *Disability:* Orthopedic impairment

A song lyric by Canadian children's entertainer Raffi lists global similarities. The rhymes have no plot structure, but the illustrations depict a microcosm of several families' experiencing a full day's cycle of activities.

Of particular interest is the integrated population of these families. Skin tones vary, cross-generational relations are established, and one child is dependent on a wheelchair and adult assistance for some of the activities.

Illustrations with simple shapes and pure color values are reminiscent of a child's crayon drawing but incorporate realistic detail.

Analysis: The ecumenical text is full of images children can relate to. Presenting them with lively views of family life extends the book's usefulness. The casual inclusion of a person with a disability is welcome in a format that often wrongly assumes its audience cannot pick up such subtle elements. Raffi's overt message for global acceptance of our common situation sensitively includes the visual portrayal of a child who happens to use a wheelchair.

■ Reuter, Bjarne. *Buster's World.* Trans. by Anthea Bell. Dutton, 1989. 112pp. (0-525-44475-0) Reading Level: Grades 4–7. (BCCB S89) *Disability:* Orthopedic impairment

Buster Oregon Mortensen is in and out of trouble in his Danish community. Buster's sister, Ingeborg, is lame and has been plagued by a bully to the point of asking for Buster's help. He hands Ingeborg a stone and tells her to throw it at the cruel pest. This starts a sequence of chase, encounter, and revenge that introduces Buster to new areas of the neighborhood and a love interest.

Mr. Mortensen is a street magician with few parenting skills, so Buster exercises his own brand of ruse and persuasive speech to make his way.

Analysis: This award-winning import seems formulaic when compared with American young adult novels. Beyond pat elements common to "problem" novels, the characterization of Buster is engaging because of Buster's disregard for rules and his unique world view. The little romance and challenges of adolescent insecurities are nicely presented. Ingeborg is one member of an unorthodox family, and her disability is just one of the differences portrayed. Recommended for large collections.

■ Richmond, Sandra. **Wheels for Walking.** Atlantic, 1985. 195pp. (0-316-74439-5) Reading Level: Grades 7–10. (BCCB N85)
Disability: Quadriplegia; Paraplegia

"Oh, Jake, I just want to be normal again. If only there was a chance. I can't believe this has happened. One day you wake up and your life is over." These feelings and other observations of life in a rehabilitation center are presented by 18-year-old Sally Parker in the present tense in Part One of the book. Paralyzed from a broken neck, she hates interacting with doctors who humiliate her on their rounds and therapists who goad her into trying to use her seemingly useless body. She has lashed out at her family and Brian, her old boyfriend, rejecting their love along with their encouragement. Instead, Sally establishes a relationship with Jake, a paraplegic who resents most of the care they are receiving at the center. Jake was injured while driving drunk and still uses rebellious behavior to prove his independence.

Part Two of the book is a past-tense account of Sally's injury and early treatment. "It was the physiotherapist who finally told me the truth and I hated her for it." Sally describes how she sent Brian away because she did not feel a "gimp" was worthy of his love; he responded, "How can you be so selfish? You're not the only one who's hurting."

Part Three returns to the present tense at the center, where Sally feels that "Like my veins, punctured and weak from all the blood tests, my emotions are exhausted." When Jake breaks so many of the rules that the staff refuse to readmit him, Sally realizes that she must set a different course for herself. She learns that her disability has not interfered with her ability to have children, she learns to roll over and sit up by herself, and she is asked to be maid of honor at the wedding of a nurse she met after the accident. With these new insights about herself and her future, she risks calling Brian. Next, Sally tells her parents she is amenable to coming home for a weekend visit.

Analysis: Those readers who are willing to sort out the chronology of the story will be rewarded by a dramatic and convincing portrayal. The slow physical and emotional recovery that Sally faces are all part of the author's own experience. When characters say things such as, "There are lots of people who live perfectly normal lives in a wheelchair, and many are worse off than you," Sally has a natural, unforgiving reaction. Nevertheless, the information is there for the reader, just as it is there in Sally's memory when she is ready to see beyond her limitations to what her life can still offer.

■ Riddell, Ruth. *Shadow Witch.* Atheneum, 1989. 208pp. (0-689-31484-1) Reading Level: Grades 5–7.
Disability: Orthopedic impairment

Drew injured his spine while "flying" on LSD and must face the Shadow Witch's curse on his family before he can make a new life for himself. *See full annotation* Chapter 6: Emotional Disturbances.

■ Rose, Karen. *Kristin and Boone.* Houghton, 1983. 209pp. (0-395-34560-X) Reading Level: Grades 6–9. (BCCB Mr84)
Disability: Short stature

Beautiful Kristin, a 14-year-old film star, has never known her father but finds a man to trust and love in her director, Adam Boone. Following a science fiction script for a *Beauty and the Beast* variation, Boone requires more than a slick and superficial performance from Kristin. Since she has been nominated for an Emmy award, she resents this demanding attitude at first but learns to respect his opinion.

When letters from her mother's past identify Kristin's father, a tentative reunion turns into his efforts to manipulate Kristin into appearing with him in a film. Boone tactfully pronounces the script as "unproduceable," and Kristin invites Boone to escort her to the Emmy awards. He declines because he has surgery scheduled for one of the complications his dwarfism causes. Kristin hears that Boone has been hospitalized, so sends her costar to the Emmy awards while she rushes to be with Boone. Just before he dies, Kristin reveals that she wishes Boone were her father.

Analysis: Boone's stature as a director is distinct from his physical stature, and this marginal plot is strengthened by presenting such a nonstereotypic character. Kristin's success and beauty do not satisfy her, so it is refreshing to see the story deal with her search for a father figure instead of a lover. Kristin learns about Boone's disability, develops empathy, and makes mature judgments that are good to expose readers to. A weak cover illustration and some difficult shifts in format may limit this book's popularity.

■ Rue, Nancy. *Row This Boat Ashore.* Crossway, 1986. 265pp. (paper 0-89107-393-0) Reading Level: Grades 8–12. (SLJ F87)
Disability: Polio; Deafness

Felix is the typical high school cheerleader until her dissatisfaction and restlessness prompt her school counselor to propose that Felix may have outgrown high school society and might benefit from night classes at college. There she meets Michael, is attracted to him, and then is put off when she sees he uses a wheelchair. Michael is independent and gets around so well in his adoptive parents' home that Felix has to revise her opinion about his disability from polio. Michael's mother was admitted to a hospital for psychiatric care while he was being treated at a state hospital. He visits the state hospital for treatment twice a week, and when Felix accompanies him, she meets a child named Alex, who is deaf and mute.

Felix is uncomfortable with religious beliefs and people who hold them, but she still falls in love with Michael. She gives no advance notice to her girlfriend, Annie, about Michael's condition. The introduction at Homecoming is uncomfortable, and a subsequent double date is worse. A hostile polio patient at the state hospital hits Felix with a crutch. Felix drives off the road in a snowstorm, Michael does his best to help her but gets hurt trying, and they are both hospitalized. Felix says good-bye to Michael, who leaves to undergo two years of treatment to learn to walk—at least with crutches. The violent girl at the state hospital is evaluated for psychiatric needs to avoid charges of assault. Seven months later, Felix has a better relationship with her family, has settled on the vocational choice of teaching deaf children, attends her church regularly, reads the Bible, puzzles through new concepts, and feels an even deeper love for Michael.

Analysis: Polio is a dated ailment, and it is unfortunate that such a pleasant book about disability and faith is set in the past. Medical and psychiatric procedures have changed a great deal since then, and readers may assume, incorrectly, of course, that this invalidates the spiritual insights Michael shares with Felix.

The scenario of a mentally unstable mother who just disappears into an institution while her polio-stricken son was garrisoned with other "cripples" until a compassionate nurse becomes his protective mother and religious mentor sounds Dickensian. The hostile polio patient with crutches may be there to counter angelic stereotypes. Michael is so-o-o-o good and refuses Felix's physical advances because of religious conviction and self-sacrificing love. This is believable as a characterization, but sweeping him off to therapy for two years does not let him grow or let either character develop self-discipline regarding celibacy to match convictions. Is there a rehabilitation program for polio that would make a difference that late in his life? In any case, at least he is mobile, competent, lovable, level-headed, and eager to have Felix face his limitations as well as let him do all he can for himself.

Felix's first-person point of view interjects humor with an edge to it, which counters some contrived elements. Readers may find the dramatic roadside rescue gripping and the bittersweet love story just what they were looking for. Selectors often ignore religious press paperback titles; this offers more than most, though less than the best in mainstream juvenile publishing.

■ Rylant, Cynthia. *A Blue-Eyed Daisy*. Bradbury, 1985. 99pp. (0-02-777960-2) Reading Level: Grades 5–7. (BCCB S85)
Disability: Orthopedic impairment; Epilepsy

By the time Ellie Farley is 11, her mother, four teenaged sisters, and father have difficulty communicating about much besides what scraps each one saved from dinner for the dog's bowl. Things were not always this bleak, and Ellie realizes that her father's injured right arm, loss of his job in the mines, and hard drinking are to blame. When their dog, Bullet, gives Ellie an opportunity to learn to hunt with her father, she becomes a good shot.

At school, a classmate has a "fit," and the ensuing discussion about "swallowing his tongue" is so confusing that Ellie calls the hospital to find out about epilepsy. Her interest and personal fears are addressed by a helpful nurse. After a boy gets shot by his own brother in a careless accident, Ellie and her father come to an understanding about her nervous avoidance of shooting practice.

After Ellie's father has an accident while driving drunk, Ellie visits with a woman whose husband had worked with Mr. Farley. Ellie hears that "He used to be a good man, your daddy." By the time Ellie turns 12, one sister is engaged, and Bullet's reputation as a good rabbit dog has Mr. Farley making plans to raise puppies.

Analysis: The writing is economical, yet insightful. A full year in Ellie's life is related strictly from her 11-year-old point of view, but the nuance in dialogue and action offers a well-developed picture of rural life and individuals changing to cope with it. Not every person who suffers an orthopedic impairment will become a drunk, but Mr. Farley's loss of strength in one arm also caused him to lose his job, his ability to use his rifle, and his role as provider for all six women in his family. Most readers will be able to discern these interactions, although the author's subtle observations do not spell it out for them. In the end, Ellie reflects that loaning Bullet out to hunters "meant Okey had more man-talk and was happier, and sober, more often."

All the characters have depth, even though they may appear briefly, and each one has a quality that teaches Ellie something about herself. When Harvey cames back to school after being treated for a seizure:

> None of the kids really talked to him, and nobody mentioned his fit. Mostly they all seemed embarrassed, too.
>
> If she hadn't been so sure she wasn't going to have any fits, Ellie would have kept away from Harvey like the rest of them. And if she hadn't known he'd been given some medicine to stop any more fits from coming, she would have kept her eyes on him like a hawk.
>
> But she knew he was all right. And she was, too.

This is a wonderful example of information and models of acceptance incorporated into a fine piece of children's literature. Its honest portrayal of characters with impairments is just one of this book's merits.

■ Sachs, Elizabeth-Ann. *Where Are You, Cow Patty?* Atheneum, 1984. 146pp. (0-689-31057-9) Reading Level: Grades 5–7. (BCCB S84) *Disability:* Scoliosis

Janie met Courtney in the hospital for their surgeries to correct spinal curvature. Janie is a tomboy and is annoyed when, on a visit, Courtney flirts with Harold Waxby. Farm events like milking a cow and witnessing the birth of a calf lighten Janie's mood. Before Courtney leaves, she admits she flirted with Harold for fur. but never meant to come between Janie and her best pal. In the end, Janie knows she can stand up to Harold's pressure that they have formal dates as practice for entering junior high.

Analysis: A sequel to *Just Like Always,* this title shows that scoliosis is just a detour in Janie's "normal" adolescent development. A silly recurring dream about a kissing bird does not detract from the reader's appreciation of other passages in this humorous story.

■ Slepian, Jan. *Getting on with It.* Macmillan, 1985. 171pp. (0-02-782930-8) Reading Level: Grades 5–8. (BCCB Mr86) *Disability:* Orthopedic impairment

Beryl Brice, called "Berry," is 13 and is aware that her parents have sent her to spend a month with her grandmother so they can complete arrangements for a separation. Grandmother lives with Agnes, a former family domestic, in a rented house on the shore of Lake Erie. Two other houses nearby belong to "Ma" Simpson, who is in failing health. Ma is cared for by her younger sister—Hortie—and Sonny, a man who has lived with them since he was a teenager in need of foster care.

An artistic Norse beauty named Wanda arrives and leases the third house. Berry daydreams about many things, pairs Sonny and Wanda in her imagination, and makes a wishful calculation on her lucky stone that if Sonny and Wanda fall in love, Mr. and Mrs. Brice will get back together also.

Berry plays along the shore and in the woods with a 10-year-old boy named Floyd. They discover a "crazy" man in the woods who traps and tinkers with electronic equipment. The man, Smitty, reveals that he acts crazy to scare off people, but Berry discovers that he is really Sonny's father, who's been drinking and drifting around ever since his wife died in a car accident he caused.

Berry saves a rabbit from a ferocious dog, and Hortie nurses it back to health. Hortie and Sonny share intimacies that puzzle Berry, because she has never seen her parents share affection in physical gestures or playful moments. When Berry spies on Wanda's flirting with Sonny, she realizes that wishes about romance for the younger couple would be at Hortie's expense.

Wanda tells Berry she plans to complete her gallery showing of batik paintings and hopes Sonny will travel with her afterward. Berry asks about the trip while Sonny and Hortie and Wanda are all together. Hortie urges Sonny to make a life with someone younger, who can give him children. Sonny professes his love for Hortie. Wanda assures Hortie that children would not have been part of her plans.

When "Ma" Simpson dies, her funeral depresses Grandmother because of suppressed memories about World War II Germany. Floyd hears that the police are looking for Smitty, and he goes to warn him. When the boy is reported missing, Berry fights her fear of the dark and finds Floyd caught in a trap. She gets to town and is credited with saving Floyd's life. Berry learns that Smitty is leaving again, though Sonny and Hortie have invited him to live with them. Berry is delighted to learn Sonny and Hortie married. She decides to set the rabbit free and to get on with reality instead of dreaming.

Analysis: Berry is a perceptive and imaginative young lady. What she discovers about others at the lake gives her insights about the flaws in her parents' relationship. Her father withdraws from trouble, like his own mother. Mrs. Brice is busy with her own agenda, like Wanda. When Berry sees that Hortie's and Sonny's relationship is based on more than their mutual love for "Ma," she learns that life should not always follow the romantic patterns of a Brontë novel.

The hazards of having imagination and few other outlets in one's life are personified by Agnes. Berry thinks, "Aggie got most of her knowledge of the world from soap operas and movie magazines." She hardly steps outside, sits in the car to avoid the bugs if she does go out of the house, crochets, makes suspicious judgments about their landlady's family, and enjoys the funerals of people she does not know. Aggie is also shown to be a loyal companion for Grandmother, an excellent cook, and a beloved member of the household. Her limp and perhaps her reclusive behavior are explained by Berry's summary of an old family story, which begins, "Poor Aggie, to have grown up when polio was still around. She was the neglected crippled daughter of a Czech mill hand and a sickly mother. . . ."

Smitty's guilt-ridden existence is summarized in a drunken groan, "Tired. Too many bars . . . too many women . . . all those years . . . all those rooms . . . bound to happen. . . ." Berry later sees Sonny comforting his father, and she reflects that the young man's tender care and infinite sadness seemed a reversal of a painting at home called "The Prodigal Son." The author is very skilled at creating characters and maintaining suspense in a story that also features a young girl's introspection and fantasy. Italics set off Berry's wishful thinking, so readers will not be confused by shifts of scene in this perceptive novel.

■ Smith, Doris Buchanan. *Voyages.* Viking, 1989. 170pp. (0-670-80739-7) Reading Level: Grades 6–8.
Disability: Paraplegia

Twelve-year-old Janessa prefers being in traction for a spinal injury to facing the world, until she has fantasy adventures with Norse gods and heroes. *See full annotation* Chapter 6: Emotional Disturbances.

■ Snyder, Carol. *Dear Mom and Dad, Don't Worry.* Bantam, 1989. 160pp. (0-553-05801-0) Reading Level: Grades 8–12. (KR 1 D89)
Disability: Spinal injury

Carly falls out of a broken hammock and fractures her spine when she is 13. Everyone gives her advice, and her friend Michelle learns not to blame herself for the incident. Carly returns to school in a brace.

Analysis: Slight characterizations and stiff dialogue weaken this story. There are many other problem novel trappings but *Izzy, Willy-Nilly* and *Wheels for Walking* would be much better choices for serious exposure to disabilities due to an accident.

■ Snyder, Carol. *Ike and Mama and the Seven Surprises*. Lothrop, 1985. 160pp. (0-688-03732-1) Reading Level: Grades 3–6.
Disability: Tuberculosis; Orthopedic impairment

Jake arrives in Manhattan, from Russia, and does not let his limp stop him from getting a job in a bakery. *See full annotation* Chapter 4: Health Problems.

■ Snyder, Zilpha Keatley. *Libby on Wednesday*. Delacorte, 1990. 196pp. (0-385-29979-6) Reading Level: Grades 5–7. (KR 1 F90; BCCB Ap90; HB My-Je90)
Disability: Cerebral palsy

Libby faces seventh-grade realities when her family decides her home-enriched education needs to be supplemented by socialization skills. Her grandfather, a novelist, is well-known, and Libby loves to write. She keeps a journal and various collections. When Libby is grouped with four other young writers for workshop meetings, the five styles and personalities clash. By sharing their works and risking criticism, the group members make progress in their writing as well as in interpersonal relations. Once their adviser cannot meet with them because of a hospital stay, the students continue to gather on their own. One member of their group, G.G., is rescued by the others from his abusive alcoholic father.

Analysis: With care, the author's narrative and Libby's journal entries reveal a *Breakfast Club*–type experience for middle-graders. After their superficial differences and biases have been exposed, the five learn to respect each other and then band together to protect one of the members. This plot element provides dramatic tension but is not so subtle as other aspects of the book.

The student characters are each identifiable "types"—from cheerleader to bully to punker to crippled genius. Alex has cerebral palsy and cannot "write" in the physical sense of the word. However, with the special education classroom's equipment, Alex produces satirical pieces that Libby is impressed with. Alex is just one of the portrayals that deepen as Libby gets "socialized." What makes the story valuable is that all of the students are shown to have more depth than first impressions of them could denote. The adult characters are as individualistic as the younger ones, making this a good selection for most collections.

■ Strachan, Ian. *The Flawed Glass*. Little, Brown, 1990. 204pp. (0-316-81813-5) Reading Level: Grades 6–8. (KR 15 S90; BCCB N90)
Disability: Neurological impairment; Speech impairment

An isolated Scottish island has been home to inquisitive Shona MacLeod, and it now has a new "laird." The American who bought the island as a tax break transplants his family there. His son, Carl, meets Shona and is interested in accompanying her on her nature explorations of the area. This is logistically difficult, for Shona lacks good motor control and cannot speak, though she can make sounds. Carl finds a way for Shona to use a computer to communicate. Once she is able to express her thoughts and clearly respond, her life changes.

Analysis: Shona's awkward gait is described, and her mobility problems seem realistic, but one wonders why there are no tasks for raising sheep that Shona's family could have adapted for their island-traveling daughter. That puzzle, together with the flat portrayal of Carl's father, constitutes the major flaw in an otherwise engrossing portrait of a contemporary child limited more by old attitudes and lack of technology than by her serious neurological impairment.

Because Shona can hear, she has good language development, but the unstructured sounds or erratic movements she makes cannot be interpreted by her family, teachers, or other islanders. Also, they do not expect Shona to be able to communicate, so their misinterpretations of her actions pile one frustration after another on the girl's efforts.

Carl's expectations, however, are open ended. The more time he spends with Shona, the more convinced he becomes that she has lots of knowledge and opinions that she simply cannot express. The physical substitute of the computer for a voice or gestures is nicely depicted. The time involved in Shona's acquisition of her new skills is not hurried. Interesting characters and setting also strengthen this novel.

■ Talbert, Marc. *Toby.* Dial, 1987. 168pp. (0-8037-0441-0) Reading Level: Grades 6–8.
Disability: Neurological impairment; Speech impairment

Toby's mother has difficulties from brain damage, and their neighbor has a stroke. *See full annotation* Chapter 6: Mental Retardation.

■ Terris, Susan. *Wings and Roots.* Farrar, 1982. 186pp. (0-374-38451-7) Reading Level: Grades 7–9. (BCCB Je82)
Disability: Orthopedic impairment

In 1955, the Salk vaccine means hope for most but has come too late to spare bitter Kit, who at 14 is being cared for in the town hospital, where Jeannie works as a volunteer. Everyone is puzzled by the occasional appearance of prose poems signed "Yeti." Jeannie suspects the writer is

Kit. During the next four years Kit and Jeannie enjoy a friendship that they feel may be love. Kit's mobility has improved, and he feels he may attain some of the goals he once thought polio had stolen from him.

Analysis: The title refers to Kit's need for wings or freedom beyond the restrictions of his paralysis and Jeannie's desire for emotional roots. Four years of ups and downs in their relationship can be tedious reading, because no other action lends drama. Considered as a piece of historical fiction, this accurately portrays the frustrations and narrow expectations of a male polio patient in 1955. Kit makes slow, steady progress in reestablishing motor pathways and reversing the atrophy that would have affected his muscles.

■ Thiele, Colin. *Jodie's Journey.* Harper & Row, 1990. 169pp. (LB 0-06-026133-1) Reading Level: Grades 5–9. (KR 15 O90; BCCB Ja91)
Disability: Arthritis, rheumatoid

Jody is nearly 12 when she starts having sore, swollen joints. At first, everyone assumes that entering competitions with her horse, Monarch, causes Jody's pain. Weeks of agony and bearing the unsympathetic reactions of her classmates and teachers follow. When her condition is diagnosed as rheumatoid arthritis, and Jody must become accustomed to the limitations of a wheelchair, her parents consider selling Monarch. A doctor points out that Monarch is Jody's friend, not just a mount for a sport she can no longer pursue. When Australia's bush area suffers a historic fire (Ash Wednesday, 1983) Jody and Monarch save each other's life.

Analysis: Thiele combines his personal knowledge of dealing with rheumatoid arthritis with his reliable skill as a novelist in this horse story. Jody has an ailment that is invisible yet debilitating. Jody has to adjust not only to her new limitations, but to the way her parents and others perceive her and the pain she is trying to cope with. The balance that Jody strikes is important, and the authentic portrayal of her struggle is not undermined by Thiele's exciting conclusion.

■ Thompson, Julian F. *Facing It.* Avon/Flare, 1983. 230pp. (paper 0-380-84491-5) Reading Level: Grades 8–12. (BCCB F84)
Disability: Orthopedic impairment

At camp, he is known as Randy Duke, because he does not want anyone to associate him with the promising left-handed pitcher who lost his chance at the major leagues when three fingers were severed from his left hand. His activities as a counselor are a distraction from his injury and crushed hopes. Randy feels drawn to a young camper and falls in love with an open young woman. When she finds out Randy lied to her, she runs away. Randy and another camper search for the girl and achieve a reunion.

Analysis: Interpersonal relationships win out over bitter disappointments in a story of summer love. Strong writing style and well-differentiated characters highlight this young adult novel. A college man's damaged self-image is the principal focus, and the author draws a stronger correspondence between Randy's aspirations and his new disability than other portrayals of this type of loss tend to establish. Recommended for secondary collections when *The Crazy Horse Electric Game* proves too sad for a given audience.

■ Voigt, Cynthia. *Izzy, Willy-Nilly.* Atheneum, 1986. 276pp. (0-689-31202-4) Reading Level: Grades 7–12. (BCCB My86)
Disability: Amputation

Isobel ("Izzy") is in an automobile accident at age 15, which results in the amputation of one leg below the knee. She views this as leaving her with part of a leg, "and her whole life changed." Suzy, Lisa, and Lauren, Izzy's friends, visit her in the hospital, but they do not stay loyal. Eccentric Rosamunde Webber surprises Izzy and prompts some changes in both the injured girl's room and her outlook.

At home, Izzy resents the physical accommodations her parents have made, because it emphasizes the permanency of her condition. Each of her older twin brothers, Joel and Jack, deals differently with her disability. Izzy tries to control her feelings, feels ashamed when she weeps, and judges herself harshly for not adjusting to her loss as well as her loved ones believe she has. Making plans to return to school is difficult for her and compounded by the secret that Marco, her date the night of the accident, was drunk.

Izzy starts school and experiences the change in her schoolmates' attitude toward her. She deals awkwardly with the silence, the stares, and the offers of assistance. Eventually, she allows a classmate to carry her up some difficult steps, and she joins the newspaper staff. She angrily interrupts Marco and a new lovely, motivated as much by envy of the girl's grace as by concern that anyone else should risk Marco's recklessness.

Analysis: Isobel Lingard has a hard adjustment to make, an issue that often overshadows the elements of a plot that could make this a well-rounded story. The character of Rosamunde provides an attractive foil for the other teens, who seem like stock characters. It is never made clear why all her former friends desert Izzy. This implies that her previous popularity was earned by her cheerfulness, and that physical injury precludes Izzy's ever being cheerful again.

This book is more successful in portraying Izzy's adjustment to her new self-image and social status than the physical demands of losing her lower leg.

■ Wahl, Jan. *Button Eye's Orange.* Illus. by Wendy Watson. Warne, 1980. 42pp. (0-7232-6188-1) Reading Level: Grades PS–2. (BCCB Mr81) *Disability:* Orthopedic impairment

Bonzer must stay in bed, but he does not mind so long as his favorite toy, Button Eye, is there too. Bonzer's mother sits at his bedside sewing many stuffed animals like Button Eye, but she then takes them away to sell. Button Eye has a leg that is sewn on backward, so he and the boy with a leg that does not "walk right" have a special bond.

Bonzer wants an orange, and Button Eye has an adventure at the market while getting one for him. Bonzer and his mother come to the market to find Button Eye, and the boy is sure his toy has bought him the orange.

Analysis: An odd mixture of fantasy and reality is illustrated in pastel-colored compositions that hint at the skill Wendy Watson has developed since this venture. Wahl has less control of the characters and plot elements in this book than in other allegories that maintain the author's poetic flow. Lots of good ideas and budding talent do not mesh in this picture book, which is indexed in *A to Zoo.*

One of the best illustrations shows both Bonzer's walking with a brace on his leg and that this is evidently a single-parent family. Therefore, it is unfortunate that Button Eye's marketplace adventure intrudes more than expands on the loving little tale of mother and son.

■ Weiman, Eiveen. *It Takes Brains.* Atheneum, 1982. 276pp. (0-689-30896-5) Reading Level: Grades 5–6. (BCCB Jl82) *Disability:* Epilepsy; Learning disabilities

Barbara Brainard cannot either avoid or live up to her nickname of "Brains." Her parents are both doctors, and students often borrow her homework to copy, but Barbara gets disappointing report cards, and the teachers at her expensive private school are unpleased. When the family moves to a big house in Ohio, things change for Barbara.

One teacher thinks that Barbara's impulsive behavior and inattentiveness make schoolwork hard for her but that placement in a special program where students choose their own projects might challenge her to do her best. A classmate, Ned Ferris, is the nephew of the Brainards' housekeeper, and Barbara has fun sledding with Ned and scouting for shopping carts to return for pay. Ned's little sister has epilepsy; Barbara asks her parents to describe what may cause the problem.

Barbara develops projects for school, friendships, and outside interests but is still unhappy because her busy parents do not seem to love her enough to make time for her. When Barbara is watching over Emily, the little girl falls from a swing. Barbara's father discovers Emily has a nonmalignant tumor, and he operates to remove it.

Analysis: Several plot threads and a dog wander around Barbara's life the year before her twelfth birthday. She comes to understand her weaknesses and strengths, and she adjusts her expectations of her parents. The episodes with Emily show the 4-year-old as a protected doll who needs help. The pat ending of surgery to remove Emily's tumor gives Barbara something specific to appreciate about her busy, learned father to balance her feelings of neglect.

■ Woolverton, Linda. *Running Before the Wind.* Houghton, 1987. 152pp. (0-395-42116-0) Reading Level: Grades 6–9. (BCCB Ap87)
Disability: Orthopedic impairment; Emotional disturbance

Kelly Mackenzie enjoys running and hopes to train for junior high track, but her father is adamant that she not join the team. His mood swings can be triggered by Kelly's slipping below an A grade in algebra or a mispronounced word. His anger shifts to relaxed comaraderie and good humor when the family takes a sailing trip to Catalina. When they return home, he finds out he has been passed over for promotion. He claims that management does not "want a gimp representing the company." Kelly assumes: "Her father was talking about his polio leg. He'd contracted the disease when he was a teenager. But he wasn't a cripple. One of his legs was a little shorter and skinnier than the other; that was all."

Kelly's father overturns the dinner table in a rage because Kelly was picking at her food with little appetite. Kelly's sister and mother try to maneuver themselves out of his way, and Kelly finds out from her mother why he is so furious about Kelly wanting to run track. His own promising record as a miler was interrupted by the bout with polio. The next time he gets angry at Kelly about her interest in running during summer school, she confronts him with her new knowledge of his past: "Why do you have to take running away from me just because the polio took it away from you?" His rage is evident when he calls Kelly to him, she hesitates, and he promises not to hit her. But when she comes near, he strikes her so hard that she falls to the floor.

The next morning, he tries to speak to Kelly before he sails on someone else's boat to Baja California but she refuses to let him into her room. He is killed in a boating accident, and during her period of grief, Kelly has to deal with the additional guilt over her last day with her father. Kelly's depressed mother is in bed all day every day, and Kelly's sister resists the necessity to sell the family's boat.

Kelly begins her summer school training for track and appreciates the coach's low-key praise of her stamina in a long-distance run. Kelly competes well but nearly strikes a teammate who did not give up her position in a race. The coach assumes Kelly's hostility stems from the usual anger sometimes brought on by grief and asks if Kelly has ever talked with a counselor about her father. Kelly says no but tells her coach "the whole horrible truth" and the "awful secret" that she is glad her father is not around anymore.

Kelly invites her mother and sister to see her cross-country race. When her mother claims she lacks the strength to attend, Kelly speaks out about her father. "Let's stop pretending that he was Mr. Perfect! Dad was crazy and we all know it!" Kelly gets slapped by her mother, fights back her own rage, and then vows that "No one is ever going to touch me like that again. Not ever!"

When Kelly lines up for her event, she sees her mother and sister in the stands. She struggles for first position and nearly loses within sight of the finish line when she thinks of her father. Kelly visits the sailboat, removes the sale sign, and cleans up the recent evidence of neglect. She decides that she misses her father, though she probably never can forgive him for the things he did. "There was a hole in the world now that he was gone. And she would give anything to have him back, no matter what."

Analysis: Mr. Mackenzie's uncontrolled rage is triggered by Kelly's independent behavior, which her father sees as defiance, and the father's bout with polio, which is blamed for any disappointment that occurs in his life. His competence and enjoyment in sailing activities usually elevate his mood. Early in the story, Mr. Mackenzie is overbearing and irrational toward Kelly's boyfriend; later, the youth talks about Kelly's crazy dad at school. This unkind act helps sketch in two minor characters when Kelly's boy-crazy best friend provides a loyal defense. Less believable portrayals are the roles of Kelly's passive/petrified mother and sister.

Domestic violence and its emotional ramifications are the focus of this story. Mr. Mackenzie's shorter and weaker leg do not compose his disability so much as his polio-stricken self-image. There is a bit of explication when Kelly's mother says, "His mother died when he was an infant and he was practically raised by the family housekeeper, who was . . . very abusive." He may also be a manic-depressive, but Kelly's ability to control her own temper is credited to her use of some inner strength that her father must have lacked.

Coming to terms with her father's memory is Kelly's challenge, and her characterization is well drawn. The supportive coach initiates needed counseling, but no foreshadowing of continued professional help is given. Instead, Kelly's last-page admission that she would put up with anything again to have her father back sets her in the same camp as her passive mother and sister. This is a disappointing resolution, with Kelly willing to return to an abusive pattern and even establishing one by committing to spend her time maintaining the boat that her uncle has suggested they sell. What is presented as a happy ending by a shift of tone in Kelly's soul searching could be simply the start of another problem for this wounded 13-year-old girl.

■ Wright, Betty Ren. *Rosie and the Dance of the Dinosaurs.* Holiday, 1989. 136pp. (0-8234-0782-9) Reading Level: Grades 4–6. (BCCB F90) *Disability:* Orthopedic impairment; Depression

Rosie and her mother are alone in the house, because Papa has been transferred to Milwaukee. It seems that someone is entering their house and disturbing their belongings. Rosie, who is a piano player, meets a new girl, Angela, who also plays piano, and her undisciplined younger brother. Rosie practices her recital piece, called "Dance of the Dinosaurs," and imagines a story about a dinosaur family, separated and reunited. The day of the recital, Rosie is able to concentrate on her playing instead of her fear that having only nine fingers makes the ending quite difficult to play. Rosie learns that there can be more than one star at a recital. The obnoxious boy who nearly ruined her piece feels cheered up when Rosie shares her "magic trick" of counting only four fingers on her right hand.

Analysis: Strong storytelling and vivid events, such as a bat under the couch-bed and worms all over a house, enliven this book. Rosie is adjusting to various stresses and sees her mother's depression deepen with respect to the imminent move to Milwaukee. Skill in art and a challenging piano piece do not serve to bolster Rosie's self-image when the new girl in town says, "Oh, yuk! Your fingers—what's wrong with your hand?" Angela's response, "So she's got nine fingers. So what?" is the kind of flip acceptance Rosie used to be able to show when her father was home. Since she is feeling vulnerable, without him, she acts more withdrawn during the current period of adjustment. This title could supplement collections in which bratty younger brothers and their outrageous pranks are appreciated.

■ Wright, Betty Ren. *The Summer of Mrs. MacGregor.* Holiday, 1986. 160pp. (0-8234-0628-8) Reading Level: Grades 5–8. *Disability:* Cardiac disorder; Cerebral hemorrhage; Emotional disturbance

Mr. Jameson, a neighbor who has hired Caroline to help him after his stroke, falls because he refuses to rely on his walker. *See full annotation* Chapter 4: Health Problems.

■ Yep, Laurence. *The Serpent's Children.* Harper & Row, 1984. 288pp. (LB 0-06-026812-3) Reading Level: Grades 5–8. (BCCB Mr84) *Disability:* Orthopedic impairment

Cassia's mother and father have been dedicated to the "work" of revolting against Manchu domination, but first "the demons" who bring opium and firearms to nineteenth-century China's Middle Kingdom must be repelled. Their mother dies when Cassia is just 8, but the headstrong girl defies clan members by staying on her family's land with her younger brother. Their father does return, but his leg has been injured, and he must rely on crutches until it heals. His dedication to the "work" focuses on training his children in the ways of warriors, and he is disappointed that his son, Foxfire, does not show skill in martial arts the way Cassia does.

In a confrontation with a mercenary who used to fight for the "work," Cassia's father is humiliated because of his weak leg. Famine strikes the land, and all Cassia's efforts to do what her mother would have done in order to save the family fail. When they have been reduced to eating grass soup, Foxfire hears of a way to get to the Golden Mountain. His father disowns Foxfire as a dreamer who has abandoned the "work," and the boy leaves for California. Since their home and lands are already confiscated for debt, and a friend has placed himself as assurance for repayment of Foxfire's passage, Cassia and her father force the clerk to substitute themselves as potential slaves should Foxfire be unable to pay on his three-year loan. Cassia is stunned when the clerk who she thought was coming to take them as slaves delivers twenty strings of cash. A learned uncle reads Foxfire's dictated letter, which indicates his hope that the money will be used to fight the cycle of poverty at home.

Foxfire's success inspires other clan members to pledge their lands or themselves for men's passage to the Golden Mountain. Cassia uses Foxfire's money to buy land, and she takes out a loan to plant crops in the tired soil. An early rain ruins the clan's rice crop, and relatives are indeed taken as slaves in payment of debt when their son dies while crossing to California. To avoid the same fate, Cassia suggests her father ask Foxfire to get a loan in California, where the repayment would not be so impossible. Another letter from Foxfire describes the hardships of his crossing and the dangers of his work so that other peasants who intend to become a

"Guest of the Golden Mountain" will be forewarned of their choice between two kinds of death rather than a promise of riches.

Analysis: Yep's deep feeling for the characters he portrays in a distant Chinese clan helps establish a unique point of view and vision. Peasant life is demonstrated in compelling scenes such as the binding of Cassia's feet to ensure that she would be fit as a wife instead of a field worker, the prying of Mother's story window from the wall when there was no food and nothing left to sell, and Peony's crying as her parents took her to a brothel to be sold as a slave so the three of them would not starve.

Oppression by the white "demons" is not as direct a burden on these people as what Foxfire recognizes as a cycle of bad harvests, indebtedness, and corruption. Father's injury makes him more demanding with Foxfire and as a military instructor, because a lame man cannot be in the fight himself. His prowess as a fighter compensates for his injured leg against untrained attackers, but he cannot best his old associate, Dusty. Father regains part of his self-esteem when he takes leadership of the clan's guard. Finally, Cassia's fighting skills and Father's shotgun, which is purchased thanks to Foxfire's work and advice, drive the mercenary out of their valley.

The cover is a symbolic portrait of the family: Crutches abandoned in the corner to represent Father, Cassia firmly seated with one knee drawn up, Foxfire standing in an attitude of defiant thought, and Mother's carved story window spilling a pattern of shadow and light upon both of "The Serpent's Children." Few historical novels deal this clearly with why the immigrant population of the United States faced the dangers of nineteenth-century travel and American pioneer days. This is a highly recommended title that can broaden understanding of one ethnic group's heritage while portraying the physical and emotional strength of a family in very hard times. It might be a transitional book for maturing readers before they try Buck's *The Good Earth.*

5

BOOKS DEALING
WITH SENSORY PROBLEMS

This chapter contains titles classified in two sections: Hearing Impairments and Visual Impairments.

Citations are alphabetical by author in each section.

Short entries describe secondary characters or additional disabilities discussed at length in a full annotation that has been classified in some other chapter. "See" references are noted.

HEARING IMPAIRMENTS

■ Andrews, Jean F. *The Flying Fingers Club.* Kendall Green, 1988. 100pp. (Paper 0-930323-44-0) Reading Level: Grades 3–5. (BCCB F89) *Disability:* Deafness; Learning disabilities

Donald was in third grade last year and is bitter about having to repeat it while attending special classes for certain subjects. He meets Matt, who comes to class with an interpreter because he is deaf and wants to try regular class assignments. Matt teaches Donald to finger spell and sign. They play together and share clues about who may be stealing papers from the newspaper route that Donald's sister delivers.

Analysis: Some suspense is provided by the boys' attempt to solve a mystery. The characters reveal a lot of information about their disabilities and accommodations, which can slow down the story line. All in all, it is nice that Gallaudet is distributing a work of juvenile fiction that portrays friendships being built in a mainstreamed educational setting.

■ Aseltine, Lorraine, Evelyn Mueller, and Nancy Tait. *I'm Deaf and It's Okay.* Illus. by Helen Cogancherry. Whitman, 1986. 39pp. (0-8075-3472-2) Reading Level: Grades K–4. (SLJ Ag86)
Disability: Deafness

A boy in elementary school narrates present-tense episodes from his life and shares his feelings and expectations that are related to the use of hearing aids. In bed, with his instruments off, and in the dark, "I feel alone. I am afraid. I start to cry." When Mom comes in and "signs and talks to me about how dark it seems when my hearing aids are on the night table, instead of in my ears, I put my hand on her throat and feel her voice purring as she speaks."

During dress-up with his little sister, Molly, he feels left out by telephone call interruptions that he cannot take part in because "I need to see someone's lips to understand what the person is saying." Later, he pushes Molly off Grandma's lap when their laughter over a picture book made him afraid that Grandma likes "Molly better than me because Molly can hear and talk better than I can. I feel angry! I hate Molly!"

At school and with his friends the boy is able to do fun things like listen to the librarian tell a story or make plans for a Halloween costume. He also has to figure out why his school hearing aid stops working and to wait for his mother to find him when he no one else in the store can understand his signs about being lost.

He expects to grow out of his hearing impairment, because none of the adults he knows wear hearing aids. After his parents and teacher explain that that will not happen, he is very angry. He meets a 17-year-old named Brian, who visits the class. "Brian says it's okay to be grown-up and wear hearing aids. Really, it is." Brian understands how the boy feels, describes all the activities and friends he enjoys, then rides the bus home with the little boy.

Analysis: Trying to keep an authentic point of view and tone often makes this text awkward. Complex sentences alternate with bald statements of the boy's emotional reactions. The most significant plot element is Brian's intervention in the boy's negative reactions to facts about the permanency of his hearing loss.

Expressive drawings in sepia and gray pose this little boy in each situation that he describes. Nice variety of layout, the use of figures that extend beyond the picture border, and characters shown using appropriate signs and expressions add to the illustrations' effectiveness. When the text reads, "Grandma says she loves both me and Molly a lot. She hugs me hard. I love Grandma a lot, too, and I feel better now," the picture shows Grandmother signing "love."

Readers can match up a two-page spread of signs in the back of the book with earlier illustrations in the story. Alert audiences will interpret Brian's classroom signing of "fine/okay" while he taps his hearing aid. That is the real message of this pleasant book, and the boy signs the same statement on an inviting color cover.

■ Bunting, Eve. *A Sudden Silence.* Harcourt, 1988. 107pp. (0-15-282058-2) Reading Level: Grades 8–12. (BCCB Je88)
Disability: Deafness

"Could I have grabbed Bry in time? Could I have pulled him with me? How far ahead HAD he been?" These questions and anger over his deaf brother's hit-and-run death hound Jesse Harmon. He feels guilty when he feels attracted to Chloe, the girl Bry introduced Jesse to that fateful night. Jesse is determined to find the killer. He pursues every clue and hint, with help from the police and Chloe, then recognizes her parents' car as the one involved in the accident. His first suspicions that it was Chloe's father who caused the drunk driving accident are wrong—it was Chloe's mother. When Jesse confronts Chloe with his evidence, she concedes that it fits the pattern of her mother's alcoholism.

The young people go their separate ways, never free of whispers associating them with the accident. "It's hard for people to accept that a hit-and-run driver can be rich and respectable. And that an alcoholic isn't a bum drinking wine out of a bottle in a paper bag."

Analysis: This romance has mystery and emotional tension relating to the death of a hearing-impaired teenager. The characterization of Bry is provided through Jesse's memories, his loneliness for his brother, and comments that other people who knew Bry make while Jesse is investigating. The arcade worker recalls how good Bry was at video games: "Man, was that bozo a whiz, or what? I never saw a more coordinated kid, and him as deaf as a dish."

One of the most unusual characters is a homeless drunk called Sowbug, who liked Bry. Bry was an active, compassionate young man, and though his hearing impairment made it impossible for him to avoid the swerving car, it is not depicted as a "handicap" to the boy when he was alive. Bunting's slim novel has the added appeal of California's surf scene that even includes a riot at an MTV contest.

■ Christian, Mary Blount. *Mystery at Camp Triumph.* Whitman, 1986. 128pp. (0-8075-5366-2) Reading Level: Grades 4–6.
Disability: Deafness

Nate helps solve the mysterious accidents that have been happening at his camp by reading people's lips and cooperating with Angie, who is blind. *See full annotation* Chapter 5: Visual Impairments.

■ Guccione, Leslie D. *Tell Me How the Wind Sounds.* Scholastic, 1989. 224pp. (0-590-42615-X) Reading Level: Grades 7–9. (KR 15 N89; SLJ O89)
Disability: Deafness

Amanda is 15 when she meets Jake on Clark's Island, off the coast of Massachusetts. She misses all the amenities and social aspects of her mainland life and feels trapped into baby-sitting with her 8-year-old half-brothers. She is angered by every encounter with Jake until he tells her that he is deaf.

> Amanda blinked hard. The boy's voice was nasal and muffled, as if he had a bad cold, but the word was painfully clear.
> Jake made a V at his eyes and twisted his wrist to her, touched his left fist with his index finger, and tapped his chest. "Look at me," he interpreted. "I can read your lips."
> Jake continued as the girl stared. Let her see what it felt like not to understand!

During the weeks after that, Amanda and her brothers learn signs. She and Jake become close, working through the obstacles in communication and their differences in personality. A Fourth of July celebration bonds their friendship. Jake knows Amanda has a boyfriend on the mainland but hopes to express his own feelings for her. He is coaxed to "Caterham, in the hearing world," for an errand with Amanda, but their time ends in misunderstanding and an argument.

Chris arrives to visit Amanda, and his disdain for the rugged island is equal to his outrage that "the deaf kid" is six feet tall and 16. Amanda wants to make Chris happy, but none of the things the island offers appeal to him. She realizes that Chris is not a good listener and that she likes the things he dismisses. Amanda's stepmother understands her confusion, and the family leaves Amanda alone for the day.

While out in Jake's lobster boat, Amanda begs him to speak again instead of relying on her limited knowledge of signs. A storm requires Amanda to use the radio to summon help. After saving each other's life, they enjoy a summer romance. Amanda's choice for their last date is a dance in town, where Jake will have to reach out more to his classmates.

They return to Clark's Island, and Jake leads a farewell dance on shore "with no music at all."

Analysis: Jake had meningitis at age 6, which left him profoundly deaf and altered his speech. He is defensive and independent, so seeks shelter in "his world" on the island. He recognizes his deep feelings for Amanda and sums up her disappointment in Chris with personal insight: "It hurts—hurts—when you make up people in your head. When they don't love what you love." In the end, Amanda and Jake are prepared for a relationship that may or may not survive as love instead of a hollow promise of forever.

The author incorporates signs, spoken dialogue, and thoughts by consistent use of italics and quotation marks. This unique romance has a vivid setting, action, and well-developed characters. Recommended for most collections, the book tells adolescent readers about the many types of communication skills that develop here. Sweet Valley fans will enjoy this better offering from a veteran series writer.

■ Hess, Lilo. *The Good Luck Dog.* Photos by Lilo Hess. Scribner, 1985. 44pp. (0-684-18344-7) Reading Level: Grades 3–5. (BCCB Je85)
Disability: Deafness

In ancient times a Tibetan terrier was thought to bring good luck to its owners. In this story, a dog is stolen, taken to a laboratory, and then turned over to an animal welfare shelter. He is adopted by a careless owner. The dog is injured and then is given to a lonely deaf girl who begins to give him an education. First obedience classes, and then a program in the Sound Alert School, prepare the terrier to help his new owner.

Analysis: Unique for its incorporation of Sound Alert training, this is still a weak story. The photographs are of uneven quality, so the shaggy dog's adventures are sometimes blurred. Perceptive children may note that the deaf girl is much like any other child.

■ Holman, Felice. *Secret City, U. S. A.* Scribner, 1990. 208pp. (0-684-19168-7) Reading Level: Grades 5–8. (BCCB Ap90;HB My-Je90;KR 15 Ap90)
Disability: Deafness; Emotional disturbance

Benno is 13 when he and his friend Moon try "pioneering" in their poverty-stricken neighborhood. They reclaim an area to shelter a growing community of homeless youths. An old man is rescued from a cellar, which brings Benno's friends into contact with a nurse who intends to resolve their various needs.

Analysis: Benno is interested in "pioneering" as a legacy from his grandfather, whose death Benno is still dealing with. Moon's parents are deaf, which has an effect on his life in the barrio and on the way he expresses himself. Moon's mental skills and the attributes of each outcast that comes into Benno's shelter are demonstrated during the story. If the ending is too optimistic, it helps soften the bleak look at Benno's crowded family circumstances, his brushes with street dangers and gangs, and the various circumstances or emotional disturbances that have limited the other characters' options for shelter. A vivid novel, some readers may be put off by the author's philosophical comments at each chapter head or the dialogue's frequent contractions and phonetic merging of words to represent authentic speech patterns. For most collections, it can provide another look at survival on the streets.

■ Jones, Rebecca C. *Madeline and the Great (Old) Escape Artist.* Dutton, 1983. 112pp. (0-525-44074-7) Reading Level: Grades 4–7. *Disability:* Hearing Impairment

Madeline meets 94-year-old Mary Gibson in the hospital, and they share secrets, even though Madeline has to yell them sometimes because Mary is so hard of hearing. *See full annotation* Chapter 4: Orthopedic/Neurological Impairments.

■ Knox-Wagner, Elaine. *An Apartment's No Place for a Kid.* Illus. by Rodney Pate. Whitman, 1985. 29pp. (0-8075-0373-8) Reading Level: Grades 2–3. (BCCB F86) *Disability:* Deafness

Kelly and her mother move to the city when her mother gets transferred. They live in an apartment, where Kelly dislikes the different smells and noises, resists talking to any of the neighbors because they are strangers, and misuses her time in the apartment after school. Mom calls several times to check on her bored daughter. Kelly is frightened when someone knocks on the door and does not respond to her when she asks, "Who's there?" Kelly calls her mother but has to leave a message with a coworker, who calls the police. The police, Kelly's mother, and Mrs. Welch from across the hall determine that Kelly was in no danger. Mrs. Welch had come to offer some cookies and did not answer Kelly because she is "a bit hard of hearing lately."

Mrs. Welch offers to spend time after school with Kelly and has many ideas about having fun in an apartment.

Analysis: A reassuring story, told in awkward phrases at times, this presents some of the stresses and decisions that face latchkey children.

Mrs. Welch has all the time in the world for Kelly, and they become a pleasant intergenerational match. Mrs. Welch's hearing loss does not interfere with playing computer games, doing crossword puzzles, or exploring the basement and the neighborhood with Kelly.

■ Miller, Frances. *Aren't You the One Who . . . ?* Atheneum, 1983. 209 pp. (0-689-30961-9) Reading Level: Grades 7–10.
Disability: Deafness

Matt was accused of killing his deaf sister after their parents died in a car accident. *See full annotation* Chapter 6: Mental Retardation.

■ Moore, Robin. *The Bread Sister of Sinking Creek.* Lippincott, 1990. 154pp. (LB 0-397-32419-7) Reading Level: Grades 5–7. (KR 15 Ap90; BCCB S90; BL J190)
Disability: Deafness

Maggie Callahan is 14 when she rides out to find Aunt Franny on the Pennsylvania frontier. However, the cabin is abandoned, and Maggie finds work baking bread that earns her the nickname "Bread Sister." Through fire, snow, flood, and injury, Maggie is the plucky heroine. She learns that being a "Bread Sister" to the community includes social interaction and benevolence.
Analysis: This story unfolds in one near-miss after another with little leavening of truth. Recipes at the end may tie it in with a curriculum on 1776, but there are many better historical novels available. A self-constructed sign language that is too successful and modern feminism are two of the flaws in credibility that are not overcome by lively characters and story-telling skill.

■ Nelson, Theresa. *And One for All.* Orchard, 1989. 182 pp. (LB 0-531-08404-3) Reading Level: Grades 7–12.
Disability: Hearing impairment

Geraldine's father is deaf in one ear from a World War II injury that earned him a Purple Heart. *See full annotation* Chapter 6: Learning Disabilities.

■ Pace, Betty. *Chris Gets Ear Tubes.* Illus. by Kathryn Hutton. Gallaudet, 1987. 44pp. (paper 0-930323-36-X) Reading Level: Grades PS–K. (BL J188)
Disability: Hearing impairment

Chris cannot hear well because there is fluid in his ears. His doctor recommends that Chris go to the hospital to have ear tubes inserted. Chris is shown around and rides on a gurney and a wheelchair. His family is there to encourage him, and the operation is a success.

Analysis: Implants of this type are common, and drains may be prescribed to avoid additional hearing loss from scars due to repeated ear infections. A lot of information is presented without condescension. Preparation for the operation is conveyed in four-color settings with realistic detail. The figures are drawn in a stiff style, but their interaction, like Daddy giving his son a high-five, is believable.

A unique offering from a reliable source, this title will be useful in many communities.

■ Pollock, Penny. *Keeping It Secret.* Illus. by Donna Diamond. Putnam, 1982. 110pp. (0-399-20934-4) Reading Level: Grades 4–6. (BCCB Ja83) *Disability:* Hearing impairment

When Mary Lou is 11, she moves from Wisconsin to New Jersey. She is very defensive about her new classmates' reaction to the fact that her nickname is her home state's name, and she determines to keep her hearing aids a secret. Although her former classmates and teacher had shown interest in her equipment when her hearing loss was first diagnosed, Wisconsin does not trust these new students to understand or accept her. When she dislodges the hearing aids in her sweater, she bumbles through the rest of her day without them rather than admit to anyone that she needs to use instruments to hear. Spelling bees, swimming parties, and the school field day seem ominous events to Wisconsin as long as she is "keeping it secret."

The teacher informs the other class members about Wisconsin's hearing aids, suggesting that they not mention the issue until Wisconsin is ready to bring the subject up herself.

Wisconsin tries to please her father with success in math. Eventually, her big brother, Will, and her father help her improve her softball skills, though at first they try to discourage her interest. Another girl, who seems to have a perfect life, is paired with Wisconsin for an event on Field Day, and Wisconsin learns that parental pressure can be as bad as overprotection. Wisconsin determines to do her best when it is her turn at bat, even after her hearing aid falls out onto Jason's foot.

Analysis: Wisconsin shares a lot of specifics about her hearing loss during the course of her adjustment story. Her father is overprotective because of guilt associated with the genetic weakness that caused Wisconsin's deafness. Even though the doctors warned that surgery could fail to correct her trouble, Wisconsin's family members still have not resolved their feelings about her total loss of hearing in one ear.

Once Wisconsin abandons her secretive, defensive ways, she can respond to the friendly overtures she has been ignoring from the start. Part of her adjustment consists of finding an easier way of relating with her parents and older brother since the disappointing surgery and move. The new-girl-in-school plot is familiar, and here it serves as a vehicle to present unique adjustments in the life of a sixth-grader who uses the BICROS system of hearing instruments to compensate for her hearing loss. Portraits of the principal characters and Wisconsin make this a nonthreatening, slim novel for reluctant upper-grade readers.

■ Pople, Maureen. **The Other Side of the Family.** Henry Holt, 1987. 176pp. (0-8050-0758-X) Reading Level: Grades 6–9. (KR 15 My88) *Disability:* Deafness

Kate is evacuated from London to Australia during the blitz of World War II, but when a torpedo hits Sydney Harbor, she is sent to her Grandma Tucker's home. Kate finds out that her grandmother is deaf and has to work to just get by, which is certainly not what she was led to believe about the uncommunicative old woman. Kate makes good friends during her time there and brings together estranged people in her family and her circle of acquaintances.

Analysis: This lively story has a firm setting and an appealing protagonist. Several plot turns and misunderstandings hinge on the fact that Grandma is deaf, and few people know it. The portrayal is well-rounded, however, so this title is a good supplemental choice for large collections.

■ Richemont, Enid. **The Time Tree.** Little, Brown, 1990. 96pp. (0-316-74452-2) Reading Level: Grades 4–7. (KR 1 My90; BCCB My90; HB S-090) *Disability:* Deafness

Joanne and Rachel enjoy playing in a tree in London. One day, Anne silently appears there, dressed in Elizabethan clothes. The girls use broken speech to communicate with Anne, become friends, and experience time travel to Anne's historical era. There, Anne's deafness causes her to be deemed a freak, unable to speak intelligibly even to her family. With patient tutoring, Joanna and Rachel teach Anne to write. Years later, Anne's visits to the time tree stop, but a sampler in a museum is evidence that Anne existed and benefited from her lessons in the time tree.

Analysis: The mood of this fantasy, with its dappled light and leafy setting, is stronger than its inner logic. How Anne can time travel from the tree's sapling past is not explored, but why she feels more comfortable with her future friends and their modern acceptance of her disability is clear. The Elizabethan episode implies that Anne is considered a halfwit or an evil, imperfect creature, which is accurate for that time and social setting. Simplistic in many ways, this is a pleasant story of friendship but for larger collections and a younger audience than *The Flawed Glass*.

■ Schatell, Brian. *The McGoonys Have a Party*. Illus. by Brian Schatell. Harper & Row, 1985. 32pp. (LB 0-397-32124-4) Reading Level: Grades 2–3. (BL 15 D85)
Disability: Hearing impairment

Mr. McGoony has poor hearing, and Mrs. McGoony is so forgetful that things go wrong at every opportunity.

Analysis: This original tale uses the same premise as many folktales, so the malaprops and misunderstandings that are generated in the McGoony household are for humorous effect only. The slapstick presentation is not as well matched in illustrations as Marshall's pictures of the Stupids, but the audience will be the same. Ridiculous action should not be criticized for its insensitivity toward people who have these weaknesses but are merely farces that should be balanced by realistic portrayals in a collection.

■ Scott, Virginia M. *Belonging*. Illus. by Judith Blair. Gallaudet, 1986. 200pp. (0-930323-14-9) Reading Level: Grades 6–10. (SLJ My86)
Disability: Deafness

When Gustie Blaine is 15 she contracts meningitis, which affects her hearing and leaves her too weak and dizzy to attend school in the fall. Every day Gustie seems to have a different hearing level, and several specialists give their opinion. Eventually, she returns to school, has difficulty with balance and following class discussions, and realizes her friends avoid her. A hearing aid is no solution, for it just amplifies noise, and voices are still unintelligible. Gustie loses her residual hearing as well, and her parents are distraught.

Classes in speechreading are helpful, but Gustie experiences the limitations of this communication method. The special education counselor at her school helps Gustie, one note-taker becomes a friend, and Gustie dates a boy she met before she lost her hearing. The boy, Jack, has an older brother and sister-in-law who deal well with their own deafness by using teletypewriters and closed-captioned decoders. Gustie writes her parents a letter, has a reunion with her cheerleading friend, and celebrates her sixteenth birthday with new self-knowledge.

Analysis: Overprotective parents and uncomfortable friends are realistic elements in this story of adjustment. There is no driving plot other than Gustie's new self-awareness and the emotional roller coaster her recovery presents. Like *Izzy, Willy-Nilly* this is a close examination of one girl's trauma. Other students in Gustie's school have congenital deafness, and this book makes sensitive distinctions between various degrees of hearing ability and the technological and communication options that suit each impairment. Since Gustie still has her speech patterns intact, this is an excellent complement to *Tell Me How the Wind Sounds.*

■ Terris, Susan. *Baby-Snatcher.* Farrar, 1984. 170pp. (0-374-30473-4)
Reading Level: Grades 6–8. (BCCB Mr85)
Disability: Deafness

Laurel's older brother and sister take turns chaperoning her for the summer at their vacation cottage. At 13, Laurel would rather be considered responsible enough to be on her own. She takes a job baby-sitting for Ivan's baby. Ivan is an artist and Laurel is sure she loves him. The baby is not responsive, so Laurel suspects that the child may be deaf. Ivan does not pay attention to her concern, and Laurel becomes suspicious that he is concealing other things about his child as well. Laurel helps reunite the baby, who has been kidnapped, with its mother.

Analysis: Kidnapping was one of the hot topics of the 1980s. This story lets readers project what their action might be in the face of such a discovery. The baby's hearing impairment is only a slight detail here; the tale concerns a young teen's budding confidence in her own perceptions and judgments.

■ Windsor, M. A. *Pretty Saro.* Atheneum, 1986. 200pp. (0-689-31288-6)
Reading Level: Grades 6–8. (BL 15 N86)
Disability: Hearing impairment

Sarah lives on a horse farm in Kentucky. She has twice won the grand championship for five-gaited ponies at the state fair, but her third chance is foiled when her pony's leg gives out. At 14, Sarah is cool toward the new students whose new homes have changed and crowded the land she has always known. When others speak to her, she does not respond, so classmates think she is a snob. After a teacher discovers her hearing impairment and a doctor fits her with a hearing aid, Sarah gets used to the instrument and enjoys the difference it makes.

Ellen Schneider becomes Sarah's friend, and her older brother, John, nicknames Sarah "Pretty Saro." When Sarah wants to train horses and teach riding instead of go to shows, her mother refuses to allow it. Sarah's mother pushes her daughter to try winning for the third time, in spite of the pony's hoof that has no feeling. The pony's prize-winning performance is followed by a storm that makes the horse bolt and then throw Sarah. John locates the unconscious girl and tells her he loves her, while Ellen runs for help.

Analysis: One of the reasons Sarah has trouble making friends is her seemingly aloof body language; another is snobbery patterned after that of her supercompetitive mother. The emotional dilemma of weighing parental values and choices against one's own preferences is the major theme, and it nicely accommodates the information about Sarah's hearing impairment. This is a good title for horse fans and those who feel that their mother just doesn't understand them.

VISUAL IMPAIRMENTS

■ Bess, Clayton. *Story for a Black Night.* Houghton, 1982. 84pp. (0-395-31857-2) Reading Level: Grades 5–8. (BCCB Je82)
Disability: Blindness

A Liberian father tells his children a story from his own childhood: Called Momo then, he and his baby sister, Meatta, and blind Old Ma were cared for by Ma. One evening, two women beg for shelter with the family. The women abandon a sick baby, smallpox claims Meatta, Ma and Momo recover from the disease, and the stranger's mother comes to claim the baby, who survived. Ma will not give up the child, whom she nursed at such risk to her own family.

Analysis: This story offers a vivid presentation of village life and family interaction. Old Ma has her firm opinions and is accorded respect, but Ma's insistence on offering shelter and then care for the strangers and the baby overrides the blind woman's wishes. Recommended for its distinctive use of language and strong story telling.

■ Christian, Mary Blount. *Mystery at Camp Triumph.* Whitman, 1986. 128pp. (0-8075-5366-2) Reading Level: Grades 4–6. (BL 15 N86)
Disability: Blindness; Deafness; Orthopedic impairment

Angie was blinded in a car accident one year before her psychiatrist recommends her for a grant to attend Camp Triumph. Her mother has assisted Angie with everything since her injury, so being left to find her own way around camp is difficult for Angie. Angie meets her roommate, who wears leg braces, and falls into the water while following ropes that were supposed to lead back to her cabin. The camp has been beset by mishaps, but this is the first time that tampering was evident. Angie calls home, leaving a message on her parents' phone that insisted she be taken home, especially because she believes she saw a flash of light when she fell off the bank.

An examination by the small-town doctor does not convince Angie that what she saw was like "seeing stars" from a blow on the head and not restored sight. She overhears comments in the alley that seem related to her accident at camp and loses her cane. She pieces together clues about who would profit from the camp's closing, and she enlists the help of other campers in solving the mystery, because any of the adults at camp could have been the one who returned her cane as a warning.

Angie learns to listen more carefully, coordinate her own outfits, improve her mobility skills, lift her feet with confidence, and turn her face instead of her ear toward people who are talking. She finds out that losing her sight has no bearing on her art and horseback riding. On the trail, a wire causes the horses to rear and bolt. Angie has to go for help, and on the way she encounters the craft leader. When the director says he is ready to close the camp because of this latest accident, Angie insists it was more sabotage.

Angie gets the craft leader to admit her involvement, and the mayor is exposed as a villain ready to profit from real estate speculation and the city's right to the camp property once it can no longer function as a special camp.

Analysis: Plenty of Nancy Drew fans will be pleased with this little mystery. All of the portrayals of campers are from Angie's point of view, which results in their limitations' being revealed after the dialogue has established other character traits. It is rather interesting when Angie has to correct her assumption that the advice-giving camp psychologist is sighted.

During a rap session the campers talk about mainstreaming, each with their own concern. Many of the clues about the mystery are available from Nate, whose ability to read lips is often overlooked by people who think of him only as a deaf boy. Finally, Angie gains perspective on her injury when she is told that rest cannot help Wheels, who "is determined to go until he can't. He has muscular dystrophy, Angie. All his muscles are wasting away—including his heart. The heart is a muscle, too, don't forget."

It is clear that, at 16, Angie has not adjusted to her disability. She is handicapped by her father's attitude, her mother's overprotection, and her own resentment. As her cabinmate says, "A handicap is something that gets in your way. I'm impaired, not handicapped. Boy, you really haven't done much toward getting yourself back into the real world, have you? Anybody blind ought to be able to hear these braces. They squeak, but they get me around."

This plot may squeak, too, and the style is clumsy, but the story is filled with good portrayals of special need kids.

■ Clifford, Eth. **The Man Who Sang in the Dark.** Illus. by Mary Beth Owen. Houghton, 1987. 112pp. (0-395-43664-8) Reading Level: Grades 3–5. (BCCB 087)
Disability: Blindness

In Philadelphia during the depression, Leah and her brother, Daniel, move to an apartment over a grocery store. Their mother is widowed and works at home on her sewing machine. At 10, Leah tries to be brave in the new situation, facing both loneliness for her father and the hardships of poverty. The elderly couple who owns the building is friendly to them, and their nephew, Gideon Brown, introduces himself. The tall young man is blind and uses a cane, so the first time Leah sees him in the building, she is frightened. When he introduces himself to the family, he mentions that he plays the guitar and sings for a living.

Mother makes dresses for Mrs. Alpert, but the rich woman also enjoys taking care of Daniel when his mother is busy. Mrs. Alpert tries to adopt Daniel until Leah reclaims him. Leah shares with Daniel and Gideon a poem she wrote, and she ends up describing colors to the musician in fanciful images.

> "Black is darkness. It's the shadows in the hall, and being lonely, and afraid. It's not being able to see." She clapped her hand to her mouth. "I'm sorry."
> "But you are right. To be blind is to live in unimaginable darkness."
> " . . . the darkness is not in my soul. Do you understand?"

Leah does understand because there was a darkness in her mother's soul for a time after Father died. Gideon gets a job and orders the sewing of two formal shirts and a black tie by Mother. Gideon and Mother attend a concert together, and Gideon's aunt baby-sits with Leah and Daniel. The Safers insist on being called Grandpa and Grandma.

The Alperts move to California and adopt an infant boy.

Gideon gets a radio job, and the Safers sell their building to buy a house. Gideon suggests that it will be easier for them to find an apartment if the blind man and the widow marry. Leah's mother accepts his proposal, because they have all come to love each other.

To celebrate the purchase of a big house where the six of them can live together as a family, Gideon sings Leah's poem set to music.

Analysis: This warm story allows Leah to change her opinion of Gideon and realize that the man's blindness does not stop him from getting to know her for the creative dreamer she is. The little girl's bias is dispelled when she considers her mother's marriage plans: "Mama married? To a blind man? No, Leah told herself, not to a blind man. To Gideon, who was kind and understanding, who had given her courage, a man who could sing in the dark."

Clifford's slim historical novel is recommended for upper-elementary readers, who will enjoy the frequent pencil drawings that complement this book's episodes.

■ Cohen, Miriam. *See You Tomorrow, Charles.* Illus. by Lillian Aberman Hoban. Greenwillow, 1983. 32pp. (0-688-01804-1) Reading Level: Grades PS–2. (BCCB Ap83)
Disability: Blindness

Charles joins his first-grade classmates in play. Danny avoids roughhousing with him because classmates have warned that Charles is blind and will not know who is punching him. Charles gives a correct response in class, and Anna Marie roots for him instead of considering him a threat to her status as top student.

Jim unconsciously invites Charles to look at his clay project, and Charles turns aside Anna Marie's literal criticism of Jim's casual phrase. Charles has braille instruction with a special teacher. The children discuss Charles's abilities and project that his career options are limited. The teacher points out to Anna Marie that Charles can find his way back to his desk without the little girl's solicitous assistance. Later, Charles leads three classmates out of the dark basement.

Analysis: Here, Cohen and Hoban introduce a visual impairment into their charming mix of first-grade personalities who star in several books about adjusting to school. The scruffy little individuals learn that Charles's blindness may make some tasks difficult but that Charles can do a lot for himself and should be treated the same as other students. Charles is imaginative and intelligent, and his classmates adjust to his special abilities and needs at the same time as he adjusts to mainstreamed experiences. Hero for the day, Charles is given the limelight at the end, which makes the story even more satisfying for its read-aloud audience. This humorous book is an outstanding choice for all collections.

■ Collura, Mary-Ellen Lang. *Winners.* Dial, 1986. 129pp. (0-8037-0011-3)
Reading Level: Grades 6–9. (SLJ Ja87)
Disability: Blindness

Jordy Threebears was orphaned and placed in eleven different foster homes before his fifteenth birthday. He is taken in by his grandfather, Joe Speckledhawk, and lives on the Ash Creek Blackfoot Reserve in Alberta. It is hard for him to adjust to school until the physical education instructor encourages him to participate in athletics. He also gets some welcome information about his father and mother from Mr. Cambell. However, his newfound pride in his family is destroyed when someone calls him a "dirty Indian," and he storms off campus for two days in the wild. He comes to the cabin of Erasmus Watermedicine and has to be air-lifted to a hospital for treatment for pneumonia and frostbite. Jordy's heretofore suppressed memories of his mother's death and a visit from Mr. Cambell reveal that she was attacked by drunks and died of her injuries after running away to hide.

Jordy and his grandfather exchange Christmas gifts, and Jordy's new horse is given a corral by members of the Siksika tribe. The physical education instructor recruits Jordy to help train a blind girl for a challenging trail ride in exchange for his own riding lessons. Emily MacKenzie works hard on her sport despite her disability. Jordy is hassled by the prejudiced ranch foreman, Fred Brady. Mr. MacKenzie fires Brady for his behavior, and that night Jordy's horse is stolen. Jordy recovers his horse weeks later at a rodeo. Erasmus helps Jordy nurse the horse after all the abuse it has been through. Two months of training allow Jordy and Emily to enter an endurance race, but Emily gets injured and they finish in last place.

Jordy studies by correspondence course and keeps working on his riding. He locates clippings about his mother's death and discovers that his grandfather killed one of the men responsible—the brother of Fred Brady. Jordy rides against Fred Brady in another endurance race; the man falsely accuses him, then attacks him on the trail. Jordy saves Brady's life and completes the race, winning first place.

Analysis: Jordy's adventures and his effort to connect with his past make for an engaging story. The character of Fred Brady is as villainous as can be. Emily is active and lovely and does not simper at Jordy's romantic attentions. The vivid setting and sensitive introduction of tribal people and customs make this a worthwhile addition for most collections. For another treatment of blind competitors on long-distance horse trails, see Hall's *Half the Battle*.

Interestingly, neither of the disabled characters finishes the race.

■ Corcoran, Barbara. *The Sky Is Falling*. Atheneum, 1988. 185pp. (0-689-31388-8) Reading Level: Grades 7–9. (BCCB Ja89)
Disability: Blindness

In 1931 Annah saw the depression take her dad's job and her brother's college hopes. With dad looking for work in Chicago, and mother in Florida with her own parents, Annah is sent to stay in New Hampshire with Aunt Edna. A classmate, Mabel, makes school unbearable until another newcomer, Dodie, makes friends with Annah. Things are even worse for Dodie at home, where she cares for her blind brother, deals with her alcoholic mother, and is treated harshly by her stepfather. Annah is invited to live with a family servant whom she loves but offers the opportunity to Dodie.

Analysis: Disappointments and adjustments caused by financial reversals show why Annah felt as though "the sky is falling." But theatrical overkill in characterizations such as evil Mabel, cruel stepfather, drunken mother, and blind brother flaw this historical fiction. The good writing about a particular period will still attract readers.

■ Coutant, Helen. *The Gift*. Illus. by Vo-Dinh Mai. Knopf, 1983. 45pp. (LB 0-394-95499-8) Reading Level: Grades 3–5. (BCCB Je83)
Disability: Blindness

Anna misses her next-door neighbor, Nana Marie, while the old woman is in the hospital. Nana Marie moved in with her son and daughter-in-law, Rita, during Anna's fifth-grade year. Rita invites Anna to a welcome home party and reveals that Nana Marie is now blind. Anna is angry, skips school, and takes a walk through the woods. The girl gathers potential presents for the party but worries that a stone, fern, or pod will only remind Nana Marie of things she can never see again: "There had to be a way to bring the whole woods, the sky, and the fields to Nana Marie. What else would do? What else would be worthy of their friendship?"

The party is over by the time Anna gets to Rita's house, but she goes up to her friend's room. It is a joyful reunion, and Anna recounts her walk, saying that her gift is a promise to share these wonders and delights every day with Nana Marie.

Analysis: Gentle, but not subtle, this story uses Nana Marie's sudden loss of vision to explore a little girl's accommodation of change. The flashbacks of their six-month-long friendship include disjointed but pleasant images. Action may seem too flat to some readers, because the story is mostly Anna's recollections and reflections about Nana Marie. For example, Anna wonders, "how Nana Marie had felt waking up blind." She also ponders "what if" doctors had to remove Nana Marie's pretty blue eyes and "only two black holes were left?" The girl is reassured to see that Nana Marie's appearance is unchanged.

Part of Anna's concern comes from the abrupt way she learned of Nana Marie's blindness: "Drop by after school. She'll be looking for you." Rita's voice, suddenly lower, caught Anna's attention. "She won't really be looking for you, Nana Marie won't. But come to see her anyway. She'll need your company now that she's blind."

Rita is blunt with the child about Nana Marie's return, condition, and need for company, but this trait is consistent with her character. The only explanation Rita gives about the blindness is that it "Just happened, just like that. It's a pity. It's terrible." Anna thinks of Rita as a television-watching recluse, so the woman's pitying opinions have little bearing on Nana Marie's open relationship with Anna. "Even though something as terrible as going blind had happened to Nana Marie, she really hadn't changed. She could still marvel at the world, she could still feel the moonlight. Anna knew she was going to be all right." Each spread of this simple tale has pencil illustrations that feature an Asian girl in hazy compositions that complement the text. Recommended for an audience older than the one targeted by *A Gift for Tia Rosa*, readers will see an intercultural and intergenerational friendship nicely portrayed.

■ First, Julia. *The Absolute, Ultimate End.* Franklin Watts, 1985. 156pp. (0-531-10075-8) Reading Level: Grades 6–8. (SLJ F86)
Disability: Blindness; Epilepsy

Maggie Thayer is in eighth grade, when her father is asked to run for the school committee on a platform of cutting waste in school. Maggie is in the drama club, where she can be close to her long-time crush, Stevie Garber. Her good friend Eloise enjoys sports activities. These two areas, and monies for the special education needs of mainstreamed students, are all threatened by the proposed cuts. Maggie is disgusted by the thought of helping to tutor in the special education room because she knows some of the students sometimes have seizures. She is paired with a blind student,

Doreen, who has no braille materials or recorded texts for social studies. Maggie overcomes her dislike of associating with handicapped students, finding out that Doreen manages well in the cafeteria, in music studies, and in recreational activities.

When Maggie discusses with her father the intended cuts, she expresses concern that they will be unfair to her school friends. She is elected chairperson of a student protest to take place at City Hall. The "normal" students keep their own efforts a secret, as a surprise for their differently abled classmates. The mainstreamed students show up with signs of their own and have organized, in addition, a successful protest effort. Maggie's father clarifies that his efforts have been directed at reducing waste so that the special education programs could be saved. He and Maggie's mother are proud of their daughter's efforts in this respect. Doreen gives a piano recital, Maggie campaigns for her father, and Stevie helps.

Analysis: Maggie's change of heart is showcased in this pat little plot. The dialogue is humorous and the characterizations adequate. Doreen's abilities are well presented, and Maggie is suitably impressed with her new friend's mobility skills and musical talent. Some specific areas, such as playing braille monopoly and the staging of the protest *for* the special students instead of planning *with* that competent group of classmates, are especially insightful.

■ Fleischman, Paul. *Finzel the Farsighted.* Dutton, 1983. 48pp. (0-525-44057-7) Reading Level: Grades 3–5. (BCCB Ja84)
Disability: Visual impairment

Finzel is famed in his village for an ability to tell the details of anyone's past or future by examining some produce the person has raised. Unfortunately, he is also so nearsighted that he puts flowers in the candlestick and eats a lemon he is supposed to "read" for the town simpleton, Pavel. Each visit from Pavel results in a mix-up, and Finzel tells Pavel that he has a cold, which progresses to whooping cough and, finally, pneumonia. All the symptoms of these ailments actually belong to the woman who sells Finzel much of his food. Finzel's poor eyesight has led him to substitute the ill person's produce for Pavel's, and Pavel is so dim-witted that he believes he must be sick.

Pavel's brother discovers the confusion and hopes to steal Finzel's money by presenting Finzel's own flower to be read. The location of Finzel's strongbox is revealed, as is the prophecy that two thieves will come, but only the first one will get away. Pavel's brother is discovered, and he finds out that the first thief was a mouse who made off with a bit of cheese.

Analysis: This original tale is done in the simpleton tradition. Because it is not an adaptation, most collections will display it with the author's other carefully crafted prose, instead of with folklore. The mishaps of Finzel and Pavel depend on their impairments, and this is the intent of such folktale variants. Readers will enjoy the soft illustrations, and listeners will delight in any retelling.

■ Getz, David. *Thin Air.* Henry Holt, 1990. 120pp. (0-8050-1379-2) Reading Level: Grades 5–8.
Disability: Blindness

Jacob has a chronic health impairment, expresses disdain of his brother's attentions and his mother's inescapable precautions, and makes friends with a blind newspaper vendor. *See full annotation* Chapter 4: Health Problems.

■ Giff, Patricia Reilly. *Watch Out, Ronald Morgan!* Illus. by Susanna Natti. Viking, 1985. 24pp. (0-670-80433-9) Reading Level: Grades K–3. (SLJ Mr86)
Disability: Visual impairment

Ronald Morgan cannot tell the labels on the gerbil food and the fish food apart, he does not play kickball well, he can not read his own book report without blinking, and his snowflake has not been cut out properly. A note from the teacher suggests that Ronald have an eye exam, and a pair of corrective lenses in blue frames is ordered. Ronald is disappointed when he is still clumsy and confuses the pet food boxes, so he takes off his glasses. Another note from the teacher points out that throwing well depends on practice as well as good vision and that being able to see is not the same as learning to pay attention and "watch out!" Ronald feels better about his new glasses because his teacher says she thinks he is a super kid. His next art project of a snowman is cut out neatly, and he adds a pair of blue glasses to make it "super."
Analysis: Beginning readers enjoy book series, and another story about Ronald will please many. Colorful, lively drawings have the same humorous tone as the text. Ronald's impression that the glasses will solve all his problems at school and make him the best student in every subject is sensitively deflated. This seems a more age-appropriate concern than the self-image/appearance themes developed in other titles for the lower grades.

■ Hall, Lynn. *Half the Battle.* Scribner, 1982. 160pp. (0-684-17348-4)
Reading Level: Grades 8–10. (SLJ Ag82)
Disability: Visual impairment

Blair is preparing to take a grueling, hundred-mile horseback ride called
the Sangre Trek. His younger brother, Loren, will be guiding Blair, because the high school senior has such a severe visual impairment that he
is nearly blind. Loren resents Blair's dependence, the way he takes Loren's
assistance for granted, and all the praise Blair gets for any accomplishment. During the endurance training, Loren pushes his brother and his
brother's horse to their limits, hoping Blair will drop out. Loren hopes to
win in his own age class if he does not have to keep a slower pace with
Blair.

Blair's horse is injured, but he trains another. Loren leads Blair off the
trail on the second day, assuming that Blair will be able to finish on his
own. However, Blair's horse bolts, Blair feels the tracks back to the trail,
he falls, screaming, then climbs up again. Loren's horse is startled, kicks
Blair in the head, and throws Loren off. Blair stays in the hospital with
Loren, who is treated for a concussion, a broken leg, and other injuries.
When Loren regains consciousness, the two brothers plan for next year's
trek, and the recognize both the conflicts and the affection in their relationship.

Analysis: Alternating points of view in the narration allow readers to
see the complexities in this sibling situation in which a disability has
affected the lives of two active boys. The way Blair uses his impairment to
manipulate Loren is also described in their dating patterns. Loren resents
Blair for many things and feels frustrated because he is swayed by the view
of Blair as too "sweet and helpless and brave" to defy. It is simplistic that
one crisis could serve as a common turning point for both brothers, but
Hall tells a fast-paced story, and horse fans will not mind the quick
resolution.

Since these brothers pursue a rugged sport, romances, and rivalries, this
book is a good antidote to older, pity-full portrayals of blind young men.

■ Hall, Lynn. *Murder at the Spaniel Show.* Scribner, 1988. 128pp. (0-684-
18961-5) Reading Level: Grades 5–8. (BCCB N88)
Disability: Blindness

Tabby is a kennel girl for Turner Quinn, a blind, autocratic dog breeder.
Tabby puts a lot of effort into preparing Quinn's dogs for a spaniel show.
She is also determined to find out why someone does not want Ted Quinn,

Turner's twin brother, to judge Best of Show. Tabby finds out that Turner hates his brother, and she solves the mystery.

Analysis: As a dog story, this provides a goodly amount of information on dog breeding and showing. Turner is a privileged person, despite his visual impairment, and his unpleasant personality is not blamed or excused by this impairment. Hall does not bring all the mystery elements together without stretching believability, but animal story fans can count on her books for entertainment.

■ Hellberg, Hans-Eric. *Ben's Lucky Hat.* Trans. by Patricia Crampton. Crown, 1982. 122pp. (0-517-54825-9) Reading Level: Grades 3–4. (BCCB Ja83)
Disability: Visual impairment

Ben is so farsighted that, without his glasses, the colors on his artwork all blur together. He also is clumsy and gets picked for sports only because his friend Sammy is a good athlete. Sammy dies in an accident by being careless. Ben is confused by certain of his parents' and teachers' comments. He finds a hat, regards it as magical, has some mishaps, and hides from the police in a garage with a classmate named Barbie. Barbie takes him home for lunch. Ben notices that her mother wears glasses, and he tries on the mother's lenses for farsightedness. At once, he relaxes, because everything is in focus. Barbie says he looks silly, but her father counters, "People who wear glasses look smarter than anyone."

Bossy Barbie casts Ben as the priest in the children's funeral for a bird. He wears his hat and says a prayer that is dedicated to Sammy. To settle the hat's ownership, Barbie has Ben and Kevin prove their courage by climbing a tree. Wearing the hat, Ben reaches the goal.

Analysis: Ben's vision is so poor that it is a strain to read in bed, and he has been told not to. Only when he seems tired in the mornings does his mother restate the rule against reading in bed. There is humor in this thwarted parental effort, because the boy knows his parents know he reads almost every night. Barbie also lends humorous moments since she is such an original personality.

Ben lost his best friend, and because he was shy and awkward, the loss was hard. "It had been easier when Sammy was alive" is a frequently used statement as the action follows Ben's adjustment and interaction with new friends. The ending is satisfying without being too sweet.

> Tomorrow everything would probably be the same as before, and he would be the one who was not allowed to join in and play because he was so clumsy and saw so badly, but it was a long time till tomorrow. And he had a vague

suspicion that the situation had changed. His friends no longer regarded him as a dunce. He had succeeded in beating Kevin.

This was originally published in Sweden in 1965, but the characterizations and tone are not old-fashioned at all. The cover shows a self-satisfied Ben, wearing his hat, looking to his higher goal from an upper branch of the tree. Too nice to miss, the older title will be a good addition to most collections.

■ Johnson, Emily Rhoads. *Spring and the Shadow Man.* Dodd, 1984. 160pp. (paper 0-396-08330-7) Reading Level: Grades 4–6. (SLJ S84) *Disability:* Blindness

Imaginative sixth-grader Spring Weldon moves to a new home. Delia, the housekeeper, sends the girl door-to-door, selling garden seeds so she will meet the neighbors. Next door, a man answers the door, and Spring thinks he must be crazy. Later, she brings a wounded kitten to him for help, and finds out that he was recently blinded by glaucoma. She learns that Mr. Lincus and Delia danced and corresponded before he lost his vision, that he now wants to keep his blindness a secret, that his sister wants him to move to Ohio to stay with her, and that tubby Howard's father will reward his son if Mr. Lincus sells his house for commercial development.

Spring visits with Mr. Lincus and is comforted when he tells her a lively imagination is a gift. She accidentally reveals that Mr. Lincus is blind and Howard booby-traps the yard with an upturned rake. Spring acts as matchmaker for Delia and Howard, and they marry, open a tearoom, hire Howard, and credit Spring's imagination with good problem solving.

Analysis: Large collections may want to offer this contrived story as a quick read about an inventive heroine. Spring is clever as well as imaginative, and at one point she devises a system of marking Mr. Lincus's canned goods so he can tell them apart. Mr. Lincus's poor adjustment to his loss of vision and his need for secrecy seem to further the plot rather than naturally develop his characterization. The happy-together-forever ending is too sweet, but Spring is shown establishing friendships and coming to terms with her imaginative nature.

■ Levinson, Marilyn. *Fourth-Grade Four.* Illus. by Leslie Bowman. Henry Holt, 1989. 57pp. (0-8050-1082-3) Reading Level: Grades 3–5. (BCCB Ja90) *Disability:* Visual impairment

"Los Tres Amigos" consists of Alex, Steve, and Billy, fourth-grade buddies who follow Billy's lead in bullying kids who are overweight or wear glasses. Now, Alex is having difficulty reading the chalkboard, seeing across the hall, and playing soccer. Glasses will be helpful, but Alex does not know how to admit that he is getting them. His worries are lightened when he decides that a fourth classmate is not so bad, even though he wears glasses, and when it is disclosed that Billy has to repeat first grade.

Analysis: Anxieties about peer opinion and how eyeglasses might affect a fourth-grade boy's friendships are the themes of this slight story. Part of the Redfeather series, this is intended for new readers who are making a transition to chapter books and is designed to be comfortable rather than challenging.

■ McDonald, Megan. *The Potato Man.* Illus. by Ted Lewin. Orchard, 1991. 32pp. (LB 0-531-08514-7) Reading Level: Grades PS–2.
Disability: Visual impairment

Grandfather tells how, as a child, he and the neighborhood kids were frightened of the vegetable seller, Mr. Angelo, who had lost an eye in the Great War. *See full annotation* Chapter 7: Various Disabilities.

■ Mark, Michael. *Toba.* Illus. by Neil Waldman. Bradbury, 1984. 105pp. (0-02-762300-9) Reading Level: Grades 4–6. (BCCB Je84)
Disability: Blindness

In 1913, Toba lives in Poland. Her father is a blind tailor, and Toba thinks the world of him. Toba has several microadventures such as going to the dentist, finding a robin's egg, taking a trip with her family, and going shopping with her mother.

Analysis: This graceful period piece presents a Jewish family headed by a skilled man who is blind. Toba's affection, naive observations, and sensitive perceptions make for a tender story that can be recommended to upper-grade readers.

■ Martin, Bill, and John Archambault. *Knots on a Counting Rope.* Illus. by Ted Rand. Henry Holt, 1987. 32pp. (0-8050-0571-4) Reading Level: Grades K–2. (BCCB N87)
Disability: Blindness

A southwestern landscape is the backdrop to a campfire that silhouettes a Native American man and a boy who requests an often repeated story.

The boy interjects details as his grandfather tells of the stormy night a weak boy was born; how the boy responded when two blue horses came by; and how tribal ceremony gave the boy a strong name, which had already helped him cross some of the dark mountains of life that make people feel suddenly afraid.

> Will I always have to live in the dark?
>> Yes, Boy.
>> You were born with a dark curtain
>> in front of your eyes.
> But there are many ways to see, Grandfather.

The boy describes how he "sees" with his hands; he understands abstract concepts like time and colors by the emotions and images they elicit from him. Grandfather continues the story of how a foal was born, that the boy trained this horse, and how the boy learned the trail by "counting her gallops." One tribal day there is a race that Grandfather encourages the boy to try.

> And what did the people say, Grandfather?
>> They said,
>> "Who is that boy riding bareback . . .
>> racing the race with all of his heart?"
> And you said,
>> "That is Boy-Strength-of-Blue-Horses . . .
>> He and his horse are together like one."
> But I didn't win, Grandfather.
>> No, but you rode like the wind. . . .
>> You were crossing dark mountains, Boy!

Once the story is told, another knot is tied in the counting rope. "When the rope is filled with knots, you will know the story by heart and can tell it to yourself."

Analysis: Some anthropological anomalies undermine the ritual story telling and tribal philosophy attempted in this book. The setting is roughly the Navajo Nation during this century.

Children will notice that not all of the Indians wear regalia; one of the racers uses a baseball cap. Text blocks are at one side of the spread so that the illustrations have impact and the figures have expression. The child is shown alert and open-eyed, a good shift from the convention of identifying blind characters by drawing their eyes shut or covered with dark glasses. Some gutters swallow details (a rider's face, a horse's head, etc.), but most of the illustrations arc as impressive as this fine story.

■ Pearson, Susan. *Happy Birthday, Grampie.* Illus. by Ronald Himler. Dial, 1987. 32pp. (LB 0-8037-3458-1) Reading Level: Grades PS–3. (SLJ MS87)
Disability: Blindness

Martha has prepared a special card for her grandfather's birthday. She cut the letters from textured paper to spell out an English message, "Happy Birthday, Grampie. I Love You." Grampie is blind and lives in a nursing home. On recent family visits, he has been speaking only in Swedish.

The drive out to the nursing home after church is pleasant. Martha repeats her one Swedish phrase and gives her gifts. Grampie puzzles over the card for a time and then smiles and responds in English that he loves Martha too.

Analysis: Gentle watercolors accompany this well-written text and support the loving tone of Martha's efforts to communicate with her grandfather. Her memories are handled without sentimental sweetness, and there is suspense before the satisfying ending. Martha is ready to accommodate her grandfather's lost sight, and her character is defined enough that readers can project what she may feel when Grampie is "even older than 89" and having more difficulties.

This excellent book reverses the sexes of the roles played in Fox's picture book *Wilfred Gordon Partridge.*

■ Phipson, Joan. *The Watcher in the Garden.* Atheneum, 1982. 228pp. (0-689-50246-X) Reading Level: Grades 6–9. (BCCB D82)
Disability: Blindness

Kitty is 15 when she visits a hilltop garden, senses an evil presence there, and befriends Mr. Lovett. Mr. Lovett is an elderly blind man who fears a 17-year-old tough named Terry. Terry's malicious and vengeful plans include Lovett's murder. The garden recognizes Terry as a violent intruder and tries to harm him. Kitty knows Terry's hostile thoughts and intervenes.

Analysis: This fantasy includes good characterization and builds suspense, but frequent introspection slows the pace. When telepathic communication and sentient plants in the garden are introduced into the story, readers will be willing to suspend their disbelief. Mr. Lovett is aware of Terry's hostility, but since he is not the only one with a "sixth sense" in this story, it does not foster the stereotype of a disability's automatically being accommodated by special skill in another area.

■ Sargent, Susan, and Donna A. Wirt. *My Favorite Place.* Illus. by Allan Eitzen. Abingdon, 1983. Unp. (paper 0-687-27538-5) Reading Level: Grades PS–3.
Disability: Blindness

One day at the beach is presented in a sequence of observations, some quite poetic. Paired with brown-and-blue duo-tone color separations that use double-page spreads to show action at the beach, the first-person text gives a lively view of a family trip to this child's favorite place. Only on the last pages does the dark-haired girl reveal:

> The ocean is the only place where we go that I can hear and smell and taste and touch all the things I like. The wind, the water, the seagulls, the salt, the sand, and the sun—all these at one place, for me to experience!
> I cannot see. I have never been able to see. But I have my other senses.

Analysis: Careful plot structure shows the attitude of the parents and the enthusiasm of the child rather than telling readers what to think. The story progresses at a good pace, with excellent balance between revealed observations, interactions, and information. The child describes her feelings in simple statements such as:

> I wanted to run and touch everything I heard.
> But my mother's firm grip would not let me go. And that made me angry.
> But my anger went away when my mother picked me up and threw me into the ocean.
> "Swim to me," she called.
> And I did.

This is an appealing presentation of a family enjoying a day at the beach, with the incidental detail that the girl who is specifically having so much fun has been blind all her life.

The family could be Hispanic, but skin tone and the father's mustache do not create a caricatured stereotype. The illustrations use white space, bleed off on all sides, and incorporate texture for variety. The simple but realistic human figures are graceful and expressive. This stapled paperback deserves a better binding, because it has the strengths that picture books need, as well as the spirit that is lacking from many stories that show characters with disabilities in only passive roles.

■ Sorenson, Jody. *The Secret Letters of Mama Cat.* Walker, 1988. 122pp. (LB 0-8027-6791-5) Reading Level: Grades 5–8. (BCCB Je88) *Disability:* Deafness

Chicago is familiar to Meredith and is where her grandmother recently died, so the sixth-grader disagrees with the family decision to move to San Antonio. Her older sister, Tina, was not comfortable in public school and is now enrolled in a boarding school for the deaf. Meredith writes about her feelings, new experiences, and new friends in letters addressed to Grandma. Mom finds the letters, reads them, and persuades Meredith to stop being obsessed with her grandmother.

Analysis: Meredith has dilemmas that readers will recognize, such as moving before seventh grade and not having any friends, being interested in a special boy, and feeling lonesome for her sister and grandmother. What her mother views as an abnormal obsession with Grandma's death could be seen as one girl's way of easing her way through big changes in her life while still grieving. Tina is happy in her new environment, which may have more to do with the author's bias against mainstreaming in education than with reality. This short novel is a mixed bag that only large collections will find useful.

■ Tusa, Tricia. *Libby's New Glasses.* Illus. by Tricia Tusa. Holiday, 1984. 28pp. (0-8234-0523-0) Reading Level: Grades PS–2. (BCCB N84) *Disability:* Visual impairment

Libby hates the way she looks in her new glasses, and she runs away from home. She meets an ostrich, hiding its head in the sand. When the ostrich comes up, wearing glasses, Libby invites it to take a walk, saying, "maybe things will look different through our new glasses." The two ramble along the shore, reassuring each other that glasses are no reason to hide forever.

Analysis: Libby "stared at her new face" behind a locked door and decided that "All the kids at school will tease me!" This very real reaction is awkwardly paired with the fable of the ostrich. Although the pictures are lively and humorous, the text and the fantasy transition are flat. As a reassuring book for little ones whose self-image is more important to them than their improved vision, this title can be useful.

■ Ure, Jean. *After Thursday.* Delacorte, 1987. 181pp. (0-385-29548-0) Reading Level: Grades 7–12. (BCCB My87) *Disability:* Blindness

Marianne and her mother move to an apartment. Abe Shonfeld is seven years older than Marianne and teaches music at a girl's school. Abe and

Marianne date and belong to a vocal ensemble, the Thursday Group. When Marianne takes Abe through the new apartment, he coaxes her out of a jealous, injured mood. "It wasn't very often he pleaded blindness as an excuse; more often he stubbornly did his best to ignore it. It was easier when he ignored it. On the rare occasions when he took advantage (like now), she went all crumbly and couldn't resist."

Besides her possessive streak, Marianne is defensive toward others with regard to Abe's visual impairment. "There were some people who seemed to think that simply because a person was blind he must also be deaf, or dumb, or feeble-minded." Abe's roommate has a brother, Peter, who is visiting. An ugly-duckling schoolmate of Marianne's, named Debbie, has bloomed into a raven-haired songstress, whose recital plans captivate Abe and leave Marianne out one evening. Still, Marianne avoids invitations to go riding, and she will not make weekend plans that exclude Abe.

Visiting Abe, Marianne gets to know Peter better, and Donald warns her that he would be upset to see Abe hurt again by a girlfriend. Marianne spends the night at Abe's apartment, because Peter gets too drunk to drive her home. Both Donald and her mother warn Marianne that Abe is the vulnerable one in the relationship and that "feelings you have now aren't necessarily going to be the feelings you have this time next year."

Marianne is shocked when Abe says he wants a guide dog. When he comments on her "nursemaid" activities, she regrets the social activities she has turned down. "It wasn't worth making sacrifices for someone who just flung it all back in your face." Abe's sister, Jessica, confides, "I think sometimes he feels stifled even when we're all falling over backward to keep out of his way and let him get on with it." Jessica also points out that a 17-year-old girl is likely to change and not to want to spend the rest of her life with a person whose blindness makes situations and relationships complicated. Debbie needs an accompanist for her recital, and Abe spends three weeks away from town with her to prepare.

Marianne gets involved with school events and spends time with Peter. She misses several calls from Abe, and Peter kisses her. The night before Debbie's recital, Peter tries to seduce Marianne during a drunken bash at Abe's appartment. She tries to protect the piano from the intoxicated guests. Debbie's and Abe's first two performances are well received, but Marianne overhears that their reception is to serve as an informal engagement party as well. Her fears that Abe and Debbie have fallen in love are dispelled when Debbie's fiancé is introduced. Abe wants Marianne with him, but his success makes Marianne self-conscious and insecure. She literally falls into his arms at the reception, upstaging the soloist and her fiancé.

Analysis: Marianne's good intentions and romantic weaknesses make for a realistic characterization. When she is clear sighted about Abe, she gives good advice: "Mostly it's just common sense," she said. "If you see he needs help, then you help him; if it looks as though he can manage, then you leave him to get on with it. But it's easy enough to ask. All you have to do is say, are you okay or do you want a hand? Or most likely he'll ask you. The important thing is not to be scared."

When she is being wishful though, "she had these secret dreams that one day, in the not too distant future, a brilliant eye surgeon would perform some miracle operation on Abe and make him able to see, and then he WOULD be able to drive, and ride, and go skiing, and do all the other things that now he couldn't. She knew it wasn't possible, for he had already told her so, but it didn't hurt to fantasize just a little bit, did it?"

Marianne enjoys Peter's attention because it gives her "normal" outings and new attention from her peers. In his own way, Abe is as protective of Marianne as she is of him, and because he is older, he does not pressure her about sex. It is clear in the story that this is the responsible decision of a loving man, not an asexual situation that may stem from his disability.

Abe often asks what people look like and has his own ideas about colors and the mood each one has. At one point he chides Marianne for not knowing about Passover, since he knows about Easter, and their religious differences compose another area that Marianne has to find answers for. Ure is skilled at writing books that have interesting characters in situations that stretch their self-image and preconceptions. This sequel to *See You Thursday* is an excellent selection for any young adult collection.

■ Ure, Jean. **See You Thursday.** Delacorte, 1983. 194pp. (0-385-29303-8) Reading Level: Grades 7–12. (BCCB D83)
Disability: Blindness

Marianne's mother rents a room to Mr. Shonfeld. At 16, Marianne is sensitive about not having a date for her school's Easter party and fears that their blind tenant will be an intrusion on her life. Abe Shonfeld instructs piano students, and he swaps lessons with Marianne when she offers, in turn, to help him learn to cook. Abe is her guest at the Easter party and begins accompanying her on country walks to her "kingdom," an abandoned building she uses as a hideaway.

Marianne joins Abe's singing group as an alto, and she learns to relax with the members. After exchanging invitations to concerts with Abe, Marianne turns down a date from someone her own age. Marianne's mother asks Abe to move out because of the blooming relationship, but Marianne visits Abe anyway. She becomes distraught because Abe refuses to make love to her and because her mother forbids her to see him again.

She runs off to her "kingdom," and Abe comes looking for her, but he falls into a quarry and is slightly injured. Abe locates a new apartment, and the couple hope to be reunited after he has a visit with his sister in London.

Analysis: As in *Butterflies Are Free,* Abe has set an independent course for his life when he gets surprised by a romance with a unique young lady. Marianne had biased ideas about blindness that are dispelled as she gets to know Abe. When she wants him to leave his cane behind and use her as a guide, he points out that blindness cannot be disguised and that limitations dictate certain accommodations. One theme deals with the difference in age, another with the difference in religious background. Abe's disability is nicely presented as just another difference. Recommended for young adult collections, along with its sequel, *After Thursday.*

■ Wartski, Maureen Crane. *The Lake Is on Fire.* Westminster, 1981. 130pp. (0-664-32687-0) Reading Level: Grades 5–8. (SLJ N81) *Disability:* Blindness

Ricky is in his mid-teens when an automobile accident kills his best friend, Leo. Ricky is blinded in the accident. He slashes his wrists in a suicide attempt, but he survives. At a rented mountain cabin, Ricky is supposed to spend time fighting his depression, but memories of time spent there with Leo make this difficult. Family friends have brought a dog, King, whose snarling and history of abuse intimidate Ricky. When a thunderstorm causes a tree to smash into the cabin, Ricky relies on King to help him flee from the dangers of the wild and a forest fire. The rescue helicopter drops a line for Ricky only, but he holds on to King, and they are both saved from the inferno.

Analysis: This is a doggy bit of melodrama so unlikely that it undermines the potentially realistic aspects of Ricky's grief and his needs for adjustment. If already in a collection, this title can be suggested to Lynn Hall fans. If not, less sentimental fare can be chosen that explores the reestablishment of trust after a serious physical or emotional loss.

■ Wilde, Nicholas. *Into the Dark.* Scholastic, 1990. 176pp. (0-590-43424-1) Reading Level: Grades 5–8. (KR 1 S90; BCCB N90) *Disability:* Blindness

Matthew is 12 when a vacation in coastal England enables him to experience the scents and sounds of the countryside. He is blind, but once he meets Roly at the cemetery, together they explore salt marshes, the shore, and an abandoned manor house. Matthew wonders why Roly sounds so sad and will not speak to Matthew's mother. Comments from townsfolk also make Matthew realize that Roly is not simply the local lad he had assumed his friend to be. Matthew can hear Roly, but no one else can, and since he is blind, Matthew was unaware that others could not see Roly either. One hundred years before, Roly was involved in a tragedy and has come back to ask for forgiveness so that he can pass over to eternal rest.

Analysis: Because the third-person text maintains Matthew's point of view, description is limited to the senses he uses. This is a unique aspect to a ghost story that in other ways is a bit predictable. Readers will love the familiar foreshadowings and moody developments of the plot. Matthew and his mother are clearly drawn characters, and it is exciting to think of Matthew being able to tramp about as he pleases because of Roly's mysterious presence. Matthew is clever and able to resolve his ethereal friend's problem. A strong choice for most collections.

■ Wisniewski, David. *Elfwyn's Saga.* Illus. by David Wisniewski. Lothrop, Lee & Shepard, 1990. 32pp. (LB 0-688-09590-9) Reading Level: Grades K–4. (KR 1 Ag90; HB N-D90)
Disability: Blindness

In Iceland, long ago, Elfwyn was born blind because her father had been cursed by the Viking, Gorm. When covetous Gorm brings a magic crystal as a gift, only Elfwyn is safe from the visions it plagues each member of the household with. Elfwyn destroys the crystal and restores her family's prosperity.

Analysis: With historical sources and legendary roots noted, the author frames an inviting original story. Elfwyn is self-reliant, and the tone of the tale is beautifully matched by the author's intricate cut-paper illustrations. A first choice for collections.

6

BOOKS DEALING WITH COGNITIVE AND BEHAVIOR PROBLEMS

This chapter contains titles classified in four sections: Emotional Disturbances, Learning Disabilities, Mental Retardation, and Speech and Language Impairments.

Citations are alphabetical by author in each section.

Books under Emotional Disturbances refer to autism, chemical dependency, mental illness, psychosis, and schizophrenia.

Learning Disabilities includes dyslexia and perceptual and other problems.

Books that deal with problems caused by brain injury, developmental disability, and Down's syndrome are annotated in the section on Mental Retardation.

Speech and Language Impairments contains titles portraying communication problems such as aphasia and stuttering.

Short entries describe secondary characters or additional disabilities discussed at length in a full annotation that has been classified in some other chapter. "See" references are noted.

EMOTIONAL DISTURBANCES

■ Adler, C. S. *Fly Free.* Coward, 1984. 159pp. (0-698-20606-1)
Reading Level: Grades 6–8. (BCCB Je84)
Disability: Emotional disturbance

Shari is 13 when she works on a bird-banding project with Mrs. Wallace. The older woman likes Shari and helps her deal with her confusion when

Shari's abusive mother reveals that Zeke is not her real father, and Pete is a half-brother.

Analysis: Shari is shy and sensitive to the cruel names and blows her sulky mother rains down on her. Since Zeke is always on truck runs much of the time, Shari's mother vents her frustrations and resentments on her oldest child.

Shari likes to go into the woods, climb trees, and watch birds. Her dreams of flying free are symbolic of her trapped feelings that generate from being called "Ape Face" or receiving a beating from her mother. At times this book is too broad in contrasting the good Mrs. Wallace and bad old Mom. However, Shari does make an adjustment and set goals for herself, so some readers will enjoy this look at stressful family scenes.

■ Adler, C. S. *One Sister Too Many.* Macmillan, 1989. 176pp. (0-02-700271-3) Reading Level: Grades 5–7. (BCCB Mr89)
Disability: Emotional disturbance

Case is outgoing and resilient, but she seems to attract trouble. Her baby sister is crying all the time, her parents are always tired, and the babysitter, Charlene, acts strangely. At school, Case's teacher seems unreasonable, and her older sister gets mad at the least little thing. When Case and her friend Willie foil a kidnapping, Case is the heroine.

Analysis: Charlene is portrayed as a suspicious, opinionated person whose perceptions are out of balance with reality. This is a sequel to *Split Sisters* and may offer a bit of action for upper-elementary readers who like Case and do not mind if the plot gets melodramatic.

■ Adler, C. S. *The Shell Lady's Daughter.* Coward-McCann, 1983. 140pp. (0-698-20580-4) Reading Level: Grades 7–9. (BCCB Je83)
Disability: Emotional disturbance

Kelly Allgood and her mother share a special love and friendship, because Mr. Allgood is a pilot and must be away from home a lot. When Kelly becomes 14, she starts to spend more time with friends her own age, so her mother spends more time alone. Kelly notices that her mother sleeps a lot, gets distracted from projects she begins, and unconsciously pricks at her hand with a needle. Kelly calls her father about it, but no action is taken until Mrs. Allgood must be hospitalized after a suicide attempt.

Sent to Florida for the summer, Kelly is unaware of her mother's medical condition and is not allowed to see or speak to her. Kelly stays with her grandparents, unhappy because Grandmother makes cruel remarks about Kelly's mother all the time. Kelly's memories of her mother include several stories her mother used to tell about common girls who marry a prince, only to be abandoned and then to waste away until the Sea King sets their spirit in a seashell for protection. Kelly wished the sad endings could have been changed so that the Sea King would take care of the ladies instead.

A neighbor explains that severe depression is caused by a chemical imbalance and that people who are coping with depression need lots of love and support. Kelly decides she failed her mother and is the cause of Mrs. Allgood's hospitalization. Kelly's grandmother reveals that an overdose of sleeping pills was the reason Mrs. Allgood had to be admitted to the hospital. Kelly works through her shock over the suicide attempt and her anger at her father and grandparents. She interacts more openly with her grandparents and grows closer to them during her visit. Instead of attending the boarding school her father had arranged, Kelly insists on coming home to provide love and support when her mother returns from the hospital.

The family has a happy reunion, mother is on medication and will continue to see her psychiatrist, and Kelly sees herself as "the king of the sea" who would care for the sad lady now.

Analysis: Kelly tells her first-person account, interjecting "shell lady" stories, in this perceptive novel. Since it is from Kelly's point of view, her "happy ending" of dealing with guilt by resolving to be the savior of a situation is believable. Unfortunately, it is a flawed resolution. Grandmother warns Kelly that she cannot be responsible for a sick, dependent woman, but her advice is undermined by a bitter-tongued characterization. Mrs. Allgood's psychiatrist insists that Kelly's mother has to help herself, but Kelly gets her own way. Unless Kelly buys into the doctor's opinion, she will be caretaker and codependent very soon. Readers cannot be expected to anticipate these hazards, so this story is weakened by implying that Kelly's choice is healthy and helpful.

■ Aiello, Barbara, and Jeffrey Shulman. *On with the Show!* Illus. by Loel Barr. Twenty-First Century, 1989. 56pp. (0-941477-06-1) Reading Level: Grades 4–6. (BCCB 089)
Disability: Emotional disturbance

The fifth-grade students at Brenda's school are putting on a musical. Brenda tells her therapist about the trouble she is having with other children involved in the project. Her feelings are related to emotions about her parents' divorce, which her counselor has been helping her understand. Brenda agrees that her reactions are connected and that she can achieve success in getting along with others once she understands how she feels.

Analysis: Middle elementary readers rarely meet a character through first-person exchanges with a therapist, though young adult novels use this voice. The comments are authentic and the story unreels at a good pace for its audience, but the illustrations are distracting. Part of a series that interjects special needs information into first-person fiction, the title's bibliotherapeutic value is clear for collections that include other Kids on the Block books.

■ Allard, Harry. *Miss Nelson Has a Field Day.* Illus. by James Marshall. Houghton, 1985. 32pp. (0-395-36690-9) Reading Level: Grades PS–2. *Disability:* Emotional disturbance

Everyone at Horace B. Smedley School has been down in the dumps because the football team is really bad. The children are subdued, the principal is "so depressed he hid under his desk," and the big Thanksgiving game against Central is coming up. Miss Nelson hears wild laughter coming from the teachers' lounge: "Coach Armstrong had cracked up."

Once Miss Nelson fixes coffee, calms the coach down, takes him home in a taxi, and convinces him to take a "nice long rest," Miss Viola Swamp appears on the scene to whip the team into shape. When the Smedley Tornadoes win, 77 to 3, Miss Nelson celebrates with her sister, Barbara.

Analysis: Allard needs Coach Armstrong to be indisposed so that Miss Nelson can come to the rescue in this sequel to two earlier classroom farces. The touch of mystery in the Miss Nelson books is heightened by views of the demure teacher grading papers at the same time that "the Swamp" is on campus.

Marshall's illustrations show the inappropriate behavior of Coach Armstrong when he stands on one foot on a table, then blows his whistle to signal a play in the taxi on the way home. One element of subtle humor in this book comes from the principal's inept way of covering up the coach's emotional collapse: "The next day it was announced over the PA that Coach Armstrong would be out for a long time with the measles." Coach Armstrong's illness is necessary to the humorous plot, helps develop Miss Nelson's characterization, and acknowledges that stress can affect the entire population of a school in different ways.

■ Ames, Mildred. *Who Will Speak for the Lamb?* Harper & Row, 1989. 224pp. (LB 0-06-020112-6) Reading Level: Grades 7–10. (BCCB Ap89) *Disability:* Emotional disturbance

Julie is new at her school in Santa Delores. Her father has taken an appointment at the university, and Julie has escaped the pressures of being a top teen model. She and her boyfriend, Jeff, each have trouble with their mothers. Julie's mom is so ambitious for her daughter that she caused her nervous breakdown. Jeff's mother is widowed and clings to her son. The students' romance develops with their joining animal rights protests and investigations. Julie's father is conducting research that Jeff infiltrates.

Analysis: Julie is trying to make her own decisions and form her own opinions—difficult tasks for someone recovering from a recent emotional disturbance. The story has momentum, from the teacher's demonstration of how to kill a sheep, to Jeff's spying at the lab. Sometimes information on animal rights and abuses intrudes on the dialogue. Often, novels trace the decline of a character into emotional illness, but this one shows readers that the road back to health can offer independence, romance, and, maybe, adventure.

■ Arrick, Fran. *Nice Girl from Good Home.* Bradbury, 1984. 160pp. (0-02-705840-9) Reading Level: Grades 7–10. (BCCB D84)
Disability: Mental illness

The Hewitt family experiences a drastic change that affects each member when Father loses his job. The mother, Deborah, rejects any decisions that would save money, because she has based her adult self-image on being able to buy "pretty things" and maintain an attractive, carefree public face. One example occurs when Dory, 15, and her mother purchase for the Sadie Hawkins dance an expensive dress that Dory hides from her father when he insists they return what they cannot afford. Deborah's violent reaction to the suggestion that she might sew Dory a dress like the new one is early evidence of her total rejection of reminders of the way her own mother provided substitutes for "the best" during a deprived childhood.

Deborah's decline into psychotic behavior is hastened when the house is put up for sale. She can hear music no one else hears and will not talk rationally with her husband. Soap operas fill her days, and her husband stays out job hunting, watching movies, or drinking in bars. Dory has shifted her attention from socially acceptable choices for dates that so pleased her mother, to Steve Hill, a known delinquent. Jeremy, eager to earn money for college, has come up with a job as a house painter and the constructive suggestion that his father and he accept an order for making cabinets. Deborah is horrified that her family would be changing from amateur carpenters to "workmen" as her father had been. When Dory is arrested at home for calling in a bomb scare, Deborah calls her the "pretty girl" who was taken away and she does not recognize family members.

The closing scene takes place a few weeks after Deborah has been hospitalized. Dory tells her unresponsive mother all the news of Jeremy's graduation, Dory's probation and summer school plans, and the efforts to begin the new family business.

Analysis: The author's skilled construction of this plot is interesting: "Family has everything—Family loses everything—Family regains something worthwhile" is rarely presented with development of all of the involved characters. Usually, only the teen protagonist experiences growth, and the adults are attributed rigid traits to sustain them through the changes. That Deborah's rigid materialistic trait actually defeats her rather than sustains her offers an uncommonly honest portrayal.

This entire family experiences emotional stress related to their financial shifts. The presentation of four people who cope with stress in constructive or destructive ways makes this a well-rounded view of adjustment disorders. The father's depressed drinking, the daughter's reckless risk-taking, and the mother's withdrawal from reality are all symptomatic. The ending might have been improved by indicating that not only the mother but the entire family would need time and therapy to work up to a healthy emotional foundation for home life under the new circumstances.

■ Avi. *Wolf Rider: A Tale of Terror.* Bradbury, 1986. 202pp. (0-02-707760-8) Reading Level: Grades 7–10. (BCCB D86)
Disability: Emotional disturbance

Andrew Zadinsky is at home with a friend when the phone rings in his new apartment. A stranger, who calls himself Zeke, describes a college student he claims to have murdered. Andy reports this to the police, who treat it as a prank. The school counselor interprets Andy's claims about the call as a manifestation of grief triggered by the first anniversary of Mrs. Zadinsky's death in an accident. Andy follows up on the clues himself and calls the student Zeke named. Since Nina exists, Andy visits campus to see if she matches the caller's description. When Andy tries to speak with Nina to warn her of Zeke's violent delusions about her, she decides that Andy's efforts constitute harassment and threatens a morals charge.

Mr. Zadinsky sides with the police, the counselor, and Nina. Andy determines to trace back who could have had the Zadinsky's brand-new phone number. He calls his father's colleagues in the math department, identifies the voice of Zeke as Paul Lucas, and pressures the unbalanced man by making phone calls to "Zeke." Andy's father is distracted by a budding romance, distrusts his son for the first time in their relationship, and makes plans for Andy to visit an aunt. Andy has no intention of leaving town before he can prove Paul Lucas is a threat to Nina.

Andy sneaks on campus to "unmask" Lucas outside one of Nina's classes but is forced into a car at knife point. While driving into the hills, Paul Lucas makes comments that Andy recognizes as a shift into Zeke's personality. Lucas parks at the edge of a cliff, and Andy takes the knife away and opens his door. In the struggle, Lucas releases the hand brake, unable to get out of his seat belt before the car goes off the cliff. Andy hitchhikes to town and covers his absence with a story about running away. When Mr. Zadinski looks for Andy's baseball mitt for last-minute packing, he finds a monogrammed cuff link, evidence that Andy was with Paul Lucas the night of the professor's "suicide." He secretes the item in his pocket as he and his son part at the airport.

Analysis: This thriller uses a third-person account that shifts focus between Andy and Zeke/Lucas. There are some indications that Lucas has escaped grinding poverty in the hills to build a life at the college. He is obsessed with details about other instructors' lives, as well as his student Nina. The ambiguous ending leaves readers wondering whether Nina or Andy was really in danger of being killed by Zeke.

This work is dark and calculated to remain a mystery even when the reading is done. The cover is a mystical view of a boy with a lance, riding a wolf out of a phone dial. Avi fans or fantasy readers may be misled by the supernatural tone of the title and the look of the cover. This title is recommended for middle grade audiences, who can identify with the 15-year-old protagonist as he struggles against the adults in his life. They will find it an engaging mystery that does not place all the blame for wrongful death on a villain too easy to dismiss as "criminally insane."

■ Bates, Betty. *The Great Male Conspiracy.* Holiday, 1986. 165pp. (0-8234-0629-6) Reading Level: Grades 4–6. (BCCB Ja87)
Disability: Emotional disturbance

When Maggie is 12 she sees little good in the men and boys she knows. Her father is distant and preoccupied. A boy at school is pestering her and clumsy. And, worst of all, is the way her sister's husband, Burl, ignores Alicia and their baby son. Maggie tries to help her sister and then learns that Burl has left with all their money.

Alicia moves back home to get help with the baby. She gets a job at a bank. Burl calls collect to demand money, and Father tells him off. For several months, Alicia dates a fellow named Keith. Maggie anticipates Keith will prove as unreliable as all "males" and wonders why her sister risks being hurt again.

When Father wins an award, the family celebrates. Alicia divorces Burl and makes plans to marry Keith and move to Baltimore. Maggie's resentment of all males is softened by Alicia's point that the adorable baby is going to grow up to be a man too. Keith reassures Maggie that he wants the baby to know his aunt, and he invites her to visit. Maggie admits that Burl first got everybody to like him and then betrayed them all. Keith says not all men are like that. When Burl calls again, Maggie feels pity instead of hatred. She accepts that her father is indeed preoccupied with important business and that her schoolmate's teasing is evidence that he really likes her.

Analysis: This first-person account of Maggie's difficult year is filled with incidents and interesting ideas. At first, only Alicia knows how backward her husband's emotional skills are. His adolescent behavior includes bragging, lying, smoking, drinking, wasteful spending, and inability to keep a job. His irresponsibility has been masked by charismatic, manipulative charm. If this sounds like the Peter Pan syndrome, readers can be glad that Maggie learns only vicariously about betrayal and that Alicia finds someone who wants to be a husband and father instead of a childish grown-up.

■ Bawden, Nina. *Kept in the Dark.* Lothrop, 1982. 160pp. (0-688-00900-X)
Reading Level: Grades 5–7. (BCCB Ap82)
Disability: Emotional disturbance

Noel, Clara, and Bosie go to stay with their grandfather, whom they have never met. Clara feels they are being kept in the dark about their father's hospitalization and the reason why they have never met their mother's parents before. It is hard enough to get along with gruff Grandfather, but when their half-cousin David moves in, things get dangerous. The children play along with his "happy families" game after fights and threats. Then, police bring Bosie home, suspended for a prank at school, and David runs off, assuming he has been reported to the authorities. Mr. and Mrs. Jacobs come, and Clara realizes that the couple is being left in the dark about David's bullying: "She had good reason, too. It would upset her parents to know the children had been so frightened. In danger. And it would hurt Grandpa terribly. He would hate them to know that he hadn't been master of the house, always."

Analysis: As in *Henry,* Bawden's family is under stress because the father is absent. Mr. Jacob has suffered a nervous breakdown, is not recovering, and his treatment even includes basketweaving, so no new insights come from that portrayal. When he is alert to Noel's comment that David was "Rather a crazy man, but he did try to help," Mr. Jacobs is immediately excluded by everyone's desire to put the experience behind them and not cause worry. Too bad, because it closes this story well yet leaves David without a likely ally for psychiatric care. "She thought how much David would have liked to be here, and how very glad we felt that he wasn't."

David calls himself a genius and uses fear to control the family and create a "happy" home for himself. He alienates all the family members in the process, because he has no model for real love and caring in his life:

> Clara said, "Were your parents out all the time, David?"
> He shrugged his shoulders. "Came home when they'd got enough drink inside them. A good steaming fight and then bed, that was the setup. Not much room for me in it. Except to bash me to hell and gone if I got in the way."

There is no denying that this is a well-written, suspenseful story, but the father's emotional disturbance is glanced over, and David's is exploited for the menace it introduces. Clara is all compassion at the beginning but hardens against David like her grandmother. A more hopeful resolution for the child of alcoholics is available in *Up Country,* where self-recognition and therapy are available. Stress over family secrets is presented in *The Sunday Doll* and *Secret of the Sacred Hula Hoop,* so this title would be a supplemental recommendation.

■ Bawden, Nina. *The Outside Child.* Lothrop, 1989. 230pp. (LB 0-688-08965-8) Reading Level: Grades 5–8. (KR 15 S89)
Disability: Emotional disturbance

Jane is 13 when she finds out that her father has a second family. He has left her to be raised by two aunts while he is away at sea. She and her friend Plato have life-styles that make them each an "outside child," but Jane determines to meet her half-siblings. She unravels the mystery that she was abandoned by a weak father and an emotionally disturbed stepmother. Jane learns that her eccentric aunts, distant father, and other adults are not perfect.

Analysis: This is an excellent story, written with Bawden's controlled pace and full characterizations. The foreshadowing of Jane's discovery about her family's painful secret is well done. This portrayal of disability helps the mystery along more than it offers any new insights on how an emotional disturbance in the family can make people pursue a fresh start. Still, it is a highly recommended reading experience for all of its other qualities.

■ Behrens, Michael. *At the Edge.* Avon, 1988. 201pp. (paper 0-380-75610-2) Reading Level: Grades 9–12. (BCCB D88)
Disability: Emotional disturbance

Dan is in his senior year of high school when he meets Terri. He is uninterested in most things but becomes obsessed by this blonde with a "hard glint" in her eyes that "is not entirely rational." Dan recalls many incidents of his childhood reflecting on always being second best on the school swim team. Terri has also experienced big disappointments by way of her ambitions to be a dancer. Terri breaks off with Dan, leaving him with smoldering memories.

Analysis: This plot blends romance, sports action, and problem-novel elements for a story that will appeal to teen readers. Terri's heartless behavior is attributed to a manic-depressive condition. Other books deal with love interests who help their ill partner work through to recovery. This one can serve only as a hotter variant of the love-em-and-lose-em teen romance.

■ Bograd, Larry. *Bad Apple.* Farrar, 1982. 152pp. (0-374-30472-6) Reading Level: Grades 8–10. (BCCB A83)
Disability: Emotional disturbance

Nick has a hard life with his parents, an older brother, and an emotionally disturbed uncle, who lives with them. Nick sees a counselor at school and recalls several events from his life that make him feel abused, criticized, and falsely accused of his sister's accidental death. Things do not get better, and when he and a tough friend rob a couple, his hostility flares up and he beats the elderly pair. He regards his arrest as positive attention that will make him famous.

Analysis: Nick's hostile behavior and his uncle's inappropriate behavior are two problems glimpsed in this vivid but uneven story of sordid lives. Flashbacks and emotions are presented, which create a choppy case study of an unhappy delinquent rather than a well-plotted novel.

■ Bradley, Virginia Jonas. *Who Could Forget the Mayor of Lodi?* Dodd, 1985. 199pp. (0-396-08504-0) Reading Level: Grades 7–9. (BCCB My85)
Disability: Emotional disturbance

Lois narrates the story of her summer in a small Nebraska town during the depression era. She has come home after one year of teaching but hopes to go back to college and study geology. Her best friend, Dev Skinner, has problems with her mother, who has regressed to the behavior of a 20-year-old and does not recognize her daughter. The mystery of the summer consists of the appearance of a handsome young man who identifies himself as the mayor of Lodi. Lois met him when she had a flat tire but discovers that he has also paid a visit to Mrs. Skinner. When the mayor of Lodi visits again, he and Lois are attracted to each other. He urges Lois to accept his mother's invitation to live with her while attending Northwestern University. Lois arranges for a meeting that brings Mrs. Skinner back to reality and to an acceptance of the daughter she has denied.

Analysis: These characters are not as well developed as the setting and the time period are. Reunion with an old college roommate that restores sanity is a pat plot device. Still, much of the book has to do with Dev's efforts to deal with the bizarre behavior that Mrs. Skinner's delusion causes. Dev has a sympathetic assistant in Lois, and the story provides some historical perspectives on mental problems.

■ Brancato, Robin F. *Sweet Bells Jangled out of Tune.* Knopf, 1982. 200pp. (0-394-94809-2) Reading Level: Grades 5–8. (BCCB My82) *Disability:* Dementia

Ellen Dohrmann has not been allowed to see her paternal grandmother for seven years. Ellen recalls the incident when her deceased father's mother came for her at school and entertained her in the old woman's fine home until police found them there while investigating a jewelry story theft. Ellen is now 15 and she defies her mother's wishes in order to seek out Grandma Eva, by now the town "character" and outcast. The elderly woman is weak and disoriented, living in a mansion cluttered with several years' worth of accumulated trash and unopened mail.

When Ellen visits again, with a friend, Grandma Eva locks the young stranger in a closet and runs off with the key. Ellen gets two acquaintances to release her girlfriend, and she fights the hatred she begins to feel because of Grandma's behavior. Ellen also recalls other times that Grandma Eva's eccentric comments were frightening.

Ellen coaxes her grandmother out of the hospital parking entrance, where she has been blocking traffic. Eva tells Ellen that the health department is taking action and will be investigating. Ellen gets her mother to relent and tours the hospital's psychiatric ward as a likely option for Eva's future care. Grandma Eva tries to burn down the mansion when she recalls that her father said it should never be turned over to strangers. Ellen intervenes, tricks Eva into signing papers to commit herself, feels bad about the deception, and rationalizes that her grandmother can always sign herself out later.

Analysis: Ellen's ambivalence, loyalty, and developing sense of responsibility are well defined, but the characterization of Eva is not rounded out enough by Ellen's flashbacks and reflections. Grandma Eva's current bizarre behavior is life threatening, and so Ellen's use of deception for establishing institutional care is unnecessarily dramatic. Ellen's need to be the hero depends on the tenuous plot turn that allows her mother and social agencies to ignore the woman for years, even after she has stolen property, kidnapped her granddaughter, and stopped communicating with all utility companies. One strength of the story is that Ellen also has a relationship with her maternal grandparents, which balances against Eva's geriatric decline and avoids stereotyping old people as prone to decreased mental soundness.

Brancato has a flare for capturing the attention of teens and developing sympathetic protagonists. This is a useful novel, although it lacks the depth of others published in the late 80s.

■ Bridgers, Sue Ellen. **Permanent Connections.** Harper & Row, 1987. 320pp. (LB 0-06-020712-4) Reading Level: Grades 7–10. (BCCB Mr87) *Disability:* Emotional disturbance; Orthopedic impairment

Rob overhears his parents as they discuss his sullen behavior and the trouble he has been courting for two years. At 17, he resents his capable little sister; relies on pot, alcohol, and sex to "float" beyond parental expectations; and backslides to just above failure in his classwork, applying himself to nothing. When his musical aspirations do not pay off in expert guitar-playing ability within a month and his teacher gives him a low grade on an "inspired" paper he wrote while stoned, Rob continues his pattern of angry withdrawal.

Rob accompanies his father to North Carolina when Uncle Fairlee breaks his hip in a fall. Grandpa is ornery and speaks his mind about any changes in the family farm and about his youngest son's "Yankee" family. Rob is required to stay and help with Fairlee's personal care for the first three months of school. Rob's Aunt Coralee suffers from agoraphobia, so he must help with the grocery shopping, also. Aunt Rosalie lives in town and nags everyone, including Rob's cousin Lorraine. Lorraine and her boyfriend Travis are friendly toward Rob, encourage him to date another newcomer, Ellery, and try to help him fit in at school. Ellery has her own hurts from her parents' recent divorce. She is attracted to Rob, and one evening they even make love, but she then asks him to leave her alone. Rob has been suppressing most of his rage and completing his tasks on the farm, for which his father pays him. He gets drunk on bootlegged liquor one night, then has Travis locate some pot for him. Rob is charged with possession after he runs the truck off the road while under the influence.

Ellery's mother recommends a lawyer. The local police hassle Rob for information about his supplier. Travis's farm is raided, and Rob is sorry for the trouble he has brought on people he cares for. When Rob leaves the house during a storm, Grandpa gets injured while looking for him. Rob recalls quotes from his childhood and goes to a church, where a priest helps him talk out his remorse and self-hate. Rob's father comes to the farm to check on Grandpa and stand by Rob during court proceedings. The charges are dismissed because of lack of evidence. Fairlee recovers, and Coralee regains her interest in outside activities. Ellery and Rob intend to keep in touch, though he will go back home with his father.

Analysis: Coralee's condition is dismissed by her sister as foolishness. Ellery's mother, though, knew that the three-year-old pattern had to be dealt with slowly. "It didn't happen all at once, . . . Ginny Collier's been coming over every day helping her to walk out on the porch.

"Ginny stays beside her, talking to her all the time while they walk. She's been a good friend to Coralee."

Uncle Fairlee summarizes both the incident that triggered Coralee's obsession and Rob's and Coralee's emotional problems when he says, "That's the worst kind of thing to be afraid of. Something in your head. Who can tell you it ain't there?"

All of the characters and the plot elements are joined with perceptive skill. The troubled teenagers are clearly acting out, and the peers and adults in their lives are doing their best to love them through it. Yet, all the characters know their own weaknesses, and all are drawn coping in their own ways with life.

■ Brooks, Bruce. *The Moves Make the Man.* Harper & Row, 1984. 280pp. (LB 0-06-020698-5) Reading Level: Grades 7–10. (BCCB F85)
Disability: Emotional disturbance

In a southern town, a newly integrated junior high school is the setting for a unique friendship between Jerome Foxworthy, black, bright and articulate, and a white boy called Bix. Jerome rambles through first-person recollections, impressions, and colorful expressions to present his role as the head of his household after his mother falls ill. He meets Bix in home economics class, and can tell by the condition of the boy's clothing that something must be wrong with Bix's mother too. Jerome wants to learn to cook healthy food, so he resists the assignment to make mock apple pies from crackers. This "lie," consisting of serving wet crackers and cinnamon, touches off a psychotic episode with his partner, Bix.

Jerome establishes a friendship with Bix and coaches him in basketball. Bix refuses to learn to fake or to make any moves, although he improves in other ways. Bix accepts a challenge from his stepfather to a one-on-one, his reward to be a visit with his mother, who is in a psychiatric care institution. Encounters at the hospital overwhelm him, and he runs away to Washington, D.C. Jerome helps in the search for Bix.

Analysis: Jerome has keen insights and biting language to express them with. His mature role at home and the warm relationships there are well developed. The sports action scenes are detailed, and Bix's peculiarities are revealed with skill. In class, Jerome recognizes Bix as an athlete whose confidence and style had caught his eye earlier. When Bix acts withdrawn, Jerome realizes there is something wrong. After their mock apple pie outshines all others, and a teacher is invited to taste some, Bix becomes so distressed that Jerome says, "He was slipping back fast into the slinker, right while I watched. His eyes kept getting deeper in their holes and looking more confused."

Not only is this book a popular choice because of its black male point of view and sports emphasis, but also it is a worthwhile exploration of an emotional disturbance that is being treated and one that is undiagnosed. Bix's opinion of his mother's condition or his own emotional imbalance shows in Jerome's quote, " 'I'm not crazy,' he said, like he was disgusted." The story has no pat conclusions, and the dramatic events at the psychiatric hospital bring it to a jarring end, but readers may feel just as disoriented by these stylistic choices as Jerome is by the loss of a friend.

■ Brooks, Bruce. *No Kidding.* Harper & Row, 1989. 224pp. (0-06-020723-X) Reading Level: Grades 8–12. (KR 1 Mr89)
Disability: Emotional disturbance

In the twenty-first century, adults are often alcoholics under the guardianship of their children or are regimented members of a religious sect. Either way, few children are born due to the deleterious effects of cathode ray tubes on fetuses, and even those have little childhood. Sam is 14 when he commits his mother for rehabilitation and allows a couple to adopt his younger brother, Ollie. Sam then organizes things for his mother's release, new living quarters, and new job. He has a plan to reunite her with Ollie also. However, all his plans and preconceptions are given new perspective when his mother introduces Sam to functional family life where there are "kidding," commitment, and love.

Analysis: As in *Up Country* and *Captain Coatrack Returns,* therapy introduces changes for a youngster who has had no childhood. The futuristic setting is well established, but Brooks stays true to psychological patterns that would still affect his scenario. Most adults' lack of a sense of responsibility and their arrested emotional development plague this futuristic society, but the novel focuses on one sympathetic character dealing with a painful past and tentative love. Readers will be rewarded with many insights about society's flaws, human weakness, and the coping behavior of children of alcoholics. This is an excellent choice for any young adult collection.

■ Bunn, Scott. *Just Hold On.* Delacorte, 1982. 160pp. (0-440-04257-7) Reading Level: Grades 8–10. (BCCB 082)
Disability: Emotional disturbance

Charlotte returns from a hunting trip with her father, her parents quarrel, and her mother walks out. Charlotte is raped by her father, who is a doctor. Charlotte meets Stephen, whose father is also a doctor. Stephen is shy and lonely and is coping with his father's alcoholism. Over two years, Charlotte and Stephen become friends, then lovers. On a class trip to New York, Charlotte has an emotional breakdown. Stephen has a homosexual experience with a classmate.

Charlotte writes a letter with no return address to Stephen saying that she is in another hospital and expects to be under care for a long time. Stephen's father has died, and he lives and works in New York.

Analysis: The sexual abuse of Charlotte and her subsequent emotional collapse are presented in tragic waves that buffet the well-drawn but poorly developed characters. If this book is already in a collection, it may ease V. C. Andrews fans toward less lurid young adult fiction like Davis's *Sex Education.*

■ Burch, Robert. *King Kong and Other Poets.* Viking, 1986. 123pp. (0-670-80927-6) Reading Level: Grades 5–7. (BCCB 086)
Disability: Emotional disturbance

Andy and Marilyn share a sixth-grade classroom. When one of her poems wins a newspaper contest, she is elected "poet laureate." Her whimsical, humorous verse is all she shares with others at first. Andy discovers why Marilyn seems sad, despite living in a resort and getting everything she wants. Marilyn is lonely because her mother has died and her father has had a nervous breakdown. As her father improves, Marilyn's outlook brightens.

Analysis: Andy is persistent with his overtures of friendship. When Marilyn confides in him, a supportive relationship is established. Though the story is only a vignette about this brief friendship, it is a pleasant offering for readers. Marilyn's father has chosen to do work that is more physically demanding than California's computer industry. He has found a way to cope, and Marilyn has used her poetry for a healthy release during this time of healing.

■ Byars, Betsy. *The Burning Questions of Bingo Brown.* Viking, 1988. 166pp. (0-670-81932-8) Reading Level: Grades 5–7.
Disability: Emotional disturbance

In middle school, Bingo is beset by many questions about life and love and why his best teacher ever is so weird lately. His classmate, Melissa, is able to find out about the girl named Dawn that Mr. Markham is so in love with. But what Dawn says about the relationship does not match the obsessive comments Mr. Markham makes to his class. When Mr. Markham gets injured in a motorcycle crash, Bingo and the class's "Rambo" investigate. It sure looks intentional to them, and Melissa knows that "Mr. Mark" was not wearing his helmet. But what could the students have done to stop Mr. Markham if he "flipped his lid" and then tried suicide?

Bingo has very supportive parents to help him work things out, and his new ability to carry on a "mixed-sex" conversation with Melissa doesn't hurt either.

Analysis: Humor tempers the serious theme of accepting and coping with adult fallibility. Bingo is charming and his small troubles ease readers into the big problem of seeing someone you care for lose all perspective on their own life. Mr. Markham's odd assignments include writing a letter to someone thinking of suicide. Bingo feels burdened that "maybe we were writing the letters to him, and maybe our letters weren't good enough." Mrs. Brown has the opportunity to respond: "A person is given a wonderful gift, Bingo—life. Life! And if he throws it away—as your teacher may have tried to do—if he throws it away, he's never going to get it back. Never! You can't change your mind next month and say, 'Well, I'm tired of being dead. I think I'll pop back into the world.' It doesn't work that way. You slam the door shut, and you're never going to open it up again. To me, slamming that door is betrayal to everybody you slammed the door on, and it is the cruelest betrayal in the world."

Bingo had been accused of "swirling around in his own personalized tornado," but by the end of the story, he is not just spying on classmates, daydreaming about burning questions, and jotting amusing drawings down in his journal. Bingo becomes observant and appreciative of the people he has interpersonal interaction with, and readers will be glad they spent time with him. This portrayal also shows "Mr. Mark" on the way to recovery and glad to have a visit from Bingo and Melissa.

■ Calvert, Patricia. *The Hour of the Wolf.* Scribner, 1983. 148pp. (0-684-17961-X) Reading Level: Grades 7–9. (BCCB F84)
Disability: Emotional disturbance

Jake lives with his father's old friend in Alaska after attempting suicide. The Doc is supportive, and Jake makes friends with Danny Yumiat. When Danny dies, Jake and Danny's sister compete in the dogsled run from Anchorage to Nome called the Last Great Race.

Analysis: Jake has felt pressure from his macho father but becomes able to reconcile at the end. *Black Star, Bright Dawn* is a stronger piece of writing, but this adventure is well plotted, and the characterizations are adequate.

■ Cannon, Bettie. *A Bellsong for Sarah Raines.* Scribner, 1987. 192pp. (0-684-18839-2) Reading Level: Grades 7–10. (BCCB Je87)
Disability: Emotional disturbance

Fourteen-year-old Sarah lives in Detroit during the depression. When her alcoholic father becomes so distressed about not having a job that he commits suicide, Sarah and her mother move back to Kentucky. Sarah's parents grew up in this mining community, and Sarah faces the fact that everyone knows about her parents' past as well as the circumstances of her father's death.

Having an extended family is both novel and stressful for Sarah. She adjusts to rural living and meets her first love.

Analysis: Sarah's reflections on the changes in her life include her coming to terms with her father's suicide. Many other subplots and themes crowd the story line, and the ending is melodramatic. Historical fiction collections could be supplemented with this piece.

■ Carter, Alden R. *Up Country.* Putnam, 1989. 224pp. (0-399-21583-2) Reading Level: Grades 8–12. (BCCB MS89)
Disability: Emotional disturbance

Carl Staggers is 16 when his mother's pattern of drinking and arrests results in the police's coming to announce that she has assaulted her latest lover. To pay her bail, Carl uses money he has saved from fixing stolen stereos, but she goes straight to another bar. Carl is tempted to run away, but he sticks to his plan of getting only A's to be awarded a good scholarship and of saving toward training in electrical engineering. His mother is in a hit-and-run accident and tries to have Carl take the blame for her when police come to the house. She is remanded to an alcoholic treatment center so Carl is sent from Milwaukee to stay with his mother's brother Glen and Aunt June "up country."

Adjustment to a small school and "hick" entertainment is hard for Carl, but what is more difficult is letting himself care about the people he meets. This includes his cousin Bob and a girl named Signa. Signa lives and works hard on a nearby farm and starts dating Carl. When Carl has fun, he feels guilty about his mother facing the horrors of drying out in some padded cell. He almost runs off when the family goes to church, and he is constantly worried that the stolen equipment in his mother's basement will be discovered.

Aunt June has standards that Carl chafes against; while Carl tries to figure out her motivation for riding him, Uncle Glen says:

"Oh, she figures if we'd been more like family to you and my sis, maybe we would have seen the trouble coming. You know, been able to help before things got so bad."

"That's the dumbest thing I've ever heard," I blurted. "I've been trying to help her for years. If it's anybody's fault what's happened, it's mine."

Carl's mother graduates to a halfway house, and their plans for a visit get postponed week after week. The stereo thief calls to inform Carl that the basement full of equipment was found by the police. When Carl is ordered to return to Milwaukee, the school principal says he regrets he did not get to know Carl better.

"I want to tell you one thing straight out. And, believe me, I say it as one who's been there. You don't understand what's happened to you growing up in an alcoholic home. It warps a person's outlook. Right now, you don't understand the real reasons for what's happened to you. But there are books that can help you, there are organizations that can help you, and there are people who can help you. I hope you find them."

Carl's social worker is influential in returning him to the farm after a suspenseful criminal investigation. There Carl does research and finally confides in Signa:

"We've got a name," I said. "All the stupid bastards like me are called C.A.'s—children of alcoholics. We've been studied, tested, and had books written about us."

In court, Carl pleads guilty and has to make restitution but asks to live with his aunt and uncle instead of his mother. Bob and Carl start a firewood-cutting business. One weekend, Carl helps his mother pack up to move into an apartment, returns up country, and dismisses one of his favorite fantasies.

Analysis: Carl's experiences, fantasies, problems, and realizations make compelling reading. When Carl discovers that his defensive and calculating personality is one that exhibits classic coping behavior, he is distraught. Instead of outlining a case study, this novel carefully develops realistic situations and characterizations that will move young adults.

■ Cassedy, Sylvia. *Lucie Babbidge's House.* Crowell, 1989. 243pp. (LB 0-690-04798-3) Reading Level: Grades 5–7. (BCCB S89)
Disability: Emotional disturbance

Lucie Babbidge attends a girls' school where she croaks, "I don't know" to her teacher's every question and bears the brunt of classmates' jokes. But in Lucie's house she is the well-loved daughter of a privileged family. Not until everyone else's science project sprouts does it become evident that Lucie's bean has been used as the new baby in her imaginary family adventures with a dollhouse hidden deep in a forgotten corner of the school.

Lucie is assigned to write a letter and establishes correspondence with Delia, a descendant of the dollhouse's original owner. Delia's letters detail a kidnapping after classmates take the dolls away from Lucie's hidden play area. Lucie is ill for three weeks and then steals the dolls from a classmate's desk. Finally, Lucie makes a pun in class instead of responding to her teacher with the customary "I don't know."

Analysis: Like Sachs's *The Bear's House,* this novel alternates somber action with the solitary fantasy life of a child. Because readers must be well into the book before Lucie's play world is defined, the story may be difficult for some children to complete. Ambiguous fantasy elements together with true memories of Lucie's dead parents wash over the complex plot. Lucie's characterization is skillfully developed, and readers will realize that all the playfulness, wit, artistic longings, and love that the dolls express are really aspects of Lucie's personality that she cannot bring herself to apply in the bleak world of her school. The letters from Delia (real or created by Lucie?) and the feeling of power that Lucie gets from retrieving the dolls help her to integrate her fantasy self and her "school" self.

■ Cavallaro, Ann. *Blimp.* Dutton, 1983. 156pp. (0-525-67139-0) Reading Level: Grades 7–9. (BCCB Ap83)
Disability: Emotional disturbance

Kim considers herself a blimp. When Gary, a handsome new senior at school, pays attention to her, she wonders why. Gary tells Kim that his twin brother died the year before. Kim learns that Gary was driving, could not avoid a skid, and blames himself for the death. Gary borrows from Kim an important paper but does not show up on the due day. Gary has had his phone number changed, so Kim's father takes her to his house to retrieve her paper. Gary has a bandaged wrist and gives Kim his new number on the back of a business card for crisis intervention.

Kim dates Gary until she learns that he got an A on her book report. He contacts her, and she realizes that she loves him despite his flaws. When she goes to visit him at his house, an ambulance is there, taking Gary away for treatment for another suicide attempt. Gary reveals that his mother is an alcoholic and that his father is very hard on him. Kim has made an appointment with a psychologist to discuss her weight problem, and Gary is encouraged to do the same to discuss his own problems.

Kim diets with water pills and loses 66 pounds in five months. Gary uses antidepressants but neither notices the change in Kim nor returns her romantic interest. Gary works for Kim's father, and Kim dates a classmate named Mack. Gary's mother admits that she was the one who turned in Kim's paper for credit for Gary. Kim is ready to go to the prom with Mack and intends to suppress her feelings for Gary when he gives her a note that expresses how much he loves her. She says she loves him too, even with the problems he must work out.

Analysis: There are some rambling passages to this story, but the characters are well defined. Kim's diet is problematic, but it is encouraging to follow a protagonist through successful therapy to the point where the doctor says sessions can stop. Gary's family has so many dysfunctional elements that it is hard to believe that Kim will be able to love him through all that lies ahead. This teen romance with a touch of the problem novel is for large collections with insatiable middle school readers.

■ Christiansen, C. B. *A Small Pleasure.* Atheneum, 1988. 134pp. (0-689-31369-1) Reading Level: Grades 7–12.
Disability: Emotional disturbance

Wray Jean admired her successful Uncle Raymond until he became so depressed he went to live at Hearthhaven Home. *See full annotation* Chapter 4: Health Problems.

■ Cleaver, Vera. *Belle Pruitt.* Lippincott, 1988. 176pp. (LB 0-397-32305-0) Reading Level: Grades 5–7. (BCCB 088)
Disability: Emotional disturbance

Belle has a baby brother named Darwin, who dies from pneumonia. Her mother is crushed by grief and withdraws. Aunt George comes to help but seems to foster her sister-in-law's dependence instead. Eleven-year-old Belle has a literal view of life and death until she hears a tree talking to her.

Creative insights come to Belle after this, and she begins to accept the loss of her brother.

Analysis: Characters are developed skillfully, and the theme of acceptance of death is balanced by passages that show the character's other dreams and ambitions that are either achieved or lost. Belle's mother cannot be comforted and withdraws into her grief to a point where the family becomes dysfunctional. Aunt George supersedes the physical role of Belle's mother and fosters her emotional absence as well. Yet, there is no villain. Each character is allowed her own aspirations, which the reader can consider beyond the last page.

■ Cleaver, Vera. *Moon Lake Angel.* Lothrop, 1987. 135pp. (0-688-04952-4) Reading Level: Grades 5–7. (BCCB Je87)
Disability: Emotional disturbance

Kitty Dale has grown up in many different foster homes while her mother marries and remarries. When Kitty is 10, she tries to find her father, who left the family when she was very young. Her efforts fail, so she rejoins her mother and is introduced to her latest stepfather. The man is so conventional that Kitty is tempted to shock him with news that one of her former stepfathers is now under care for insanity. Kitty abandons her plan because of her instinctive compassion. She realizes that her true sources of affection are her foster family and friends, not her self-indulgent mother.

Analysis: This summer trek through memories of Kitty's odd upbringing, her flirtation with emotional blackmail, and her emotional arrival in the bosom of her substitute family can be an additional choice for Cleaver readers and fans of "child against the world" plots.

Kitty's impressions of the adults in her life and her persistent drive toward an alternative to the life she has had are appealing. Kitty's reflections on her "insane" former stepfather and the true causes of his condition are slight. His character becomes a pawn, sacrificed in Kitty's mother's incessant pattern of serial marriage.

■ Clements, Bruce. *Coming About.* Farrar, 1984. 185pp. (0-374-31457-8) Reading Level: Grades 6–9. (BCCB Je84)
Disability: Emotional disturbance

Preposterous ideas are part of Carl's appeal for his friend Bob. It is easy to label Carl as a weirdo, but when a school administrator tells Bob that Carl once attacked a faculty member and was "hospitalized for mental illness," Bob is shocked. Bob has his own interests in student body campaigns and in renovating an iceboat, but Carl's home life concerns him too. Carl's father is physically abusive to his wife, and Carl defends this. When Carl's mother is injured so badly that she moves out, Carl goes to stay with Bob. Then Carl runs away, asks Bob to help falsify some school records, and joins the Navy to be a photographer.

Analysis: Bob's narration of his friendship with Carl is well written. He finds out that the account of Bob's attack on a teacher was exaggerated. However, Bob's reaction to the possibility that his garrulous friend could have a serious mental illness may be of interest. Carl's problems outweigh plot elements about Bob's family and girlfriends, but the characters will hold reader interest.

■ Colman, Hila. ***Nobody Told Me What I Need to Know.*** Morrow, 1984. 165pp. (0-688-03869-7) Reading Level: Grades 7–9. (BCCB N84)
Disability: Emotional disturbance

Alix is 16 before she becomes dissatisfied with the cultured, refined, and privileged pattern of her life with her intellectual-snob parents. A new boy next door makes Alix reevaluate her preferences, and she comes to desire closer relationships within her peer group. Nick's father makes bad business decisions and commits suicide by carbon monoxide poisoning. Alix is shaken from her preconceptions, and when Nick's family moves away, Alix introduces his talented girlfriend to the art treasures that Alix has always taken for granted.

Analysis: Alix is not as personally affected by this suicide as the characters in *The Last April Dancers,* and Mr. O'Carney's vulnerable personality is not as well developed. However, this is a well-written story and will be a good additional title in young adult collections.

■ Conrad, Pam. ***Prairie Songs.*** Harper & Row, 1985. 176pp. (LB 0-06-021337-X) Reading Level: Grades 6–8. (BCCB S85)
Disability: Emotional disturbance

At the turn of the century, in Nebraska, farmers spread their sod houses miles apart on the flat prairie. Louisa loves this life, and she wants the new doctor and his wife to enjoy some wildflowers when they arrive. She overhears some comments about city folk not being able to last the winter, and her little brother, Lester, associates this with the death of their pretty baby sister, Delilah. Dr. and Mrs. Berryman arrive, and Louisa has never seen such a beautifully dressed woman or so many books.

Neighbors introduce Mrs. Berryman to tasks, such as collecting "chips"—the cow droppings that burn. She insists on wearing gloves for this duty and has trouble adjusting to other realities of prairie life. Mrs.

Berryman spends time reading with Louisa and Lester, sharing her books. Louisa notices how disappointments, like a broken cradle, and shocks, like a scene with another student and a gun, unsettle Mrs. Berryman's nerves. When her baby is stillborn, Mrs. Berryman loses interest in everything and makes odd comments about city life, as if she does not know where she is. A bad rain drips through the muslin roofs of sod houses, and Louisa witnesses Mrs. Berryman's distracted efforts to wrap all her books in clothing, piling them up and then spreading her skirts over the odd collection to protect them.

A train accident requires Louisa's father and the doctor to travel, but, totally withdrawn now, Mrs. Berryman refuses to leave her fireside to join Louisa and her mother and brother. Two Lakota men come to the soddy, demand food, discover Lester under the bed, and leave with the family horse. Next morning, Louisa's mother walks through the snow with both children to check on Mrs. Berryman. The doctor's home is empty, and the children discover Mrs. Berryman seated outside, frozen to death in a pose of terror.

Louisa recites a poem for the Fourth of July celebration. "Maybe it was a kind of thank-you to her, or maybe just a small sign to everyone else, telling them that a lady had come to Nebraska once and died, but that first she had taught me some poems and read me some books." When she falters, her usually silent brother prompts her along.

Analysis: The triggers of Mrs. Berryman's emotional disturbance are presented from Louisa's point of view. Every shock registered by the unstable woman is softened by the girl's knowledge of prairie life and by the experiences or expectations shared by Louisa's mother. Mrs. Berryman's tragic death completes her withdrawal from a harsh landscape and a life that was too foreign to the environment she knew how to cope with. When she teaches Louisa to use empathy toward Lester's quiet nature and works hard through her difficult childbirth, Mrs. Berryman is shown using her natural strengths. These strengths are undermined by a sequence of change and circumstance that she cannot control.

The writing is direct, yet uses poetic imagery and descriptions. This title won the 1986 IRA Children's Book Award and can be highly recommended to a wide range of students.

■ Conrad, Pam. *Taking the Ferry Home.* Harper & Row, 1988. 192pp. (LB 0-06-021318-3) Reading Level: Grades 8–12. (KR 1 Je88)
Disability: Emotional disturbance

Ali and Simone are 16 the summer they meet on Dune Island. Ali's father is a novelist and recovering alcoholic. Her mother is away, working on a dissertation, so Ali is open to spending time with Simone. Simone is beautiful, rich, and seriously disturbed. Simone's mother is an alcoholic, and a childhood tragedy has taken its toll on Simone. Simone moves in on Ali's relationship with a boy, so Ali drops her as a friend. When Simone's mother drives Simone to desperate action, Ali comes to the rescue.

Analysis: Alternating points of view in each chapter allow readers to experience Simone's troubles and to watch Ali's opinions shift. At first, Simone is the "Princess," with everything going for her. Later, her grasping, callous personality is revealed, but it is also balanced by scenes of emotional neglect and the harsh memories that haunt her. Ali's characterization is enhanced by the compassion and courage she exhibits toward Simone, but Simone's portrayal stands on its own as well. This title offers more than many problem novels that present the same themes.

■ Cooney, Caroline B. *Don't Blame the Music.* Pacer, 1986. 172pp. (0-448-47778-5) Reading Level: Grades 7–9. (BCCB MS86)
Disability: Emotional disturbance

Susan has always considered her older sister, Ashley, as a loving protector. When Ashley comes home after a failed career as a rock singer, she spoils personal property, insults the family, and remains bitter and sullen. Susan has school dynamics to cope with, as well as questions about the boys she likes. Stress is generated by Ashley's aggression and hostility until her parents finally suggest therapy.

Analysis: It is unclear whether these parents delay in getting Ashley to a counselor because they are patient or because they are unnerved by her personality shift. This title could be valuable as a sustained picture of hostility that is totally disrupting a family.

■ Corcoran, Barbara. *Annie's Monster.* Atheneum, 1990. 188pp. (0-689-31632-1) Reading Level: Grades 5–8. (KR 15 Ag90; HB N-D90; BCCB N90)
Disability: Emotional disturbance

Annie MacDougal is the oldest child in a family with four talented children. Annie does not feel talented herself, but she compassionately crusades for an accident-prone Irish wolfhound and a homeless woman, Cora, who is mentally disturbed. When townspeople in their small Maine community want to do something about Annie's gigantic pet, she reminds them that the dog saved Cora's life.

Analysis: The family and townsfolk are well-established characters in this dog story. The issues of humane treatment of animals and the parallel concern for finding Cora an appropriate living situation do not overburden the plot. Since Annie's entire family is involved in helping Cora, the solution is not as simplistic as is found in many books for children. A recommended purchase, by a prolific author.

■ Craig, Mary Francis. *The Sunday Doll.* Dodd, 1988. 138pp. (0-396-09309-4) Reading Level: Grades 5–8.
Disability: Emotional disturbance

Emmy stays with her Aunt Harriet when her sister's boyfriend commits suicide. *See full annotation* Chapter 4: Health Problems.

■ Cross, Gillian. *On the Edge.* Holiday, 1985. 170pp. (0-8234-0559-1) Reading Level: Grades 5–8.
Disability: Emotional disturbance

Two fanatics kidnap a newswoman's son, then reveal the roots of their hatred for family ties. *See full annotation.* Chapter 7: Various Disabilities.

■ Crutcher, Chris. *Chinese Handcuffs.* Greenwillow, 1989. 202pp. (0-688-08345-5) Reading Level: Grades 8–12. (BCCB MS89)
Disability: Emotional disturbance

Tragic events and heartbreaking revelations surround Dillon Heminway after his brother commits suicide. He deals with his distress by writing long letters to his dead brother. He also spends time with his brother's girl, falls in love with her, and discovers that the new baby in her family is actually her son by his brother. Another girlfriend is cold toward Dillon, and he finds out that sexual abuse by her father and now her stepfather has caused this reaction.

Analysis: Though good writing and solid insights distinguish this book, the subplots lack cohesiveness. The story is intriguing, for emotional disturbances can be rooted in events that seem as slight as a woven bamboo toy. Also, a person who is dealing with abuse, grief, shame, and anger is likely to be as immobilized as one who pulls and pulls at a Chinese handcuff instead of relaxing and considering why it has such a hold. This story touches on four teenagers' serious problems and their potential as roots of emotional disturbance.

■ Davis, Gibbs. *Swann Song.* Bradbury, 1982. 192pp. (0-87888-198-0) Reading Level: Grades 7–9. (BCCB Je82)
Disability: Emotional disturbance

By tenth grade, Prudence and Mary Tess are best friends, but once Elliott Swann and Prudence become a couple, the girls spend less time together. Mary Tess is overweight and has a crush on Tim. Swann lets Prudence know that Tim is using Mary Tess for help in schoolwork and has made crass comments about sexual experiences with Mary Tess. Prudence tries to keep her generous friend from being hurt, but at their secret place at the top of a cliff, Mary Tess insists that she has "messed up."

Mary Tess is missing the next morning, and Prudence and Swann find the girl's book manuscript torn to pieces at the top of the cliff above a quarry. Later, Swann punches Tim out after Prudence hears a news report that Mary Tess was found dead in shallow water below the cliff. Prudence dumps the remains of the novel on the desk of a supercritical teacher whom Mary Tess had idolized as a published author. Realizing that Mary Tess had always been there for her during her troubles, Prudence broods until her own little sister offers comfort. Also, 'Prudence couldn't remember ever seeing Mrs. Opie sober and wondered if it had taken the death of her only child to get her to dry out."

Swann wants to take Prudence to his special retreat in the wild, but she asks to return to the cliff to dispose of things stored in a secret tree hollow she used to share with Mary Tess. There they discuss the possibility that Mary Tess had jumped from the cliff, and Prudence determines that people do not simply grow out of their insecurities, but they have to face them with courage.

Analysis: This romance offers perceptive interactions between many of its characters. Mary Tess uses caretaking behavior and individualistic flare to cope with her poor home environment and her self-consciousness. Prudence is so tall, she has the same type of self-image problems, but Mary Tess always was there to push Prudence to trust her own potential.

When Mary Tess both loses her scholarship because she has spent so much time on her novel and realizes that Tim's attentions were self-serving, the girl is ready to run away. Prudence blames herself for not being a good friend when Mary Tess needed one, but Swann helps her think through her true responsibility.

> "Mary Tess always acted like she never needed anyone," she said, speaking her thoughts. Swan walked over to her and sat down. "After a while we believed that, and I think we neglected her. She was always helping everyone else. She seemed so strong."
> "I should have realized how upset she was. I could have saved her if—"
> "If what!" Swann said loudly. "No one destroys another person's life. If it was suicide, and I'm not saying it was, then it was Mary Tess' life and she chose to give it up. It was her decision, not yours."

Though the ending is more ambiguous than Peck's *Remembering the Good Times,* this story makes the same subtle point that young people get caught up in the bad times they are experiencing, and they lose perspective on the permanence of suicide.

> "Did you know that even a handful of water like this is affected by the moon's pull?" Swann said. He sucked the water from his hand and reached down for more.
> "You mean even a thimbleful of water has a high and a low tide, like the ocean?" Swann nodded and wiped his hands dry on his jeans.
> People have high and low tides too, she thought, pressing her cool, wet hands against her face. One day she was in love with herself and the next day she was her own worst enemy. If only Mary Tess could have seen that and ridden out the tide.

Most collections will benefit from the addition of this successful novel, which does not slight its serious subplot yet captures special friendships and a blissful first love.

■ Davis, Jenny. *Sex Education.* Orchard, 1988. 150pp. (0-531-08356-X)
Reading Level: Grades 7–10. (BCCB S88)
Disability: Emotional disturbance

Olivia became emotionally paralyzed when she was 15 because of the death of her study partner, David. She has been under psychiatric care for a year, "which is something of a record for this place. You're supposed to get well and go home or get worse and go to State. From what I hear, the state hospital is a real pit. This place is not. Actually, it's very nice. Rugs, curtains, windows."

Olivia's doctor has suggested she write this story because "there is healing in telling, telling even the worst. But what he doesn't understand is that I don't want to get well. So. There. Now I've said it."

Dr. Hirsch also counsels Olivia's parents, who blame themselves for her sudden retreat into seven months of sleep and unresponsiveness followed by five months of tranquilizers and therapy. "I would rather go back to being blind and crazy. At least then I didn't remember."

Olivia then tells how her unconventional teacher gave a sex education class assignment. She and David met and helped a new couple in the neighborhood. The woman was pregnant and had difficulties. She was also endangered by her husband's abuse. David and Olivia kept their discoveries to themselves and tried to coax Maggie away from her home. In a confrontation with Maggie's husband, David was pushed down the steep front steps and dies of a broken neck at Olivia's feet.

In conclusion, Olivia recites what Dr. Hirsch told her about Mr. Parker's arrest—that he served one year for homicide and that his wife could not give testimony but disappeared after the trial. Olivia appends a note about her teacher's visit, which prompted Olivia to offer comfort as David would have:

> "The blame is not yours. Dean Parker killed David, not you. Not even me. And I was there and agreed to it all. It was Mr. Parker. Don't blame yourself for this."
> She stared at me, her green eyes wide open. "Do you believe that?" she asked in a whisper.
> "Yes. I know it." And I did. Suddenly I did. "You did the best you could. So did I. So did David. Even Maggie, in her way. The blaming is of no use."

Olivia makes up her mind to use the hurt she has experienced along with what David and her teacher taught her about sex, love, and life.

Analysis: Olivia regrets that she and David never made love but recognizes that they shared all the elements in David's "recipe" for sex: "Sex is in the joining, the mixing, the blending of two people." Caring about someone else was necessary for that blend, and though the assignment to care went out of control at the Parkers' house, resulting in David's death, Olivia learns not to let it result in her own.

Powerfully written, this novel touches on teen pregnancy, wife abuse, romance, and emotional disturbance.

■ DeClements, Barthe. *No Place for Me.* Viking/Kestrel, 1987. 136pp. (0-670-81908-5) Reading Level: Grades 5–7. (BCCB Ja88)
Disability: Emotional disturbance

Copper Jones is 12 when her mother is institutionalized. Her stepfather has a new job, so Copper stays with her Aunt Dorothy for a while. The routines and rules of this family are more than Copper can adjust to, so she is sent to another relative's home. Copper has heard that her father's sister was a witch, and it is true. Aunt Maggie practices white magic and is part of a coven. Copper gets to visit her mother and learns some things about life and her mother's outlook that are in constant conflict. Copper gains insight from Aunt Maggie and determines to abandon some of the behaviors and values that she learned from her alcoholic mother.

Analysis: Though it is simplistic to assume that Copper can untangle her childhood traumas with only Aunt Maggie's patient love and empathy to guide her, this book depicts how skewed perceptions and motivations can affect a child raised in a home where substance abuse is common. Since her mother is under psychiatric care and Copper has experience with her mother's immediate family, readers may recognize some of the causes of Mom's instability. When Copper is ready to take positive action, instead of continuing the self-destructive pattern she has learned from Mom, the story line and characterization can seem written to formula. However, DeClements has a way of endearing to many readers her underdog heroines in search of a little happiness.

■ Delton, Judy. **Near Occasion of Sin.** Harcourt, 1984. 152pp. (0-15-256738-0) Reading Level: Grades 8–12. (BCCB D84)
Disability: Emotional disturbance

Tess was named for St. Therese the Little Flower of Jesus and was raised in Milwaukee during the depression. She has a parochial education, stays a virgin, and becomes a teacher alongside the same nuns who had taught her. She meets a handsome stranger whose kisses and vows of love excite her. Concerned that his aggressive intimacy puts them in danger of eternal damnation, she agrees to a short engagement. Within moments of the wedding, Duane claims a husband's right to be the only person a wife needs. Stating his sexual demands and starting an insensitive and unwise pattern of repeated love-making, Duane intimidates Tess. By the time they drive from Milwaukee to his California home, she is pregnant.

A man who claims Duane is his brother appears at the door, but the name he uses is different from the one she was married by. After Tess puts pressure on Duane to tell her the truth, he loses his job and blames it on her. She feels her prayers are answered when he suggests that they return to her home town and that she take back her old job.

Whenever Tess notices that family responsibilities are being ignored, he manipulates her with church dogma so that she will give in to his authority. She is even warned by staff at the parochial school she works in that she must honor her husband's wishes no matter how irresponsible they seem because that is how he will learn to be strong.

Duane is offered a fourth-grade teaching assignment at the same school as Tess and gets paid more because he is the head of a household. He refuses to socialize with other couples, and when Tess goes out with girlfriend, he harasses them with obscene phone calls. She confronts him with this, and his response is that she is in need of psychiatric care and that her irrational behavior is driving him crazy. When the school principal has to let Duane go because his students are unruly and their mothers have complained of obscene calls from Duane, Tess packs her bags and goes home to her parents.

Her daughter is born and baptized in the Catholic church. Named after St. Therese the Little Flower of Jesus, they nickname the child Terri.

Analysis: This depressing little novel presents a vivid picture of Catholic education and male-female relations in the middle of this century. Duane has apparently established a new persona for himself, as a pathological liar. His comments about enrolling in graduate school and his superficial commitment to Tess and the church are all aimed at satisfying his sexual and physical desires. "What a jerk!" readers will think when he exercises his supremacy by taking groceries out of the refrigerator to make room for all his beer, by spending on magazines and cigarettes money Tess earns, by nearly raping her and then rejecting her once she is pregnant, and by digging up the bulbs she plants because he has claimed the yard work as his private and appropriate domain. Readers may feel the story is too bad to be true, but the author tells it so powerfully they will be moved.

■ Dines, Carol. **Best Friends Tell the Best Lies.** Delacorte, 1989. 213pp. (0-385-29704-1) Reading Level: Grades 7–10. (BCCB MS89) *Disability:* Emotional disturbance

Leah is 14 and has a best friend named Tamara. Leah's mother feels that Tamara is too wild and that Leah has become rebellious by spending so much time with her. Tamara says and does outrageous things, such as hinting that her mother is a murderer and making sexual overtures toward a classmate named Caesar. Leah has a boyfriend named Miguel, and disagreements abound when Miguel's uncle, José dates Leah's mom. There are general outbursts between all of the characters, often centering on Tamara's unconventional actions and Leah's loyal defense of her friend.
Analysis: Tamara's self-destructive behavior puts Leah's other relationships at risk, and arguments seem to swamp the story at times. The ending is handled well, though its transition to quiet revelations of the friendship's painful end does make for a sudden shift of tone.

■ Dragonwagon, Crescent. **The Year It Rained.** Macmillan, 1985. 213pp. (0-02-733110-5) Reading Level: Grades 7–10. (BCCB Mr86) *Disability:* Schizophrenia

Seventeen-year-old Elizabeth Stein reflects on her family situation and other elements of her difficult life. Her mother was loving and responsive, but her father was alcoholic and irresponsible. She has made three suicide attempts and has been hospitalized several times for schizophrenia. A friend of hers is also ill, and this worries her. When Elizabeth meets a sensitive and sympathetic poet, she realizes her driving goal to be a writer.
Analysis: Elizabeth shares numerous details and shifts from current observations to retrospective comments. This may be characteristic of her

mental impairment, but it can obscure incidents for the reader. Her recent recovery is based in part on megavitamin therapy, which offers a new insight into medical options.

■ Duffy, James. *Missing.* Scribner, 1988. 144pp. (0-684-18912-7) Reading Level: Grades 4–6. (BCCB Mr88)
Disability: Emotional disturbance

Ten-year-old Kate is kidnapped. Children aged 10 know about the dangers of strangers, but both Mr. Atwood and his wife had offered a ride, saying that they knew Kate's mother. Kate has run away twice before, so the search for her is taken up by her sister, Sandy, and retired policewoman Agatha Bates. They are the only ones convinced that Kate is in danger this time. Kate is not abused, but the kidnapper attempts to convince her that she will be happy as his child. The police and Agatha Bates piece together the facts about another girl's disappearance some years before with the assumption that the father of that child saw in Kate a resemblance to his daughter and so kidnapped Kate.

Analysis: This author's contrivance of extreme grief over a missing child fills the need for a villain motivated to kidnap but not kill the victim. Several suspense stories for upper-elementary and middle school soften the denouement of their pulse-quickening plots by presenting the perpetrator as emotionally unstable instead of criminally insane. Though this device may evoke compassion for the book's characters and spare the reader's sensibilities; it can create an unfortunate stereotype in children's literature. This thriller should be complemented with portrayals of parents who do not go to illegal lengths to cope with grief over a lost child.

■ Duncan, Lois. *The Twisted Window.* Delacorte, 1987. 192pp. (paper 0-385-29566-9) Reading Level: Grades 7–10. (BCCB MS87)
Disability: Emotional disturbance

Tracy meets Brad and is suspicious of his claim to be a new student at her high school. He pays attention to her though, then confides that he needs her help to rescue his little sister who was kidnapped by their own stepfather. Because Tracy is staying with her aunt and uncle due to an unusual custody decision, she is open to Brad's story about his stepfather's crime. Tracy baby-sits for the couple who Brad insists is concealing his sister. The evening they take Mindy, Brad has to use a gun to force the homeowner into the pantry. Brad drives Tracy and Mindy from Texas toward Albuquerque. Tracy doubts Brad's stories because of the little girl's reactions to him and her consistent use of the name "Cricket."

When Tracy places a call to Brad's mother, she finds out that Mindy died four months earlier. She also finds out that Cricket is Brad's former stepfather's niece. Brad leaves with Cricket when he sees Tracy on the phone. She calls her aunt and uncle and finds out that her father is on his way back from Rome because Tracy is missing. Brad's best friend, Jamie, picks Tracy up, and the two girls track down the disturbed young man.

Brad takes "Mindy" to the family cabin and plans to get custody of her with Jamie's help. Tracy tries to sneak Cricket out of the cabin while Jamie talks to Brad. When his rifle discharges, he is shocked to see "Mindy" fall. The fear that he has hurt the little girl forces him to recall the day he really did kill his 2-year-old sister when she ran into his path as he drove away from her birthday party.

Jamie is there to help Brad with his realizations. Kate assures Cricket that they are going home.

Analysis: This thriller has better structure in its foreshadowing and shifting points of view than Duffy's *Missing* or Kehret's *Deadly Stranger*. There is no villain, which readers learn as Jamie shares her side of the story.

"Don't you *dare* call Brad crazy!" Jamie said angrily.

"What term would *you* use for someone who threatens to kill people?"

"He's been pretending too long, that's all," said Jamie. "You don't have any idea of all that Brad's been through. It's enough to make any-body act sort of—different."

Among Brad's devastating memories are his mother's accusations that Brad's father never would have died of a heart attack if he had not gone into the woods with Brad, leaving medical attention three hours away. The driveway collision that killed Mindy was an accident, but "Mom says it's the same as murder." Instead of casting a flat-out bad guy to reveal in a clever twist of plot, Duncan creates a plausible scenario for Brad's emotional disturbance and gives him a supportive girlfriend who will see him through the pain he has been avoiding with denial.

Duncan fans will not be disappointed, and this novel is recommended for most collections.

■ Eige, Lillian. *Cady.* Illus. by Janet Wentworth. Harper & Row, 1987. 183pp. (LB 0-06-021793-6) Reading Level: Grades 5–7. (BCCB F87) *Disability:* Emotional disturbance

Cady has never had a real family and Thea, the lady with whom he goes to live when he is 12, does not answer his questions. There is some secrecy about his being there that is not made clear to him. "Sometimes Cady thought an invisible line divided her down the middle into two people, one happy with him, the other nervous and afraid for him."

He meets Pete, whose mother has sent her son to live with his Uncle Ingvald. Pete misses his sister, Velda, until their mother gets a new boyfriend and sends Velda to Uncle Ingvald's as well. Cady observes both a man who lives by himself in the woods and an injured fox. Thea invites the recluse to a holiday meal, and Cady sees that the adults resemble each other and that Cady looks like both of them.

Mr. Lowell takes back to his cabin a blank journal he got from Thea for Christmas. Thea explains to Cady, "It isn't healthy to turn your back on the world entirely. It's one way of ending your life." Velda stays past the holidays, starts school, and makes friends. Cady has a crush on her and thinks working on a science project with Pete will give the three students more time together. Cady asks Mr. Lowell and his tame fox to help. Velda does sketches for the project, and the frequent visits this requires establishes a delicate relationship between the man and the children.

Cady finds out Mr. Lowell has decided to stay. Cady tells Thea what he has guessed and she confirms his suspicions that Mr. Lowell is Cady's father, and her brother. Cady's mother died, and his father was too overwhelmed with guilt and grief to keep the boy with him. He joined the service, then was under treatment in a veterans hospital. He still represses memories and is fearful of Cady, but the boy determines to hang onto him so that the man cannot get away.

Someone kills the fox and when Cady blames himself, his father offers comfort, recognizes Cady as his son, and breaks through the block his sorrow had placed on his memory. The family members come together slowly, and they see a vixen with her kits in the spring.

Analysis: This is a well-written story with a touch of mystery. Cady and his friends are from differently dysfunctional families, but which create the same emotional needs in all of them. The veterans' hospital could not address Mr. Lowell's deepest scars, and Thea did not have the resources to help her brother earlier. His slow reentry into human relationships is paralleled by the healing and taming of the fox.

Cady was actually kidnapped by Thea from his mother's extended family, who had been concealing him by shifting him from one home to another. Lowell had been called a murderer and had been told the son was not his at a time when he was most vulnerable and apparently believed it enough to drop out of Cady's life. The loneliness is palpable in this empathic tale.

■ Evernden, Margery. *The Kite Song.* Lothrop, 1984. 192pp. (0-688-01200-0) Reading Level: Grades 5–8. (BCCB 084)
Disability: Emotional disturbance; Amputation; Muteness

When Jamie's mother dies, his half-brother, Ron, takes him into his family of four. Ron has lost his job but washes windows with his cousin, Clem. Clem reads his poem, "Kite Song," to Jamie and gets a rare reaction out of the withdrawn 11-year-old. Teased as a dummy at school and determined not to return, Jamie is enrolled in a school for children with disabilities. His first friend there is April, a black girl who cannot speak. He recites Mother Goose rhymes and Clem's poem for April instead of reading a book for class. Jamie's teacher, Kate, uses a copy of "Kite Song" to discover that Jamie can read.

Clem's artificial leg causes him to fall and injure himself, and money pressures make Ron lash out at his wife. Jamie is so burdened by guilt from many unrelated events, that he runs away when Clem leaves the family. Kate finds Jamie with Clem, explains that Ron has arranged to get counseling, and assures Jamie that he is ready to be in a regular classroom again.

Analysis: Jamie's unresponsiveness to family and educators thaws as he learns to care for new people in his life and to release his guilt about his father's and mother's deaths. Veteran Clem has his own impairments from the war, the least of which seems to be his artificial leg.

The character of April is interesting; she and Jamie form a friendship and work to present "Kite Song" in a school program. Her healthy attitude helps readers to see that being "colored" and mute does not stop this character from learning to sign and communicate caring for another person. Lots of extraneous elements, like racial bias and wife abuse, clutter the story at times. However, Jamie's interactions with his teacher are constructive, and they do address the way an emotional limitation can interfere with all other aspects of a person's life.

■ Forman, James D. *The Big Bang.* Scribner, 1989. 160pp. (0-684-19004-4) Reading Level: Grades 8–12. (KR 1 S89)
Disability: Emotional disturbance

Chris Walker is in therapy after being the only survivor of a van full of partying high schoolers that was hit by a train. He is concerned that his older brother, Jeff, may have indeed intended to stop on the tracks in a suicide attempt. After all, his mother had driven into a tree and killed herself earlier. Chris recalls his father's pride in a successful business, his brother's football victories, and his mother's problem with alcohol. After their mother's suicide, Jeff's behavior became erratic, his drinking increased, and his driving got wild. Though Chris sees that there was a suicidal pattern to his brother's actions, he finally remembers that drunken

Jeff had Chris drive the van the evening of the accident. Chris and his counselor address the confusion and guilt this memory causes.

Analysis: Like *A Year Without Friends*, this story is told from the affected teenager's point of view. As in *Sex Education*, the patient sorts out the realities of the situation so a therapist can help to address the deepest problems. Believable details and straightforward presentation of symptoms make this a strong choice for young adults.

■ Forman, James D. *Cry Havoc.* Scribner, 1988. 196pp. (0-684-18838-4)
Reading Level: Grades 9–12. (BCCB MS88)
Disability: Emotional disturbance

Research Grant 4387-J-1 has been terminated, but an "unstable" survivor of the genetic experiment is responsible for the death of an infant and a teenage girl in Sandy Cliffs. The community's leading attorney is trying to puzzle through the meaning of his life. His daughter, Cathy, has been suspended from the private academy that members of his family have attended for generations. His wife, Joan, has been in a psychiatric institution for nine years, after an ugly suicide attempt that involved puppies from her kennel business: "Ten years of therapy and self-pity had left Joan as miserable now as she had been in the beginning. How many times had he heard her say, 'Why was I ever made alive?' All those years—guilt, suffering, and money—and there was not much he could do about it except get a divorce and make her more unhappy." Joan's best friend, Pat, is the logical choice for remarriage according to Joan.

Cathy fears she will also develop a mental illness and finds it hard to settle on the ambitious educational path her father has in mind. Her boyfriend, Bruce, comes to visit and praises one of Joan's drawings. Joan seems stressed out by the dinner, then takes many pills that her husband counts out so she can "do just fine." However, Joan attempts suicide again and is returned to the hospital, which she now considers her home.

The town is in turmoil from terrifying attacks by what seems to be a pack of dogs. Joan is found dead in her sleep at the hospital. Jim senses a "vacuum in their lives," because even through Joan's absence, "Hope had been living in the house long after she had left."

Analysis: Frequent soul searching and intercut scenes detract from the pace of this story. Guilty reflection on the possibility of postpartum depression or too many drugs and not enough love occupy Cathy and her father. Pat's character is admirable but unconvincing. A disturbed Vietnam vet, who was freed by the father's legal defense only to haunt the man's life serves as a red herring in this story, which is an uneasy stew of terror and family-problem novel: pretty bleak on the human side and rather pat with the evil of a scientific-tampering theme. Recommended for large collections or in paper for horror shelves.

■ Fosburgh, Liza. *Cruise Control.* Bantam, 1988. 217pp. (0-553-05491-0) Reading Level: Grades 7–10. (BCCB 088)
Disability: Emotional disturbance

Gussie, Jimbo, and Annie know that their mother drinks too much. Gussie is 16 and has suspicions about the amount of time Dad spends with a woman from work. Dad is kind toward Mom most of the time but is unhelpful with respect to her drinking behavior or Annie's obsession with food. Ten-year-old Jimbo is very clever and has earned a bankroll by gambling.

A girl named Ethel visits for a while, insisting on being called "Flame." A dangerous situation prompts Gussie and Jimbo to take their mother's car to transport Flame to safety with their aunt and uncle. There, "Miss Baby" comforts her nephews and the waif and offers Flame a job. Mom is hospitalized after a breakdown. Gussie and Jimbo find their father to be more loving once they return home.

Analysis: In depicting how each member of a family responds individually to the stress of living with an alcoholic, this story succeeds. Unfortunately, the plot is cluttered with other elements and coincidental solutions that weaken its effectiveness. Large collections may want to consider this as an additional title.

■ Fox, Paula. *The Village by the Sea.* Orchard/Watts, 1988. 148pp. (LB 0-531-08388-8) Reading Level: Grades 5–8.
Disability: Emotional disturbance

Father describes his sister, Bea, as "a terror," and mother summarizes the cause as envy, but there is no one else whom Emma can stay with while her parents are concerned with father's heart surgery. *See full annotation* Chapter 4: Health Problems.

■ Franco, Marjorie. *Love in a Different Key.* Houghton, 1983. 160pp. (0-395-34827-7) Reading Level: Grades 7–9. (BCCB Mr84)
Disability: Emotional disturbance

Neenah has devoted years to become a concert pianist, but during her senior year at a new school, she sets some new social priorities. She meets Michael, who plays the guitar in a group that performs regularly. Occasionally Michael makes paranoid comments, but he keeps such a busy schedule that Neenah simply thinks it is sleep that he needs in order to clear up his bizarre perceptions. When Michael's grandmother dies, he has to be hospitalized for his emotional disturbance.

Though Neenah has been preparing for a recital, she performs badly and believes she must choose between music and her love for Michael. She gives up piano and has regular visits with Michael, during which she sees small improvements in him. As he recovers, he shares with Neenah that it is wrong to quit because of one mistake and that he is determined to stay well.

Neenah returns to her music professor to continue her studies; the professor says that musicians need to recognize beauty and pain without being blinded by either. This level of emotional maturity was what the professor felt was lacking in Neenah's earlier performances, but she plays beautifully at her next concert. Michael copes well enough with his fears to be there, waiting in the wings.

Analysis: Romances often use emotional disturbances to challenge the main character, then end on too sunny a note. This book allows readers to consider how different loyalties can make decisions difficult in such a situation. Neenah tries to eliminate the conflict by choosing Michael over piano but discovers that music is too big a part of her life. Michael has been very ambitious, but it makes him ill. In the end, Neenah realizes it will be hard to find a balance between Michael's fears, their love, and their talents. Perceptive writing in a fluent style creates a strong novel here.

■ Freeman, Gail. *Out from Under.* Bradbury, 1982. 166pp. (0-8788-8188-3) Reading Level: Grades 6–10.
Disability: Emotional disturbance

Emily Corson and her mother are working out a new relationship after the death of Mr. Corson one year ago. Emily has a crush on the school bus driver, Tank, and is surprised to learn he is to be her instructor in a weaving class her mother encouraged Emily to take.

Emily's best friend, Carla, attempts suicide after being rejected for a school play and assaulted at a party. Emily writes letters to Carla at the hospital where she is being treated for depression. Emily visits Carla, and Tank gives her a lift home. Tank and Mrs. Corson establish a relationship that makes Emily jealous and angry. Carla comes home for the weekend and keeps up her suicide game to manipulate everyone around her.

Emily has been involved with the school play and feels closer to Ernie than Carla by springtime. Tank moves to California, and Emily feels more sympathetic toward her mother.

Analysis: Emily's grief has her in an emotional tunnel but "after a year's time she could see pale light seeping in." So many feelings have to be resolved that they could have bogged down the story line, but this author keeps things clear. Carla's depressive state is manifested in obsessions such as suicide and a dramatic craving for attention. Emily calls her own perceptions "crazy" when she considers Carla's personality and emotional disorder.

> It was crazy, all the things she was thinking in that short time. She felt afraid that Carla would die, and sad that she might lose her, angry at her for going so far with her suicide game, and annoyed at her for always wanting to be the center of attention, and then suddenly suspicious of Carla's motives.
>
> Emily sighed, feeling both defeated and relieved. Trying to guess what Carla wanted was like playing a complicated chess game and not knowing if your pieces were white or black.

Emily is much healthier by the end of this story, perhaps because she has distanced herself from the drain of Carla's complicated needs. Supporting the recovery of a mentally ill person who is under professional care is taxing enough, but trying to help the patient with friendship or love alone can endanger one's own mental health. This is a valuable portrayal to add to collections that already have Riley's *Crazy Quilt*.

■ French, Michael. *Us Against Them.* Bantam, 1987. 151pp. (0-553-05440-6) Reading Level: Grades 8–10. (BCCB Mr88)
Disability: Emotional disturbance

Seven kids feel so out of place in their small town, that they form a club. Reed is their leader, who has a way of building up the confidence and solidarity of misunderstood loners. When their clubhouse in an abandoned gas station is scheduled to be torn down, Reed decides the group should go into the Adirondacks for a few days. When it is time to go home, Reed pressures all of them to vote unanimously to stay. A worried father locates their wilderness home and is killed while struggling with Reed.

Analysis: Like Duncan's *Killing Mr. Griffin,* this novel presents a charismatic young man whose obsessions cause the death of an adult. Reed's positive traits are many, but his fatal flaw is his need to be in control. He manipulates his friends, challenges the wilderness, and defies the father of two of the girls in the group. If there has to be an unstable villain in a melodrama like this, at least he has some good traits too. The other characters are flat, and interactions that could substantiate their great bond and the high regard everyone has for Reed are lacking. Believability is not a critical element in escapist reading, so stock this if an additional title is needed.

■ Gaeddert, Lou-Ann. *A Summer like Turnips*. Henry Holt, 1989. 71pp. (0-8050-0839-X) Reading Level: Grades 5–8. (BCCB MS89)
Disability: Emotional disturbance; Depression

Bruce goes for his annual visit with Gramps. Gram died earlier in the year, and Bruce expected Gramps to be sad but sees that Gramps is surly and does little besides watch TV. Bruce tries to cheer Gramps up but gets yelled at. With patience, Bruce makes suggestions that overcome Gramp's lack of interests. Slowly, they reestablish their rituals and relationship.

Analysis: This brief book cannot delve deeply into its characterizations, but the emotional content is genuine. Gramps's withdrawn behavior is classic, and Bruce's mature persistence is loving. Readers can learn about emotional recovery from depressive disorders.

■ Graber, Richard. *Doc*. HarperCollins, 1986. 160pp. (0-06-022064-3) Reading Level: Grades 7–10.
Disability: Alzheimer's disease; Emotional disturbance

Lance has been under psychiatric care but foolishly mixes his medication with alcohol. *See full annotation* Chapter 4: Health Problems.

■ Grant, Cynthia. *Hard Love*. Atheneum, 1983. 206pp. (0-689-30985-6) Reading Level: Grades 9–12. (BCCB D83)
Disability: Emotional disturbance

Stephen is a high school senior when he falls for a 23-year-old divorcee named Molly Doyle. He drives his father's expensive car and looks so mature that Molly falls in love with him, too, before he reveals their age difference. Stephen can talk comfortably with Molly.

One of his main concerns is his friend Paulie. Paulie's mother committed suicide, Paulie blames his cold father for it, and he is in a cycle of substance abuse and risk-taking that has lost him all his friends but Stephen. All of Stephen's efforts to tell his parents about Paulie's problems are turned aside until Paulie throws a potted plant through a glass door at their Thanksgiving gathering.

Paulie's father gives him a trained Doberman attack dog. Paulie takes the dog to a New Year's party with his old friends but gets so drunk that he shouts commands and is attacked by the dog. Stephen uses a shovel to stop the dog, and it dies. Paulie is treated, loses one eye, and begins psychological treatment with the support of his father. Stephen and Molly relax about the future and their age difference and enjoy being in love.

Analysis: Paulie's father is so harsh that he views the boy's erratic behavior as laziness and irresponsibility. The pattern of a parent giving material things to a child to substitute for emotional needs is dramatically presented. Stephen, also, has a privileged life-style and is at odds with his own father because Stephen wants to study nursing. Stephen's steady goals and loyal concern for his pal are nicely developed. This story has depth, is well written, and stands out from other titles in which the teens cannot get the adults to recognize the emotional disturbance of a friend or family member.

■ Guy, Rosa. *New Guys Around the Block.* Delacorte, 1983. 199pp. (0-440-06005-2) Reading Level: Grades 8–10. (BCCB Ag83)
Disability: Alcohol, problems with

Imamu wants to get a job and paint their apartment in Harlem before his mother returns from the institution where she is being treated for alcoholism. It is difficult for Imamu to get work, because the police suspect him of recent burglaries. Olivette, Imamu's new friend, helps with the painting, and the two find clues about the burglaries as well as the violent beating of a girl on the block. Imamu's other friend, Iggy, is suspected of harming the girl, but the police cannot solve the crimes. Imamu figures it all out.

Analysis: Guy establishes characters that react and interact believably within their disadvantaged environment. Prejudice and suspicion are part of the overwhelming emotional tension portrayed. Alcoholism and hostility are two of the coping patterns revealed. Olivette serves as a foil to the bleak and hopeless patterns in Imamu's life in this sequel to *The Disappearance.*

■ Hahn, Mary Downing. *Daphne's Book.* Houghton, 1983. 177pp. (0-89919-183-5) Reading Level: Grades 5–7. (BCCB Ja84)
Disability: Emotional disturbance; Dementia

In seventh grade, what you wear and who your friends are are important, so Jessica does not want to be paired with Daphne for a project. She describes how Daphne became the butt of jokes because of her name, because of her odd clothing, and because she is uncommunicative.

While they write and illustrate a book together on the project, Jessica discovers that Daphne lives in unsanitary, unheated housing with her grandmother and kindergarten-age sister, Hope. Jessica honors her promise not to reveal the situation, until the grandmother's delusions that her son is back from Vietnam and her senile behavior are beyond Daphne's best efforts to cope. Daphne and Hope are cared for in a shelter until their grandmother dies. Then they are to go live with others of their mother's relatives in a welcoming environment.

Daphne's book, written with Jessica, wins a prize that prompts a meeting where the girls are able to mend their friendship.

Analysis: The story implies there are obtuse school and city authorities who would not be aware of a child's month-long absence from school or the condition of her home. Jessica's narration includes dramatic impressions of the grandmother's demented perceptions and her hostility. It is made clear that the old woman's distrust and uncooperative actions hasten her physiological decline. Daphne feels she does not deserve to be liked because sometimes she hated her situation enough to wish her grandmother would die. When she admits these feelings to Jessica and is reminded that a child should not have to deal with all the complications she had been trying to solve on her own, Daphne begins to heal her self-image and release her guilt. This is a sober story for children who may be looking for pathos or an underprivileged but artistic soul to empathize with.

■ Hall, Lynn. *The Boy in the Off-White Hat.* Scribner, 1984. 87pp. (0-684-18224-6) Reading Level: Grades 5–7. (BCCB F85)
Disability: Emotional disturbance

Skeeter spends her first summer in Arkansas living with Shane and his mom Maxine. Nine-year-old Shane has never had a father, and his mother is busy running the Okay Corral. Skeeter enjoys the time she spends with Shane but feels uncomfortable when Burge Franklin starts coming by to visit.

Burge takes Shane on an all-day outing that triggers changes in Shane's behavior. First, he throws away a cowboy hat that Burge had given him, and then he acts secretive and anxious at Burge's visits. Maxine is hospitalized with a broken leg, and Burge stays overnight with the children. Skeeter shares her room with Shane and wakes to hear him crying. He refuses to tell her why, but when Burge loses his job and Maxine offers him a place to stay, Shane runs away. Skeeter finds Shane, who tells her that his name is John and that he had done bad things with Burge, so he had to be sent away. Skeeter informs Maxine that Burge has been molesting Shane, and Maxine beats Burge up. County counselors help Shane, and a social worker reunites the family.

Analysis: This perceptive novel allows 13-year-old Skeeter to make believable observations about a devastating situation. Shane's reactions are convincing yet, paired with the social worker's explanation of his probable experiences, distance the reader from the actual sexual offense. Burge is revealed to have a criminal record comprising four convictions, jail sentences, and broken parole for molestation of children. Skeeter and Maxine are frustrated at not sensing earlier what was wrong. The ending indicates that Shane's emotional disturbance could recur, and it acknowledges that both mother and son will need counseling for some time.

This is a recommended title, because it describes the roots of an emotional disturbance in the life of a lovable boy and does not ignore the potential for psychological problems past the "happy" ending of the story.

■ Hall, Lynn. *Fair Maiden.* Scribner, 1990. 122pp. (0-684-19213-6) Reading Level: Grades 7–10. (KR 15 Ag90; BCCB D90) *Disability:* Emotional disturbance

Jennifer is a senior in high school, when, for six weekends, she plays the role of a fair maiden at Minnetonka, Minnesota's Renaissance Fair. That fifteenth-century atmosphere and the lute-accompanied love songs of John are an escape for vulnerable Jennifer. Her busy mother is increasingly distracted because Jennifer's brother will be returning home soon. He has received treatment at a psychiatric hospital for his violent psychotic episodes. Pretending with her mother that everything will be fine and missing her father and stepfather, Jennifer seeks some security from John. Jennifer realizes that making love and acting out a romantic relationship with John are not satisfying, once her friend helps her consider other aspects of a loving commitment.

Analysis: Jennifer's harsh life includes the inescapable drain that her brother's emotional disturbance has placed on the family. In one scene, Jennifer's brother attacks his mother and sister. Within a pleasant romance, Hall dramatically shows several of the ways in which love cannot conquer all.

■ Halvorson, Marilyn. *Cowboys Don't Cry.* Delacorte, 1984. 160pp. (0-385-29374-7) Reading Level: Grades 6–8. (BCCB Je85) *Disability:* Emotional disturbance

Shane Morgan is new in town because he has inherited his grandfather's farm in Alberta. His father, Josh Morgan, a rodeo clown and former bull riding star, has established residency to comply with the will. Shane is embarrassed by his father's drunken outbursts, and he resents the man's refusal to let him train his mother's horse, Angel. Their first full year in one place goes poorly for the estranged pair.

"I'm hooked on books about as bad as Dad is hooked on booze, and for the same reasons. I've always liked reading and, since Mom always had her nose in a book, I picked up the habit pretty young. But it wasn't till after Mom was gone that I really got into reading so much. As long as I kept reading, I could just make myself disappear into the story and not be scared or worried or lonesome, nothing—I didn't even have to be myself anymore."

Fourteen-year-old Shane tries to get involved in school, meets Casey Sutherland, nurses his mother's horse, and tries running track. His father keeps drinking and uses bull riding prize money to buy Shane a motorbike. Shane is perceptive about the grief and guilt that have prompted his father's behavior since Mrs. Morgan was killed in a car her husband was driving. The boy knows he needs his father more than the farm Josh is supposed to sacrifice his old life-style for or the motorbike. When Shane argues with Josh and then is injured in a motorbike crash, his father is devastated and misunderstands Shane's request that he stay away.

Shane lives with the Sutherlands, who receive an encouraging letter from Shane's father. At the local rodeo, Shane is saved from a charging bull by the rodeo clown—whose costume cannot mask Josh Morgan's blue eyes. Shane and his father begin to train Angel together.

Analysis: When four years of grief and unresolved guilt are exposed, Shane and his father can start to share their feelings for each other. Josh cannot bring himself to address the letter to Shane but reveals to Mrs. Sutherland that "I don't really understand why I ran off that night. Except that I seem to be real good at running when the going gets tough. I know I've got an awful lot to make up for, and it's not going to be easy. But I've quit drinking. And I'm working now. P.S. If you think he's ready to hear it, tell Shane I'm sorry. And I miss him."

When Josh is knocked out by the bull, Shane calls out, "You can't die! I need you. I love you, Dad." This scene avoids total cliché when Josh responds, "Quit yellin' in my ear, Shane. I ain't dead," then whispers, "I love you too, kid."

A well-written novel, this also has the appeal of Shane's memories of life with the rodeo, his first romance, and his desire to train his mother's horse. Balanced against the heart-wrenching drama, these subplots enhance the story with well-drawn characterizations.

■ Hamilton, Virginia. *The Mystery of Drear House.* Greenwillow, 1987. 217pp. (0-688-04026-8) Reading Level: Grades 5–7. (BCCB My87) *Disability:* Emotional disturbance

The Small family discovered a nineteenth-century abolitionist's Underground Railroad station for runaway slaves in *The House of Dies Drear.*

Now they hear of a treasure hidden a century ago in a hillside cavern. Great-Grandmother comes to live with the Smalls, and each member finds a way to make her welcome. A secret passageway is discovered, and they also come upon a neighbor with delusions about being an Indian woman who cared for runaway black orphans. An old man called Mr. Pluto has been the "treasure-keeper." Part of the treasure goes as a reward to a despicable character who had planned to keep it all, and Mr. Pluto goes to live with the Small family.

Analysis: Hamilton's writing is well crafted, but readers will need to be familiar with the setting and characters of *The House of Dies Drear* to understand this conclusion. Here, the encounter with a neighbor who is reliving a tale from the past has shiver value, but little more. Every reader should access to Hamilton's first, outstanding story about the Smalls and should be aware of the emotional disturbance that figures in this plot.

■ Hermes, Patricia. ***Nobody's Fault.*** Harcourt, 1981. 107pp. (0-15-257466-2) Reading Level: Grades 4–6. (BCCB Ap82)
Disability: Emotional disturbance

Emily was often at odds with her brother, and if she had not been putting a snake in his bedroom when he was injured by a riding mower, she might have heard his calls for help in time to keep him from bleeding to death. She writes in her diary that he is recuperating in the hospital, thus creating a reality she can cope with. She gets too ill to attend the funeral, refuses food, and sleeps on and on.

Dr. Weintraub offers psychiatric help, listing decisions her mother and father made on that day that might have affected the outcome of the accident. Emily defends her parents by pointing out, "It's nobody's fault." Once she can accept that and dismiss her self-blame, she visits her brother's grave, wears his baseball cap, and makes up with her best friend.

Analysis: The character of the sympathetic therapist is one of this book's strongest assets. Though the plot summary may be melodramatic, the story is rather flat in its presentation of insights into the psychological stages of grief and mourning.

■ Hermes, Patricia. ***You Shouldn't Have to Say Good-bye.*** Harcourt, 1982. 117pp. (0-15-299944-2) Reading Level: Grades 5–7.
Disability: Emotional disturbance

Robin admits that her mother has agoraphobia and may not be well enough to attend a gymnastics show. *See full annotation* Chapter 4: Health Problems.

■ Holland, Isabelle. *The Empty House.* Lippincott, 1983. 128pp. (LB 0-397-32006-X) Reading Level: Grades 7–9.
Disability: Emotional disturbance; Orthopedic impairment

Betsy meets Ellen Whitelaw, who secretly keeps her disabled daughter at home in a spooky house on the Jersey shore. *See full annotation* Chapter 4: Orthopedic/Neurological Impairments.

■ Howard, Ellen. *Gillyflower.* Atheneum, 1986. 106pp. (0-689-31274-1) Reading Level: Grades 6–10. (BCCB N86)
Disability: Emotional disturbance

Gilly's little sister, Honey, depends on her because their mother works nights at the hospital and their father spends most of his time drinking beer and complaining about not having a job. Gilly makes up many stories to tell and also uses the fantasies to help her cope with sexual abuse from her father. When new neighbors move in, Gilly makes friends with Mary Rose. Gilly's father forbids her to play with the "stuck-up" neighbors after school, so Gilly bends the rule and plays with Mary Rose on Saturday instead.

Honey makes a comment that Gilly interprets as evidence that her father is also molesting his younger daughter. Gilly speaks to her mother about the incest, and they move to an aunt's home. Gilly tells police and a counselor about her father's abusive behavior. Returning home, Gilly sees two types of flowers blooming in Mary Rose's renovated garden and they have the same names as the two friends.

Analysis: This very sensitive novel allows readers to see how Gilly defends herself from her father's sexual attacks and from tremendous feelings of guilt by creating a fantasy life for "Juliana." Juliana fills Gilly's mind with dangerous scenes during her father's sex acts, and then Gilly tells the resolution of the danger as a fairy tale for Honey. Because this could be the root of a multiple personality disorder, the author adds at the close of the book that Gilly gets competent counseling. Gilly also learns by interacting with her neighbors that fathers can touch their daughters in a way that is not "sexy".

The father lives alone and is in therapy by the end of the story. Gilly is told, "It's OK to be angry when someone hurts you. It's OK to be sad."

"Your dad is a grown-up, Gilly," Mrs. Paul said. "He should know what's right. He should know what's wrong. Grown-ups don't have the right to hurt kids, not even their own kids. Grown-ups don't have the right to make kids do wrong things. Your dad is mixed up. Perhaps it will help to understand that's why he molested you, but you mustn't blame yourself. The molesting was his fault, and all that has happened since is his fault, too."

Not my fault?

"Telling was the right thing to do," Mar said.

"The brave thing," said Mrs. Paul.

Like Hall's *The Boy in the Off-White Hat*, this novel is an important addition to most collections.

■ Howard, Ellen. *Sister.* Atheneum, 1990. 160pp. (0-689-31653-4) Reading Level: Grades 5–7. (KR 1 N90; HB N-D90; BCCB D90) *Disability:* Emotional disturbance

In 1886, 13-year-old Alena is a fine student and may earn a scholarship to go to normal school. When her mother goes into labor, Alena helps deliver the child because her father is away. The newborn dies, and Mother is devastated. Besides Alena's own grief at the baby's death, she must cope with the disappointment of giving up school so she can help her mother. When Alena's menstrual cycle begins, the naive girl fears that she is dying. Though Alena hoped to return to school once Mother's depression lifted, she realizes that the birth of a new sister, who raises her mother's spirits, will require Alena to stay at home. Alena comforts herself by setting domestic goals.

Analysis: A prequel to *Edith, Herself,* in which Mother's death uproots Edith and sets her back in Alena's care, this fine historical novel deals fairly with a situation that truly affected the author's ancestors. Characterizations have depth, and the details of farm responsibilities are interesting. A recommended addition to most collections.

■ Hyland, Betty. *The Girl with the Crazy Brother.* Franklin Watts, 1987. 128pp. (0-531-10345-5) Reading Level: Grades 7–10. (BCCB Ap87) *Disability:* Schizophrenia

Dana and her brother move to California and attend a new school. She makes friends in the sophomore class, but her brother Bill, a senior, has certain trouble. He is a soccer star and a National Merit Scholar, but his behavior becomes more and more embarrassing. His illness is diagnosed as schizophrenia. Besides the problems his condition causes his parents, Bill's behavior makes Dana feel awkward with her friends and guilty about her embarrassment.

Analysis: Bill's loneliness and distress escalate to hospitalization and treatment for schizophrenia. The characterizations show in a candid and credible manner a family's anguish and eventual adjustment. This perceptive story is recommended for middle school and public library collections.

■ Jensen, Kathryn. *Pocket Change*. Macmillan, 1989. 171pp. (0-02-747731-2) Reading Level: Grades 7–10. (BCCB Ap89)
Disability: Emotional disturbance

Josephine Monroe is a gun enthusiast, who lived alone with her Vietnam veteran father for seven years before he remarried. She likes her stepmother, Marsha, and enjoys her baby brother, Chrissy. She has a boyfriend named Brian, but they have trouble socializing with both her classmates and his, because they attend rival schools.

Dad starts acting moody, says Josie should get rid of her gun, gets suspicious of Brian, stops working, rages at Marsha because she takes a job, and even confuses his wife with a Vietnamese woman from the past. His flashbacks increase and he intimidates the family of Josephine's best friend, Mary Chang, so much that the family moves away. During a standoff with police, Josie is unable to shock Dad into the present and barely saves Chrissy from being shot by their father. After he is hospitalized, Josie sends him a glass dove she hopes will make him happy, and she makes plans to attend college.

Analysis: This stiffly written thriller offers accurate, well-researched information on readjustment disorders of veterans. The Monroe family's story will involve readers as Josie tries to be the strong one but finds she must let others help. In the end, Josie characteristically declines the group counseling that Marsha invites her to join. Instead, she resolves on her own: "I don't hate my father. How can you hate someone who—even though he tears up your life—loves you enough to do the one thing that scares him more than anything?"

■ Jones, Penelope. *The Stealing Thing*. Bradbury, 1983. 179pp. (0-02-747870-X) Reading Level: Grades 3–5. (BCCB My83)
Disability: Emotional disturbance

Hope feels abandoned by her parents, her favorite baby-sitter, and her best friend one summer. She introduces herself as "Lee" at camp and takes things from shops and another girl at camp. One day she comes home and finds her new baby-sitter dressed in her mother's clothing and drinking. Hope and her parents are invited to stay at a lake cabin for their first real vacation together.

Analysis: Eight-year-old Hope has surprised herself by stealing and pretending to be someone else all summer. Her parents turn about at the end, but Hope works through her feelings of neglect on her own for the most part. The baby-sitter is sympathetically described as a troubled girl in one of the scenes of closeness between Hope and her mother.

■ Kehret, Peg. **Deadly Stranger.** Dodd, 1987. 166pp. (0-396-09039-7) Reading Level: Grades 5–7. (BCCB MS87)
Disability: Emotional disturbance

Katie goes to school in a new location and makes friends with Shannon. Their plans to go shopping together are delayed when an older boy at Shannon's house says his sister is having a piano lesson. Shannon disappears. Katie is injured by a hit-and-run driver and hospitalized.

Shannon has been kidnapped by a young man who believes she is his sister. Sometimes he treats her well, and other times he is cruel. Katie finds out that Shannon has no brother and provides information about the young man. He lived in Shannon's house before, and his sister had been killed in a car crash.

Analysis: Like Duncan's *Twisted Window* and Duffy's *Missing,* this novel depends on a mentally disturbed kidnapper for its suspense and comforting ending. Duffy and Kehret alternate scenes between the kidnapper and the friend who is trying to puzzle out a rescue. Duncan's book is more convincing and stylish, so the story of Shannon's kidnap should be added to a collection only if more titles are needed in this genre.

■ Klein, Norma. **Learning How to Fall.** Bantam, 1989. 182pp. (0-553-05809-6) Reading Level: Grades 8–10. (BCCB S89)
Disability: Emotional disturbance

Dusty has a girlfriend named Star, whose best friend is Amelia. While Dusty is under psychiatric care, Amelia's visits him. Dusty's father is a recovering alcoholic, his mother lives with a female lover, and Star seems to have written him off since his father put him in the hospital. After his discharge, Dusty gets to know Amelia's family and believes he is falling in love with her. Dusty and Star get together once, which undermines Amelia's budding love for him.

Analysis: Dusty is in the hospital at his father's insistence, but it is evident that all the characters have difficulty with interpersonal trust and interaction. The complications are based on so many fashionable problems—alcohol abuse, homosexuality, fear of commitment—that the story does not flow as well as the stylish writing.

■ Klein, Norma. *Older Men*. Dial, 1987. 226pp. (0-8037-0178-0)
Reading Level: Grades 9–12. (BCCB S87)
Disability: Emotional disturbance

Elise is 16 when her mother is committed to a psychiatric hospital for
depression. A visit with her grandmother gives Elise insights on her
mother's vulnerability and the loveless, overbearing relationship that the
woman has with Elise's father. When her mother wants to leave the
hospital, hoping to avoid shock treatments, Elise's father refuses to allow
the discharge.

Elise meets Kara and Tim, her father's stepchildren from his first
marriage. Kara reveals that there is a pattern of exclusive love between
Elise's father and his little girls that warps the lives of everyone in the
family. Kara's brother has been under psychiatric care and has undergone
shock treatments. He and Elise become lovers, partly as a way to defy their
controlling father.

When Elise's mother escapes from the hospital in a cab and hides out
for the required 72-hour period to end the facility's right to readmit her
without two doctors' opinions, Elise stands up to her father to ensure that
the woman remain free.

Elise starts college. Her mother picks up her own previously incomplete
course of college studies and lives on her own. Elise's father comes to visit
with a widowed woman who has a boy and a girl. Elise verifies for herself
her father's pattern of doting on a daughter and warping the emotions of
the excluded family members.

Analysis: Elise learns how to perceive her programmed motivations and
her father's manipulative ways in this unusual coming-of-age story. She
has more trouble than many teens in relationships with the opposite sex
and feels jealous of Kara due to their father's obsessive love. Since her
father speaks with authority and is a health care professional, it takes the
evidence of her step-sibling's psychological quirks to help Elise grow
beyond his self-centered kind of love.

Elise does a lot of soul searching but does not seek counseling to gain
insights on her relationship with Tim or her step-siblings' seemingly
stunted lives. When evaluating her mother's recovery, Elise says, "What
I see now that I had lost sight of before is her strength, her sense of irony,
her capacity to love. At times she still has that expression of wonderment
at the world that she had when she got out of the hospital. She's not seeing
a psychiatrist or taking any drugs. Instead she jogs and indulges in things
that she enjoys."

Recommended for large young adult collections.

■ Lasky, Kathryn. *Home Free.* Macmillan, 1985. 245pp. (0-02-751650-4)
Reading Level: Grades 8–10. (BCCB F86)
Disability: Autism

Sam is 15 when his father dies in an auto accident and he moves with his
mother from the Midwest to New England. He meets an old man who
defends a reservoir for the bald eagles that use the game reserve. The valley
was flooded at the turn of the century, and commercial development
threatens it now. Sam watches the birds and photographs them. He becomes friends with an autistic girl named Lucy. She not only has some
type of communication with the eagles but also is connected to the past.
Lucy and Sam have time-travel experiences, and they learn of an orphan
who died in 1892. Lucy seems to be that girl's reincarnation.

The old man dies of cancer, but his dream of a wilderness reserve is
carried on by Sam and Lucy. They can "talk" to the eagles, and they
witness a pair that establish a nest.

Analysis: This hybrid plot relies on Lucy's disability for its time-fantasy
elements and the mystical communication with eagles. She gets well too
quickly and fits into Sam's household with little regard for true aspects of
autism. The more realistic portrayal of an old man with terminal illness
who is fighting for his principles and finding young apprentices to carry on
the effort strengthens the book.

■ Levitin, Sonia. *Silver Days.* Atheneum, 1988. 192pp. (0-689-31563-5)
Reading Level: Grades 6–10. (KR 1 Mr89)
Disability: Emotional disturbance

In 1940 the Platt family arrives in New York, reunited after fleeing Nazi
Germany. Though they face prejudice and economic trials, they find a way
to relocate to California. Lisa resumes ballet instruction, but her teacher
is a strident German whom she finds it hard to put up with. Their Japanese
neighbors are interned after the 1941 bombing of Pearl Harbor. Ruth falls
in love with a departing soldier. When the Red Cross confirms that Lisa's
grandmother is dead, Lisa's mother experiences severe depression. Lisa
makes the adjustments that are necessary and determines that those years
that were not good enough to be considered golden can be at least silver.

Analysis: A sequel to *Journey to America,* this has authenticity and
bittersweet revelations about war refugees during the 1940s. Fears about
the concentration camps could be kept at bay with hope for a time, but
depression results when bad news reaches the family. Highly recommended for most collections, this portrayal is credible and nicely incorporated in an excellent work of historical fiction.

■ Levoy, Myron. *Pictures of Adam.* Harper & Row, 1986. 218pp. (LB 0-06-023829-1) Reading Level: Grades 6–9.
Disability: Emotional disturbance

Adam insists that he comes from outer space and shows Lisa both his ability to hold his breath underwater and a portion of his "space capsule." *See full annotation* Chapter 6: Speech and Language Impairments.

■ Levoy, Myron. *Three Friends.* Harper & Row, 1984. 187pp. (LB 0-06-023827-5) Reading Level: Grades 7–10. (BCCB My84)
Disability: Emotional disturbance

Karen and her best friend, Lori, are 14 when they meet Joshua. The three "weirdos" have their own interests that set them apart from other school-mates. Karen is an energetic feminist, eager to have her friends be as socially active as she is. Joshua's grandfather was a Grand Master in chess and encourages Joshua to study for world-class competitions. Lori is a shy girl whose moods shift dramatically.

When Karen and Joshua pair up for a date, Lori dances off with a boy and gets drunk. She flees from his physical advances, and he accuses her of being a lesbian. Lori confides in Karen that she is confused and wants to be the one holding and kissing somebody—sometimes Karen. Karen encourages Lori to see a therapist, but Lori's parents have already said no to Lori's earlier requests for the same.

Joshua almost gives up his chess match with the American champion because Karen claims he is addicted to the game. Lori is given a sleeping pill prescription, which she abuses. She nearly dies of an overdose, and her friends visit her in the hospital. Joshua confronts the girls with the way the three friends have been manipulating each other. Karen warns him that five days of study in psychology do not equip him to analyze Lori, and he is not prepared when Lori's doubts about her sexuality are revealed. The interaction gives Joshua the same mental challenge and sense of accomplishment that chess does, so he agrees with Karen that psychology is a field he would like to study.

Lori feels comfortable enough to confide that one of her daydreams is to "start a farm somewhere, with friends like you, and raise vegetables and things, and live off the land. A place where we could really be ourselves. And then, if the H-bomb fell, we would have been happy up til then, doing things, and being together."

Analysis: Three misfits in the school scene have their own outlets and form a three-way friendship. When Lori's depressive moods focus on the betrayal and desire she feels toward Karen, she acts in reckless ways. She wants to talk to someone about it, and when her parents do not get professional help for her, Lori confides in Karen.

Focusing on Loris' repressed anger and the hate she feels she cannot show without losing the love she wants so much, the three friends make one breakthrough. The presentation of three interesting characters in a vividly drawn situation is believable. Less suspenseful than *The Girl in the Box* by Quida Sebasteyan, this story offers readers the same type of love triangle with a more satisfying ending.

■ Lichtman, Wendy. *Telling Secrets.* Harper & Row, 1986. 243pp. (LB 0-06-023885-2) Reading Level: Grades 7–10. (BCCB Je86) *Disability:* Emotional disturbance

Toby is sworn to secrecy about her father's imprisonment for embezzlement. Keeping this secret disrupts her freshman year of college, undermines her friendship with her roommate, and makes her uncomfortable with the lover she reveals it to. Guilt builds until Toby hears from her cousin that "secrets" and denial are a family sickness. The cousin had attempted suicide, was hospitalized for two months, uses antidepressants, and goes to counseling several times a week. Toby swaps her secret for this revelation. She visits her father and tells her mother about Arnie's suicide attempt. Toby's father is released, and she contacts her friends.

Analysis: Chapter 18 discusses Arnie's condition and treatment. He says of his depression, "It's like I'm dissolving, or I don't exist. Or it doesn't matter if I do." Toby's stress is manifested in various ways, and her father admits that he stole the money to prove he was more than just a boring accountant, but that the secrecy was overwhelming. This is a strong story with an honest look at the value of honesty.

■ Lisle, Janet. *Afternoon of the Elves.* Orchard, 1989. 122pp. (LB 0-531-08437-X) Reading Level: Grades 5–7. (BCCB O89) *Disability:* Emotional disturbance

Hillary knows that her neighbor wears odd clothing and is repeating fifth grade. She is surprised when she discovers that Sara-Kate's yard has an elf village in it. Sara-Kate shares stories about the elves and teaches Hillary to "go slowly and quietly, and look deep." Hillary enters Sara-Kate's ramshackle home and finds Sara-Kate comforting her mother in her lap. Later, Hillary learns that Sara-Kate forged a note so she could stay home and look after her mother.

Hillary understands that Sara-Kate does all the shopping and a lot of stealing to make do. Sara-Kate insists, "My mother used to get upset all the time. Her mind's not always right, so then she gets sick. See, sometimes the envelope comes and sometimes it doesn't come. I learned what to do when it doesn't come." The "envelope" is support money from Sara-Kate's father, who is "not exactly rich" and left a year earlier.

Sara-Kate insists on making her own way because "Nobody knows how to take care of my mother except me. They've tried to do it. Even my father tried, but he couldn't so he left. Now I'm doing it. I've done it for a year so far and nobody even knows. People are stupid. They can't see a thing. They don't have a clue to what's going on right under their noses, in their own backyards."

Hillary's mother visits and gets past Sara-Kate's stories to see what conditions they are living in. Rumors and a news article and conversations with her mother make Hillary question Sara-Kate's motives in striking up a friendship with the younger girl. Hillary transfers the elf village onto her family's property.

Analysis: Sara-Kate's inventiveness extends to survival skills and the elf village. Her friendship with Hillary is complex, and the ending shows that Hillary has become more observant and "shrewd" due to her friendship with Sara-Kate. Sara-Kate's mother needs care, but her daughter distrusts authorities who she fears will "put her someplace far away, out of sight."

As in *Daphne's Book,* out-of-town relatives come to provide a home for the child who tried so hard to be caretaker for a seriously disturbed adult guardian. Hillary does not have an opportunity to speak with Sara-Kate, but by protecting the elf village she makes peace with her guilt over betraying a friend.

■ Lowry, Lois. *Rabble Starkey.* Houghton, 1987. 192pp. (0-395-43607-9)
Reading Level: Grades 5–8. (BCCB Mr87)
Disability: Emotional disturbance

Parable (Rabble) Starkey has country roots, a very young mom, and a deep desire for stability in her life. The Bigelow family hires Rabble's mother to help out, because Mrs. Bigelow is not well enough to care for her infant son. Rabble and Veronica Bigelow are in the same sixth-grade class. They are such good friends that Rabble loans Veronica some cousins for their family tree projects. When Mrs. Bigelow becomes so disturbed that she nearly drowns her son, she is placed in a hospital for several months of treatment. Veronica says her mother is "crazy" and makes a new family tree because "I'm not going to have my mother on my new one at all."

Rabble enjoys her months of living inside the Bigelow home, with Veronica so close they are almost sisters. Mr. Bigelow shares books with

Rabble and encourages her mother, Sweet Ho(sanna) to continue her own education. Many changes in the interpersonal relationships occur that must be resolved before Mrs. Bigelow returns home. Rabble accepts her mother's study and teaching career plans, decides to use standard English more often, and helps Veronica resolve feelings about her own mother's weaknesses and love.

Analysis: Rabble's narration is lively and involving. She is proud of her grandmother's country legacy, and readers will enjoy the regional flavor of Rabble's ungrammatical style. Sweet Ho was only 14 when she married, got pregnant, and was abandoned by Rabble's father. This novel shows Sweet Ho's maturation as well as Rabble's and Veronica's development. Lowry also constructs a particularly vivid scene of Mrs. Bigelow's nervous breakdown.

This excellent novel touches on Mr. Bigelow's and Sweet Ho's attraction to each other during the difficult time of Mrs. Bigelow's hospitalization. Subplots about a cranky old neighbor who dies and a delinquent boy down the street add depth. The ending is a new beginning for everyone, satisfying but not pat. When Rabble discovers that Veronica also is "scared" about Mrs. Bigelow's return, Veronica explains, "I am glad. But I'm scared because what if she gets sick again? What if she doesn't remember to take her medicine? Daddy says she won't, but I keep thinking what if—."

■ McDonnell, Margot B. *My Own Worst Enemy.* Putnam, 1984. 192pp. (0-399-21102-0) Reading Level: Grades 7–9.
Disability: Heart disease; Emotional disturbance

Todd recalls the year his father had heart bypass surgery and, in addition, had to be admitted to a psychiatric hospital for depression. *See full annotation* Chapter 4: Health Problems.

■ MacLachlan, Patricia. *Mama One, Mama Two.* Illus. by Ruth Lercher Bornstein. Harper & Row, 1982. 32pp. (LB 0-06-024082-0) Reading Level: Grades K–2.
Disability: Emotional disturbance

Katherine and Maudie care for a wakeful baby, then Maudie asks for the story of Mama One, Mama Two. Katherine tells how a little girl and her mother lived happily, until the woman became so unhappy that her paintings were dark, and the chores did not get done. Maudie interjects details as Katherine continues about Tom, the social worker, who took Mama One to a place where she could find out what made her sad. He also took the girl to a new home with Mama Two. When Katherine puts the baby in its crib, she sleeps with Maudie for a while.

Analysis: Katherine is clearly the Mama Two of the story, and her efforts to comfort Maudie and serve as a foster parent do not undermine the affection Maudie has for her mother. This is an outstanding text, by the Newbery Award–winning author of *Sarah, Plain and Tall.* The illustrations are pastels smudged with evening shadows that match the understated progression of this story within a story. Few books for this age group are as successful as this fine title.

■ MacLean, John. *Mac.* Houghton, 1987. 175pp. (0-395-43080-1)
Reading Level: Grades 8–12. (BCCB D87)
Disability: Emotional disturbance

Mac is comfortable with his skills as a skier and soccer player but uncomfortable around girls. He is surprised that beautiful Jenny likes him enough to suggest going together to a school dance. They enjoy intimacies and being a couple until Mac's behavior changes drastically. He cannot sleep, has nightmares, is hostile toward everyone, and lets months go by without showing any interest in sports. He is distracted when he is with Jenny, forgets about her even if they are kissing, and begins to avoid her at school.

A meeting with a male counselor ends up in Mac's vomiting on the man's shoes. His experiences with a female counselor are quite different. She seems to barely have time for him but helps him break through to a painful memory he has been suppressing. She suggests that he may want to confide in a man about the way in which he has been hurt. Mac finally becomes able to reveal that a doctor who was to perform a sports physical molested him. The fears of being accused of homosexual tendencies and the guilt that he had done something to deserve the accusation are settled with his counselor. However, Mac is still distant with Jenny. She yells at him, her mother comes home, he hides under Jenny's bed, and they wind up kissing all night. When they sneak out of the house, Mac tentatively guesses that they must be "going together again."

Analysis: Mac's first-person story is divided into three passages. The reader is excluded from details of the sexual abuse but given insight into the confusion and terror Mac feels. The female counselor manipulates Mac's first sessions by pretending to have errands to run, but he cuts through the pretense. She includes a lot of psychological information in the final sessions and tries to protect Mac from particularly probing questions. For an older audience than *The Boy in the Off-White Hat,* this is a recommended title.

■ McNair, Joseph. *Commander Coatrack Returns.* Houghton, 1989. 188pp. (0-395-48295-X) Reading Level: Grades 6–9. *Disability:* Emotional disturbance

Lisa is used to her parents' depression, but when her new friend, Robert, will not stop using other identities at school and at home, she decides that he needs help. *See full annotation* Chapter 7: Multiple/Severe Disabilities.

■ Magorian, Michelle. *Good Night, Mr. Tom.* Harper & Row, 1982. 304pp. (LB 0-06-024079-2) Reading Level: Grades 6–9. (BCCB Mr82) *Disability:* Emotional disturbance

During World War II, Will is evacuated from London to live with "Mr. Tom." Tom Oakley discovers that Will has been emotionally and physically abused by a mother who considers the boy incapable of being good. She sent a belt and a note along with him to be sure Will was properly punished. Tom coaxes Will into sleeping in the bed instead of under it, though Will wets it every night. Will makes a friend, 9-year-old Zacharias, who has also been evacuated.

Will goes to school and has lessons with younger children because he cannot read. On his ninth birthday, he is stunned by gifts and a celebration in his honor. His mother sends letters, but they are full of warnings about Will's evil behavior. After two months, Tom and Will rely on each other for acceptance and love that had been lacking in their life.

Will's mother sends for him because she is ill; the boy returns to the apartment, finding a baby girl there with her mouth taped shut. Will is beaten for asking about the baby and finally chained to a pipe, where Tom and a warden find him. The lifeless body of the baby is taken from Will and he is sedated and placed in a hospital to recover enough to go live in a children's home. Tom kidnaps Will and nurses him with Zach's assistance. After a holiday at the shore, Will studies art with Geoffrey Sanderton. Will is informed that his mother has committed suicide, and Tom adopts the boy.

Zach tries to visit his wounded father in London but is killed in the bombings. Will mourns for four months until a comment by Geoffrey about his own dead friend comforts the boy. Will repairs Zach's bike and begins to enjoy life again with Mr. Tom, his dad.

Analysis: This tense story is clearly set in a time period when mental illness and child abuse received little attention from authorities, whose only option was to send children to institutional facilities. Mr. Tom knows that Will needs more individual encouragement and love than an institutional environment would offer. Tom also knows that Will's needs have forced himself to change the reclusive patterns the 60-year-old man established after his wife's death.

Will's mother is beset by religious fears and lacks any nurturing skills, so her characterization serves to present a deranged villainess, whose behavior leads to the death of an infant, the nightmarish suffering of her son, and her own suicide.

■ Mahy, Margaret. *Memory.* McElderry, 1988. 278pp. (0-689-50446-2) Reading Level: Grades 8–12.
Disability: Emotional disturbance

Jonny Dart looks for the only witness to his sister's death, haunted by fears that he caused the fatal fall five years ago. *See full annotation* Chapter 4: Health Problems.

■ Miklowitz, Gloria D. *Close to the Edge.* Dell, 1984. 160pp. (paper 0-440-91381-0) Reading Level: Grades 7–9. (BCCB My83)
Disability: Emotional disturbance; Arthritis

Jenny feels depressed with her life and is shocked when a classmate named Cindy attempts suicide. A school counselor suggests that Jenny do some volunteer work by accompanying a senior citizens' kitchen band that performs regularly at hospitals and nursing homes. Jenny admires one of the members, Hannah, who is active and upbeat despite her arthritis. Jenny is less and less satisfied with her social outlets and is worried that Cindy is not getting psychological counseling but still has suicidal intentions. One boring Friday evening, Jenny and her younger sister get out the Sabbath candles and create their own ceremony.

Their grandmother is injured and the family decides to have her move nearer so they can spend time together. Cindy gives Jenny a brooch before committing suicide, so Jenny blames herself for not intervening. Jenny learns to value her loving family and follows the example of her elderly friends who do not give up on life without a struggle.

Analysis: Jenny flirts with suicide at the opening of this perceptive novel. Her characterization has depth and she develops the insight that she has been "close to the edge" of self-destruction. Cindy confides that her mother is impossible to please and is too concerned about what people will say if she puts Cindy into counseling. This is a very subtle revelation of Cindy's deep emotional disturbance. Readers may not recognize the fundamental differences between Cindy's unmet needs in her relationship with her mother and Jenny's period of isolation and purposelessness.

■ Miklowitz, Gloria D. *Goodbye Tomorrow.* Delacorte, 1987. 192pp.
(0-385-29562-6) Reading Level: Grades 7–12. (BCCB My87)
Disability: AIDS

Alex is a high school student, busy with classes, friends, athletics, plans for
college, and special moments with Shannon, the girl he loves. Twice his
plans get put on hold because of severe bouts with the flu. An examination
reveals that transfusions following an accident years ago resulted in exposure to AIDS. Alex is scared by the news that he may develop the disease.
As more people hear of Alex's health problem, he is ostracized from
extracurricular activities such as the swim team, he experiences discrimina-
tion, and he loses his job. Bereft of his usual pursuits, Alex receives
support from his family and the friends who remain loyal to him.

Analysis: Candid exposure to the stresses of living with the physical and
social realities of AIDS is provided in this young adult novel. The point
of view shifts between Alex, Shannon, and Christy and so explores the
shock, fear, and conflicting feelings of several characters. This is a good
complement to Klein's *Night Kites,* for it deals with a case of AIDS that
is not related to homosexual activity.

■ Miner, Jane Claypool. *Day at a Time: Dealing with an Alcoholic.*
Illus. by Vista III Design. Crestwood, 1982. 63pp. (LB 0-89686-167-8)
Reading Level: Grades 4–9.
Disability: Emotional disturbance

Ellen Russell wishes she could tell her father what she thinks about his
drinking and the fights it causes between her parents. When things get so
bad that Mr. Russell attacks her mother with a broken bottle, he is placed
in an institution. Mrs. Russell goes to Alanon meetings and applies the
guidelines she has learned, but when Mr. Russell is released, he begins
drinking again. Ellen does not agree that Alanon methods make anything
better, and she refuses to go to Alateen.

Ellen's father demands the car keys when he is drunk, and Ellen realizes
she has just taken up her mother's old pattern of confrontation and
manipulation. Her father strikes her, and she heads off to Alateen.

Analysis: A case history of alcoholism and the applications of Alanon
guidelines are dramatized in this book from the Crisis series. Reluctant
readers will enjoy each illustrated spread, and straightforward text will
encourage them. The two points that no one but themselves can prevent
alcoholics from drinking and that the guilt felt by family members over an
alcoholic's behavior cannot "help" are clearly incorporated into the dialogue and plot. If a pamphlet from Alanon cannot serve your needs, try
this book.

■ Miner, Jane Claypool. *Miracle of Time: Adopting a Sister.* Illus. by Vista III Design. Crestwood, 1982. 63pp. (LB 0-89686-172-4) Reading Level: Grades 4–9.
Disability: Emotional disturbance

A 5-year old Vietnamese orphan is being adopted by Shirley's family. Shirley has moved her dance things out of her room to prepare to share it with the little sister she has been anticipating. When Kim wakes, screaming, and will not be comforted by family members, a doctor says that only love, rest, and time can bring about a change. Kim continues to be aloof and destroys a rag doll Shirley offers her. Shirley is distracted at school and feels guilt about her own harsh anger and disappointment over Kim.

After months without a breakthrough, the family decides to place Kim in a home for disturbed children. Just before the scheduled trip, Shirley dances for Kim in hopes that the music may bring a response. Instead, Kim laughs at Shirley's frustrated mime action of banging her head against the wall. Shirley, her mother, and Kim share a smile that seems like progress.

Analysis: Kim's trauma is never defined but implied. Shirley's emotional groping is presented believably, though the dialogue and description are written with a remedial reading audience in mind. Illustrations are profuse but flat, as in all the Crisis series books. *Mail Order Kid* is a better choice for chapter book readers, but this title can serve in resource collections for students who read far below their grade level.

■ Miner, Jane Claypool. *Mountain Fear: When a Brother Dies.* Illus. by Vista III Design. Crestwood, 1982. 63pp. (LB 0-89686-166-X) Reading Level: Grades 4–9.
Disability: Acrophobia

Don Murphy dies in an accident while hiking in the mountains with his twin brother, John. Besides grief for a loved one, John must adjust to becoming an individual now that his twin brother is gone. John is withdrawn when he returns to school, then is paralyzed with fear when he finds himself high up in the bleachers in gym. He cuts school and meets a pickpocket at the zoo. John calls the 10-year-old "Bozo" and accepts his offer to be like a little brother.

One day, John catches himself overreacting to the boy's climb up a jungle gym. John avoids several camping invitations, and they go to an amusement park at the beach as a substitute outing for the disappointed Bozo. When Bozo panics and begins to climb out of a stuck Ferris wheel's seat, John scales the machinery to join the hysterical boy until a worker frees the operator's lever.

Analysis: John's self-image is disrupted when his twin brother dies in a tragic outing. The fear of heights that he has experienced is dismissed in one heroic act. This is too superficial to benefit readers who can cope with real juvenile novels. Part of the Crisis series, it is slim, heavily illustrated, and useful for reluctant readers.

■ Naylor, Phyllis Reynolds. *The Dark of the Tunnel.* Atheneum, 1985. 216pp. (0-689-31098-6) Reading Level: Grades 7–10.
Disability: Cancer; Emotional disturbance

A reclusive artist, called Cougar, protects his mountain from townspeople who support nuclear emergency practice drills. *See full annotation* Chapter 4: Health Problems.

■ Naylor, Phyllis Reynolds. *The Keeper.* Atheneum, 1986. 228pp. (0-689-31204-0) Reading Level: Grades 6–10. (BCCB My86)
Disability: Emotional disturbance

Nick Karpinski is in eighth grade, just starting to date Lois, and sharing activities with his friend Danny and Danny's girl, Karen. Jacob Karpinski, Nick's father, walks off his job, and Nick tries to convince his mother that something is wrong with his father's paranoid perceptions. Stress affects Nick's health, he gets information from the school nurse, and he saves his father from a suicide attempt. Nick's mother remains optimistic because Jacob has a new job. However, her husband then announces he wants to become a priest but gets turned away at the church. Jacob refuses to go to a hospital, and Mrs. Karpinski and Nick must find out what steps to take to commit him. They anticipate that taking this action will destroy any trust Jacob has in them, and they try to change his behavior as it becomes more and more bizarre.

When Jacob has a delusion that he has been poisoned, he goes to the hospital willingly, but it is up to Nick, Jacob's wife, and the school nurse to provide the appropriate statements that will get Jacob treatment for mental illness. When Nick admits his father's condition, Lois cancels their dance date, but Karen stays loyal.

Analysis: Jacob's delusions and irrational acts accumulate and affect his family at a dramatic pace, which represents an accurate picture of some mental illnesses. Naylor gives each character depth in range of emotion and dawning understanding of the problem.

Of special interest is the plot element that shows how the legal process can become as defeating as the mentally unstable person's actions. The hard choice that two psychiatrists must examine Jacob to declare him mentally ill and the option that someone must prove to police that he is a danger to himself or others defeat Mrs. Karpinski's first resolve to get help for her husband. Nixon's suspenseful writing does not become melodramatic, though the family fears mount, knives are hidden away each night, Jacob buys a gun, and, finally, he drives in a dangerous rush to the hospital when he fears poisoning.

This is a riveting story, well written and sensitive and clearly portraying all characters affected by a loved one's emotional disturbance and the social complexities surrounding their experience.

■ Newton, Suzanne. *I Will Call It Georgie's Blues.* Viking, 1983. 204pp. (0-670-39131-X) Reading Level: Grades 7–10. (BCCB N83)
Disability: Emotional disturbance

Neal Sloan is 15, has an older sister, Aileen, and a 7-year-old brother, Georgie. Their father, Reverend Sloan, keeps rigid rules and is protective of his family's reputation because it has bearing on his position at the Gideon Baptist Church. Aileen dates the most rebellious boy at school and feels her father's precautions and strictures make everyone in their family weird. Neal has a different type of personal outlet, because for two years he has been learning to play jazz piano. Neal uses a neighbor's instrument or the piano at church to practice in secret, because he knows his father would insist that jazz is not an appropriate style of music for a minister's child to pursue. Georgie is insecure and constantly worried about being as perfect as his father wants him to be. One day the boy disappears on the way to school, but Neal checks on him and finds the boy arrived safely. After a run-in with a tough classmate, Neal fears retaliation, then gets suspended for fighting.

Mrs. Sloan is advised that Georgie needs counseling, but Reverend Sloan has heard a rumor that makes him adamant about avoiding any psychiatric clinic. The rumor is traced to Georgie, and the little boy is so distressed by his father's angry remarks that he hides out in a chicken coop. When Neal finds Georgie, the boy will not communicate or respond to anyone. The family takes Georgie to a clinic in a nearby town. When they return, Neal vents his worry and establishes his individuality by pounding out at the church his piano piece called "Georgie's Blues." Townsfolk join him in the tearful event and applaud his performance.

Analysis: Dramatic action and consistent tension between the characters make this an involving book. Reverend Sloan's single-minded need for preservation of appearances is believable, and the classic "preacher's kid" reactions of defiance and deception are played out by Aileen and Neal. Georgie's needs are ignored to the point where he believes that his family's bodies have been taken over by strangers who do not love him. Psychiatric counseling for the entire family will follow the action of the story because Reverend Sloan is remorseful enough to address his cycle of setting impossible standards and then blaming his family for not meeting those expectations.

■ Nixon, Joan Lowery. *Secret, Silent Screams.* Delacorte, 1988. 180pp. (0-440-50059-1) Reading Level: Grades 7–10. (BCCB D88)
Disability: Emotional disturbance

In a suburban community outside of Houston, Marti visits the police station and speaks with a young policewoman. "Barry Logan is—was—my friend. His funeral was this morning. The police said he committed suicide and everyone believes it, but I know Barry didn't kill himself. It's important to me that people know the truth because Barry was my friend."

Marti was a junior in high school when Robin committed suicide, followed by her guilt-ridden boyfriend's crashing his car at 90 miles an hour. The song "Sudden Death" was associated with both suicides and was in the VCR at Barry's when he was found. A note that read "The thought of suicide is a great consolation" was found and was confirmed as being in Barry's his handwriting. The officer reads the report: "Barry shot himself with a Rossi .22 handgun. He shot himself in the right side of the head." Marti retorts, "He couldn't! He wouldn't have shot himself like that! Barry was left-handed!"

Other elements also do not fit the profile of a suicide. Barry had just been informed that he qualified for early acceptance at A&M. Mrs. Logan says, "It's our fault that Barry died. The doctor and the police asked if we'd recognized the signs." Marti insists that there were no signs. Marti tries to enlist help from Barry's closest buddies, so they all know she is looking for evidence. This endangers her own life, and the murderer places Barry's baseball cap on her bed as a warning.

Marti sees a TV show on teen suicide that refers to the suicides in May and a national experience "called the copycat syndrome, meaning that a young person who is depressed commits suicide because others have." Another doctor blames Barry's death on the hopelessness induced by the song "Sudden Death." Marti's call-in comments to the program are cut off, but the murderer rings her immediately and whispers, "Nice going, Marti."

Marti deduces that Emmet is the murderer, because he tries to manipulate her into writing a phrase that could double as a suicide note. "Sudden Death" is playing on the VCR when she comes home, and Marti confronts the vengeful brother of one of Barry's friends who has been sent to prison.

Analysis: Nixon includes lots of information on the true suicides that took place in Marti's community. Marti's comments on the television show stressed that parents may be too busy to see signs of depression, but teen friends should be alert to changes in behavior that are meaningful as suicide warning signs. As further encouragement, the book carries the following dedication: "This book is for you because you are unique and important and special. Hang on to your dreams. Hold tight to hope. Someone rejoices in your joy. Someone cares about your sorrows and your fears. I do, too. I care."

Though the adults are wrong about Barry's death, their advice to Marti about her grief is still valid. She even accepts her mother's suggestion that she go for counseling—but first she has to make police reports about Emmet's assault. Emmet's murderous plans are fueled by his delusions that Thad's imprisonment for robbery can be blamed on "disloyal" friends. This skillfully developed and credible suspense thriller can be recommended to a wide range of readers.

■ Nixon, Joan Lowery. *The Specter.* Delacorte, 1982. 184pp. (0-440-08063-0) Reading Level: Grades 7–10.
Disability: Emotional disturbance

Julie has been abused and is in constant fear of a man she calls Sikes. *See full annotation* Chapter 4: Health Problems.

■ O'Dell, Scott. *Black Star, Bright Dawn.* Houghton, 1988. 134pp. (0-395-47778-6) Reading Level: Grades 6–9. (BCCB Je88)
Disability: Phobia; Orthopedic impairment

Bright Dawn is treated like a son by her Eskimo father and allowed to drive the sled when he goes hunting. He is lost on the ice for days, and the doctor must remove all the fingers on his right hand. When that injury heals, the man still is so haunted by his experience on the floating ice that the doctor suggests the family move inland. Bright Dawn does well at the bigger school, and her father is offered a year's employment to train for the Iditarod as the representative of the town's cannery. Bright Dawn records all the coach's comments, because her father cannot read or write. When a practice run breaks her father's shoulder, Bright Dawn is allowed to substitute for him in the race.

Bright Dawn faces the hazards of the trail with an old-timer who shares tribal tales. Bright Dawn is in the lead at the halfway point and wins a cash prize. Her lead dog, Black Star, senses danger when a white-out keeps them on a piece of ice so long that they lose the lead. Her father rescues them near their old home. Bright Dawn is able to complete the race and earns recognition for her sportsmanship and accomplishment. Bright Dawn's mother encourages her to study to become a teacher and return to the village to help other children caught between the white and Eskimo ways. Instead of sending the dogs back by plane, Bright Dawn and her father hitch them up for another overland run.

Analysis: The grueling Iditarod from Anchorage to Nome crosses two mountain ranges and the Yukon River. O'Dell's well-researched plot and practiced skill with characterization make this a fascinating story. Bright Dawn gains maturity, especially by focusing on doing her best instead of being the best—a quality needed by her dog as well. Courage, love, and determination not only see Bright Dawn through the race but also draw her father back to face his horror of the open sea.

It is good to have an additional title of such high quality to offer readers of *Island of the Blue Dolphins* and *Julie of the Wolves.*

■ O'Dell, Scott. *The Spanish Smile.* Houghton, 1982. 182pp. (0-395-32867-5) Reading Level: Grades 7–10. (BCCB Ja83)
Disability: Emotional disturbance

Lucinda de Cabrillo y Benevides is 16 and the beautiful, rich, cultured prisoner of her insane father on an island off the coast of California. The non-Hispanic women who kept her father company from time to time have all been murdered, and their bodies are in crystal coffins, guarded by a poisonous snake. Her father's hatred for twentieth-century literature is coupled with his intent to force California to be returned to Spanish rule. When the crazy man dies of snakebite, his estate and its gold mines go to Lucinda.

Analysis: O'Dell played Gothic writer here and pulled out too many stops. A Nazi doctor who experimented on the "gringas" and Benevides's threat to take a reactor plant by force are only two of the plot's many melodramatic devices. Benevides's delusion should be taken as it was developed—for outrageous impact with no hint of realism at all.

■ Osborne, Mary P. *Love Always, Blue.* Dial, 1983. 188pp. (0-8037-0031-8) Reading Level: Grades 7–10. (BCCB Ja84)
Disability: Depression

Blue Murray is bored by life in Layette, North Carolina, where her family moved two years earlier to take possession of her mother's inheritance. In February, her father moves to Greenwich Village, to pursue playwriting. By June, Blue knows that her mother is dating, confronts her mother about the separation, and blames her for loving their new, monied, lifestyle more than the happy family life Blue recalls.

Blue's father forgets her birthday through his preoccupation with having a play read for possible production, but Blue begs him to let her come visit when school is out. When Blue arrives, she spends time with her father and meets Nat and his mother, Annie. Annie had dated Blue's father, and when conflict with the director causes Blue's father to act distant, Annie comments that Mr. Murray never recovers well from disappointments. Blue resents this and tells Nat that everybody at home behaved as though something were really wrong with her father.

Mr. Murray returns, sleeps all afternoon, then begs Blue not to leave him alone. He calls himself a loser and wakes her with his crying. The scene escalates, with items being thrown, and the two rushing out of the apartment. Without keys, and lost, Blue calls her mother, who suggests that she call the police. Instead, Blue contacts Annie, who lets her back into the apartment. Blue's father calls, ashamed to return, but she tells him she will be waiting for him. Her Uncle Walter arrives to take Blue home, and her father agrees she should go and not worry about him.

Back home, Blue is ready to make the most of life in Lafayette and hopeful that her father will be happier once he gets promised therapy.

Analysis: Blue's character is well developed, as she goes from the petulant 15-year-old who wants to blame Mother, to a mature young adult who can see her parents as individuals struggling to deal with weaknesses and complex personal relationships. Blue's point of view is maintained, and it is true to life that family members will deny stress caused by an emotionally disturbed person, until they witness an episode of extreme behavior. Mr. Murray has refused therapy, and it is supposed to be this incident of frightening his child that makes him promise to seek help. It is an honest touch that Blue is hopeful but no longer unrealistic about her father's future. The portrayal and characterizations in this book are stronger than its story line, so it would not be a good first choice.

■ Passey, Helen K. *Speak to the Rain.* Atheneum, 1989. 160pp. (0-689-31489-2) Reading Level: Grades 7–10. (KR 1 N89)
Disability: Emotional disturbance

The Miles family is in distress over the death of Mrs. Miles in an accident caused by a drunk driver. One year after her death, the family moves to a forest home in Washington State. Seventeen-year-old Janna is the responsible member because her father is retreating into alcoholism. Her new friend, Kyle, also has a father with a drinking problem.

Karen is 9 but suffers depression and guilt because she was in the accident that killed her mother. Mysterious spirits from Native Americans drowned at the lake beckon Karen. Janna rouses her father to help in dispelling Karen's grief before the little girl is destroyed.

Analysis: There is suspense in the struggle against restless spirits, and the realistic elements of the plot hold interest as well. Janna is assisted by a teacher and a shaman in confronting the flood victims who haunt the lake. Three injurious situations due to alcohol abuse are portrayed, yet a lasting solution is not presented. This is a supplemental choice.

■ Paulsen, Gary. *Dancing Carl.* Bradbury, 1983. 105pp. (0-02-770210-3) Reading Level: Grades 5–7. (BCCB MS83)
Disability: Emotional disturbance; Neurological impairment

In 1958, the people of a small Minnesota town socialize during winter at an iced-over parking area. Carl, who has been emotionally disturbed since World War II, tends the grounds and sleeps in the warming sheds near the skating and hockey rinks. Marsh and his buddy Willy are 12 years old when they see Carl dance alone on the ice. The boys wonder about Carl's behavior, and they sense he has a mythic power to stop trouble or offer comfort. When Carl dances, then leaves a rose on the ice for Helen, his successful courtship fascinates Marsh.

Later, Marsh hears that Helen was brain damaged, that the two lived together but never married, and that Carl's alcoholism killed him. But Marsh decides that those details are not important compared with the special moment when Carl's silent dancing drew Helen to him.

Analysis: Older people with special needs are rarely portrayed as sexual, social beings. Paulsen uses skillful prose to make one moment stand out in the memory of both his protagonist and his readers. Marsh and Willy may not react believably to Carl's drunken moods or odd ways, but the story makes a special point about acceptance and love.

■ Peck, Richard. *Princess Ashley.* Delacorte, 1987. 208pp. (0-385-29561-8) Reading Level: Grades 7–10. (BCCB Je87)
Disability: Emotional disturbance

Chelsea enters a new school her sophomore year and is flattered to be singled out by lovely Ashley, whose circle of friends constitute the social apex of her class. If Ashley proposes any party, dance, or pairing off of couples, it happens. Her boyfriend Craig joins and then undermines the success of a larcenous group of upperclassmen. By getting alcohol to sell for underage social events, Craig establishes a reputation and a bad drinking problem. Chelsea is at odds with her mother, a counselor at the school, over most of Ashley's decisions for two years. Chelsea's boyfriend, Pod, stands by her when Ashley makes it clear that the main reason she became friends was that Chelsea's mother was in a position to help if and when Craig got in trouble.

Chelsea's mother cannot be bribed to help with Craig's upcoming court appearance. Ashley tries to manage a dance in competition with the senior prom. Craig is out of control and gets injured in a drunk driving collision. He is hospitalized with brain damage and paralysis. Too late, his teachers, counselors, friends, and family reflect on ways they could have intervened when Craig's behavior first gave evidence of his emotional needs.

Analysis: A bit of a shocker, the social and emotional power plays in this novel have credibility. Pod's parents are wealthy throwbacks to the 60s, Chelsea's father is a recovered emotional casualty of the Vietnam war, and Ashley's stepmother has been outmaneuvered. Chelsea's mother is frustrated that many of the kids she should be counseling are rarely referred to her office. When Chelsea suggests that Ashley could get help if her mother stays at the school, it shows she has gained insight on the unhealthy values her peers have. Tragedy in the form of a disabling accident strikes the story's golden boy: "They say he's hooked up on machines that breathe for him, that he weighs ninety pounds now, that somebody ought to pull the plug. But nobody really knows."

The emotional healing between Chelsea and her mother lends a hopeful note to this hard-hitting picture of adolescent life.

▉ Peck, Richard. *Remembering the Good Times.* Delacorte, 1985. 181pp. (0-385-29396-8) Reading Level: Grades 7–10. (BCCB Je85) *Disability:* Emotional disturbance; Geriatric impairment; Hyperactivity

Buck tells the story of his three-way friendship with Kate and Trav. From various locations such as Kate's special place in her family's pear orchard, Trav's affluent suburban home, and Buck's trailer, the friends share many growing pains and activities. A hyperactive boy named Skeeter was soothed by Trav the day he met Buck and Kate. Trave explained that he was a hyperactive child and recognized the signs. Skeeter says, "I think maybe I'm redirecting a lot of that energy or anger or fear or whatever it was. I can still get pretty keyed up over things. I have to watch myself."

Years later, Skeeter beats up Buck and harasses a teacher. Trav is distressed by the revenge that Kate takes on Skeeter. "It could just as well have been me. Skeeter acts out all his aggressions, and I just keep mine in and let them eat at me."

Friends and family are stunned when Trav's perfectionism drives him to suicide. Buck and Kate regret the suicidal signs that they missed, and the school sponsors a meeting to warn "how teenagers get caught up in what essentially can be a fad. We see it, but there is no mechanism to inform young people of the finality of death, that suicide is a permanent solution to a temporary problem." Trav's father resigns from the school board. Great-Grandmother Polly Prior wheels herself forward and helps the audience stop casting and dodging blame. The emotions her comments elicit from Kate and Buck "won't bring him back." Yet Buck's father responds, "This brings you back."

Analysis: Outstanding young adult books with deep characterizations are a pleasure to recommend. Peck's polished style keeps dialogue and action moving to the inevitable conclusion. The foreshadowing stand side by side with humor that is so needed for "remembering the good times." Academic mediocrity and parental shortcomings as well as Trav's troubled nature lead to his desperation. Polly's geriatric needs and feisty use of her wheelchair are natural. Through Trav's insights, readers learn why Skeeter bullies and intimidates everyone.

Recommended for all collections serving teens, this is an important book.

■ Pevsner, Stella. *How Could You Do It, Diane?* Clairon, 1989. 192pp. (0-395-51041-4) Reading Level: Grades 7–9. (BCCB S89)
Disability: Emotional disturbance

Bethany finds her stepsister on the couch, dead of an overdose of barbiturates. In a struggle to find the reasons why Diane committed suicide, Bethany interviews the girl's friends and associates. Andrea lost her brother in an accident, and Bethany can tell "she wasn't over her brother's death by a long shot." Younger siblings are a distraction for Bethany's parents, and they try to suppress the fact of the suicide incident. But conversations and odds and ends at the house include vivid memories of Diane for Bethany.

There are hints that Bethany was upset over breakups with Steve, and then Max. Max describes a time when Diane dramatically broke Steve's picture, then scraped a glass shard across her arm to prove that Max was the only one who mattered to her and that she wanted to get back together. When their little brother gets in trouble for fighting and the little sister has nightmares and wets the bed, Bethany's parents finally seek counseling. They learn both to place in the past Diane's unknown motives and the possibility that it was an impulsive act instead of calculated suicide and to get on with their own life.

Analysis: This companion to *And You Give Me a Pain, Elaine* includes the characters Andrea and Elaine but is not actually a sequel. Shared grief and confusion are revealed through Bethany's first-person, present-tense story. Diane's characterization emanates only from everyone else's reminiscences about her and boils down to that of an immature, insecure girl who "could get riled up and rant and rave, but then after she'd gotten it out of her system she'd be pleasant, almost casual." The only truth about suicide is that it does not just get things out of your system: "There was no going back, no coming back."

If a collection already includes *Remembering the Good Times,* this title can be supplementary.

■ Phipson, Joan. *Bianca.* McElderry, 1988. 168pp. (0-689-50448-9)
Reading Level: Grades 8–12. (BCCB S88)
Disability: Emotional disturbance

A 17-year-old named Hubert, his sister, Emily, and 5-year-old brother, Paul, discover a mother duck and then a girl rowing alone near an island. Farmers bring a distracted woman named Frances to a doctor, and she is admitted to the hospital. She recalls events that involved her daughter, Bianca, and her husband, who died in a farming accident. Robbers recently threatened their home, and Bianca had been missing ever since Frances had warned her daughter away from the house.

Hubert, Emily, and Paul are the doctor's children. When Hubert and Emily return to the island, they find the solitary girl. She tries to avoid them, but Emily becomes interested in her. "Now I'm going to find out who she is. She looks quite bonkers to me."

Bianca's suppressed memories of the day she had news to share with her mother, was reminded of her father's funeral, and was met with screams that she should go away are presented. "She was balanced precariously on a mental peak, one side of which fell to black depths, the other to the daylit present and stability. It was Frances who tipped the balance. It took Bianca a moment to understand that she was being rejected for a second time, that the one person in whom she had learned to have total faith had turned against her.

Bianca's flight and her days on the island up until her encounter with Hubert and Emily are described.

Again, Hubert and Emily corner the girl to offer help. Bianca nearly drowns and is cared for at the doctor's fishing trailer. Hubert is able to help Bianca regain her memory and establish trust. Bianca provides her name first, then tells about the day she saw her cat eat its kittens. Emily wants to take Bianca to her father for treatment, but Bianca grows hysterical at that suggestion. Emily slaps the girl, shakes her, and settles her in bed.

The doctor is angry when he finds out that his patient has left the hospital. Frances persuades a cab driver to take her home, stops for news of Bianca, and realizes searchers have tracked her to the lake. Emily and Hubert tell their parents about Bianca, and Hubert accompanies his father to get the girl. She was frightened by her returning memories and left. Hubert pulls her to safety at the dam again. Later, Hubert confronts her about her lack of trust and her self-destructive behavior. Hubert goes to tell Bianca's mother that the girl is being cared for at his home but needs to recover more before seeing her mother. Emily has little success reaching Bianca, but Hubert is able to help the disturbed girl gain perspective on the circumstances that made her feel so rejected. A reunion of mother and daughter is staged at the music teacher's home.

Analysis: Careful intercutting of scenes and shifts of points of view make this demanding reading. Characterizations are well drawn, and Hubert is a rather sympathetic character whose dreamy, introspective style is quite different from Emily's pragmatic approach to things. Bianca and her mother have been in shock, and Bianca's amnesia is credible. The weakest point in the plot is Hubert's intuitive ability to provide effective therapy for Bianca. As in *Three Friends,* this enables the teen protagonist to accomplish something special but is stretching the fabric of an otherwise well-woven tale. Recommended for larger young adult collections or for mystery fans who may be lured to another genre by this psychological drama.

■ Pinkwater, Daniel. ***Uncle Melvin.*** Illus. by Daniel Pinkwater. Macmillan, 1989. 32pp. (0-02-774675-5) Reading Level: Grades K–3. (BCCB N89; SLJ Ja90)
Disability: Emotional disturbance

Charles's Uncle Melvin comes every day from "the Looney Bin" to fix breakfast for Charles, accompany the boy to and from school, work in the garden, and fix things up around the house. At night Uncle Melvin returns to "a special place for crazy people."

Uncle Melvin says odd things to Charles and the boy's parents. One time "he mowed the lawn, but he left a big X unmowed in the middle" with a stone message to flying saucers that he was a friend. Uncle Melvin has a theory that the president is a disguised iguana, is convinced he can speak with animals, needs to wear a green derby to bounce his thoughts back into his brain if they get away before he is finished with them, and turns right or left to control rain and rainbows.

Twice Charles talks to his father about Uncle Melvin's claims. Charles's father insists that no one can control the weather, that Uncle Melvin is a special person: "He sees the world in his own way." Then, he says:

"I don't want you to argue with Melvin—and I know you won't make fun of him."

"You mean because he's crazy?"

"Charles, I have never though of Melvin as crazy. In many ways he is the least crazy person I know. He has his ideas—that's all."

The pattern of their weeks is described, and Charles recalls one rainy Saturday when he saw Uncle Melvin digging in the garden under four rainbows.

Analysis: An ambivalent ending is in Pinkwater's style but may not be in the best interest of readers. "What is real?" is hard enough for 4- to 6-year-olds to determine, so teachers should discuss the characters fully with kindergarten and first-grade students. Charles is confused by Uncle Melvin's delusions, but he has witnessed the man's competence at fixing breakfast and performing household tasks. This accepting attitude and the tolerant parents are the most valuable parts of this quirky story. As a boy, Uncle Melvin had wild birds come perch on his fingers; he whistles with the birds as if they are having a conversation. This mildly steretoyped trait and Melvin's own use of the term "Looney Bin" are balanced by the accessible format and childlike point of view maintained in this title. Splashy colors and scratchy black drawings complement each revelation about Uncle Melvin.

■ Piowaty, Kim Kennelly. *Don't Look in Her Eyes.* Atheneum, 1983. 179pp. (0-689-50273-7) Reading Level: Grades 6–8. (BCCB Mr83) *Disability:* Emotional disturbance; Cosmetic impairment

Jason has been caring for his 15-month-old brother, Chad, since he was born, and for the last year the 12-year-old has not attended school. His manic mother is sure the government wants to take Chad and insists that if they learn Jason skips school so she can work, they will take the older boy away. Her delusions worsen, she is abusive to Chad, and she threatens Jason with physical harm. When she disappears, Jason does all he can to cope with each day.

Jason makes a friend, Brant. A secluded treehouse is not enough shelter for the boys, and Jason feels his mother's rage has trapped him into hurting Chad himself. Brant's parents try to intervene, but Jason cannot let go of the convictions that he is evil and his mother has cast a spell over him. On visiting his mother in a psychiatric institution, Jason observes her desperate, incoherent condition and is persuaded to think of her as sick with an illness that is not contagious. Jason prays for his mother to be forgiven and gives thanks for a new family.

Analysis: Alcoholism may have deepened the mother's psychosis, and other triggers are hinted at in this story. However, there is no hope of recovery, and Jason thinks his mother is pathetic, pulling her hair out and saying nonsensical things. Brant's parents indicate that the ill mother left her children because she was afraid of hurting them, but this protestation rings hollow. A better portrayal here is Brant's cosmetic impairment of an oddly shaped eye and mouth. Brant assures Jason he expects his appearance will be corrected by surgery once he is old enough. Jason's insensitive laughter at Brant's features initiates a fight, the friendship, and eventually a family bond. Like *Afternoon of the Elves* and *Goodnight, Mr. Tom* in content, but not as well written, this is for large collections only.

■ Rabinowich, Ellen. **Underneath I'm Different.** Delacorte, 1983. 180pp. (0-440-09253-1) Reading Level: Grades 6–8. (BCCB My83)
Disability: Emotional disturbance

Amy is 16 when she enrolls in ballet class to lose some weight. She meets Ansel, another high school student who accompanies the dancers and sculpts. On their first date he shows her the studio/barn near his parents' mansion. He admires the plump ladies in older artists' work, and tells Amy he believes that people who may look alike on the outside can still be quite different within.

Ansel's womanizing father wants him to go into business, but Ansel plans to attend Pratt for art studies. Amy models for Ansel's college entrance project, but it does not go well, and Ansel is moody. After Ansel is missing for a week, Amy goes to speak with his father. The evasive man finally reveals that Ansel is in the locked ward of a psychiatric hospital in Connecticut. Later, visits are allowed, but Ansel refuses to see Amy, although she takes the train there every evening. She sneaks in, and he warns her that he is no good for the people he loves. Amy writes letters after that and receives news that Ansel is to go to live with his aunt in Paris. Amy involves herself in her feminist friend's campaign to include more women writer's in the school curriculum, gets a job, and loses weight because she is no longer hiding her frustrations about her mother in cravings for food.

Analysis: Very much the problem novel, Amy's parents bicker about money, and her mother wants to make her daughter over into an ad for the family beauty shop. Ansel's troubles stem from suppressed grief over his mother's suicide six months earlier. His father is dating, but it is unclear if that is the behavior that motivated Mrs. Pierce's death.

This patterned story is an additional selection for times when *Love in a Different Key* and *The Pig Out Blues* are off the shelf.

■ Rappaport, Doreen. *"But She's Still My Grandma!"*. Illus. by Bernadette Simmons. Human Sciences, 1983. 29pp. (0-89885-072-X) Reading Level: Grades 6–9. (BCCB Je83)
Disability: Dementia

Jessica visits her grandmother in a nursing home. Her father has warned Jessica that Grandma does not remember and may not recognize family members. When Grandma sees Jessica, she says, "Pretty girl." Jessica is disturbed by Grandma's vacant look and the unresponsive residents sitting in a row. When the family goes outdoors for a walk, Jessica begins a poem, and Grandma continues it with the next line. Jessica understands that this is still her grandma, and she loves her.

Analysis: The illustrations in this book are its biggest weakness. Pencil drawings with a yellow tint do not hold the interest of a picture book audience. The stiff text may serve lower-elementary readers, but a more appealing presentation of this situation and a deeper examination of disorientation and its effect on family members are available in Nelson's *Always Gramma*.

■ Reading, J.P. *The Summer of Sassy Jo.* Houghton, 1989. 182pp. (0-395-48950-4) Reading Level: Grades 6–9.
Disability: Emotional disturbance

Sara Jo was abandoned by her alcoholic mother, but eight years later goes to spend the summer with her. *See full annotation* Chapter 4: Health Problems.

■ Riddell, Ruth. *Shadow Witch.* Atheneum, 1989. 208pp. (0-689-31484-1) Reading Level: Grades 5–7. (SLJ N89)
Disability: Emotional disturbance; Orthopedic impairment

A 1960s LSD-related accident injured Drew MacCaslim and haunted him with dreams of the Shadow Witch. He goes to Nova Scotia and discovers his family curse. Getting to know old Angus Corkum helps Drew find a power over the witch's eternal trap of hatred.

Analysis: A scramble of Gothic elements and unbelievable details crowd this story. Drew uses a walker and is resentful toward his able-bodied brother and uncle. In real time, and in dreams, Drew wanders ancient passages to confront Mamgu the witch, who has enslaved the first-born MacCaslims for generations.

Drew's nightmares and delusions have been going on for five months, and at 16, his mother and uncle "had arranged his life into hour-long sessions with doctors and psychiatrists, and short stints in private hospitals." He pretends to control the dreams because he does not want to be sent "to the loony farm." Doctors have the opinion that Drew "could not possibly help himself back to health." Though this convoluted plot finds a way for the wise Scotsman, Angus, to help Drew recover, his unlikely path to forgiveness of a hateful father is hardly worth following.

■ Riley, Jocelyn. *Crazy Quilt.* Morrow, 1984. 215pp. (0-688-03873-5)
Reading Level: Grades 6–9. (BCCB N84)
Disability: Emotional disturbance

Merle, at 13, gives a first-person account of school and family life one month after her mother has been hospitalized for yet another episode of "weirding out all over the place." Merle has trouble readjusting to school, because her classmates have shifted and she is not in the WB, "white bread," social crowd. A defiant, new girl at school interests Merle, and when the WB slam book reveals that "Jinx" is in a foster home, Merle gains insights about the problems other families face.

Merle has stressful interactions both with her mother at a court hearing to extend hospitalization and with a domineering grandmother at home. There is constant bickering with her younger brother and sister, who have their own problems coping with this dysfunctional family situation.

After writing a poem for the newspaper and communicating with her mother by letter, Merle feels better about herself. Though her mother's first home visit dissolves into arguments, Merle decides that every life has its own pattern. Like a crazy quilt made from the best scraps, she must create something useful from the ragged elements in her life.

Analysis: This sequel to *Only My Mouth Is Smiling* shows how, without intervention, a dysfunctional family stagnates within its cycle. At the end of the first book, Grandma was hoping new medication would stop her daughter's paranoid flights from reality. Family counseling was prescribed, and, though Grandma was not open to admitting her own flaws, she speaks disdainfully of the hospital staff when home visits are authorized before group therapy for the family is available.

Merle relinquishes some of her guilt when she comforts her mother at the end.

It was a good thing I was getting grown-up, because Mother never would be; I could see that now. Even when I was six and needed a valentine box she'd let me down, and all the other times since then. But as long ago as junior high she'd been backing away from situations she couldn't deal with; that was before I was ever even born.

That the sequel disproves the happy ending of the first book is a valid reason for recommending this book. It may be disjointed reading at times, but this forces the reader to experience some of the stress that affects the characters. Merle is not the classic "caretaker" oldest child, because the grandmother inserts herself into that role. Perceptive readers will see that Merle needs more than either reading about Francie in *A Tree Grows in Brooklyn* or meeting an abused teen to gain a healthy perspective on her life.

■ Riley, Jocelyn. *Only My Mouth Is Smiling.* Morrow, 1982. 224pp. (0-688-01087-3) Reading Level: Grades 6–9.
Disability: Emotional disturbance

Three children are taken to live in a tent at Lake Lune when their mother feels threatened by their living situation. Merle, the oldest, gives a first-person view of the cycles of emotional disturbance that interrupt their life.

When she started to get sick she'd always lose her job right off. First she'd save up some money while she was working, then she'd start staying up all night and talking about *They* and the FBI, then she'd lose her job and tell Grandma that she couldn't afford to pay the rent, then she'd use her savings to do crazy things, then she'd go to the hospital and we'd live alone with Grandma, and then she'd come back, clear-faced and uncrazy, and get a job again. It was like a merry-go-round.

Merle and her younger brother and sister make the best of their time at a rural school and find friends. Mrs. Hauser, the mother of one of Merle's friends, helps Merle learn to crochet a belt and encourages her to stop ignoring her mother's problems, hoping they will go away. The authorities step in, and Grandma retrieves the children.

Analysis: The insights that Merle gains about her mother's progression from mental stability to "nervous breakdowns" are quite accurate. It is hard to believe that she does not know her mother should be taking medication, but the author is consistent in portraying how that ignorance is fostered by Grandma's optimism and Mother's railing against any mention of "crazy" or "drugs." The ending is a blend of disclosures and prophecies that offer hope for Merle's future. However, the institutionalized treatment followed by family counseling that Grandma describes can give a false impression to readers that this serious and complex disability is easy to work through, once identified.

■ Rinaldi, Ann. *The Last Silk Dress.* Holiday, 1988. 348pp. (0-8234-0690-3)
Reading Level: Grades 7–10. (BCCB MS88)
Disability: Emotional disturbance

Susan is inspired to support the Confederate cause, and she often dresses in clothing left in her older brother's room to go around Richmond. Her father leaves his position as editor of the newspaper in order to assist the southern army, so he can no longer protect Susan from her mother's rages.

Mama is a volatile tyrant with her slaves and her daughter, sensitive to social disfavor regarding her son, Lucien. Lucien left home after some argument with his father and now operates a gambling hall, supplying it with high-priced produce and contraband. Lucien recognizes his old clothes and beats Susan as a thief because they have never met before. When she reveals her name, he inquires after Charlotte, their mother, who is "still quite mad," but he refuses to tell Susan why.

Instead, Lucien helps Susan and her friend complete their task of gathering enough silk dresses to supply material for an observation balloon. Susan is impressed by the enthusiastic and generous support of this southern cause by ladies who work in a brothel.

Lucien introduces Susan to a Yankee newspaper artist who sketches Susan as an example of a southern belle. When Charlotte sees Susan's portrait in the Yankee paper, she mistreats Susan and refuses to let her see the balloon that has been completed and deployed in the area. Notice comes that Susan's father has been killed and has given Lucien guardianship of his sister. Spitefully, Charlotte returns home from the reading of the will and tells Susan that Lucien's father was not Susan's natural father. This explains why Charlotte reviles Susan as a "Yankee Brat" all the time.

The story comes out that Lucien was fond of a servant girl, and his father intervened by revealing that the slave was Lucien's half-sister. Disgusted by his father's double standards and hypocrisy, Lucien left home and was befriended by townsfolk who helped him earn his own way. Corrupt southern morals and social conventions also led Charlotte to lash back at her husband by having an affair with Susan's Yankee father. Emotionally unstable from the death of three children, betrayed by her husband, and estranged from her surviving son, Charlotte refused to forgive her husband and vented her frustrations on Susan, her "Yankee Brat."

Susan goes to Lucien, preferring to share social ostracism with him than corrupt gentility with her mother. He tells her that it doesn't matter to him if they had different fathers and that Hugh Chilmark loved her and considered himself her father.

Susan loves the Yankee artist, Timothy, and feels her loyalty swinging away from white slaveholders. She provides information that leads to the Yankee capture of her balloon.

Analysis: Social pressures in the unique setting of America's historic South are well integrated in this Civil War adventure. Susan is unlike those in her mother's circle of respectable southern ladies, and she proves herself to be as passionate and resourceful as her father seemed to be. Charlotte hurts her daughter deeply with the revelation that there was no blood connection between the intelligent newspaper man they are mourning and Susan. Charlotte also hopes her vengeful truths will drive a wedge between Lucien and Susan, who has just come to know her brother as a person instead of the mysterious, absent owner of various things in a sealed-off room.

Action, romance, period details, and military history are pieced together with plausible supposition to make an impressive historical novel.

■ Rodowsky, Colby F. *The Gathering Room.* Farrar, 1981. 186pp. (0-374-32520-0) Reading Level: Grades 4–6. (BCCB Ap82)
Disability: Emotional disturbance

Mudge is 9 years old and lives with his parents, Ned and Serena, in an old graveyard. His companions are the ghosts that linger near their gravestones. His father tends the graves and teaches Mudge daily in the gathering room, where mourners once came for funerals. Mudge thinks his life constitutes a natural pattern and is comfortable with his parents' reclusive ways.

His mother helps Mudge recall when Ned "would sit and stare and not say anything at all" and cried so much that Mudge ran away to hide in his room. Mudge understands that his mother and father came to live in the gatehouse and become caretakers instead of following the doctor's advice about hospitals or Aunt Ernestus's maxim that "You do what you have to do." But when elderly Great-Aunt Ernestus and her dog intrude and then preservationists buy the property, things change quickly.

Mudge learns that his father was a lawyer and had a nervous breakdown after his friend the governor was murdered. Aunt Ernestus and Mudge have some fun together, and she explains why she tracked the family down. Making decisions about looking for work or a new place to live overwhelms Mudge's parents. Mudge's mother busies herself packing but says that if they had had a quieter time to decide to leave on their own,

Mudge's father would not be so distracted. Mudge uses the newly installed phone to call Aunt Ernestus, because he can see that his parents need help with "the dragons" in their life. Mudge takes leave of his new friend, Marcus, and the ghosts.

Analysis: At first, Mudge resents any changes in his life and does not want to participate in the care of Aunt Ernestus. Later, he relies on Aunt Ernestus to help his father when decisions get so difficult it is "as though Ned has gotten to the end of the high diving board and isn't able to jump."

Aunt Ernestus tactfully arrives and offers to stay with Mudge while Ned makes plans and investigates jobs and apartments. Having a moderator helps Ned work through things, though he is defensive at first. Mudge decides he has not betrayed his parents but has helped them get the assistance they needed when their coping skills were overtaxed.

This is a worthwhile book, with a sensitive portrayal of a vulnerable couple facing the challenge of returning to a life-style that requires more social interaction. They realize that Mudge has missed out on common childhood friendships and pranks but are unaware of his mystical experiences with the ghosts. This is another ghost story for fans of *The Court of the Stone Children* and *Beloved Benjamin is Waiting*.

■ Rosen, David. **Henry's Tower.** Illus. by Lynne Feldman. Platypus, 1984. 28pp. (0-930905-01-6) Reading Level: Grades 2–4. (BCCB Je85) *Disability:* Neurosis

Henry is building a tower of blocks. His father knocks it down twice. When Henry retreats to the attic, he thinks about how Dad has changed from a nice parent into one who growls. When he asks his mother what is wrong, she replies, "His feelings were deeply hurt in the war." Henry is told that time and love will help Dad. This information helps Henry affirm that he does love his father. Henry recalls that his father always enjoyed licorice, and he shares some with Dad.

Analysis: When Henry experiences his father's hostility, he feels threatened and confused. When he asks mother about the change in Dad, he gets a vague answer about hurt feelings, love, and time. These terms seem too abstract to heal the hurts described. If the limited language is indication that the audience should be K–2, then the illustrations make a poor match. Therapy is never mentioned, so this book should not be a first choice for family counseling unless war-related neurosis is specifically an issue.

■ Ruby, Lois. **This Old Man.** Houghton, 1984. 192pp. (0-395-36563-5) Reading Level: Grades 7–10. *Disability:* Emotional disturbance

Greta lives at a group home and is given counseling so as to avoid following her mother's life-style of prostitution. *See full annotation* Chapter 4: Health Impairments.

■ Sachs, Marilyn. *Fran Ellen's House.* Dutton, 1987. 97pp. (0-525-44345-2)
Reading Level: Grades 4–6. (BCCB N87)
Disability: Emotional disturbance

Fran Ellen's mother, older brother, and three sisters are reunited after the children have been circulated to several different foster homes. Mama dislikes the cockroach-ridden apartment they move into, but she is trying to restore a home for her children. The older children know that "Mama has to take a pill to keep her cheerful. If she doesn't take her pill, she will get sick and have to go back to the hospital again." Fran Ellen is hopeful that the 3-year-old, Flora, will readjust to being with her real family and stop weeping for her foster care providers. Fran Ellen is resentful when Flora prefers to be with 7-year-old sister Felice because Felice is close to the age of Flora's foster sister. Felice is a slow learner and the brunt of teasing at school.

Fran Ellen tries to distract Flora with the bears' house that she retrieved from a shelter. The beautiful gift from Fran Ellen's teacher has been ruined, and the Goldilocks is missing. Fran Ellen makes up conversations between the three bears that help her deal with the disjointed feelings she has about her mother's hospitalization and the family's uneasy readjustment. Flora starts wetting the bed, and her mother is overwhelmed by caring for the distressed preschooler. The social worker suggests that Flora be allowed to return to her old foster home, which turns out to be a relief for the child and her mother. Fran Ellen feels devastated about this.

Felice is excluded from Fran Ellen's efforts to fix up the bears' house at first, but as Fran Ellen gets involved with school and friends, Felice takes over the refurbishment. When so many little things that have been missing are found serving as furnishings in the bears' house, Fletcher, Florence, and even Mama begin to create special additions to the dollhouse. Fran Ellen realizes that the bears' house has become Felice's game to help her deal with changes.

Felice likes to hear Fran Ellen tell about the time she was in elementary school and played with the bears' house. Felice has decided that it is good that Goldilocks is gone and that the bears forgive Fran Ellen for letting their house become so scruffy. By Christmas, the bears' house is lovely, with a picture of Fran Ellen in it, thanks to Felice. Felice has her own imaginary conversations with the bears now.

Analysis: This sequel to *The Bears' House* is as touching as the first novel. The author is skilled at establishing character and showing development in brief episodes. The use of italics for Frank Ellen's fantasy follows the style of the first book.

Felice is a well realized character though this is Fran Ellen's story. At one point, Felice says that Mama Bear's appearance is "weird. She looks like this girl in my class, Valerie Johnson, who has a big scar on her mouth, only it's in the middle, and she talks funny." Such realistic details, credible emotions, and honest impressions enhance this short novel.

Fran Ellen makes friends in her junior high classes, her older brother and sister do well in high school, and the outlook for Mama's reentry into the work force is good. Highly recommended, especially because fans of the first book had to wait sixteen years to read more about Fran Ellen.

■ Sachs, Marilyn. *Just like a Friend.* Dutton, 1989. 154pp. (0-525-44524-2) Reading Level: Grades 6–9.
Disability: Emotional disturbance

Patti is 14 when her young, spoiled mother cannot cope with Dad's heart attack. *See full annotation* Chapter 4: Health Problems.

■ Sallis, Susan. *Secret Places of the Stairs.* Harper & Row, 1984. 151pp. (LB 0-06-025142-5) Reading Level: Grades 7–10.
Disability: Emotional disturbance

Cass's mother warns her that she will kill herself before she lets Cass cause her another nervous breakdown. *See full annotation* Chapter 7: Multiple/Severe Disabilities.

■ Shreve, Susan. *Lucy Forever and Miss Rosetree, Shrinks.* Henry Holt, 1987. 121pp. (0-8050-0340-1) Reading Level: Grades 4–5. (BCCB Je87)
Disability: Emotional disturbance

Lucy Childs and her friend Rosie Treeman play an after-school game in which they report to work at Shrinks, Incorporated, and maintain elaborate case histories for seriously disturbed patients. When a patient calls for advice, it may be Mrs. Parks, who fears her husband wants to eat her, or Samantha, who is developing zebra stripes on her belly. The girls use professional names—Lucy Forever and Miss Rosetree. Lucy's father is a psychologist who specializes in helping children and has an office on the same property as the girls' play area. Dr. Child has made it clear that his office and his patients are strictly off-limits to Lucy and Rosie.

A silent child stops by at Shrinks, Incorporated. Rosie offers the little girl a doll to dress. Their visit is cut short when a large woman comes to get "Cinder." Before the child turns to leave, she pulls down the collar of her frilly dress to show a recent red scar across her throat. Rosie supposes that Cinder had her throat cut and that is why she cannot speak. Lucy believes Cinder could talk if she wanted to.

As the weeks continue, Lucy tells lies to her piano teacher to gain time to investigate Cinder's mysterious background. Rosie sees Cinder in a car with Mr. Van Dyke, Lucy's piano teacher. Lucy decides to risk sneaking a look at Cinder's file in Dr. Childs' office. Besides finding Cinder's address, Lucy reads, "Diagnosis: child abuse" before replacing the confidential record.

Lucy finds Cinder tied to a tree in the yard of a group home just as Mr. Van Dyke comes along and asks how Lucy came to be so far from home. Mr. Van Dyke explains that he teaches Cinder piano three times a week because she is very talented. Mr. Van Dyke unties Cinder and tells the nurse, Miss Brill, that he will take Lucy home and return for Cinder's lesson. Mr. Van Dyke sees through Lucy's excuse for being at the home and warns Lucy to stay away from Cinder.

After her next appointment, Cinder returns the doll, but it is in a fancy new dress and has had its neck slashed. When Lucy interrupts her next piano lesson by asking Mr. Van Dyke why Cinder had a scar, he warns her again, "We are all working hard to help Cinder overcome her fears so she can talk again . . . and you could ruin everything."

Lucy confides in her father that she has quit piano and is surprised that he does not try to make her reconsider. Dr. Childs discusses Cinder's background and gives Lucy permission to try to get Cinder to talk. Rosie and Lucy forge a note to extend Cinder's visits so that they will have more time after the 5-year-old's appointment with Dr. Childs. Rosie tries to use hypnotism the next time Cinder comes down to Shrinks, Incorporated. Cinder says "No Rope," but the girls do not reveal this to Dr. Childs and they both have dreams about Cinder being in danger. Cinder is bruised, scratched, and dirty when she next visits, and then she disappears. Lucy is worried that her father will discover the forgery when he compares information with Miss Brill. She leaves home, finds Cinder down at the creek, and they decide to run away together. Miss Brill finds them in a shop, takes Lucy home, and warns her to stay out of Cinder's business. Cinder's look of terror as Miss Brill drives off convinces Lucy that a rescue is necessary, but Rosie is too sick to help.

Lucy witnesses Miss Brill kicking a little boy and then is herself captured by the woman. Her release is aided by Rosie's persistence. When Cinder is found, Lucy proposes that the Childs adopt her, and they agree.

Analysis: This award-winning mystery has a notable cast of characters and maintains its momentum through clever dialogue, consistent role-playing, and clever plot turns. Cinder is often called the "mute child," and when Lucy tells the police what Cinder has recounted, she says:

"She was cutting a piece of rope to tie Cinder in bed at night since she had threatened to run away, and Cinder came into the kitchen. Apparently Miss Brill flung out her hand with the knife in it and said 'Go away,' and the knife accidentally cut Cinder's throat. Then she told Cinder if she ever told anyone, especially the social worker, how her throat was cut, Miss Brill would strangle her with the rope."

"And so she decided not to talk," Dr. Childs said.

"Maybe she decided and maybe she simply couldn't," Lucy said. "But she certainly is talking now."

The book gives a sympathetic view of psychiatric counseling in that Lucy and Rosie not only emulate the therapists they know, but Lucy also recognizes the special skills and ethics her father applies to sort through his patients' secret sorrows. Readers will learn that therapy can help people adjust to life's problems, and it is clear that Cinder's life held more terror than most children will ever experience. This upper-grade thriller is highly recommended for its writing style and unusual plot. Fans of *Anastasia . . .* will relate to Lucy's and Rosie's enterprise.

■ Silsbee, Peter. *The Big Way Out.* Bradbury, 1984. 180pp. (0-02-782670-8) Reading Level: Grades 8–10. (BCCB Ap84)
Disability: Emotional disturbance

The MacNamara family is struggling with violent outbursts and erratic behavior that their father displays after the suicide of Dr. MacNamara's brother. As the one-year anniversary of the funeral nears, Dr. Mac-Namara strikes his wife, Kelsey, who then flies from California to her home town in the Adirondacks with Paul. Paul's older brother, Tim, accompanies their father to Kansas City for the "funeral," and it becomes obvious from persistent phone calls that the obsessed man will continue across country to reclaim his wife and 14-year-old.

Paul was in town during the previous summer and has cousins who try to help him adjust to school. He is intimidated by his father's pursuit, confused by his mother's apparent capitulation, and resentful of his brother's ability to influence their father's rages yet stay loyal. Paul takes a rifle, fights his fear of failure at climbing the water tower in town, and positions himself to await his father's arrival in town. However, he does not shoot his father, or himself, and returns to his grandmother's home.

When some local toughs pick on Paul, Dr. MacNamara becomes increasingly hostile, causes a scene, drives recklessly with the whole family in the car, and runs up the curb, ordering his wife out of the car. Paul grabs his father across the throat and demands that the man swear on his brother's grave to leave his wife and sons alone. Once again, his father's cleverness and his mother's submissiveness defeat Paul's efforts.

> Dr. MacNamara looked into the back seat at his son's face. "I'm sorry I hit your mother," he said abruptly. "Now let's shake hands like men and we'll forget about it."
> "You're crazy." Paul said through his teeth. "Do you know how crazy you are?"
> Dr. MacNamara's eyebrows went up; his eyes glinted.
> "No," Paul answered his own question. "You don't know how crazy you are, do you?" . . .
> Kelsey reached over and touched his arm. "I'm all right," she said, her eyes full.
> "Can't you see how crazy he is?"
> "It's all right. We're just having an argument."
> Paul pulled his arm away. "You're all crazy!"

Paul, Tim, and Dr. MacNamara run off for a while, and police arrive at the car. Dr. MacNamara exhibits paranoid behavior, and Paul leads him to believe that the police are there to take him back to the hospital and that dead Uncle Jake told Paul what has to happen. Dr. MacNamara and his wife leave together in the police car.

Analysis: This dramatic novel has a serious theme and intensely realized characters. Readers will be as frustrated as Paul with the secrecy and denial that surround Dr. MacNamara's condition. Not only the guilt and grief that triggered Dr. MacNamara's emotional disturbance but also his treatment with electric shock and repeated institutionalizations are described. No indication is made that family counseling was offered, and it stretches belief that several secret hospitalizations, ten electric shock treatments, and a summer cover-up trip to the Adirondacks all took place in the one year since Jake's funeral.

Manipulative behavior, erratic mood swings, and superficially rational arguments are convincingly portrayed. Uncle Jake's suicide and the motivations for it are alluded to. Paul's contemplation of patricide versus suicide is gripping. In the end, Paul assures his father, "You have to go back to the hospital because we want you to come out well again." Earlier, Paul and Tim agreed that every visit to the hospital seemed to result in their father's "just getting worse" but that this is "the right thing" to do. This complex story can be recommended along with *Only My Mouth Is Smiling.*

■ Skurzynski, Gloria. *Dangerous Ground.* Bradbury, 1989. 160pp. (0-02-782731-3) Reading Level: Grades 4–6. (BCCB My89)
Disability: Dementia

Angela stays with her Great-Aunt Hilda until she is 11. Her parents have saved up enough from working in oil fields so that they can settle down and have Angela and "Ant Hil" join them. Aunt Hilda becomes distressed and takes Angela on a trip through Wyoming. The old woman's behavior is so erratic that Angela believes it could be caused by Alzheimer's disease. In Yellowstone Park, a bear frightens Aunt Hilda near a thermal springs area.

Angela helps medical examiners determine that her great-aunt has been taking medication prescribed for somebody else. This hazardous choice has created a chemical imbalance in Aunt Hilda that is the cause of her mental disturbance. After treatment, Aunt Hilda decides to join Angela's parents in their new home.

Analysis: This novel is an additional choice for collections. The concern that Angela has for her great-aunt is genuine, and the information about the symptoms of Alzheimer's disease that may be mimicked by taking unprescribed medications is accurate. This book offers a characterization that portrays an organic cause for emotional dysfunction that is successfully resolved for a happy ending.

■ Smith, Doris Buchanan. *Voyages.* Viking, 1989. 170pp. (0-670-80739-7) Reading Level: Grades 6–8. (BCCB F90)
Disability: Emotional disturbance; Paraplegia

Twelve-year-old Janessa is taken hostage during a minimarket robbery and breaks her back when forced out of the getaway car. She prefers being in her hospital bed, working origami, and looking out at the blank sky as a retreat from the violent world. Her psychologist removes a tube from her television to stop well-meaning staff and family from turning it on.

A visiting teacher helps Janessa do her work for seventh grade, continuing a unit on Norse mythology and Viking lore. Janessa has a "quick, strange, daytime dream" about being in Freyr's boat, with a whole body and seeing her injured self in the hospital bed.

Janessa hates having to be fed, and she accepts no visits and reads no notes from friends, not even her best friend, Lynn. "She wanted to get well, be off this bed. She did. But she wanted to live in this hospital room forever." Many of her worries are dealt with in adventures with her origami boat, which she calls Freyr. Crossing time bands and interacting with mythological characters climax when Janessa arranges to give sunglasses to the elves so they can go aboveground.

Her fantasy travels help her open up to psychological counseling. She recognizes that her confused feelings about her father come from memory of the hairy arms that shoved her from the car. She asks her father to bring Lynn for a visit. "Lynn looked at Janessa, then glanced at the apparatus, the traction, the Crutchfield tongs, and winced in pain." Janessa's tearful response turns into relieved laughter for all.

Analysis: Emotional recuperation is the theme of this fantasy. How relevant the subplots are to each other is debatable. Janessa's flashbacks are incorporated with dialogue to good effect, because readers will understand how intrusive her memories of the senseless violence are.

Janessa can fold paper into precise figures but lacks shoulder control for feeding herself most items. The ability to use hands but not arms may surprise some readers. Unlike *Wheels for Walking,* little prognosis is given, except that Janessa is scheduled to have a cast put on before her discharge. Like *A Year Without Friends,* the counseling scenes are detailed from the patient's point of view.

Smith is a skilled writer and knows how to create good characters. This vivid story implies that Janessa's recovery from trauma associated with her injury will be a good foundation for her adjustment to the physical limitations and complications that are her new reality.

■ Smith, Nancy Covert. *The Falling-Apart Winter.* Walker, 1982. 112pp. (LB 0-8027-6465-7) Reading Level: Grades 5–7. (BL 1 S82)
Disability: Emotional disturbance

Their first month living in Washington, D.C., is miserable for Adam Hanley. His father is busy with a new job, seventh-grade schoolmates are hard to make friends with, and Mrs. Hanley has unpacked nothing. She fixes more and more food for him but cannot get dressed and is always too tired to accomplish anything in the new apartment. When Mrs. Hanley is admitted to a hospital for psychiatric care, Adam tells others that she is away on important state business.

When Mrs. Hanley comes home, the parental arguments that most bothered Adam continue. Mrs. Hanley points out that her medication is to make her more reasonable, not just obedient. Family counseling is begun with a female doctor at a local clinic. Thanksgiving follows the pattern of Mrs. Hanley's waiting on the two fellows and getting superficial offers of "help." This leads to a counseling session that Mr. Hanley walks out on, refusing to return with Adam.

An essay assignment on freedom inspires Adam to continue his research on mental health, and his essay is selected for contest finals. Adam panics when he realizes that he must read the essay aloud and that it will be obvious he has written from personal experience, especially because the class bully saw Mrs. Hanley Halloween night, before her treatment began. Adam reads his essay, makes a hostile closing remark to the bully, and finds out that the lonely boy really only wants advice about his own mother, who has a drinking problem.

Analysis: The language used in this work places it in the years before the women's movement and before mental health advocates had had much impact on social roles or labels. At least the term "mental illness" is preferred to the term "crazy," and one of the solutions for Mrs. Hanley's depression is that she will go back to school and take advantage of the now greater opportunities available to women. As an easily accessible problem novel for middle school students, this has appeal. The theme is developed in an obvious progression, with an odd inclusion of dream sequences about founders of the mental health profession.

Adam will be a sympathetic character for readers to encounter, even if his speech and counseling sessions are a heavy-handed way to include information in a fictional work.

■ Snyder, Zilpha Keatley. *And Condors Danced.* Delacorte, 1987. 216pp. (0-385-29575-8) Reading Level: Grades 4–7. (BCCB N87) *Disability:* Emotional disturbance

Carly wishes she could be invisible. She is ignored enough at home to feel invisible, what with her older sister, Nellie, running the household and romantic Lila daydreaming of her thwarted love for a Spanish boy. When the Harwick family came from Maine to mild, southern California, Carly's mother was distressed to leave her relatives and became weakened by bouts of pneumonia. Then her 2-year-old son Petey died. Carly's "birth had not been the cure for her mother's deep depression, as everyone had hoped it would be, and instead had nearly resulted in her death."

Great Aunt M. (for Mehitabel) and Woo Ying, her Chinese ranch hand, cared for Carly. Carly likes to recall all this family lore while visiting Petey's grave to coax out a good cry. She loves to read tragic tales and enjoys riding donkeys into the canyon in hopes of seeing condors dance after their wide-winged courtship flight. Even the local bully cannot dim Carly's lively enjoyment of her eleventh year of life, 1907.

But, when Mama dies, Carly is burdened by guilt. Her dog, Tiger, had gotten killed earlier, and she had felt awful. But when her own mother died, she could not even cry. Carly sympathetically supports the grief of her family but becomes more and more subdued. Nellie, who had shouldered the physical burdens of running a house because of her mother's persistent tragic posing, confronts Carly, then summarizes the real problem.

"Anna Hartwick was not your mother, Carly. Oh, I don't mean she didn't give birth to you, because she did, but your mother was Aunt M. And Woo Ying. Woo Ying is much much more your mother than Mama ever was.". . .

"But she was a mother to you, and to Charles and Arthur and Lila?". . .

"Yes. When we were little. Mama was good with little babies, I think. At least until Petey died. And then—well, after that I guess things became reversed. After that it was as if I were the mother and she became my child."

"Oh, Nellie," Carly said. She was thinking that when Mama died Nellie had lost both her mother and her child.

Carly feels like exploring again, and the last of her dark mood passes when a long day of waiting to see condors dance is rewarded by the sight of three of them soaring above. At the end of the story, she is ready to accept a puppy to replace Tiger, because she is no longer afraid to count on future happiness.

Analysis: Period detail, description of the countryside, and social constraints of the time all add to this charming historical novel. Since the last wild condors were captured for breeding shortly after this book was published, it offers a unique picture of a California legend. The emotional drama allows readers to determine for themselves if Mama was ill, homesick, or heartless. So many well-characterized personalities are affected by Mama's invalid life-style that this novel succeeds in presenting a strong picture of physical and mental disability at the turn of the century.

At one point Carly has to deal with the taunt: "Everybody says your pa's the orneriest man in Santa Luisa. And that what ails your ma is mostly in her head, and—and all of you Hartwicks think you're so high and mighty."

Carly's fascination with tragic tales is in line with the fashionable sentimentality of the day. Her active imagination and free-ranging adventures are barely curtailed by social proprieties. Sometimes so much remembering, thinking, and doing clutters the story, but this Newbery Award–winning writer has created a convincing picture from her own family history. Young fans of *Anne of Green Gables* would like meeting Carly too.

■ Strasser, Todd. *Wildlife*. Delacorte, 1987. 224pp. (paper 0-385-29560-X)
Reading Level: Grades 7–10. (BCCB Je87)
Disability: Emotional disturbance

After two years of success on the rock scene, Gary is between a concert tour and a new album. His old girlfriend, Allison, is pursuing her education and wants to cool the romance, because Gary's life-style is so constrained by fame. On an MTV interview, neurotic Oscar feuds with stoned drummer Karl. Internal troubles dissolve the band, called Coming Attractions, and Gary goes on to produce records. He is able to reconcile with Allison.

Analysis: Consistent with the characterizations established in *Rock 'n Roll Nights* and *Turn It Up,* Karl's substance abuse and risk-taking are fueled by the money gained from his success. Oscar's egotistical obsessions are fueled by fame, as summarized by the band's manager: "Look, you and I both know we're dealing with a conceited, hypersensitive, and sometimes irrational person," Mike said. "But the band still needs him."

Gary and his cousin Susan survive the world of rock music with fewer scars than Karl and Oscar. Oscar starts his own band to star in, and Karl leaves a treatment center for a Buddhist monastery. Karl's mother is also an unstable character, clearly drawn. The story has a high-interest setting and is honest in its presentation. The ending is satisfying, and, like Gary, readers will see that performers need a combination of talent, drive, and luck to be successful as professional musicians, but survival is something beyond financial success.

■ Stretton, Barbara. ***The Truth of the Matter.*** Knopf, 1983. 213pp. (LB 0-394-96144-7) Reading Level: Grades 7–9. (BCCB D83)
Disability: Emotional disturbance

Jenny is a senior in high school with a boyfriend away at Yale. Her friend Andrea dates Peter, who assumes he will be accepted at Harvard. Jenny's father does not want her to plan on college, afraid that she may grow dissatisfied like her mother, who ran off six months earlier and has remarried. Letters arrive from Jenny's mother, but the girl refuses to read them. Peter tries to disrupt his classes and confirm scandalous accusations about the new history teacher. Jenny's research on Richard III leads to a script for Andrea to star in.

Peter's brooding about Andrea's seeming lack of interest in him coincides with Jenny's knowledge that Andrea has a crush on the history teacher. When Jenny makes a sympathetic comment to Peter, his angry mood over a bad grade focuses on violence against Jenny. Peter has lost his chance at Harvard, gets kicked off his team, and tries to run down Andrea and the teacher. Peter and Andrea are hospitalized, and Peter is scheduled for psychiatric care. Peter's irrational behavior and the analogy of the wrongly judged Richard III make Jenny open her mother's latest letter so she can get answers she needs about her mother's decision to leave home.

Analysis: In most cases, the convincing characters and relationships save this melodramatic plot. Jenny thinks that Peter's unpredictability is attractive at one point, but in the end is glad to count on steady, insightful Sam. Peter and his obsessions are revealed with subtlety, but not the roots of his problem, which may be attributed to a materialistic home life, high parental expectations, and peer pressure to plague teachers. This book can serve best in large paperback collections when readers are looking for someone else's problems to distract them for a while. For the same stressors in another fine novel, readers may be referred to Peck's *Remembering the Good Times.*

■ Sweeney, Joyce. *Center Line.* Delacorte, 1984. 246pp. (0-385-29320-8) Reading Level: Grades 7–10. (BCCB Je84)
Disability: Emotional disturbance

Five teenage brothers run away from their abusive father. On their way through the Midwest to Florida, they panhandle, nurse a sick sibling, and squabble. Their leader is Shawn, who, at 18, pushes himself to drive night after night, focused on the center line of the highway and afraid he may drift off the road or react too slowly to oncoming traffic. An artistic brother finds a home with an older lover, and the remaining four continue their trek.

Shawn intends to support his younger brothers once they arrive in Florida, but Rick rebels. They find out that no charges for car theft have been made, and the remaining three sons establish a new home.

Analysis: This fast-paced adventure offers a balance between humorous scenes, tragedy, and a touch of romance. It presents five male characters affected by the death of their mother and the alcoholism of their father. Shawn and Chris share the adult roles of father and mother. Rick is so guilt ridden about his defiance on the day his mother died, that he assumes a tough-guy persona. Even after they are safely away from their father, Rick cannot abandon his attitude of defiance, which precipitates a beating by Shawn. Shawn is devastated to realize he may be following his abusive father's pattern.

The boys all have their own escapes: responsibility, reading, art, music, drugs. A hopeful note results from Shawn's investigations into securing guardianship of his brothers and getting professional help with his emotional scars. The female characters lack depth, but S. E. Hinton fans will appreciate this addition to any young adult collection.

■ Sweeney, Joyce. *Right Behind the Rain.* Delacorte, 1987. 192pp. (0-385-29551-0) Reading Level: Grades 7–10. (BCCB MS87)
Disability: Emotional disturbance

Carla is 17 the summer her older brother comes home with news that he has been promised a movie role. Until filming starts, he is involved in production of a local musical comedy. Carla has always believed her brother was a gifted performer and has enjoyed his friendship as well. Soon, however, Kevin starts to say and do things that are out of character, and Carla recognizes some of the symptoms of suicidal depression. When he buys a gun, Carla confronts him and consults a hotline for advice. Carla presents the idea of getting therapy as an alternative to Kevin's intention to shoot himself.

Analysis: Like the progression of emotional disorder described in *Don't Blame It on the Music,* this novel portrays the parents as inattentive and ineffectual so that the adolescent protagonist can win the day. Aside from this flaw, the book has consistent characterization and shows a believable depth of affection for an ill sibling. It is unusual for such portrayals to explore relations between different sex children. Besides the concern Carla has about Kevin, a bit of romance for her helps lift this tale from being merely an uninventive case history.

■ Talbert, Marc. *Pillow of Clouds.* Dial, 1991. 208pp. (0-8037-0901-3)
Reading Level: Grades 7–9. (KR 1 Mr91; BCCB Ap91)
Disability: Emotional disturbance

Chester lives with his mother and is visiting his father and stepmother when he turns 13. A divorce court agreement calls for Chester to decide, now, which parent he wants to live with. Chester's mother is emotionally unstable and abuses alcohol, yet, when Chester returns to tell her his decision, he feels that she needs him too much for him to leave. Chester's father calls, Chester announces that he wants to go back to Santa Fe, and then he enjoys the friendship of José and Arturo. Chester's mother attempts suicide, and Chester must deal with guilt and his confused interpretations of his mother's love for him and his for her.

Analysis: This is a demanding decision for a 13-year-old, yet the author manages to present it with compassion and credibility. As in *Up Country,* a teenager has to face the emotional tangle his mother's abnormal patterns have established for him. Unlike that story, poverty is not one of the things Chester must run away from. His mother is rich, and she clearly loves him in a controlling, self-centered way. Instead, a happy home life and self-acceptance are things that prove hard for Chester to run toward. This is an impressive book that will be good for most collections.

■ Tamar, Erika. *Blues for Silk Garcia.* Crown, 1983. 161pp. (0-517-54671-X) Reading Level: Grades 7–10. (BCCB Je83)
Disability: Emotional disturbance

Linda Ann is a high school student who takes lessons at the Guitar Institute. She learns that her father was called "Silk" Garcia, was a guitarist who composed a piece called "Blues for Linda Ann," and has died recently. Lin's mother will not tell her anything, so Lin and her friend Jeff locate musicians who knew Silk. Anthony "Silk" Garcia is remembered as a disturbed person who had offered his baby girl for sale and was dependent on drugs. Even the song that appeared to be dedicated to his daughter had actually appeared earlier under another title.

Lin has been so involved with the search for information about her father and her own career as a guitarist, that she ignores Jeff, betrays her boyfriend Michael, and resents her mother's secretive attitude. In the end, Lin gains perspective on her mother's silence and begins to value the people in her life.

Analysis: There is a very appealing cover on this book showing a dark-haired girl playing guitar. The mysterious elements and Lin's disillusionment will interest young adult readers. The characterizations are convincing, but the story about a self-destructive artist who manifests emotional disturbances and substance abuse is pretty trite.

■ Terris, Susan. *The Latchkey Kids.* Farrar, 1986. 167pp. (0-374-34363-2) Reading Level: Grades 4–6. (BCCB Mr86)
Disability: Emotional disturbance

Callie has a little brother named Rex. She is only 11, but Callie must pick up Rex, unlock their apartment, watch over her brother, and do chores. Her parents depend on Callie, but she does not feel that they appreciate her.

Callie enjoys her new friend, Nora. Nora introduces Callie to her Chinese family. Callie's father has been so depressed lately that it is a strain on the whole family. Callie tells her parents how angry her latchkey responsibilities make her, and her parents resolve to make improvements in their situation.

Analysis: Callie drifts into imagined scenes at times without sufficient signals to the reader. Otherwise, this is a well-written story with skillfully defined characters and fluid dialogue. Father's difficulties are indicated, and their impact on the entire family is described for upper-elementary readers in this recommended title.

■ Thesman, Jean. *The Last April Dancers*. Houghton, 1987. 224pp.
(0-395-43024-0) Reading Level: Grades 8–12. (BCCB S87)
Disability: Emotional disturbance

Catherine St. John writes letters to a mysterious Sheila, because her father
has mistakenly called her by that name. "Cat" is very concerned about her
father's forgetful behavior and the "crazy" garden that fills much of his
time since his unemployment began. His distraction and restlessness have
resulted in scrambled rows of plants that wander into the lawn. Cat's
mother is a real estate salesperson with firm opinions about her 15-year-
old daughter's appearance and the type of boyfriend she should encourage. Cat cannot get her mother to talk about Mr. St. John's forgetful, odd
behavior. "Sometimes I think that she is as crazy as he is. She got that way
pretending that nothing is wrong with him."

Cat adores Cameron, the gifted boy next door, but they are both
avoiding conflict with protective mothers by enjoying their long-standing
friendship and dating only other schoolmates. One activity that Cameron,
Cat, and her father share are evening drives out to the St. John farm.
Lately, the drive is stressful because Mr. St. John's driving is so erratic.
The country home has been abandoned, but its cherry orchards still bear
fruit. Here, Catherine shares memories and dreams with her father and
Cameron. On one visit, they dance together in the orchard, and Mr. St.
John reminisces about "April Dancers."

Increasingly worried about her father, Cat calls her grandmother from
school. But the woman warns that she will tell Cat's mother she is being
upset by Cat's questions about Mr. St. John's "tired" state. A visit to the
doctor results in two prescriptions for Mr. St. John—one for bronchitis,
the other a mystery no one will discuss with Cat.

Against her better judgment, Cat agrees to leave her father alone on the
Saturday of her birthday to help with a dance. He has given her pearls that
belonged to his grandmother but then forgets to pick Cat up for her
driving test. Cameron's father takes her instead, and Cat loses her temper
when she arrives home and her father is there. His groping expression
cannot diffuse her anger, and she rushes out of the house for her celebration date with Cameron. They have a picnic at the farm. On their way
home, Cat sees her father's car by the bridge and learns that he has
committed suicide. She blames herself and is sent to stay with her Aunt
Leah.

Leah shares memories of Cat's father and brother. Cat learns that her
father had been hospitalized before she was born and that bottles of
untaken pills proved that he had forgotten or avoided his medication

before his suicide. Cameron comes to Leah's for a visit when his parents think he is at music camp. Assured that Cat is better and that their love is mutual, he goes on to his music studies.

Cat had seen a kite escape from its owners earlier in the summer. Once she resolves her feelings about her father's death, she flies a kite herself and cuts the string to release it. "I watched it until it soared away, and then I cried. It's so hard to let go and say good-bye." Cat never asked Leah about Sheila but writes the delusion/lost love phantom a last note: "I'm not sure all of my tears were for my father. Maybe some of them were for the St. John women. We did the best we could, and maybe if we remember that, we can forgive each other. Sometimes the kite gets away."

Analysis: This perceptive story impressively deals with the denial and destructive patterns that can foil treatment of a depressive condition. Mr. St. John's mother dithers, his wife works hard and cleans forever, his doctor shields the daughter, and his daughter cannot assert herself or express her fears. The foreshadowing is not heavy-handed, yet it follows the sequence of the symptoms of suicide. The sweet, romantic theme of Cat and Cameron's maturing relationship lightens this serious novel. Strong imagery like dancing in the orchard, pearls splashing off the fatal bridge, and a red kite ceremoniously cut free will touch readers.

■ Thesman, Jean. *Rachel Chance.* Houghton, 1990. 175pp. (0-395-50934-3) Reading Level: Grades 6–9. (KR 1 Ap90; BCCB Je90)
Disability: Emotional disturbance

Rachel's mother was widowed, so she brought Rachel to Grandpa Chance's farm near Seattle. When Rachel's baby brother was born, there was no known father and local opinion judged the Chances pretty harshly. When the little boy, Ryder, is 2, he is kidnapped by a revivalist group. Rachel's mother suffers an emotional collapse. Granpa Chance, Rachel, their neighbor (Druid Annie), and the hired boy (Hank) form a rescue party. While tracking Ryder, Hank and Rachel become close. Rachel also locates Ryder's father, who had no idea that a child had been born.

Analysis: Rachel's character, 1940s morality, poverty, and serendipity make up this story. A talented writer, Thesman keeps suspense going, and most readers will be satisfied. Rachel's mother has been overstressed by her unconventional life-style as well as the sudden disappearance of her son.

Rachel is a tenacious and loving person, but her mother's recovery from shock, grief, and social ostracism should require more strength of character than even Rachel Chance has to offer.

■ Thompson, Julian F. *Goofbang Value Daze*. Scholastic, 1989. 261pp.
(0-590-41946-3) Reading Level: Grades 8–10. (BCCB MS89)
Disability: Emotional disturbance

Gabe attends high school in a dome-covered community. He and his girl,
Dori, become involved in several censorship issues: AIDS testing, student
behavior restrictions, and school-athletic pressures. Gabe's protests are
within legal limits, but he comes into conflict with the authorities from
school and the Congress. Gabe achieves some of his goals, but Doris's
father commits suicide and she leaves town.

Analysis: The futuristic elements of the story do not detract from its
social commentary or humor. Gabe has a solid relationship with his
parents, though many of the adult characters are stock types. Dori's father
is presented as limited, tense, and overserious. His suicide serves mainly as
a dramatic turn of plot. There is little interaction between Dori and Gabe
after her loss, but some insights on coping with a loved one's emotional
disturbance are offered in this piece of fiction.

■ Ure, Jean. *If It Weren't for Sebastian*. Delacorte, 1985. 185pp. (0-385-
29380-1) Reading Level: Grades 8–10. (BCCB Je85)
Disability: Emotional disturbance

Maggie Easter decides against college and a medical career. She breaks
family tradition and feels compelled to live on her own while going to
secretarial school. Her boarding house is full of young people, including
Sebastian, who's "mad as a flaming hatter." Sebastian takes risks, makes
scenes, pursues causes, and gets himself thrown out of good schools.
Maggie admires Sebastian and is intrigued by the tenant that others say
makes "a flaming exhibition of himself." One time she leaves gossipers
wondering about his sexual orientation and finds him pondering suicide
by drowning—like Ophelia.

> "People who talk of it," he said, "never do it, do they?"
> He made it sound as if it were a serious question.
> "No," said Maggie. She said it very firmly. "People who talk of it don't."
> "That's what I thought." He turned back to the water. "That's why I talk
> of it."

They recite poetry back and forth as a game and become closer while
caring for an abandoned cat that they name Sunday. Maggie sees three full
bottles of aspirin at Sebastian's and removes them to protect the cat. She
assumes Sebastian's obsession with death and suicide keeps him too busy

posing to really use one of the options he has presented. On a trip to a rural park, Sebastian talks about his fearful visions of Sunday cut and bleeding like a butchered animal. He recounts his childhood on a farm, where he used to dream that his pet rabbit had its throat cut. Maggie assembles Sebastian's comments into a "picture of how it must have been, Sebastian having meat forced upon him and promptly being sick and his father saying he was a driveling idiot and ought to be put away."

After a test in class, she gets home and sees Sebastian's work boots, then discovers that the young man has disappeared for days at a time before. Sebastian's mother briskly recounts Sebastian's "fits" and "games" and asks if he had been going to a clinic as he was supposed to. When Sebastian is found wandering barefoot in traffic, the boarding house residents feel guilt stricken because all the casual comments about him being "bonkers" turned out to be true. Maggie decides that she wants to start up studies to become a psychiatrist.

Analysis: "If it weren't for Sebastian," Maggie may have followed her friend Val to America and never found her true calling in life. But the pat-sounding summary does not hint at the otherwise fully drawn characterizations, complex revelations, sensitivity, and appeal of this romance. Sebastian's parents think of him as "silly," have no idea how long ago was the last time they last saw him, and have left it up to him to keep his clinic appointments.

After Sebastian is placed in psychiatric care, Maggie imagines herself being responsible for him and seeing him through successful treatment, because "You couldn't let a person go around being unhappy. Not as unhappy as Sebastian sometimes was."

Maggie's brother assures her that medication and psychiatric methods can be helpful. His realistic viewpoints and encouragement that Maggie go to college and medical school ring true and give the ending a hopeful tone.

■ White, Ellen Emerson. *Life Without Friends.* Scholastic, 1987. 256pp. (LB 0-590-33781-5) Reading Level: Grades 8–12. (BCCB Mr87)
Disability: Emotional disturbance

Beverly came to live in Boston with her father, young stepmother, and preschool half-brother after her mother's depression and alcoholism resulted in a fatal accident—perhaps suicide. The friends she established at a coed prep school partied recklessly, led by her lover, Tim. Beverly has just testified against Tim, whose substance abuse, drug dealing, and psychotic behavior led to the murder of two classmates. When she returns to school, Beverly is intent on maintaining academic excellence and feels isolated by her passive role in the death of the school's popular top student. Beverly suffers from an ulcer, flashbacks about sexual and physical abuse by Tim, and nightmares.

When she begins therapy with a new doctor, Beverly is hostile and caustic in her remarks. One day in the public gardens, she meets Derek, a groundsman who has just graduated from high school and has only vague plans about going into the service. He counters Beverly's rebuffs with wit, and she sets the limits of a friendship she is sure her father will disapprove of. When her father puts pressure on her to decide which college she will go to in the fall, Beverly selects the one she is least likely to share with students who know about the murders.

After finals, Beverly is second in her class but does not participate in graduation ceremonies because she is haunted by the absence of the dead girl who would have been valedictorian. In addition, Beverly regrets not telling her father about her mother's condition before the accident.

During the summer, Beverly works at an ice cream shop, and her family meets Derek. Weekly sessions with her doctor continue, with Derek gently probing to discover why just getting through each day is so hard for Beverly. Beverly's dad accepts Derek, her stepmother trusts him, and 5-year-old half-brother Oliver enjoys playing with him. Beverly is afraid Derek will hate her if he knows the truth, but she is surprised by his reaction, which is indignation that Tim would hurt her. Derek tells Beverly that he loves her and that there are lots of other people in her life who want to help her as soon as she lets them.

Before Beverly goes away to college, she takes up running, stops smoking, has some successful sessions with her doctor, and makes friends with her stepmother. Derek gets a job as a carpenter's apprentice, and assumes Beverly will grow away from him at college, but she is able to tell him she loves him and that he makes her happy.

Analysis: This sequel to the suspenseful story *Friends for Life* examines how a girl's self-hatred causes her to push friends and family away while she puzzles through the roots of her destructive school year. It is surprising that she could have maintained her high grades and extracurricular activities while drinking, doing drugs, and partying with Tim. However, her sharp retorts and evasive humor show that she is a very intelligent girl. Most revelations about Beverly are made in halting, incomplete sentences, peppered with ellipses and the teen pause word "like." These devices make introspection and dialogue lurch forward, but they sound genuine and parallel Beverly's own hesitant progress in gaining a clearer perspective on events in her life.

This title can be recommended to a mature audience that can appreciate the psychological drama and light romance that give Beverly hope she will recover from severe emotional scars.

■ White, Ruth. *Sweet Creek Holler.* Farrar, 1988. 215pp. (0-374-37360-4)
Reading Level: Grades 6–8. (BCCB 088)
Disability: Emotional disturbance

Ginny Shortt moves with her mother and sister, Junie, to Sweet Creek
Holler after her father is killed in a mining camp. Their grandfather
promises to bring things by to help out, but seeing their troubles always
makes him procrastinate and become unreliable. Ginny's best friend
through six years of Appalachian childhood is Lou Jean Purvis. Ginny
takes joy in the land, her dog, candy parties, risky swings on a vine, and
her family. By sixth grade, fickle schoolmates, gossip, and social disfavor
affect Ginny's life and destroy Lou Jean.

Mrs. Shortt is not hired as postmistress because a mean-spirited gossip
pulls political favors. Mr. Purvis, a genial drunk who saves Ginny from a
snake, is rumored to have gotten his own daughter pregnant. Really, the
girl was desperate for affection because of her mother's difficulty with
dealing with an alcoholic husband. When Lou Jean becomes depressed
about the abandonment by her lover and the humiliation resulting from
gossip about incest, she sets her clothing on fire and dies.

Ginny and Junie break through the isolation of rich Mrs. Clancy and
help her. The old lady is called a "witch" because of her reclusive behavior, which started when her two daughters died of typhoid fever and her
husband's grief led to suicide a few weeks after. Mrs. Clancy gets Mrs.
Shortt a job in a bookstore. Ginny is glad to move away from the small-
minded and unforgiving people in the community and assumes her mother
will marry Mrs. Clancy's son.

Analysis: Many events and regional qualities are developed in this
account of six years in Ginny's life. The characterizations are complex,
and the scope of the book is ambitious. That the mother falls in love with
the mine owner and that Ginny and her sister are likely to settle in the lap
of luxury constitute a satisfying ending, even if a bit contrived.

Ginny is not sure whether Lou Jean intended suicide, but it is clear that
Lou Jean's unnatural fascination with fire and her distracted ways led to
her death. The community's unyielding opinions about characters who
have weaknesses or emotional disturbances due to circumstance are
strongly portrayed.

■ Willey, Margaret. *Finding David Dolores.* Harper & Row, 1986. 150pp.
(LB 0-06-026484-5) Reading Level: Grades 6–9. (BCCB My86)
Disability: Emotional disturbance

When Arly Weston turns 13, she feels irritable, avoids her mother and old
friends, and strikes out on long walks to heighten her lonely brooding. On

one walk, she sees David Dolores and later discovers he is a musician, a senior, and an only child whose father has died. Arly does not speak to David but fantasizes about him as the important "someone" she has found to give her life meaning.

An even more dramatic character is Regina Miller, who dresses outlandishly, is scornful about seventh grade at her new school, and carries hatred for her mother as "a secret every single day of" her life. Regina is so rude when Arly dines with the Millers that Arly can only see her friend's hostility in high contrast with Mrs. Miller's kindness and Regina's sister's tolerance.

Regina becomes friends with Mrs. Delores and rejects Arly's advice that Mrs. Miller should be told about the relationship. When Mrs. Miller finds out how much time Regina has been spending with the artistic Althea Dolores, she is concerned. When Regina turns to Althea for help with personal hygiene questions because her period starts, Mrs. Miller goes to visit Mrs. Dolores. Althea realizes that Mrs. Miller is not the uncaring parent Regina made her out to be.

David returns from summer music camp and resents the way Regina monopolizes his mother. Arly feels that Regina has manipulated Arly's fantasy about David into a relationship for herself without thinking of the people or emotional costs involved. Regina runs away and locks herself in Althea's studio after an argument with her mother. Arly is able to pierce Regina's obstinate hatred by pointing out that Regina's cruelty toward her mother is really rooted in anger toward her father. The girls are able to laugh together, but know that their friendship has altered significantly.

The Millers return to Minneapolis, and David goes off to study music. Two years later, Althea and Arly share a clipping that shows Regina winning an art contest.

Analysis: Three families weather adolescent adjustments in interpersonal and parent-child relations. The adult characterizations are as three-dimensional as the teen protagonist and her disturbed friend. Arly's withdrawal is part of her maturation process, but Regina's rejection of her mother shows a profound emotional disturbance. Arly is manipulated into the position of sole friend and ally for Regina, until she trusts her own observations of the Miller family. Regina's caustic opinions and lies are shown to be based on warped perceptions instead of reality.

Regina's pursuit of artistic expression is evident in the ending, but there is no indication that professional intervention aided the Millers in their reconciliation. Since Regina had been so out of touch with reality, it is a bit hollow to assume she could recover with only one peer comment about misplaced anger. On the whole, though, this is a highly recommended title for middle school.

■ Willey, Margaret. *Saving Lenny.* Bantam, 1990. 160pp. (0-553-05850-9)
Reading Level: Grades 7–12. (KR 15 Ap90; BCCB Mr90; HB Jl-Ag90)
Disability: Depression

Jesse and her best friend, Kay, find a way for Jesse to meet the attractive
new boy, Lenny. Jesse and Lenny become devoted to each other, but Kay
recognizes that the romance has shut out old friendships. Lenny has
second thoughts about college and convinces Jesse to live with him in a
cottage after high school. As the couple withdraw into a codependent
relationship, Lenny's behavior becomes less rational. Jesse believes that
only she can restore Lenny to his sensitive, smart self, until she recognizes
his advanced depression; Kay is there to help out.

Analysis: Obsessive behavior and its progression constitute the focus of
these plot turns, yet the author keeps the sad case study from falling into
melodrama. By alternating the narrative between Jesse and Kay, two
perspectives and deeper characterizations get presented. Lenny is first seen
as a figure of romance, with classic dark moods from brooding on the
unknowns of life. His exclusive kind of love isolates Jesse emotionally, so
that any accusations or demands he throws at her are very powerful. This
relationship collapses much sooner than many codependent situations,
but the portrayals are authentic enough to appeal to young adult readers.

■ Windsor, Patricia. *The Sandman's Eyes.* Delacorte, 1985. 271pp.
(0-385-29381-X) Reading Level: Grades 7–10. (BCCB MS85)
Disability: Emotional disturbance; Speech and language impairments

Mickey (Michael) returns to his grandfather's home after two years in a
special school and under psychiatric care. At age 16 he had witnessed a
murder, was the major suspect in the crime, and became so disoriented
that he had "mental laryngitis." During sixth grade, when he was called
"Mouse," a classmate died from a long fall at the park. His girlfriend,
Lindsey, has been warned away from Mickey because of the murder he
witnessed in Monrovia Park and the court action that followed.

A reporter named Gary wants to write about Michael, and he reviews
with Mickey the details of the murder and the investigation. He summarizes that Mickey cast suspicion on himself by being uncooperative:

> "You wouldn't talk!"
> "I couldn't," I told him. "There's a difference."
> Something happened to my voice and I didn't have any control over
> it. . . .
> "What beats me," Gary said, getting sympathetic again, "is why they

didn't get a psychiatrist to diagnose it. Hundreds of kids develop problems like that when they're in a traumatic situation like a courtroom. They stutter or go mute. Some of them even have epileptic seizures."

Gary supports Michael's readjustment and helps unravel the mystery of missing letters by using as resources Lindsey, conflicting eyewitness reports, and replays of scenes where "Michael sees a woman get pushed off the wall. Nobody believes him." On a date with Mary Ann, Michael claims that someone tried to kill him and that his memory of who it could be became lost because of a blow to his head. Mary Ann enjoys the date and reveals that Lindsey's father had been the witness who saw Michael run out of the park too quickly to have been responsible for the murder.

Gary hypnotizes Michael to elicit the name of the assailant but winds up telling Michael the boy's mother, Allison, is not dead but was sent to a psychiatric institution years ago. Mike sees Gary's notes and throws Gary out for wanting to investigate him as a serial murderer. The next day, Michael finds out his mother was disowned as a hippie-influenced unwed mother whose child had been taken away because she neglected him. He ponders the roots of his mother's nervous breakdown and his own feelings of abandonment and concludes that when he illegally entered other people's houses, he was really only looking for his parents. Gary tells Michael his mother's address and alias, and the boy has a reunion with the young woman on her farm.

Michael gets a mysterious message to meet someone at midnight at the wall. He does not report this to the police, thinking they would assume he was crazy enough to write it himself. Lindsey's mother says she is there to warn him but is revealed as the jealous killer. The secret that Michael keeps is that Lindsey's womanizing father is Michael's father as well.

Analysis: This thriller has strong episodes and self-analysis. The first-person account includes comments from "the smirker" within Michael's personality, which becomes his own reasoning after he meets his mother. Allison is fearful and vague, drinks but seems happy and plans to continue her artwork. The two psychiatrists have different therapy styles, and, although the first one's perceptions are wrong, his methods do help Michael integrate all the information that comes forward in the course of the story. Complex and exciting and romantic, this will appeal to the same readers who enjoy Davis's *Sex Education* or the Nixon mysteries.

■ Woolverton, Linda. **Running Before the Wind.** Houghton, 1987. 152pp. (0-395-42116-0) Reading Level: Grades 6–9.
Disability: Emotional disturbance

Mr. Mackenzie had polio as a teenager and had to quit running; out of abnormal envy, he beats his daughter when he learns she is training secretly for track. *See full annotation* Chapter 4: Orthopedic/Neurological Impairments.

■ Wright, Betty Ren. *The Summer of Mrs. MacGregor.* Holiday, 1986. 160pp. (0-8234-0628-8) Reading Level: Grades 5–8.
Disability: Cardiac disorder; Cerebral hemorrhage; Emotional disturbance

Lillian spends the summer as "Mrs. Lillina MacGregor," shoplifts, steals money, then gets hysterical when confronted with her lies. *See full annotation* Chapter 4: Health Problems.

■ Yep, Laurence. *Kind Hearts and Gentle Monsters.* Harper & Row, 1982. 192pp. (LB 0-06-026733-X) Reading Level: Grades 7–9. (BCCB My82)
Disability: Emotional disturbance

Charley is a sophomore at Loyola High School when a poison pen chain letter makes him confront Chris Pomeroy. The two amend their opinions of each other and become friends. Mrs. Pomeroy is a volatile person with a history of emotional disturbances and suicide attempts. Her psychiatrist has advised Chris to try to live her own life, and Chris and Charley retreat to the zoo or library for time together away from Mrs. Pomeroy. When Charley invites Chris and her mother for a Christmas celebration, Mrs. Pomeroy refuses to go and later attempts suicide.

Chris views this as part of a hopeless cycle that has made the last ten Christmas seasons miserable and worn down Mr. Pomeroy until he had a heart attack three years ago. Charley comforts Chris when she feels she has nothing left to offer her desperate, grasping mother. Charley promises to support Chris during counseling and in making some hard choices.

Analysis: Yep establishes clearly defined characters in a difficult situation. The plot is more a progression of personal revelations than events, but it provides another view of the stresses an adolescent experiences when a parent is emotionally dysfunctional. Mrs. Pomeroy's behavior is revealed in dramatic interactions when Charley is present, like the day she saws on her wrist with a file until Chris makes her stop. Like Riley's *Crazy Quilt* and Silsbee's *The Big Way Out,* this novel discusses the strain caused by a pattern of emotional disturbance in a family. Chris's challenge is to find a balance between supporting her mother and living her own life. This is a realistic romance that can lead readers to look beyond the abrasive surface of "monstrous" behavior.

■ Zindel, Paul. *Harry and Hortense at Hormone High.* Harper & Row, 1984. 151pp. (LB 0-06-026869-7) Reading Level: Grades 7–9. (BCCB D84)
Disability: Emotional disturbance

Harry and Hortense have always been friends, but when they include Jason Rohr in their close relationship, tragedy and farce are equal possibilities. Comic dialogue and interaction at high school point out other people's foibles. Jason's differences are that his idealism and self-giving attitudes are combined with a delusion that he is Icarus, a god. He wants to save the world and is willing to start with improving Hormone High.
  Analysis: First-person observations by adolescents can be too flip for characterizing Jason's tentative hold on reality and his personal identity. Harry and Hortense like Icarus, the god, and also feel compassion for lonely Jason, who obviously needs friendship and acceptance. This novel skirts a worst-case scenario and portrays Jason as an altruistic soul worth getting close to.

LEARNING DISABILITIES

■ Adler, C. S. *Eddie's Blue-Winged Dragon.* Putnam, 1988. 144pp. (0-399-21535-2) Reading Level: Grades 4–6.
Disability: Learning disabilities

Gary expects to drop out of school when he is 16, feeling he will know enough to run his father's store. *See full annotation* Chapter 4: Orthopedic/Neurological Impairments.

■ Adler, C. S. *Kiss the Clown.* Clarion, 1986. 178pp. (0-89919-419-2) Reading Level: Grades 7–9. (BCCB MS86)
Disability: Learning disabilities; Dyslexia

Viki Hill lives in a village in Guatemala, where her father is a missionary. Her decision to pose nude for an artist triggers family discord, and she is sent to live with an aunt in upstate New York. Attending high school and trying hard to fit in, Viki has her first steady dates with Marc. But Marc has an older brother, Joel, and Viki finds herself attracted more and more to him.

The contrast between the brothers is profound: Joel is the class clown, his dyslexia addressed in special education classes with little success. Marc achieves in honor courses and is planning on law school. When Marc's campaign for class president ends in defeat, he is crushed. Viki realizes he has a self-centered and impatient nature, and she recognizes how the boys' highly educated and ambitious parents put pressure on both their sons. Joel is always in arguments at home over his lack of concern for the future, but he does keep an after-school job at a stable. Viki feels that Joel is a nicer person—generous, kind to all, and very loyal to Marc, even when Viki points out their differences.

Viki develops a relationship with her aunt as well. Their conversations help Viki to sort out her feelings about her father's total involvement in his work, and the ways her mother seems apathetic, aloof toward the villagers, and happy only when house guests engage her in conversation. Viki fears that her parents' marriage will break up because of her mother's flirtations. Father sees no family problem other than that Mother seems depressed, so Viki wonders if her return to Guatemala will be requested soon.

In winter, Viki goes on a cross-country skiing trip with Marc's family and is rescued during a blizzard by Joel. They confide their mutual attraction. Joel responds candidly to Viki's questions about his dyslexia. Viki breaks up with Marc, but Joel waits to date her until his brother has had time to stop grieving about this loss. Meanwhile, Joel intends to try again to learn to read and makes progress this time, motivated by the idea that he does not deserve a girl like Viki unless he builds this skill.

Marc announces that Viki is leaving for Guatemala, and Joel is furious when he learns that Marc has a new girlfriend but did not let his brother know until it was too late to do anything more than say good-bye to Viki. Viki and Joel tell each other of their love, kiss, and plan that Joel will work on his reading while they both wait for Viki's return.

Analysis: Since the point of view shifts between Viki, Marc, and Joel, some readers may have to struggle to keep up with the shared perceptions. The characterizations do come across though, uniquely inserting a character with a learning disability as part of a love triangle. Also, it is obvious that Joel has been handicapped by his parents' attitudes and the competitive pressure at home as much as by his dyslexia. That he has found satisfying part-time employment in the face of parental conflict is far from the stereotype of learning-disabled workers' preparation by parents and programs for success-ensured positions. Conversely, Marc's personality flaws are seen in such high contrast to Joel's easygoing nature, that the book could imply that all kids in special education have learned to turn their discouragement into kind, generous, and loyal attitudes. Readers should enjoy this love story portraying characters in several different relationships where one person is motivated by an ambition that the other person cannot identify with.

■ Aiello, Barbara, and Jeffrey Shulman. *Secrets Aren't Always for Keeps.* Illus. by Loel Barr. Twenty-First Century, 1988. 48pp. (0-941477-01-0) Reading Level: Grades 3–5. (SLJ Mr89)
Disability: Learning disabilities

Jennifer Hauser is hosting her pen pal from Australia, Kay. Fourteen letters in the exchange were dictated by Jennifer to her best friend, Melody, because LD, "learning difference," makes Jennifer's writing difficult to read, and Melody has excellent handwriting. Jennifer wanted to impress Kay with her first letter, then kept her LD and special classes secret by sending tape-recorded letters. Jennifer hatches several plans to avoid telling Kay about her disability. She makes up a game when Kay arrives, and they exchange sealed notes that have their biggest personal secret in them. Jennifer hopes Kay will read her note about having LD so she will not have to tell her friend face-to-face and risk rejection.

At Jennifer's school, her visitor and her "down under" vocabulary bring Jennifer popularity. But Melody confronts Jennifer in the bathroom about the "pillow talk" game that Jennifer lies about to keep Kay from thinking Jennifer is "retarded or something." While Kay is answering the class's questions about Australia, Jennifer slips out to study in the resource room. Kay joins her there to say she was aware of Jennifer's learning disability because the girls' mothers had shared the information. Kay insists that such secrets are for sharing, especially with a friend.

Analysis: This plot is much flatter than the other titles in The Kids on the Block series. The father is a psychologist, always nudging Jennifer to do the right thing. There may have been foreshadowing of communication between the mothers, but there is no explanation for Mother's having read Jennifer's letter from Kay before her daughter got home to open it. Juvenile characters deserve more respect than that, especially if the point of the story is to show how capable a child can be despite disability.

This book follows the series format of questions and answers in the back and will be useful in large collections for information. A better reading experience may be offered by Giff's *The Girl Who Knew Everything,* but cartoonish illustrations make this short work pleasant for students who are enjoying Giff's easier Polk Street School episodes.

■ Andrews, Jean F. *The Flying Fingers Club.* Kendall Green, 1988. 100pp. (paper 0-930323-44-0) Reading Level: Grades 3–5.
Disability: Deafness; Learning disabilities

Donald repeats third grade and makes a new friend, Matt, who is deaf. *See full annotation* Chapter 5: Hearing Impairments.

■ Cassedy, Sylvia. *M. E. and Morton.* Crowell, 1987. 312pp. (LB 0-690-04562-X) Reading Level: Grades 5–8. (BCCB MS87)
Disability: Learning disabilities

Mary Ella is 11 and likes to make up games and fantasies, but when a new girl moves into the neighborhood and becomes her friend, M. E. finds new interests. She also is amazed that Polly spends time playing with M. E.'s 14-year-old brother, Morton. He is repeating seventh grade and has no playmates at all. When M. E. meets Polly's grandmother for the first time, she can tell that Morton has already been a frequent visitor and is puzzled: "The only time anybody had ever invited Morton to their house, it was to play a trick on him."

At school Mary Ella is excluded from social groups, so she is delighted to have stories of an "outside friend" who does not attend classes there. Polly says outrageous things and lives under difficult conditions, but M. E. is enchanted with the girl's stories and invention. By August, M. E.'s mother is alert to the changes in her daughter and starts including M. E. in the complaints she usually reserved for Morton. There are plans to send Morton away at the end of summer.

One day Morton falls from the roof and is hospitalized. M. E. sees her parents in the hall during a visit and wonders, "Were they secretly glad, I wondered, that such a terrible thing had happened to Morton, so that at last they could love him and want him to live?"

Polly visits also, and she and M. E. bring gifts for Morton. When they place one in his hand, he wakes. M. E. and her parents set a new family pattern of appreciation of Morton for what he can do instead of demeaning him.

Analysis: Embarrassed by Morton's differences and sure that their son is too stupid to expect much of, M. E.'s parents ignore him most of the time and denigrate him in his presence the rest of the time. M. E. follows their lead and even taunts him along with others as "Morton without the T!" Polly gives M. E. perspective because she has fewer material or social resources than the private school classmates M. E. is used to. M. E. also admires Polly. On learning that Polly has a sister who stays at home with her mother because that girl was the favorite child, M. E. lies and says that Morton is her parents' favorite.

Morton is "nice"—meaning he does not defy or argue with anyone. His portrayal is faithful, because his plodding logic and narrow experiences have indeed not allowed him to develop many skills. Cassedy's girl characters use complex fantasy to help decode the world around them. Morton is a victim in this story as surely as the boy in *Goodnight Mr. Tom.* An audience for either that title or *Lucie Babidge's House* may also enjoy this title as an alternative choice.

■ DeClements, Barthe. **Sixth Grade Can Really Kill You.** Viking, 1985. 146pp. (0-670-80656-0) Reading Level: Grades 4–7. (BCCB D85) *Disability:* Learning disabilities

"Bad Helen" is disruptive in sixth grade, and her grades are so poor that she may not enter junior high. Tests have shown her intelligence to be above average, so her mother feels justified in refusing to enroll Helen in special education classes. Though her mother spends time tutoring Helen at home, Helen excells only in math, gym, and music. Her frustration at not being able to read, in addition to her pranks to cover up the fact that she cannot, results in her placement in another teacher's class at the end of the semester.

Mr. Marshall, the new teacher, introduces Helen to the special education classroom and lets her decide if she might like to try it. When Mother is out of town, Father supports Helen's decision to try the special class. He points out that Mother worries about what other people might think but that that is not a good reason to refuse help. Helen is teased, but most of her friends stay loyal. She works with the school psychologist, struggles a bit with the principal's suggestion that this should be the end of "Bad Helen," and finally admits to Mr. Marshall that misbehaving is a habit she is willing break—at least until junior high.

Analysis: The author captures classroom dynamics and natural dialogue so well that the story's uneven pace is easy to overlook. Helen is unique, knowing she is not "dumb" but simply needs to face her reading problem before other things in her life can sort themselves out. Her overprotective mother is told by the principal that learning-disabled students cannot survive in the school system without special help. When Helen's father encourages her not to worry about being labeled "dumb," Helen starts gaining the skills that allow her to prove she can succeed in a mainstreamed school setting. During that very semester, she relinquishes the self-image of "Bad Helen" and pays for spray paint damage that she did to the school. That she has saved her third firecracker for junior high is the type of detail that keeps a serious subject from overpowering an entertaining school story.

■ Dereske, Jo. *The Lone Sentinel.* Atheneum, 1989. 176pp. (0-689-31552-X) Reading Level: Grades 4–8. (KR 1 S89)
Disability: Neurological impairment; Mental retardation

The planet Azure is a source of biosote for the alien Helgatites. Fourteen-year-old Erik helps man the Lone Sentinel to protect the growth. His mother has died, and a fierce storm kills his father. Eric conceals this from authorities because he does not want to be moved to a crowded city. Augusta and her brain-damaged twin sister Willa take refuge with Erik, because Augusta fears Willa will be sent to an institution back in the city. When an alien called Maag arrives ahead of schedule, Eric gets suspicious. The girls and Eric foil Maag's attempts to destroy the biosote. Grateful Helgatites offer medical help to Willa, and trust between the children and the aliens is rewarded.

Analysis: Invention and characterization are stronger than pace in this science fiction novel. It becomes a survival story when the young protagonists outwit the villain. Willa's impairments are judged harshly by her society but not by her sister or the aliens who can both accommodate and correct it.

■ Dixon, Jeanne. *The Tempered Wind.* Atheneum, 1987. 224pp. (0-689-31339-X) Reading Level: Grades 7–9. (BCCB 087)
Disability: Short stature

In the 1940s, Gabriella was overprotected as a child and often isolated because of her dwarfism. At age 13, she became orphaned, was taken in by an aunt, and was awarded a scholarship to the Young Ladies Christian Academy. Unhappy there, she responds to an ad for a farm-chore girl in Montana. However, she lacks the skills required for the position. Facing prejudice, Gabriella finds an appropriate career, an admirer, and friends.

Analysis: Gabriella is 17 when she recounts these events. Her physical limitations are depicted in a candid manner, and the emotional content of the story is realistic. Bitterness and resolution are made equally clear in Gabriella's characterization, though minor characters are not as well drawn. Recommended because it allows the protagonist to determine her own way and shows both her adaptability and courage.

■ Foley, June. *Falling in Love is No Snap.* Delacorte, 1986. 139pp. (0-835-29490-5) Reading Level: Grades 6–9. (SLJ D86)
Disability: Attention deficit disorder

Alexandra Suskind lives with her divorced mother, attends private school, and wants to become a famous photographer. She appreciates that her mother works hard to provide social and educational opportunities for her daughter, who cannot find a way to inform her mother that photography is her vocational choice, not business. Alexandra is shooting pictures of her neighborhood when she falls in love at the first sight of Heracles Damaskinakis, whose father owns the local Greek deli. They get to know each other, Heracles confides that he wants to be a scientist and not the next operator of the deli, and they share a kiss. Then Heracles tells Alexandra he has a girlfriend, so Alexandra fabricates a boyfriend similar to one of her wealthy classmates.

Heracles wants to present his father a picture of Theo, Heracles's younger brother. Alexandra agrees to take the picture but has a lot of trouble getting the restless boy to cooperate. Finally, she has Theo start on a portrait of Alexandra so he will stay put long enough at one activity for her to get him in focus.

Alexandra and Heracles encourage each other to tell their parents what their life goals are, but neither teenager finds a way to communicate. When Mr. Damaskinakis falls ill and Heracles is overwhelmed with responsibilities for the deli and Theo, Alexandra offers to take the boy home with her. Mrs. Suskind has worked before with students with attention deficit disorders, sends Alexandra back for Theo's medicine, and helps Theo settle down enough to hear a story.

Alexandra tells her mother her plans for a career in photography. Mr. Damaskinakis follows the teacher's instructions so well that Theo becomes able to help in the deli, and Heracles makes plans to attend Stanford. In addition, he has broken up with his girlfriend, and Alexandra admits her deception so they can be together.

Analysis: A light romance in easy-to-read first-person narrative deals nicely with the theme of living up to someone else's expectations. The family assumption that Heracles would stay on at the deli is strengthened by Theo's learning disability. Once the disability is under control, Heracles feels free to seek his preferred career path. Since communication is so difficult between the Damaskinakis males that they ignore discussion of Mrs. Damaskinakis, her death, or Theo's problem, it shows consistent characterization that Heracles is reluctant to speak up about his hopes for college.

Theo is not the central character but is certainly the catalyst for change in both families. Alexandra's mother has skills and knowledge about hyperactivity that her daughter never knew about. Theo is shown to be energetic and restless instead of incorrigible, and his suggested medical regimen is credible. Middle school readers and older students with reading difficulties will be interested in this romance.

■ Froelich, Margaret. *Reasons to Stay.* Houghton, 1986. 181pp. (0-395-41068-1) Reading Level: Grades 6–9. (BCCB D86)
Disability: Learning disabilities

Three children grow up in poverty in 1906. The oldest girl, Florence, does not like to go to school because she cannot read. She is also obsessive about the hand-me-down dresses a do-good neighbor brings by. When 12-year-old Babe's best efforts to give her mother food and rest fail, the reclusive pregnant woman dies. Their drunken father lashes out at his 7-year-old son, Rivius. When authorities threaten to place the children in a county home and bring charges of theft against the father, he runs off with the children and all their belongings in a mule-drawn wagon. The wagon breaks down near a mill in a storm, and the children stay with the family that owns the mill.

Babe pieces together the facts that Florence's and Rivius's father is not her father and that her mother had been married to another man in a nearby community. She leaves Florence and Rivius in the care of the family at the mill and goes to seek her own grandparents. She talks to her great-aunt and aunt, then realizes that relatives can be hateful and unforgiving but that loving strangers can create a family. Babe resolves her feelings about her mother's life and death, and she enjoys gardening with her foster grandmother as a legacy from her paternal grandmother.

Analysis: Babe never thinks of Florence as "slow" but always assumes a protective role with her. At 13, Florence gets male attention that Babe hopes the girl is intimidated by enough to avoid. When Babe wishes for a nicer father, she chooses her best friend's father, who sits in a wheeled chair and plays checkers with his daughter.

This well-written historical novel uses old-fashioned expressions that add to its clear sense of place and time. Babe is something of a female Huckleberry Finn, trying to work out her grief, anger, and shame. The happy ending shows Florence to be teasing her new foster sister but does not indicate any change in her learning disabilities. The foster parents' patience and tolerance of Rivius imply that the children will be accepted for what and who they are without the harsh treatment they were once subject to.

■ Giff, Patricia Reilly. *The Beast in Ms. Rooney's Room.* Illus. by Blanche Sims. Dell, 1984. 76pp. (paper 0-440-40485-1) Reading Level: Grades 2–4. (SLJ D84)
Disability: Learning disabilities

Ms. Rooney's second-grade class includes Richard Best—for the second year in a row. He calls himself "Beast" and has firm opinions about his classmates, especially Matthew, who has a baby-wet-the-bed smell. Richard sticks to his lie about Ms. Rooney's records being mixed up when someone says he was left back "by dumbness," not by accident. He has special reading time with Mrs. Paris and a classmate named Emily Arrow. He feels self-conscious reading from a skinny book, but for the first time, words look familiar and he can figure out how to spell what he hears. Matthew is the most helpful person with spelling, and Richard decides that maybe Matthew hates wetting his bed as much as Richard hates still having his baby teeth. The class wins a banner for good behavior, and Richard's artwork makes a fine gift for Mrs. Paris's faded bulletin board.

Analysis: Shorter than Shreve's *The Flunking of Joshua T. Bates,* this book is just the type Richard drew for himself, "Not a big fat book. But not a little skinny book either. Kind of an in-between book." Once his impulsiveness is better controlled and his maturity level improves, Richard is able to focus better on his assignments and curb his behavior. He has a breakthrough in reading readiness when he notices that "arrow" with a lowercase "a" and Emily Arrow's last name look the same. He also applies his younger classmate's clues that in spelling, "All you have to do is stick some little words together. Turn them into big ones."

Originally offered in paperback, this series is now available in hardcover editions because of its popularity.

■ Gould, Marilyn. *The Twelfth of June.* Lippincott, 1986. 183pp. (LB 0-397-32130-9) Reading Level: Grades 5–8. (SLJ N86)
Disability: Cerebral palsy

Janis, who has cerebral palsy, is 12 years old in this sequel to *Golden Daffodils.* Her good friend Barney calls her "Daff" and confides that he wants to run away from home. She distracts him from his family pressures with an invitation to come play a new video game at her house. Classmates ooze about a boy who wears after shave, and when Janis responds unenthusiastically, another girl says,

> "It's not just imagination, Janny. It's sexuality. But . . ." Her eyes scanned my less than perfect body. "I guess you don't have those kinds of fantasies or personal feelings."

I wanted to bop her. I mean, what does cerebral palsy have to do with sexuality or personal feelings or fantasies?

Fantasies about Barney and worries about "zits" and discomfort with the giddy romances swirling around her make the next few months hard on Janis. Barney is preparing for his bar mitzvah, and after a misunderstanding at Janis's home, he joins up with the class punkers. Janis is miserable and lonely but when the family invitation to Barney's bar mitzvah arrives with her name omitted, she is devastated. Barney appears immediately with a bunch of daffodils and an explanation that his mother sent the invitation early and that Janis's invitation is separate and personal because he is asking her to run away on the train with him. Their "betrothal" has been discussed before, but Janis writes a song about flowers blooming at the proper time in order to tell Barney they need to wait. Barney has been able to reform the punkers and lure them into learning via video games. Janis has learned to make the most of her strong arm and dramatic longings by performing her song with guitar accompaniment at the bar mitzvah.

Analysis: Janis made progress with her physical limitations after the first book's account of her fifth-grade year. She no longer wears a leg brace, and medication controls her big seizures. She has a facial twitch, one arm is weaker than the other, and small seizures threaten her if she is overtired. Also, during the course of this plot, her grandmother recovers from a stroke, but physical limitations and a patronizing caregiver do not stop the clever lady from intervening when Janis and her mother need a neutral facilitator for their "summit" on sex.

The most significant theme is Janis's right to adolescent longings and sexual stirrings. Her accusations that "Dr. Fuchs told you all about the wonderful special activities where handicapped girls can meet handicapped boys so they don't bother little normal boys like hers" are very accurate. However, Barney himself does not seem so normal in this book, even though he is consistently portrayed as a precocious boy. His scheme to skip town seems a mixture of teen delusion and stressed-out desperation. The adults in his life have high expectations of him in school, in music, and in life, and preparing for his ceremonial rite of passage puts the vulnerable thinker at the edge of reason.

Janis is more credible in her musings on relationships and her forthright questioning of her father: "Do you think a person like me should ever get married?" When her father responds that people who love each other and want to spend their lives together should marry—even if they have disabilities or if the situation is "one with and one without"—Janis presses him to tell how he would feel if her sister, Stella, married someone with cerebral palsy. These important issues are embedded in serious, well-written passages that clash with the valley slang dialogue of other scenes. The casual tone is welcome, and southern California is as valid a regional setting as Manhattan or Appalachia; however "pretty darn good speech," "Gye!" and "damn" this or that seem self-conscious rather than natural expressions here.

Fans of the DeClements books will like meeting Janis in *Golden Daffodils* and following her into middle school by reading *The Twelfth of June*.

■ Greenwald, Sheila. *Will the Real Gertrude Hollings Please Stand Up?*- Little, Brown, 1983. 162pp. (0-316-32707-7) Reading Level: Grades 4–6. (BCCB D83)
Disability: Dyslexia

Gertrude is 11 when her parents go on a three-week trip to Greece. She dreads staying with her aunt and uncle and her cousin Albert. He calls her "dumb Gertrude" because she needs a tutor to keep up in school due to dyslexia. Albert is only 10, but a superachiever, and dinner conversation at his home is a preassigned topic. Gertrude goes to the library with a friend to help prepare for one evening's discussion of Greek mythology. Albert is impressed with all Gertrude can share about Athena and Arachne, and she leads him to believe she has arcane powers like the oracles of old. During a hike, she warns him that the baby his mother is expecting will take his place.

Albert spends the next days in bed, unresponsive to a doctor's treatment, so Gertrude is frightened that she has gone too far. The next weekend in the country, while in her "trance," she speaks of the benefits of being a sibling, but Albert is doubtful and they get lost for a while. When the frantic parents decide Gertrude is too much trouble, they send her to stay with friends. Albert runs away and Gertrude finds him at the museum. The children go to Albert's home, a neighbor calls the police thinking they are robbers, Gertrude's parents come home early from Greece, and in the hubbub Gertrude finds out she is going to have a baby in the family too.

Analysis: Greenwald is skilled at keeping her books busy and filling them with lively characters and humorous dialogue. A contrived ending is countered with Gertrude's character development. Her mother is supportive and sympathetic about Gertrude's learning problems, because she has dyslexia herself and can point out famous people who also had to compensate for that weakness.

Gertrude is tired of the teasing she gets and sets out to gain Albert's respect, in the process gaining self-respect. Her story-telling talents draw Albert, because his parents have been so strict in encouraging his gifted-ness that they have stifled his imagination. Fiction is out-of-bounds, and dinner is a time for serious discussion in order to edify the children in Albert's household. Readers can hope that that pattern will be revised with the advent of Albert's sibling.

■ Hansen, Joyce. *Yellow Bird and Me.* Clarion, 1986. 155pp. (0-89919-335-8) Reading Level: Grades 4–6. (BCCB Ap86)
Disability: Dyslexia

Doris misses Amir, who has been placed in a group home in Syracuse. She writes him letters that discuss her progress in school, and he replies. Doris wants to visit her friend, but her parents do not want her to work to earn the money for a trip to Syracuse from the Bronx. Yellow Bird, a boy whose clowning has always masked his need for special help with school assignments, asks Doris to help him study, because he cannot read. Amir advises that "You got to see inside of Bird to see who he really is. I bet if you helped him, Doris, he'd be a good student. Remember how he was beginning to change?"

Their teacher accuses Bird of cheating on a test when she sees him using a prompt sheet with the dates of important events written on it. He insists that it was just to keep the numbers in the right order, not to give him the answers to test questions. His explanation is not accepted, and Mrs. Barker warns Doris, "Let's not forget which of us is the teacher."

When Bird is placed in the special education class, Doris is stunned, the teacher looks overwhelmed, and Bird is humiliated. The drama production that Bird has been looking forward to is cast with Bird as the lead. Doris fills in another role at the last minute, because she has practiced so often with Bird that she knows the lines. Bird helps Doris with her lines when her nervousness sets in. Doris summarizes for Amir:

"Mr. Washington explained to Barker what was wrong and now he gets special tutoring in reading. He's got something called dyslexia. It's real hard for him to read even though he's really smart. Barker doesn't pick on him anymore. She lets him tell her the answers to written tests and then he writes them down later. Bird does everything we do except it takes him a little longer."

Analysis: Doris learns that she can keep her friendship with Amir and feels closer to him when she lets herself help Yellow Bird. Amir was the gentle hero of *The Gift-Giver,* and this story shows Doris's resisting peer pressure and valuing relationships just as he encouraged her earlier to do. Doris exercises some deception, with Bird as a lookout, in order to work at the beauty parlor, but her parents and the shop operator come to an understanding in the end.

The special education class teaches time with a plastic clock, and "some of the the kids could hardly speak" so Bird's classmates can distinguish that his placement there is more punishment than accommodation. Characterization of the harsh sixth-grade teacher, Mrs. Barker, is flat. However, believable interactions between children and adults in a black community strengthen this novel for upper-grade readers.

■ Kennemore, Tim. *Wall of Words.* Faber, 1983. 173pp. (0-571-11856-9)
Reading Level: Grades 5–7. (BCCB MS83)
Disability: Dyslexia

Kim has three sisters. Their father has been gone over a year, trying to complete a book for publication. Kit is 13 and usually at odds with her youngest sister, Anna. The other girl, Kerry, has visited psychologists to determine why school makes her so upset that she becomes ill. One of Kim's teachers is dyslexic and helps Kerry acknowledge that she is not retarded but has a special learning disability. Once Kerry's dread of failure is lessened because she has been diagnosed with dyslexia, her health improves as well.

Analysis: This amusing story has strong dialogue and a pleasant cast of characters. As some problems are resolved, other friction between the sisters is believably left unresolved, without a pat solution. This will enhance many collections.

■ Kline, Suzy. *Herbie Jones.* Illus. by Richard Williams. Putnam, 1985. 95pp. (0-399-21183-7) Reading Level: Grades 2–4. (BCCB S85)
Disability: Reading problems

Herbie is in third grade and the lowest reading group, called the Apples. He is also reading *Charlotte's Web* because he likes spiders, but he gets very low scores on his phonics worksheets. After a visit with the reading supervisor, Herbie is promoted. This still does not solve his buddy's problem about being stuck in a group with a dumb name. So, they get the girls to change the name to Spiders.

Analysis: This is written at the right level for children who are ready for chapter books but who may lack confidence because of placement in a low-level reading group. Herbie can read, if he is motivated, and phonics does not motivate him. His buddy can read hard words that he sees a lot, like those on the fast-food menu. These two problems can be identified early enough that the boys' reading problems do not become learning problems.

Herbie feels good when Miss Pinkham promotes him out of the Apples. This may be believable, but the sentence that summarizes Herbie's emotions is a bit heavy-handed. "She thought he was capable, and THAT made Herbie feel warm inside." It seems inconsistent with the introspection of a boy who is crushed when the two spiders he named get cleaned to death. The story is funny and is just the beginning of the adventures of Herbie for eager new readers looking for a series.

■ Lewis, Marjorie. *Wrongway Applebaum.* Illus. by Margot Apple. Coward, 1984. 63pp. (0-698-20610-X) Reading Level: Grades 3–5. (BCCB F85)
Disability: Learning disabilities

Stanley Applebaum is in fifth grade when his awkwardness and inability to tell left from right conflict with his family's interest in baseball. His grandmother Sophie agrees to sponsor a fifth-grade team if Stanley is on the roster and she can be the coach. Though practice helps Stanley gain running coordination and speed, he gets confused about plays and even runs the bases backward once he hits the last pitch in the ninth inning of the big game. The umpire calls the game a tie and "Wrongway" Applebaum considers track as a more suitable sport for his combination of strengths and weaknesses.

Analysis: Stanley's parents and grandmother try to help him with skills and his self-image, but there is little diagnostic assistance. He is feeling left out at school and considers himself a disappointment to his father even before the team is formed. When the rest of his team is doing so well, Stanley assumes he will mess up the championship game in front of everyone in town. Stanley's determination and persistence pay off in an unexpected way. Since the humorous elements and upper-grade squabbles ring true, Stanley's little adventure will please many.

■ Lowry, Lois. *Us and Uncle Fraud.* Houghton, 1984. 148pp. (LB 0-395-36833-X) Reading Level: Grades 4–6.
Disability: Learning disabilities

Uncle Claude comes for a visit, and Louise learns not to judge him only on his extravagant stories and promises or on his poor spelling and rootless wandering. *See full annotation* Chapter 4: Orthopedic/Neurological Impairments.

■ Marek, Margot. *Different, Not Dumb.* Illus. by photos by Barbara Kirk,. Franklin Watts, 1985. 30pp. (0-531-04722-9) Reading Level: Grades 2–3. (BCCB Ap85)
Disability: Learning disabilities

Mike is in a second-grade class, and math is no problem, but reading is quite difficult. His learning disability is addressed once he begins a special class for remedial reading exercises. Mike makes progress and stops worrying that his classmates may think he is "dumb." One day a box falls off a truck, and it has a long word on it that Jeff cannot read. Mike sounds the word out the way he has learned in his special class, so the "EXPLOSIVES" are removed by police officers. Mike is a hero and gets complimented as a good reader.

Analysis: This story is more encouraging than realistic, despite the use of photographs that dramatize the action. The black-and-white images are in focus and do have enough contrast to please lower-grade readers. The big problem about this type of plot is that Mike's achievement in reading and accommodations made for his learning differences are overshadowed by the hero ending. Becoming an overachiever with unrealistic expectations is a real hazard for disabled people, and this book may not help dispell the message.

■ Mark, Jan. **Handles.** Atheneum, 1985. 162pp. (0-689-31140-0) Reading Level: Grades 6–9. (BCCB My85)
Disability: Learning disabilities

Erica is bored when she first goes to stay with her aunt in the country. She likes motorcycles, and when she meets the owner of the local cycle repair shop, she helps him out. Auntie Joan is upset by Erica's apparent shift in behavior that stems from hanging around the shop, and Erica is sent home.

Analysis: A well-written story line and clearly developed characterizations highlight this book. Erica's cousin, Robert, has limited understanding, yet his portrayal is sympathetic. The title derives from nicknames that are given to people once a level of camaraderie is established. This is a strong selection for middle school collections.

■ Martin, Ann M. **Yours Turly, Shirley.** Holiday, 1988. 133pp. (0-8234-0719-5) Reading Level: Grades 3–5. (BCCB D88)
Disability: Dyslexia

Shirley is starting fourth grade with a lot of insecurities about performing well. She clowns around to cover her inadequacies and is offered special help by Mr. Bradley, her new teacher. Shirley also has an 8-year-old adopted sister, named Jackie. Shirley enjoys having Jackie to love and help, but when the Vietnamese child makes so much progress in her studies that she catches up to Shirley, jealousy divides the sisters. Shirley's dyslexia does not hamper her artistic efforts, and she is unanimously elected class artist. Shirley is able to mend her relationship with Jackie.

Analysis: Sibling conflict complicated by a cognitive disability is presented by the author of *Inside Out*. This time the point of view is that of the affected child, and the children are sisters instead of brothers. Mr. Bradley tries to help Shirley understand that she is not stupid but lacks the skills necessary to compensate for her dyslexia. It is nice to have this portrayal of a war-zone adoptee who establishes a loving relationship to balance against the characterizations in this volume that focus on adjustment disorders and emotional scars.

Light humor adds to Martin's sympathetic treatment of a disability in a warm, family story.

■ Nelson, Theresa. **And One for All.** Orchard, 1989. 182pp. (LB 0-531-08404-3) Reading Level: Grades 7–12. (BCCB Ja89)
Disability: Learning disabilities; Hearing impairment

In 1968, Geraldine Brennan is traveling by bus to Washington and recalling the year 1966, when she started seventh grade, and her brother, Wing, was a senior in high school. Wing had always had trouble reading, but his poor grades got him suspended from the school basketball team. Because of the draft and the Vietnam war, Wing's best friend, Sam, and his classmates were focused on getting into college.

Geraldine had usually tagged along with her older brother and Sam, but she introduced her kindergarten-age brother and his pal to the haunts and stories of an old carved-on tree. She had no close friends her own age but enjoyed reading and did well in her Catholic school. She was comforted when Sam tried to tutor Wing so he could get back on the team. Sam also talked Wing into apologizing after a fight by challenging the boy to face his midterm exams and not be a quitter.

The day Wing turned 18, he enlisted in the Marines. Sam blamed it on Wing's impulsive reaction to freezing up on an English test and his senseless anger at being suspended from the team. Wing showed Geraldine that he did get passing marks for the semester but that he had already been sworn in and so reported for Marine training at Paris Island, South Carolina.

Geraldine's family found Sam in town, handing out protest flyers about the war. Sam was regarded as a traitor, and when he graduated with honors, Geraldine's family made excuses not to attend. Wing visited home, had a fight with Sam, and came home drunk.

Letters exchanged between July 1967 and April 1968 trace Wing's experiences in the armed services and the changes in life at home. Two

Marine officers came with news of Wing's death in a mortar attack at Khe Sanh. It was Easter break, so Geraldine went to Sam's house to tell him that Wing was dead, but Sam had returned to Washington for a peace march.

Geraldine ends her memories and her bus trip, arriving in Washington. She sees all the people involved in the peace march and understands that, far from being traitors, they are motivated by love for "Our Boys." Sam is organizing a candlelight demonstration, and Geraldine senses the little glows and cries for peace that are coming up around her as she tries to tell Sam about Wing. The marchers leave without Sam, but he tells Geraldine, "It doesn't matter. We were too late, anyhow."

Sam drives Geraldine back home, telling her about his father, who died in World War II, and the man's last talk with Wing. Sam had tried to convince Wing to desert and go to Canada with some contacts Sam had made. After the funeral, Sam and Geraldine and the little boys carve new initials in the old tree.

Analysis: This outstanding novel presents a vivid picture of a particularly difficult phase of Geraldine's life and the history of the United States. Wing's reading problems were so pronounced that even when he was a preschooler, Geraldine thought it must just be harder for her big brother's brown eyes to let light in. Wing is shown being tutored by his mother in second grade, focusing on achievement in sports instead of academics, and being impatient with Sam's explanations. When his parents become upset over his deception, Wing explains that grades are simply not more important to him than the basketball team is.

Wing is volatile and gets especially angry if anyone implies that he is dumb. He is motivated to go through boot camp and places in the top 10 percent of his group. His letters contain spelling and grammatical errors that are consistent with his characterization. He is pleased to receive a promotion in the field to lance corporal. After Wing's funeral, his little brother overhears another veteran bragging how "he made it back safe from Nam because he passed some smartness test and got a desk job. Just like he didn't think Wing was smart or something."

This is a well-rounded portrayal, and the story includes perceptive observations on the way Wing limits his own options and misreads his best friend's concern about Wing going into combat. The father's hearing impairment is a result of one of two injuries that earned him purple hearts in World War II. The disability is a minor aspect of the story, but the medals are an important parallel for Sam's characterization. His mother was sent a purple heart after Sam's father was killed, by mistake, "on this bridge that was scheduled to get blown up just then." This novel is highly recommended for a broad audience.

■ Peck, Richard. *Remembering the Good Times.* Delacorte, 1985.
181pp. (0-385-29396-8) Reading Level: Grades 7–10.
Disability: Hyperactivity

Trav feels an affinity for Skeeter, the bully, because they are both troubled
boys. *See full annotation* Chapter 6: Emotional Disturbances.

■ Rylant, Cynthia. *Children of Christmas: Stories for the Season.* Illus. by
S. D. Schindler. Orchard, 1987. 38pp. (LB 0-531-08306-3) Reading Level:
Grades 5—12. (SLJ 087)
Disability: Learning disabilities

Several short stories about the Holiday Season focus on characters with
bleak expectations for their community's celebration. The final tale is
about Mae, a bag lady who has forgotten what a home has to offer. She
wanders the streets with three dogs, only one of which has a name. She is
hungry and ill and too confused to locate the "sick place," where she has
been helped in the past. She finds a door that opens into the staff area of
a library. She makes a feast of the leftover treats and goes through the
"book place" to an area that has inviting seats and colors.

> There are pictures all over the walls, full of color, and things hang down
> from the ceiling, paper things on strings. Mae wants one but she can't reach
> it. There is a Christmas tree in the room. Mae knows what that is but she
> is afraid of them. Marty and the dogs sniff at it, though. . . .
> On the floor next to her cushion, Mae sees a basket of books. They are
> very shiny and at first she is afraid. But finally she picks one up.
> It is a book about a snowman, Mae can see that. It is easy for her since
> it has no words, only pictures.

After viewing the adventures of a flying snowman and a boy, Mae picks
up the next book: "It has words, so Mae nearly puts it back down, but the
pictures of the woman and the baby and all the stars in the sky hold her
and Mae turns the pages slowly, curled into her cushion, and breathes
deep and quiet, and looks."

Mae leaves early the next morning to avoid being found, but the streets
are empty and shops are closed: "Mae walks with her dogs, her stomach
full, not sick anymore. A sign in a store window says 'Merry Christmas!'
But Mae sees only a snowman flying and a woman and a baby and stars
and stars and stars."

Analysis: This highly praised collection will cause readers to reflect on
what they have and what they take for granted. Since Mae is only one of
several portrayals of emotionally and physically needy people in this

book, the author avoids stereotypic sentimentality. Mae's limitations are well realized and, although present tense is used throughout the book, it is especially fitting in this piece.

Everyone in town knows Mae: "She's been on the streets for years. She has wild eyes and nobody trusts her. She wears stinking clothes and nobody approaches her. She enjoys garbage cans and nobody likes her." Mae might be mentally retarded and/or emotionally disturbed, but she is definitely functioning at a different mental capacity level than some of the other homeless characters referred to in this story. The large, picture book format will fool readers so the book should be introduced as several different read-alouds, or as a book talk with a socially astute audience.

■ Rylant, Cynthia. *Every Living Thing.* Illus. by S. D. Schindler. Bradbury, 1985. 81pp. (0-02-777200-4) Reading Level: Grades 5–7.
Disability: Learning disabilities

Twelve short stories feature animals and the impact they make on the lives of children and adults with different physical and emotional needs. *See full annotation* Chapter 7: Various Disabilities.

■ Shreve, Susan. *The Flunking of Joshua T. Bates.* Knopf, 1984. 82pp. (LB 0-394-96380-6) Reading Level: Grades 2–4. (BCCB My84)
Disability: Reading problems

The day before school starts, Joshua gets the bad news that he will have to repeat third grade. He makes threats, bears insults, lies to people, and gets into a fight during the first weeks of school. He also gets to know his new teacher, helps the other third-graders with their work, and practices his reading in the hopes of being promoted to fourth grade before the year ends.

During a baseball game challenge between the third and fourth grade, Joshua's best friend loyally misses the ball, allowing Joshua's class to win. Joshua reads aloud at his teacher's house and learns that the woman's husband has just moved out and is getting a divorce. By October, Joshua is ready to take a placement test, and his score is high enough to let him join the fourth-graders. He feels "homesick" at the change, and his teacher admits that she feels the same.

Analysis: Mother explains to Joshua that "he was one of those slow-developing children who hadn't learned to read well enough to keep up with his classmates." Joshua doubts it is "a question of eye-hand coordination," because he was the best baseball player in his class. Joshua is convinced that his teacher last year hated boys and that other fellows who read worse than he were promoted.

In one academic quarter, Joshua gets all A's and gains the reading skills he needs to succeed along with his age-mates. Perhaps the busy summer at the beach provided the maturation time he needed, and perhaps daily attention from his teacher in her home fostered the self-confidence Joshua lacked. Joshua asks his teacher to make him "as smart as anyone in the fourth grade." She responds, "You are already smart, Joshua. What you need to do is learn to read."

The illustrations are natural and expressive pencil drawings in black and white. The straightforward title is paired on the color cover with a straight-on view of Joshua, arms crossed in a determined attitude. The text includes terms like "brain-damaged" and "formerly retarded" in Joshua's musings. For children who have learning disabilities that cannot be dispelled so readily as Joshua's, this book may be limited to vicarious wish fulfillment. For children who are tempted to judge their classmates, and their teachers, this may be a humorous lesson in recognizing others as people first.

■ Swenson, Judy Harris, and Roxane Brown Kunz. *Learning My Way: I'm a Winner!* Illus. by Lynne J. Kratoska. Dillon, 1986. 39pp. (LB 0-87518-351-4) Reading Level: Grades 3–6. (SLJ Mr87)
Disability: Hyperactivity; Learning disabilities

"I wonder if other kids think much about how they learn. I know I do. But, I have to. It usually takes me longer to learn than others in my class, because I am learning disabled.

"My Grandpa John, who lives with us, doesn't understand my learning problems. He always says, 'Dan Peters, I think you're the smartest, quickest kid ever. Don't you forget it!' "

Dan continues to recount how his learning differences caused him to repeat third grade, and how anxiety and stress made him too ill to attend fourth-grade classes. After his doctor, teacher, principal, and school psychologist ask questions and use tests to determine why Dan has so much trouble in school, he is given special help during classmates' reading time.

"Dan, everyone's different. People learn in many ways. You're a smart boy, but you need to be taught in a special way because you have a learning disability. That means there's a gap between how smart you are and how fast you learn."

Mom's explanation and Dan's experiences introduce the terms hyperactive, cope, individual educational plan (IEP), appropriate behavior, resource room, resource teacher, attitude, depressed, occupational and physical therapy, speech therapist, and special education. Dan asks why he is unlike his brother or his sister, who is in a gifted class. Grandpa points out that the 8-year-old sister may be able to read much better than Dan but that Dan has greater artistic skill.

"Everyone can learn to compensate. To compensate means that you use other ways to get what you want. If you can't learn addition and subtraction facts, you can learn to use a calculator. If you can't read a story, then listen to a tape of the story. If your handwriting isn't good, you can learn to use a typewriter or computer."

Dan concludes by summarizing, "My life is mostly positive and good. I have a family who loves me, teachers who care, my own special program at school, and some good friends. I know my learning difference is not my fault. I'm not dumb. I try hard and I do many things well. I'm not a quitter. I believe I'm a winner!"

Analysis: An expository piece on learning disability as it is experienced by one 11-year-old boy is illustrated on every other spread. Part of the Understanding Pressure series, it is called "An Up Book"—supposedly for its upbeat overview of a complex disability. Dan's emotions and interactions with adults are clearly expressed.

Dan's relations with other students are only alluded to: "Once in a while I still feel nervous at school. Sometimes the bigger kids act like bullies. They call me names and make fun of me because I go to my resource class. They don't understand how my special class helps me. It's quiet, and I always know what is expected. I feel smart in my resource class."

This "fiction" has slight story line and characterization and can be properly classified with nonfiction books on special education. If considered fiction, it can supplement upper-grade collections that include DeClement's *6th Grade Can Really Kill You* and Hansen's *Yellow Bird and Me.*

■ Thomas, Ruth. **The Runaways.** Lippincott, 1989. 297pp. (LB 0-397-32345-X) Reading Level: Grades 6–8. (KR 15 My89)
Disability: Learning disabilities

Julia is 11 years old and has a learning disability. In addition, she is a tattletale and often at odds with schoolmates like Nathan, a black boy with poor vision. The two children cut school and find an envelope of money in an empty house. They show their treasure off on the playground, then run away from home to avoid an interview with the principal or condemning parents.

Argumentative, clumsy, and unprepared, the children eventually build cooperation and enough new skills to acquire food, shelter, and clothing.

For weeks, they pay their way and get by, until clumsy Julia breaks her leg. Nathan goes for help, which requires that the children reveal their whereabouts.

Analysis: This story shifts from unsympathetic descriptions of the little outcasts to humorous accounts of their misadventures. Julia has her good points and a talent for attending to details that often escape imaginative Nathan. Nathan is nearsighted but has a store of ideas from the many books he has read. This romp through the English countryside is harmless to them, and it certainly will not bother middle-grade readers either.

■ Van Raven, Pieter. *Harpoon Island.* Scribner, 1989. 150pp. (0-684-19092-3) Reading Level: Grades 7–10. (BCCB Ja90)
Disability: Developmental disability; speech and language impairments

Newcomers to a small coastal community in the days before World War I, Frank Barnes and his son Brady meet and stand up to prejudice. Brady is small and slow for a 10-year-old, and talking seems beyond his capability. Ethnic suspicions are fueled by the local preacher, but when Brady spots a German sub, the community is willing to accept the Barneses, despite their German background. Frank refuses to accept their hypocritical shift of opinion, because it is based on a violent act.

Analysis: Brady's skills have always been impaired, but his inability to communicate verbally may also be due to trama from his mother's recent desertion of the family. Because the author uses Brady's limitations to create dramatic tension, little can be learned about muteness or developmental disorders from this plot. The social interrelationships are more clearly developed. Collections that need additional historical novels for middle school readers may find this useful.

■ Voigt, Cynthia. *Dicey's Song.* Atheneum, 1982. 204pp. (0-689-30944-9) Reading Level: Grades 5–8. (BCCB O82)
Disability: Learning disabilities

The four Tillerman children live with their grandmother because their mother is in a psychiatric institution. Gram begins adoption procedures because the children were abandoned and had to make their way to Maryland on their own. The children adjust to life with Gram but have various problems in school. Eight-year-old Maybeth has been placed in third grade but has so much difficulty reading that she needs special tutoring. Her musical talents are encouraged though by 13-year-old Dicey's earning the money for Maybeth's piano lessons.

Seven-year-old Sammy is well behaved but withdrawn in class; he then comes home with evidence of being in fights with teasing classmates. James is a gifted student, and at 10 years old designs a remedial reading program for Maybeth to help her with phonetics. Dicey is aloof and hardly knows how to accept her grandmother's care or Mina's and Jeff's offer of friendship. The adoption is finalized just before word comes that the children's mother is dying.

Gram and Dicey are with the unconscious woman when she dies, they arrange to have her cremated, and they bury her ashes under a tree on family property.

Analysis: A sequel to *Homecoming,* this Newbery Award–winning novel is an in-depth portrait of a unique family in transition. Dicey is changing physically as well as emotionally, as the drive and self-reliance that helped the children find their grandmother soften so that Dicey can reach out to friends and find new ways to express affection for her siblings and ill mother. Dicey always insists that Maybeth is shy and slow, not retarded. James is able to work with Maybeth on reading problems that teachers could not or would not address. The author is so skillful in presenting these complex characters that she maintains credibility and will engage the sympathy of many readers.

■ Voigt, Cynthia. **Seventeen Against the Dealer.** Atheneum, 1989. 192pp. (0-689-31497-3) Reading Level: Grades 8–12.
Disability: Learning disabilities

Dicey Tillerman is as goal oriented and focused on being her family's main source of support as ever. Instead of pursuing a college career like her boyfriend, Jeff, and her brother, James, Dicey wants to make boats. She never has done that type of work but collects tools, books, and a boat order from a wealthy man who is impressed with her independent drive and confidence. The money advanced for the boat has to go toward materials and new tools after a break-in at the shop.

When Dicey takes a boring job refinishing boats for her landlord so that she can retain her commissioned job, a drifter, Cisco Kidd, exchanges work with her for a place to stay. He is talkative and disarming, and he waxes philosophical when Dicey loses her order for the boat she has been busy designing. Dicey has been so absorbed in her plans, financial struggles, and taxing labor on the boats that she loses contact with Jeff and is unaware of her grandmother's health problems. Maybeth and Sammy are high school students with their own academic concerns, but they help Dicey become alert to Gram's need for a doctor. Cisco helps out at the shop while Dicey nurses Gram's pneumonia.

Dicey trys to cash a check to pay Cisco, even though salary was not part of their original agreement. The teller explains that no money is available, because Cisco had earlier presented a countersigned check for over $800 in cash. His explanation at the bank seemed plausible, and Dicey cannot recover the amount because she had not written "for deposit only" on the check. She analyzes this setback and decides to paint the last boats and use the barn on the Tillerman property as a shop. She also decides to put more time into her personal relationships while pursuing her new goal, which is to use the lumber and her design to build a boat for herself.

Analysis: Dicey is a complex character, introduced to readers through the Newbery Medal winner, *Homecoming.* Besides continuing the characterizations from other stories about the Tillerman family and friends, this title examines how valuable traits like determination and independence can undermine a person's success if they are out of balance with interpersonal needs.

Dicey never discovers the secret that Cisco is "Kidding" her with as he gains her trust; the name is a cover-up because he is her father. Not only does the charming vagabond drift into and out of her life again, but he takes money he believes he has a right to. Before he decides to keep her money, he assures her that she cannot claim bankruptcy because she never earned enough to live on. Dicey's obtuseness and the glaring mistake of endorsing a check without designating an account for deposit stretch the plot's believability.

Maybeth may have trouble both expressing herself and achieving in academic pursuits, but she has lots of opportunity to date, and she likes one fellow in particular. This subplot demonstrates a pleasant social aspect of Maybeth's character. Also, Dicey values her sister's competencies and thinks Maybeth's limitations have given her a special ability to deal with failure, "like marsh grass, being there, being what she was, high tide or low tide, winter cold or summer warmth, being who she was."

When Maybeth is pleased to be doing the best that she can and Gram gives up some of her feisty drive, Dicey gains insight. There is some idealization of the characters who have physical and mental challenges in their life, but Dicey has the same admiration for Sammy's tennis scholarship endeavors and James's decision to audit a difficult course. It is clear that these portrayals underline Voigt's themes regarding the value of work, pleasure from effort, and the importance of realistic expectations to complement ambition.

■ Webb, Sharon. *Earth Song.* Atheneum, 1983. 190pp. (0-689-30964-3)
Reading Level: Grades 7–10. (BCCB Mr83)
Disability: Down's syndrome

Human beings have colonized space and learned to prevent death. In the settlement of Renascence, children are educated and encouraged to develop their creativity until they are 16. Then they must choose between continuing to use their creative abilities and sacrificing them to attain immortality. David and Liss are lovers, but David decides to be a composer and face mortality. Liss leaves for her home, pregnant with David's child, and marries Kurt.

Kurt and Liss become aware of Silvio's efforts to control people's minds. Children with Down's syndrome are found to possess a psychic power that defeats Silvio.

Analysis: MacCaffrey's *To Ride Pegasus* and *The Ship Who Sang* create scenarios where special needs people serve society in a future existence. This novel is not as successful as those titles because there is not enough foreshadowing of either Silvio's fatal flaw or the significance of the children with Down's syndrome. For younger science fiction fans, this is an additional choice.

■ Weiman, Eiveen. *It Takes Brains.* Atheneum, 1982. 276pp. (0-689-30896-5) Reading Level: Grades 5–6.
Disability: Learning disabilities

Barbara Brainard cannot avoid or live up to her nickname of "Brains" until an enrichment class helps her concentrate, become less impulsive, and assume responsibility for her own learning contracts. *See full annotation* Chapter 4: Orthopedic/Neurological Impairments.

■ Wolff, Virginia Euwer. *Probably Still Nick Swansen.* Holt, 1988. 144pp. (0-8050-0701-6) Reading Level: Grades 6–10. (BCCB D88)
Disability: Learning disabilities

Nick Swansen is 16 and attends high school classes in Room 19. Other special education students there include two "Downs kids," some "hyperactives," and students whose troubles with reading and spelling keep them out of regular classes. Nick does not know if there is a word for his placement in special ed, and when students leave Room 19 because they are "Going Up," he ponders "Where is Up?" During Shana's "Going Up" party, he wonders what it means when she stands next to him for the class picture, takes his hand, and makes a private joke. He decides it probably means that she likes him, maybe enough to still be friendly after she leaves Room 19.

Nick wishes he could ask his sister some of his questions, because she used to explain things, or she asked him questions that he had not thought of yet. But this sister, who would have been 19, drowned when she was 10. Nick has learned from his teacher to make lists to help him decide what to do, so he plans out the extra work required at the greenhouse to pay for prom tickets and to purchase a rose corsage for Shana. He counts the days until the prom, and he practices dancing. Nick's and Shana's parents have a long telephone conversation to plan transportation to the prom and to the marina for a boat ride and breakfast.

When Nick takes Shana's corsage over to her house before the date, he meets her mother. The woman is so preoccupied with a magazine layout of her newly remodeled kitchen that Nick decides she is "a hyperactive," so he is as patient with her as he has learned to be with his classmates. He notices that the rest of the house is in disarray and that the sewing area that Shana works on her dress in is dark and crowded. At home, Nick's father helps him dress in his tux and talks about "rites of passage." Then, Nick's mother takes pleasure in driving him to the prom.

While waiting and waiting for Shana, Nick tries to keep warm by dancing in the shadowed parking lot. Two men come out and talk about their children, the prom queen and twin boys who will be graduating. One of the boys has trouble with math but was not put in with the "droolers," because "It'd be a handicap. You put a kid with the droolers, he'll end up a drooler."

Nick goes straight home after the dance. The next morning his parents find out that Shana said Nick had canceled the date, and Nick broods about Shana's lie to get out of dating a drooler.

Nick avoids his school locker to be sure not to meet Shana, then runs laps at the track. A girl with short hair waves at him, and he waves back. She comes closer, and Nick is surprised to see it is Shana with her long hair chopped off. Shana wants to tell Nick what happened and that she wears his corsage all the time at home. Nick listens to Shana's account of the evening her dress was not ready and of the resultant confusion with her mother and conflict with her father that made her lie about Nick's canceling the date.

Shana admits that she is grounded and will get yelled at for staying to talk to Nick, then exclaims, "It's my minimal brain dysfunction that's got me into all this mess." Nick is interested in this phrase that probably describes the reason for his placement in Room 19. Nick is noncommittal when Shana asks if she can run with him the next day.

The next day, Nick run laps with Shana. She knows a word for the way Nick can remember everything about amphibians—savant. Shana wonders if Nick's interest in amphibians that can breathe in and out of the water is connected to the tragedy of his sister's death. Nick gets dizzy thinking about that suggestion. He thinks of Shana, his sister Dianne, liking amphibians, his mother's Beethoven music, and his father's promised driving lesson. Nick dismisses some of the worries he has been preoccupied with by deciding, "Probably he was still Nick Swansen."

Analysis: This consistent character study of a teenage boy in special education classes since the fourth grade includes credible portrayals that help to distinguish his minimal brain dysfunction from other learning disabilities and from mental retardation. As in *First Your Penny,* the point of view is that of a protagonist whose perceptions are constrained by his unique differences. Nick is very literal, yet has difficulty integrating all his observations, knowledge, and memories.

Subtle differences in social interactions are obvious to Nick, but, though he ponders their significance, he does not know the right terms to express his confusion, questions, or concern. When he overhears the fathers at the prom, he follows their conversation and marvels that they "knew so much, they didn't stop between words and look in their brains for the right ones; they had the right ones in their mouths already." Nick has good reasoning skills when he is not under pressure, and Shana does too, but she was overwhelmed by the chaos at her house the night of the prom. After hearing Shana's account, Nick reflects, "Somewhere in that big old house she could've found a dress to wear. She didn't have to make up a lie and make me wait for hours and hours like a drooler while everybody danced to the music." When Shana introduces the phrase "minimal brain dysfunction," Nick is excited to have an appropriate label for his problems.

This novel is highly recommended and has been given the International Reading Association Award. The hardback's cover is an evocative view of Nick as he bends some blinds just enough to look out of a window. The separated and shadowed portrait this presents is a symbol for Nick's unsentimental narration and challenged characterization. Browsers may assume it is a suspense novel, so the paperback cover of Nick as he waits in his tux may prove more inviting to series and teen romance readers.

MENTAL RETARDATION

■ Alcock, Vivien. *The Monster Garden.* Delacorte, 1988. 134pp. (0-440-50053-2) Reading Level: Grades 5–8.
Disability: Mental retardation

Frankie blackmails her brother into sharing a tissue sample he has secreted away from their father's lab. Lightning strikes, and she accidentally creates a baby monster. She enlists the help of a classmate, the girl's older brother, another girlfriend, and the gardener. They create a hutch in the backyard, where "Monnie" develops at an alarming rate.

The disloyal classmate tells Frankie's father about the monster in the garden, and Frankie makes a desperate trek to the shore with Monnie. Monnie runs off toward the ocean, and Frankie is found and taken home. Her father and brothers and housekeeper act solicitous, and Frankie learns that her friends have created a cover story for her. Frankie returns to the shore occasionally and, as a teenager, gets to see Monnie again—grown into a beautiful creature of the sea.

Analysis: Alcock's skillful writing creates a sympathetic character in this inventive fantasy. The gardener, Alf, is the only adult in on Frankie's secret, and his limited understanding of the source of the tissue sample leads him to assume that Monnie is an exotic pet: "I like Alf. He is a slow, cheerful man who always wears a straw hat, summer or winter. He has one of those curved mouths like a child's drawing of a smile, and fingernails full of earth. He knows all about plants and animals, and they seem to know him, too, and brighten up when he's there. People say he is simple. I don't know. He can read the *Daily Mirror* and do the football pools and whistle like a robin. I don't believe he's as simple as they think."

Alf has dignity and a sensible approach to Frankie's desire to care for Monnie. When they have to invent a story for Frankie's father, Alf's contribution is a cryptic card that reads, "Dear Frankie, Get better. Your dad sees you can hav the rabit wot I told him about, you know, the one we made the hutch for—"

This excellent book includes the portrayal of a very capable man whose mental limitations enhance his bond with animals and children. Since Frankie's observations are genuine and are incorporated into the story line so well, some use of stereotypic attributes for Alf can be forgiven.

■ Brown, Kay. **Willy's Summer Dream.** Gulliver/Harcourt, 1989. 32pp. (0-15-200645-1) Reading Level: Grades 5–7. (BCCB 089)
Disability: Mental retardation

Willy lives in Brooklyn with his mother, whom he thinks of as "ole Bertha." His father does not even visit. At 14, Willy cannot read or write, and he assumes being retarded is why he has no friends and why his father avoids him. An older girl, named Kathleen, lives next door while visiting her aunt. She helps Willy study, and they become friends. Willy also makes friends with a boy he meets at Sag Harbor. Willy helps the younger boy avoid abuse by his caretaker. Willy gains confidence about his social abilities, though he still cannot read or write.

Analysis: This is not a well-written book, and the events do not unfold in a well-organized plot. The theme is nice, but it uses the stereotype of a dull, black adolescent male who is being reared by a poor but devoted mother. The title will not fill the need for portrayals of minority characters with impairments, but it does provide exposure to a sympathetic character's making the most of his limitations.

■ Carrick, Carol. **Stay Away from Simon!** Illus. by Donald Carrick. Clarion, 1985. 64pp. (0-89919-343-9) Reading Level: Grades 3–6. (BCCB N85)
Disability: Mental retardation

During the 1800s, in a village where the miller's son is taunted as "simple Simon," Lucy has several experiences that give her a more accepting attitude toward the retarded teenager. Her first interactions with Simon are colored by the rumor that Simon was responsible for a little boy's drowning. She has heard the townspeople say that Simon is "no more than an animal, like the big, dumb oxen he cared for." But Simon is clever enough to make toys for the children. He tries to join in the fun of a snow fight, then follows Lucy and her brother into a snowstorm. Lucy had been chanting a counting rhyme to Josiah, and though they hide from Simon, he finds them just when they realize they are lost and likely to freeze to death. Simon instructs Lucy to put Josiah "under" his clothing so the boy can be carried piggyback. They encounter Lucy's father, and Lucy is surprised that Simon knew to lead them toward their parents' land.

Lucy makes negative judgments about Simon's table manners and his preference to sleep in the barn. When her mother asks her to go into the barn to take out some cider, Lucy discloses her fear, blames Simon for their getting lost in the first place, and quotes a friend who says Simon is "the child of the devil." Lucy's parents provide information about Simon's family and the truth about the drowning, and Lucy has their model of acceptance to follow. When she takes out the cider, she is surprised by Simon's request that she "No go!" until he has recited the counting rhyme she had been teaching Josiah.

Analysis: This early chapter story has illustrations to help readers who are new to extended plots to understand the action. The historical view both of retardation as a mark of the devil and of disabled people as outcasts to be suspicious of is clear. When the protagonist's preconceived ideas are challenged by acquainting herself with Simon, this becomes an important aspect of her character development. That Simon is shown in an active—even heroic—role offers a dramatic, perhaps too purposive, story, but one which is written well for its intended audience.

■ Crutcher, Chris. *The Crazy Horse Electric Game.* Greenwillow, 1987. 160pp. (0-688-06683-6) Reading Level: Grades 7–12.
Disability: Mental retardation

Jack graduates from One More Last Chance High School, where they call him Telephone Man. *See full annotation* Chapter 4: Orthopedic/Neurological Impairments.

■ Dubelaar, Thea. *Maria.* Trans. by Anthea Bell. Illus. by Mance Post. Morrow, 1982. 128pp. (0-688-01062-8) Reading Level: Grades 2–4. (BCCB A82)
Disability: Mental retardation

Maria stays with Mrs. Bloom, because her father is a ship's captain and her mother is in the hospital. Her older brother, Erik, is mentally retarded and has been placed in a home with other special needs boarders. He comes to Mrs. Bloom's on the weekend, which cheers Maria because she loves him very much. Maria gets to visit the zoo and her mother. She meets a new friend and makes the best of her run-ins with unfriendly, cross Mrs. Bloom. Papa's ship docks, and everyone reunites at home.
Analysis: This story is translated from the Dutch, and some social elements may seem odd to readers. Erik is an important member of the family, and only the circumstances of mother's illness force the children to be separated. The story's episodes are presented with adequate pace, but its repetitive structure makes the overall effect rather static.

■ Froelich, Margaret Walden. *Hide Crawford Quick.* Houghton, 1983. 168pp. (0-395-33884-0) Reading Level: Grades 5–8.
Disability: Mental retardation

During World War II, Gracie discovers that the slow girl at school can remember all the words of songs she hears on the radio, and she helps her take part in the school's Christmas program. *See full annotation* Chapter 4: Orthopedic/Neurological Impairments.

■ Hansen, Joyce. *Yellow Bird and Me.* Clarion, 1986. 155pp. (0-89919-335-8) Reading Level: Grades 4–6.
Disability: Mental retardation

Doris finds that classmates take part in joining her in defense of Yellow Bird, a sixth grader placed with special education students because he cannot read and goofs off in class. *See full annotation* Chapter 6: Learning Disabilities.

■ Hermes, Patricia. *Who Will Take Care of Me?* Harcourt, 1983. 99pp.
(0-15-296265-4) Reading Level: Grades 4–6. (BCCB MS83)
Disability: Mental retardation

Mark and his younger brother, Pete, were orphaned when their parents
were killed in an accident. Since then, they have lived with their grandmother on a farm. Once, Pete was taken to a special class, but he was
laughed at, and Mark had to come in to calm him. Grandmother has kept
Pete home with her all day ever since, and Mark has been responsible for
Pete's whereabouts because the 10-year-old has the mind of a 5-year-old
and often wanders off.

Grandmother uses a cane to get around, but then becomes so ill the first
month of summer vacation, that Mark cannot have any fun with the few
friends he has. Grandmother dies, and Aunt Agnes makes plans with the
doctor to place Pete in a special school. Mark knows his grandmother
wanted to keep Pete out of an institution, so he and Pete run away to the
family's lakeside cabin.

Pete loves animals, and he takes a duck with them when they run away.
They also get acquainted with a man named Eric, who feeds wild deer. The
boys work together to open the cabin, but when Mark wakes up, Pete is
gone. The doctor arrives to claim the boys and admits that Mark should
have been consulted about plans for Pete's care and education. Eric and
Mark search the far side of the lake, where deer hide during the day. Pete
has found an injured fawn, and the boys are returned to the cabin. Aunt
Agnes cares for the boys, and when school starts, Pete has his own interests for the first time. Mark realizes that Grandmother may have been too
protective of Pete, and he is ready to play with his school friends by the
end of the story, sure that Pete will be okay without him.

Analysis: This plot has good pace and reveals how overprotection of a
disabled child can hamper every member of the family. The boys have a
lively downhill ride at the beginning of the story that helps define Grandmother's loving concern for her boys. The suspense of searching for Pete
is also well constructed.

The cover shows a wide-eyed Pete, holding a duck in the foreground,
with his older brother watching in the distance. Descriptions of Mark's
impressions of institutional care and of Pete's negative experience in a
special class are dismissed by the doctor's explanations that things are
different now and that Pete's original class was one of many experimental
methods that educators were trying out.

Pete's communication style is consistent with his mental limitations.
Readers will appreciate that the boy has an interest in animals, can learn

to distinguish one duck from another when his brother cannot, and skill-fully carves figures once he is given an opportunity to learn to safely use a knife. This story is highly recommended as an enjoyable drama about a child who learns to compromise between protective and responsible pat-terns of interaction with his disabled brother.

■ Hill, Donna. *First Your Penny.* Atheneum, 1985. 207pp. (0-689-31093-5)
Reading Level: Grades 6–9. (BCCB Je85)
Disability: Mental retardation

Like other 16-year-olds, Richard Downing hates when his sister, Claire, uses his nickname "Dicky," and he struggles with his mother over how he should spend his time. Unlike other 16-year-olds, Richard does not attend school. In addition, his learning disability makes it difficult to do some of the jobs he is interested in trying. He pursues several types of employment, including work at a supermarket and a florist, but he cannot cope with reading and numbers. He gets frustrated with the babyish things in his room and removes them. When Claire explains to her escort, Hugh, that Richard has a mental age of about 7 in most areas, Richard overhears them. Hugh helps Richard get a job as a stockboy, but Mrs. Downing makes him quit. She feels Richard's behavior is getting to be too taxing, and a friend suggests that Richard be sent away for institutional care.

Richard has a friend named Pompeyo, who helps him forge a permis-sion slip for a lifeguarding course. After Richard admits this to his instruc-tor, the gentleman explains that a work program could find Richard a job he is suited for and give him training in it. Pompeyo is killed when his bike hits a car, and Richard learns his sister will be moving out of town. Richard tells people what he thinks, and this time Claire supports him so that Mrs. Downing calls for an appointment regarding the special work program.

Analysis: Because it is Richard who shares this story, it is a challenge for readers to piece together the reasons for people's behavior toward him. It is possible that readers will feel the same frustrations that Richard expresses until they gather enough details to understand his special needs.

This is a rewarding narrative that shows how protective love and too much help can limit a disabled person more than physical or mental impairments do. Richard wishes for independence, is at odds with his family members until they see that he needs that measure of self-reliance, and is highly motivated to have a job. This is an excellent portrayal to counter the pitiable, lower-class, mentally retarded stereotypes that fill minor roles in order to show another character's benevolence.

■ Hooks, William H. *A Flight of Dazzle Angels.* Macmillan, 1988. 176pp. (0-02-744430-9) Reading Level: Grades 7–10.
Disability: Mental retardation

In 1908, southern townfolk call Annie Earle's brother "feebleminded." *See full annotation* Chapter 4: Orthopedic/Neurological Impairments.

■ Hunt, Irene. *The Everlasting Hills.* Scribner, 1985. 192pp. (0-684-18340-4) Reading Level: Grades 6–8. (BCCB MS85)
Disability: Mental retardation; Arthritis; Heart disease

In the mountains of Colorado, Breck Tydings has a ranch, a daughter, Bethany, and a son, Jeremy. Breck has been harsh with Jeremy since an older brother died. Jeremy is slow, cannot read, and has trouble pronouncing certain sounds. When Jeremy is 12, Bethany falls in love with Adam, so the boy feels abandoned to Breck's cruelty. Jeremy runs away and spends a year with an old man named Ishmael.

Ishmael has a weak heart that requires medication. Jeremy helps the old man with chores and drives him to town. These new responsibilities help Jeremy build skills, and Ishmael encourages Jeremy to correct his speech. Breck demands that Jeremy come back to help on the Tydings's ranch, now that Bethany is ready to marry Adam and leave. Jeremy refuses and expresses the bitterness he feels toward Breck.

There is a deserted village that Ishmael wants to visit, though his health is failing. Jeremy locates a gravestone to help Ishmael remember his family name just before he dies. Breck visits Jeremy, who has inherited Ishmael's cabin, and they discuss Ishmael's wish to restore the village. Jeremy sees that his father's arthritis will make life alone, on the ranch too difficult once Bethany has her baby to tend to. When Jeremy tells Breck of the baby's birth, he also announces that he will be returning home with his "father."

Analysis: This story of overcoming limitations and low expectations can be recommended, though it depends on characterizations with narrow emotional range. Breck is so cold and abusive, Bethany is so good, and Jeremy is so bitter that the final reunion may seem melodramatic. While Jeremy is gaining physical and emotional strength under Ishmael's patient encouragement, readers will realize that the boy's fear of failing is more a handicap than his brain damage due to oxygen deprivation at birth.

The resentments between Breck and Jeremy are resolved once Jeremy's self-image has been built up to the point that he can call Breck "father" without mispronouncing it or feeling their old hatred. Perhaps Breck is more approachable because his own impaired physical abilities have given him insight about Jeremy, but it also seems that Breck sees Jeremy's improved skills as something a father can take pride in, whereas before, he had called Jeremy a "nothing." The author's writing skill can keep readers involved in the actions and interactions enough to accept sketchy motivations for such big changes between the main characters.

■ Laird, Elizabeth. *Loving Ben.* Delacorte, 1989. 183pp. (0-385-29810-2)
Reading Level: Grades 7–10. (BCCB 089)
Disability: Down's syndrome; Hydrocephalus

Anna is 12 when her mother gives birth to a baby boy at home and the boy is rushed to the hospital. The doctor tries to explain to Anna "in that stupid voice grown-ups never use to each other," but Anna's father makes it clear that "Your brother's not quite right . . . Dr. Randall thinks he may be handicapped." Father chooses the name Benedict, because it means "blessed," and when the baby comes home, Anna is glad her mother feels tender toward the boy: "I felt dreadfully afraid that she wouldn't love him. And if she didn't love Ben, perhaps she would stop loving me, too."

When Anna sees that "His head was far too big," it does not stop her from falling in love with Ben. "I don't care how handicapped you are. I'll always love you. I'll protect you and look after you."

For two years Anna tries to keep her home life and school life separate. Mom is often up at night with Ben, who has respiratory problems and a weak heart. The 9-year-old sister, Katy, feels ignored and sometimes lashes out. Anna knows that Ben is developmentally delayed but goes against her mother's advice to get him to play with some of Katy's old baby toys. Anna teaches Ben to kiss, and he is delighted to repeat the action. Katy expresses her jealousy of Ben, and Anna evaluates why she prefers to play with the little boy.

"I really did like Ben much better than her. But did that mean I actually preferred him to be handicapped? That would be twisted and selfish. Still, when I thought about it, I decided it was okay. It was best to love Ben just for himself. Wishing couldn't make him any better, but loving him would make him happy."

Wise Mrs. Chapman runs a corner newsstand and helps Anna sort out her feelings and reactions to classmates who see Ben. "People are only scared of handicaps because they're not used to them," the older woman says, and she encourages Anna to let her friends get to know and love Ben. Anna's former best friend visits Ben and is intrigued that he can learn and relate to people.

Anna develops a crush on Tony, whom she sees at the tennis courts, then is flattered when she thinks another boy from the church youth group wants to meet with her.

Katy and Anna get the flu, and Ben dies of complications from the virus. Debbie's probing questions help Anna verbalize her questions about Ben's handicap, life, death, and God. Katy regrets keeping her favorite toy away from Ben, and she places it in Ben's coffin. Strained relationships between Katy and Anna, and Mom and Dad have time to heal.

One day at work Anna meets a handicapped little girl. The little girl is named Jackie, and her mother explains that she is a Down's syndrome child. Anna teaches Jackie to brush her own hair and be more independent. Jackie's big brother turns out to be Tony. The handsome, spoiled young man shows his resentment about Jackie's birth and the way it disrupted his family. After showing Tony that Jackie could do much more if his mother did not protect her so much, Anna blurts out that her own brother, Ben, died.

Anna decides to introduce perfectionist Debbie to "impeccable" Tony. Anna hears that she has been missed at church by the fellow in the youth club.

Analysis: The emotional authenticity of this story is impressive, and its straightforward tone counters sentimentality. So much of Anna's story happens after Ben's death that the characterizations avoid the Victorian trap of "a blessed release" that edifies all concerned. The setting is 1980s England with tea, Princess Di, and spandex clothing, but there is an odd limbo to it, because other British terms and calling mother "Mum" have been changed to expressions familiar to readers in the United States. Perhaps English medical procedures of that decade are accurately represented, but they do not match the efforts that would have been made in the United States to avoid Ben's hydrocephalus from causing extreme brain damage and continued pressure on his developing skull. The cover shows Anna playing with her brother in profile and his oversized head is obvious, matching the honest tone of the story. Though this story seems awkwardly transplanted in time and location, its flaws are minor compared with the insights it can offer.

■ Levin, Betty. *Brother Moose.* Greenwillow, 1990. 213pp. (0-688-09266-7) Reading Level: Grades 5–8. (KR 1 My90; BCCB My90; HB S-090)
Disability: Mental retardation

Nell and Louisa are orphans, but they care for each other like sisters. Louisa, who is slow to understand things, is placed with abusive caretakers, and Nell is also "farmed-out" to help at the Fowlers. The Fowlers leave their farm to winter in Maine. Their hired man Joe, a Native American, helps Louisa and Nell seek shelter with Mrs. Fowler when danger threatens them in New Brunswick. With Joe's grandson, Peter, the four make a wilderness trek through Canada.

Analysis: An adventure story set in the nineteenth century, this provides a consistent portrayal of a child with limited mental abilities. The way Louisa is treated is accurate for the period, but the author sensitively reveals Joe's and Nell's concern for her. There is dignity in Joe's character as well. Glooskap stories, a moose's good example of survival, and the forging of this temporary family are just some of the rich story telling here. An outstanding choice.

■ Lipsyte, Robert. *Jock and Jill.* Harper & Row, 1982. 153pp. (LB 0-06-023899-2) Reading Level: Grades 7–10. (BCCB Ap82)
Disability: Mental retardation

Jock is set to play in championship baseball finals at Yankee Stadium when he falls in love with Jill. He hates learning that she uses drugs, and he questions the wisdom of use of his own pain-killer injections given by the team doctor. The tragic scene of small children tied to radiators in decrepit buildings while their mothers get piecework haunts Jock. He meets Hector and supports the young Puerto Rican's efforts to convince the mayor of New York to improve things. The team coach pushes his players to the big game.

Analysis: Social weight and credible characters make this novel stand out from most of the stories about maturity catching up to a high schooler. Jock loses another girlfriend and accommodates the needs of his retarded younger brother along the way. Audiences will find lots going on to keep them reading in this novel.

■ Martin, Ann M. *Inside Out.* Holiday, 1984. 160pp. (0-8234-0512-5) Reading Level: Grades 4–6. (BCCB My84)
Disability: Autism; Health impairment

Eleven-year-old Jonno and his sister, Lizzie, help out a lot at home with their 4-year-old brother, James. James is unable to speak or dress himself or do other things preschoolers learn. The Petersons have spent a lot of time going to doctors to find out why James acts as if other people do not exist, and they now know he has autism. A special school may have an opening for James, but it will be costly to send him there.

Jonno has two buddies at school and wonders why he and his friends seem "inside out" with their feelings showing, unlike the "cool" boys. Since the impassive boys constitute the "in" crowd, Jonno is lured into their teasing of an older boy, "Edweird," who has missed a lot of school and gained weight due to a health impairment. When James causes a scene at the playground and throws a destructive tantrum at home, Mrs. Peterson enrolls him in a half-day program. Teachers observe James at home, and they work on having him make eye contact and name family members in pictures. Jonno is excited by the small improvements he sees in James and is distressed to hear his parents discussing institutionalization as a possibility for James in the future. Jonno, Lizzie, and Pete plan a successful backyard carnival, and Jonno's donation of some of the profits to James's school is featured in the newspaper.

Analysis: Descriptions of life with someone as seriously disabled as James are hard to integrate in a plot, but here the episodes are presented from a loving brother's point of view. Honest perceptions and maturity beyond his 11 years mark Jonno's observations at times, but the embarrassment, anger, money worries, school dynamics, and loyalty his character experiences are on target. The concerns that Jonno has about his own social position and his brother's abnormal behavior are legitimate but sometimes intrude on the story line. It is hoped that readers may gain the same insight that Jonno does when he helps Edward and his mother avoid public ridicule, knowing how he felt when James was laughed at for removing his clothes at the playground. A misleading, comic-style cover may lack appeal for the readers most likely to respond to this unique family story.

■ Miller, Frances. *Aren't You the One Who . . . ?* Atheneum, 1983. 209pp. (0-689-30961-9) Reading Level: Grades 7–10. (BCCB Ap83)
Disability: Mental retardation; Deafness

Matt lives in Los Angeles with the police officer who investigated a murder charge that Matt has been cleared of. Because the highly publicized case concerned the death of his deaf sister, Matt is haunted by the likelihood that strangers will recognize his name. He is hurt when his hometown friend Gary admits that he believed the charges and destroyed all Matt's track awards and personal treasures.

Matt runs around his neighborhood to train and meets a motherless family of four kids. The oldest boy and Matt become friends, and the oldest sister, Meg, takes Matt out to the stables to help exercise the horses. At first, Matt, who grew up on a ranch in Idaho, pretends to be a novice rider, but Don sees through the pretense. Don is a slow learner in math and reading, and his foster careperson, "Aunt Cora," has insisted that he stay in school as long as he is a minor. After his eighteenth birthday, she will not get funds for his support and will make him move out.

Matt has trouble running track, and when he finally settles down to do his best, the coach accuses him of using drugs. Don is sure that he needs a job to avoid being sent to an institution for the rest of his life, and Meg and Matt try to help. Matt feels things are too tough to make a new start, and he plans to run away with Don. Don gets a live-in job as a vet's assistant on his own and moves his things from his abusive home. Matt stands up for Don but gets punched in the face and hurts his head on the wall.

Matt smoothes over the misunderstandings with his own new family that stem from his week of trying to work things out for Don. He also tells Meg he is sorry, gets her father to see how unfair it is to count on Meg to mother the rest of the family, and calls his friend Gary to mend that friendship with an invitation to visit during spring break.

Analysis: This story is recommended for most collections, because it has depth and consistent development of complex characters. Don's home life is harsh, yet he is sympathetic toward his friends' family problems. His skill with animals and with tasks that he can learn by repetition instead of written directions is accurate and consistent with the learning limitations Meg describes. The derogatory use of "dummy" and the brutality of Aunt Cora's boyfriend are flatly villainous, but Aunt Cora is allowed to show a flicker of love and pride in Don's achievement along with her weak capitulation to her boyfriend's demands.

Though Matt locates the same job earlier in the day, Don is able to read through the want ads on his own, and he interviews successfully without Matt's intervention. Matt and Meg are more than advocates for Don—they are touched by things he does for them as well. Since the three friends are allowed to learn about each other in believable episodes, small contrivances are easy to excuse.

The memories that Matt shares about his hearing-impaired sister are few, but telling. She learned to say his name aloud at age 3, attended public school, and enjoyed many activities before their parents died in a car accident. Matt's aversion to institutionalized care facilities caused him to run away with her, which inadvertently led to her murder. The same aversion caused him to put his relationship with his foster family, his coach, and Meg at risk when Don's eighteenth birthday became the deadline for independence. This biased view of special education facilities could have been tempered by other opinions without undermining Matt's motivation.

■ Mills, Claudia. *At the Back of the Woods.* Four Winds, 1982. 86pp. (0-590-07830-5) Reading Level: Grades 3–6. (SLJ Ja83)
Disability: Mental retardation; Emotional disturbance

Clarisse is 10 years old when Emily moves into town. Some of the girls who play in the woods across from Mrs. Spinelli, the witch's house, do not like Emily, but Clarisse is in awe of the newcomer's bravery. When a birthday party comes up, Inga, whose mother is under treatment for an emotional disturbance, brings a can opener, because it was the only thing available at home. Emily replaces her gift with Inga's and takes all the ridicule for the peculiar present.

One girl shares her father's magazines of nude photographs, and Clarisse is mortified, but Emily proves how casual she can be about nudity by jumping, naked, from a tree. Emily also surprises Clarisse by crossing the brook to touch Mrs. Spinelli's chicken coop, by defending Inga against cruel comments about her mother's return after electric shock therapy, and by taking Mrs. Spinelli's cat to prove it is not a witch's familiar. A hurricane drowns the cat, and Mrs. Spinelli sets out a notice that she has put a curse on the person responsible.

Clarisse sees Emily's self-confident ways decay and realizes that true courage comes from facing a known fear, not from some naive sense of invulnerability. The next summer, Clarisse and her parents go to visit her brother Davey, who was placed in special care because of mental retardation. Emily moves away before Clarisse returns.

Analysis: Clarisse tells a first-person account of maturing and gaining insight on other people's motivations and complexities. Emily is a memorable character for Clarisse, but readers will also understand that Inga has a special challenge that takes true bravery. One of the things Clarisse likes about Emily is the way she accepts Davey and plays with the little boy despite others' reactions to his mental retardation.

Davey's parents do not discuss sex or bathroom secrets with Clarisse, so it is possible that they are as guarded in what they say about Davey's condition and "new treatment" in Tulsa. This attitude is real enough, but it leads to Clarisse's confusion.

■ Miner, Jane Claypool. *She's My Sister: Having a Retarded Sister.* Illus. by Vista III Design. Crestwood, 1982. 63pp. (LB 0-89686-171-6) Reading Level: Grades 5–9.
Disability: Mental retardation

Sixteen-year-old Mary Lou is adjusting with little grace to the changes at home and school, now that her older sister, Judy, has returned after ten years in a special school for mentally handicapped children. To avoid having peers learn that Judy is her sister, Mary Lou makes plans to transfer to another school and live with her single aunt. That arrangement fails within the first week. Mary Lou returns home, where she surprises herself by being glad to see Judy, and she helps her mother more around the house.

When school starts, Mary Lou curtails her social life and worries about any brush with the "special kids" that might inform her friends that she has a retarded sister. When Judy is teased by two boys in the hall, Mary Lou watches long enough to decide she should interrupt and come to her sister's defense. The action ends with a hallway hug between the sisters.

Analysis: Classic aspects of Down's syndrome are used in a description of Judy, but the illustrations serve to simply present her with a very immature appearance. "Though Judy looks more normal than many of the other children in the school where she lived, she does look different. She is short, and her face is very round. Her eyes are different too. But the main thing is that Judy would never be very smart. She is 18 and has the mind of a 6-year-old."

The new special education classes on campus are referred to by one of Mary Lou's friends as "a whole load of retards." Once, at home, Mary Lou "wondered again what life must be like for Judy. Was it awful? She didn't think so, Judy usually seemed happy and cheerful." Readers of this book will still be wondering because of superficial characterizations of Judy and her family.

The writing is stilted, and an exchange between Mary Lou and Aunt Helen seems like stressed-out analysis instead of dialogue.

> "All you think about is yourself," Mary Lou answered. "You never think about me."
>
> "That's just the point," Helen answered. "I do think about you but I think about myself, too. Your mother never thinks about anyone but her children. I'm afraid you're really very spoiled, Mary Lou. And you only care how things look, not how they really are."

Reluctant readers may respond to this petulant protagonist and the uneven, fashion-ad style sketches that give clues about Mary Lou's interpersonal relations. Stronger titles in the Crisis series are available for curriculum support, and *Welcome Home Jellybean* or TV episodes of *Life Goes On* will be better discussion starters about mainstreaming in education.

■ Naylor, Phyllis Reynolds. *A String of Chances.* Atheneum, 1982. 244pp. (0-689-30935-X) Reading Level: Grades 7–9. (BCCB O82)
Disability: Mental retardation; Cerebral hemorrhage; Dementia

Evie is 16 when she goes to spend the summer with a pregnant cousin. Evie's parents always open their home to those in need. Evie's older sister, Rose, complains about the mentally retarded man, senile woman, and stroke victim currently at the house. But Evie is more upset by the idea of her enemy, Matt, staying in her room while she is away.

Evie and Donna Jean enjoy crafts and plan to start a shop called "The Cousins." When the baby is born, Donna Jean has a hard delivery at home, and the parents and Evie are devastated when the charming infant dies of "crib death."

Since Matt has been challenging Evie's faith, she talks to her father about her doubts after the baby's death. He is supportive instead of dogmatic in offering her his own beliefs. Evie, the boarders at her parents', and the family rally the spirits of Donna Jean and her husband. "The Cousins" is likely to be a reality, and if Evie and Matt are unmarried at age 30, they may consider making a match.

Analysis: Character development in this story is very effective. A death in the family and a crisis of faith are dealt with sensitively. The presence of people with special needs in Evie's home is not introduced merely to prove her father is a virtuous man. The people are fully integrated into the family's activities and concerns. Tolerance and self-understanding are ambitious themes to present to middle school readers, but Naylor does a skilled job of it.

■ Rabe, Bernice. **Where's Chimpy?** Illus. by photos by Diane Schmidt. Whitman, 1988. 32pp. (0-8075-8928-4) Reading Level: Grades PS–2. (BCCB O88)
Disability: Down's syndrome

It is Misty's bedtime, but she cannot get to sleep without her stuffed monkey companion, Chimpy. Daddy helps her recall all of the things she did during the day. They check all the locations in which Chimpy may have been mislaid, and often they find other toys, but no Chimpy. At last, Chimpy is found in the bathroom, one of the last places Misty was in while getting ready for bed.

Analysis: Rabe has created a picture book text that has less story line than *The Balancing Girl* but the same subtle approach to featuring a child with a specific impairment. Though the text does not mention that Misty is a child with Down's syndrome, the condition is specified in an author's note that describes how the story and its photographic illustrations evolved. At times, the illustrations are confusing, because Misty's memory of the day appears on one side of the spread, framed with a different color, but reproduced as clearly as the present action on the other side of the spread. If a visual convention from the movies could have been used to either blur or distinguish the flashback, the use of photographs would not have been problematic.

Just as children learn to recognize differences and to feel reassured by similarities between themselves and children featured, for example, on unnarrated "Sesame Street" segments, readers and read-aloud audiences of this book will gain casual exposure to a child with Down's syndrome.

■ Ruby, Lois. *Two Truths in My Pocket.* Viking, 1982. 137pp. (0-670-73724-0) Reading Level: Grades 7–10. (BCCB Je82)
Disability: Mental retardation; Geriatric impairment

Six short stories about growing up in Jewish families include two portrayals of females with physical impairments. Fifteen-year-old Tracy is featured in "Forgetting Me, Remember Me." Her father teases her as "Little Miss Super Jew," because she puts so much store in ceremonies such as her brother's upcoming bar mitzvah. She is minimally brain damaged but wants to take a role in the ceremony and intends to memorize all the passages for her own bat mitzvah.

The last selection, "Frail Bridge," enables 16-year-old Rochela to see her great-grandmother as someone other than a suffering invalid whose needs for weekly visits and medical attention cut into Rochela's social life. After she hears relatives recalling the woman's compassionate life, Rochela can grieve and accept her inheritance of Bubbie Yetta's wedding ring and pearls.

Analysis: Minor roles in long works and supportive characters in this type of short fiction often lack depth. However, this collection offers a unique focus on the Jewish experience and can supplement collections that hope to build intercultural understanding.

■ Rylant, Cynthia. *A Couple of Kooks and Other Stories About Love.* Orchard, 1990. 112pp. (LB 0-531-08500-7) Reading Level: Grades 8–12. (KR 15 Ag90; HB N-D90; BCCB N90)
Disability: Mental retardation

A collection of eight stories featuring assorted characters in loving relationships. "A Crush" tells of Ernie, a young man with mental retardation. He uses seed packet mementos from his mother to raise secret bouquets for Delores, the woman who runs a hardware store.

Analysis: Rylant presents well-crafted short stories around a theme of love triumphant. As in *Children of Christmas* and *Every Living Thing,* characters with disabilities are integrated in her skillful examinations of human nature. Ernie's seeds are his only tie to his mother, yet his sacrifice has rewards.

■ Slepian, Jan. *Risk n' Roses.* Putnam, 1990. 176pp. (0-399-22219-7)
Reading Level: Grades 5–7. (KR 15 J190; HB Ja-F91; BCCB N90)
Disability: Mental retardation

In the Bronx during 1948, tough, abused Jean plays pranks on Mr. Kaminsky and leads a club called The Dares. Skip Berman and her older
sister, Angela, move into the building across the street. Angela's mental
retardation is a source of conflict between Skip's parents, and Skip resents
the custodial role she must assume with Angela. Skip makes friends with
Mr. Kaminsky and learns how the Holocaust has taken many of his loved
ones and separated him from his wife.

Angela is given a cruel "dare" to complete before Jean will allow her
to join the club. Though Skip admires Jean in many ways and wishes there
were fewer rules in her own life, her conscience makes her resist Jean's
manipulations. Skip determines that her relationship with Angela is worth
the limits that caring for someone imposes on behavior.

Analysis: Slepian's period novel sensitively discloses various characters
and the stresses that motivate their actions. Mr. Kaminsky's anxiety and
grief and Jean's vindictive anger are shown realistically. Angela is a believable portrayal, and Skip's dilemma is one that still faces siblings of special
needs children. In a thoughtful novel for middle-grade readers, this author
once again incorporates a well-rounded description of how a disability can
affect the life of a person.

■ Smith, Lucia B. *A Special Kind of Sister.* Illus. by Chuck Hall. Holt, 1979.
24pp. (0-03-047121-4) Reading Level: Grades 2–3. (BCCB S79)
Disability: Mental retardation

Sarah is 7 and has a younger brother afflicted with mental retardation. He
gets attention she is jealous of. He embarrasses her in public. Her new
friend left as soon as he saw Andy, and Sarah worries about losing other
friends. Mom tries to help Sarah focus on the ways she is special too. "I
told my Mom that I was glad I wasn't Andy. She said, 'I'm glad that
you're you, too.'"

Analysis: The illustrations in this book are flat drawings of Sarah that
never show Andy's face. Since there are other titles in which the central
character is affected by the mental retardation of a sibling, this can be
considered a supplemental book useful for portraying the family stress
brought on by dealing with disabilities. It is older than most titles in this
volume but was not covered in the Baskin/Harris works. Since it is indexed in *A to Zoo,* it is annotated here to help with collection development
decisions.

■ Talbert, Marc. *Toby.* Dial, 1987. 168pp. (0-8037-0441-0) Reading Level: Grades 6–8. (BCCB D87)
Disability: Mental retardation; Neurological and speech impairments

Toby likes to curl up under the porch with his dog, where he overhears his mother being told that Toby urinated on the minister's son, Harold. It was in retaliation for weeks of persecution by the other fifth-grade boys, but Reverend Olsen would never believe his son is a hateful, bullying liar. Toby likes to visit "ol' lady Bertram." The December before, a stroke "slowed Mrs. Bertram down for a couple of months. But she seemed fine now—except that she believed that she was dead."

Toby's father, Paul, works at the slaughterhouse next to the school. Paul and Mary are affectionate parents, who defend Toby as a good boy, but their opinion carries little weight because Paul is "slow," and Mary speaks haltingly due to brain damage. After Toby dines out with his parents, his maternal grandparents, and the minister's family, Harold threatens Toby. He says he hates the "whole retarded family," then mentions Reverend Olsen's suggestion that Toby come live with Harold's family. Toby ducks under the porch in time to hear his grandparents discussing foster care for Toby. They say things that indicate Toby was born despite a vasectomy Paul had had at the insistence of Toby's grandparents.

Harold badgers Toby, steals things from Mrs. Bertram, starts a fight at school, and tells his father that Toby was the one who set up the hideout in the church basement for smoking and vile rock posters. Harold's stories are backed up by John, Pete, and the new girl, Robin. When Toby returns the stolen things to Mrs. Bertram, her son accuses Toby of being the thief. Harold's gang throws rocks at Toby's house, breaking windows and injuring Paul. Mr. Bertram helps Toby, his dog, and Paul to capture the vandals and make them admit what they did to Reverend Olsen.

Paul and Mary ask Toby if he might like to go live with Paul's parents, because "Ma-bee we aren' good enough pair-ants fer you." Toby replies that he would rather stay with his momma and poppa. "We can take care of each other." His mother turns down Toby's offer to get a job and to help more around the house. "You jes' wor-ray 'bout bean a boy. We'll wor-ray 'bout mon-aie."

Analysis: Toby's suffering through this unusual family story is the result of Harold's bullying and his jealousy. Only the principal shows insight about Toby's innocence and Harold's schemes to blame Toby for vandalism and brawls. Toby is cut off every time he tries to explain to adults what the real situation is. He lacks the ability to speak persuasively for himself, but it is unclear if he is emotionally disturbed (lots of fetal positions under the porch and a bed-wetting nightmare) or just over-whelmed by Harold's quick "explanations" that always shift guilt from the minister's son to the "retarded" family's boy.

Ironically, the terrible sequence of events is initiated by Reverend Olsen's guilt-ridden assistance to Mary—his injured high school flame—and her family. Harold focuses his alienated feelings and evident hatred of his father on the man's commitment to help "the re-turds." The more concern Reverend Olsen shows for Toby's family, the more Harold perse-cutes his classmate.

These motivations are subtle and require mature insight on the reader's part. Most of the characterizations seem shallow because Toby's enemies are so bad and his allies (wanted or not) are so good. Toby's impressions of his parents range from an analogy of his mother as a dented can of still-sweet-on-the-inside peaches to the hog-blood smell of his father after work. Their home life, playful affection, sexuality, and concern for Toby are nicely revealed.

The three disabled adults are in ineffectual positions in most scenes. This book shows that mental and neurological impairments can make fitting into a community difficult but need not undermine the fundamental love and care available in a home.

■ Teague, Sam. *The King of Hearts' Heart*. Little, Brown, 1987. 186pp. (0-316-83427-0) Reading Level: Grades 6–9. (BCCB D87)
Disability: Mental retardation; Multiple disabilities

Until age 4, next-door neighbors Billy and Harold were as alike as two playmates could be. Their accident on a tire swing changed that, because Billy fell into a coma for three weeks and suffered brain damage. "The day after Santa had dropped off Billy's toys, they were too old for him." By the time the boys are 13, their interests are so far apart that Harold resents the times his parents "volunteer" him to do things with Billy. The girl of Harold's dreams gets knocked down when Harold takes Billy skating, and although Harold is humiliated, eventually he and Kate become close. Kate has a severly disabled younger brother, named Mike.

Track takes up Harold's afternoons, but Billy is a constant presence in Harold's life. Kate invites both boys over to meet Mike, and Harold is surprised to see the child is very small and has to be tied into a wheelchair. Billy's reaction to news that Mike can't talk is:

> "Then what's he good for?" Billy asked.
> "He's good for me," Kate said, "just like you are good for Harold."

Mike hurts himself, and Harold and Billy are moved to see Kate's and her parents' routine efforts to comfort the screaming boy. Billy wonders if he will ever be like Mike, and Harold assures him to the contrary. Billy continues:

> "I won't never be like you, neither, will I, Harold?"
> "No, never," I answered.
> "Something to think about, huh?"
> "Something to think about."
> "Something not to think about, too, huh, Harold?"
> "Something not to think about, too," I answered.

When Kate's brother, Mike, dies, she comes to Harold, saying, "I wanted to talk to you because you'd understand." Harold recalls the day his dog died and how Billy made a necklace out of the pet's tag to comfort Harold. The two boys attend Mike's funeral.

Billy is coached in track by Harold and Kate, and he improves his performance by wearing an ankle weight. He qualifies for the state competition and then places second in an out-of-town race. Harold, his parents, Billy's parents, and Kate drive together to the International Summer Special Olympics Games. Billy stays with his teammates and becomes a popular leader among the special athletes. Billy is injured in his race but crosses the finish line. After the closing ceremonies, Harold meets Billy at the gate and takes his friend up to the winner's stand to present him with the prized dog tag medal.

Analysis: Teague's story of a friendship that survives adolescent strains includes very well realized characterizations. Harold's first-person account is in natural-sounding dialogue and male musings but has oddly ornate descriptive passages. Readers may wonder if the point of view has shifted to an older Harold using sage perception and dramatic rhetoric or whether the author is intruding with his own opinion. The subplots consisting of a romance with Kate, competition in track, and middle school peer pressure are carefully connected in each fast-paced scene.

Billy is consistently depicted, and his unique communication style and naive logic are revealed in engaging dialogue. Kate's relationship with Mike is less complex but still believable.

The adults are supportive of the boys' friendship, and Harold's parents present altruistic motives, ethical choices, and even financial options during the story, so Harold's maturation and sense of responsibility are never glossed over simply as innate goodness. Part of Harold's lesson in love is to be glad of Billy's independence so that both boys can take chances in new activities and new friendships without damaging their own relationship. This theme is also developed in *Commander Coatrack Returns,* when a girl Harold's age shifts from being the principal caregiver for her brother, and in *Who Will Take Care of Me?* when a boy and his brother make the same adjustment.

This is highly recommended because of the growth of all the characters and the many little insights that are included such as defeating nervous "butterflies" before running track, facing heroes or bullies, knowing how to lose, and experiencing a first kiss. The boys are comfortably scruffy too, with treatment of subjects like padded bras and wet beds worked into the right places in the story. Readers will respond to this book and to the big-hearted characters they meet here.

■ Thrasher, Crystal. *End of a Dark Road.* Atheneum, 1982. 228pp. (0-689-50250-8) Reading Level: Grades 6–8. (BCCB N82)
Disability: Mental retardation

During one of the years of the depression, Seeley is a 15-year-old sophomore in high school. Her bus driver, Mr. Avery, helps her solve some of her problems. Her friend Russell is shot by an abusive father. The brunt of everyone's joke is Peedle, a retarded boy whom Seeley tries to protect.

When Seeley's father dies, she is employed in Mr. and Mrs. Avery's store. By moving to town, Seeley and her brother plan to be able to attend better schools, and their mother can earn a living.

Analysis: This period story continues events after *The Dark Didn't Catch Me* and *Between Dark and Daylight.* Like Carrick's *Stay Away from Simon,* this title gives a historical view of attitudes regarding mental retardation. Seeley's characterization includes a model for acceptance that is mildly flawed by its irritating load of goodness. Recommended for vivid depiction of a particular place and time, it lacks the strength of story line that is found in the first two titles.

■ Truss, Jan. *Jasmin.* Atheneum, 1982. 196pp. (0-689-50228-1) Reading Level: Grades 5–7. (BCCB A82)
Disability: Mental retardation

Sixth-grader Jasmin Stalke is the oldest girl in a crowded family of nine. She fears that she will be held back in school and runs away from her responsibilities at home, into the Canadian wilderness. One of her brothers tries to follow her, but his efforts are complicated by mental retardation. Their parents assume the children are together, but Jasmin lives alone in a cave until the family is reunited.

Analysis: This suspenseful survival tale offers clear characterization. Jasmin's parents are loving, and her relationship with her mentally impaired sibling is warm. Descriptive passages sometimes layer adjectives and phrases in an awkward manner. Also, the slow pace and pat ending undermine this book's plot enough to make it a supplemental choice only.

■ Wright, Betty Ren. *My Sister Is Different.* Raintree, 1981. 31pp. (0-8172-1369-4) Reading Level: Grades 2–4. (BCCB Mr82)
Disability: Mental retardation

Carlo has a lot of resentment about being in charge of his sister, Terry. Terry is older but acts younger than Carlo due to mental retardation. Other children make fun of Terry, and Carlo sometimes finds it hard to follow his grandmother's advice to love his sister.

At Christmastime, the children go shopping and become separated. Terry has not followed Carlo's directions to the bathroom successfully, and he regrets not taking time to show her exactly. He remembers the good things about Terry and nearly bumps into her in his panicked search for his sister. Terry is complimented by the mother of a fussy baby for being so good at calming the child. When his resentment builds again, Carlo recalls when Terry got lost. He gives Terry a nice birthday card, and his grandmother indicates she is pleased with his loving heart.

Analysis: The book's illustrations are marginal, and the story presents an implied message that siblings should be able to love special needs children in every situation. Carlo's dislike for the caretaker role his family gives him is more realistic than the resolution presented in this story. If Carlo can gain parental approbation only by taking Terry everywhere he goes, and Terry can have social outlets only when Carlo is willing to share, the two will have an unhappy childhood.

SPEECH AND LANGUAGE IMPAIRMENTS

■ Adler, C. S. *Eddie's Blue-Winged Dragon.* Putnam, 1988. 144pp. (0-399-21535-2) Reading Level: Grades 4–6.
Disability: Speech impairment

Eddie thinks his speech is clear and that his teacher is just crabby, until a classmate honestly points out that he sometimes talks too fast for others to understand the words slurred by his cerebral palsy. *See full annotation* Chapter 4: Orthopedic/Neurological Impairments.

■ Crutcher, Chris. *The Crazy Horse Electric Game.* Greenwillow, 1987. 160pp. (0-688-06683-6) Reading Level: Grades 7–12.
Disability: Neurological disabilities; Speech impairment

Willie Weaver refuses to speak much after his accident, because brain damage makes it so hard for him to form the words. *See full annotation* Chapter 4: Orthopedic/Neurological Impairments.

■ Evernden, Margery. *The Kite Song.* Lothrop, 1984. 192pp. (0-688-01200-0) Reading Level: Grades 5–8.
Disability: Emotional disturbance; Amputation; Muteness

Amy attends a special school, because she cannot speak, but she learns to sign a poem to perform with her friend Jamie. *See full annotation* Chapter 6: Emotional Disturbances.

■ Hopkins, Lila. *Eating Crow.* Franklin Watts, 1988. 135pp. (0-531-10499-0) Reading Level: Grades 4–6.
Disability: Speech impairment

Croaker Douglas, a black boy, feels indebted to God and the local root woman, Miss Sophie, when his dog, Beauty, heals after a bobcat attack. Croaker torments the new white boy at school but is willing to "eat crow" once he finds out that the boy is mute instead of just too proud to talk. Zeke used to talk and was a "happy, good student" until he was in a plane crash that killed both his parents.

Zeke lives with his aunt and his gabby crow, Piccolo, a survivor of his father's last experiment. Croaker and Zeke become friends. One day, Bobby Broder shoots Piccolo with a shotgun. The boys climb up a water tower to rescue the injured bird. The bird falls, and Beauty runs off with it in her mouth. Croaker fears heights and the lightning storm that approaches but is calmed by Zeke's whispering "Don't be afraid, Croaker. Shhh, brother, shhh." Zeke and his friends find Piccolo recovering in the home of Miss Sophie.

Analysis: Zeke's teacher describes his trauma this way: "Ezekiel's body is defending him against something his mind cannot handle." Then she assures Croaker that "one of these days, when he really needs to, or wants to, Zeke will overcome his mutism." This makes a pretty contrived resolution seem scientific—after all, the teacher and the doctor said it would happen.

Soda, one of the classmates who helps rescue Piccolo from the water tower, stutters under stress. He is certain that Miss Sophie is responsible for Zeke's cure. Zeke's inability to speak is replaced by a stilted observation that Miss Sophie "is really a fine old woman who seems to know the rudiments of medical technique." Some may praise the story for its treatment of interracial friendship and the theme of kindness to animals, but overall it lacks style.

■ Klein, Norma. *My Life as a Body.* Knopf, 1987. 304pp. (LB 0-394-99051-X) Reading Level: Grades 9–12.
Disability: Speech and language impairments

Sam was hit by a car, so Augie tutors him until his problems with concentration and language clear up suddenly. *See full annotation* Chapter 4: Orthopedic/Neurological Impairments.

■ Levinson, Nancy Smiler. *Your Friend, Natalie Popper.* Lodestar, 1991. 128pp. (0-525-67307-5) Reading Level: Grades 5–7. (KR 15 D90; BCCB F91; SLJ Mr91)
Disability: Stuttering; Polio

In 1946, Natalie and Corinne attend Two Tall Pines Camp. Corinne has been to camp before, but it is a new experience for sixth-grade graduate Natalie. When Arlette and Corinne become swim buddies, Natalie feels abandoned. An informed naturalist named Gretchen, who stutters, becomes the brunt of Natalie's discomfort when they are thrown together. Marlys angers Natalie with anti-Semitic remarks and then is stricken with polio. Everyone is sent home.

Analysis: A crowded camp story, the period details provide some additional interest. Natalie learns that awkward Gretchen is worth getting to know and that her stutter is related to shyness. Marlys is offensive, but in a way gets her comeuppance because polio was the scourge of the era. Although well written and accurate in detailing an adolescent experience of the postwar years, this is not essential when budgets are limited. As an additional camp story, it is fine.

■ Levoy, Myron. *Pictures of Adam.* Harper & Row, 1986. 218pp. (LB 0-06-023829-1) Reading Level: Grades 6–9. (BCCB Ap86)
Disability: Speech impairment; Emotional disturbance

Adam is transferred from a special class to Lisa's science class. He is so shy and put upon by other students that Lisa feels sorry for him and tries to strike up a friendship. He insists that he comes from outer space and shows her both his ability to hold his breath underwater and a portion of his "space capsule." Lisa takes pictures of Adam's derelict home and family for a contest. Their simple life-style makes a big contrast with Lisa's lavish home. Lisa's mother dislikes Adam and argues with Lisa about the relationship.

Lisa finds out more about Adam when he disappears for a few days, then confronts him with his fantasy and helps him bury memories of his abusive father.

Analysis: Adam's behavior and delusions stem from being beaten with a chain by his father. Adam's history of violent behavior has apparently been addressed while he was in a class for special students. Once he is mainstreamed, he exhibits timid behavior and comforts himself with his fantasy about being an alien. Lisa's mother is drunk and/or depressed, so she overreacts to Adam's poor clothing, his stutter, and finding the teens (after they kissed) in Lisa's room.

When Lisa muses about Adam's emotional disturbance, she unknowingly summarizes the problem she is also having with her mother: "He LOOKED perfectly normal. But somewhere in all the delicate things that make up a brain, and a person, and a personality, there was this streak or scar, like on a photo negative. And you can't get it out, no matter how you try. Every time you make a print, it's still there. And the way the world is, it always happens to the pictures you love the most."

Recommended for most collections and for book talking because the cover makes Adam look so young it might not attract the right readers.

■ Namovicz, Gene Inyart. *To Talk in Time.* Four Winds, 1987. 156pp. (0-02-768170-X) Reading Level: Grades 5–8. (BCCB Je87)
Disability: Speech impairment

Luke grows up in a small island community, but he moves to the big city when he is 12. His family had hoped that Luke would be forced to speak, despite his paralyzing shyness, once they changed his environment. Luke returns to the island for vacation with his older brother, Paul. When it is learned that rabies may have been transmitted to a friendly stranger, Luke overcomes his shyness in order to find the traveler and determines "To Talk in Time."

Analysis: Luke speaks to the members of his family, so when outsiders perceive him as mute, it is an incorrect assumption. The emotional block that Luke deals with is called shyness; no withdrawal-causing trauma is blamed. Like the younger brother in *Prairie Songs,* Luke has supporters who feel he will talk, in time, if left to develop social skills at his own pace. But Luke's story depends too heavily on his extreme silence and sudden change, for heroic reasons, to be plausible. There are few novels that focus on the pain a character may experience due to difficulty in communication skills, so this may be an adventure worth stocking.

■ Sanders, Scott R. **Badman Ballad.** Bradbury, 1986. 241pp. (0-02-778230-1) Reading Level: Grades 7–9. (BCCB N86)
Disability: Muteness; Mental retardation; Short stature

In 1813, Ely searches for his brother on the Ohio Valley frontier. He is sent to capture a murderer by the townsfolk of Roma. The murdered man was a dwarf. Ely's companion is Lightfoot, a lawyer who has no knowledge of outdoor survival. The person they are seeking is a giant of a man who is mute and retarded. Ely falls in love with a French-Shawnee girl named Rain Hawk. She had been persecuted by the vicious dwarf until he was murdered.

Analysis: The theme of prejudice and its attendant societal viciousness toward anyone who is different is introduced here. With so many "outsider" characters and a slow-going plot, the story loses its intrigue, though. A gentle giant and a mean-spirited dwarf are stereotypic roles for characters with these disabilities. The murderer, though mute, must deal with the townspeople's accusations, so there is an original element to these portrayals.

■ Slepian, Jan. **The Night of the Bozos.** Dutton, 1983. 152pp. (0-525-44070-4) Reading Level: Grades K–3. (BCCB N83)
Disability: Stuttering

Thirteen-year-old George and his Uncle Hibbie meet a carnival worker named Lolly. She invites them to the fairgrounds, and later they come for dinner. George prefers music, junkyards, and his Uncle Hibbie's company to meeting people, and he is almost overwhelmed by the strangers and lively banter of carnival workers. When "the Bozo" wants to quit his job of taunting people into buying tries to dunk him in the tank, Uncle Hibbie is interested in the job. Hibbie feels that his stuttering will not be a problem if he is pretending to be someone else.

The annual clubhouse gala needs George to set up the lighting and sound equipment, but he must work without Hibbie, who is working successfully at the carnival. When George plays a tune, the manager and guests enjoy the impromptu performance. Lolly comes to George but runs away because she feels her parents care more for their trained animals than for her. She jumps from a boat in the middle of the lake, even though she cannot swim. George amplifies his personal encouraging message to her, and her screams enable her to be rescued. Lolly's father hires Hibbie to help with the animals, Lolly promises to see George when the carnival comes back next year, and George knows he will miss his uncle but can do things on his own now.

Analysis: George, at 13, is impressed by 14-year-old Lolly's outgoing ways and threatened by Hibbie's interest in trying something new. This highly recommended title has both style and perceptive dialogue. The way Lolly tries to get her parents' attention is believable, and the added flavor of carnival life will interest readers. The isolation and insecurities that affect George, Lolly, and Hibbie are part of well-rounded characterizations. Hibbie knows himself well enough to see that his stutter arises from self-consciousness. However, instead of a pat "cure," he realizes that he is capable of entertaining and communicating with people as himself—not just as Bozo.

■ Strachan, Ian. *The Flawed Glass.* Little, Brown, 1990. 204pp. (0-316-81813-5) Reading Level: Grades 6–8.
Disability: Speech impairment

Shona lacks good motor control and cannot speak, so Carl finds a way for Shona to use a computer to communicate. *See full annotation* Chapter 4: Orthopedic/Neurological Impairments.

■ Talbert, Marc. *Toby.* Dial, 1987. 168pp. (0-8037-0441-0) Reading Level: Grades 6–8.
Disability: Speech impairment

Toby's mother was in an accident during her high school days, which left her with mobility and speech problems. *See full annotation* Chapter 6: Mental Retardation.

■ Windsor, Patricia. *The Sandman's Eyes.* Delacorte, 1985. 271pp. (0-385-29381-X) Reading Level: Grades 7–10.
Disability: Speech and language impairments

Mickey cannot respond when he is accused of murder, then spends two years in a special school before he is released and finds the real murderer. *See full annotation* Chapter 6: Emotional Disturbances

■ Yolen, Jane. *Children of the Wolf.* Viking, 1984. 136pp. (0-670-21763-8) Reading Level: Grades 6–9. (BCCB Je84)
Disability: Language impairment

Mohandas is 14 and lives in an orphanage in India. He goes with the director, Mr. Welles, to a village that has two ghosts; he and Mr. Welles capture two girls that have been raised by wolves. One girl dies after the missionary gives Mohandas the task of taming Amala and Kamala. Mohandas's roommate, Rama, makes a jealous comment about all the time Mohandas spends with Kamala.

Kamala responds to Mohandas, speaking a few words and understanding directions. This is far from the stories of the jungle that he had hoped for or Mr. Welles's intention to convert her to Christianity. Rama's interest in Kamala, once she has learned some words and develops a figure, elicits another girl's retaliation. Kamala runs away and is rescued by Mohandas, but she stops speaking and regresses to animallike behavior. He goes to school in England and returns to find Kamala has died.

Analysis: Based on accounts from the 1920s, Yolen has created vivid scenes and credible interactions. The taunts by other children and the children's cruelty seem harsh, but because all the orphans have physical and emotional scars and their culture orients them to establishing a pecking order, their treatment of the "dog-girls" is believable. Mr. Welles considers the girls "miracles" at the beginning but dismisses Kamala after her use of simple language implies that she is mentally retarded and can never respond to his ideology. Mohandas shares insights about the relationships between language, thought, and memory.

This unusual historical fiction has an inviting cover that shows the two girls, naked, in in the wild and Mohandas's observing one's characteristic howl at the moon.

7

BOOKS DEALING WITH MULTIPLE/SEVERE AND VARIOUS DISABILITIES

This chapter contains titles classified in two sections: Multiple/Severe Disabilities and Various Disabilities.

Multiple/Severe Disabilities groups portrayals of complex impairments and genetic differences that affect one character.

Various Disabilities classifies portrayals of single characters with impairments that do not fall into the material in previous chapters (e.g., Cosmetic impairment) and portrayals of groups of four or more characters who each have distinct physical, mental, or emotional disabilities.

Short entries describe secondary characters discussed at length in a full annotation that has been classified in some other chapter. "See" references are noted.

MULTIPLE/SEVERE DISABILITIES

■ Dickinson, Peter. *Eva.* Delacorte, 1988. 219pp. (0-440-50129-6)
Reading Level: Grades 8–12. (KR 1 F89)
Disability: Health impairment; Emotional disturbance

Eva is 13 when she is injured so badly it should be fatal—but the ultimate transplant replicates her brain patterns and memory in the brain of a chimpanzee. Waking in the hospital, she is allowed to see herself and says, "Hi Kelly," to the body of an ape she had known. Eva grew up with her father's research reserve full of chimpanzees, and she is familiar with their animal behavior, so she also realizes that the dreams she has of the forest may be an inherited memory from her chimpanzee host. At first, Eva has the same adjustments to make as an amputee, because the chimpanzee body is so much shorter. She also has to learn to operate a portable speech synthesizer to communicate with humans. She hears another chimpanzee call out in fear at the hospital and ponders the ethics of the procedure she has undergone. Further attempts fail because the patients go insane, unable to integrate their human mind with their chimp body.

When Eva goes home to her parents, the expenses of the experimental procedure and public interest lead her to work with a troop of trained chimps on commercials. In the studio, she helps the director get the acting needed from the animals and meets the director's son. He campaigns to return to their native habitats the few animals that remain alive in the world. A location shoot in one of those wilderness remnants is Eva's opportunity to lead the troop to freedom. She is the alpha female of the troop for generations. Human apathy becomes so widespread that mass suicide is frequent and technological relics like Eva's synthesizer cannot be repaired or reproduced by the time Eva dies of old age.

Analysis: Outstanding futuristic invention by Dickinson never leaves psychological or physical adjustments out of the story. What physical disability could be greater than to lose your entire body? Eva has to accommodate every possible physical and sensory difference. She also spends a lot of time helping her mother deal with the identity conflict that results from the merger of human and ape. Eva wears a jumpsuit and uses the voice tool to communicate with her family and humans. However, she also likes to enter the ape enclosure "naked" and be groomed and accepted by the troop. Stunning fiction like this should be available everywhere, and the beautiful cover with human eyes in closeup with tree silhouettes is a grabber.

■ Doherty, Berlie. *Granny Was a Buffer Girl.* Orchard, 1988. 160pp. (LB 0-531-08354-3) Reading Level: Grades 6–10. (BCCB Mr88)
Disability: Multiple disabilities; Mental retardation

Jess is ready to leave England for a year of university study in France. Her farewell party may be embarrassing, especially because her boyfriend will be exposed to her extended family's oral histories—the traditional entertainment at such a gathering. Granny was a buffer girl who felt like Cinderella when the owner's son singled her out at a company dance. Other family reminiscences include a troubled marriage and Jess's interactions with a disoriented, mentally retarded man she originally feared.

Jess's own story is that her seriously disabled brother wanted a baby sister, and so her parents had taken the chance and the additional responsibility of having another child. She always loved to be with him, even when she saw that people at the park reacted to his special needs in a negative way. All the stories teach lessons of love that help Jess face the upcoming separation.

Analysis: Outstanding writing, accurate historical details, and moving emotional content make this an excellent choice for collections. Like Rylant's short works, each story has resonance and emotional veracity. Jess's brother is sweet but not wimpy in dealing with his vulnerabilities. The family can seem indulgent, but the motivation is clearly lovingly supportive, not guilt ridden or ultragood. Winner of the Carnegie Award, this is a highly recommended title.

■ Ethridge, Kenneth E. *Viola, Furgy, Bobbi and Me.* Holiday, 1988. 160pp. (0-8234-0746-2) Reading Level: Grades 5–9. (KR 15 F89)
Disability: Orthopedic impairment

Steve tells of the year he did yard work for Viola and saved her from her villainous daughters. His friend Furgy got thrown out of the house by an alcoholic father just in time to move in with Viola after a lawyer protected the old woman's independence. Bobbie is the pretty girlfriend that rounds out the rescue after Viola breaks her hip.

Analysis: Viola is a Detroit Tigers fan and a friendly little lady, but she went wrong as a mother. Her daughters pull a "Hush, Hush, Sweet Charlotte" routine, hiding glasses and messing around with Viola's walker. Money is the goal, and placement in a nursing home is the tragedy that is avoided by intervening teens. Slang diction dates it.

■ Laird, Elizabeth. *Loving Ben.* Delacorte, 1989. 183pp. (0-385-29810-2) Reading Level: Grades 7–10.
Disability: Hydrocephalus

Anna enjoys caring for her baby brother, Ben, and helps him learn as much as he can despite his birth defects and poor health. *See full annotation* Chapter 6: Mental Retardation.

■ McNair, Joseph. *Commander Coatrack Returns.* Houghton, 1989. 188pp. (0-395-48295-X) Reading Level: Grades 6–9. (1 KR Ap89)
Disability: Multiple disabilities; Emotional disturbance; Mental retardation

Lisa is 13 when things change at her house; she blames it on her parents' psychologist, whom she has never met. Her mother is a real estate salesperson, and her father evaluates peanut butter and experimental crops. When her 5-year-old brother, Cody, was born with serious birth defects due to a drug his mother had taken, the family relied on Lisa to care for the boy every afternoon. There was domestic help, but Lisa had also taken care of her parents because their guilt sometimes pushed them into "a really bad depression."

Once the adults start therapy, they take over household chores and enroll Cody in special education classes at the hospital. Lisa feels at loose ends, with so much time to be a kid now, and wants to play old games with Cody and his private spaceship made out of the family coatrack. Instead, her mother occupies Cody with reinforcement activities that the teacher at the hospital has assigned.

At school, Lisa's best friend is a fierce feminist who dyes her hair and dresses as uniquely as possible. The new boy at school captures Lisa's attention when he pretends to be other people so as to be able to deal with stressful situations. At first, Lisa thinks it is brave of him to talk back to the school bully that way. Then she enjoys the witty exchanges she can have if she acts along with Robert. She visits Robert and finds out that his parents and a military background have pressured him into playing with alternate identities. Sometimes Robert talks about himself in the third person, and when he speaks for himself it is usually to complain about his parents.

Lisa sees that her parents are trying to make improvements in their "family unit." Cody is growing, and Lisa admits that perhaps he would have been able to learn more even sooner if the family had been in better balance.

Lisa's mother helps her daughter see that Robert's imagination and game playing are appealing to Lisa because they resemble Cody's. Lisa had found someone else to create a ritual of pretend with after Cody's schooling gave her free time she was unaccustomed to. The doctor describes Lisa's parents' actions as a flip-flop that went from placing too many demands on their seventh-grader to excluding her from all her usual activities and roles.

Lisa is invited to join her parents in counseling and in making family decisions. She also enjoys being known at school as the friend of the two most interesting individuals on campus.

Analysis: Cody's special needs require several operations that have put financial stress on the family. Though his internal organs are corrected, his appearance and inability to speak are evident differences, and in public places Lisa is aggressive toward "rude" strangers. Her mother reprimands

Lisa and in the final chapters shares a lot of hand-me-down insights. This is a bit heavy, but it is integrated with humorous asides from Lisa, her girlfriend, and the amusing bits with the coatrack.

Robert's withdrawal into his fantasy personalities is pieced together from Lisa's experiences and conversations with Robert and his mother. Present-tense accounts lend immediacy and help pull readers over some lumpy places in the plot. This is an excellent choice for exposure to several emotional disturbances, counseling, behavior modification, and a hopeful instead of an ultrasweet impression of a severely disabled child who is greatly loved.

■ Mayne, William. *Gideon Ahoy!* Delacorte, 1989. 155pp. (0-440-50126-1) Reading Level: Grades 5–10. (BCCB F89)
Disability: Deafness; Language impairment; Mental retardation

Twelve-year-old Eva interprets her older brother Gideon's experiences and the unique way he perceives life due to the deafness and mental retardation that resulted from a childhood illness. Language and sense of time are the biggest contrasts between Gideon and the world around him. Eva thinks her whirlwind toddler siblings, Mercury and Tansy, are closer to Gideon in many ways because the twins have a secret communication language as well.

Grandpa Catt, Eva, and Mum do what they can to deal with new developments as Gideon gets a job on a canal boat, injures his hand, loses his job, runs away, and nearly dies from fumes near a kiln. After being in a coma that agonizes the family, Gideon revives—his hearing restored. There is good news that the canal boat job is still available if Dad leaves his open-sea sailing to captain a boat with Gideon as his crew.

Analysis: More than a story, this is a challenging experience in reading. Mayne's creative use of language includes Gideon's limited expressions for pleasure ("Dththth"), distress ("Rauh"), and hunger ("Hyagh"). When Eva is sharing something from Gideon's experience, she uses his present-tense-only viewpoint. Even her impressions of family uproar are condensed in a way that makes reading difficult but that enhances the communication of experience and feeling. Because it is difficult to understand what goes on in Gideon's family, persistent readers earn their insights on how difficult it is for Gideon to deal with his disabilities.

When Gideon is confused or hurt, he is given sympathy without coddling. When outsiders are judgmental, the family has plenty of loving tolerance to balance it. Most details, like Grandpa Catt's building with bricks that melt, add to the firm setting and rich characterizations, but the plot turn of Gideon's restored hearing seems redundant. With Dad home from long voyages and a family business to run, could sounds and the confusing convolutions of language really make life better for Gideon? That aside, the book is outstanding and recommended for children who can handle inventive writing.

■ Sallis, Susan. **Secret Places of the Stairs.** Harper & Row, 1984. 151pp. (LB 0-06-025142-5) Reading Level: Grades 7–10. (BCCB Ap84) *Disability:* Down's syndrome; Multiple disabilities; Emotional disturbance

Catherine is visiting with her best friend, Nadine, when their silliness gets out of hand in a market. Cass, as she is called, curls up in a shopping cart, musses her hair, sucks her thumb, and chews through a package of cheese before a woman comes up and exclaims, "Dearie! How did you know I needed cheese?" Mortified that "They thought you were mental!" and suspicious because a woman mistook her for some "nutter" she knew, Cass abandons her joke.

Cass is 17 and in college, but she splits her weekends between her father's farm and her mother's comfortable home in town. Her half-brother, age 10, wants to spend more time with Cass, but their mother seems to keep them apart, reveals that she would rather kill herself than let Cass trigger a second nervous breakdown, and accuses Cass of trying to break up the marriage. Cass had been alone with her father from the time she was 3, until he remarried and fathered twin girls. Now she feels excluded from both of the families and rebuffs her wealthy stepfather, pregnant stepmother, and the twins' grandmother.

Nadine urges Cass to make plans for a spring-break trip to Sweden. Their efforts are helped along by Gideon Jones, who seems attracted to Cass. When Cass refuses her stepfather's money for the trip and stays with the twins so her stepmother can go away and rest during break, Gideon stays to be with her. They go to a fair, but Gideon misinterprets Cass's verbal fencing and forces himself on her in an open field. She assumes he is motivated by guilt and fear that she was not on the pill when he tracks her down at the farm to propose marriage. She refuses the marriage proposal but enlists Gideon's help in locating information on a younger sister, named Deirdre, whose birth announcement has just been found. Since no death notice exists to substantiate her father's story that Deirdre died of pneumonia, Cass follows her intuition, and another contact with the lady from the market, to Worrall Hall, a hospital for the "terminally ill."

Pretending to be a raffle volunteer delivering a prize, Cass goes into

Deirdre's room but runs out in hysterics. Gideon catches up to her, calms her down, and explains that he already knew "that Deirdre is alive. You were right. I know that she is handicapped, and I know this hospital is for terminal cases." Cass returns with a gift but is ashamed of herself for not wanting to touch her sister. Once Deirdre becomes too ill for visitors, Gideon uses his asthma as a ruse to help Cass get in to the hall. Cass's father rushes from the farm to be with both his daughters, and their mother arrives just before Deirdre dies. Mother, Gideon, and Nadine help Cass talk out feelings to gain perspective on her two families and the stresses that her father and mother had covered over with secrets.

Analysis: Cass recalls the events that led her to discover that a sister, born 16 years ago, is still alive, in an institution, though no one ever told Cass about it. The portrayal incorporates clear descriptions of the family's "horror" at the sight of Deirdre's fetal position, lack of arms, and "mongoloid" features.

What is supposed to be a compassionate mystery of life, loss, and love often leans toward soap opera. Too much contrivance, such as Gideon's abiding love born of a glance, a bus ride, and some time at the fair, weakens the story for mature readers. On the other hand, Cass's clowning, giggling, obtuse wordplay, insecurity, judgmental bitterness, and sexual responses are recognizable adolescent traits. Until the secret of Deirdre's birth, Mother's mental illness, and Father's style of expressing love for his children are revealed, Cass cannot dismiss childhood guilt regarding her parents' split and her own resentment toward the stepparents and half-siblings who already care about her.

One of the problems Sallis's books pose for American audiences is the use of British slang, which slows conversation and introspection. Another flaw is the indiscriminant use of "mongoloid" to describe Deirdre's multiple disabilities and deformities. The author is much more sensitive to the mother's history of emotional disturbance and the self-pity she had to learn to deal with before starting a second family.

It is clear in this book that Deirdre was severely disabled yet loved by her mother, her health care providers, and a frequent visitor.

If a collection already includes *Why I'm Already Blue,* and for fans of Sallis's other special needs characters, this title can be a supplementary choice.

■ Teague, Sam. *The King of Hearts' Heart.* Little, Brown, 1987. 186pp. (0-316-83427-0) Reading Level: Grades 6–9.
Disability: Multiple disabilities

Kate's brother, Mike, has many special needs, but she loves him, and his death makes her turn to Harold for comfort. *See full annotation* Chapter 6: Mental Retardation.

■ Voigt, Cynthia. *Tree by Leaf.* Atheneum, 1988. 208pp. (0-689-31403-5) Reading Level: Grades 5–9. (BCCB Ap88)
Disability: Cosmetic impairment

Clothilde inherited the Maine peninsula where her mother set up house during World War I. When father left for the war, he was sure he would make a grand reappearance on a fine horse, and he flaunted his own father's advice. Now he is back, with such a disfigured face and uncertain self-image that he sleeps in the boathouse. Nate is lured back to the grandfather's privileged life-style, so 12-year-old Clothilde is left with most of the responsibilities and concern for her parents' continued estrangement.

Clothilde hears a voice of encouragement in the woods and appreciates her father's sketches of the wildlife. Their tentative relationship encourages Father to risk being rejected by Mother. There is a loving reunion between Clothilde's parents. Years later, Clothilde meets the stepchild of some fawning relative and decides to bequeath the peninsula to the forlorn girl.

Analysis: Setting and dialogue for this period piece are convincing, but the element of a "voice from beyond" that imparts wisdom to Clothilde becomes intrusive. The relationship between this sensitive girl and her disabled and disillusioned father is not rushed. He records his haunting memories of the war in some of his sketches as well as the restorative woodland scenes and studies. Clothilde observes that her mother has changed a lot by learning to survive hard times with neither a man nor wealth to rely on. The element of Mother's character that remains is love for her husband that was not based on the material comfort his family guaranteed her or the social regard his previously dashing appearance lent her.

■ Willey, Margaret. *The Bigger Book of Lydia.* Harper & Row, 1983. 256pp. (LB 0-06-026486-1) Reading Level: Grades 7–10.
Disability: Short stature

Lydia begins The Bigger Book when her father's death convinces her that small stature makes a person vulnerable. *See full annotation* Chapter 4: Health Problems.

VARIOUS DISABILITIES

■ Alcock, Vivien. *Travelers by Night.* Delacorte, 1985. 182pp. (LB 0-385-29406-9) Reading Level: Grades 4–6. (BCCB O85)
Disability: Cosmetic impairment; Cerebral hemorrhage

Belle and Charlie are cousins who have grown up as circus performers. To earn money, they dance and do magic in costume on the roads around the circus compound. Their secret efforts are to pay for surgery to correct a scar that Belle got from a high wire accident. Charlie was able to save her life, but the experience has undermined Belle's talent for acts that require a head for heights.

The circus closes, and an aunt arranges to keep Belle and Charlie in school while Belle's parents perform with an American troupe. Belle has a special affection for an old trainer and his elephant, Tessie. When the trainer suffers a stroke, Tessie is scheduled to be destroyed. Charlie and Belle execute a plan to take Tessie through the woods to a wild animal reserve. A group of runaways who live in the woods ambushes the children, but Tessie comes to protect Belle. One boy goes to the police and the newspaper with his story of an elephant in Yald Forest. By the time Charlie and Belle get Tessie to the reserve, public opinion has rallied to Tessie's defense, and they are all offered a place at the safari park.

Belle and Charlie arrive at their new school and make friends. Belle plans to study and work with animals, but she and Charlie do their old routines during school breaks. He hopes to establish circus-style performances, without animal acts, at a safari park someday.

Analysis: This adventure story offers consistent characterization of someone who has lost self-confidence as well as vanity in a foolish accident. Belle's talent and beauty could not protect her from a fall from the high wire when she was not supposed to go near the equipment. At first, Charlie supports her plans to restore her appearance, but by the end of their trek, he is encouraging her to pull back her hair and stop hiding the scar.

They spend all of their savings to get Tessie to a safe home, and Belle feels so good about her ability to handle the elephant that she focuses on a new life's goal instead.

This well-written tale for upper-elementary students includes a child's unpleasant reaction to the scar and an adult's insightful response.

At 12 years of age, the cousins have an odd mixture of innocence and maturity that may be explained by the unique environment of their upbringing. An even younger boy gives an artless description of stroke impairments that will benefit readers.

Accurate portrayals of adult and child reactions to impairments are part of what builds believability into the otherwise unlikely plot of this recommended title.

■ Asimov, Isaac, ed., Martin Greenberg, ed., and Charles Waugh, ed. *Young Mutants.* Harper & Row, 1984. 256pp. (LB 0-06-020157-6) Reading Level: Grades 6–10. (BCCB Mr84)
Disability: Various disabilities

Twelve different authors' short stories share the theme of genetic mutation, featuring children with a wide range of differences that are usually portrayed as beneficial adaptations. There are humor, suspense, eery invention, and heartfelt insight in the collection.

Analysis: This science fiction anthology introduces noted writers and a broad variety of tales. Each chapter has a short introduction, for example:

> "During childhood, days sometimes seem to last forever. But what would it be like if childhood lasted forever?"
>
> "Children often use their parents' behavior as a model for their own actions."
>
> "This is a story of a man receiving his future as a result of a boy's present."

From genetic tampering to a future psychologist's prescription of a friend for an incorrigible child to a man recovering from a heart attack to a boy who can write only in a lost language to communicate, this book has many special characterizations.

■ Brown, Irene Bennett. *Before the Lark.* Atheneum, 1982. 191pp. (0-689-30920-1) Reading Level: Grades 5–7. (BCCB Ja83)
Disability: Cosmetic impairment

In Kansas during 1888, Jocey convinces her grandmother to come to the farm Jocey's father deserted. Together they struggle to make the farm prosper. Jocey's mother died earlier, and Jocey is self-conscious about her harelip. Jocey is offered a free operation as a medical school demonstration. Her father comes to see her in the hospital.

Analysis: This historical novel features a winning protagonist, who allows her cosmetic impairment to isolate her but who proves she can accomplish what she determines to do. Her father lacks that kind of emotional strength and shows up at the end as a weak solution to Jocey's longing for his return. The free surgery to repair Jocey's lip is a bit pat, but this impairment is unusual in juvenile literature. The novel focuses on Jocey's strength of character more than the compassion of strangers. The book has good style and structure, but its uneven pace and contrived ending make it an additional selection.

■ Byars, Betsy. *A Blossom Promise.* Illus. by Jacqueline Rogers. Delacorte, 1987. 145pp. (0-385-29578-2) Reading Level: Grades 4–6. (BCCB N87)
Disability: Amputation; Emotional disturbance; Heart attack; Orthopedic impairment

Two weeks of rain postpone Junior's plans to spend the night in Mad Mary's cave. Junior's mother and older sister, Maggie, are part of a trick riding team out on the rodeo circuit for spring break, and Pap is in charge of his grandsons, Junior and Vern.

Vern Blossom and his best friend have built a raft, and the flooded river lined with spectators seems to offer the perfect opportunity for a one-mile voyage. When the raft capsizes, Pap is there to rescue the boys, but he suffers a heart attack. Junior desperately tries to waken Pap when Mary appears and orders Junior to call an ambulance. The Blossom family gathers to find out about Pap's recovery. Pap's big dog grieves and goes into a coma, and the Blossoms and Maggie's boyfriend, Richie, sneak the animal into Pap's hospital room. Pap stirs and places his hand on the dog's head, eliciting a response. Maggie doubts her mother's promise that this summer will be the last time the Blossoms travel with the rodeo before settling down, because she has heard it all before. Maggie promises to make her flighty mother's talk of opening a riding school a reality.

Analysis: The three Blossom children are busy as ever in this book, with each chapter looking in on their actions and memories from one location to another. Their exceptional friends are worth meeting. Maggies beau uses an artificial leg, is active and sensitive and in love. Mary fixes varmint stew, "can't sleep under a roof," and lives below the vultures, but she has dignity. Junior anticipates his visit with admiration: "Mary would be in front with her cane. He would be behind with his stick. It was amazing the way the forest and bushes seemed to part for Mary, like something out of the Bible."

Pap's rodeo days are gone, but his skill with a rope is still evident. The crisis of his heart attack is followed by uncertain days that give authenticity to this drama. Byars's skill at combining serious themes with humor and family feelings shines through.

■ Cohen, Barbara. *Roses.* Lothrop, 1984. 192pp. (0-688-02166-2) Reading Level: Grades 6–9. (BCCB My84)
Disability: Cosmetic impairment

Izzie is the adolescent narrator of a variation of *Beauty and the Beast.* Here, a wealthy and learned man runs a floral business. He is hideously scarred from a fire and has kept himself in social isolation for years. He hires Isabel, becomes her mentor, and is desolate when Izzie's father makes her quit her job. Izzie and her boyfriend visit the gentleman in the hospital. They persuade him to have plastic surgery. He accepts the fact that Izzie is in love and that he should return to society.

Analysis: There seems to be a lot of contrivance in the "The Beast's" reasons for avoiding surgery or society before this encounter, but other elements of characterization are good. Cohen is a skilled writer, and her dialogue is particularly strong.

■ Cormier, Robert. *The Bumblebee Flies Anyway.* Pantheon, 1983. 241pp. (LB 0-394-96120-X) Reading Level: Grades 7–10. (BCCB S83) *Disability:* Health impairment; Neurological impairment

At the Complex, experimental drug therapy from the "Handyman" often includes "merchandise" and "doodads" that would "scare the hell out of" Barney Snow if he thought about them in medical terms. Barney has no sense of taste or smell, Billy the Kidney defies orders to stay in his wheelchair, quiet Allie has tics and muscle spasms so that "when he did speak he stammered, the words emerging torturously in a shower of spit," and Mazzo is a quick-witted nasty person. All the others are being treated for terminal illnesses, but Barney is involved in different types of tests. Spotting a red sports car in the junkyard next door, Barney relives a dream/ memory of losing control of an MG and running into a girl.

Barney tries to stay uninformed and indifferent about the people at the Complex, but he meets Mazzo's twin sister, Cassie. She wants him to help reunite her family and Mazzo, who refuses to see them and has entered the experimental program in hopes of a quick death. To introduce the topic of Cassie, Barney breaks his rule about staying aloof from the other patients. Mazzo describes his athletic past and wishes he were killed in one of his daring close calls instead of wasting away plugged into equipment. Evidence of decay, Mazzo's plea, and anger "at whatever brings people to a point in their lives that they prefer dying to living" make Barney promise to help Mazzo "go out in a blaze of glory . . . . One big wild ride."

Barney takes a car apart and rebuilds its shell up in the attic of the Complex. Allie suggests that parts be moved in spare wheelchairs he had found. Allie and Billy stand guard to assist. When Barney tests the freight elevator to be sure they can use it in the plan, he stops at a fifth floor office. There he finds simulation equipment for his nightmare about the car accident. The memory suppression tests he volunteered for started at a hospice with a "screen" for his knowledge that he was dying. Barney tries to integrate information about his remission, details of his life from the doctor, and his unspoken love for Cassie. He tells Cassie about his fake car; she says the car is like a bumblebee that flies no matter how many laws of aerodynamics its design breaks.

Since Barney's experiments are over, the lab authorities arrange for his departure. He does not want to leave, because all his memories and friendships have to do with the Complex: "Barney felt as if he had been manufactured here, like some kind of Frankenstein's monster, but of pieces of tape and film, images printed on a screen, sounds burned into his ears."

Barney plans his last day and the flight of the Bumblebee. He gets a kiss from Cassie when she guesses that he built the Bumblebee for her brother. Barney tells Mazzo about the car, and the young men disconnect Mazzo's intravenous tubes so that he can walk up to the attic. Billy follows and watches them push the Bumblebee into position. On the roof, Barney changes his mind about going in the car and holds Mazzo's failing body so they can see its descent. As Mazzo dies, his twin sister feels his emotions and then her own reactions. The flight of the Bumblebee is Barney's comfort, and he replays it in his mind when everything around his death bed seems to be gray, sad, unsmiling faces.

Analysis: Relentless as the situation it portrays, this novel can grab readers with its dark cover of a transparent boy doubled over in pain. Mysteries abound, yet the setting is convincing. Pain, courage, compassion, fear, desperation, and even religious conviction are realized in the characterizations. Barney's last-minute revision of his suicide plan gives the tragedy resonance, for his defiance against the laws of nature does not force him to abandon what life he has left.

Billy and Allie keep pushing their limits and vicariously enjoy as much as they can. Mazzo's despairing death wish is transformed into a final physical challenge of positioning the Bumblebee for launch. There is nothing easy about this book, but junior and senior high school students deserve a go at such a well-written heartbreaker.

■ Cross, Gillian. *On the Edge.* Holiday, 1985. 170pp. (0-8234-0559-1)
Reading Level: Grades 5–8. (BCCB Jl85)
Disability: Amnesia; Emotional disturbance

Tug wakes with dim memories of a persistent woman named Hank but cannot recall anything else. Neither does he recognize the man and woman who say they are his parents. He knows the clothing and especially the running shoes are his, but his reflection seems wrong. The adult couple is treating him like a prisoner as well, so Tug's efforts to remember who he really is are hampered. He establishes a bit of trust and affection with the woman and thinks of her as "Ma." When he recognizes a famous news-woman as "Hank" and concludes that he is her son, Liam Shakespeare, who is being held for terrorist demands, Tug also learns that his captors belong to a group devoted to destroying the family as a social unit.

Poachers on nearby property include a girl named Jenny. She pieces together the mystery of Tug and his captors and is taken as a second hostage while attempting a rescue. The terrorist gives Tug the choice of turning to "Hank" for confirmation of his identity or running toward freedom before he is to be killed. Tug weighs both the arguments his captors have made against family ties and his limited memories of Hank and experiences with "Ma." He chooses to run. When Jenny sees "Ma" hesitate with the gun, she speaks about the love the woman is feeling. Tug hears a gunshot that hits "Ma" and shouts of encouragement from both women. He continues running.

Analysis: This suspense story, set in England, uses two viewpoints to reveal elements of mystery and intriguing characterizations. The plot has particular strength, never slighting the emotional conflicts of self-actualization and family interpersonal relationships that motivate the action. The terrorists reveal the ghosts that have driven them to hate their own family units and to be motivated toward violent social demands against being "brought up to please other people. Forced into jobs they don't like. Trained to conform to the million tiny rules that each family makes for itself."

The antisocial actions are clear-cut in their role in the story, but the author spends time exposing the roots of the characters' emotional disturbances. In recounting the various challenges that members of the movement set for themselves to prove devotion to the cause, "Ma" and the male leader reveal personal histories of child abuse and hatred for a father. These unresolved emotional disturbances lead to their actions and the questions that Tug withstands. "They were both staring at him. Fierce eyes. Mad eyes, thought Tug. Mad questions. Why should I play their games?" Tug rebuilds an identity from the exercise, tastes, or activities that give him pleasure and from imaginary admonitions from "Hank." Since some of the comforting moments come from "Ma," Tug ironically establishes a bit of family with the family-hating terrorists.

This well-written story will grab readers, and Tug's literal identity crisis will give them more to think about than a formula whodunit.

■ Dickinson, Peter. *Healer.* Delacorte, 1985. 184pp. (0-385-29372-0)
Reading Level: Grades 6–9.
Disability: Various disabilities

Many ill and disabled people come to the Foundation's Harmony Sessions to be healed by 10-year-old Pinkie Proudfoot. *See full annotation* Chapter 4: Orthopedic/Neurological Impairments.

■ Edwards, Page. *Scarface Joe.* Four Winds, 1984. 122pp. (0-590-07899-2) Reading Level: Grades 6–8. (BCCB MS84)
Disability: Cosmetic impairment

Joe enjoys little during his summer visit to Colorado. Then his cheek gets scarred during a freak accident in an abandoned mine. Joe's family returns home. Joe keeps his scar covered with a bandage for a long time. Finally, he meets a girl who convinces him to remove the gauze.
Analysis: The misleading title implies that Joe has been fully identified with this facial mark. If the novel had stronger characterization, readers could gain some insights about adjusting to change. As it is, Joe seems at first ultrasensitive, then too easily soothed by a persuasive girl's gentle, accepting touch on his scar.

■ Giff, Patricia Reilly. *Candy Corn Contest.* Illus. by Blanche Sims. Dell, 1984. 76pp. (paper 0-440-41072-X) Reading Level: Grades 2–4. (SLJ F85)
Disability: Enuresis; Learning disabilities

Second-grader Richard Best is going to host a sleepover, but one by one, his guests refuse to come if they have to be near Matthew, the classmate who smells like a baby who wet the bed. Until then, Richard enjoyed planning to share a prize jar of candy corn with Matthew, despite the struggle they would have earning guesses by reading pages in their library books. Richard becomes angry with Matthew because of the incurred social stigma yet is puzzled by his friend's news that he will be going out of town instead of attending the sleepover.

After Richard absentmindedly plays with the contest candy and eats three pieces, he sneaks into the classroom to revise the secret number on the bottom of the jar. Matthew comes in and convinces him to leave the number alone. Richard realizes that Matthew lied about going out of town in order to avoid problems at the sleepover, and he accepts his friend's offer of three replacement candy corn pieces. The boys make accommodations for Matthew's attendance at the sleepover, and Richard resists using the correct candy corn count that he saw earlier as his guess.
Analysis: Richard's feelings about his outcast friend, Matthew, rise and fall as social opinion aimed at Matthew rubs off on his friend. When the guests cancel out, Richard gets angry because his party is being ruined.

Then Richard makes Matthew the brunt of a jeering remark about germs and regrets the hurt he causes.

There is no exploration of the emotional or physical roots of Matthew's bed-wetting problem, but his mother suggests he use an alarm clock at the party for two nighttime trips to the bathroom. This is a reasonable step in the management of enuresis. The hygiene problems related to Matthew's enuresis are addressed when he resolves both to use the bubble bath that his reading teacher gave him for erasing her board and to bathe more often, as Richard suggests. This topic is difficult to deal with at a young child's level of understanding, but it is in the context of an engaging classroom story. The illustrations and slim format are fine for children who are in second grade themselves or just beyond beginning reading materials.

■ Herlihy, Dirlie. *Ludie's Song.* Dial, 1988. 224pp. (0-8037-0533-6) Reading Level: Grades 6–8. (BCCB 088) *Disability:* Cosmetic impairment

Martha goes to visit her Uncle Ray and Aunt Letta in rural Georgia some years after World War II. She is 13, and her ideas about racial equality are challenged when she gets to know an artistic black girl named Ludie and her brother, Chili. Several white boys accuse Martha of being a "nigger lover," and they threaten to rape her and lynch Chili. Martha helps defend Chili, tricks one of the perpetrators into confessing, and gains Uncle Ray as an ally in improving life for Ludie and her brother.

Analysis: Martha learns that her Uncle Lonnie got Ludie pregnant and then nearly burned the black girl to death in a fit of rage. The event disfigured Ludie, and Martha muses about the physical and emotional scars that do not hamper Ludy's artistic skill. Experience with violence against blacks and evidence of Ludie's artistic abilities cause Martha to reevaluate and dispel her racial bias. A lot happens in this novel, and many characters appear by description instead of development through scenes that reveal their traits. As historical fiction, this creates a vivid setting and presents a clear theme of individual worth over social prejudices.

■ Holland, Isabelle. *Perdita.* Little, Brown, 1983. 225pp. (0-316-37001-0) Reading Level: Grades 7–9. (BCCB 083) *Disability:* Amnesia

Perdita has lost her memory in an accident—she was found in a well. Nuns nurse the teenager back to health. She gets a job at a horse farm, where the owner is a handsome fellow with a stepsister named Nancy, who is terrified of her mother. Nancy works with Perdita on her show riding. Perdita gets past the owner's surly manner, and they fall in love. Perdita's memory returns, and she identifies her attacker and the murderer of her mother.

Analysis: This tale has been included in reading lists for students who need to be lured from comics to classics. It is definitely on the low end of the scale, contrived, stereotypical, and predictable. Holland's writing experience is what makes it a good transition title for adolescents who have not developed leisure reading habits and desire soapy plots.

■ Howe, James. *A Night Without Stars.* Atheneum, 1983. 178pp. (0689-30957-0) Reading Level: Grades 4–7.
Disability: Cosmetic impairment

Maria Tirone meets Donald, whom the other patients call "Monster Man" because of his injuries from a fire. *See full annotation* Chapter 4: Health Problems.

■ Jacobs, Paul Samuel. *Born into Light.* Scholastic, 1988. 147pp. (0-590-40710-4) Reading Level: Grades 6–10.
Disability: Health impairment

Roger Westwood is 10 in 1913, when a burst of light heralds changes in his life. A naked boy runs wild near their farm until Roger's sister, Charlotte, and his mother bring the child into the family. Roger finds a burnt clearing, a metal canister, and an embryonic corpse that he shares with the local doctor. The boy is named Benjamin, and he learns and grows at a tremendous rate. The doctor takes Roger's family to visit a little girl in an asylum. They remove the silent child, Nell, from that harsh place, and she establishes empathic contact with Benjamin. Benjamin uses mud from the burnt clearing to heal a wound, and, later, Nell swallows some of it. It heals her vocal chords and some internal incompleteness, but both children continue to mature at an accelerated rate at which they catch up to their foster siblings in physical development.

The doctor marries Roger's mother and advances the children's studies. Away at school, Roger sees that Benjamin outshines everyone in intellectual and physical pursuits. One day Benjamin is well matched in a race against another school's champion, but the other youth dies at the end of the run. Benjamin marries Charlotte, and they have two children. Roger loves Nell, but she points out that her alien body is aging prematurely.

Benjamin makes plans for his children and other second-generation-alien seed to continue their trip to a distant settlement. Some Earth parents cannot bring themselves to let their offspring go; others see the separation as the completion of a pattern and the legacy of spouses they have lost to terminal illnesses.

Roger recalls all this during his own old age, speculating about Earth's explosion of invention and progress once the second-generation children who remained behind had matured.

Analysis: What seems a suspenseful story of the rural past turns into a unique work of speculative fiction. Every detail is precise, and each development well forshadowed. Benjamin and Nell are seen as different, offering a combination of strengths and weaknesses that lead the doctor to say, "They will be like meteors, bright and full of light, but quick expiring."

These aliens are given physical and intellectual superiority with a liability, and their presence on Earth is only a stage in their star course goal, not the focus of conquest. What a nice change. Highly recommended.

■ McDonald, Megan. *The Potato Man.* Illus. by Ted Lewin. Orchard, 1991. 32pp. (LB 0-531-08514-7) Reading Level: Grades PS–2. (KR 15 Ja91; BCCB F91)
Disability: Cosmetic impairment; Visual impairment

Grandfather tells how, as a child, he and the neighborhood kids were frightened of the vegetable seller, Mr. Angelo, who had lost an eye in the Great War. Distrusting the man's looks and taking advantage of his limited vision, the children built a myth of bad luck around the "Potato Man" and kept the produce that fell off the wagon. When Grandfather returned a pomegranate, the old man made a Christmas gift of it to the remorseful boy.

Analysis: Never showing the face of the vendor, which "was as lumpy as a potato itself," the illustrations capture the period and inner turmoil of Grandfather's reminiscences about the "Potato Man." The pleasant rituals of taunting Mr. Angelo sour once Grandfather thinks of him as a person. Such rehumanizing constitutes a valuable device making this title worthwhile to include in most collections. Though some readers may have difficulty with the many contractions in dialogue, such as "He couldn'a saw us," a read-aloud will make the most of this lovely book. Effective watercolor compositions introduce the 1920s from a child's point of view.

■ Mahy, Margaret. *The Blood-and-Thunder Adventure on Hurricane Peak.* Illus. by Wendy Smith. McElderry, 1989. 144pp. (0-689-50488-8) Reading Level: Grades 4–7. (BCCB O89)
Disability: Various disabilities

Wicked industrialist Sir Quincey Judd-Sprocket tries to kidnap beautiful scientist Belladonna Doppler. This would devastate Heathcliff Warlock, resident magician and deputy principal of the Unexpected School on Hurricane Peak. The six students at the school join with Sir Quincey's mysterious aunt and two hired villains in farcical adventures, magic, and absurdity. In the end, Belladonna and Heathcliff join for romantic and academic purposes to keep the Unexpected School operating. Sir Quincey's plans to develop the mountain for mining are foiled, and he buys computers for everyone at the school.

Analysis: Nonsense and witty twists on melodramatic conventions mark Mahy's inventive spoof. Busy sketches of the principal players show evil Sir Quincey in his wheelchair with many attachments; the chair always need repairs. Faithful helper "Amadeus was weedy and wore a large hearing aid that whistled and howled like a banshee." The silliness softens these stereotypes; they were never intended to be taken as role models so evaluation standards should not be applied to these inept, disabled characters. They are just as bad at being bad as they can be.

Aunt Perdita suffers from amnesia but is the real founder of Unexpected School and was swept away with young "Bottomley Quince" years ago. She has been with Sir Quincey ever since, "doing all his mechanical repairs," unaware of the grown villain's past or her own. What could one expect from a place high in the Pigweed Mountains?

■ Mattingley, Cristobel. *The Miracle Tree.* Illus. by Marianne Yamaguchi. Harcourt, 1986. 28pp. (0-15-200530-7) Reading Level: Grades 4–8. (BCCB D86)
Disability: Radiation sickness; Cosmetic impairment; Emotional disturbance

After the bombing of Nagasaki, a soldier comes to the ravaged town to seek his wife. He spends years helping to clear rubble, reestablish plants in the city, and apprenticing himself to an old gardener. One pine tree that he plants and visits twice a year becomes a symbol of hope for two women. The older woman has come to Nagasaki to reunite with her daughter, who married a soldier without family permission. The mother cannot find her, but she folds a thousand paper cranes for the well-being of her daughter and visits church regularly.

A younger woman has lodgings near the pine tree and observes life through a window overlooking it. She survived the bombing, "but her hair fell out, her skin was scarred and ridged from burns, and her eyes were dull and blank." She does not speak but begins writing poems once she notices the pine tree, the gardener, and the woman with the paper cranes.

One Christmas, the young woman's strength is fading, and she folds her poems, written over the years, into paper cranes. The gardener finds one in the boughs of the pine tree and goes with the old woman to locate the writer. He recognizes the disfigured poet as his wife, Hanako, and she acknowledges, "You are my Taro. . . . And you are my mother." Taro goes with the women to the church, where Hanako places her plain white cranes in the Christ child's hands. Her prayer is "Let peace prevail on earth."

Analysis: The bombing of Nagasaki tragically injured Hanako and others. Taro's description of and search for his lovely young bride meet the chilling statement, "No one is beautiful who has suffered atomic blast." When Hanako sees her reflection at the hospital, "She did not know herself. When they asked her name, she said, 'I am a withered leaf.' And when they asked about her family, she said, 'My husband was killed at the war. My mother is dead.' Then she did not speak again."

The author skillfully shifts point of view between the three mournful characters as they cope with their loneliness in different ways. Flashbacks are full of clues about how the war changed their life, as well as poetic insights about the love each has for the other. This makes the ending credible instead of melodramatic.

Yamaguchi's illustrations are cloudy charcoal drawings (metaphors in themselves for beauty that can still exist within something that has been burned and hardened). The drawings not only portray action but also enhance the text layout with pine bough and crane garland motifs. This is an excellent choice for most collections, because the emotional cost of war is portrayed as well as the physical destruction. A picture book format may put off some of the upper-grade audience who will be mature enough for this story; conversely, middle-graders will have to be led to this holiday gift.

■ Mayne, William. *All the King's Men.* Delacorte, 1988. 182pp. (0-385-29626-6) Reading Level: Grades 4–6. (BCCB Mr88)
Disability: Multiple disabilities; Orthopedic impairment; Short stature; Various disabilities

The first of the three stories in this collection is about a 44-year-old who belongs to a medieval king as part of a group of dwarfs. Joachim "was the responsible one, the only one with my full senses, so I had the driving of the horse and the finding of the way, and all else to do for the five of us, or seven if you count the animals." Hubert has chronic allergies, Roberto is clever at making things, malicious Rafe cannot hear or speak, and Fonso is "one of God's children and an idiot."

The queen has died, and, because "dwarfs are a woman's plaything," the king has sent the little men to the winter palace, where the majordomo ignores their needs. "A dwarf has privileges direct from the King, but no esteem from the rest of the court. . . . We are nothing without the King . . ." Without fire or enough food, the dwarfs take rations and are punished in the stocks for a day. The first stone thrown is cast back by Roberto; by mid-day the stocks are broken and kept at hand so that all but Fonso can pretend to still be imprisoned. Fonso runs off with the dogs, and the other dwarfs leave the stocks when the Infanta throws a 6-year-old's fit during a key ceremony to celebrate royalty's arrival. She also causes mischief that the dwarfs are beaten for. A queen arrives, bringing her own dwarfs: a woman, a black dandy, and his white counterpart. The cardinal archbishop, whose kindness and love are appreciated by the band, arrives for a week and promises to visit them.

After the wedding of the king and queen, the archbishop brings the dwarfs' story of neglect to the king. While investigating the living arrangements, they all find Hubert and the dwarf woman kissing.

"My Lord Bishop," says the King, "do dwarfs then love?"

"Sire," says the Archbishop, "do Kings?"

There is a second marriage, between Hubert and Elise. All the new couples have a happy ending, even the Infanta and her new stepbrother, "the Dolphin."

In "Boy to Island" a lonely little girl is rescued from an enchanted island. The fantasy of "Stony Ray" includes Kirsty's grandfather, who "thought I could be mad all these years, because I knew it happened but it couldn't."

Analysis: Outstanding writing style and depth of characterization make these easy to recommend. The social and personal insights contained in the title story contribute to an excellent addition to children's literature. Joachim provides an alert (though uneducated, as in the consistent use of "Dolphin" for "Dauphin") point of view on court dynamics and social roles. His own orthopedic disabilities are made clearer when he recalls showing his unbending legs to the archbishop after being admonished about humbling himself for worship. "For a time, among all the kneeling servants and courtiers I was the tallest." The King is just, and the Queen proves loving, but grief and affairs of state apparently made it easier than usual to ignore the needs of their special courtiers. Only *Little Little,* with a contemporary setting, does a fuller job of humanizing stereotypes of little people, but this provides a firm historical view of the segregated life they lived.

■ Rostkowski, Margaret I. *After the Dancing Days*. Harper & Row, 1986. 217pp. (LB 0-06-025078-X) Reading Level: Grades 5–8. (BCCB Ja86) *Disability:* Cosmetic impairment

Annie Metcalf is 13 when her father returns home from his World War I assignment of caring for injured veterans. Mrs. Metcalf wants her husband to take up his private practice and shuts out reminders of the war that her brother died in. Dr. Metcalf works instead with disfigured and wounded soldiers admitted to St. John's hospital. On a visit to the hospital, Annie is horrified by the appearance of Andrew Crayton, who was burned by mustard gas. She hears other people say it would have been better if "they had died in Europe" but becomes convinced she should return to the hospital to help with the patients no one else wants to see. Annie's grandfather reads to a blind patient while Annie gets past Andrew's aloof bitterness. Mrs. Metcalf causes a scene when she observes Annie and Andrew together. The woman insists that Annie's association with such injured men will have a bad effect on her daughter.

Grandfather falls ill and Mrs. Metcalf cares for him out of town. In her absence, Annie continues visiting the hospital and becomes close to several of the patients. Andrew is awarded the Purple Heart but considers it a joke because there was no heroic action connected with his injury. Investigating her uncle's death, Annie finds out that he did not get a Purple Heart, because his death was due to untreated measles. Andrew helps Amy sort out her feelings about this and her disobeying of Mrs. Pierce's rule against visiting the hospital. Andrew gets a job helping at another hospital and gives his medal to Annie as a memento of her friendship, which helped him readjust to life.

Analysis: Historical fiction can convey the universality of life, and this title is recommended for its view of the damage done by war and of adolescent striving for values and ethics that conflict with parental ones. Mrs. Metcalf's reactions may seem shallow, but the motivations are complex. Other characters revise their biased view as does Annie's mother, so gossip and harsh first reactions are balanced by scenes and dialogue that reveal the injured characters more fully. Recommended, this would follow Montgomery's *Rilla of Ingleside* nicely for a fuller view of the homefront during World War I.

■ Rylant, Cynthia. *Every Living Thing*. Illus. by S. D. Schindler. Bradbury, 1985. 81pp. (0-02-777200-4) Reading Level: Grades 5–7. (BCCB Mr86) *Disability:* Learning disabilities; Health impairment

Twelve short stories feature animals and the impact they make on the lives of children and adults. The first piece, titled "Slower Than the Rest," is about a learning-disabled boy whose pet turtle helps him make a prize-winning presentation on forest fire prevention. In "Papa's Parrot," Harry's father suffers a heart attack, and the boy takes care of the family candy shop while the man is hospitalized. There, the parrot that has been keeping Papa company says, "Where's Harry? Miss him," and the son understands how much a younger Harry's afternoon visits to the store had meant to his father.

"Drying Out" is about Jack Mitchell, a veteran whose wife left him before he became an alcoholic. While in the veterans' hospital for treatment, Jack feeds the three squirrels that come to his window. Having them there to care for helps him decide to stay for therapy, and, when he is released, he returns to feed them each week in thanks for seeing him through.

Mr. Willis cares for his invalid wife in "Planting Things." When a robin lay eggs near the house, he keeps watch and coaxes Mrs. Willis to get out of bed to observe the new family with him. After the robins fly away, he saves the nest. "Mr. Willis would look after his wife all winter. Then come spring, he would put the nest, ready-made, in one of his apple trees. He was a man who enjoyed planting things."

Analysis: As in *Children of Christmas,* Rylant uses short, revealing episodes around one theme in people's lives. This book examines various human needs and how animals help fill them. Sensitive sketches of each character are graceful yet pithy, and chapter decorations and drawings illustrate each story in a complementary tone.

Animal stories have great appeal, and the writing is very accessible, so this is highly recommended.

■ Sieruta, Peter D. *Heartbeats and Other Stories.* Harper & Row, 1989. 224pp. (LB 0-06-025849-7) Reading Level: Grades 8–12. (KR 1 D89) *Disability:* Various disabilities

Nine stories about teenage characters touch on many of life's disappointments and joys. One story is about a race in which a disabled student in a wheelchair is pushed through the course by an athlete who had the skill to have won on her own. Overweight, shy, nerdy, overconfident, withdrawn, or affectionate, these characters make choices and consider their feelings in each story.

Analysis: Humor and self-knowledge come in equal parts in this book. The point of view changes for each story and establishes distinct characterizations. A girl who has trouble with her own weight and would love to excell at something athletic is impressed by the wheelchair pushing. Readers may align themselves with her admiration of the able-bodied sportswoman or may form their own impressions of the athlete with special needs. An enjoyable collection like this should be available for circulation in many young adult collections.

■ Turner, Ann Warren. *Time of the Bison.* Illus. by Beth Peck. Macmillan, 1987. 54pp. (0-02-789300-6) Reading Level: Grades 3–5. (BCCB Ja88) *Disability:* Cosmetic impairment

Scar Boy knows that his childhood name that relates to his physical self will be replaced in a ceremony with his adult name. He is not allowed to draw, sculpt, or paint, because his cave-tribe fears the power of such images. When Scar Boy makes a mud horse, his father takes him to a clan gathering. Painter of Caves takes the boy as an apprentice and promises him the name of Animal Shaper.

Analysis: Set in a vague, tribal past, cave-man trappings like the name "Mammoth Man" may be superfluous. A dark-skinned tribe with a less developed society seems stereotyped. For a picture book that is comfortable, transitional reading, this may have appeal.

PROFESSIONAL BIBLIOGRAPHY

Compiled by Steven D. Robertson.

Anderson, Winifred, Stephen Chitwood, and Deidre Hayden. *Negotiating the Special Education Maze: A Guide for Parents and Teachers.* Prentice-Hall, 1982.

Azarnoff, Pat. *Health, Illness, and Disability: A Guide to Books for Children and Young Adults.* Bowker, 1983.

Baskin, Barbara and Karen Harris. *Notes from a Different Drummer: A Guide to Juvenile Fiction Portraying the Handicapped.* Bowker, 1977.

——. *More Notes from a Different Drummer: A Guide to Juvenile Fiction Portraying the Handicapped.* Bowker, 1984.

——. *The Special Child in the Library.* American Library Association, 1976.

Blacher, Jan. *Severely Handicapped Young Children & Their Families: Research in Review.* Harcourt Brace Jovanovich, 1984.

Bleck, Eugene E. and Donald Nagel, eds. *Physically Handicapped Children: A Medical Atlas for Teachers.* 2nd ed. Grune, 1981.

Boy Scouts of America. *Handicapped Awareness.* Boy Scouts of America, 1986.

——. *Scouting for the Physically Handicapped.* Boy Scouts of America, 1971.

Bradway, Lauren C. *A Systems Approach to Handicapped Children: Helping Children Grow.* Charles C. Thomas, 1984.

Brennan, Wilfred K. *Changing Special Education Now.* 2nd rev. ed. Taylor & Francis, 1987.

Buscaglia, Leo. *The Disabled & Their Parents: A Counseling Challenge.* Holt, Rinehart & Winston, 1983.

Callahan, Charles R. *Since Owen: A Parent-to-Parent Guide to Care of the Disabled Child.* Johns Hopkins University Pr., 1990.

Chaney, Sky and Fisher, Pam. *The Discovery Book: A Helpful Guide for the World Written by Children with Disabilities.* United Cerebral Palsy of the North Bay, 1989.

Coombs, Jan and Frederick Sard. *Living With the Disabled: You Can Help.* Sterling, 1984.

Dickaman, Irving and Sol Gordon. *One Miracle at a Time: How to Help Your Disabled Child—From the Experience of Other Parents.* Simon & Schuster, 1985.

Dreyer, Sharon S. *The Bookfinder.* 4 vols. American Guidance Service, 1981–89.

Fadiman, Clifton. *The World Treasury of Children's Literature: Book Three* Little, Brown and Co., 1985.

Featherstone, Helen. *A Difference in the Family: Living with a Disabled Child.* Penguin, 1981.

Fink, Dale. *School-Age Children with Special Needs: What Do They Do When School Is Out?* Exceptional Parent, 1988.

Friedberg, Joan Brest, et al. *Accept Me As I Am: Best Books of Juvenile Nonfiction on Impairments and Disabilities.* Bowker, 1985.

Froschl, Merle, et al. *Including All of Us: An Early Childhood Curriculum, about Disability.* Educational Equity Concepts, 1985.

Gillespie, John and Corinne J. Naden. *Best Books for Children: Preschool Through Grade 6.* Bowker, 1990.

Gliedman, John and William Roth. *The Unexpected Minority: Handicapped Children in America.* Harcourt Brace Jovanovich, 1980.

Gloeckler, Ted and Carol Simpson. *Exceptional Students in Regular Classrooms: Challenges, Services & Methods.* Mayfield, 1988.

Goldberg, Steven. *Special Education Law: A Guide for Parents, Advocates and Educators.* Plenum, 1982.

Goldfarb, Lori A., et al. *Meeting the Challenge of Disability or Chronic Illness.* P.H. Brookes, 1986.

Good, Julia P. and Joyce C. Reis *A Special Kind of Parenting: Meeting the Needs of Handicapped Children.* La Leche, 1985.

Gurney, Peter W. *Self-Esteem in Children with Special Educational Needs.* Routledge, Chapman & Hall, 1988.

Hearne, Betsy, Zena Sutherland, and Marilyn Kaye. *Celebrating Children's Books.* Lothrop, Lee and Shepard, 1981.

Heddell, Fred. *Children with Mental Handicaps: A Guide for Parents and Carers.* David & Charles, 1989.

————. *Children with Physical Handicaps: A Guide for Parents and Carers.* David & Charles, 1989.

Hughes, James and Joicey Hurth. *Handicapped Children and Mainstreaming: A Mental Health Perspective.* National Institute of Mental Health, 1984.

Hume, Maggie. *A Mandate to Educate: The Law and Handicapped Children.* Capitol Publications, 1987.

Jones, Monica. *Home Care for the Chronically Ill or Disabled Child: A Manual and Sourcebook for Parents and Professionals.* Harper & Row, 1985.

Knoblock, Peter. *Understanding Exceptional Children.* Scott Foresman, 1987.

Kroth, Roger L. *Communicating with Parents of Exceptional Children.* 2nd ed. Love Publishing Co., 1985.

Lima, Carolyn and John A. Lima. *A to Zoo: Subject Access to Children's Picture Books.* Bowker, 1989.

Lindeman, James E. and Sally J. Lindeman. *Growing Up Proud: A Parent's Guide to the Psychological Care of Children with Disabilities.* Warner, 1991.

McKaig, Kathleen, et al. *Beyond the Threshold: Families Caring for Their Children Who Have Significant Developmental Disabilities.* Community Service Society of New York, 1986.

Melton, David. *Promises to Keep: A Handbook for Parents of Learning Disabled, Brain-injured, and Other Exceptional Children.* Franklin Watts, 1984.

Meyen, Edward L. and Thomas M. Skrtic, eds. *Exceptional Children & Youth.* 3rd ed. Love Publishing Co., 1988.

Miezo, Peggy. *Parenting Children with Disabilities.* Phoenix Soc, 1983.

Mobility International. *Persons with Disabilities, 1985–86.* Mobility International, 1985.

Murray-Seegart, Carola. *Nasty Girls, Thugs and Humans like Us: Social Relations between Severely Disabled & Nondisabled Students in High School.* P.H. Brookes, 1989.

Newson, Elizabeth and Tony Hipgrave. *Getting through to Your Handicapped Child: A Handbook for Parents, Foster-Parents, Teachers & Anyone Caring for Handicapped Children.* Cambridge University Pr., 1983.

Odom, Mildred and Diane Clark. *The Exceptional Child in a Regular Classroom.* Master Teacher, 1983.

OECD & CERI. *Young People with Handicaps: The Road to Adulthood.* Organization for Economic Cooperation & Development, 1987.

Patton, James R., et al. *Exceptional Children in Focus.* 4th ed. Merrill, 1987.

Pearlman, Laura and Kathleen Scott. *Raising the Handicapped Child.* Prentice-Hall, 1981.

Phillips, William R. and Janet Rosenberg, eds. *The Origins of Modern Treatment & the Education of Physically Handicapped Children: An Original Anthology.* Physically Handicapped in Society Series. Ayer, 1980.

Powell, Thomas H. and Peggy Ogle. *Brothers and Sisters—A Special Part of Exceptional Families.* P.H. Brookes, 1985.

Pueschel, Siegfried M. and James C. Bernier. *The Special Child: A Source Book for Parents of Children with Developmental Disabilities.* P.H. Brookes, 1988.

Quicke, John. *Disability in Modern Children's Fiction.* Brookline Books, 1985.

Riddick, Barbara. *Toys and Play for the Handicapped Child.* Routledge, Chapman & Hall, 1982.

Rosenberg, Maxine B. and George Ancona. *Finding a Way: Living with Exceptional Brothers and Sisters.* Lothrop, Lee & Shepard, 1988.

Ross, Bette M. *Our Special Child: A Guide to Successful Parenting of Handicapped Children.* Walker & Co., 1981.

Routburg, Marcia. *On Becoming a Special Parent: A Mini-Support Group in a Book.* Parent/Professional, 1986.

Sanford, Doris. *Don't Look at Me: A Child's Book about Feeling Different.* Multnomah, 1986.

Schleifer, Maxwell J. and Stanley D. Klein, eds. *The Disabled Child and the Family: An Exceptional Parent Reader.* Boston: Exceptional Parent Pr., 1985.

Scwede, Olga. *An Early Childhood Activity Program for Handicapped Children.* Exceptional Pr Inc., 1977.

Segal, Marilyn. *In Time & With Love: Caring for the Special Needs Baby.* Newmarket, 1988.

Seligman, Milton. *The Family with a Handicapped Child: Understanding and Treatment.* Grune, 1983.

———. *Strategies for Helping Parents of Exceptional Children: A Guide for Teachers.* Macmillan, 1979.

Seligman, Milton and Rosalyn Darling. *Ordinary Families, Special Children: A Systems Approach to Childhood Disability*. Guilford Pr., 1989.

Shore, Kenneth. *The Special Education Handbook: A Comprehensive Guide for Parents and Educators*. Teacher's College Pr., 1986.

Simons, Robin. *After the Tears: Parents Talk about Raising a Child with a Disability*. Harcourt Brace Jovanovich, 1987.

Stigen, Gail. *Heartaches and Handicaps: An Irreverent Survival Manual for Parents*. Science and Behavior Books, 1976.

Sutherland, Zena. *The Best in Children's Books*. University of Chicago Pr., 1973.

————. *Children and Books*. Scott, Foresman, 1986.

Sygall, Susan. *A World of Options: A Guide to International Educational Exchange, Community Service and Travel for*

Thomas, Carrol H. and James L. Thomas, ed. *Meeting the Needs of the Handicapped: A Resource for Teachers and Librarians*. Oryx Press, 1980.

Thompson, Karen and Julie Andrzejewski. *Why Can't Sharon Kowalski Come Home?* Spinsters/Aunt Lute Book Co., 1988.

Wheeler, Bonnie. *Challenged Parenting: A Practical Handbook for Parents of Children with Handicaps*. Regal Books, 1983.

Zang, Barbara. *How to Get Help for Kids: A Reference Guide to Services for Handicapped Children*. Neal-Schuman, 1980.

Ziegler, Carlos R. *The Image of the Handicapped in Children's Literature*. William R. Phillips and Janet Rosenberg, eds. Physically Handicapped in Society Series, Ayer, 1980.

AUTHOR INDEX

The Author Index covers all entries in this volume and annotated entries from *Notes from a Different Drummer* (1977) and *More Notes from a Different Drummer* (1984). All numbers refer to page numbers. Page numbers preceded by an N indicate a page number in *Notes from a Different Drummer;* page numbers preceded by an M indicate a page number in *More Notes from a Different Drummer.*

TITLE INDEX

The Title Index covers all entries in this volume and annotated entries from *Notes from a Different Drummer* (1977) and *More Notes from a Different Drummer* (1984). All numbers refer to page numbers. Page numbers preceded by an N indicate a page number in *Notes from a Different Drummer;* page numbers preceded by an M indicate a page number in *More Notes from a Different Drummer.*

SUBJECT INDEX

The Subject Index covers the annotated entries that appear in this volume. Please see the bibliographic listing at the end of Chapter 1 for a subject breakdown of books included in *Notes from a Different Drummer* (1977) and *More Notes from a Different Drummer* (1984).